CW01266295

JESUS' WORDS

ON SALVATION

DOUGLAS J. DEL TONDO, ESQ.

Copyright © 2008 by Douglas J. Del Tondo

ISBN 978-0-7414-4357-1

Published by:

PUBLISHING.COM

Info@buybooksontheweb.com
www.buybooksontheweb.com
Toll-free (877) BUY BOOK
Local Phone (610) 941-9999
Fax (610) 941-9959

Printed in the United States of America

Published December 2012

TABLE OF CONTENTS

Preface

Have you ever wondered what Jesus taught was the means to be saved? What was Jesus' Gospel if you summarized only Jesus' words on salvation?

Bonhoeffer's Claims

In 1937, the famous Lutheran Pastor named Dietrich Bonhoeffer did just that. He summarized the gospel only relying upon Jesus' words. He ignored all other sources. Do you know what Bonhoeffer found in *The Cost of Discipleship* (1937)(reprint Simon & Schuster: 1995)?

Bonhoeffer claims to have discovered Jesus taught a Gospel of Costly Grace. Bonhoeffer says we have somehow been misled to accept an opposite gospel. The message of what Bonhoeffer first coined as the gospel of cheap grace.[1]

Bonhoeffer threw down quite a challenge. The response? Essentially, because Bonhoeffer died as a martyr at Nazi hands, he is often spoken about with great respect. Yet, his critique of modern Christian doctrine is largely ignored.

In fact, some believers even read *Cost of Discipleship* but still do not somehow realize Bonhoeffer is calling for a new reformation. It is not for lack of bluntness. Bonhoeffer in one passage said we had developed a "Christianity without Christ." (*Id.* at 59.) He says our salvation doctrine emphasizes belief to the neglect of Jesus' repeatedly-stated requirement of repentance and that a Christian observe all Jesus' teachings and commands.

Bonhoeffer argued that Jesus always insisted such costs were *necessary* for salvation-sake of a disciple. Bonhoeffer said we have shifted *away* from what Jesus taught. If

---

1. For a summary of Bonhoeffer's arguments, see page 234 *et seq.*, and pages 127-132.

Christ returned and preached today the same gospel He preached 2000 years ago, Bonhoeffer said most in the church would dismiss His words on doctrinal grounds. (*Id.*, at 35.)

Bonhoeffer says we have employed disparaging labels for what Jesus taught, making social pressure to conform to cheap grace doctrine more important than Jesus' words. As a result, Bonhoeffer said "if Jesus Himself — alone with His word — could come in our midst at sermon time," a significantly large group would "reject" His message. (*Id.*, at 35.)

What more could Bonhoeffer do to get our attention. He was saying we had developed within the mainstream a false doctrine on salvation.

Thus, this book charts out a course to test Bonhoeffer's claims. He offered up proofs. He explained them in pastoral style. He set forth Jesus' teachings, parables and similes.

However, Bonhoeffer unfortunately has failed so far. Bonhoeffer assumed using Jesus' plain-speaking passages would be enough for Christians to reject the gospel of cheap grace. Bonhoeffer assumed Christians would simply recognize the Master's voice and follow it. However, Bonhoeffer overlooked the bewitching and beguiling effort of Satan, just like Satan worked in the garden.

A Change In Approach From Bonhoeffer's Method

What will be different here from Bonhoeffer's approach?

First, we will systematically identify all of Jesus' direct statements and parabolic statements on salvation.

For example, it is a direct statement when Jesus says "all those who obey My Teaching should never ever die." (John 8:51.) It is a direct teaching when Jesus says "every tree without good fruit is cut down and thrown in the fire." (Matt. 7:19.) It is a direct statement when Jesus says you have two choices: you can go to "heaven-maimed" or "hell-whole." (Mark 9:42-47.)

The reason to focus on direct statements is they are all powerful tools to assist in unlocking any alleged ambiguity in a parable. For example, some misconstrue parables to wrong conclusions. We know they are wrong conclusions by comparing them to Jesus' direct statements on salvation. Thus, we can detect and expose such error by familiarizing ourselves with Jesus' direct statements pertinent to salvation. Hence, direct statements by Jesus have a priority, for they serve as building-blocks to understand parables.

This relationship between direct statements and parables is mentioned by Mark in his gospel. The Gospel of Mark notes Jesus gave direct statements to His disciples to clarify meanings of parables which He spoke to a general audience. At the end of a group of parables (4:33), Mark writes: "With many such parables he spoke the word to them [*i.e.*, the crowds] as much as they could understand." Then in verse 34 Mark adds: "He did not speak to them without a parable, but *privately to his own disciples he explained everything.*"

Therefore, these direct statements represent Jesus' plain explanation of His principles to His disciples. Accordingly, we will prioritize Jesus' direct statements as spelling out clearly the terms of salvation. These passages are clear enough on their own, and need no or little elucidation. However, they help elucidate the parables if we had any doubt about the parables.

My Beliefs

As you read, please remember always that I am directing you to follow Christ, and His teaching. I love the Lord Jesus Christ, and pray I would always be willing to do and follow anything and everything He asks. I believe in His resurrection; Jesus died for our sins; He is Lord and Messiah; divine (God-from-true-God) and one with the Father; and He will return to Judge the Living and the Dead.

The question in this book is not about the *facts* regarding Jesus, which I assume every reader accepts. The question is whether if you accept these facts means you now "sit back, relax and enjoy your salvation," as J. Vernon McGee insists is true.[2] Or is something else certainly required, just as William Tyndale — the great English Reformer — said?

A Parade of Witnesses Includes Tyndale and Shockingly The (Mature) Luther Too

The Lutheran pastor Bonhoeffer was not alone in attacking cheap grace. He had many predecessors. The earliest rebuttals to cheap grace included Apostles Matthew,[3] Peter,[4] and John,[5] as well as James[6] and Jude.[7] There also was Tertullian (207 A.D.)[8] and Augustine (413 AD).[9]

Furthermore, as we discuss below at page vi *et seq*, there were many who attacked cheap grace among the leading Protestant Reformers. This included William Tyndale, Erasmus, and Melancthon (Luther's closest confidant). To the surprise of many, we can even say Luther radically but quietly changed his salvation-doctrine by 1541. At that point, he too rejected faith alone as sufficient for believers.[10] (Calvin too criticized faith alone doctrine sometimes.)[11]

---

2. See J. Vernon McGee, *How You Can Have the Assurance of Salvation* (Pasadena: 1976) at 12.
3. See page 518 *et seq.*
4. See page 500 *et seq.*, and page 521 *et seq.*
5. On Apostle John, see page 14 *et seq.*, and page 417 *et seq.*
6. See page 492, page 522-23.
7. See page 537 *et seq.*
8. See page 538.
9. See page 538 *et seq.*
10. See page xiii *infra.*
11. See page 232, page 236 *et seq.*, and 470.

Among the many other predecessors who shared Bonhoeffer's view were John Locke, Jeremy Taylor and Menno Simons of the Netherlands. There was also William Paley,[12] John Wesley,[13] and Charles Finney.[14] Finally, there was Kierkegaard and Bonhoeffer himself. Thus, the road tread here has been covered before. Yet, this time, we hope by examining all counter-arguments and speaking clearly, the debate can finally end.

Encouragement From Tyndale: His Stunning Reversal On Faith Alone

The English Reformation began principally with William Tyndale (1494-1536) — a scholar in ancient Greek, trained at Oxford and Cambridge. He became proficient too in Hebrew to perform his translation work on the 'Old Testament.' Tyndale died a martyr, strangled and then burned at the stake. He was the first to publish the New Testament in English. At the time of his first English translation of the New Testament in 1526, Tyndale had already firmly converted to Luther's doctrine of Faith Alone.

In fact, in 1528, Tyndale had publicly endorsed justification by *faith alone* after his meeting Luther in 1524. Yet, beginning in 1530 and continuing until his death in 1536, Tyndale made a stunning reversal on faith alone doctrine. When he did so, Tyndale was at the height of his Bible translation work, and was still only age 34.

What was this change? Tyndale adopted what the first reformer — a Dutchman named Erasmus (1466-1536) of Oxford[15] — had christened in 1530 as *duplex iustitia.* In English, this means *double justification.* Tyndale's elabora-

---

12. See page 515 *et seq.*
13. See page 73 *et seq.*
14. See page 42 *et seq.*

tion on Erasmus' doctrine lived on in the minds of famous men such as John Locke, Jeremy Taylor, George Horne, William Paley, and Charles Finney.

Recognition Of Tyndale's Stunning Rejection Of Faith Alone

There is absolutely no disagreement among the leading scholars about Tyndale's final views on salvation. Cross, for example, explains: "Increasingly in his last years....[Tyndale was] moving away from the doctrine of *faith alone*, [and] emphasized the covenant [and] *works*...."[16]

Another evangelical scholar admits Tyndale "certainly did not" remain "loyal" to Luther's "doctrine on justification."[17] Tyndale's later doctrine was "overthrowing the whole basis of the [German] Reformation: which is to say justification by *faith alone*."[18] Tyndale's lessons are clearly

---

15. Erasmus' work *Handbook of A Christian Soldier* was released in English in 1503, and found an Oxford scholar, William Tyndale, as one of its earliest avid readers. Erasmus in a series of books heroically battled errors by the Catholic Church, including its doctrine of Mary; its traditions not found in Scripture, etc. Erasmus, one of the best scholars of Europe in ancient Greek and Latin, was subjected to persecution and indictment by the Inquisition. One can still hear the unmistakable bitterness in the *Catholic Encyclopedia* article "Erasmus" about this very first reformer. (Luther emerged only in 1517.) In 1516, Erasmus published the New Testament for the first time in Greek with his own Latin translation. This violated Catholic prohibitions which claimed the Latin Vulgate had become the official text. The Erasmus Greek text was the one Luther used to translate the Bible into German in 1522. Erasmus also gave the English-speaking world the first quasi-translation of the New Testament entitled *Paraphrases of the New Testament* in 1516. The *Paraphrases* were amplified and revised in reprints in 1519,1522,1527, and 1535. (Tyndale's English New Testament first appeared in 1526.) As a result, Roman Catholic officials in Spain brought articles of indictment against Erasmus to bring him before the Inquisitor but the process ended in deadlock. (Henry Charles Lea, *A History of the Inquisition of Spain* (MacMillan: 1907) at 414.) Upon Erasmus' death, "his works were [placed]...on the Index of prohibited books" by the Roman Catholic Church. (Johann J. Herzog, *The New Schaff-Herzog Encyclopedia of Religious Knowledge* (1909) at 166.)

recognized as reflecting Erasmus' doctrine of 'double justification.' Tyndale is described pejoratively, accordingly, as allowing "works a decisive role in salvation," which made the "theology of Tyndale...legalistic."[19] Claire Cross concludes the idea of "double justification" is "the position which Tyndale eventually reached."[20]

Tyndale's Biography

There is no doubt of the spiritual journey that preceded Tyndale's stunning reversal on salvation doctrine. In 1524, he went to Germany, and met with Luther. When Tyndale came back, he published in English in 1528 Luther's sermon *Justification by Faith*. Tyndale did so by putting his own name to it, with some original embellishments. It was entitled *Parable of the Wicked Mammon*. Luther and Tyndale were obviously collaborating at this juncture.

Doctrine of Double Justification

Something happened to Tyndale by 1530. He had second thoughts on Luther's doctrine. He developed ideas which ultimately led him to reject as dangerous Luther's youthful ideas on faith alone. Tyndale endorsed in substance what Erasmus had first proposed in 1530 — the doctrine of *double justification*.[21] It was Erasmus' solution to reconcile Paul's Gospel of faith alone to Jesus' Gospel. It was ingenious, to

---

16. Claire Cross, *Church and People: England, 1450-1660* (Blackwell Publishing, 1999) at 45.

17. Paul D. L. Avis, *Anglicanism and the Christian Church: Theological Resources in Historical Perspective* (Continuum International Publishing Group, 2002) at 16.

18. David Broughton Knox, *The Doctrine of Faith in the Reign of Henry VIII* (London, 1961) at 6.

19. Carl R. Trueman, *Luther's Legacy: Salvation and English Reformers, 1525-1556* (Oxford Univ. Press, 1994) at 55.

20. Claire Cross, *supra*, at 45.

say the least. One can affirm, as Bonhoeffer does too, that "faith alone justifies," but then append, as Bonhoeffer does, "but love perfects." (Bonhoeffer, *Testament* (1995) at 251.) As elaborated by Tyndale, this doctrine teaches that justification begins by faith alone for the non-Christian, but thereafter further justification requires obedience, works and stern repentance for a Christian to remain justified. The way William Tyndale put it was that faith alone initiates your salvation and brings salvation, but "if thou wilt not go back again, but continue in grace, and come to that salvation and glorious resurrection of Christ *thou must work and join works to faith in will and deed too....*" (William Tyndale, *The Works of the English Reformers: William Tyndale and John Frith* (Ebenezer Palmer: 1831) at 8.)

Double Justification: Best Set Forth By John Locke

John Locke provided one of the clearest statements of Tyndale's doctrine — an elaboration and tightening up of what Erasmus first dubbed as *double justification*. Locke said Paul in Romans 8:13 implies that from those who "are actually under the covenant of grace, *good works are strictly required*, under the *penalty of the loss of eternal life.*" What then of Paul's 'faith, not works' (Eph. 2:8-9) doctrine? John Locke says grace initiates without works, but once in grace, works are required. "Thus, grace and works [coexist], without

---

21. Erasmus' commentaries on the Psalms were partially devoted to this theme of double justification. They were published as an ongoing series of commentaries between 1528-31. In these commentaries, Erasmus explained that there is a synergy between faith and works. The bones are faith while the flesh is good works "which are inseparable from faith and love." This is not based on human merit, but God's desire to save those who ask for salvation. See Erasmus, *Exposition on the Psalms* (Univ. Toronto Press, 2003) at 9. In his treatment of Psalm 22 (started late 1529), he calls this doctrine *duplex iustitia*, or *double justification.* There Erasmus explains the idea of *duplex iustitia*: "Righteousness is of two kinds, the first being the innocence to which we are restored through faith and baptism and the second the righteousness of faith *working* through love," citing Galatians 5:6.

any difficulty." Locke says this solves the *perplexity and seeming contradiction*" within Paul's doctrine. Locke says that without this solution, many are led to a "mistake concerning the kingdom of God." Locke then summed up by saying what initiates by faith translates us into the kingdom, and into the "way of eternal life" but thereafter we are only "sure to attain" it if we have "persevered in that life which the Gospel required, *viz.*, faith and *obedience*."[22]

Biography of Tyndale. Early in his career, Tyndale endorsed with one qualification Luther's core doctrine on *Justification by Faith* in a book entitled *The Parable of the Wicked Mammon* (1528). This book is a sermon of Luther on justification delivered in the mouth of Tyndale. However, it also contains Tyndale's explanations and qualifications. These gave the "matter... a perfectly original" meaning.[23]

Thus, in *Parable of the Wicked Mammon*, Tyndale echoes all of Luther's youthful salvation principles, such as justification by faith alone and the lack of any need to strive to do good works for salvation-sake. Tyndale added just one significant qualifier to Luther. Tyndale merely insisted *repentance* is a distinct means of how a Christian remains forgiven of later sin. Tyndale writes in the *Parable*: "So that if through fragility we fall a thousand times in a day, *yet if we do repent again*, we have always mercy laid up for us in store in Jesus Christ our Lord."[24] Luther originally had said the same thing,

---

22. *The Works of John Locke* (London: Thomas Tegg, 1828) Vol. VIII at 415 (emphasis added.) Calvin tried to spin double justification to mean something quite different. He claimed there is one justification before God and one before man. Thus, before God it is always faith alone. (*Institutes* iii.11.2.) Obviously, Calvin's interpretation is not what Tyndale nor Erasmus was saying.

23. F. L. Clarke, *The Life of William Tyndale* (W. Swan Sonnenschein, 1883) at 77-78.

24. William Tyndale, John Frith, Thomas Russell, *The Works of the English Reformers: William Tyndale and John Frith* (Ebenezer Palmer 1831) at 90.

---

but without "*if we do repent again.*"[25] This was purposeful by Luther. The youthful Luther taught contrition was irrelevant to forgiveness. (Luther, *Sermon on Indulgences*, 1517.) Faith alone was all that was required to receive God's forgiveness at all times, according to the young Luther.

Hence, one can see at this juncture, Tyndale was drawing a very fine and single line *against* Luther's doctrine. Tyndale was insisting ongoing justification, distinct from initial justification, depended on repentance from sin. As time progressed, and as Tyndale was engaged in more and more translation, this single line of difference ended in the rejection of Luther's ideas of faith alone as dangerous for at least a believer.

After Tyndale's first English New Testament was printed in 1526 when he was age 30, Tyndale embarked on translating the 'Old Testament' in 1530. Tyndale's commentaries on Moses' writings at this juncture put him at complete odds with the youthful Luther. (As we shall see, Tyndale was firmly on Jesus' side. See Matt. 5:19.) Rather than any idea of the Law receding into oblivion, or of separate covenants, Tyndale's view now was that the "Old Testament and New Testament comprised one covenant, and a covenant was understood as a contract." In this, "God had revealed what man can and cannot do." Thus, while "justification by faith" was the solvent for sin, still "the justice perceived by Moses set the forgiven sinner into a path of unswerving obedience."[26] The "Old and New" make "one gospel."[27]

---

25. Luther's statement was "[N]o sin will separate us from the Lamb, even though we commit fornication and murder a thousand times a day." Martin Luther, *Luther Works*, I Letters (American Ed.) Vol. 48 at 282.
26. William A. Clebsch, *England's Earliest Protestants, 1520-1535* (Yale University Press, 1964) at 201,203 (paraphrasing Tyndale).
27. William Tyndale, *Tyndale's Old Testament* (Ed. David Daniell) (Yale University Press, 1992) at xxiii (describing Tyndale's doctrine).

In 1534, in Tyndale's *Preface to the New Testament*, the break with Luther's early ideas was final and irreparable. Yet, this divorce was based on reading Jesus' words in Matthew in their superior right over anyone else's doctrine. Tyndale, now age 38, was at his most mature in knowledge of Biblical languages, with the best training of that day — from Oxford and Cambridge. He was also at the height of his mental faculties. Yet, undoubtedly, Tyndale was also a verifiable reformer and a hero of unquestioned stature against the errors of Catholicism. But now in the *Preface to the New Testament*, Tyndale began bit by bit to allow Jesus' words to demolish faith alone doctrine.

Tyndale began by saying that God's mercies only apply to those who "meek" themselves before God and "keep His Laws."[28] Tyndale in the very next sentence then vigorously denounced faith alone doctrine: "Now if any man, that submitteth *not* himself to keep the commandments, do think that he hath *faith* in God, the same man's faith is vain, *worldly, damnable, devilish, and plain presumption*, as is above said, and is *no faith that can justify*, or be accepted before God. And that is it that James meaneth in his epistle. For "how can a man believe" [and be justified without works]." (Tyndale, *Doctrinal Treatises, id.*, at 470.)

Tyndale goes on to explain: "Now read all the scripture, and see where God sent any to preach *mercy* to any, *save unto them only that repent, and turn to God with all their hearts, to keep his commandments*. Unto the disobedient, that will not turn, is threatened wrath, vengeance and damnation, according to all the terrible acts and fearful examples of

---

28. After explaining the Parable of the Unmerciful Servant, Tyndale concludes: "The general covenant, wherein all other are comprehended and included is this: If *we meek ourselves* to God, to *keep all his laws*, after the example of Christ, *then* God hath bound himself to us, to keep and make good all the *mercies in Christ* throughout all scriptures." (Tyndale, *Doctrinal Treatises and Introductions to Different Portions of the Holy Scripture, by William Tyndale, Martyr, 1536* (Henry Walter ed., The Parker Society, Cambridge, 1848) at 470.)

the Bible." Tyndale then says some *read the promises* of salvation for faith *out-of-context* of the entire covenant of God. "Moreover, where thou findest a promise, and no covenant expressed therewith, *there must thou understand a covenant; that we, when we be received to grace, know it to be our duty to keep the law."* *Id.*, at 471.

Tyndale then severly warns those guilty of reading the promises of God about grace out-of-context — without the conditions of obedience. Tyndale is alarmed at the contrary doctrine (faith alone), saying: "This have I said, most dear reader, to warn thee, lest thou shouldest be *deceived*, and shouldest not only read the scriptures *in vain* and to *no profit*, but also unto thy *greater damnation."*[29]

Tyndale insisted: "For God offereth mercy upon *the condition that he [the listener] will mend his living."*[30] Tyndale then gives the same series of discussions of Jesus' words that you will read in this book *Jesus' Words on Salvation.*

For example, Tyndale says the Parable of the Unprofitable Servant proves those Christians who "live [obediently] thereafter" according to the commands receive life, but servants who do not do so but are unprofitable "shall *lose the grace* of true knowledge, and be binded again...." Tyndale goes on: "And [in] Luke xii [:47]), the servant that knoweth his master's will, and prepareth not himself, shall be beaten with many stripes, that is, shall have *greater damnation.*" Tyndale thereupon keeps beating the stick on faith alone's head: "And Matt, vii [:26-27], all that hear the word of God, and do not thereafter, build on sand: that is, as the foundation laid on sand cannot resist violence of water, but is undermined and *overthrown*, even so the *faith of them that have no lust nor love to the law of God*, builded upon the sand of their *own imaginations*, and not on the rock of God's word, according to his covenants, turneth to desperation in time of

---

29.*Id.* at 471.
30.*Id.* at 472.

tribulation, and when God cometh to judge."[31] Tyndale goes on and on, traversing much the same ground you will be reading in this book.

Interestingly, Tyndale was even a terrible 'legalist' by today's standards when he satirized those who justified moving the Sabbath from Saturday to Sunday![32]

Tyndale for all his intellectual honesty was also spiritually honest. Tyndale's 1530 work *The Practyse of Prelates* condemned King Henry's divorce. King Henry's bitter anger thereafter caught up with Tyndale. By liege of the authorities at Brussels, Tyndale was strangled and then burned at the stake in 1536.

Yet, the lesson in all this is that a brilliant reformer — one fully cognizant of every argument of Luther and who had become a friend and collaborator of Luther's (so much so Tyndale penned Luther's ideas on justification as his own in 1528) — did in fact by 1530-1534 completely reject Luther's youthful faith alone ideas.

Tyndale Causes Luther To Quietly Abandon Faith Alone

Did Tyndale turn Luther around to accept double justification, and abandon faith alone as justification of a believer? Yes, he did.

---

31. *Id.* at 472-73.

32. Tyndale responded to More's defense of Catholic Sunday-Sabbath practice, saying "a great matter, we be lords over the Saboth; and may yet change it into the Monday, or any other day, as we see need; or may make every tenth day holy day only, if we see cause why. We may make two every week, if it were expedient, and one not enough to teach the people." *An Answer to Sir Thomas More's Dialogue... by William Tyndale, Martyr, 1536* (H. Walter ed., The Parker Society, Cambridge, 1850) at 97. Tyndale says the Roman Catholic change in 363 A.D. from Saturday to Sunday was solely to spite the Jews. Tyndale writes: "Neither was there *any cause to change it from the Saturday*, than to put difference between us and the Jews; and lest we should become servants unto the day, after their superstition." He means this was the Catholic reasoning which Tyndale was satirizing.

Let's remember that Luther and Tyndale became associates in 1524 when Tyndale visited Luther in Germany. Tyndale could easily impress Luther as a man of greater learning in Greek and Hebrew than Luther himself. Their common bond was unique, and could provide a deep linkage few men will ever share. They were co-venturers in Bible translation, battling Catholic errors. This shared partnership of purpose and outlook would presumably have become solidified in 1524 when the two men met. In fact, one might think Luther regarded their intimacy as entirely special because he knew Tyndale was at least his equal, if not his superior, in learning. Luther would know better than anyone that Tyndale proved his friendship and solidarity. This was proven to Luther by Tyndale publishing as his own work Luther's sermon entitled *Justification by Faith*. It was entitled *The Parable of the Wicked Mammon* (1528). No doubt Luther welcomed this spreading of the 'gospel.' Hence, the bond of respect by Luther for Tyndale must have been tremendous.

Could that tremendous respect have moved Luther to himself change his own doctrine on faith alone? It most certainly appears to be the **best explanation** for what happened to Luther in mid-1531 to the end of his life. The evidence can be found in four primary places: (1) the *Catechisms* of 1531; (2) Luther's revolution on his view of the Mosaic Law in 1537; (3) the Lutheran agreement proposed at the *Regensburg Diet of 1541*; and (4) the actions of Luther's close aid, Melancthon, in 1548 after Luther's death, where he led the Lutheran Church to accept *double justification* as official doctrine from 1556 to 1580. (It was overturned in 1580.)

i. The Catechisms (1531) and the Antinomian Theses (1537)

If one examines carefully the change by Luther in the 1531 *Catechisms* (and thereafter), you can see Tyndale must have similarly influenced even Luther himself to accept *double justification*. The *Catechisms* written by Luther are all about a Christian's duty to obey the Ten Commandments and repentance as the means for forgiveness. (This is a salvation doctrine because without forgiveness, how could a Christian otherwise be saved?) You cannot find the word justification in the *Shorter Catechism*. You hear no mention of salvation by faith alone for the non-believer. Hence, Luther's Catechisms are a precise reflection of what a believer in *double justification* would present as the believer's *path* for forgiveness and salvation with God. It is as if Tyndale were writing the *Catechisms* for Luther.

Evangelicals who have discovered this change in the *Catechisms* condemn Luther for it. For example, Miles Stanford said in the *Catechisms* the "Lutheran Church" turned into "legalism" by adopting an "unscriptural application of 'the law as the rule of life' for the believer."[33] Likewise, Pastor Dwight Oswald regards Luther's *Catechism* as having made Luther a heretic. Oswald says Luther in the *Catechism* is so at odds with Paul's doctrines that even Luther must be deemed lost and responsible for having led countless numbers to perish in hell.[34] Similarly, Calvinists at Calvin College skewer Luther's 1531 edition of his catechism for departing from the faith he previously taught so boldly.[35]

Yet, Luther at some point prior to his death in 1546 insisted his followers put greater stock in his *Catechisms* over anything he wrote previously. Luther's biographer states: "Luther said that he would be glad to have all his works per-

---

33. Quoted in Bob Nyberg's *Covenant Theology Versus Dispensationalism A Matter of Law Versus Grace,* reprinted online at http://4himnet.com/ bnyberg/dispensationalism01.html.

34. See Pastor Dwight Oswald, "Martin Luther's Sacramental Gospel," *Earnestly Contending For The Faith* (Nov-Dec. 1997). See also, *Lutheran Heresy* at http://www.jesus-is-savior.com.

35. Calvinists thereby find the 1531 *Catechism* defective spiritually: "It gives undue importance to the sacraments by making them co-ordinate parts with the three great divisions; and elevates private confession and absolution almost to the dignity of a third sacrament [*i.e.*, salvific.]." (Calvin College at http://www.ccel.org/s/schaff/hcc7/htm/ii.v.xiv.htm.)

ish except the reply to Erasmus and the *Catechism*."[36] Why would Luther say this unless he himself felt some particular doctrines had changed for the better in the *Catechisms*? Furthermore, the mature Luther likewise in his *Antinomian Theses* (1537) demonstrates he rejected his own earlier view of the Mosaic Law. In 1537, Luther favored precisely what Tyndale had come to teach about the Law from 1530 onward.

Prior to Tyndale's 1530 revolution on the Mosaic Law still applying to a Christian, Luther in a sermon entitled *How Christians Should Regard Moses* given August 27, 1525 wrote this disavowal of any need to follow any part of the Mosaic Law:[37]

> The sectarian spirits want to saddle us with Moses and all the commandments. We will just skip that. We will regard Moses as a teacher, *but we will not regard him as our lawgiver — unless he agrees with both the New Testament and the natural law.*

> So, then, we will neither observe nor accept Moses. Moses is dead. His rule ended when Christ came. He is of no further service....*[E]ven the Ten Commandments do not pertain to us.*

Luther even in mid-1531 still held the same view — just before Tyndale's English treatises would arrive in German. Luther gave this speech in early 1531:

> The scholastics think that the judicial and ceremonial laws of Moses were *abolished* by the coming of Christ, but not the moral law. They

---

36. Roland H. Bainton, *Here I Stand: The Life of Martin Luther* (Abingdon Classics, 1990) at 263.

37. Martin Luther, "How Christians Should Regard Moses," *Luther's Works: Word and Sacrament I* (Philadelphia: Muhlenberg Press, 1960) Vol. 35 at 161-174.

are blind. When Paul declares that we are delivered from the curse of the Law *he means the whole Law*, particularly the moral law which more than the other laws accuses, curses, and condemns the conscience. The Ten Commandments have no right to condemn that conscience in which Jesus dwells, for Jesus has taken from the Ten Commandments the *right* and power to curse us.[38]

Then Luther experienced just as dramatic a reversal on the Law as took place for Tyndale in 1530. First, if you look at Luther's *Catechisms* of late 1531-early 1532, you can see that the *Longer* and *Shorter Catechism* are both dominated by an exposition on each of the Ten Commandments. Even the Sabbath appears, albeit moved to Sunday.[39]

Why this emphasis on the Law for a believer?

Five years later, Luther's rationale would be clearly explained in his *Antinomian Theses* (1537).[40] In this and the *Smalcald Articles* (1537), Luther says a Christian can spiritually die and become like a non-Christian for violation of the Ten Commandments. (Tyndale's *Double Justification* doctrine.) Luther's new teachings startled his faithful pupils. In *Antinomian Theses*, Luther echoes Tyndale's new ideas on the Mosaic Law as well, saying: "To abolish the Law is therefore to abolish the truth of God."[41] Leaving the young Luther's abandonment of the Mosaic Law out-to-dry, the

---

38. Martin Luther, *Epistle on Galatians* 4:25 (delivered 1531, printed 1535), reprint at http://www.biblehelpsonline.com/martinluther/galatians/galatians4.htm (last accessed 2005).

39. Here is the only difference between Tyndale and Luther at this point in their lives. Tyndale said it was wrong to move Sabbath from Saturday to Sunday. Luther implied a one-in-seven principle is all that matters.

40. Martin Luther, *Don't Tell Me That! From Martin Luther's Antinomian Theses* (Lutheran Press: 2004).

41. Martin Luther, *Antinomian Theses* (1537), reprinted as *Don't Tell Me That From Martin Luther's Antinomian Theses* (Minneapolis: Lutheran Press, 2004) at 33-34.

mature Luther said anyone who would "discard the Law [given Moses] would effectively put an end to our obedience to God." (*Don't Tell Me That (Antinomian Theses)*, *id.* at 32.) Yet, as we saw above, the young Luther earlier said in 1525 that Paul "abolished the Sabbath" and declared all the Law "abolished," even the moral law.

What can explain the mature Luther's reversal on salvation doctrine (done without fanfare) and the Mosaic Law (done with some fanfare)? Tyndale. Only a man of that character and influence over Luther can explain the sudden and major shift made by Luther. This earthquake in Luther's thinking followed in *precise synchronization* the fundamental shift in Tyndale's thinking which preceded shortly before each of Luther's major shifts.

ii. The Regensburg Diet of 1541 Proves Luther's Switch

The story of the Regensburg (aka Regensberg) Colloquy (Diet) of 1541 proves that Luther materially changed his doctrine on salvation. To this conference Luther sent as his agents only two men: Bucer and Melancthon. What they proposed and obtained agreement on from the Roman negotiator was Tyndale's doctrine of *double justification*.

Could Luther conceivably be surprised at this?

First, let's look at Martin Bucer (1491-1551). He was a Lutheran pastor and a very early supporter of Luther — starting in 1518. During the 1530s, while still a Lutheran pastor, Bucer wrote several works to defend *double justification*.[42] He used that term, first coined by Erasmus.

Let's next look at the second agent Luther sent to Regensburg—Melancthon. He was the perpetual right-hand man of Luther at Wittenberg. Philip Melancthon (1497-1560) was a Professor of Greek and second only to Erasmus in excellence in Greek translation in all of Europe.[43] He was also a Latin scholar. Most important of all, Melancthon was indubitably Luther's closest aid since the early days of the movement until Luther's death. In 1521, with unmistakable zeal, Melancthon advanced justification by faith alone vigor-ously in a commentary on Romans.[44] This work was the first systematic commentary by the Lutheran party to defend their doctrines. Clearly, Melancthon was a knowledgeable, faithful zealous Lutheran reformer.

In fact, Luther and Melancthon were inseparable part-ners, working side-by-side constantly at Wittenberg until Luther's death in 1546. When Luther died, his final directions were given at his death-bed to Melancthon. "On the death of Luther, Philip Melancthon...was placed *at the head of the Lutheran church*." (R. Adam,*The Religious World*: 358.) No matter what change in doctrine Melancthon went through, Luther never once criticized this man. Luther obviously knew Melancthon was of superior knowledge and intellect to him-self.

Yet to the shock of many around Luther, in 1536, Melancthon left behind his firm hold on faith alone. He now deemed it only saved the non-believer. The believer was under the obligation of obedience and works for salvation's-sake. He had adopted double justification. This is first men-

---

42.Martin Bucer was a personal follower of Luther in 1518, later excom-municated by Rome. In 1522, Bucer became a pastor in the Palatinate. By the 1530s, he advocated "double justification." As McGrath explains, "The most significant exposition of justification within the early reformed church is due to Martin Bucer...Bucer develops a doc-trine of *double justification*." (Alister E. McGrath, *Iustitia Dei: A His-tory of the Christian Doctrine of Justification* (Cambridge: 1998) at 221.) Bucer's double justification was identical to Tyndale's. McGrath summarizes it: "Although man's primary justification takes place on the basis of faith alone (*sola fide*), his secondary justification takes place on the basis of *works*." *Id.* Thus, there is "an initial justification by faith, and a subsequent *justification by works*." *Id.*, at 222.

43.In 1518 Melancthon was offered, on Reuchlin's recommendation, a professorship of Greek at Wittenberg. "I know of no one among the Germans who is superior to him," wrote Reuchlin to the Elector of Saxony, "save only Erasmus Roterodamus, and he is a dutchman."

44.Melancthon in his 1521 exposition on Romans entitled *Loci communes rerum theologicarum* clearly taught faith alone. This was the first sys-tematic summary of Luther's doctrine.

---

tioned in a 1536 letter about pastor Cordatus of Niemeck. Melancthon writes: "*New obedience* is necessary by necessity of order of the cause and effect; also by necessity of duty or command; also by necessity of *retaining faith*, and *avoiding punishments*, temporal and *eternal*." Then Melancthon says of Cordatus, having heard this teaching, he "stirs up against me the city, the surrounding countries, and the court itself, because, in explaining the controversy concerning *justification*, I said that *renewed obedience was necessary to salvation*."[45]

Words could not be clearer than that Melancthon adopted Tyndale's and Bucer's doctrine of *double justification*. This was no temporary change in heart. In 1552, Melancthon urged his pupil George Major to publish a book entitled *On the Necessity of Good Works* (1552). This book insisted good works are necessary for the *salvation* of the believer. Faith alone justification is only true for the non-believer. (Again, this is *double justification* doctrine.) Melancthon used the controversy from this book to convene a Synod to resolve the issue. Using that forum, in 1556 the Lutheran Synod resolved the point in favor of *double justification* which stood firm until 1580. See page xxviii *infra*.

Thus, as of 1539, the double justification views of both Bucer and Melancthon were open for all to see.

What was Luther's response to Melancthon's change in outlook? Luther "was anxious to avoid any rupture or discord with Melancthon" and "knew also how to keep silence...."[46] Yet, Luther did more than that. In 1539, Luther chose Melancthon to work out a rapprochement with Catho-

---

45. John Scott, Joseph Milner, Isaac Milner, *The History of the Church of Christ: Intended as a Continuation of the Work* (R.B. Seely and W. Burnside, 1829) at 125, citing *Epistles [of Melancthon]*, vi at 438: item, 403. See also this letter in John Fletcher, *The Works of the Reverend John Fletcher* (B. Waugh & T. Mason, 1833) at 515, quoting from Richard Baxter, *Confession of Faith* (London: 1655) at 330, 334.

46. Julius Köstlin, *Life of Luther* (Scribner's 1893) at 501.

lics on a variety of doctrines, including justification. On behalf of Luther, Melancthon obtained agreement in a 1539 conference from the papal representatives on this double justification doctrine.[47] Then Luther's friend and co-pastor Martin Bucer drew up the list of agreed points in what later became known as the Regensburg Book "with its important article on justification."[48]

This *Regensburg Book* was to be used in preparation for a scheduled conference in April 1541 at Regensburg. This book reflected the prior oral agreements between Melancthon and the Roman party, including on double justification. As McGrath says, the double-justification wording was no surprise because Bucer must have written it. He was a strong public advocate of double justification among Lutherans.

Next, we move ahead two years. These negotiations from 1539 were ready to reach a final stage of approval on all points. Two months prior to the conference, on February 13, 1541, Luther had "in his hands the *Regensburg Book.*"[49] This is the same book which in material part was written by Luther's friend Bucer.

Could this idea of double justification have been written into the *Regensburg Book* by the Catholic side? Only the naive would think so. First, the entire idea originated with Protestants. It was never a Catholic notion. Double justifica-

---

47. "In 1539, Herzog George of Saxony and his chancellor, George von Karlowitz, convened a colloquy in Leipzig to discuss the differences between *Melancthon's confession* and Roman doctrine. Although they found common ground concerning *justification and good works*, the participants failed to achieve overall consensus." (Michael Stephen Springer, *Restoring Christ's Church: John A Lasco and the Forma AC Ratio* (Ashgate Publishing, 2007) at 21.) The meetings continued on other issues in November 1540, with Melancthon alone representing Luther, and Eck alone representing the Catholic Church. *Id.* The contentious issues then were the mass and sacraments. *Id.*, at 22.

48. Alister E. McGrath, *Iustitia Dei: A History of the Christian Doctrine of Justification* (Cambridge: 1998) at 222.

49. "Conference of Regensburg," *Wikipedia.*

Jesus' Words On Salvation

tion was first proposed by the anti-Catholic reformer Erasmus, then by Tyndale and then finally by Bucer — one of the drafters of the Regensburg Book — the very book we are trying to determine who originated its language on double justification.

The second proof this language originated with Bucer-Luther is that a Catholic would not have invented double justification doctrine. To Catholics, justification is solely by baptism, which for a baby neither involves faith nor works. See Footnote 53 on page xxv. To Catholics, a sacrament saves. They claim justification needs neither faith nor works as long as the Church dispensed baptism to you.

Thus, it is obvious that Luther, Melancthon and Bucer must have thought double justification was close enough that it could be the basis for reconciliation with the Catholic church. Hence, the proposal at Regensburg on double justification was of a totally Protestant origin: it was a doctrine first formulated by the anti-Catholic reformer Erasmus in 1530, then advanced by the reformer Tyndale in 1530, and pushed by the Lutherans Bucer and Melancthon in the mid-1530s. That's why the language appears in the Regensburg Book in the first place, before the congress was even held.

Next, the Regensburg Diet began on April 5, 1541. Luther's representatives were Melancthon and Martin Bucer who, as noted already, were both open advocates of double justification.

To this conference, the Landgrave of Hesse also appointed Johannes Pistorius to represent the Protestant side. He "stood loyal to Melancthon."[50]

After a series of negotiations, on May 2, 1541 both Melancthon on behalf of Luther and the representatives of the Pope announced an agreement on justification doctrine at Regensburg. "The participants at Regensberg Colloquy

---

50. See "Johannes Pistorius," *The New Schaff-Herzog Encyclopedia of Religious Knowledge* (1911), *supra*, at 74. This says "he stood loyal to Melancthon."

forged [agreement on] *a double justification* formula...."[51]
They agreed on "double justification," saying a sinner is only
justified by a "living and effectual faith" rather than a dead
faith, *i.e.*, one lacking works (hence requiring secondary justification of a Christian).[52] Mere faith alone was discarded.

Tyndale's salvation doctrine had triumphed!

However, it is often uncritically implied that Luther
rejected on *principle* what Melancthon brought back from
Regensburg. Typically, we read "Luther was [not] satisfied"
with the article on *justification*, but the specifics are always
sketchy. The truth is that before rejecting it, Luther in a letter
defended the justification article to the Elector who was
angry that it had abandoned faith alone. (Scott, 1828: 277,
281.) The Elector vented his anger particularly at Melancthon. Luther told the Elector not to be too hard on him. Luther
said the justification article would only go into effect if all the
other points in the conference were accepted by the Catholic
church. (Scott: 281.) Luther encouraged him to let the issue
alone because the conference would prove embarrassing to
Catholicism, and weaken it. Luther then conceded faith alone
was still an important principle, but many historians do not
realize Luther was speaking of *initial* justification of an *unbeliever*, where this was still true. Luther was being coy with the
Elector by not explaining how salvation for the Christian
believer would be seen in a new light. (*E.g.*, Scott: 278.)

---

51. Joseph A. Burgess & Jeffrey Gros, *Building Unity: Ecumenical Dialogues with Roman Catholic Participation in the United States* (Paulist
Press, 1989) at 234.

52. See James M. Kittelson, *Luther the Reformer: The Story of the Man
and His Career* (Fortress Press, 2003) at 278. The actual text was two
sentences: "It is secure and wholesome teaching that the sinner is justified by a *living* [not dead] and *effectual* faith, for through such faith we
will be acceptable to God and accepted for the sake of Christ. A living
faith, therefore, appropriates the mercy in Christ and believes that the
righteousness which is in Christ will be freely reckoned for nothing
and also receives the promise of the Holy Spirit." (See "Diet of
Regensburg," *Oxford Encyclopedia of the Reformation* (New York:
Oxford University Press, 1996) (bracketed text: mine).

In fact, to think Luther truly objected to secondary justification of the believer simply makes no sense. First, Melancthon and Bucer were long-time confidants of Luther. They were no renegades. Second, Luther had to know in advance their *open* and *notorious* views on double justification. In fact, the only thing that makes sense is they were chosen particularly because of their shared view on that issue. Third, there was far too much preparation for this meeting to suggest Luther had not understood the *Regensburg Book* in advance. There had been two years of negotiation on the point of justification. Also, Luther's friend Bucer wrote much of the *Regensburg Book*. Finally, and most important, the language on double justification was a Protestant idea from beginning to end, and was never a Catholic concept.

Thus, it begs all credulity to believe that Luther had not authorized the *double justification* agreement reached by his agents at the 1541 conference. In fact, Luther's agreement with that doctrine is the only explanation why Luther chose these two men in the first place. Luther knew these two men, more than any of his other allies, sincerely believed and could defend the doctrine of double justification to the Catholics. It would take a lot to convince Catholics that justification was not by means of the sacrament of baptism.

Consequently, Luther must have given Melancthon permission in 1541 to accept *double justification* at Regensburg. It is not shocking therefore to consider the possibility that Luther himself had changed his salvation doctrine. Unmistakably, double justification was previously endorsed by Tyndale — someone in whom Luther was reposing great trust. Thus, it would not be at all surprising that Luther too had shifted in Tyndale's direction.

So, if it was not *principle* that led Luther to reject the Regensburg agreement *after the fact*, what other reason than principle could explain Luther's decision?

Timing of events plays a key role in proving what forces operated upon Luther. A deputation from the conference arrived at Wittenberg on June 9th to see Luther's reactions to the final agreements on several points. Luther acknowledged to them that he previously had seen the article on justification. (Scott: 287.) Luther said he was willing to accept it even though it used Paul's words in Galatians in a manner that he would not utilize. (*Id.*) Luther said that, however, he would do nothing to interfere with the acceptance of the articles. (Scott: 288.) For this, Lutherans praised Luther for his "prudence" and "temper" on this occasion. (Scott: 288.) Then before that deputation returned to Regensburg, Cardinal Caraffa (later a pope) told his Catholic negotiator, Contarini, that he had "betrayed the cause of the church, especially on the question of justification." (Scott: 289.) For Catholics, justification would always be by baptism.[53]

"Before the deputation [to Luther] had returned, the Roman party had destroyed all hope of union."[54] Luther and everyone else had learned that the Roman higher authorities rejected the Tyndalian compromise on justification.

Thus, Luther now knew before the deputation returned that he would be sticking his neck out unnecessarily if he himself continued to openly defend *double justification.* Only at this juncture did Luther then "demand... that even the articles agreed upon should be rejected."[55] Consequently,

---

53. Most Protestants misapprehend Catholicism as teaching justification by works. Instead, baptism is what matters. In 1545, the Roman Catholic church convened the Council of Trent to restate Catholic positions against Protestant doctrines. Its final decree was that baptism is the sole instrument of justification. See *Canones et decreta concilii Tridentini* (Leipzig, 1860) at 28 (decree VI:vii). A translation appears in C. F. Allison, *The Rise of Moralism: The Proclamation of the Gospel from Hooker to Baxter* (London, S.P.C.K., 1966) at 213ff. Thus, in Catholicism *faith* plays no role in justification. Nor do *works of obedience* by a baby play any role. Rather, the sacrament of baptism on a faithless baby who has done no good works makes a baby supposedly justified.

54. "Conference of Regensburg," *Wikipedia.*

---

only after Luther knew the Roman rejection of the justification article did Luther call back his agents' agreement on justification and every other agreement.

Moreover, how do those who portray Luther's decision was based upon principle explain away the fact Luther had the Regensburg Book long before the 1541 Conference began? They disingenuously claim Luther only belatedly "had become fully acquainted with the contents" of the "Regensburg Book" after his agents reached the accord at Regensburg.[56] How naive!

Justification was the key issue going into the conference. Are we to believe Luther did not read the Regensburg Book on that point ahead of time? Or that when he did so, he did not understand its *two* sentences on justification? And even though his friend and ally Bucer obviously is the person who drew up this language months in advance, are we to think Bucer never discussed and worked over the language with Luther? Only the gullible could ever believe such nonsense.

Thus, what instead explains Luther pulling back if it was not on principle?

We must remember what risk Luther had of being lynched by his own troops and lose support of his Elector if the word spread of his change in such a core doctrine. As Dr. Samworth says, the agreement reached by Melancthon (Luther's closest aid) at Regensburg on May 2, 1541 "*rejects* the Protestant concepts of sola fide or *faith alone*...." (More correctly, it rejects it as true for the believer; it maintains faith alone is true for the non-believer.) Yet, we already established, Luther must have approved this dramatic change in

---

55. "Conference of Regensburg," *Wikipedia*. Others put it this way: "At the last minute both parties backed away from their tentative rapprochement...." Andrew Purves, *Pastoral Theology in the Classical Tradition* (Westminster: John Knox Press, 2001) at 79.

56. "Conference of Regensburg," *Wikipedia*. The *Liber Ratisbonensis* can be found in *Melanthonis Opera, Corpus Reformatorum* 4:190-238.

advance. Luther must have accepted Tyndale's case for *double justification*. But when Melancthon returned, the heat from Luther's other less-informed supporters would obviously make it difficult — nay perhaps impossible — for Luther to come out in the open. Why bother doing so when the higher-ups in the Roman party already announced their rejection on the justification clause? Thus, Luther's decision to reject the 1541 agreement after the Roman party withdrew its concurrence must have had to do with politics, not principle.

In other words, Luther had created his own hornet's nest where the Queen can no longer leave without the hive stinging her to death. If he backed down, he could legitimately fear that his own troops would oust their old Master, treating him as a traitor. The Elector had in fact declared those feelings to Luther about Melancthon's acceptance of the article on justification during the Regensburg conference itself. (Scott,1828:278-279.) This is not a unique example of Luther's coyness. Indeed, it similarly explains Luther's obscurely placed reversal of his previously vociferous position on the alleged bondage of the human will.[57]

Thus, we have not mistaken what transformation has taken place in Luther's mind on salvation under Tyndale's obvious influence. Luther made strenuous efforts to escape the trap of his own devices prior to his death in 1546. Luther did so in 1541 by seeking to re-connect with Catholicism on this one key issue. It ended in frustration because the Catho-

---

57. See Thomas Yardley How, *A Vindication of the Protestant Episcopal Church: In a Series of Letters* (Eastburn, Kirk, & Co, 1816) at 397, quoting Erasmus, 1528, *Epistolae*, book xx, ep. 63. See the language of that 1527 Lutheran confession in Richard Watson & Nathan Bangs, *A Biblical and Theological Dictionary: Explanatory of the History, Manners and Customs of the Jews* (Carlton & Porter, 1832) at 646. Melancthon later expanded this into a doctrine of synergy of man's free will cooperating with God's energy. "Synergism," *New Schaff-Herzog Encyclopedia* (1911) at 224. Before his death, Melancthon fully renounced the whole idea of bondage of the will. See Watson & Bangs, *supra*, at 647.

lics were the first to express dissatisfaction with the justification clause. Luther thereby left it to Melancthon to make the effort after Luther died to fix the justification doctrine of the Lutheran church. We shall see that double justification later triumphed for over twenty-years within the Lutheran church.

iii. Two Years After Luther Dies, Closest Aids Successfully Push Double Justification As Official Lutheran Doctrine

Luther died in 1546. Melancthon — true to his master Luther — advanced double justification in 1548. It was an effort that met with success despite vociferous faith-alone opposition within the Lutheran church. What explains such a dramatic reversal? The highest leaders of the Lutheran church must have known Luther's true view had come to accept double justification. That is the best explanation why for 24 years *double justification* became, at Melancthon's instigation, the *official Lutheran doctrine.* This was from 1556 to 1580. Only the *Book of Concord* of 1580 finally repealed this revolutionary switch. It unraveled Melancthon's efforts which taught faith alone does not maintain justification. The *Book of Concord* reversed Melancthon's principle effectuated in 1556 despite his being the closest confidant of the deceased Luther.

This account begins in 1548. Upon Luther's death, Melacanthon was the new head of the Lutheran church. And in Europe, his role was bigger: "After Luther's death he became the theological leader of the German Reformation." He was Luther's closest aid and confidant. Melancthon led a group of Luther's closest aids to meet in 1548 at Leipzig. They openly endorsed *double justification.* They chose one of their number — George Major (1502-74), a Lutheran theology professor at Wittenberg — to publish a book entitled *On the Necessity of Good Works* (1552). He clearly wrote that "no one will be saved...without good works."[58]

A furious response came from a vocal minority within the Lutheran church. These were obviously less intimate with Luther's change of heart. They were adamant on faith alone as sufficient to save even a believer. They called Major the "devil" and "godless" and his work a "mark of the Antichrist."[59] Melacanthon too was called a "turncoat." Flacius, one of his students, denounced Melancthon as a heretic.[60]

To resolve the dispute, the Lutheran Synod of 1556 convened. Its final decrees firmly endorsed *double justification*. It said in evangelism to non-believers, they would still teach justification by faith alone. But the necessity of works for believers for salvation is true as both an abstract and legal matter. (*Double Justification.*) Yet, the Synod ruled that when the Christian believer would be told in a sermon that "works were necessary," the pastor should omit "for salvation" to avoid giving canon-fodder to the Catholics to criticize Lutheranism. Hence, this is precisely the doctrine of *double justification*, simply truncated for political, not spiritual reasons.[61]

This ruling stood within Lutheranism until 1580 when the *Book of Concord* wiped it out. The *Book of Concord* said faith alone was the doctrine of justification applicable to both the believer and unbeliever.

iv. The Enormous Implication About The Leading Reformers

Thus, Tyndale had changed Luther's mind on the most fundamental of issues: faith alone's salvific effect for a believer. And if Tyndale truly did so — the case that this hap-

---

58. Melancthon gathered trusted members of the Lutheran leadership in 1548 to meet at Leipzig where they agreed on the salvific necessity of good works for believers as a truth "conformable to the truths in the [four] gospels." (Johann Lorenz Mosheim & George Gleig, *An Ecclesiastical History, Ancient and Modern: From the Birth of Christ to the Beginning of the Eighteenth Century* (London: 1811) Vol. IV at 312.) See also Philip Schaff, *Creeds of Christendon* (1919) at 276.

59. Many in the Lutheran camp called Major and the others involved of the "devil." Flacius called Major "godless." Wigand said this idea was the "pillar of popery and a mark of Antichrist." (See Philip Schaff, *Creeds of Christendon* (1919) at 276.)

60. Patrick W. Carey, *Biographical Dictionary of Christian Theologians* (Greenwood Press, 2000) at 359.

---

pened is very strong — then this means the four leading minds of the early reformation — Erasmus, Tyndale, Luther, and Melancthon — had each come to conclude *double justification* was the correct salvation formula. It would be five if you include the father of the reformation in the Netherlands —Menno Simons.[62] Double justification doctrine says a non-believer must believe to be saved (faith alone), but a Christian must repent of sin, do good works and obey Christ or otherwise perish everlastingly (double justification).

Tyndale Is A Respectable Hero For Those Who Dissent From 'Faith Alone' As Cheap Grace

Even if we were not convinced about Luther conforming to Tyndale's idea, then, if nothing else, we can affirm Tyndale's ideas were accepted by the Lutheran party who represented Lutheranism at the Regensburg Diet of 1541. We can also say Tyndale's double justification doctrine became the official doctrine on salvation of the Lutheran Church from

---

61. Here is Schaff's synopsis: "A synod, held at Eisenach in 1556, decided in seven theses that Major's proposition was *true only in abstracto and in foro legis*, but not inforo *evangelii*, and *should be avoided* as *liable to be misunderstood* in a popish sense. Christ delivered us from the curse of the law, and faith alone is necessary both for justification and salvation, which are identical. The theses were subscribed by Amsdorf, Strigel, Horlin, Hugel, Stossel, and even by Menius (although the fifth was directed against him). But now there arose a controversy on *the admission of the abstract and legal necessity of good works*, which was defended by Flacius, Wigand, and Morlin; opposed by Amsdorf and Aurifaber as semi-popish. **The former view** [*i.e.*, the abstract and legal necessity of good works for salvation] **prevailed**. Melanchthon felt that the necessity of *good works for salvation* might imply their meritoriousness, and hence proposed to drop the words *for salvation*, and to be contented with the assertion that good works are necessary because God commanded them, and man is bound to obey his Creator. This *middle course* was adopted by the Wittenberg Professors and by the Diet of Princes at Frankfort (1558) [*i.e.*, the majority ruling], but was rejected by the strict Lutherans [*i.e.*, the defeated minority]." (Philip Schaff, *The Creeds of Christendom: With a History and Critical Notes* (Harper: 1919) at 276.)

1556 to 1580. We can also affirm double justification was held by the highest Lutheran official next to Luther: Melancthon. That's enough to conclude even a good Lutheran and a pre-eminent Greek scholar, like Melancthon, can recognize Tyndale's doctrine is more correct than faith alone doctrine.

Moreover, even if we could not cite Luther as an ally, we do not need to feel we are at a great loss. Tyndale was his own man and is a great ally anyway. By himself, Tyndale can stand up to anyone, including Luther, when it comes to defending the truth of what Jesus *truly* taught. Tyndale was a great figure in the Reformation all by himself. He thus becomes *a hero for those who believe modern salvation doctrine misses Jesus' points.* Tyndale was *the* Reformation in England! Tyndale for a time was Luther's pupil, but it appears quite clearly that Luther in the end, true to Christ, let Tyndale lead him later to follow Christ's words on salvation.

Why did Luther and others like Melancthon accept this input from Tyndale? Because both Luther and Melancthon knew Tyndale was an independent thinker with deep knowledge of Scripture in its original language. Both men

---

62. "The first wave of Reformation, initiated by Martin Luther, did not come to the Netherlands." ("History of Religion in the Netherlands," *Wikipedia.*) Instead, the reformation in the Netherlands started with the Anabaptists, principally Menno Simons (1496-1561). He was the founder of the Mennonites. In 1556 he wrote a treatise in favor of double justification, entitled *Van het rechte Christen geloove.* He criticized the (pre-1541) Lutheran idea that "faith is alone necessary to salvation." Instead, Menno contended the "faith that justifies is a faith that 'worketh by love'" — taken from Erasmus. See Hardwick:281-82. In English, one can find Menno's work *A Foundation and Plain Instruction of the Saving Doctrine of Our Lord Jesus.* Two snippets give the direction of his thought: "Namely, that no one can... glory in the grace of God, the forgiveness of sin, or the merits of Christ, unless he has truly repented. It is not enough to say, we are Abraham's children, that is, that we profess to be Christians and be esteemed as the followers of Christ. But *we must do the works of Abraham*, that is, we must walk as all the true children of God are commanded to walk." *Id.* at 23. "True faith that is acceptable to God is not *dead faith*....It works and wills righteousness.... 'Every tree that does not bring forth good fruit is...is accursed and consumed by fire." (Matt. 3:21.)" *Id.* at 28-29.

---

also knew that Tyndale was honest and full of integrity. Thus, no amount of friendship would permit Tyndale to cower to any monolithic "Reformation." His integrity instead required that he even question Luther's doctrine. Tyndale's only Lord was Christ. And to our dear Lord, brother Tyndale was true!

Perhaps it was also Tyndale's single hearted devotion to the *words* of the Master that could influence Luther and Melancthon to both regret their prior writings. Someone with monumental influence like Tyndale was necessary to move men like Luther and Melancthon to such a stunning change of previously published doctrine.

Hence, Tyndale is a spiritual hero in every respect. He upheld Christ's doctrine on salvation against both the pressure of German reformers and Catholic counter-reformers. He did not resist Luther's deductions precipitously. He had fully comprehended them. In fact, Tyndale had clearly accepted them in the *Parable of the Wicked Mammon* (1528). Nor had Tyndale cavalierly rejected Luther's youthful faith alone idea as

Tyndale's last words: 'Lord open the eyes of the king.'

sufficient to save believers. Instead, he had the fullest knowledge possible of both New and 'Old Testaments.' How else can 82% of the English in the King James Bible of 1611 be the words of William Tyndale from 1534? Nor was Tyndale any personal enemy of Luther. Rather, they were friends after 1524. Tyndale travelled specifically to Wittenberg to see Luther that year. This led to an intimate association with Luther's ideas on justification. Tyndale published in 1528 Luther's sermon on justification by faith. Tyndale even put it under his own name with minor embellishments!

Thus, with an educational background and experience unparalleled by any Bible student before or since, and with unimpeachable evangelical credentials, *Tyndale elected to hold the pure line of Jesus' words against all comers*. He rejected faith alone doctrine for the believer. In all of this mess of men mangling God's word, Tyndale stands head and shoulders above them all. For this he lost his life in this world, but he gained it for the next.

> "[Jesus] said to the Judeans who had **believed** in Him, 'If you **obey** [*meno*, continue in] my teaching, then you are my disciples indeed. And you shall know the truth, and the truth shall make you **free**. [The Judeans said they are not slaves. Jesus responded.] Whosoever **practices sin** is a **slave** to it." Jn 8:30-34

Hence, let's examine Jesus' doctrine with the very same courage that Tyndale had. Let's be willing to put all our reputation in this world at stake if that is what it costs to accept all of the teachings of Jesus Christ.

Yet, just because the story of Tyndale and his impact is an encouraging story does not mean this book is about his or Luther's doctrine. Instead, this book is about what Jesus taught. What obviously impelled Tyndale to submit to the doctrine of double justification had mostly to do with his belief that Jesus' words are more important than anyone else's words. Thus, we intend to follow his more mature realization that he had to emphasize Jesus' words to determine doctrine. He must have realized Jesus said He was our "*Sole* Teacher." (Matt. 23:10.) Jesus *alone* is the source of truth.

Therefore, we start with a clean slate. We are open to find whatever Jesus taught on salvation, even if it were not exactly double justification. Even if it were faith alone, we would accept that too.

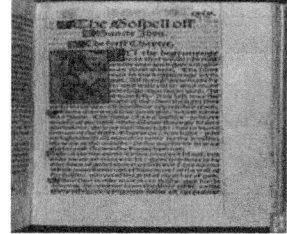

Tyndale's 1534 New Testament: why did Tyndale at first accept but then by 1534 reject faith alone doctrine?

Hall of Fame of Dissenters from Faith Alone

"Any many that submitteth not himself to keep the commandments [yet] do think he hath faith in God, the same man's faith is vain, damnable, devlish, and plain presumption...and is no faith that can justify." (*Doctrinal Treatises.*)

William Tyndale
1494-1536

"New obedience... is necessity of duty or command: also by necessity of retaining faith...and avoiding punish-ments...eternal...[C]oncerning justification, renewed obedience [is] necessary to salvation." (1536, *Letters of PM* #403.)

Philipp Melancthon
1497-1560
Successor to Luther as head of Lutheran church in 1546

At Melancthon's request, in 1552, he wrote a book entitled *On The Necessity of Good Works* in which he wrote: "No one will be saved with-out good works." The controversy that ensued was used by Melancthon to rectify Lutheran justification doctrine which stood firm until 1580.

Georg Major
1502-1574, ordained by Martin Luther in 1537, Professor & Pastor

"No one can glory in the grace of God, in the forgiveness of sins, and the merits of Christ unless he has truly repented. It is not enough to say we are Abraham's children, that is we profess to be Christians...but we must do the works of Abraham, that is, we must walk as all the true children of God are commanded to walk. True faith...is not dead faith." (1556)

Menno Simons
1496-1561
Founder of reformation in the Netherlands

1   *Atonement: Be Reconciled First To The One You Sinned Against Or Otherwise No Effect*

Cheap Grace Claims You Receive An Irrevocable Covering Of All Future Sin Upon Faith Alone

The standard faith alone view is that once you believe in Jesus, His atoning blood washes you permanently. There is no other condition to acquire and/or retain atonement than simply a belief in Jesus as Lord and Savior. Typically, this belief is expressed in a sinner's prayer, either silently or out-loud. After being said, the sinner is told that if truly said from the heart, they are now saved forever, and cannot lose their salvation. Christ's blood was shed for them. They are permanently saved.

Hence, based on atonement, God not only erases your prior sin, but God also will never supposedly see any sin you commit in the future. An example of this common view is expressed by Don Fortner, the Pastor of Grace Baptist Church in Danville, Kentucky. He writes in *God Sees No Sin*[1] that once atonement is applied, then God never sees you sin again: "God *sees no sin* in His people...The Son of God... made an end of our sins, and justified and sanctified us by His blood." This cheap grace teacher directly applies this to our current state of ongoing (unrepentant) sin: "I rejoice to declare to every *believing sinner* that God will *never punish* you for

---

1. Dan Fortner, *God Sees No Sin* at http://www.pristinegrace.org/media.php?id=297 (accessed 8-25-07).

your sins, *hold you accountable at His bar for your sins*,... *because of your sins*. For Him to do so, He must violate His own justice and overturn the satisfaction of His own Son."

Charles Stanley, two-time president of the Southern Baptists and familiar radio-tv personality, makes it even more explicit. He insists that once you receive Christ's atonement based on faith alone, God never sees you sinning again. You are permanently covered. You need never worry again about sin costing you your salvation. Charles Stanley explains that no sin he can commit can "deprive me of my forgiveness God purchased in my behalf through Christ's blood at Calvary." (Stanley, *The Gift of Forgiveness* (Thomas Nelson, 1991) at 104.) Stanley writes that once God's forgiveness is given, no sin thereafter can change the atonement previously granted:

> But a man or woman who has been rescued once from a state of unforgiveness *need not worry*. For once 100% of a man's or woman's sins have been forgiven, *the potential for being unforgiven has been done away with*. The risk factor is zero. There are *no more fires* from which the believer needs to be saved. (Stanley, *The Gift of Forgiveness* (Thomas Nelson, 1991) at 36.)(Emphasis added.)

Are Fortner and Stanley correct? *No.*

Jesus' Doctrine On Conditions To Acquire Atonement

First, let's address the question of *acquisition* of atonement. Is it solely based upon faith alone? *No.*

Jesus says atonement has no application until and unless you reconcile with the one you offended. (Matt. 5:23-24.)

Be Reconciled Before Sacrifice

Jesus taught:

(22) but I say unto you, that every one who is ***angry with his brother*** shall be in danger of the judgment; and whosoever shall say to his brother, Raca, shall be in danger of the council; and whosoever shall say, Thou fool, shall be in danger of the ***hell of fire***. (23) If therefore thou art ***offering thy*** ~~gift~~ *[atoning sacrifice, doron in Greek and Hebrew] at the [place for sacrifice]* ~~altar~~, and there rememberest that ***thy brother hath aught against thee***, (24) ***leave there thy*** ~~gift~~*[atoning sacrifice] before the [place of sacrifice]*~~altar~~*, and go thy way, first be reconciled to thy brother, and then come and offer thy [atoning sacrifice]*. (25) Agree with thine adversary quickly, while thou art with him in the way; lest haply the adversary deliver thee to the judge, and the judge deliver thee to the officer, and thou be cast into prison. (26) Verily I say unto thee, thou shalt by no means come out thence, till thou have paid the last farthing. (Matt 5:22-26, ASV with modifications in brackets.)

In Matthew 5:23-24, Jesus says that before you bring the "sacrifice"[2] (often translated as 'gift') to the "sacrifice place"[3] (typically translated as 'altar') make sure you are "reconciled to your brother" who has something against you.

What was this sacrifice to which Jesus referred? Throughout the year, the people brought to the priests a variety of sacrifices. Each offering can be called a gift to God, but each gift was intended as an atoning sacrifice — blotting out sin and cleansing the individual. In its article on "Atonement," *The Encyclopedia of Judaism* explains: "Every sacrifice may thus be considered a *kofer*, in the original sense a

---

2. Barnes and Clarke both concur the meaning here is "sacrifice."

proprietary gift, and its purpose is to 'make ***atonement*** ('le kapper') for the people. Lev. 9:7; 10:17."[4] Atonement is intended to "***cleanse*** the person from his guilt" ('mehatao,' Lev.iv.26, v.6-10)." ("Atonement," *Encyclopedia of Judaism*.)

Thus, Jesus' reference is to a sacrifice at the Temple's altar. He was talking about atoning sacrifices which the priests received and then made on behalf of the people to grant them cleanness from their prior sin in God's eyes.

Jesus in Matthew 5:23-24 was thus telling His audience that receipt of atonement had to be post-poned when there was still an unresolved sin problem between you and someone else. What does this mean?

Jesus means you must leave your atoning *sacrifice* at the *sacrifice-place* if someone has something against you because you sinned against them. There is nothing defective in the sacrifice offered. It is perfect to atone for you. Yet, you are not able to receive its effect because of a defect in your past behavior. Jesus says you must first go home and ***be reconciled*** to those you offended. You must come to terms with your adversary while you are still in the way with him or oth-

---

3. The Greek word is *thusiasterion*. It literally means "sacrifice place." (*Interlinear Scripture Analyzer.*) Barnes concurs that this meant the "altar... in front of the Temple, and was the place on which ***sacrifices*** were made." Jesus uses this identical expression in Matthew 23:18, typically translated as "gift upon the altar." Barnes says in that verse Jesus means the "altar of burnt offerings" in the court of the priests. "It was made of brass, about thirty feet in length and breadth, and fifteen feet in height." He continues, saying here were "offered all the beasts and bloody oblations of the temple." See Albert Barnes, *Notes Explanatory and Practical on the Gospels: Designed for Sunday School Teachers* (Harper & Brothers, 1853) at 262.

4. The word *atone* in Hebrew is related to the word *kofer*, to ransom. ("Atonement," *Jewish Encyclopedia*). There were various *kofers* to make for various sins. For example, if a man was killed by an ox, there was a special *kofer* for that. (Ex. 21:30, *kofer*.) The kofer was sometimes the blood of sacrifice. (Lev. 17:11.) Other times it was a money offering, called a *kesef kippurim*. (Exodus 30:15-16.)(*Id.*) http://jewish-encyclopedia.com/view.jsp?artid=2092&letter=A&search=atonement.

---

erwise, the debt you owe him will come back to haunt you later. You will end up in prison. (Matt. 5:25-26.) Instead, *only* after you appeased your adversary, can you come to the sacrifice-place and offer up the gift God has provided (Jesus) for you as the atoning sacrifice. (Matt. 5:24.)

Hence, asking for atonement to apply to you must be postponed *unless and until you have repented from your wrong and taken action that accomplishes reconciliation* with the one you sinned against.

Such actions to appease the one you wronged are what the Prophet John-the-Baptist called *works worthy of repentance.* This topic is also addressed at pages 296 and 339-340 *infra* and in an online chapter.[5] This pre-condition for atonement will become abundantly clear as we find more corroboration that Jesus meant atonement in Matthew 5:23-24.

Commentators Who Get It Right

Barnes Sees Sacrifice Is Unacceptable Without Repentance

Albert Barnes (1798-1870), a famous commentator and Presbyterian pastor, says this passage means Jesus was saying that repentance in the heart had to come first before the atoning sacrifice would be acceptable to God. Barnes explains:

> If therefore, says he, a man has gone so far as to bring his gift to the very altar, and should remember that any one had any thing against him, it was his duty there to leave his offering, and go and be reconciled. While a difference of this nature existed, *his offering could not be acceptable.*[6]

---

5. See online chapter 'Works Worthy of Repentance."

Barnes explains the meaning of what is translated as *gift* really meant the *sacrifice* you would give the priest to offer on your behalf under the Mosaic Law. And the *altar* really meant the *sacrifice place* at the Temple of Jerusalem:

> *Thy gift.* Thy **sacrifice**. What thou art about to devote to God as an offering. *To the altar.* The altar was situated in front of the temple, and was the place on which **sacrifices** were made.

Barnes then explains what it means that another *has anything against you.*

> *Hath aught.* Is offended, or thinks he has been injured by you in any manner.

Barnes finally comments on the all important command of Jesus that you must be *first reconciled.*

> *First be reconciled.* This means to settle the difficulty; to make proper acknowledgment, or satisfaction, for the injury. It you have wronged him, **make restitution**. If you owe him a debt which ought to be paid, pay it. If you have injured his character, confess it, and seek pardon. If he is under an erroneous impression; if your conduct has been such as to lead him to suspect that you have injured him, make an explanation. Do all in your power, and all you ought to do, to have the matter settled.

In other words, Jesus meant you must take all steps necessary to reconcile with the party offended. These works are typically called works-worthy-of-repentance. The sacrifice offered at the sacrifice place for you was *unacceptable* until these personal steps at repentance and works were done

---

6. Albert Barnes, *Notes Explanatory and Practical on the Gospels: Designed for Sunday School Teachers* (Harper & Brothers, 1853) at 69-70.

first. Barnes did not so clearly draw out the necessity of works-worthy-of-repentance in such stark terms, but that implication is self-evident from what he just admitted.

Campbell Correctly Understands Jesus

Alexander Campbell (1788-1866), the American Baptist reformer of Irish descent, founder of Bethany College and inspiration for the Disciples of Christ congregations,[7] had the same view of this passage in his work *The Christian System* (2d Ed. 1839):

> We sin against God always, when we sin against man; and therefore, ***after making all things right with man, we can only, through sacrifice, which makes the matter right with God, obtain forgiveness***. To the same effect, Jesus speaks, Matt. v. 23, 24, "Be reconciled to your brother," ***first make the matter right with him***, "and then come and offer your gift." *Id.*, at 55. (Emphasis added.)

Thus, our forgiveness from God is contingent on His accepting a sacrifice on our behalf.

Campbell then interprets Jesus as saying the effectiveness of sacrifice as atonement is in turn contingent on "making the matter [of earlier sin] right with God."

---

7. Campbell's doctrine of "no creed but the Bible" sought unity by relying only upon the teachings of Jesus and the apostles, thereby dispensing with formal creeds. This also required dispensing with denominational names such as "Baptist," because it did not follow the original depiction of Christ's followers. Campbell said they were known as a "disciple of Christ." This effort to restore primitive Christianity led to the founding of the Disciples of Christ and Churches of Christ. In 1880, there were 592 Disciples of Christ churches with 592,000 members. For more on the background of this movement, see http://www.mun.ca/rels/restmov/texts/wlhayden/etc/TCCODOC.HTM (last accessed 5/7/2007). In soteriology, they teach the necessity of "faith and repentance." They also emphasize obedience. See "Disciples of Christ," *A Religious Encyclopedia* (Ed. Philip Schaff)(1894).

Campbell is thus understanding Jesus without being confused by the vague "gift" translation within the KJV version of Matthew 5:23-24. Jesus says first make the matter right with the one you offended, and then offer your gift (sacrifice). Otherwise, *the sacrifice is ineffectual, and you have no forgiveness with God.*

Jesus Is Simply Repeating The Prophets

What corroborates that Barnes and Campbell are reading Jesus correctly is that Jesus is simply repeating a common lesson in the Prophets. The Prophets often had to correct a false notion that atonement was solely based on the act of sacrifice. The Prophets repeatedly insisted atonement only could cover a person who had truly first repented and took steps of reform. Otherwise the atonement had no effect. Atonement was not magic. (Jer. 7:20-25; Mic. 6:6-8,[8] Joel 2:13, Hos.14:1-2;[9] and Mal. 1:10,[10] 3:3-4. Cf. Isaiah 27:9.)

One good synopsis of these prophetic passages says: "The Prophets disparaged sacrifices that were offered without...a determined turning from sin and returning to God by striving after righteousness."[11]

---

8. "Wherewith shall I come before Jehovah, and bow myself before the high God? shall I come before him with *burnt-offerings*, with calves a year old? (7) will Jehovah be *pleased with thousands of rams*, or with ten thousands of rivers of oil? shall I give my first-born for my transgression, the fruit of my body for the sin of my soul? (8) He hath showed thee, O man, what is good; and what doth Jehovah require of thee, but to do justly, and to love kindness, and to walk humbly with thy God?" (Micah 6:6-8 ASV.)

9. "Take with you words, and return unto Jehovah: say unto him, Take away all iniquity, and accept that which is good: so will we *render as bullocks the offering of our lips*." (Hos 14:2 ASV.)

10. "Oh that there were one among you that would shut the doors, that ye might not kindle fire on mine altar in vain! I have no pleasure in you, saith Jehovah of hosts, *neither will I accept an offering at your hand*." (Mal 1:10 ASV.)

Treating Atonement Like Magic Condemned in 1 Samuel 15

God gave us an illustration from the life of King Saul of this principle. It demonstrates how abhorrent it is to God that people treat atonement as effectual for those who are sinning and unrepentant. God was incredibly angry with Saul for thinking bringing atonement to God had some magical power for even a disobedient person to receive forgiveness.

Who was King Saul? He was a Benjamite who assumed he could use God's sacrifice system without any condition of obedience. Saul was told to take no booty from an enemy of God. He was supposed to destroy their livestock and possessions. Saul did not do so. He had the intent of offering it to God in a sacrifice. God's response was not to accuse Saul of hypocrisy. God never suggests that Saul had no intent to make a sacrifice offering with the war booty. God's response takes Saul at his word in that respect. Rather, God rejects the Benjamite Saul's idea that a disobedient person's sacrifice has any value. *Obedience* must come before sacrifice. Obedience is the indispensable condition to bring an effectual sacrifice offering. This is the same lesson Jesus was teaching in Matthew 5:23-24.

This illustration is found in 1 Samuel 15:22-23. Saul disobeyed God but was planning on offering ***an atoning sacrifice*** using the booty he recovered. God said this was pure abuse of the principle of cleansing from atonement. The prophet Samuel on behalf of God rebukes the Benjamite Saul's logic.

> 22 Has the LORD as great delight in burnt offerings and sacrifices, as in ***obeying the voice of the LORD***? Behold, ***to obey is better than sacrifice, and to listen than the fat of rams***. 23 For rebellion is as the sin of divination, and presumption is as iniquity and idolatry. Because ***you have rejected the word of the***

---

11. "Korban," *Wikipedia Encyclopedia.*

LORD, He has also rejected you from being king.

Hence, God places obedience ahead of sacrifice. The gift of an atoning sacrifice from the disobedient is rejected. Thus, the Prophet Samuel taught when you disobey the Lord, you "have rejected the word of the Lord." The fact you intend to later ask for atonement from the Lord by some sacrifice you call upon (*e.g.*, the gift of Jesus' sacrifice) does not wipe out the disobedience. It makes it worse.

It is equivalent to the sin of *where man tries to control God*: *divination.*

The Prophet Samuel says this is also *presumption* on your part. You are presuming on God's good nature that He will accept such sacrificial atonement even when you disobey God in expectation you can cleanse such acts by atonement.

Finally, Samuel says it is *idolatry* because your sin is worshipping your own power to set the terms of what God must accept. *You become your own idol.* You become your own demi-god, if you will, who can set the terms of when God must apply atonement to you.

Consequently, God does not accept atonement, even of an innocent lamb, on behalf of the disobedient. To think so is to practice *divination, rebellion, idolatry* and *iniquity.*

Jesus Was Also Actually Quoting A Common Temple Doctrine of His Day

Jesus' teaching on leaving your sacrifice at the altar and being reconciled first with the one you sinned against (Matt. 5:23-24) was a deliberate paraphrase of a common temple teaching of that day. This lesson was given in relation to atonement. To implement the prophets' lesson that atonement was not magic, but conditional on repentance and reform, the Levite priests created the Days of Ten.

What were the Days of Ten?

In Judaism of Jesus' day, there was a ten day period leading up to the Day of Atonement. (The Day of Atonement was one special day where the entire people were simultaneously to submit to atonement procedures in the Law. Other personal atonements took place during the year.) This ten day period "was designated for seeking forgiveness between individuals."[12] Brad Young explains what this means:

> A person was not prepared to seek divine mercy during the great fast on the Day of Atonement *if he or she had not first sought reconciliation* with his neighbor....The preparation for this [Day]...focused on the *necessity to forgive one another* on a personal level so as to approach God without a bitter heart. *Mercy from above* depended upon *showing mercy to those below*.[13]

The temple teachings from Jesus' era on the Days of Ten used almost identical language as used by Jesus. The teachings said that for "transgressions that are between a person and his or her neighbor, the Day of Atonement effects atonement *only if one has first appeased his neighbor*."[14] It specifies that the Day of Atonement cannot effect atonement unless a person first makes amends for transgressions against his or her neighbor.

Therefore, Jesus was clearly paraphrasing this temple principle on the atonement. Jesus laid down the identical condition:

- before an atonement offering, go be reconciled to the one you offended (Jesus in Matthew 5:23-24).
  is the same as

---

12. Brad H. Young, *The Parables:Jewish Tradition and Christian Interpretation* (Massachusetts: Hendrickson, 2000) at 123.

13. *Id.*, at 123-24.

14. Quoted in *id.*, at 124.

- before an atonement offering, go and first appease the neighbor you offended (Temple lessons on Day of Atonement).

Jesus was obviously extending the principle from the Days of Ten to every sacrifice you bring to the priests *throughout* the year. There were many atoning sacrifices throughout the Biblical calendar year. Jesus did not restrict the principle of the Days of Ten simply to the Day of Atonement. Jesus made it an every-sacrifice principle.

Therefore, once you recognize Jesus' effort to expand temple doctrine to an every-sacrifice principle, you see Jesus is talking about a condition to atonement.

Jesus' meaning is clear: before you can bring your sacrifice (*i.e.*, any one of the many atoning sacrifices throughout the year), you must follow the Days of Ten principle. You must first seek reconciliation with the one you sinned against. It is implied that absent such action, the atonement would be ineffectual to cleanse you from sin.

Is There Any Necessary Maintenance Of The Atonement Covering?

As we quoted at the outset, the second claim by the cheap grace doctrine of Stanley and Fortner was that once the atonement covering applies, God never sees you sinning again. You are supposedly never in jeopardy of losing the forgiveness of God once the atonement initiates to protect you. Is this correct?

Once again, cheap grace has the wrong answer.

John 15:1-6: How Are Those Clean Now Kept Clean in the Future?

Remember that atonement is intended to "*cleanse* the person from his guilt" ('mehatao,' Lev.iv.26, v.6-10)." ("Atonement," *Encyclopedia of Judaism*.)

Jesus in the Metaphor of the Vine (John 15:1-10) is going to pick up on that *cleansing* theme. We will learn, by comparing it to 1 John 1:7-9, that Jesus means to refer to the cleansing of *atonement* in the Metaphor of the Vine.

First, in the Metaphor of the Vine, Jesus is speaking to eleven of the twelve. Judas has left. Jesus says right now they are all "***clean***." (John 15:3, *katharos*.) Jesus explains why: "You are already ***clean*** through the *teaching* I have already given you." (John 15:3.) Such teachings included "repent or perish" (Luke 13:5)[15] and the "heaven maimed" or "hell whole" principle, which clearly makes salvation 100% conditional on repentance and reform. (Mark 9:42-47.)[16] These principles would, if followed, make the eleven *clean* under the atonement principles we discussed above. We shall see, when we examine 1 John 1:7-9, that this is precisely what Jesus meant about *clean* in John 15:1-6.

Assuming for now that Jesus means they were *clean* because of an initial repentance, did Jesus ever also explain how they would remain *clean*? Yes.

Jesus then says that "every branch that bears fruit (*i.e.*, obeys), He (God) is keeping clean." (John 15:2, *katharei* in present active indicative — continuous tense.)

Does this lesson on present *cleanness* and subsequent *cleanness* when bearing fruit have anything to do with atonement? It most certainly does.

For the very same Apostle John who penned those words in John 15:1-6 also used identical words in 1 John 1:7-9 to explain a two fold atonement principle:

1. An *initial* cleansing (katharei) by the blood of Jesus through repentance; and

2. A *subsequent* cleansing (katharei) by the blood of Jesus by ongoing obedience.

15.For full discussion on that passage, see page 87 *et seq.*

16.For full discussion on that passage, see page 45 *e seq.*

Apostle John's Two-Fold Atonement Principle.

In line with Jesus in John 15:1-6, Apostle John tells us the blood of Jesus' *cleansing* applies to a Christian *only after initially* confessing and repenting from sin and then *subsequently* only as we are walking in the light:

> (7) but **if we walk in the light**, as he is in the light, we have fellowship one with another, and **the blood of Jesus his Son cleanseth** [*katharei*, present active indicative] **us from all sin**. (8) If we say that we have no sin, we deceive ourselves, and the truth is not in us. (9) **If we confess our sins**, he is faithful and righteous to forgive us our sins, and [should have] **cleans[ed]** [*katharei*, aorist active subjunctive] **us from all unrighteousness**. (1 John 1:7-9, ASV.)

The exact same vocabulary used in John 15:1-6 is used here: the active form of *katharei*, to cleanse. Apostle John directly lifts out the verb *cleaning* from John 15:1-6. He then uses it in 1 John 1:7 in conjunction with the *blood of Jesus his Son,* saying it keeps us *clean.*

Apostle John thus says if we "confess our sins," then the blood of Jesus should have cleansed us. If we keep on obeying Jesus, then as "we walk in the light," *i.e.*, obey God, the *blood of Jesus* keeps us clean from all sins.

What does *walking in the light* mean here? It is unquestionable that *walks* in 1 John 1:7-9 means *obedience.* This is how it was used a few verses later. In 1 John 2:3-6, John talks about "if we keep his commandments" versus "keepeth not his commandments." Apostle John stresses the importance to "keepeth his word." He then sums up his point, saying he who "abides in him ought himself also to **walk** even as he **walked**." (1 John 2:3-6, ASV.) *Walking in the light* in 1 John 1:9 must therefore mean obeying God's commandments.

Hence, Apostle John takes the same vocabulary and structure of John 15:1-6 on *cleans*, and applies it to *atonement*. John unquestionably then says it initiates by repentance ("confessing") and is maintained by *walking in the light*. John then equates this *walking in the light* with "keeping his commandments."

TABLE 1. **John 15:1-6 Compared to 1 John 1:7-9**

Initial Cleansing (by Blood)	Subsequent Cleansing (by Blood)
Jesus tells apostles right now they are all "**clean**." (John 15:3, *katharos*.) Jesus explains why: "You are already clean through the teaching I have already given you." (John 15:3.) Such teachings included "repent or perish" (Luke 13:5).	Jesus then says that "every branch that bears fruit (*i.e.,* obeys), He (God) is keeping **clean**." (John 15:2, *katharei* in present active indicative — continuous tense.)
"If we confess our sins, he is faithful and righteous to forgive us our sins, and [should have] **cleans[ed]**[*katharei*, aorist active subjunctive] us from all unrighteousness." (1 John 1:9)	"if we walk in the light, as he is in the light, we have fellowship one with another, and the blood of Jesus his Son **cleanseth** [katharei, present active indicative] us from all sin." (1 John 1:7). *Cf.* 1 John 2:3-6.

Impact Of Disobedience & Lack of Contrition On Atonement

A positive requirement always has a negative implication. If you must do something to be clean, the failure to do that something means you will in that situation not be clean.

Here, Apostle John necessarily implies if you do not confess your sins, atonement does not apply in the first place. This gets back to Jesus' statement that you must first 'be reconciled to the one you offended.' (Matthew 5:23-24.) Absent works worthy of repentance, atonement is out-of-the question. As Apostle Peter identically states, "Repent ye therefore, and turn again, that your sins may be ***blotted out***...." (Acts 3:19 ASV.)

The second implication from what John says is pretty clear. He says as "we walk in the light," *i.e.*, obey God, the *blood of Jesus* keeps us clean from all sins. It follows directly that disobedience would mean the atonement is rolled back. We are seen as sinning. Without atonement covering you, you lose God's cleansing of you of sin.

This directly ties back to Jesus' words in John 15:1-6. Jesus says that "every branch that bears fruit (*i.e.*, obeys), He (God) is keeping clean." (John 15:2.) The negative implication would mean that any fruitless branch, *i.e.*, one not walking in the light, will not be kept clean in God's eyes. Just as Apostle John implies in 1 John 1:7-9, atonement ceases its effectiveness upon disobedience.

In fact, Jesus does not leave this to simply implication. Jesus in the Metaphor of the Vine specifically warns the eleven apostles who are "clean right now" of the loss of salvation of even a "branch in me." Jesus says a "branch in me" that is not producing fruit is "taken away" (John 15:2.) The branch taken away Jesus later says is "thrown outside" and burned. (John 15:6.) This is obviously a picture of final condemnation in hell.[17]

Obedience Doctrine of Jesus Matches His Maintenance-Atonement Doctrine

We can corroborate further we are correctly understanding the continuous nature of the condition to atonement by examining Jesus' doctrine on obedience. We can be sure that indeed Tyndale was right about this aspect of double-justification—the necessity of a believer to *walk in the light* to remain clean in God's sight. This will then vindicate the other reformers who held this same view as Tyndale: Erasmus, Melancthon, Bucer, Menno Simons, and the mature Luther.[18]

---

17. For extensive discussion on the Metaphor of the Vine, see the chapter beginning at page 343.

18. See "A Parade of Witnesses Includes Tyndale and Shockingly The (Mature) Luther Too" on page iv *et seq.* of the Preface.

What was Jesus' doctrine on obedience? Jesus was adamant that professing belief in Him as Lord is meaningless unless you also obey Him. Jesus said those who call Him 'Lord, Lord' but "do not do what I say" have a flawed concept of what it means to say that He is Lord. (Luke 6:46.)[19] If you call Him Lord "but do not do His will" Jesus will tell you "I never knew you." (Matt. 7:21.) Jesus said those who profess to want to obey Him, but do not actually do so are lost. But those sinners who repent and obey will enter heaven instead of those who merely profess they will obey Him but do not do so. (Parable of the Two Sons. Matthew 21:28-31.)[20]

Jesus means obedience is not optional for those who call Him Lord. Salvation is gained or lost depending on actual obedience to Him, not mere profession one way or the other.

Reverend William Paley (1743-1805), a famous Christian preacher in his day, gave an excellent exposition in accord regarding Jesus' doctrine on obedience in Matthew 7:21-22.

Who was William Paley? "He was the greatest divine of the period," gifted with "remarkable vigor and clearness of intellect, and originality of character."[21] His "perspicacity of intellect and simplicity of style are almost unrivaled." Paley formulated in 1802 the famous watchmaker argument in favor of God as designer of the universe.

In Paley's Sermons in *The Works of William Paley* (1825) volume six at page 201 *et seq.*, we find this excellent analysis of Matthew 7:21. Paley explains what Jesus had to mean on the role of obedience and faith in salvation:

---

19. "And why call ye me, Lord, Lord, and do not the things which I say?" (Luke 6:46 ASV.)

20. For full discussion, see page 105 *et seq.,* and page 566.

21. *The Chambers Cyclopedia of English Literature* (1844) under "Dr. Paley" at page 651 *et seq.*

For instance, what words can be **plainer, more positive, or more decisive of this point** than our Saviour's own? "Not every one that saith unto me, Lord, Lord, shall enter into the kingdom of Heaven, but he that doeth the will of my Father which is in Heaven." [Matt. 7:21.] **There can be no doubt but that they who are here introduced as crying out to Jesus Christ 'Lord, Lord,' are supposed to believe in him**; yet neither their devotion, **nor their faith** which prompted it, **were sufficient to save them**. Id., at 214-215.

As the *Free Will Baptist* (January 1860) at 78 likewise comments on the same passage: "[In] Matthew 7:21-27...[n]o fault is found with the *faith* of those that were cast out, but for disobedience they were condemned."

After discussing Matthew 7:21, Paley next explains how Jesus re-emphasizes the same point in the very next sentence. Jesus speaks unquestionably of those who had faith, *i.e.*, workers of prophecies and miracles in Jesus' name, but whose faith alone did not suffice:

Nay, farther our Lord, in the same passage, proceeds to tell his hearers, that many will say to him in that day, "Have we not prophesied in thy name, and in thy name have cast out devils, and in thy name done many wonderful works?" [Matt. 7:22.] **It cannot be questioned but that they who do these things in Christ's name believe in Christ**. Yet what will be their reception? "I will profess unto you I never knew you."[22] And who are they who shall be

---

22. The expression "I never knew you" is an axiom in that culture. A parent who did not want to see their child killed due to wilful disobedience (under the Mosaic Law) in this life would deny ever knowing the child. The effect of such temporal relief was that the child was cut off from any inheritance from the parent. See my prior book, *Jesus' Words Only* (2007) at 208 fn.13.

thus repulsed and rejected? No others than **the workers of iniquity**. "Depart from me, ye workers of iniquity." [Matt. 7:23.] *Id.* at 215.

Apostle John's Doctrine On Obedience

To uncover Jesus' 'walk in the light' requirement in John 15:1-6, it is likewise helpful to compare Apostle John's doctrine on obedience. After all, Apostle John is the one penning these words in John 15:1-6. Who better than John to give us insight on their meaning. The first proof, of course, is John's view that as we *walk in the light*, the blood of Jesus keeps us clean in God's sight. (1 John 1:7-9, ASV.) The second, and conclusive proof, is we find John saying the same thing in 1 John 2:3-6. As you read this, ask yourself whether Christ's blood can conceivably apply to a disobedient Christian:

> (3) And hereby we know that we know him, *if we keep his commandments*. (4) He that saith, I [deeply] know [*egnoka* Gk.] him, and **keepeth not his commandments**, is a **liar**, and the truth is not in him; (5) but **whoso keepeth his word**, in him verily hath the **love of God been perfected**. Hereby we know that **we are in him**: (6) he that saith he abideth in him ought himself also to **walk** even as he **walked**.[23] (1 John 2:3-6)(ASV)

As mentioned before, this passage involves Apostle John speaking again of *walking*. Thus, when he said as "we walk in the light" the "blood of Jesus" cleanses us (1 John 1:7), we see 1 John 2:3-6 identifies what *walking* means. It clearly means "keepeth his word" which is equated with "keepeth... his commandments." (1 John 2:3,5.)

23.*Cf.* "[The man who] hath **walked** in my statutes, and hath kept mine ordinances, to deal truly; he is **just**, he shall surely live, saith the Lord Jehovah." (Eze 18:9 ASV.) For more on justification, see page 34.

What John also clearly says in 1 John 2:3-6 is that if you disobey Jesus, then you do not *thoroughly* know Him. The Greek word *egnoka* is formed by the prefix *epi* plus *ginoska*. The prefix *epi* here means *above the norm, intensely.* Thus, Vine's says its primary meaning is "to know thoroughly (epi, 'intensive' [of] ginosko, 'to know.')"[24]

Thus, you do not *thoroughly* know Jesus if you do not obey Him. Your lack of obedience is not merely a reflection of your never having *faith* in Christ. Rather, it shows your faith is the same shallow belief that demons have. Your disobedience proves you do not **thoroughly** know Jesus. As a result, your disobedience demonstrates the "love of God has [not yet] been perfected in you." (1 John 2:3-6.)

Hence, be careful to note that if you are disobedient to Christ, John does not say it proves you never believed in Jesus. John knew those religious rulers who had "truly believed [*epi-pisteousin*] in Him but would not confess Him." (John 12:42; see page 445.) John wrote prior to his Gospel that such "cowards...will be thrown into the lake of burning sulfur" with "unbelievers." (Rev. 21:8.) Thus John knew disobedience is proof you do not know Jesus well enough. It is proof that the love of God has not yet been perfected in you.

In that light, 1 John 2:4 adequately explains what happens in 1 John 1:7-9 to the Christian who is not walking in the light. Such a Christian needs to repent and confess to have the blood of Christ cleanse them anew. You may have believed in Jesus but it ended there because you disobey Him. Disobedience makes your acceptance vain: "He that saith, I [deeply] *know* [egnoska] him, and **keepeth not his commandments**, is a **liar**." (1 Jn 2:4.)

> "If we are not walking in the light, we have no warrant for believing that our sins are covered. There is no assurance of salvation while you are living in disobedience." John Piper
>
> *Let Us Walk In The Light of God* **(1985)**

24. Vine's Commentary on *epiginoska*'s usage in 2 Pe 2:20 and 22.

Isaiah Prophecy of Messiah Confirms Conditional Atonement

Remember we previously quoted Don Fortner, the Pastor of Grace Baptist Church in Danville, Kentucky? He had written in *God Sees No Sin*[25] that once atonement is applied, God never sees you sin again: "God *sees no sin* in His people...The Son of God... made an end of our sins, and justified and sanctified us by His blood."

However, in Isaiah, God warns that people will erroneously one day think when they sin that God does not see their sin. They will instead seek power over God with "incantations" — the invocation of mere words — in the hope these words protect them from God seeing their sin. Speaking of those deluded by such verbal "incantations," God says:

> You said, "no one sees me" — but your wisdom and your knowledge have misled you. (Isaiah 47:10 Dead Sea Scrolls Bible "DSSB.")[26]

In a word, people will wrongly think atonement applies so effectively that God never sees their ongoing sinning again as long as they utter an incantation. To disabuse people of this idea, God in Isaiah makes clear that the Servant who will suffer and atone for sin does not redeem those who recite incantations but only this type of person:

> And *a Redeemer will come to Zion, to those in Jacob, who turn from transgression,* says the Lord. (Isaiah 59:20, DSSB.)

God explains His principles of salvation that the Servant's sacrifice in chapter fifty-three provides:

---

25. Dan Fortner, *God Sees No Sin* at http://www.pristinegrace.org/media.php?id=297 (accessed 8-25-07).

26. The Isaiah text was recovered in the 1950s at the Dead Sea town of Qumran. It was finally translated in 1999 by Abegg, Flint and Ulrich as the *Dead Sea Scrolls Bible: The Oldest Known Bible Translated for the First Time Into English* (DSSB.)

(7) Let the wicked *forsake his way,* and the unrighteous person his thoughts; let him return to the Lord, and *He will have mercy upon him, and He will freely pardon*. (Isaiah 55, DSSB.)

Deducing what this means is not difficult. If you "turn from transgression" and "forsake" your sinful ways and return to the Lord, God will *freely* pardon. Messiah will come to redeem those who do so.

This redemption by Messiah was synonymous with atonement. In Hebrew, the word for *atonement* (*kapper, kipper*) derives from the noun *kofer*, which means *ransom*.[27] The activity of *ransoming* is also called *redeeming*.

Thus, the very prophecy of Messiah in Isaiah teaches the same principle of atonement, redemption and ransom as Jesus did. Atonement initiates for and belongs to the humble and contrite.

This principle only becomes stronger the more you read all the Messianic passages in Isaiah. After promising the suffering servant would come to take sins away (atonement), God repeats His salvation principles in Isaiah 66:2 (DSSB): "This is the one whom I will look upon: the one who is *humble* and *contrite in spirit* and who *trembles at my word*...." God explains it is these alone who will "inherit my Holy Mountain." (Isaiah 59:13). The words *humble* and *contrite* (about sin) are synonyms for repentance from sin. The words *trembles at my words* are a synonym for obedience.

Two verses later, God says of this inheritance: "For thus says the high and lofty One who inhabits eternity, whose name is Holy: he will dwell in the height and the holy place, and also with the *one who is of a contrite and humble spirit*, to revive the spirit of the contrite, to revive the spirit of the humble...." (Isaiah 59:15 DSSB.)

27.See "Atonement," *Encyclopedia of Judaism*. It explains: "The root ('kipper'), to make atonement.... seems to be a derivative from the noun 'kofer' (ransom) and to have meant originally 'to atone.'"

This is the same message as Jesus gives in the instruction to leave the sacrifice at the altar and go be reconciled to anyone you offended. Only the repentant and contrite about sin will receive an effective atonement.

Ezekiel's Prophetic Message on Salvation

A further confirmation of what Jesus is saying is by finding the parallel doctrine in Ezekiel. The Prophet has the identical logic to what Jesus says in Matthew 5:23-24.

Ezekiel teaches when you are sinning, but repent (and do works worthy of repentance), you have (eternal) life, and all your sins are forgotten. (Note the order: repentance including works-of-reconciliation followed by wiping out of past sins.) However, when you are righteous but sin again, you (spiritually) die, and all your good deeds are forgotten. Life and death, in the spiritual sense, hence turns on obedience. Failure of obedience means death. Repentance and continuing to obey (maintenance) keeps you abiding in life. Despite Prophet Ezekiel delivering this message direct from God Almighty, few Christians have read this. Let's listen:

> And thou, son of man, say unto the children of thy people, "The righteousness of the righteous shall not deliver him in the day of his transgression; and as for the wickedness of the wicked, he shall not fall thereby in the day that he ***turneth from his wickedness***; neither shall ***he that is righteous be able to live thereby in the day that he sinneth***. (13) When I say to the righteous, that he shall surely ***live***; if ***he trust to his righteousness***, and ***commit iniquity***, none of his righteous deeds shall be remembered; but in his iniquity that he hath committed, therein shall he ***die***. (14) Again, when I say unto the wicked, Thou shalt surely ***die***; if he turn from his sin, and do that which is lawful and right; (15) if the wicked ***restore the***

> ***pledge, give again that which he had taken
> by robbery****, walk in the statutes of life, com-
> mitting no iniquity; **he shall surely live**, he
> shall not die. (16) **None of his sins** that he hath
> committed **shall be remembered** against him:
> he hath done that which is lawful and right; he
> shall surely **live**." (Eze 33:12-16 ASV.)

What could be more plain? What could be more decisive on what Jesus teaches? Ezekiel's sequence in verses fifteen and sixteen precisely match the command of Jesus to be
reconciled to the one you offended before atonement applies:

TABLE 2. Parallel Ezekiel 33 to Matthew 5:23-24

First Be Reconciled	Then Atonement
"if the wicked restore the pledge, give again that which he had taken by rob- bery, walk in the statutes of life, committing no iniq- uity...." (Ezekiel 33:15).	"None of his sins that he hath committed shall be remembered against him...." (Ezekiel 33:16).
"leave there thy [atoning] sacrifice before the altar, and go thy way, first be rec- onciled to thy brother" (Matt 5:24a)	"and then come and offer thy [atoning] sacrifice." (Matt 5:24b)

*Cheap Grace Commentators On Leaving
Your Sacrifice At The Temple*

The message of Jesus on atonement is not welcomed
by faith alone doctrine. It would imply a condition other than
faith is necessary to have atonement apply. Jesus would
require first, just as the prophets had claimed, repentance

from sin and works-worthy-of-repentance — what Jesus describes as making reconciliation with the one you offended. You are to do what it takes to allay the righteous anger of anyone you offended.

How do cheap grace commentators deal with Matthew 5:23-24? Do they elucidate its meaning by any plain reading? No. They do everything possible to downplay that this passage has anything to do with atonement.

Clarke: A Commentator In Turmoil

Clarke makes a commentary on this passage. He gets this right initially. Clarke says Jesus means "Do not attempt to bring any offering to God while thou...hast any difference with thy neighbor, which thou hast not used thy diligence to get adjusted."

However then Clarke tries to spin this to be about repentance prior to an "act of religious worship." He does not want you to see Jesus is talking about *sacrifice* — Atonement.

Clarke next tries to take the focus off the need for you to obtain forgiveness from sin against another. He says that the real problem is you have "enmity in your heart" and this needs to be removed. ***Clarke's claim is false***.

Rather, Jesus says the problem to overcome is that someone else has "something against you." ***It is not at all that you have some burning anger against the other***.

However, toward the end of his commentary, Clarke correctly restates Jesus' point. "My own obstinacy...must render me ***utterly unfit to receive*** any good from God's hands...." Yet, Clarke cannot bring himself to acknowledge this obstinacy impacts salvation. Clarke cannot say Jesus refuses atonement until one resolves their obstinacy about sin. So at the last second, Clark spins this again away from such a conclusion. He repeats the idea that my worship (not atonement) is unacceptable prior to repentance. What Jesus supposedly is talking about is not atonement but whether we bring to God "worship...in an acceptable manner."

One can see that faith-alone commentary is in turmoil as it tries to explain this passage. The reason is this passage utterly destroys faith alone doctrine. Tyndale was right.

Conclusion

Hence, while most today claim someone can come to Jesus in an ungodly state and be justified by faith alone, they do not understand the nature of atonement in the age of Christ. They think Abraham's faith is alone sufficient in the era of Christ. Yet, Abraham would have known that God put the atonement system in effect through Moses *after Abraham*. In fact, God says He deliberately delivered orders on "sacrifices or offerings" for the *first* time only after He first gave the Law (principally the Ten Commandments) to obey. (Jer. 7:22-23.) God says He did so to prove the priority of obedience over sacrifice. *Id.* Hence, when Jesus came to "fulfil the (Mosaic) Law" and not to "abolish it" (Matt. 5:17), Jesus did not come to fulfill any pre-Mosaic principle of atonement alive during Abraham's age. *Jesus' atonement was only under the Mosaic Law.* His atonement is hence subject to all the clarifications made by the Prophets on the *conditional effectiveness* for atonement under the Mosaic Law. Thus, in a *post-Abrahamic age*, even Abraham would know that no one who seeks that atoning sacrifice of Jesus to apply to them can accept the *free gift of God* on the altar and also imagine it has unconditional effectiveness. Abraham can read that the Mosaic principles are "eternal for all generations." (Ex. 27:21; 30:21; Lev. 6:18; 7:36; 10:9; 17:7; 23:14, 21, 41; 24:3; Num. 10:8; 15:15.) Hence, if you want the benefit of Jesus' atonement to apply to you, you have to accept it on Jesus' terms. His atonement only has a conditional effectiveness. You may not plea His blood until you "go thy way [and] first be reconciled to thy brother, and then come and offer thy [atoning sacrifice]." (Matt. 5:24.) As Apostle John said, "confess your sins" and "keep walking in the light," and the "blood of Jesus will keep cleansing you." (1 John 1:7-9.)

2 *The Repentant Goes Home Justified & The Shallowly Righteous Does Not*

Who Goes Home Justified? Who Does Not?

Jesus taught how one *is* justified and *not* justified in the Parable of the Publican and the Pharisee. Jesus uses the same word for *justified* as Paul used everywhere that Paul taught about justification. Jesus clearly ties initial justification to repentance from sin. Jesus then ties the lack of justification to a similar lack of repentance — this time over the failure to recognize an incomplete obedience. Hence, Jesus means by justification God's standards for imputing atonement to you, as discussed in the prior chapter.

Is there any way to square this parable with the idea that Jesus teaches justification initiates and is maintained by a moment of faith, let alone by faith alone? We will explore the arguments that try to square it that way.

First, let's listen to Jesus alone.

> (9) And he spake also this parable unto certain **who trusted in themselves that they were righteous**, and set all others at nought:[1] (10) Two men went up into the temple to pray; the one **a Pharisee, and the other a publican.** (11) The Pharisee stood and prayed thus with himself, **God, I thank thee, that I am not as the rest of men, extortioners, unjust, adulterers, or even as this publican. (12) I fast twice in**

---

1. Luke is clearer: "To some who were confident of their own righteousness and looked down on everybody else...." (Luke 18:9.)

---

the week; I give tithes of all that I get. (13)
But the publican, standing afar off, *would not
lift up so much as his eyes unto heaven, but
smote his breast, saying, God, be thou merciful to me a sinner.* (14) I say unto you, This
man went down to his house *justified rather
than the other*: for every one that *exalteth
himself* shall be humbled; but he that *humb-
leth himself* shall be exalted. (Luke 18:9-14
ASV.)

This parable is not hard to discern, particularly if you
recognize that Jesus uses a Pharisee as the religious ruler to
contrast against a Publican.

Let's put the comparisons and contrasts side-by-side
in a table so the meaning is inescapable.

TABLE 1. Jesus' Doctrine of Justification

Justified	Unjustified
"publican" (v. 10)	"Pharisee" (v. 10)
"humbled himself" (v. 14)	"exalted himself" (v. 14)
"smote his breast, saying, God, be thou merciful to me a sinner"	"(11) God, I thank thee, that I am not as the rest of men, extortioners, unjust, adulterers, or even as this publican. (12) I fast twice in the week; I give tithes of all that I get."
"standing afar off, would not lift up so much as his eyes unto heaven" (v. 13)	"trusted in themselves that they were righteous" (v. 9)

Thus, the Publican *does something different* than the
Pharisee. The only difference is the Publican repents from sin
he committed. The Publican sees the Law which he has failed
to obey and he confesses his wrong. Thus, he "humbles" himself, as Jesus puts it. The Pharisee does not *act* similarly. He
fails to humble himself. He does not see how his shallow
knowledge of God's Law causes his conduct to fall below the
Law's standards. Instead, he *exalts* himself. He praises himself and his *two relatively insignificant good deeds* of *fasting*
and *tithing*.

Is the Pharisee's problem in the parable that he has sufficient good deeds and *no sin*? Is the Pharisees' problem that he thinks he is justified by obedience, but that is a wrong salvation formula (even an heretical one)?

The Modern Faith-alone gospel asserts, as we discuss below, that the Pharisee's flaw which causes lack of justification is he in fact had *no sin* and was *one-hundred percent obedient.* The Pharisee supposedly did not realize this is not enough to be saved. This way faith-alone advocates can maintain works of obedience supposedly do not justify. By contrast, the Publican was supposedly *disobedient* and because he had faith alone, the cheap grace proponents insist this is why he went home justified. This interpretation is shocking to say the least.

Before we give time to the Cheap Grace Gospel proponents to argue these two points, let's do our own careful analysis.

First, what did Jesus really intend us to see was the error of the Pharisee? What also did Jesus want us to recognize as the *cause* of the Pharisee's failing?

Pharisees' Flaw Was Failure To Repent Of Sin

First and foremost, it is obvious Jesus wants us to understand that *had* the Pharisee repented from sin, he too would be justified. This was the missing piece in the Pharisee's visit to the temple. It is the only behavior different between the two men. Jesus calls it here *humbling* yourself. The Pharisee instead *exalted* himself.

Yet, this simple truth would destroy 'justification by faith alone' doctrine if the truth of what Jesus taught were ever spread far and wide. Thus, this obvious reading is ignored. Or the passage is twisted, as we shall see.

Pharisees Are Jesus' Example Of Shallow-Law Keepers

Second, Jesus says in the parable that the cause of the failure of the Pharisee in the Temple to repent was his incomplete knowledge and adherence to God's Law.

Jesus says the Pharisee in the Temple praises himself for tithing. Jesus elsewhere said Pharisees were good about following this less important command to tithe. However, Jesus faulted the Pharisees for ignoring the weightier commands of the Law. (Matt. 23:23). The Pharisee in the Temple also was right that he followed the fasting rules twice a week. However, that was a command from the Oral Law,[2] not the written Law given Moses. Jesus said elsewhere that the Pharisees negated the written Law by requiring obedience to their Oral Law — "mere commandments of men." (Matt. 15:9.)

Thus, the cause of the Pharisee's failure to repent was his sect's shallow knowledge of God's Law. In other words, the Pharisee was being destroyed by his shallow *belief* in what laws applied to himself. This was precisely what God said destroyed the people in Hosea 4:6. God said in Hosea that because the religious leaders were no longer teaching the full Law, the people were being destroyed.[3] This is why Jesus elsewhere taught only when your "righteousness exceeds the righteousness of the Pharisees can you enter the kingdom of heaven." (Matt. 5:20.) Their righteousness was shallow.

Hence, contrary to what faith alone doctrine insists, Jesus was not teaching justification was lacking because the Pharisee was perfectly obeying the Law but lacked faith. Rather, Jesus is pointing precisely at someone who does not

---

2. The Pharisees fasted twice a week — on Mondays and Thursdays. This is deducible from an early Second Century document — the *Didache*, sometimes called the *Teaching of the Twelve Apostles*. It instructs: "Be careful not to schedule your fasts at the times when the hypocrites fast. They fast on the second (Monday) and fifth (Thursday) day of the week, therefore make your fast on the fourth (Wednesday) day and the Preparation day (Friday, the day of preparation for the Sabbath-Saturday)." (*Didache* 8:1.)

3. For full discussion, see 151 *et seq.*

---

keep the Law but merely *thinks* he does so as he **waters it down**. The Pharisees had replaced the written Law with their **oral** traditions. Hence, the Pharisee's doctrine was so off that as he stands in front of the temple he can assure himself that he is obedient without realizing he was not obedient to God's true Laws. He may have been faithful in keeping the oral law which his compatriots invented. This permitted himself to engage in self-justification by means of shallow doctrines. But it did not make the Pharisee truly obedient to God's Law and hence justified.

Hence, this parable is not saying one is lacking justification if one obeys the Law perfectly.

Smug Self-Righteousness: What It Represents In Jesus' Lesson

The Pharisee in the parable also thanked God that he was not like those who were "extortioners, unjust, and adulterers" such as the Publicans. Yet, was this true? Or was it a smug self-righteous attitude?

Jesus elsewhere said the Pharisees taught a diluted doctrine on adultery, permitting lust for a married woman if it did not end up in the act of adultery.[4] By having a wrong view of the Law on adultery, this Pharisee's self-examination ended up shallow and defective on the very issue of adultery which this Pharisee was congratulating himself that he obeyed.

Thus, the danger for the Pharisee was two-fold. He thought obedience to the Oral Law pleased God when in fact it had the opposite effect.

Second, when the Pharisee in the parable prayed to God, he did not have an adequate and clear *knowledge* of the Law. He could not do a proper self-examination. Such knowledge of Scripture is crucial to repent in favor of obedience to obtain justification in God's sight. (Deut. 6:25.) Without knowledge of the Law, this leads to self-righteousness. You

---

4. See page 165 *et seq.*

are left to rely upon your own perceptions of right and wrong. Indubitably, due to self-interest, this leads to self-affirming thoughts. In a word, smug self-righteousness will result.

The Pharisee's mistake was thus two-fold: he trusted in obedience to the Oral Law would impress God. He was also smug in his knowledge of the Law, assuming incorrectly that he kept it perfectly.[5] This closed his mind to repentance.

This smugness is thus clearly what led the Pharisee to fail to repent. Jesus wanted us to see his blindness was about the Law's provisions. With a mind closed against the Law's principles, the Pharisee became smug about his right standing with God. The Pharisee was unable to even repent properly about adultery because of wrong doctrine on when it takes place. The Pharisee's law-negating doctrines doomed him to never be able to properly repent. His resultant smugness locked him into a false sense of being right with God.

Was The Pharisee Being Scolded On His Doctrine Of Justification By Jesus?

The faith alone advocate, we shall see, is going to claim Jesus was scolding the Pharisee instead on his doctrine of justification. Allegedly, Jesus wants us to realize the Pharisee erroneously thought that he could maintain justification by works of obedience.

However, if Jesus taught that no one is justified by obeying the Law, Jesus would contradict *numerous* Scriptures, including provisions in the Law of Moses. (Deut. 6:25, discussed in the next section.) Jesus would therefore become a false prophet under Deuteronomy 13:1-5. This says anyone with signs and wonders who seduces us from following the Law is to be regarded as a false prophet even if their signs and wonders "come to pass." But Jesus did not teach justifi-

---

5. Paul reflected having precisely this self-image of his time as a Pharisee. He said: "as touching the law, [I was] a Pharisee; (6)... as touching the righteousness which is in the law, found blameless." (Phillipians 3:5-6 ASV.)

---

cation was without obedience to the Law. Only the Modern Gospel of Cheap Grace does so. It tries to impress such an heresy on top of Jesus' parable. To do this, they must engage in a highly distorted reading.

To answer this issue, we need to look at the Law and the Prophets, and what they teach on justification.

Justification In the Law of Moses

Deuteronomy 6:25 states:

> And it shall be righteousness unto us, if we observe to do all this commandment before Jehovah our God, as he hath commanded us. (ASV).

This teaches that ongoing justification is from *observing to do all the commandments* God had given to Moses. Notice this is not explaining how justification *initiates*. This is talking about how justification is *maintained.*

The Lutheran scholars Keil & Delitzsch in their *Commentary on the Old Testament* agree on this meaning of Deuteronomy 6:25:

> [O]ur righteousness will consist in the observance of the law; we shall be **regarded** and treated **by God as righteous**, if we are diligent in the observance of the law.

Plaut, a Jewish commentator, concurs. (See Footnote 10 on page 137.) Thus, God taught in Deuteronomy 6:25 that if we obey the law it will impute righteousness to us. It was the identical principle Jesus had for when atonement applies, as demonstrated in the prior chapter.

The same is found in Leviticus 18:5.

> Ye shall therefore **keep my statutes**, and mine ordinances; which **if a man do**, he shall **live** in them: I am Jehovah. (Lev 18:5 ASV.)[6]

Justification In The Prophets

We will see the same principle again in this quote from Ezekiel:

> But if a man be *just*, and do that which is lawful and right (Eze 18:5 ASV.)
>
> .... [and] hath walked in my statutes, and hath kept mine ordinances, to deal truly; he is *just*, he shall surely live, saith the Lord Jehovah. (Eze 18:9 ASV.)

Hence, the obedient is *just* and he will *live*.

Likewise, the correct translation of Habakkuk 2:4 is that the "just shall *live* by his faithfulness." In Hebrew, this means *obedient living*.[7] The fact the Septuagint of 247 B.C. translated this passage with an ambiguous Greek word *pistis*, which can mean either *faithfulness* or *faith*, has led commentators to shallow out Habakkuk's meaning of justification. They have often opted to translate it as *faith*, not *faithfulness* in several English translation.[8] However, we cannot permit a

---

6. Paul quotes this verse and understood this is as "righteousness of the law." (Romans 10:5; Gal. 3:12.) Paul then appears to say after Christ, righteousness is no longer by obeying the Law, but now is by having *pistis,* typically translated as *faith.* Paul says "the Law is not of faith (*pistis*)." (Gal. 3:11-12.) However, unless Paul meant *faithfulness* by *pistis* in his doctrine, Paul would be contradicting *inspired* Scripture. If so, Paul would be a false prophet. (Deut. 13:1-5; Isaiah 8:20.) Thus, if Paul meant to suggest that Leviticus 18:5 were ever superseded in the NT, this would nullify God's word that these words given Moses were "***eternal for all generations***." See Ex. 27:21; 30:21; Lev. 6:18; 7:36; 10:9; 17:7; 23:14, 21, 41; 24:3; Num. 10:8. Therefore, either we have mistranslated or misunderstood Paul or, by the Bible's very blunt and harsh rule, Paul is a false prophet. This is fully discussed in my prior book, *Jesus' Words Only* (2007). As we shall see, Paul often meant *faithfulness* (obedient living) by *pistis. See* page 468. If translated that way, Paul is fully consistent with the Law and Prophets. Yet, the dilemma of what Paul teaches when tension exists with Jesus' words or the Law & Prophets is non-existent for the *true* Christian. The true follower of Jesus obviously follows whatever Jesus teaches and wherever He leads. See *Jesus' Words Only* (2007).

Greek translation like the Septuagint to change God's word in Habakkuk 2:4. Nor would that translation error — no matter what respected figure was misled by such a mistranslation[9] — ever let us ignore Deuteronomy 6:25 and Ezekiel 18:5, 9, and a host of other passages on justification. Especially, when the Lord Jesus has the identical view of justification as we find in the Law and the Prophets.

What About Genesis 15:6?

There are no other passages in the Scripture that deal with justification. What about Genesis 15:6? It was another Septuagint mistranslation that misled respected New Testament figures to see that verse as dealing with justification. *Genesis 15:6 had nothing to do with justification whatsoever in the original Hebrew text.* An erroneous understanding was born solely due to a defect in the Septuagint Greek

---

7. In most English texts where Paul quotes Habakkuk in its Septuagint translation, *pistis* is rendered as *faith* rather than *faithfulness.* This translation would make it appear Paul was duped by the ambiguity in the Greek word *pistis.* However, no such ambiguity is present in the Hebrew original word *emunah.* The Hebrew word *emunah* in Habakkuk 2:4 is derived from *aman,* "to be firm, last." When used as a personal attribute of man, it means fidelity in word and deed. See Jer.7:28; Jer. 9:2; Psalm 37:3. However, for doctrinal reasons, many English translations of Habakkuk 2:4 go back and alter the Hebrew translation to the impossible rendering of *faith.* Only a few evangelical translations of Habakkuk 2:4 are faithful to the original Hebrew text. For example, we read: "by his **steadfastness** liveth" (YLT); "faithfulness" (God's Word); and "faithful to God" (Good News Bible).

8. Professor Dunning, Professor of Theology at Trevecca Nazarene College in Nashville, Tennessee, did a thorough analysis of the inappropriate ambiguity injected into Habakkuk 2:4 by the Septuagint Greek Translation. See *Jesus' Words Only* (2007) at 272-76.

9. On the fact of this misleading translation and how it has impacted NT doctrine, including in how it advances a doctrine of justification at odds with Jesus, see my prior book, *Jesus' Words Only* (2007) at 272-73, 297-98, 507-08.

Jesus' Words On Salvation   **35**

translation of 247 B.C. That translation alone created the possibility that justification of an individual was in view. However, in the original Hebrew, such a reading is missing.[10]

Hence, Jesus' teaching of justification by repentance from sin is completely consistent with all prior scripture. Nothing refutes it. And nothing impels us to abandon Jesus' lessons.

TABLE 2. **Justification In Ezekiel 18: Good Deeds Lose Value When You Sin. A Mirror Of The Parable Of The Publican And The Pharisee**

Justified	Unjustified
Again, when the wicked man *turneth away from his wickedness* that he hath committed, and *doeth that which is lawful and right*, he shall save his soul alive. (28) Because he considereth, and *turneth away from all his transgressions* that he hath committed, he shall surely live, he shall not die. Eze 18:27-28 ASV	But when the righteous turneth away from his righteousness, and committeth iniquity, and doeth according to all the abominations that the wicked man doeth, shall he live? *None of his righteous deeds that he hath done shall be remembered*: in his trespass that he hath trespassed, and in his sin that he hath sinned, in them shall he die. Eze 18:24 ASV

---

10. See "Does Genesis 15:6 Support Paul's Dispensing With Repentance?" on page 485 *et seq*. A brief synopsis is provided here. The meaning in Hebrew of Genesis 15:6 is unquestionable. When it says that "he believed the Lord, and [he] counted it to him for righteousness" (KJV), the second *he* is interpolated. In normal Hebrew syntax (and English too incidentally), the second *he* is to be identified with the *he* in the first clause: Abram aka Abraham. Thus, it was Abraham *counting* it (*i.e.*, the promise of 15:5 of children in old age) to *Him* (the Lord) as a righteous deed. But the Septuagint Greek gnarled terribly Genesis 15:6. (This is what Paul quotes.) It said, "and it was counted to him for righteousness." What was being counted? And who was counting? The Septuagint Greek translation opened up ambiguities that are simply not present in the Hebrew. The passage from beginning to end had nothing to do with the doctrine of justification. For further discussion, see *Jesus' Words Only* (2007) at 251-53, 272, 506-07 and xxix.

TABLE 2. Justification In Ezekiel 18: Good Deeds Lose Value When You Sin. A Mirror Of The Parable Of The Publican And The Pharisee

Justified	Unjustified
Publican - turned from wickedness	Pharisee - recites obedience to lesser command of tithing and to oral law on fasting.
Publican - repented from sin	Pharisee - failed to repent from sin

MacArthur's Spin To Prove This Parable Teaches Justification By Faith Alone

John MacArthur defends a faith alone reading of the Parable of the Pharisee and the Publican.

Thus, when MacArthur discusses Jesus' doctrine of justification in this passage, he claims it is compatible with faith alone doctrine. To accomplish this, MacArthur claims the Pharisees were legalists. As proven in the later chapter on the Pharisees, this is a false depiction of the Pharisees.[11] The faith-alone interpretation of Jesus' parable, such as MacArthur offers, collapses when we correct the wrong view of the Pharisees upon which his argument relies.

MacArthur begins with a wise approach:

> But the one occasion where ***Jesus actually declared someone 'justified'*** provides the ***best*** insight into the doctrine as He taught it.[12]

This is absolutely the case. The best source of the doctrine on justification should be Jesus. When Jesus declares someone *justified*, we need to find out why.

---

11. See "Exceeding The Righteousness Of The Shallowly Righteous — Matthew 5:20." on page 147 *et seq.*

12. John MacArthur, "Jesus' Perspective on Sola Fide," (2004) at http://www.biblebb.com/files/MAC/sf-solafide.htm (last accessed 4/8/2007).

However, as we shall see, MacArthur will impress on top of Jesus' words foreign ideas to make the foreign ideas palatable, and allegedly consistent with what Jesus teaches. Yet, those foreign ideas supplant and destroy Jesus' message on justification.

To save belief-alone-for-justification, MacArthur commits two misrepresentations. He falsely depicts the publican (tax-gatherer) and the Pharisee. Yet, MacArthur initially summarizes this parable accurately.

> He [Jesus] also told this parable to certain ones who trusted in themselves that they were righteous, and viewed others with contempt: 'Two men went up into the temple to pray, one a Pharisee, and the other a tax-gatherer. The Pharisee stood and was praying thus to himself, "God, I thank Thee that I am not like other people: swindlers, unjust, adulterers, or even like this tax-gatherer. I fast twice a week; I pay tithes of all that I get." But the tax-gatherer, standing some distance away, was even unwilling to lift up his eyes to heaven, but was beating his breast, saying, "God, be merciful to me, the sinner!" I tell you, this man went down to his house *justified* rather than the other; for everyone who exalts himself shall be humbled, but he who humbles himself shall be exalted." (Luke 18:9-14, emphasis added).

To this point, MacArthur is correctly summarizing the parable.

So why was the man who repented of sin justified but the man who failed to do so unjustified? The answer is blaring and obvious: *repentance is key*.

However, MacArthur will claim that the one who is unjustified is so because he had *successfully engaged in complete obedience* to the Law. And with that presupposition added to the parable, Jesus means supposedly to expose that perfect obedience cannot impute righteousness (justification) to you.

Then the justified Publican is supposedly justified — according to MacArthur — because he had been disobedient but now has faith, and hence is justified despite disobedience. Yet, *faith* is never once alluded to or mentioned in the parable. MacArthur therefore makes a highly improper superimposition of faith-alone doctrine upon the text.

MacArthur wants us to believe (at least here) that faith alone is what Jesus is implying justified the Publican.[13] First, MacArthur says:

> That parable surely shocked Jesus' listeners! They "trusted in themselves that they were righteous" (v. 9) — the very definition of self-righteousness. Their **theological heroes were the Pharisees, who held to the most rigid legalistic standards**. They fasted, made a great show of praying and giving alms, and **even went further in applying the ceremonial laws than Moses had actually prescribed**.

Let's stop there. MacArthur is saying that the Pharisees held to the "most rigid legalistic standards," and they did not merely keep the Law perfectly, but "*exceeded*" the Law to the fullest extent possible. MacArthur is building a case that the Pharisee's error was he thought his *perfect* obedience to the Law would justify himself. MacArthur is never implying they were wrong that they had indeed perfectly obeyed the Law. *Jesus is therefore supposedly telling us someone who perfectly obeys the Law is unjustified.*

13.MacArthur previously had taught repentance-from-sin (not merely a change in one's mind) is a key to salvation and compatible with faith alone. (John MacArthur, *The Gospel According to Jesus* (Zondervan: 1994) at 33.) Thus, it is likely here that MacArthur believes the Publican's repentance is what justifies. However, in MacArthur's unique worldview, he feels free to define repentance-from-sin as faith. This is unjustifiable. See page 87 *et seq.* Most evangelicals also disagree that repentance-from-sin is justifying. They even claim such an idea is heretical. See my prior book, *Jesus' Words Only* (2007) at 399 fn. 23.

Incidentally, if Jesus indeed taught that as true, then Jesus would contradict Deuteronomy 6:25.[14] Jesus would become a false prophet by virtue of Deuteronomy 13:1-5. That passage says any prophet who seduces you from following the Law's teachings is a false prophet.

But Jesus is not teaching this — not even remotely. In the Parable of the Publican and the Pharisee, the contrast is clear. The publican is someone who broke the Law and *confessed.* The Pharisee is someone who focused on the few good things they did like tithing. He proclaimed himself righteous. Yet, the Pharisee would *not* otherwise *repent.*

However, MacArthur — after he has firmly established the beach-head of his wrong premise — brings home his point. Jesus supposedly teaches justification by faith alone:

> Now He [Jesus]... astounds His listeners with a parable that seems to place a detestable tax-gatherer in a better position spiritually than a praying Pharisee.

> Jesus' point is clear. **He was teaching that justification is by faith alone.** All the theology of justification is there. But without delving into abstract theology, Jesus clearly painted the picture for us with a parable.

There is now a second misdirection in the above quote. MacArthur injected one more false idea. MacArthur claims that the contrast Jesus was making was between a "detestable tax gather" and the *spiritually flawless* and obedient Pharisee.

Describing the publican and Pharisee in that way represents a slight of hand. It makes one think *obedience* does not justify and the *disobedient* are justified by faith alone.

---

14. For further discussion on this passage, see page 33.

Yet, in truth, the publican *turned to obedience* by his repentance while the Pharisee was a sinner following Oral law and the lesser Written law. The Pharisee had a shallow obedience, which thereby made the Pharisee a sinner. The Pharisee was smug in his self-made and shallow righteousness.

What should we conclude from MacArthur's analysis?

It's rather simple. MacArthur has set up a *false contrast*, misrepresenting both figures in the parable. MacArthur has described the Publican too narrowly — omitting his repentance activity. MacArthur also has falsely depicted the Pharisee as perfectly law-abiding despite (a) the elements in the parable pointing to only obedience to two commands and (b) Jesus' many contrary lessons about the Pharisees as shallow Law-negators. (Matt. 15:6,9; 23:23.) This false re-construction of Jesus' parable by MacArthur is clearly visible in Table 3 below.

TABLE 3. Justification: Jesus' Contrasts v. MacArthur Contrasts.

Repentance Justifies (Jesus)	Faith Alone Justifies (MacArthur)
Publican "beat his breast and not look up to heaven, praying, 'Be Merciful to Me a sinner.'"	Publican "detestable tax-collector." MacArthur does not factor into the analysis the repentance-from-sin characteristic of the publican.
Pharisee 'pays his tithe', 'fasts twice a week,' and 'thanks God not an adulterer etc. like that Publican over there'	Pharisee kept Law flawlessly and even exceeded to admirable lengths.

Conclusion

In this Parable of the Publican and the Pharisee, Jesus is contrasting *a sinner who repents* against one who does not. Jesus declares justified a notorious publican/tax-collector who repents. Jesus declares unjustified a Pharisee who fails to do so. It's that simple. Smug self-righteousness about little points of Law and the Oral Law prevents the Pharisee from repenting. They have to abandon their emphasis on the oral law (Matt. 15:6,9) and their myopic focus on less weighty matters of the Law — such as tithing (Matt. 23:23).

Hence, contrary to what MacArthur implies, the Publican is not simply a "detestable tax-gather." Jesus is not declaring justified the tax-gather as one who remains detestable with no turning to obey. Nor is Jesus declaring the Pharisee unjustified because the Pharisee is supposedly perfectly obedient but lacks the alleged 'faith' of the Publican.

Instead, Jesus is *squarely differentiating* the two based upon repentance from sin. This differentiation is resisted by the Cheap Grace Gospel because it means Jesus taught justification by *repentance from sin and obedience.* Cheap Grace Gospel adherents say such a repentance requirement is *works-righteousness*. Hence, they adamantly twist Jesus' doctrine to conform to faith-alone doctrine.

However, the Parable of the Publican and the Pharisee proves justification initiates by repentance from sin. It is not by faith alone. Nor can an incomplete obedience ever justify.

Exaggerated Atonement Principle Cancels Jesus' Point.

The famous Charles Finney points out how some exaggerate the atonement to wipe out Jesus' justification doctrine. Finney explains below that Jesus' atonement only provides the blood that can wash clean another. Nothing else about the animal's life (or Jesus' life) who died as a sacrifice is imputed. The penitent under the Law was not ever excused by sacrifices from repentance or from obeying God. These personal behaviors (repentance & obedience) are the means of initial justification and remaining just and having (eternal) life. Finney says anyone who suggests atonement wipes out the need for justifying behavior has made a ludicrous error.

Therefore, Charles Finney—the famous attorney turned evangelist—explains below that personal justification is never by atonement. To ever think so demonstrates a fundamental misreading of the nature of atonement. Finney is right: atonement never imputes justification to an unrepentant sinner, just as we proved in the prior chapter.[15] Instead, atonement is only applied upon personal justification. Charles G. Finney wrote this in his sermon *Justification by Faith* (1837):

> Under the gospel, sinners are **not justified by having the obedience of Jesus Christ set down to their account, as if he had obeyed the law for them, or in their stead**. It is **not an uncommon mistake** to suppose that when sinners are justified under the gospel they **are accounted righteous** in the eye of the law, by having the obedience or righteousness of Christ imputed to them....**[T]his idea is absurd and impossible**, for this reason, that **Jesus Christ** was bound to obey the law for himself, and **could no more perform works of supererogation, or obey on our account, than any body else**. Was it not his duty to love the Lord his God, with all his heart and soul and mind and strength, and to love his neighbor as himself? Certainly; and if he had not done so, it would have been sin. The **only work of supererogation he could perform was to submit to sufferings that were not deserved. This is called his obedience unto death, and this is set down to our account**. But **if his obedience of the law is set down to our account, why are we called on to repent and obey the law ourselves**? Does God exact double service, yes, triple ser-

---

15. See *supra* at page 2 *et seq.*

---

vice, first to have the law obeyed by the surety for us, then that he must suffer the penalty for us, and then that we must repent and obey ourselves? No such thing is demanded. *It is not required that the obedience of another should be imputed to us*. All *we owe is perpetual obedience to the law of benevolence*. And for this there can be *no substitute*. If we fail of this we must endure the penalty....[16]

Thus, Finney explains that Christ's righteousness is only a cleanser of sin; it never imputes the very righteousness which is a condition to invoke its application. Jesus obeyed unto death to provide atonement for sin, not to satisfy your personal condition to even ask for atonement (*i.e.*, justification by repentance). To say otherwise is to overthrow the principle of atonement. One who claims atonement gives you *justification* has wrongly negated Jesus' requirement for *justification* that you have personal repentance and obedience. If atonement could provide the very same justification necessary to invoke atonement, then you have eviscerated atonement's condition. You thereby will give a false assurance to someone still *without* atonement that they are justified when they certainly are not justified. Finney astutely proves it could not be otherwise, for then 'why does Jesus teach justification instead is by *repentance-from-sin* in the Parable of the Publican and the Pharisee'? If atonement satisfies that principle of justification, Finney says God would be requiring supposedly what Jesus already provides by means of atonement.

Hence, it must be that justification depends on your personal repentance-from-sin, and on no substitute for you. Atonement then applies to wash *past* sins from your account. Atonement does not satisfy the very condition that Jesus says is necessary to invoke it — personal justification. Thus, Jesus says justification is not by faith but by repentance from sin.

---

16. http://www.gospeltruth.net/1837LTPC/lptc05_just_by_faith.htm (last accessed 8-18-2007).

3 *Hell Whole Or Heaven Maimed*

The Three Passages At Issue

(42) And whosoever shall cause one of these little ones that **believe on me** to **stumble**, it were better for him if a great millstone were hanged about his neck, and he were cast into the sea. (43) And if thy hand cause thee to **stumble**, cut it off: it is good for thee to **enter into life maimed**, rather than **having thy two hands to go into hell**, into the unquenchable fire. (44) where their worm dieth not, and the fire is not quenched. (45) And if thy foot cause thee to **stumble**, cut it off: it is **good for thee to enter into life halt**, rather than **having thy two feet to be cast into hell**. (46) where their worm dieth not, and the fire is not quenched. (47) And if thine eye cause thee to **stumble**, cast it out: it is good for thee to **enter into the kingdom of God with one eye**, rather than **having two eyes to be cast into hell**; (48) where their worm dieth not, and the fire is not quenched. (Mark 9:42-48 ASV.)

(29) And if thy right eye causeth thee to stumble, pluck it out, and cast it from thee: for it is profitable for thee that **one of thy members should perish**, and **not thy whole body be cast into hell**. (30) And if thy right hand causeth thee to stumble, cut it off, and cast it from thee: for it is profitable for thee that **one of thy members should perish**, and **not thy whole body go into hell**. (Matt. 5:29-30 ASV.)

(6) But whoso shall cause one of these little ones that **believe on me to stumble**, it is profitable for him that a great millstone should be hanged about his neck, and that he should be sunk in the depth of the sea. (7) Woe unto the world because of occasions of stumbling! for it must needs be that the occasions come; but woe to that man through whom the occasion cometh! (8) And if thy hand or thy foot causeth thee to **stumble**, cut it off, and cast it from thee: it is good for thee to **enter into life maimed or halt**, rather than having **two hands or two feet to be cast into the eternal fire**. (9) And if thine eye causeth thee to **stumble**, pluck it out, and cast it from thee: it is good for thee to **enter into life with one eye**, rather than having two eyes to be cast into the hell of fire. (Matt. 18:6-9 ASV.)

The literal meaning is clear. Jesus says a "believer in me" can "stumble." (Mark 9:42: Matt. 18:6.) Jesus repetitively tells "you" that if you stumble, you had better cut off the body part causing you to sin or you will go to hell whole. In its most succinct sense, this teaches 'heaven maimed or hell whole.'

In-Depth Exposition

If you sin against God's standards, Jesus required "cutting off the body parts" that cause you to be "ensnared in sin" or you will be sent to hell. (Matthew 5:29, Matthew 18:8, and Mark 9:42-48.) You can go to "heaven maimed" or "hell whole." Jesus specifically said this principle applies to "**believers in me** who become ensnared (or stumble)." (Mark 9:42; Matt. 18:6.) Jesus described the steps needed as 'cutting off the body part ensnaring you to sin.'

What does this passage mean?

First, does "cutting off body parts" mean more than merely *sorrow for sin?*

Yes, for Jesus taught one needs to actually take urgent steps to **destroy the object from which the temptation grows**. Jesus is pointing to physical steps consistent with an antecedent mental sorrow. Thus, Jesus insists that for "believers in me" who are "ensnared" that if they wish to go to heaven, they must do so actually "maimed." Clearly, in context, Jesus is not talking about merely changing your mind about sin (*i.e.*, sorrow for sin). Nor is Jesus talking about changing your mind about Himself — faith. Rather, Jesus is talking about taking **active** measures to **prevent sin** in the future. You will then become obedient.

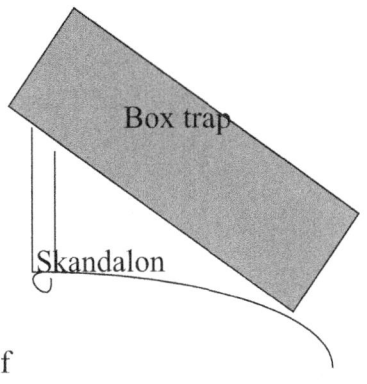

What are these steps? Are they a species of *works worthy of repentance?* Is it successful obedience? Or is it literally **separating from yourself the causes of temptation** to make repeating sin impossible? We must search this out carefully. Jesus made your salvation **absolutely indispensable** on these steps: it is heaven maimed or hell whole. There is no third option for a "believer ensnared in sin" to go to heaven by faith alone. Thus, it is imperative to find Jesus' meaning for the good of our own souls.

If you have lived with the cheap grace gospel in your consciousness as long as I have (over twenty-five years), then I venture to say this chapter will do you the most good. Why? Because Jesus is going to give you in these passages the medicine your soul needs so desperately to stay healthy and saved.

The Skandalon

We will now quote the same passages you read at the outset. However, this time, we will reveal the Greek verb *skandalizo* and the Greek noun *skandalon*. It is absolutely essential to note these words and their meaning to understand Jesus' message. So please read these verses one more time:

> (42) And whosoever shall cause one of these little ones that believe on me to stumble (*skandalizo*), it were better for him if a great millstone were hanged about his neck, and he were cast into the sea. (43) And if thy [your] hand cause thee to stumble (*skandalizo*), cut it off: it is good for thee [you] to enter into life maimed, rather than having thy two hands to go into hell, into the unquenchable fire. (44) where their worm dieth not, and the fire is not quenched. (45) And if thy [your] foot cause thee [you] to stumble (*skandalizo*), cut it off: it is good for thee [you] to enter into life halt, rather than having thy two feet to be cast into hell. (46) where their worm dieth not, and the fire is not quenched. (47) And if thine [your] eye cause thee [you] to stumble (*skandalizo*), cast it out: it is good for thee [you] to enter into the kingdom of God with one eye, rather than having two eyes to be cast into hell; (48) where their worm dieth not, and the fire is not quenched. (Mar 9:42-48 ASV.)

Jesus repeats this in Matthew. He says:

> (7) Woe unto the world because of offences (*skandalon*, plural)! for it must needs be that offences (*skandalon*) come; but woe to that man by whom the offence cometh! (8) Wherefore if thy hand or thy foot offend (*skandalizo*) thee, cut them off, and cast them from thee: it is better for thee to enter into life halt or maimed, rather than having two hands or two

feet to be cast into everlasting fire. (9) And if thine eye offend (***skandalizo***) thee, pluck it out, and cast it from thee: it is better for thee to enter into life with one eye, rather than having two eyes to be cast into hell fire. (Mat 18:7-9 ASV.)

The Picture Of A Box Trap Missing In English

To understand Jesus here it is useful to note that the Greek word translated as *stumble* is from the Greek verb *skandalizo*. Our English word *scandalized* comes from it. Its best translation here is *entrapped*. And when the passage in Matthew speaks of *offences*, it uses the plural of *skandalon*. It means here *snares*.

A *skandalon* in Greek literally meant the wooden stick that would hold up one edge of a metal box-trap. (See diagram on page 47 and photo on page 54.) Food would be put under the box. An animal would be tempted by the food to enter the trap. Then the hunter would stay a significant distance away, hidden from view. The hunter would then use a small string that was holding the *skandalon* stick. The hunter would pull on the string, causing the *skandalon* stick to collapse. The box-trap would fall, and the animal's whole body would normally be trapped inside. The animal would be *skandlizo*-ed.

It is absolutely essential to understand the *skandalon* in order to understand Jesus' message. For sometimes an animal could escape the metal trap by letting a limb be ripped off. For example, if the trap fell on a tail. Or only on a leg. Or only on an arm. The animal would be trapped only partially. Before the hunter would run over, the animal would begin a desperate struggle for its life. By a great force of will to live, the animal would release itself from the trap by using its free limbs to pull away. In that process of pulling away, the animal would tear off the body part that was pinned under the metal trap. The animal would run away, maimed but still alive.

Jesus' reference to this hunting-picture is clear from the message quoted above. In verses 43 and 45 of Mark 9, Jesus says you should "cut off" the body part ensnaring yourself. The word He uses is the verb form of the noun *skandalon*. You should behave like the animal that is ensnared (*skandalizo*-ed) by a single body part. Suffer the loss of a limb but live rather than hold onto the limb and be taken and killed by the hunter. The hunting imagery makes Jesus' meaning plain.

The Picture of Salvation At Stake For "Scandalized" Believers Is Unmistakable

Jesus is very concerned about those "believers" in him who become "skandlizo-ed." (Mark 9:42; Matt. 18:6.) Rather than Jesus telling us no Christian believer can ever become *skandalizo*-ed, Jesus bewails those who "shall cause one of these little ones that **believe on me** to stumble...." *i.e.*, be *skandalizo*-ed. (Mark 9:42; Matt.18:6.)

What is the price that one of these "believers in me" must pay for being *skandalizo*-ed? Jesus repeats three times the price is *damnation*.

TABLE 1. **The Price Of Being Entrapped (Skandalizo-ed)(Mk 9)**

SKANDALIZO-ED	RESULT
If thy hand cause thee to stumble, *i.e.*, be entrapped (*skandalizo*-ed.)	[You with] thy two hands... go into hell, into the **unquenchable fire** (43)
If thy foot causes thee to stumble, *i.e.*, be entrapped (*skandalizo*-ed.)	[You] having thy two feet [are] cast into hell where their worm dieth not, and the **fire is not quenched**. (45-46)
If thy eye causes thee to stumble, *i.e.*, be entrapped (*skandalizo*-ed.)	[You with] two eyes [are] cast into hell; where their worm dieth not, and the **fire is not quenched**. (47-48)

How Is One Saved In Jesus' Lesson?

Jesus could not be more clear about the price of salvation for the "believer in me" who has become "ensnared" (*skandalizo*-ed). It is *stern measures* of the most severe sort.

TABLE 2. **The Means of Entering Heaven In Mark 9:42-48**

CONDITION	RESULT
[If] cut it off (*i.e.*, hand causing you to be ensnared)	[You] enter into life maimed. (43)
[If] cut it off (*i.e.*, foot causing you to be ensnared)	[You] enter into life halt (45)
[If] cast it out (*i.e.*, eye causing you to be ensnared)	[You] enter into the kingdom of God with one eye (47)

What Are These Stern Measures?

The Stern Measure Given The Young Rich Man

In Jesus' answer to the young rich man's question on how to have eternal life, Jesus first tells the young man to "obey the commandments (*i.e.*, the Ten Commandments)." (Matthew 19:16-26; Mark 10:17-31; Luke 18:18-26.)

Then, when the young man says he has obeyed them, Jesus next gives the young man a heaven-maimed command:

> Jesus said unto him, If thou wouldest be perfect (*teleios*, mature, complete), **go, sell that which thou hast**, and give to the poor, and thou shalt have treasure in heaven: and come, follow me. (Matt. 19:21 ASV.)

There is no command in Scripture that one is not permitted to have wealth. But Jesus is insisting that this particular man give *all* his wealth to the poor. Why? Jesus' word choice indicates that this is how this particular young man will reach a completed and perfect state.

Isn't this a stern measure? The man was very wealthy, the text says. What problem does wealth by itself cause, even if obtained legitimately?

Jesus once said:

> No man can serve two masters; for either he will hate the one, and love the other; or else he will hold to one, and despise the other. Ye cannot serve God and **mammon**. (Matt. 6:24 ASV)

Jesus in Revelation speaks similarly, saying that riches blocked the productivity of the church members at Laodicea.

> (16) So because thou art **lukewarm**, and neither hot nor cold, I will spew thee out of my mouth. (17) Because thou sayest, **I am rich**, and **have gotten riches**, and have **need of nothing**; and knowest not that thou art the wretched one and miserable and poor and blind and naked: (Rev. 3:16-17 ASV.)

Jesus in the Parable of the Sower speaks similarly of the third seed. Its productivity is blocked by riches. Let's do a brief review of the Parable of the Sower on this issue.

In that parable, the first seed rejects the word and never believes. (Luke 8:12.) The second seed "believes for a while" but then falls into temptation and withers (dies). (Luke 8:13.) The third seed goes much farther in growth, but then is choked by thorns. Jesus tells us what are those thorns:

> And that which fell among the thorns, these are they that have heard, and as they go on their way they are **choked with cares and riches and pleasures of this life**, and bring no fruit to **perfection**. (Luke 8:14 ASV.)

Thus, repeatedly, Jesus says that riches can block productivity. Riches become thorns and hence a snare. The root problem is that riches become one's priority, causing you to not produce for the Lord.

How do these passages help us understand the heaven-maimed or hell-whole statement?

Because Jesus evidently is giving the young rich man a cure that will *prevent his serving his mammon any longer*. By giving away all his wealth to the poor, and becoming poor himself, the young man will *put an end to the source of his temptation*. The rich man if turned poor can now become rich toward God.

In this example from Jesus' ministry, the physical object that needed to be destroyed was the wealth itself. The desire for riches made the young rich man seek its service, not God's service. The young man has sacrificed productivity to God in *good works* because they often cost money to do. Thus, the young rich man may think he has not transgressed any commands among the Ten Commandments. But the affirmative commands elsewhere in the Law of charity (good works) were being ignored. Productivity in good works are being sacrificed to the god of mammon that the young man loved.

Thus, heaven maimed for this young man meant *cutting off his connection to his accumulated wealth*. Starting over will give him a new outlook where God's works are his goal rather than serving mammon.

Conclusion

Jesus' hell-whole or heaven maimed warning is in stark contrast to the Modern Gospel of Cheap Grace. Jesus says unless you buffet your body to avoid sinning you will later be rejected. (Mark 9:42-48.) A Christian believer who is ensnared has only two choices: heaven maimed or hell whole. There is no compromising idea that faith or some initial obedience is all that matters. Jesus demands *success*. The price of heaven is precisely success in avoiding sin. You must take whatever measures that achieve this or you will suffer hell forever. Jesus is blunt.

Costa Rican boy creates a classic animal trap, designed to capture birds. The stick is the *skandalon*. The corn serves to entice the bird to enter. This is the imagery Jesus meant by His use of the noun *skandalon* and the verb *skandalizo*. When the string attached to the *skandalon* is pulled, the trap is sprung. If the bird is only partially pinned, it has to let go of bird feathers or limbs in order to escape.

4 *The Parable Of The Good Servant Turned Evil*

Naming Tradition

In Luke 12:41-48 and Matthew 24: 44-50, Jesus tells us the Parable of the Good Servant Who Turned Evil. However, traditionally this has been called the Parable of the Evil Servant. Yet, that is a misnomer. It is the story of a Good Servant turned Evil. This is a very important correction in *naming.* It helps us remember the point of the message. This is about the fall of a good servant into sin. It is just like the second seed in the Parable of the Sower. That seed "believed for a while" but then "fell away" into "temptation," and thus "withered" and died. (Luke 8:6,13. See page 311 *et seq.*)

Overview

In the gospels of Luke and of Matthew, Jesus tells a story about a faithful and wise servant of the Lord. The servant is promoted over the household of his Lord. Then he gets tired of waiting for his Lord's return. Then this good servant engages in sin including mistreatment of fellow servants of his Lord. He is also partying with the drunk. Jesus says this servant who lost patience will find the Master so displeased that his Lord "will tear that servant apart and banish him with the hypocrites" and *apiston* — the "unfaithful, disobedient or unbelievers" in a place where there is "weeping and gnashing of teeth." (Matt. 24:48-50 (hypocrites); Luke 12:41-48 (*apiston* = *a* [negative prefix] + *pistos* = believer or unfaithful.)

The Lucan Text

In Luke, Jesus describes a servant who oppresses the household of his Lord. Is this the same as the good servant Jesus describes initially?

> (42) And the Lord said, Who then is the **faithful [pistos] and wise steward**, whom his lord shall set over his household, to give them their portion of food in due season? (43) Blessed is that servant, whom his lord when he cometh shall find so doing. (44) Of a truth I say unto you, that he will set him over all that he hath. (45) **But if that servant shall say in his heart**, My lord delayeth his coming; and **shall begin to beat the menservants and the maidservants**, and to eat and drink, and to be drunken; (46) the lord of that servant shall come in a day when he expecteth not, and in an hour when he knoweth not, and **shall cut him asunder**, and appoint his portion with the **unfaithful** [apiston].[1] (Luke 12:42-46 ASV)

In Luke, there is no question but that the good and faithful servant is the same as *that* servant who later turns to evil.

The Version In The Greek Matthew

The parallel passage in Matthew, based on the Greek version, reads in the American Standard Version as:

> (44) Therefore be ye also ready; for in an hour that ye think not the Son of man cometh. (45) Who then is the **faithful and wise** servant, whom his lord hath **set over his household**, to give them their food in due season? (46) Blessed is **that** [=ekeinos] servant, whom his lord when he cometh shall find so doing. (47) Verily I say unto you, that **he will set him over all that he hath**. (48) But if **that** [=ekeinos] evil servant shall say in his heart, My lord tarri-

eth; (49) and shall begin to beat his fellow-servants, and shall eat and drink with the drunken; (50) the lord of *that* [=*ekeinos*] *servant* shall come in a day when he expecteth not, and in an hour when he knoweth not, (51) and shall cut him asunder, and appoint his portion with the hypocrites: there shall be the weeping and the gnashing of teeth. (Matt. 24:44-51, ASV.)

What Verse 48 Means In The Greek Matthew

The King James and the American Standard Version read similarly in verse 48. The KJV reads: "But and if *that* evil servant shall say in his heart, My lord delayeth his coming..." (Matt. 24:48 KJV.)

---

1. Some versions say that God will "appoint his portion with the **unbelievers**." (KJV, SRV.) However, the ASV, NLT, and YLT say their portion is with the *unfaithful*. This means *disobedient*. This is probably correct due to the fact sin ends the *pistos* character of the good servant. While cheap grace proponents insist *pistis* in John 3:16 is not about obedience, they have special reasons to agree *a* + *pistos* in Luke 12:51 is talking about obedience. Dillow admits that if *apiston* means *unbelievers* in verse 51, then a once saved good servant ends up with those who never believed. This would mean a Christian can become lost for misbehavior. However this violates Dillow's belief in cheap grace (faith alone). Thus, he is compelled by faith alone doctrine to choose a meaning of *apiston* as *unfaithful* (disobedient). Dillow imagines the good servant still ends up in heaven, but just in a second tier of unfaithful (but saved) disobedient Christians. To give traction to this view that the good-servant-turned-evil ends up in heaven, he favors *apiston* rendered as *unfaithful* rather than as *unbelievers*. However, even if *apiston* means *disobedient* (which totally comports with our studies on *pisteuo* in John 3:16 at page 422 *et seq.*), Dillow has not successfully avoided that this place for the good-servant-turned-evil is hell. Jesus says in the more complete summary in Matthew that the good-servant-turned-evil ends up in a place of "weeping and gnashing." (Matt. 24:51.) Elsewhere, Jesus said at the judgment, those ensnared by sin will be sent to the "fiery furnace" — a place where there is "weeping and gnashing of teeth." (Matt. 13:42,50). Thus, the obedient *pistos* servant by later engaging in disobedience goes to hell (a place of weeping and gnashing) with the unfaithful/disobedient *a-piston*. (Lk. 12:42,46.)

Yet, we see a variance between the Greek Matthew and what we read in Luke. For in Luke, we know the faithful and wise servant is clearly the same who turned to evil. Jesus then spells out his end if that happens: weeping and gnashing.

In the Greek Matthew, this meaning is less apparent. Jesus calls this person "that evil servant," suggesting perhaps this is a *new* second servant who begins as wholly evil.

Nevertheless, even in the KJV-ASV Greek-based Matthew for verse 48, commentators agree it is the faithful and wise servant who turns to become the evil servant.

Barnes points out the literary structure of the parable dictates the good and evil servant are *one and the same*. The one who is faithful is appointed to be overseer but then later abuses that position and turns evil. Thus, Barnes says the *evil servant* is the same as the earlier *faithful and wise servant*. He explains:

> *That evil servant* — If that servant, *so appointed* [*i.e.*, the good servant], having this office, should be evil or wicked.

Likewise, Dillow admits the same at page 387 of *Reign of the Servant Kings* (1992). Dillow says the Greek and the text structure requires us to understand this servant-overseer who falls is the same as the faithful servant-overseer mentioned earlier. Jesus is saying a once faithful Christian has turned to evil. The parable then serves as a warning to us:

> In the parable of the wise servant [*i.e.*, the parable under discussion], the evil servant is after all a 'servant.' If the wise servant is saved, there is no exegetical basis for implying that the evil servant is not. In fact, **the Greek text** makes it plain that **only one servant, not two, is in view**. Then the Lord says, "But if **that** (Gr. *Ekeinos*) evil slave says ..." (24:48). He is speaking of the **same servant**, the wise one of the preceding verses. (Dillow, *Reign of the Servant Kings, supra*, at 387.)

Other Translations Of The Greek Matthew Similar To Luke

In further support of viewing Matthew 24:48 to read just like the Lucan version, we find both the NIV and NLT translate it to match Luke's version.

The NIV version of verse 48 renders the Greek of Matthew so it matches the Lucan version of that same parable. The NIV reads: "But suppose *that servant is wicked* and says to himself, 'My master is staying away a long time.'"

Likewise, the modern *The New Living Translation* of verse 48 in Matthew reads comparable to the Lucan version: "But *what if the servant is evil* and thinks, 'My master won't be back for a while....'"

Thus, in both the NIV and NLT, the Greek text is translated similarly to the Lucan version. They both evidently believe the underlying text supports saying that Jesus is warning about a good servant who turns evil.

The Hebrew Original Of Verse 48 Of Matthew 24

One final proof, but no less important, is to examine the Hebrew version of Matthew. It appears to be the correct original version of what we read in the Greek translation of Matthew. All the early church commentators said the Greek Matthew was simply a translation of an underlying Hebrew original version. That Hebrew version had been thought lost for centuries. However, Professor Howard recently published a version of the Hebrew Matthew discovered in a medieval text. It has all the earmarks of containing the original Hebrew Matthew. It has very few variants from our Greek text. Yet, those variants often unlock gnarled syntax, such as in Matthew 24:48. There and in many other places, the Hebrew Matthew reveals our Greek New Testament is surely a translation of this original Hebrew version. The Hebrew version makes sense where our Greek version sometimes does not.

Thus, it is often useful to use this medieval copy of the Hebrew text of Matthew to double-check the Greek translation which is, in turn, the basis of all English translations.

The Hebrew Matthew provides in verse 48:

But if *that servant should be evil* and should say in his heart: my Lord is late in coming.

This Hebrew version precisely matches the Lucan passage at a point where the Greek Matthew is at odds.

It hence appears once again that the Hebrew Matthew helps restore the original words of Jesus lost in the Greek translation. Even though this may appear a minutely small variance, it has an enormous impact. It answers whether this parable is about a good servant turned evil or merely about an evil servant who was never a good servant. Thankfully, God never leaves us without a path back to His truth.

Hence, using the Lucan passage, the Hebrew Matthew, and modern scholarship, we are able to unlock the gnarled syntax in the Greek of Matthew 24:48. The KJV relies upon the erroneous Greek, which causes it to have the wrong wording. The NIV and NLT are both true to the original text. The good servant later changes and turns into an evil servant, as Table 1 below demonstrates.

Table 1 compares the *Hebrew* Matthew 24:48 and Luke 12:45. They are virtually identical. By contrast, the KJV-ASV Greek text tradition of Matthew is at variance:

TABLE 1. "That Servant" Or "That Evil Servant" In Parable Of The Good Servant Turned Evil

Matthew 24:45	Luke 12:45
"But if *that servant should be evil* and should say in his heart: my Lord is late in coming...." (*Hebrew* Matthew)	"But *if that servant* shall say in his heart, My lord delayeth his coming; and shall begin to beat the menservants and the maidservants, and to eat and drink, and to be drunken;" (ASV)
"But and if *that evil servant* shall say in his heart, My lord tarrieth...." (KJV/ASV - *Greek* New Testament based on Majority Text tradition)	

In both Luke and the Hebrew Matthew, it is unquestionably clear that there are *not* two servants in view. Jesus is saying that suppose the same servant who previously had been wise and faithful becomes impatient, and rationalizes that his Lord's return justifies impudent sin. Jesus then *spells out the dire consequences as a warning to the wise and faithful servants of His day and all generations thereafter.*

However, in the Greek version of Matthew which was the basis for the KJV-ASV, it abruptly says "if that evil servant..." This opens up an ambiguity. The sudden thrust at us of an "evil servant" in the KJV-ASV tradition has led those wed to cheap grace to think this is a second and distinct 'servant' who was never a faithful and wise servant whom Jesus previously mentioned. (This was my personal solution when I too believed in cheap grace.)

Yet, some cheap grace proponents admit the Greek still means one servant is in view, as pointed out earlier. Thus, the Greek word for *that*, according to Barnes and Dillow (cheap grace proponents), strongly supports the idea that one servant is in view, and that the good servant turned evil.

Hence, there are numerous threads of proof that Matthew's version likewise means a good servant turned evil. Despite the different Greek in Matthew from Luke, it is admitted that the context proves Matthew should be translated the same way that Luke reads in Greek.

Finally, if there was any doubt, we must conclude, in light of the Lucan passage, that the Hebrew Matthew is of superior quality to the Greek text upon which the KJV-ASV was relying. The Hebrew Matthew lacks this gnarled *that-evil-servant.* The Hebrew Matthew has the simplicity which matches Luke and the parable's meaning itself: *if that good servant should turn evil and should say in his heart, etc.* Jesus was warning *wise-and-faithful* servants to be watching and waiting. Don't loose patience like Aaron did waiting for Moses to return from the mountaintop. The point of Jesus in the Lucan and Matthew passage remains identical if we use the Hebrew variant to Matthew's Gospel.

Thus, the Hebrew version of verse 48 is very helpful in reassuring us on this crucial meaning of this verse. As we shall see, some who do not like the message of this parable try to exploit the variance in the Greek-based Matthew. They do so to deny the evil servant is the same as the once good servant. Their purpose is to thereby preserve cheap grace.

Next, now that we have resolved this very important translation issue, we can begin to understand this parable. We start, like with all parables, by identifying its constituent parts. Let's break down the parable's symbolism.

The Symbolism Of The Parable

The faithful and prudent (*phronimos*) servant is elevated by his Lord over his household. Thus, because the Lord here is a symbol of Jesus Christ (Barnes), there is no doubt this faithful and wise servant is being correctly viewed as "faithful and wise" by the Lord. Accordingly, it is important to note this *servant* begins as a *true*, not a *nominal* Christian.

Then, as seen in the prior section, Jesus then explains if this faithful and wise servant should contemplate evil and starts oppressing others and revelling with the drunken, then the bad things identified in the parable will follow. Jesus explains the root cause of the fall of the faithful and wise servant into temptation. He had lost fear of his Lord's sudden return whereupon he would be held accountable for misdeeds. He "believes the day of reckoning and judgment to be far distant," thus "abandon[ing] himself to the more unrestrained indulgence of lusts." (Lisco, *supra*, at 254-55.)

Apostle Peter likewise teaches by contrast that fear of imminent final judgment — where no favoritism is shown anyone — is one which leads you to "sojourn in fear." Apostle Peter writes in 1 Peter 1:17 ASV: "And if ye call on him as Father, who without respect of persons *judgeth* according to each man's work, pass the time of *your sojourning in fear*."

Thus, this parable is clearly a warning by Jesus to those who are now truly faithful and wise servants — even those who have been elevated by their Lord to overseeing positions. Jesus is going to explain what happens if they lose fear of accountability, and thereby turn to evil.

The Fall Of The Wise And Faithful Servant

How did the good servant fall? He reasoned, in effect: "Why should I obey the Master if He will not return promptly to hold me accountable for disobedience?" This is evident in the *thought* which preceded the evil deeds:

> But if that servant should be evil and should say in his heart: my Lord is late in coming. (Hebrew Matthew 24:48)

What is this Lord's servant's end for his disobedience? He will be torn apart and cast into the place reserved for the hypocrites and disobedient. As Barnes explains:

> The unfaithful and wicked minister of God, who lives ***without expectation or fear of judgment***, shall suffer the **severest punishment** inflicted on sinners in the world of woe.

Barnes is correct. However, he somewhat eviscerates Jesus' meaning by suggesting that the only Christians who need fear Jesus' threat are ministers. Instead, any servant who loses patience for Jesus' return, and who uses such delay to justify lack of concern over accountability, is under Jesus' threat. It would be nonsense to suggest only ministers go to hell for evil deeds done by losing fear of accountability upon Jesus' return, but the rest of us can frolic in sin if we lose such fear. Moreover, to suggest the parable only applies to ministers is to undercut the context. This warning in Luke 12:45 *ff* is part of the Sermon on the Mount, where Jesus is addressing "an innumerable multitude of people." (Luke 12:1.) Hence, the warning is universal. Jesus presses His warning on all Christians.

Jesus began the identical lesson in Matthew saying its point proves the necessity to be ready and waiting when He returns. (Matt. 24:44.) Jesus wanted the crowds in Luke 12:1,51 to have the same fear of an any-time accountability if Jesus should suddenly return. This constant fear of account-ability, and loss of salvation for disobedience, would keep us from turning to debauchery and sin.

If an obedient and prudent servant subsequently changes, and commits evil, then his or her end is no different than the *apiston* (the unfaithful, the disobedient or the non-believer) and the hypocrite. Your end is in the place of weep-ing and gnashing of teeth (Matt. 24:51). This was Jesus' short-hand expression for the "fiery furnace" where all sin-ners are sent by the angels on judgment day. (Matt. 13:42,50.)

Thus, what of the faith (*pistis*) of this initially faithful and wise servant? He lost concern about any accountability for his actions which brought his prior faithfulness (*pistos*) to naught by sin. Robertson in *Word Pictures* explains this verse: "That is the temptation [that causes him] to give way to indulge in fleshly appetites or to pride of superior intellect."

Loss of fear was the root problem of the fallen wise and faithful servant. Jesus' exhortation in Matt. 24:44 signals that we must work on *our* expectations being ever vigilant. By losing fear of an imminent judgment for our personal mis-behavior, we are subject to the same temptation as the good servant turned evil. We will lose concern for our behavior. If we no longer have a fear of His return in judgment at any time, Jesus is concerned we will become lax. Then we start sinning. This is the point of the parable. It is a warning to us about ***losing concern for being accountable*** to our Lord.

The Gospel Of Cheap Grace Is Indicted By This Parable

Interestingly, the Modern Gospel of Cheap Grace feeds the precise assumption among God's servants that Jesus was condemning in the Parable of the Good Servant Turned

Evil. While cheap grace keeps up the constant hope of Jesus' coming and *rapturing us*, it then negates the impact Jesus wants from such a constant expectation. Cheap grace teaches all believers are *simultaneously* assured that they cannot miss the rapture *if they have ever once believed*. No amount of disobedience or sinfulness will separate them from the salvation God supposedly *promised* based on *faith alone*. As we will demonstrate below, cheap grace directly negates having any fear of accountability pertaining to our salvation even if Christ returned today!

Hence, the Gospel of Cheap Grace precisely feeds us with the very identical assumption which caused the good servant to turn evil and loose salvation. Cheap Grace affirms we have *no accountability for sin in relation to our salvation once in Christ*, contrary to what the Parable of the Good-Servant-Turned-Evil teaches. This is why the cheap grace (faith alone) gospel is so inimical to Christ's teachings.

Example Of Teaching There Is Nothing To Fear Once In Christ

In this passage from Max Lucado's *The Grip of Grace* (Word: 1996) at page 147, does not Lucado teach the very same fearless attitude which Jesus' message in the Parable of the Good Servant Turned Evil was combatting? Lucado says:

> The moment we begin asking those questions [*i.e.*, will I be punished for sin] we have crossed an invisible line into the arena of fear. *Grace delivered us from fear*, but watch how quickly we return. Grace told us *we didn't have to spend our lives looking over our shoulders*, but look at us glancing backward [*i.e.*, worried whether our sin will get us in trouble]. Grace told us that *we were free from guilt*, but look at us with ... guilt on our consciences [*i.e.*, over the sin we committed today].
>
> There is never a point at which *you are any less saved* than you were the first moment he

saved us. Just because you were grumpy at breakfast doesn't mean you were condemned at breakfast. When you *lost your temper yesterday, you didn't lose your salvation*. Your name doesn't disappear and reappear in the book of life according to your *moods and actions*.

Max Lucado sells millions of books on each new release. He is telling all the good and faithful servants that they have nothing to worry about. Losing your temper? Oppressing someone? Reveling with the ungodly? He says 'don't worry about it.' Lucado insists the problem is to get rid of the fear of God about sin! Oh my! God only help us!

In this way, faith-alone doctrine has removed God as One to fear. This has led to a mesmerizing effect. No counter-arguments are seriously weighed which refute faith alone. Any rationalization, even circular logic, is used by faith-alone 'Christians' to tenaciously reject Jesus' true doctrines. For otherwise, the convert would have to fear God, and that is frowned upon in sermon after sermon. "*Perfect* love casts out all fear." (1 John 4:17-19.) To them, this verse means our love is already perfected through Christ's atonement once we accept it. We must therefore supposedly remove all fear of God. Otherwise, we supposedly are still not even saved. We would be supposedly denying the very objective of God giving us salvation if we ever again experienced fear of God. Unfortunately for this view, Apostle John in the very same epistle used these identical words, and said the one who is "not keeping the commandments of Jesus" does not "have the love of God *perfected*" in them. (1 John 2:3-5.) The love of God is perfected only for those who keep the commandments. Hence, it makes a perfect fit that those who keep the commandments perfectly, and hence love God perfectly, need never fear God. Lucado and the eternal security cohorts have misread the meaning of 1 John 4:17-19. Those who perfectly love God, *i.e.*, keep His commandments perfectly, need have no fear of God. Those who do not obey God perfectly still must fear God. Lucado was wrong. Apostle John was right.

Parallel To The Second Seed In The Parable Of The Sower

The good servant hence was a Christian who fell in time of temptation. As a result, he became evil and lost, heading for hell unless he repents. This message of Jesus is precisely given again in the Parable of the Sower. Jesus describes the second seed had an identical path. The second seed "believed for a while" but then "fell away" into "temptation," and thus "withered" and died. (Luke 8: 6,13.)

The parallel is striking:

TABLE 2. Parallelism Of The Second Seed To The Good Servant Turned Evil

Christian/ Believer	Temptation	Spiritual Death and Lost
"received word with joy" "*believed*" for a while" "sprouted" (Luke 8:6, 13)	"fell away" "temptation" (Luke 8:6)	"withered away" (Luke 8:6)
"faithful and wise servant" put over Lord's household." Mat 24: 45, 47	"shall begin to beat his fellow-servants, and shall eat and drink with the drunken" Mat 24: 50	"torn asunder" and cast into a place of "weeping and gnashing" Mat 24:51

Parallel To Jesus' Exhortation To Overcomers In Revelation

In Revelation 2:10,11, Jesus said if we are faithful, we receive the crown of life:

> Be *faithful* [*pistos*] *until death*, and I will give you the *crown of life*. He who has an ear, let him hear what the Spirit says to the churches. He who overcomes shall *not be hurt by the second death*.

It follows if we are unfaithful that we will be hurt by the second death (judgment in hell). Thus, this repeats what we read in the Parable of the Good Servant Turned Evil.

Parallel To The Ten Virgins

In the Parable of the Ten Virgins, we have another parallel to the message of the good servant turned evil. In both parables, Jesus teaches that there are two kinds of Christians. First, there are those who are watching and prepared with oil burning, looking for the any-time return of Jesus. The others are those who watch for a while, are ready for a while, and have oil burning only for a time.[2]

The foolish virgins were Christians who took no heed to get the extra oil as the wise had done. The wise had more of the Holy Spirit at work in their lives. The foolish were no longer behaving as if their Lord could come at any moment.

No wonder the cheap grace church today rejects that a foolish virgin represents a Christian being threatened by Jesus with damnation for their foolishness. If we saw this as what Jesus intended, we would be more zealous for good works and obedience upon His return. Instead, evangelical Christians are far more *zealous to insist that good works are unimportant for salvation*. To avoid supposed heresy, evangelical Christians in fact *urge every believer to affirm obedience does not matter for one's salvation*. The consequence of the Fable of Cheap Grace has become a direct negation of the warnings and exhortations of the Lord of the Universe.

---

2. We discuss this parable in depth in the chapter entitled "Parable of the Virgins" on page 263.

Fable Of Cheap Grace Needs The Evil Servant To Not Lose Salvation

Dillow Contends A Good Servant Turned Evil Remains Saved

Cheap Grace says that no misbehavior of a Christian has any impact on their eternal destiny. This fable insists that if this were possible, this would be the heresy of faith-and-works.

Yet, Joseph Dillow, one of the leading defenders of the Fable of Cheap Grace, concedes that the faithful and wise servant in this parable becomes evil and then suffers weeping and gnashing.[3] Dillow makes this admission only because of the force of the underlying Greek and the logic of the passage itself.

Having confessed this fact, Dillow tells us how to square this parable with the Fable of Cheap Grace. Dillow shows us how we can resist that Jesus teaches faith-and-works. Dillow insists that this place of weeping and gnashing suffered by the once faithful and wise servant is in heaven. Dillow insists this good servant turned evil merely suffers profound regret as he enters heaven. (*Reign of The Servant Kings, supra*, at 387.)

Then what about Jesus' saying this evil servant suffers the same fate as hypocrites and "unbelievers" or "unfaithful"? Aren't they the lost? Dillow says *no*.

Dillow says the *hypocrites* can mean Christians who hypocritically judge others but still remain supposedly saved. Dillow similarly contends that the Greek word *apiston* should be translated as *unfaithful*, meaning *disobedient*. Dillow rejects the King James translation as *unbelievers* because it would imply a Christian can lose his salvation. If a Christian's fate is identical to a non-believer, then certainly a Christian would be lost. Hence, Dillow contends the good

---

3. See his quote on page 58 *supra*.

servant turned evil (Luke 12:46) shares the same fate as "unfaithful Christians" (*Id.*, at 389) rather than non-believers. Dillow imagines unfaithful (disobedient) Christians still go to heaven, yet are relegated to a non-commander role serving some alleged category of *Servant Kings-Christians* in heaven.

Hence, Dillow is saying the hypocrites and disobedient/unfaithful are references to people who actually are still going to heaven. Thus, the evil servant's fate is supposedly a guaranteed salvation. Allegedly, the good-servant-turned-evil merely suffers some regret as he enters judgment day. After that brief episode, Dillow incredibly says ***the evil servant will enter into the joy of his salvation for eternity.***

This solution will not work. We will see how absurd is such a notion.[4] Jesus says the place outside in darkness where there is weeping and gnashing is the "fiery furnace" where the "wicked" are sent on judgment day. (Matt. 13:42,50.) All the characteristics of this place as being outside in darkness are described elsewhere in Scripture as the place for those destined to go to the lake of fire on judgment day.

Yet, this bizarre idea that weeping and gnashing is in heaven is forced upon Dillow because he confessed all the other material points would, but for his bizarre solution, refute the Fable of Cheap Grace

Cheap Grace: Good Servant Is Not In View

MacArthur Blurs Evil Servant's Connection To Good Servant

John MacArthur in his *Study Bible* (1997) comments on the Parable of the Good Servant Turned Evil. MacArthur finds "the evil servant represents an ***unbeliever*** who refuses to take seriously the promise of Christ's return." (*Id.*, at 1440).

---

4. See "What is Outer Darkness Where There Is Weeping and Gnashing Of Teeth?" on page 280 *et seq.*

MacArthur thus utterly ignores that it was a good servant who turned evil. He affirms without any textual proof that the evil servant was not the good servant who was elevated. MacArthur thereby ignores that Jesus describes the evil servant as having once been a believer! Not only that — a faithful and wise one.

MacArthur's idea is an incongruous one because an unbeliever means someone who never believed in Christ. Yet, then how can Jesus fault him for not being patient for Christ's return? This is the primary fault of the evil servant.

Also, MacArthur's idea overlooks that the servant in the parable did at one time take seriously his Lord's returning, but concluded "My master is delaying his coming." (Matt. 24:48). The servant instead grew weary remaining ready for his Lord's return. Lastly, after the servant's bout of sinning, Jesus still calls Himself the "lord of that servant." (Matt. 24:48.)

Thus, MacArthur's interpretation cannot possibly be correct. It mismatches the entire tenor of the parable. It ends up with a highly incongruous warning. MacArthur asks us to believe that those who never believed are warned by Jesus to not lose patience for Jesus' return by turning to evil as leaders in Christ's church. How utterly ridiculous!

Dillow in *The Reign of the Servant Kings* (1992) at page 385 aptly critiques those holding MacArthur's views. Dillow says only "preconceptions" can keep one from seeing the evident truth that this parable is talking about a good servant turned evil — hence a Christian who falls into sin.

The Cause Of The Error Of MacArthur: A Presupposition In The Validity Of The Fable Of Cheap Grace

Then why did MacArthur insist that the *wise* servant turned evil was never a believer? Because MacArthur (a) never discussed the fact the evil servant was the wise servant at one point and (b) he used the validity of the Fable of Cheap Grace to force a meaning upon the parable to fit his preconceived belief (as of 1997) in the Fable of Cheap Grace.

John MacArthur in his *Study Bible* (1997) acknowledges the punishment for this servant is hell. This place of weeping and gnashing must be hell. Then, for that reason, MacArthur says the evil servant must be an unbeliever. "[H]e is an unbeliever ... **demonstrated by his punishment**." (Page 1440.) In other words, MacArthur deduces the *good servant turned evil* was never a believer because otherwise Jesus teaches a Christian goes to hell for misbehavior.

Why did MacArthur use this notion to read the parable? Because the Fable of Cheap Grace says *misbehavior* by Christians is irrelevant in our final salvation. Thus, if this were true, this *good servant turned evil* must be viewed as having never been a believer. But then how could a good and faithful servant not be a believer? This makes no sense.

We can clearly see that MacArthur engages in circular reasoning in the quote above. Based on the fact the servant suffers hell, MacArthur says we supposedly know this is an unbeliever. That is circular proof from a preconception. In fact, this parable calls that presupposition into question. MacArthur is drawing from outside the parable — relying on the gospel of cheap grace — to force Jesus' words to have implausible meanings. Rather than question the assumption in the validity of faith alone, MacArthur bizarrely asserts this good servant turned evil was never a true believer.

However, in this parable, we have a wise and *faithful* servant turned evil. Thus, it cannot be an unbeliever. Hence, once MacArthur admits the punishment is hell, this meant Jesus refuted the gospel of cheap grace — the faith alone of the good servant did not protect him in the day he sinned. In other words, because MacArthur admits this place where the servant goes is hell, MacArthur should concede that a believer can go to hell if disobedient. In fact, this is precisely Jesus' warning.

Breakdown In The Fable Of Cheap Grace's Ability To Solve This Parable

Thus, we see those who struggle to protect the Fable of Cheap Grace have devised two equally invalid (and contradictory) views of this parable.

One view says that because misbehavior led the *wise and faithful servant* to be damned, the wise servant must be viewed as never having believed. (MacArthur.)

The other view admits this makes no sense, and says the only palatable alternative is that the *wise* servant who turns *evil* must still end up in heaven. The place of weeping and gnashing where there are hypocrites and unfaithful is a special place supposedly for Christian sinners who were unfaithful. (Dillow). But that flies in the face of Jesus calling this place the "fiery furnace" where sinners are sent on judgment day (Matt. 13:42, 50) and a host of other obvious flaws.

When the fabulists run out of room to explain this passage, we know the faith alone doctrine — the doctrine of cheap grace — must have been clearly refuted by this passage.

John Wesley (1703-1791), the famous evangelist and inspiration for the Methodist Church, said when such self-contradictions are necessary to bolster cheap grace (in his day called 'once in grace, always in grace'), it proves its defenders have reached the limits of explanation. It proves they have a false assumption in their analysis. Wesley wrote: "When able men write such contradictions, the reason is, their mind is confused by a poor cause which they are laboring to defend."[5]

Matthew Henry: A Famous Commentator Who Understands Correctly A Christian Is At Risk Of Damnation For Misbehavior

Matthew Henry, the famous commentator, sees the evil servant as an evil Christian minister. Henry typically upholds faith alone doctrine. However, here Henry surprisingly never tries to obscure the clear meaning of this passage. He says that this servant turned evil is a Christian — although he insists only ministers are being warned — whose sin starts with doubting his Lord's return. Later, the minister's lusts draw him away from his Lord and his profession. It is not that the minister never believed. Thus, Henry correctly sees Jesus is saying this servant was once a saved believer. Henry makes

---

5. John Wesley, "Perseverance of the Saints," *Fundamental Christian Theology: A Systematic Theology* (C. J. Kinne)(1931) Vol. II, at 266-81. In this quote, Wesley was specifically dealing with the issue why Jesus gave warnings to Christians that they could become lost due to sin. Wesley insists Jesus' obvious intent was that Christians understand this is a *real* risk. However, the Calvinists said then (as they still do today) that Jesus only wanted Christians to *fear* sinning *lest they should become lost*, but never that we should fear becoming lost. While this is a self-evident contradiction (*i.e.*, the threatened risk is a mere phantom), the Calvinists to this day refuse to acknowledge their error, as they persist in this teaching. (See my prior book, *Jesus' Words Only* (2007) at 504.) Wesley in the 1700s turned the light of logic on this Calvinist claim. Wesley's critique is as follows: "Side by side with these solemn warnings of God I put this jumble of nonsense from a defender of the Calvinistic doctrine. 'Once in grace always in grace.' [The Calvinist says:] '*No true saint* who has an evidence, or an earnest of his acceptance with God, such as the true saint may have, *has a right to fear* for a moment that he shall fall nor has he a right to fear that *he shall not be saved*. I also add, that *the Bible nowhere encourages or calls upon the saints to fear, that they shall not be saved, or that they shall be lost*. It *calls on them* to fear something else, *to fear to sin*, or to apostatize, *lest they should be lost*, but *not* that *they shall sin and be lost*.' [Wesley responds:] When able men write such contradictions, the reason is, their mind is confused by a poor cause which they are laboring to defend."

---

this clear by using the very contrast that Jesus used. Henry says this person is not just a wicked man (hypocrite or unbeliever) but is a "wicked Christian."

Henry also acknowledges that Christians are the ones who are being oppressed by this Christian minister. The reason is that Jesus calls them "fellow" servants. This is another point in favor of proving that Jesus wants us to understand that the oppressing evil servant had been a true Christian.

Henry makes one further observation that is worthwhile to note. He says these wicked Christians *sear their consciences against this parable* so as to ignore the threats of Jesus' coming in judgment on them. Henry insists they will be punished *despite believing* the threat from Jesus on their salvation was *not real*:

> The *unbelief of man* shall not make that great promise [i.e., Jesus' return], or threatening (call it which you will), of *no effect*. The coming of Christ will be a most dreadful surprise to secure and careless sinners, especially to *wicked ministers*. Those that have *slighted the warnings of the word*, and silenced those of their own consciences concerning the judgment to come, cannot expect any other warnings; these will be adjudged *sufficient legal notice given*, whether taken or no; and no unfairness can be charged on Christ, if he come suddenly, without giving other notice. Behold, he has told us before.

Thus, merely because Dillow and MacArthur reassure themselves from the Fable of Cheap Grace that they are outside the reach of Jesus' warning of hell here, Henry says *not so*. Jesus will later say this parable was a sufficient legal notice to them. Henry means you can try to *slight* the warnings of Jesus. You can minimize Jesus' threat as loss of rewards (Dillow). You can claim it was aimed solely at an unbeliever and not at a once *faithful and wise* Christian minister (MacArthur). However, on judgment day, Henry says

Jesus will say *you were told beforehand* what a Christian minister must not do or otherwise he will be "cut in pieces" and be sent to hell. 'Your commentaries and rationalizations will be no defense when Jesus reads back this parable to you.' Henry signifies that Jesus will not permit any of our modern excuses to avoid its clear application to a minister's misconduct. (Its true scope is to everyone.) As Henry says, you were on sufficient legal notice by Jesus' delivery of this parable.

Aaron Is A Prior Type Of The Good Servant Who Loses Patience

One of the most interesting ways of knowing the meaning of this parable is to see the clear parallel to another *believer* — Aaron — the High Priest appointed by God in a direction to Moses!

How Aaron sins proves a believer — even one appointed personally by God to lead the people — can fall.

When Moses was on the mountain for a long time, the people became impatient.

> When the people saw how long it was taking Moses to come back down the mountain, they gathered around Aaron. 'Come on,' they said, 'make us some gods who can lead us. **We don't know what happened to this fellow Moses**, who brought us here from the land of Egypt.' (Exo 32:1 NLT.)

Aaron had previously been appointed as a faithful and wise assistant to Moses. Now, when impatience knocked at his door, he succumbed. Aaron told the people to collect their jewelry. Aaron then used it to fashion a golden-calf for them. The plan was to use its image during a Yahweh-centric worship service the next day. Aaron was trying to be syncretic — combining Yahweh-worship with images to be used in worship. Aaron presented the golden calf and told the people that the next day would be a festival to the Lord. (Ex. 32:5.) When the feast came, Aaron was surrounded by drunken revelry:

> The people got up early the next morning to sacrifice burnt offerings and peace offerings. After this, they celebrated with feasting and **drinking**, and they indulged in ***pagan revelry***. (Exo 32:6 NLT.)

Remember that in Matthew 24:49, Jesus said the servant who did evil began "to beat his fellow-servants, and ***shall eat and drink with the drunken***."

Aaron and the servant turned evil were compromised in similar ways. They were caught up with those who get drunk.

Aaron lost patience for Moses' return. Was Moses a type of Lord to Aaron? Yes. When Aaron was confronted by Moses, he calls Moses "my lord." Keil & Delitzch agree this is to signify Aaron regards Moses as his *lord*. Aaron "addresses Moses in this way on account of his office [*i.e.*, Moses' office] and his anger." This means Aaron is a perfect example of the Good Servant Turned Evil. Here is Moses' account:

> (21) And Moses said unto Aaron, What did this people unto thee, that thou hast brought a great sin upon them? (22) And Aaron said, Let not the anger of ***my lord wax hot***: thou knowest the people, that they are set on evil. (23) For they said unto me, Make us gods, which shall go before us; for as for this Moses, the man that brought us up out of the land of Egypt, we know not what is become of him. (24) And I said unto them, Whosoever hath any gold, let them break it off: so they gave it me; and I cast it into the fire, and there came out this calf (Exo 32:21-24 ASV.)

Because Moses comes back at an unexpected moment, Aaron has a particularly pathetic excuse. This reveals a lack of Aaron having planned anything realistic to explain about the golden calf. Aaron simply tries to make it sound like the golden calf supernaturally appeared from the fire. As if he could fool Moses into thinking God had a hand in this mayhem and image used in worship.

Then note that Moses calls Aaron to account when he returned. Moses is angry. (So is God.) Moses is a type of Lord. In such a role, he will call each of his own to account.

Aaron, however, was not watching and waiting. Instead, Aaron must have felt Moses was tarrying. This delay, Aaron could think, would give him enough time to pull off the image-device to soothe the people's own impatience. Aaron must never have anticipated Moses would return so soon to catch him.

What underscores this is that earlier Moses tells us that God's purpose of the thunderings and noises from the mountain was deliberately to engender fear so the people would not sin. The people begged for Moses to intervene and stop this proximity to God. They begged him to go up to meet God alone.[6] When the distance was put between Moses speaking to God and the people, they fell in sin. This then explains what is the cause of Aaron's fall: it was the *distance* and *lack of proximity to God* which led him to think he could sin and not get caught.

Hence, Aaron is *virtually indistinguishable* from the faithful and wise servant in the Parable of the Good Servant Turned Evil. Aaron is put over the household of his lord until he returned. Like the good-and-faithful servant in the parable, Aaron begins to doubt the prompt return of his master.

---

6. "(19) And they said unto Moses, Speak thou with us, and we will hear; but let not God speak with us, lest we die. (20) And Moses said unto the people, *Fear not: for God is come to prove you, and that his fear may be before you, that ye sin not.* (21) And the people stood afar off, and Moses drew near unto the thick darkness where God was." Exodus 20:19-21 ASV.

Did Aaron just like the good servant turned evil also end up participating in drunken revelry with his fellow-servants of his lord Moses? Yes. It is implied that he had put on the worship service to Yahweh using the golden calf in the midst of the service. It ended up in drunken revelry, just as befell the good servant turned evil.

Thus, it appears when Jesus tells the Parable of the Good Servant Turned Evil, Jesus is using terminology to invoke the memory of Aaron — Moses' servant. Aaron is the object lesson to illustrate the application of the parable. This is something never mentioned by commentators. Nothing seems to explain this other than lack of knowledge of the Hebrew Scriptures. Let's make a table comparison. From this, one can see Jesus is likely drawing an analogy to Aaron. Thus, no matter what status God gives you, you can fall just like Aaron did into sin — into blatant violation of God's Law, and into apostasy.

TABLE 3. Aaron Compared To The Good Servant Turned Evil

Aaron	Good Servant Turned Evil
God personally selects Aaron to help Moses.	Good and wise servant
Aaron speaks of Moses as "my lord."	"that servant" later calls the lord "my lord."
Moses leaves for the mountain to be with God, leaving Aaron in charge of the household of God.	The good and wise servant is appointed to feed and care for the household of his lord at his lord's departure.
Aaron is led into temptation by losing concern for the prompt return of his lord's return.	The good and wise servant is led into temptation by losing concern for the prompt return of his lord's return.
Aaron puts on a worship service with the people that endorses their sinful use of images (the golden calf).	The good and wise servant becomes evil by, among other things, beating fellow-servants of his lord.
Aaron ends up surrounded by people in drunken revelry.	The good and wise servant ends up drinking with those involved in drunken revelry.

Conclusion

So what happens to the once good servant — the Christian faithful servant — who later commits grievous sin? He is "cut in pieces" and assigned to a place of "weeping and gnashing of teeth" with the disobedient-unfaithful, so says our Lord. It clearly is contrary to the modern Fable of Cheap Grace. Yet, this refutation of our favorite fable comes from no less a figure than our Lord. Those who persist in faith alone doctrine as true for believers do so at their peril. For their Lord has been warning them from the pages of His word that they are to be on guard, and not forget He can come at any time and hold them to account. They must remain morally vigilant. They must not fail like Aaron did.

Why did Jesus illustrate this fall by mentioning a wise and faithful servant who was put over the household of God, like Aaron? Jesus' subtle point is that it will **not** earn you any credit that you did a good job for a long time. Aaron had a great track record too prior to the calf incident. It does not even matter you have been elevated by God's decision to be the head of His household. Indeed, Aaron was previously made the high priest over all other priests. Thus, Jesus reminds us **all the good you do is like filfthy rags when you sin**.[7] If you fall by sinning (*e.g.*, oppressing your fellow servants), you will fall very hard on the rock of God's judgment seat. Hence, you must repent and stop sinning.

---

7. Often the "filfthy rags" quote is taken out of context to suggest repenting persons who obey God have good deeds which are even filfthy to God. Not so, says Deuteronomy 6:25. Instead, Isaiah 64:5-6 must be read in its full context: "Thou meetest him that *rejoiceth and worketh righteousness*, those that remember thee in thy ways: behold, thou wast wroth, and *we sinned*: in them have we been of long time; and shall we be saved? (6) For we are *all become as one that is unclean*, and *all our righteousnesses are as a polluted garment*: and we all do fade as a leaf; and our iniquities, like the wind, take us away."

5 *Those Who Endure To The End*

A Conditional Promise Of Salvation

Where are the two places Jesus uses the strong language of a promise that you "shall" be saved?[1] One person to receive such a promise is:

> And every one that hath left houses, or brethren, or sisters, or father, or mother, or children, or lands, for my name's sake, shall receive a hundredfold, and **shall inherit eternal life**. (Matthew 19:29 ASV.) *Cf.* Matt. 25:34,46 ("inherit the kingdom" means have "eternal life.")

Jesus elsewhere makes the same promise to a person whose character is quite similar:

> If you shall endure to the end, you **shall be saved**. (Matthew 10:22 NIV.)

Even the faith-alone oriented *The Expositor's Bible Commentary* (Ed. Frank Gaebelein) (Grand Rapids, Michigan: Zondervan, 1989) agrees Matthew 10:22 discusses a condition for salvation. It says this means that the Christian must sacrifice even his life if necessary to remain true to Christ. "Otherwise there is **no salvation**." (*Id.*, Vol. 8 at 250.)

Gaebelein even emphasizes the necessity of the continuation of this action from the Greek tense used. "The verb 'endure' is in the present tense of continuous action (*hypomenomen*). It is only as we keep on **enduring** that we will be saved in time of persecution." (*Id.*, Vol. 11 at 401.)[2]

---

1. The Greek in John 3:16 is not likely a promise. See "The Final Issue: Is It 'Should' Or 'Shall' Have Eternal Life?" on page 513 *et seq.*

2. Please note that even this faith-alone commentator recognizes the present active tense signifies continuing activity.

Matthew 10:22 should therefore be revised to say: "If you keep on enduring, you shall be saved."

This is confirmed by two passages that use "shall" with "endure" that promise similar results. James teaches if we endure temptation and times of trial, we "shall" receive the crown of life. (James 1:12.)[3]

Furthermore, Matthew 10:22 is merely a parallel to what we read in Revelation 2:10,11. Jesus says there if we are faithful, we receive the crown of life:

> Do not fear any of those things which you are about to suffer. Indeed, the devil is about to throw some of you into prison, that you may be tested....Be *faithful until death*, and I will give you the *crown of life*. He who has an ear, let him hear what the Spirit says to the churches. He who overcomes shall *not be hurt by the second death*.

Jesus tells us to be faithful until death. If we do so, then we will be given the crown of life. Jesus explains further: if we overcome the testing, then we will not be hurt by the second death.

Thus, it follows by a logical corollary, that if we do not remain faithful and do not endure the testing, then we will not receive the crown of life and we will be hurt by the second death. This clearly threatens loss of salvation. Jesus proves this by actually expressly affirming this implied threatening corollary. In Luke 12:4-5,8-9, Jesus threatens hell on Christians who deny Christ:

> (4) And I say unto you my friends, Be not afraid of them that kill the body, and after that have no more that they can do. (5) But I will warn you whom ye shall fear: *Fear him, who after he hath killed hath power to cast into hell;*

---

3. *Cf.* Acts 14:21-22 (NIV): "'We must go through many hardships to enter the kingdom of God,' they [Barnabas/Paul] said.'"

yea, I say unto you, Fear him....(8) And I say unto you, Every one who shall confess me before men, him shall the Son of man also confess before the angels of God: (9) but ***he that denieth me in the presence of men shall be denied in the presence of the angels of God***. Luke 12:4-5,8-9 (ASV). (Emphasis added.)

Thus, a Christian who under persecution denies Christ will himself be denied by Christ, and be sent to hell. Instead of fearing what man can do, Jesus was exhorting you to fear God and His 'casting you into hell.'

Counter-Arguments That Negate Heavenly Salvation Is Issue In Matthew 10:22

Cheap grace advocates cannot accept there is any threat of loss of eternal life for disobedience or denial, or that there is any promise of salvation for faithfulness. This would make salvation by faith and works, which to them is a heresy. Thus, they first try to interpret *saved* in Matthew 10:22 to mean saved from *physical death* rather than from *hell*. So they teach Jesus' promise of salvation for endurance is not to eternal life. They claim it is a promise you will stay alive to the end of the tribulation period. Dave Hunt's work *In The Defense of the Faith* (Harvest House: 1996) at 330 uses some highly creative reasoning to arrive at this interpretation. Hunt like many others tries to limit the warning and the risk to only those facing persecution. They claim Jesus is promising physical salvation to those under persecution. Because physical persecution is rare in America, we are left to infer that endurance for salvation is largely irrelevant to our lives.

However, this is an unreasonable construction of Matthew 10:22. First, the word *saved* does not mean normally *saved* physically in body. Eighteen of twenty times where *saved* is used in Scripture (the Greek is *sozo*) it means to spiritual salvation. When it means saved physically, it is clear.

Moreover, when Jesus speaks of "bringing forth fruit with *endurance*" in the Parable of the Sower, it is to identify the only seed that was saved. (Luke 8:15.) Thus, "enduring" to the end in Matthew 10:22 has a striking parallel to Luke 8:15. Therefore, Matthew 10:22 should be likewise talking of salvation.

Also, other passages in New Testament writings refer to enduring, such as James 1:12 and Revelation 2:10-11. They both say if you *endure,* then it results in kingdom rewards after your physical death: you *receive the crown of life.* Whether salvation or rewards, this crown is received at a point *past* physical death. Enduring is not meant to signify merely staying alive. Thus, these two passages confirm that Jesus is speaking of endurance unto your own death and thus, even though you die in this world, you are saved in the next. (Matt. 10:22.)

Also, the cheap grace interpretation of Matthew 10:22 would make Jesus utter an illogical tautology (*i.e.*, a conditional truth whose premise is identical to its conclusion).

If Matthew 10:22 means what the cheap grace advocate says, Jesus is saying he who endures to the end of the tribulation (the premise) will be saved alive (the conclusion). Of course you would be saved alive (the conclusion) because you endured alive to the end of the tribulation (the premise). Thus, if Jesus meant those who endure alive to the end will be saved alive, Jesus would be uttering a nonsensical tautology. Tautologies are unintelligent, illogical statements, and our Lord would not talk like that.

Thus, Matthew 10:22 instead means what it says: if you keep on enduring to the end, you shall be saved.

Thus, the surest promise of salvation in Scripture is for *endurance*, and not *a one-time belief.*

How This Verse Applies To The Issue Of Denial Of Christ

Jesus means in Matthew 10:22, *among other things*, that if you deny Him, He will deny you. If you cannot withstand persecution, you will be denied being known by Jesus. Even the faith-alone pro-Scofield expositor Gaebelein (editor *Christianity Today*) concurs the warning that 'if you deny Christ, He will deny you' is a warning of loss of salvation.[4]

However, many like Charles Stanley teach the opposite. A believer supposedly can deny Christ and be saved all the while. *See,* Charles Stanley, *Eternal Security, supra,* at 93. Another who says this is Chuck Swindol, President of Dallas Theological Seminary from 1994 to 2001. He says: "You may deny Him, but He will *never deny* you....This is called the doctrine of eternal security." (Swindol, *The Problem of Defection*, audiotape YYP 6A.)

Early Church Rejected Doctrine At Odds With Matthew 10:22

Tertullian, an attorney who became an early Church leader, called this message of Stanley and Swindol the *Scorpion's Bite (Scorpiace)*.[5] He did so in a pamphlet of the same name in 202-03 A.D. Tertullian said some were relying upon Paul's words in 2 Tim. 2:13[6] to discourage potential martyrs from risking their lives if they confessed Christ. They argued

---

4. The *Expositor's Bible Commentary* (ed. Gaebelein)(1989) says regarding 2 Timothy 2:12: "If we disown him (aorist tense, arnesometha), 'he will also disown us.' This is a serious warning. We cannot reject Christ without being rejected ourselves."

5. An online copy is at http://www.tertullian.org/works/scorpiace.htm.

6. "It is a faithful saying: For if we be dead with him, we shall also live with him: (12) If we suffer, we shall also reign with him: if we deny him, he also will deny us: (13) If we believe not [*apisteo,* or *unfaithful*], yet he abideth faithful: he cannot deny himself." 2Ti 2:11-13 KJV.

Paul's words meant a believer is free to deny Christ and yet a
believer can trust God will never deny him or her later, and
thus a believer remains saved. Ironically, 2 Timothy 2:13 is
precisely the verse that Charles Stanley cites as his support to
insist a Christian can deny Christ and still be saved.

However, Tertullian was outraged because this reading of Paul contradicted Jesus. Tertullian said if this verse
said what its proponents claimed, it would contradict the Lord
Jesus in Matthew 10:22 which says "If you endure to the end,
you shall be saved." Tertullian said such a reading of Paul's
words would also violate Jesus' repeated statement that if a
Christian denies Christ, the Lord threatens him or her with
hell in Luke 12:4-5,8-9. (For the quote, see page 82 *supra*.)

Thus, the earliest Christian leaders regarded Matthew 10:22 as promising salvation only if we endure. It was
not a promise that we would be saved by a one time faith
even if we denied Christ. Such a teaching was cowardly,
anathema, accursed, and a heresy.

What This Proves About Cheap Grace In The Early Church

This digression into history also serves to reveal that
one of the earliest teachings regarded as heresy was, in fact,
cheap grace, *i.e.*, belief saves despite disobedience, denial,
etc. Indeed, this heresy arose in 202 A.D. based on the same
readings cheap grace advocates have today of 2 Tim. 2:13.

Conclusion

Thus, if you hold true to Jesus' teachings when persecuted by the "church," friends or family as a heretic, and do
not deny Him as your *true* Master, you shall be saved. If you
fold and deny Jesus is your Master of the gospel in preference
for someone else's gospel, you lose the crown of life and you
are lost. You have switched allegiances on who is the Master
to your life. Consequently, only if you "endure to the end
shall you be saved" (Matt. 10:22) still has relevance today.

6   *Repent Or Perish*

Luke 13:2-5

The *New Living Translation* of Jesus' *repent-or-perish* warning is a good place to start the next discussion:

> (2) 'Do you think those Galileans were **worse sinners** than all the other people from Galilee?' Jesus asked. 'Is that why they suffered? (3) Not at all! And **you will perish, too, unless you repent of your sins and turn to God**. (4) And what about the eighteen people who died when the tower in Siloam fell on them? Were they the worst sinners in Jerusalem? (5) No, and I tell you again that **unless you repent, you will perish, too.**' (Luke 13:2-5 NLT.)

The Greek word for *repent* in this passage is *metanoeo*. It has two meanings. Thayer's *Lexicon* says it means either *change your mind* (in the sense of a decision) or "to change one's mind for better, heartily to amend with abhorrence of one's past sins."

Metanoeo was used in the Greek Septuagint Bible to translate a Hebrew word in Isaiah 46:8 meaning "a complete change in attitude, not just a change in mind about specific acts." (G.W. Bromiley, *The International Standard Bible Encyclopedia* (Eerdman's 1995) at 136.) Likewise, in the Greek Apocrypha predating the New Testament, *metanoeo* was "frequently used...in the sense of complete **change of one's life** and a **complete turning from sin** and **to the ways (or laws) of God**." *Id.* Bromiley points out that in the 56 times it appears in the New Testament, with rare exception, *metanoeo* has the "full sense of a complete **change in one's way of life**" and "spiritual **change implied in a sinner's return to God**." *Id.*

With this prior usage, Dunn says "the call expressed in the Greek term *metanoeo* [by Jesus]...would have initially been heard as a reiteration of the call of the prophets to turn back to God, that is, by implication, from a *life in breach of God's commandments*." (Dunn, *Jesus Remembered*: 499.)

The Baptist scholar, John Broadus, in his classic *Commentary on Matthew*, explained *metanoeo* by contrasting it with other related words. The word *metamelomai* "expresses regret, and may or may not be followed by change of purpose and conduct." However, it is "quite different from the word *metanoeo* used to denote repentance unto life."[1] Hence, the contrast proves *metanoeo* means more: a change of behavior.

Hence, the NLT chose to translate *metanoeo* in Luke 13:5 as "repent of your sins and turn to God." The turning implies a change in action.

Besides *word-definition*, what in the context supports the NLT's decision? Jesus is talking about the tragedy which befell the Galileans. Eighteen of them died due to a falling tower. The audience thought this proved these eighteen were the *worst sinners*. The audience then inferred that because nothing so tragic happened to them, then they were *not* the worst of sinners and hence safe. They thought they were on the path to eternal life. Jesus says this is misreading the situation. Unless you repent from sin, you too will perish — everlastingly. Jesus is saying the Galileans were not the *worst of sinners*. The audience members *too* were *sinners who likewise needed to repent from sin*. And thus Jesus' point is they will be in the same boat as anyone else who is a sinner who has not repented from sin.

Of course, this passage merely repeats the heaven-maimed or hell-whole passage. (Mark 9:42-47.) That clearly meant you had only two choices: make a firm decision against sin and then successfully turn in the direction of that decision. Otherwise, you will perish everlastingly.

---

1. John A. Broadus, *Commentary on Matthew* (1886) (reprint: Kregel Classics: 1990) at 438.

Thus, there is little doubt that Jesus likewise has the same choice in mind when He says "repent or perish." Jesus is directing that one must repent *from sin* as the means of avoiding perishing everlastingly. Mere repentance in the sense of a *mental belief change* is not what Jesus means in context. For in this passage in Luke 13, Jesus' audience did not have a wrong idea about faith or about Jesus. Rather, they had sinned. Jesus said they were not addressing this problem. They had a wrong doctrine on what tragedies imply about their own sin. Jesus said tragedies to others implied nothing about the acceptability of their own lives. Jesus' audience thought only the Galileans who were killed were sinners because of tragedies that befell them. Jesus said *not so*.

Hence, the audience's problem was their sin (and smugness about it), not their lack of belief.

Jesus was not saying anything radically new. Psalm 32:1, 5 repeats this principle of repentance from sin for forgiveness as the first step to salvation.

> (1) Blessed is he whose transgression is *forgiven, Whose sin is covered*....(5) *I acknowledged my sin* unto thee, And mine iniquity did I not hide: I said, I will confess my transgressions unto Jehovah; And thou *forgavest the iniquity of my sin*. Selah

Other Parallel Passages

The audience's assumption about the Galileans is similar to the pride of the Pharisee in the Parable of the Publican and the Pharisee.[2]

In that parable, the Pharisee compares himself to horrid sinners. In that light, the Pharisee thought he was not half-bad. The Pharisee then interpreted this to mean he must be

---

2. For full discussion on this parable, see chapter entitled "The Repentant Goes Home Justified & The Shallowly Righteous Does Not" on page 27 *et seq.*

good in God's eyes by comparison. Yet, Jesus insisted that God does not grade *sin* on a sliding scale of comparisons. Instead, Jesus taught only the person who was repenting from sin — the publican in the parable — goes home *justified.* Only the publican who repents from sin is right with God.

Thus, when confronting the audience who thinks these Galileans are the worst of sinners, Jesus confronts them about their pride. It is the same kind of pride Jesus exposed in the Pharisee in the Parable of the Publican and the Pharisee. Both the audience in Luke 13 and the Pharisee in the parable reject personal repentance because they smugly think they are righteous "by comparison." Jesus warns that pride leads to a *shallow level of self-examination for sin*. Such shallowness will lead to perishing everlastingly. Why?

Because a *shallow self-examination* due to pride means you will *never detect the sin you need to identify* and then *repent from*.

Thus, Jesus was giving the same lesson to these people about 'repent or perish' that Jesus gave in the lesson about the Publican and the Pharisee. You cannot be right with God by making comparisons to others. You cannot infer you are righteous because nothing *bad* has happened to you yet.

Fable Of Cheap Grace Insists Repent-Or-Perish Means Nothing More Than Belief

If Jesus means we must repent *from sin or perish*, Jesus is saying the same thing He says elsewhere. Jesus elsewhere said we must mentally cut off body parts ensnaring us in sin or go to hell whole. (Mark 9:42-47.)

If, instead, one assumes a belief-change *alone* saves you (as cheap grace doctrine teaches), this process of mentally cutting off body parts would be *more* than just faith in Jesus or His work. If so, then Jesus' repent-or-perish warning destroys the prevalent doctrine of belief alone as what saves. Absent repentance from sin (which is more than just faith), Jesus would be saying you will perish in hell.

What do the cheap grace fabulists do to make one think repentance in Jesus 'repent-or-perish' warning is simply saying 'have 'faith or otherwise perish'?

First, Mark 9:42-47 (heaven-maimed or hell-whole) is ignored.

Second, these fabulists erase the primary meaning that repentance ordinarily means a decision to change one's behavior about sin. These fabulists are intent to convince Christians that a change to the **correct belief** about Jesus or His work on the cross is the only *repentance in the mind* necessary to avoid perishing everlastingly.

Thus, for the cheap grace fabulist, the word *repentance* — as Jesus supposedly used the term — was nothing more than a mental process. Once the fabulists of cheap grace embed this meaning, they then surreptitiously substitute *faith* as the meaning of *repentance*. Then they too can quote Jesus saying 'repent or perish,' but in their mind, with *repent* so redefined, Jesus supposedly means 'have a **change in belief** or perish' — have 'faith or be lost.'

To lead Christians to this conclusion, the fabulist of cheap grace will employ three methods, as we shall see in the example of the writings of the famous John Piper:

- The fabulist will never tell their listener that the primary usage of Jesus was in 13 of 20 times where Jesus used the word *repentance* that its meaning was clearly *a change in mind and behavior about sin* (not a change in faith, belief, etc.).

- The fabulist will only cite from passages where the word *repentance* is ambiguous in the sentence.

- The fabulist will never even tell Christians there is a second primary meaning to repentance: *a change from a certain behavior* — a meaning distinct from the alternative definition of *change in mind.* The fabulist will never advise the Christian in the pew that the dictionary refutes their argument.

Thus, what the Fable of Cheap Grace will do is try to draw on ambiguous passages and insist there is a possibility that Jesus means only one aspect to the word *repentance* —

an aspect which has a quality in common with faith — a mental process. Their objective is to draw the listener to think *repentance* can be equated with faith. From this groundwork, then they insist *repent or perish* means nothing more than have *faith* or *perish*. And thus **they have drawn up their case for faith alone for salvation from a passage refuting their doctrine**. For nothing is so inimical to the faith alone doctrine than Jesus' simple expression: *repent or perish*.

Hence, the fabulists do not tolerate that *repentance* in Luke 13:2-5 has any implication of a **sorrow about sin unto reformation of behavior**. Jesus in context really means you must make a change in the direction of your life from sin to obedience or you will perish everlastingly. The gospel of cheap grace cannot tolerate such a meaning.

This explains why, as we discuss next, that the fabulists of cheap grace are willing to go to any length necessary to rationalize *repentance* means only *faith*. We review this next as exemplified in the writings of the popular John Piper.

John Piper: Claims Repentance Is Merely A Change Of Mind

John Piper is a leading Reformed (Calvinist) Baptist commentator. On April 19, 2006, he wrote *Thoughts on Jesus' Demand to Repent*.[3] It is a comment on Luke 13:2-5 as well as several other quoted passages where Jesus mentions repentance. Piper will conclude that because the Greek word

---

3. See cite in bibliography. Incidentally, Piper's view in 1985 clearly affirmed at times Jesus' doctrine, even though Piper defined it as "real faith." Talking of 1 John 1:7 which says Jesus' blood does not atone unless we "are walking in the light," Piper wrote: "The message of 1 John—that **walking in the light is not optional**, but **necessary for salvation**—is good news because it creates the moral atmosphere of urgency in which serious business is done with God....It leads people to real faith instead of encouraging them to be content with a lip service that cannot change and cannot save." (See Piper, *John. Let Us Walk In The Light of God* (February 3, 1985), cited in bibliography.)

metanoeo supposedly only means *change in mind*, we can understand Jesus calling us only to have a new view of Jesus (faith) or perish. Jesus is supposedly not asking us to reform our thoughts about sin, let alone our behavior.

Piper's argument deserves very careful analysis. For Piper's argument is familiar to all evangelicals. Many others before him said the same thing. The mind-change hook is what we all have used to square 'faith alone' with what otherwise would be a very demanding principle for salvation — repent or perish.

Let's start the analysis of Piper's article by first pointing out what it omits.

Key Omissions in Piper's Analysis. Absent from Piper's quotations from Jesus about repentance is Mark 9:42-47. This is the clearest statement by Jesus about repentance. Even though Jesus did not use the Greek word *metanoeo* for repentance in that passage, the message of *heaven-maimed or hell-whole* in Mark 9:42-47 is about repentance. It erases any mystery about what Jesus means by *repent or perish* in Luke 13:5. Thus, any analysis on Jesus' usage of the Greek word translated as *repentance* which omits discussion of the *heaven-maimed or hell-whole* passage is defective.

Moreover, this is not only because Mark 9:42-47 explains *repentance.* Rather, that Marcan passage is expressed synonymously to Luke 13:5. For what is the difference between *repent or perish* and *heaven-maimed or hell-whole*? They are **mirror statements** by Jesus. They have the **identical antithesis**, which is a common Biblical method of making meaning clear. Thus, it is a travesty to never explain Luke 13:5 by making appropriate reference to Mark 9:42-47.

Second, and most important, Piper never quotes a dictionary on classical Greek on the standard meanings of *metanoeo*. One of the most commonly used Greek dictionaries in Protestant seminaries is Thayer's *Greek Lexicon*. It defines the Greek word involved (*metanoeo*) as either:

- "change in the mind;" or

- "to change one's mind for better, *heartily to amend with abhorrence of one's past sins.*"

It is in particular the latter definition that Piper omits, which is troubling, as we shall see.

Piper's Argument. Piper lays out his proposition plainly:

> One of my concerns is to show that repentance in Jesus' message is **not behavior** but the **inner change** that gives rise to new God-centered, Christ-exalting behavior.

> [R]epentance is an **internal change of mind and heart** rather than mere **sorrow for sin** or mere **improvement of behavior.**

Let's diagram Piper's point by means of Table 1:

TABLE 1. **Piper's View Of Repentance: A Mind-Only Change Versus Behavioral Change**

Repentance Means	Repentance Supposedly Does Not Mean
1. "inner change"	1. "change in behavior"
2. "internal change of mind and heart"	2. "improvement of behavior"
3."internal change of mind and heart"	3. "sorrow for sin"

How does Piper prove it is none of the meanings on the right side of Table 1? Piper does so by committing the cardinal sin of a commentator.

Cardinal Sin of A Commentator. As discussed previously, the word in Greek at issue — *metanoeo* — which we see translated as *repentance* — always has an alternative meaning of

> "to change one's mind for better, **heartily to amend with abhorrence of one's past sins.**" (Thayer's *Greek Definitions.*)

We likewise saw previously that Bromiley in *The International Standard Bible Encylopedia* (Eerdman's: 1995) said *metanoeo* was used prior to Christ to mean a "complete *change of one's life* and a *complete turning from sin* and *to the ways (or laws) of God.*" In the New Testament, with rare exception, Bromiley said *metanoeo* had the "full sense of a complete *change in one's way of life*" and "spiritual *change implied in a sinner's return to God.*"

In other words, the word *metanoeo* in Greek has each of the three meanings which Piper denies it ever has. Thus, contrary to Piper's claim, repentance *can* mean a decision to reform one's behavior and actually in sorrow reforming one's behavior. An honest commentator must tell the audience of that *possibility* even if you don't want to do so. You must then defend your alternative reading. Any other approach is *less than fair to the reader.*

Yet, by Piper denying this *possibility* even exists for any one of these other three meanings, he makes it appear the *New Living Translation* of Luke 13:5 engages in blatant mis-translation. The NLT adds that the repentance involved is from sin and toward obedience. Hence, even though Piper claims repentance *cannot possibly mean* the propositions in #1, #2 and #3 of column 2 above, these propositions are pre-cisely the meanings that the Greek word simultaneously *can* convey. Yet Piper suppresses and denies that reality.

Thus, Piper — despite all his fame and his awareness of how many people trust his every word — committed the cardinal sin of a commentator on Scripture: Piper never told the reader that his statements were directly contradicted by rudimentary Greek dictionaries and every knowledgeable expert!

Piper's Proof. Piper does attempt to justify his conclusion from a dictionary that the only meaning of the Greek word involved is *a change of one's mind.*

However, Piper does so in a completely non-conven-tional, and inappropriate manner. What is his approach?

Piper breaks the Greek word in two to its constituent parts. Then Piper tells you what those parts — when used as words by themselves — mean in a standard Greek dictionary. Then Piper claims when you put the two different parts together and add their *independent meanings* together, you then have the basic meaning of the word at issue — *metanoeo* — which is only a change in the mind.

However, the meanings of the constituent parts do not tell you always the meaning of the word when the parts are combined. For example, the word *subtraction* does not have the meaning of its two constituent parts. If you define them separately, they mean *under* (sub) and *hand(le)* (tractare). It would be foolish to then tell others the word *subtraction* means to *under hand*. Yet, that is precisely the logic of Piper. It is the sole method he employs to give *definition* to the word *metanoeo* which is the Greek word at issue. Piper writes:

> First, the meaning of the Greek word behind the English "repent" (*metanoeo*) points in this direction. It has **two parts**: *meta* and *noeo*. The **second part** (*noeo*) refers to the mind and its thoughts and perceptions and dispositions and purposes. The **first part** (*meta*) is a prefix that regularly means movement or change. So the **basic meaning of repent is to experience a change of the mind's perceptions and dispositions and purposes**.

This is highly misleading. No mention is made of the Greek dictionary definitions of the whole word *metanoeo* when the two constituent parts are combined. Why?

Because the primary usage by Jesus of *metanoeo* was overwhelmingly to mean **a change from sinful behavior to good behavior.** But if the price to avoid perishing were repentance of this type, it would offend the Gospel of Cheap Grace. This dangerous implication is precisely what Piper is resisting. Thus, Piper neglects any mention of this meaning. Furthermore, he not only ignores this alternative, but Piper also blatantly denies it is *one* possible meaning!

Yet, repentance over sin is one of *metanoeo*'s two primary meanings in any standard Greek dictionary. To repeat, while the word *metanoeo* can mean "change in the mind," its other primary meaning — and the one Jesus typically intended (as we shall see) — was "to change one's mind for better, **heartily to amend with abhorrence of one's past sins**." (Thayer).

Below in Table 2 is a list of every one of twenty passages where Jesus (including the 'Revelation of Jesus Christ') uses the word *metanoeo*. In 13 of the 20 passages, it meant **sorrowful change from sin** in the same sentence — the second dictionary meaning of 'deciding and turning from one's sin.' **Yet, seven times it was ambiguous** within the sentence.

TABLE 2. Repentance Passages (Gk. Metanoeo)

Citation	Verse [KJV]	Change or Faith?
Matthew 4:17	From that time Jesus began to preach, and to say, **Repent**: for the kingdom of heaven is at hand.	Ambiguous
Matthew 11:20	Then began he to upbraid the cities wherein most of his mighty works were done, because they **repented** not:	Ambiguous
Matthew 11:21; Luke 10:13	Woe unto thee, Chorazin! woe unto thee, Bethsaida! for if the mighty works, which were done in you, had been done in Tyre and Sidon, they would have **repented** long ago **in sackcloth and ashes**.	From sin
Matthew 12:41; Luke 11:32	The men of Nineveh shall rise in judgment with this generation, and shall condemn it: because they **repented at the preaching of Jonas**; and, behold, a greater than Jonas is here.	Ambiguous
Mark 6:12	And they went out, and preached that men should **repent**.	Ambiguous
Luke 5:32	I have not come to call the righteous but sinners to **repentance**.	Ambiguous
Luke 13:2,5	**Repent** or perish.	Ambiguous

TABLE 2. Repentance Passages (Gk. Metanoeo)

Citation	Verse [KJV]	Change or Faith?
Luke 15:7	I say unto you, that likewise joy shall be in heaven over one *sinner that repenteth*, more than over ninety and nine *just persons, which need no repentance*.	From sin
Luke 15:10	Likewise, I say unto you, there is joy in the presence of the angels of God over *one sinner that repenteth*.	From sin
Luke 17:3	Take heed to yourselves: If thy brother *trespass against thee*, rebuke him; and if *he repent*, forgive him.	From sin
Luke 17:4	And if he *trespass against thee* seven times in a day, and seven times in a day turn again to thee, saying, *I repent*; thou shalt forgive him.	From sin
Rev. 2:5	Remember therefore from whence *thou art fallen*, and repent, and *do the first works*; or else I will come unto thee quickly, and will remove thy candlestick out of his place, *except thou repent*.	From sin (for believer)
Rev. 2:16	*Repent*; or else I will come unto thee quickly, and will fight against them [sic: you] with the sword of my mouth.	From sin
Rev. 2:22	Behold, I will cast her into a bed, and them that commit *adultery* with her into great tribulation, except they *repent of their deeds*.	From sin
Rev. 3:3	Remember therefore how thou *hast received and heard*, and *hold fast*, and *repent*. If therefore thou shalt *not watch*, I will come on thee as a thief, and thou shalt not know what hour I will come upon thee.	From sin (for a believer)
Rev. 3:19	As many as *I love,* I rebuke and *chasten*: be zealous therefore, and repent.	From sin (for a believer)
Rev. 9:20	And the rest of the men which were not killed by these plagues yet *repented not of the works of their hands*, that they should not worship devils, and idols of gold, and silver, and brass, and stone, and of wood: which neither can see, nor hear, nor walk:	From sin

TABLE 2. Repentance Passages (Gk. Metanoeo)

Citation	Verse [KJV]	Change or Faith?
Rev. 9:21	*Neither repented they of their murders, nor of their sorceries, nor of their fornication, nor of their thefts.*	From sin
Rev. 16:9	And men were scorched with great heat, and blasphemed the name of God, which hath power over these plagues: and *they repented not to give him glory.*	Ambiguous
Rev. 16:11	And blasphemed the God of heaven because of their pains and their sores, and *repented not of their deeds.*	From sin
20 passages		**13** - From sin
		7 - Ambiguous

What does Piper do with these thirteen problematical passages? After all, the case is overwhelming that Jesus means by repentance that it is turning from sin.

Piper's response is to selectively base his discussion solely upon ambiguous passages.

Piper selects four of the seven ***ambiguous*** verses listed above to quote in full to make his case. He quotes them with a lead in that "here are some thoughts to help make the meaning ***more plain.***" However, quoting the ambiguous passages, as he does of Matthew 4:17, Luke 5:32, Luke 13:2-5, and Matthew 12:41, is ***precisely how to make things less plain***. It is how one would obscure and make Jesus' meaning less apparent.

It is hard to ignore Piper's intention when Piper selects none of the 13 other passages where Jesus uses the word for repentance to mean turning *from sin*.

For example, *repent or perish* in Luke 13:2-5 is ambiguous if you just look at that single sentence. You have to look to the context asking: does *repentance* mean *faith* as the mental change or *turning from sin?* It is unclear ***without*** the context. Thus, Piper elects to choose just these words "repent or perish" along with three other ambiguous verses. Then Piper ignores all of the 13 passages where Jesus clearly means by repentance a *change* about *sin*, not *faith*.

This quote selection served a clear agenda. Look at the selectivity of Piper's choices in Table 3 below. Was Piper really trying to make Jesus' point "more plain"? Or was Piper taking advantage of ambiguity in a few passages for the purpose of downplaying Jesus' *true* meaning, thereby protecting the fable of cheap grace?

TABLE 3. **Selectivity Of John Piper**

Ambiguous Passages (7)	Repentance From Sin (13/20)
Quotes in full 4 of 7 or 57%	Cites 0%

Whatever was the true purpose of such selectivity, its impact is significant. The faithful readers could never imagine a scholar like Piper would ignore there are numerous Scriptural counter-examples on *metanoeo's* meaning. They could never suspect that *metanoeo* has any meaning other than *change in mind*. So if Piper says these few passages will help make Jesus meaning 'more plain,' the trusting reader would assume these are the clearest passages. The trusting reader would assume there are no passages that refute Piper's assertion about *metanoeo's* meaning. But this natural conclusion derives only because of a poor presentation.

Piper's argumentation method proves how far the fabulists of cheap grace must go. They must bury their heads in the sand and ignore Jesus' central doctrine of repentance. Piper's desperation, when confronted by the words of Jesus, is evident in how extraordinarily strained was his alleged proof.

Piper Next Tries To Equate Repentance To Faith Alone. Now that Piper has proven (in his mind) that repentance solely means *change in mind*, Piper is going to reveal the purpose behind that limited definition.

Piper slips in that this 'change in mind' (repentance) that Jesus requires for salvation is really just about seeing Jesus in a new way. As described next, this proposition is indistinguishable from saying repentance merely means faith in Jesus. Now we are beginning to see *the agenda* behind all of Piper's preceding weak presentation. Piper says:

> Repenting means experiencing a change of mind that now sees God as true and beautiful and worthy of all our praise and all our obedience. *This change of mind also embraces Jesus in the same way.* We know this because Jesus said, "If God were your Father, you would love me, for I came from God." *Seeing God with a new mind includes seeing Jesus with a new mind*.

Thus, instead of repentance being a change in one's behavior, Piper says it is a change in the "mind" on how it "embraces" Jesus in a new way. It means we "see" Jesus "with a new mind." We now treat Jesus as a person that is "true, beautiful and worthy of all our praise and all our obedience." This 'new mind' about Jesus is obviously indistinguishable from someone now placing their faith in Jesus.

Hence, Piper has reduced "repent or perish" into having "faith or perish."

Now we see how the Fable of the Cheap Grace Gospel continues to hold onto our minds. Piper's claims are all too familiar to us. Piper is just the latest re-invention of an old saw about repentance being merely a change in your mind (akin or equal to faith). It is the same old saw which our faith-alone forefathers used to dispense with Jesus' *repent-or-perish* verses. In fact, in the *Free Will Baptist Quarterly* (Jan. 1860), it noted faith-alone adherents "make both faith and repentance occupy the same ground, give to them the same boundaries, the same characteristics, the same objects." *Id.*, at 75. But the *Free Will Baptist* denounced this as sophistry, for such is not "the sense of the words, and order of the gospel." Indeed, as we next explore, the *Free Will Baptist* is correct.

What Is Repentance In Jesus' Usage Elsewhere?

As noted above, Jesus says, "Unless you repent you will all likewise perish." (Luke 13:3.) The Greek present tense is used for *repent*. Thus, it really means "Unless you keep on repenting you will all likewise perish."

What does Jesus mean by *repentance* here? In this single sentence, without looking at the context, it is somewhat vague. Does Jesus mean a mere change in your mind? Or is it instead a call to change your sinful behaviors?

Jesus clearly elsewhere uses the same Greek word in Luke 13:3 for *repentance* to mean a **decision to turn from one's evil ways and turning from them**. This was when Jesus said the people of Nineveh "repented" at the preaching of Jonah. (Matthew 12:41.) If we turn to the passage that Jesus is referencing, will we find their repentance was a mere change in their mind to believe in Yahweh? Or was it a decision to turn from sin and doing so? What did Jesus mean by the simple word *repent* in Matthew 12:41?

Well, Jesus was summarizing an event in Scripture where the scope of the mental change is clearly identified. Whether repentance for the Ninevites meant merely faith or turning from sin is clearly addressed.

When we go to Jonah 3:4-10, we find the Bible says that when Jonah preached, the people of Nineveh gave heed, were sorry, and turned from their evil ways. (Jonah 3:8,10.) Let's read the passage in depth, for their conduct is what Jesus called "repentance."

> And he made proclamation and published through Nineveh by the decree of the king and his nobles, saying, Let neither man nor beast, herd nor flock, taste anything; let them not feed, nor drink water; (8) but let them be **covered with sackcloth**, both man and beast, and let them cry mightily unto God: yea, **let them turn every one from his evil way, and from**

> *the violence that is in his hands.* (9) Who
> knoweth whether God will not turn and repent,
> and turn away from his fierce anger, that we
> perish not? (10) And *God saw their works,*
> *that they turned from their evil way*; and God
> *repented of the evil* which he said he would
> do unto them; and he did it not. (Jonah 3:7-10
> ASV.)

Please also note that God's "repentance" involved a
change of His mind about doing a deed. This *decision by God*
was to likewise change His intended behavior. Note also
God did not make this change until "God saw their **works**,
that they turned from their evil way." Hence, God does not
relent from standing ready to punish until He sees a change in
mind reflected in *works worthy of repentance.*

Hence, this passage in Jonah proves that this
"turning" from evil by the Ninevites is what Jesus meant by
repentance by the Ninevites. This tells us Jesus intended the
word for *repentance* in Greek in Matthew 12:41 to mean a
decision in one's mind to turn from an intent and then turning.
Jesus did not mean by *repentance* the simple concept of faith
alone. Thus, this is an example overlooked by Piper. It serves
as a counter-example to his assertion. This study proves Bromiley's statement was correct that *repentance* has a primary
meaning that includes deciding to turn from sin and then
"heartily amending" your behavior out of abhorrence for it.

Conclusion

Thus, we have carefully examined the simple statement from Jesus on *repent-or-perish.* Jesus said:

> No, and I tell you again that unless you repent,
> you will perish, too.' (John 13:5.)

In response, the Gospel of Cheap Grace, in particular
its advocate Piper, insisted that the word *repent* here has no
cost element. It simply means we must embrace Jesus with a

new mind that sees Him as good, beautiful, true and worthy of obedience. In a word, we are supposedly only to have 'faith in Jesus or we will perish.'

This was precisely the argument about *repentance* by the heretic Marcion (144 A.D.) and his followers who persisted into the 400s. They taught salvation by "faith alone." (See pages 578-584.) Augustine in 413 A.D. said the solafidists argued repentance was only in the mind from "the unbelief alone" in Jesus, not by adding any obedience or good works. For this they relied upon Paul. Augustine replied: "Wonderful presumption!" Augustine showed how this violated all of Jesus' teachings. (Augustine, *Fide et operibus*, in *Seventeen Short Treatises of Augustine* (trans. Cornish)(1847) at 47,49-57.)

Marcion of Sinope

The Marcionites failed earlier but are suceeding now. Yet, we saw this passage from Jesus on "repent or perish" in Luke exactly parallels Jesus' warning that you can go to *heaven-maimed or hell-whole* in Mark 9:42-47. The antithesis in both is clear: *repent or perish = heaven-maimed or hell-whole*. There is no path to heaven Jesus offers to avoid this. There is no means to replace "repent" with "believe."

We also saw the dictionary definition from Thayer that *repent* means a decision for the better, where one turns from a specific sin or conduct henceforth. We saw too that Jesus unquestionably spoke of *repentance* the same way when He talked of the Ninevites.

Therefore, it is beyond any serious question that Jesus means by "repent or perish" in Luke 13:5 that you can go to "heaven maimed or hell whole." Jesus **specifically rejects that grace is without personal cost**. Rather, as Jesus did elsewhere, He taught again here that salvation comes at the cost of renouncing all that holds you back from obedience to God. Salvation is not by faith *alone*. **Hence, the most popular gospel of today is a false gospel**. It is not His way. Jesus' Way is bluntly 'repent or perish.'

7 *Saying But Not Doing*

*Repenting And Doing vs. Saying You Will
But Not Doing*

Introduction

In the Parable of the Two Sons, Jesus specifically taught a lesson that repentance is measured by *action* that follows. God could care less what you say if it is not followed up by obedience *consistent* with your mental belief. This lesson mirrored Jesus' citation of the example of the Ninevites as repentance (Matt. 12:41). For their mental sorrow had no validity until their words were followed by consistent action. God did not repent of His plans to punish the Ninevites until God "saw their works, that they turned from their evil ways." (Jonah 3:10.) Hence, repentance, to be valid, always implies the necessity to turn from sin. Mere sorrow for sin has no effect to stave off God's ire for your sin.

In Matthew 21:28-31, Jesus illustrates this principle in the story of two sons. One says he will do His father's will, but does not do it. The other son says he will not obey, but ultimately "repents" and *does* what His father asked.

Jesus asks: who did God's will?

Obviously, the son who repented and did what he was told. It was not the son who verbally agreed to do his father's will but then failed to do it. As P.G. Mathew said in a 1997 sermon at Grace Valley Christian Center, this parable means:

> God is not impressed with a profusion of confession ***unless*** that confession is followed by Christian ***conduct***.[1]

The German evangelical minister Friedrich Gustav-Lisco (1791-1866) likewise says, the son who makes a good profession but then is "without obedience," is "***kept out of the kingdom***" while the "publicans and harlots go in before you." (Frederick Lisco, *The Parables of Jesus* (trans. Rev. Fairbairn)(Philadelphia:1850) at 146.)

Lisco is correct that salvation is promised to the obedient one, while the disobedient is "kept out of the kingdom" despite a good profession. Jesus emphasized this was a lesson impacting salvation. Jesus equates the first son's action of doing the will of the father with "publicans and harlots." They are in contrast to the second son who symbolize the religious leaders who preach obedience, but don't obey. They are like the religious ruler and Levite in the Parable of the Good Samaritan who pass by the wounded man. (Luke 10:31-32.)

Jesus then equates the actions of the good son in the story with salvation for the ones who have repented from sin to a new life: publicans and harlots: "Verily I say unto you, that the publicans and the harlots ***go into the kingdom of God*** before you." (Mat 21:31, ASV.)

As we will explore, the Greek actually means "the publicans and harlots are ***promoted over you*** into the kingdom of God." The vague "before you" translation is apparently chosen to suggest the disobedient son still enters heaven, but in second place *behind* the publicans and harlots. This translation protects cheap grace, as we shall see.

Instead, Jesus' expression in this parable is meant to imply *exclusion* of the religious leaders from the kingdom who say they will obey but don't. As Lisco said in the quote above, Jesus means the disobedient son is "kept out of the kingdom." Moreover, this translation is more consistent with Jesus' repeated teaching that the religious leaders were blocking salvation for themselves, as well as for their proselytes.

---

1. See P. G. Mathew, M.A., M.Div., Th.M, "Self-Delusion Exposed: Matthew 7:21-23," Grace Valley Christian Center (Sermon October 12, 1997), available online at http://www.dcn.davis.ca.us/~gvcc/sermon_trans/1997/Self_Delusion_Exposed.html (accessed 7-01-07).

(Matt. 23:13-23.) Similarly, the religious ruler and Levite in the Parable of the Good Samaritan are the ones who disobeyed the command to love your neighbor, which Jesus had just said is necessary to obey to have "eternal life." (Luke 10:25,27,28,31,32.) The second (disobedient) son in the parable, who is a symbol of these religious leaders, therefore must be lost. The second son (the disobedient son) does not enter heaven merely *behind* the publicans and harlots.

Thus, the Parable of the Two Sons was not about Jesus saying the disobedient son still enjoys heaven but as a second class citizen. As we shall see below, the Modern Gospel of Cheap Grace is forced into arguing this position. Jesus does not agree with cheap grace which says sincere words rather than obedience is what matters. Thus, **many faith-alone commentators will argue Jesus meant to imply the religious leaders who are disobedient are still saved**. The religious leaders supposedly enter heaven as *second class citizens.* (This is thoroughly explored below.)

However, this reading is only to serve the Modern Gospel of Cheap Grace. But why? What explains this spin? The Modern Gospel is **always trying to destroy Jesus' point that action consistent with repentance will entitle one to heaven and not mere sincere words**. They seek to frustrate Jesus' true message that the promise of salvation does not belong to those who say they will do God's will but then *disobey.* Because Jesus' true intent destroys the doctrine of cheap grace, these commentators vigorously distort the passage. They are **actually saying with a straight-face that Jesus promises salvation for the disobedient son in this parable**! Yet that idea is a preposterous notion.

Clearly, Jesus' point was precisely the opposite. Jesus' message is that the **promise to obey without corresponding obedience is worthless**. The disobedient are lost despite a good profession. However, a true repentance with **corresponding action** gives you the right to be promoted over the disobedient into heaven.

The Fig Tree Event Sets The Context Of This Parable

This Parable of the Two Sons comes on the heels of the recent episode with the fig tree. (See Matt. 21:18-22.) John Broadus says this episode explains the Parable of the Two Sons: "The same fault had been illustrated that morning by the fig-tree, which made great *show of leaves*, but had *no fruit*." (John A. Broadus, *Commentary on Matthew* (1886)(reprint Kregel Classics: 1990) at 438.) Jesus promises the tree without good fruit is cut down and thrown in the fire. (Matt. 7:19.) Jesus is warning loss of salvation for lacking repentance unto actual obedience. This point is reiterated in the Parable of the Two Sons. Jesus is not promising salvation to the religious rulers as second-class citizens for their disobedience, as the fabulists of Cheap Grace must insist.

Let's study this passage carefully to test their reading.

The Passage

Here is the entire passage in the ASV. Jesus says:

(28) But what think ye? A man had two sons; and he came to the first, and said, Son, go work to-day in the vineyard.

(29) And he answered and said, I will not: but afterward he **repented** himself, and went.

(30) And he came to the second, and said likewise. And he answered and **said, *I go, sir:*** and **went not**.

(31) Which of the two did the will of his father? They say, The first. Jesus saith unto them, Verily I say unto you, that the publicans and the harlots **go into the kingdom of God before you**.

(32) For John came unto you in the way of righteousness, and ye believed him not; but the

publicans and the harlots believed him: and ye, when ye saw it, did not even **repent** yourselves afterward, that ye might believe him. (Mat 21:28-32, ASV.)

The Greek word translated in verse 31 as "go in before you" is a poor translation. The verb infinitive is *pro-agô*. It generally is said to mean "to lead forward, on, or onward." Here it is the Greek present participle, so it is has a continuous meaning. Because this is the linchpin word that some use to argue that Jesus means the disobedient son still enters the kingdom of God (see the next section), let's take a very close look at the word *proagô*.

Does Jesus really mean to imply the disobedient enter heaven but do so as second class citizens?

Liddell-Scott (LS) is the best Greek Lexicon. When we subtract all their cites, we get these meanings:

A. [1] lead forward or onward, escort on their way,

2. [a] carry on, produce, brought to a point

b. bring on (in age)

c. increase, raise (a dose)

3. [a] bring forward, call up (an apparition)

b. bring before a tribunal

4. lead on, induce, persuade.

5. [a] carry forward, advance; lead it on to power; carried it so far; carry on and complete;

b. of **persons**, **promote or prefer** to honor.

c. **prefer** in the way of choice

II. Intransitive.

lead the way, go before.

2. metaph., *the preceding* discourse

3. *go on, advance*

4. *excel.*[2]

Thus, in Greek, when this verb is used about *persons*, in particular between two qualitatively different groups, Liddell-Scott ("LS") says it means one group is *promoted* or *preferred* to an honor over another. (Definition 5, b above.)

There is a perfect example of this Greek usage in early Christianity. In the "canons of Nicaea" (325 A.D.) *pro-agô* meant "to *promote* in clerical rank." (Michael J. Hollerich, *Eusebius of Caesarea's Commentary on Isaiah: Christian Exegesis in the Age of Constantine* (Oxford University Press: 1999) at 184.)

If we use this meaning here, it excludes the possibility that the disobedient group is likewise *sharing* that same honor of entering the kingdom. Because this meaning in LS 5, b fits both the context and Jesus elsewhere telling us the disobedient religious leaders are going to hell (Matt.23:13-23), this must be regarded as the *correct* translation.

Thus, using the correct Greek usage here (5, b above), this key verse should have been translated:

> Verily I say unto you, that the publicans and the harlots are being **promoted over** you [or INSTEAD OF YOU] into the kingdom of God.

The obedient move up to the kingdom. The disobedient don't. That's the message of Jesus.

---

2. To pull up the Liddell-Scott lexicon, go to http://www.perseus.tufts.edu/cgi-bin/ptext?doc=Perseus%3Atext%3A1999.01.0155&layout=&loc=Matthew+21.1, and then go to verse 32, and highlight *proagusin*, and the pop up will give you this definition. (Last accessed 6/19/06).

This obvious deduction is corroborated by other commentators.

Commentaries That Agree The Disobedient Son Is Unsaved

Lectionary Bible Series

The *Lectionary Bible Series* comments on Jesus' meaning. It says Jesus' point is the one who did not obey His father is left outside of the kingdom. The disobedient are left behind the publicans and tax collectors who are permitted to go in ahead of them. It is absurd to imply Jesus means the son who disobeys is going to be saved anyway:

> Proagousin (proagw) "are entering [the kingdom of God] ahead of you" - are going before you, are preceding you. Those who never accepted God's authority over them are now accepting it in Jesus and are entering the kingdom, while those **who once accepted it**, now reject it in Jesus and **find themselves outside the kingdom**....Barclay. "Ahead of" is possibly "instead of," "in place of," but unlikely.[3]

Thus, we see the *Lectionary* say some translate the Greek to mean *instead of you.* It says this is 'unlikely,' but there is no peculiar reason why this is so. The idea of *promotion*, which Liddell Scott and early church usage supports, would mean the obedient son goes in as a promotion *over* and *instead* of the disobedient son. Thus, *instead of* would properly convey the Greek meaning.

---

3. "Matthew: The authority of Jesus. 21:23-32," *Lectionary Bible Studies and Sermons* at http://www.lectionarystudies.com/studyg/sunday26ag.html (last accessed 6/21/06.)

Even though the *Lectionary* quibbles over *how* the verse is worded, it still has the right conclusion. Jesus' point must mean the son who said he would obey but later disobeys never reaches the entry point. The Greek means he is *left* "outside of the kingdom." A crisp way of saying this is that the obedient enters *instead* of the disobedient. The *Lectionary* reached this similar conclusion without making the exhaustive analysis of the Greek, yet it has the correct conclusion.

Furthermore, the context and tenor of the parable dictate this. It would be completely incongruous to suggest Jesus is saying the only consequence of accepting God's commands but then later failing to obey is you enter heaven behind the more obedient of God's children. Such a view would be also inconsistent with all of Jesus' teachings that repentance *from sin* is essential to salvation. For example, Jesus teaches in Mark 9:42-48 that you can enter heaven maimed or hell whole. Repentance from sin that successfully *turns*, in fact, from sin, is crucial to eternal life. Thus, the *Lectionary* is correct that those left behind are left "outside the kingdom."[4]

Forerunner Commentary

This commentary correctly sees the two sons as defined by a difference in action:

> The second is a big talker, full of promises but no action. In these two men, Christ describes, on the one hand, sinners of all types, who, when convicted by John the Baptist and Himself, **turned away from their iniquities**, repented, and **obeyed God**. On the other hand are the scribes, Pharisees, and other self-righteous people who **feign a zeal for the law** but will not receive the gospel.[5]

---

4. For more on the meaning of *repentance* in Jesus' usage, see the chapter beginning at page 89.

Let's examine closely what this says about the two sons by comparing and contrasting their labels:

First Son (Repentant & Obedient)	Second Son (Disobedient)
"turned away from their iniquities"	"feign a zeal for the law"
"repented"	"not receive the gospel"
"obeyed God"	

These contrasts correctly reveal Jesus' meaning. Not receiving the Gospel is thereby equated correctly by the Forerunner Commentary with *failing* to turn away from sin, repenting and obeying God and instead feigning a zeal for the Law.

Elsewhere, the Forerunner Commentary says the second son (the religious leaders) represents

> hypocrites, those who appear or ***profess one way but act another.*** The work the father asks them to do corresponds to living God's way of life.

This is also highly accurate and informative. Yet, it has drifted a bit from the contrasts Jesus uses. These contrasts quoted above hold tighter to Jesus' point. The good son is the one who rebelled at first but then repents and obeys. The bad son is the one who says he will obey but ends up being disobedient.

Thus, the bad son is not lost because he professed insincerely or was a hypocrite *initially* in the profession. Jesus never focuses on those issues in this passage. ***Jesus never tries here to expose any hypocrisy in the profession.*** For all we know it could have been sincere by the disobedient son. Rather, Jesus makes the dividing line between the two

---

5. http://bibletools.org/index.cfm/fuseaction/Bible.show/sVerseID/23855/eVerseID/23858 (last accessed 3/22/07).

sons based on how they each *acted* differently later. The key to this passage is not to focus on whether one made a hypocritical profession. Rather, it is how the *lost are saved by being obedient after a wrong profession* which is in contrast against those who *profess correctly but later don't obey*!

In a word, Jesus has made the issue of salvation turn on *obedience* in this parable. In a sense, Jesus is saying *your profession no matter how sincere is insufficient if your obedience does not follow.*

As Jesus also said, we will be "judged" by every idle word that leaves our lips. (Matt. 12:36.) If we profess repentance from sin, but do not follow through, God will judge us for *not doing* what *we said* we would do. Matthew Henry puts it quite well: God will "judge them out of their own mouths."

This is why the Forerunner is then incorrect to suggest the second son's fault was *insincerity* in his profession. To repeat, Jesus is not drawing attention to any defect in the profession itself of the second son. It might have been with the very best of intentions and very sincere, for all we know. People can say one thing, and change their mind later.

What Jesus is pointing out is the second son's failure to subsequently *act* consistent with his profession. By contrast, the first son who initially said he would disobey (a bad profession) then repented and obeyed. Each acts differently than he professes he would do. Only the one who obeys God is saved. That's the point.

Cheap Grace Commentaries On Matthew 21:28-32: The Disobedient Son Is Saved!

Robertson's *Word Pictures*

Regarding this parable, Robertson's *Word Pictures* only has it half right. He correctly understands what Jesus means by the son who repents. "But the one who actually did the will of the father is the one who repented and went [to obey]...." Robertson agrees Jesus means *true* repentance is the one who *actually did the will of the father*. Mere words of the second son that he would obey are not enough. Robertson concedes Jesus means **mere remorse without action to follow is not true repentance**. Robertson closes: "mere sorrow is not repentance."

What did Jesus imply would happen to the Jewish leaders who were mouthing obedience but who disobeyed God? Because of adherence to the Modern Gospel of Cheap Grace, Robertson tries to imply that Jesus does not mean to say the disobedient Jewish leaders will be lost. (If Jesus did mean they were lost, then this undermines cheap grace which claims that disobedience is not the cause of damnation.) Robertson says Jesus wants us to think the disobedient *merely take second seat in heaven to the publicans and harlots*. Thus, their problem is merely complacency, not the failure to act consistent with their profession. Listen to this subtle undermining of Jesus' lesson:

> Go before you (proagousin). "In front of you" (Weymouth). The publicans and harlots **march ahead of the ecclesiastics into the kingdom of heaven**. It is a powerful indictment of the **complacency** of the Jewish theological leaders.

This is completely wrong. Robertson loses the meaning of the lesson by insisting the Weymouth translation means the disobedient son is saved but arrives in second place *inside* heaven. Robertson is suggesting that Jesus is telling the Jewish leaders they are saved. They are supposedly going to enter heaven because they accepted God's commands initially even though they later disobeyed them.

Robertson's spin is designed to say this passage is not how disobedience to your profession causes the loss of salvation. Nor is this supposedly about how only true repentance *by action* leads to salvation. Robertson turns it into a passage about rewards. So the only difference for those who *repent and actually do the will of the Father* is they supposedly march into heaven *ahead* of those believing Jewish leaders who at first accepted but later failed to do the will of God. This is a ridiculous reading!

It is amazing how commentators *nullify* Jesus' obvious messages at every turn in slavish adherence to faith alone.

Matthew Henry's Commentary: A More Conflicted Message

Henry's commentary is notable too for agreeing with Jesus but then subtly undermining it too. Henry begins correctly saying Jesus means that the work which the father  **Matthew Henry 1662- 1714** wants is obedience to do God's commands. The father asks the son to *go work today in my vineyard.* Henry says this "gospel call to work in the vineyard, requires present *obedience*.*" Henry then realizes the different outcomes is due to *action*, not beliefs or what they said with their mouth:

> Their conduct was very different. One of the sons did better than he said, proved better than he promised. His answer was bad, **but his actions were good.**

Henry then makes a very brave statement at odds with belief-alone doctrine, and properly draws out Jesus' meaning:

> Saying and **doing** are two things; and many there are that say, and do not; it is particularly charged upon the Pharisees, (Mat 23:3.) Many with their mouth show much love, but their heart goes another way. They had a good mind to be religious, but they **met with something to be done**, that was **too hard**, or something to be parted with, that was **too dear**, and so their purposes are to no purpose. Buds and blossoms are not fruit.

This is clearly Jesus' meaning. One son does, and the other says he will but does not do it. The different outcomes are because of the difference in *action* — what Henry says is fruit (*works*). Henry then correctly sees Jesus is merely repeating the principle one finds in Ezekiel 18. Henry says:

> God gives of the rule of his judgment (Eze 18:21-24), that if the sinner **turn from his wickedness**, he shall be **pardoned**; and if the righteous man turn from his righteousness, he shall be **rejected**. The tenour of the whole scripture gives us to understand that those are accepted as doing their Father's will, who, wherein they have missed it, are sorry for it, and **do better**.

But doesn't Jesus say more than the obedient merely *do better* and walk into the kingdom of heaven "before" the religious leaders who do not do God's will? The implication of Jesus is that the disobedient will be left behind, never entering heaven. The publicans and harlots who have repented are promoted to heaven *over* the disobedient religious rulers who professed a willingness to obey but then are disobedient.

Unfortunately, in the final analysis, Henry in the next quote, like Robertson, will choose to say the publicans and harlots enter heaven *before* the religious leaders. The disobedient second son supposedly still enters, but as second class citizens. Thus, Henry says Jesus means to imply the *disobedient* religious leaders *are saved*. They supposedly are not as honored because they must enter in second place. Henry means **Jesus intended us to know the son who said he would do his father's will but does not do it is still saved**. This is **nonsense**. But here is Henry saying this in the last analysis:

> These proud priests, that set up for leaders, scorned to follow, though **it were into the kingdom of heaven**, especially **to follow publicans**; through the pride of their countenance, they would not seek after God, after Christ.

Thus, for Henry the most absurd reading of Jesus is acceptable. Why? Because it matches the Modern Gospel of Cheap Grace. We do not have to obey the will of the Father to be acceptable and *enter* the kingdom. ***We supposedly can be the disobedient son, and still be saved***. We just walk in last, behind the obedient. The Cheap Grace Gospel wants us to believe Jesus intends to give *relief to* disobedient Christians from the pressure of obedience for salvation! It is amazing what nonsense people can convince themselves to believe!

Compare The Parable Of The Good Samaritan To The Parable Of The Two Sons

Introduction

There is really little doubt on Jesus' point in the Parable of the The Two Sons. We need only look a little bit ahead at other messages of Jesus to see this.

Jesus will tell a lesson to explain how to obtain eternal life to a Torah-Scholar. (Luke 10:25 *ff*.) Jesus will explain the command to love your neighbor — one of the commands Jesus will say in the same context was a command to obey to have eternal life. (Luke 10:28.)

Jesus then gives him the Parable of the Good Samaritan to illustrate the same principle we see in the Parable of the Two Sons. (Luke 10:30-37.)

The Samaritan — a member of a somewhat heretical sect (see page 122) — is equivalent to the first son in the Parable of the Two Sons. The Samaritan is a heretic everyone thinks is never going to do anything obedient to the Law. However, then the Samaritan does the right thing. By contrast, the religious ruler and Levite in the Samaritan parable are equivalent to the second son in the Parable of the Two Sons. They teach correctly obedience to the command to love thy neighbor. However, the religious ruler and Levite do the opposite of what they taught and professed.

Thus, we can see Jesus hinges the path to eternal life on obedience and not your profession alone. Only the Samaritan is obedient in the parable. The religious ruler and Levite are hence lost because they are disobedient to the command to love they neighbor (which Jesus is linking to 'eternal life' in context) despite a correct profession of faith in Yahweh. Consequently, there is an obvious parallel between the Parable of the Good Samaritan and the Parable of the Two Sons.

This clarifies the second son's fate in the Parable of the Two Sons. For the second son clearly symbolizes the religious rulers who profess God's word. The second son thus identically matches the disobedient religious ruler and Levite in the Parable of the Good Samaritan. Then since in the latter parable, Jesus is giving an exposition on how to have eternal life, and says the religious ruler and Levite are, in effect, lost from the right path to "eternal life," then it follows the disobedient second son in the Parable of the Two Sons must likewise be lost. The disobedient second son, like the disobedient religious ruler and Levite, could not conceivably be entering heaven as a second class citizen, despite the claims of Robertson and Henry above to the contrary.

The Torah-Scholar's Question Leading Into The Parable

The Parable of the Good Samaritan is an illustration designed to explain a command which Jesus says must be followed *to obtain eternal life*. Thus, we need to go back to the preceding context to know more about Jesus' doctrine on salvation.

At one point, Jesus is asked by a Torah-scholar a very good question. How does one have "eternal life"? Jesus asks this scholar what does he think. The scholar says 'obey the commandments,' and rattles off the Two Great Commandments (*i.e.*, love God with your whole heart and love thy neighbor). Jesus say the man has answered *correctly*, and says if you do these commandments from the Law upon which the whole Law hangs you will live, *i.e.*, have eternal life. (Luke 10:28.)

To this the Torah-scholar asks, 'who is my neighbor?'

The Parable Of The Good Samaritan & The Sinful Levite

Jesus is now going to answer how one obeys the command to love they neighbor versus how one violates the command. Upon proper obedience to it, Jesus just said hinges 'eternal life.' Thus, it is highly important to extract Jesus' meaning in the Parable of the Good Samaritan that follows.

Jesus explains the principle of 'love thy neighbor' in such a way that the Samaritan — a member of a sect in Judaism regarded as doctrinal heretics by the Jewish leaders — was the obedient one (and hence saved), while the Levite and the religious ruler — the ones who accept and teach God's commands weekly — pass by an injured man and do nothing. The religious ruler and Levite are disobedient to God's law, leaving a man near death to die. The religious ruler and Levite are, in effect, attempted murderers by neglecting the man in such peril. The religious ruler and Levite are not on the path to eternal life — the issue at stake in what Jesus is explaining. (Luke 10:30-37.)

Thus, the Parable of the Good Samaritan teaches us that obedience is *not in what you believe and teach (whether good or somewhat heretical)*, but in *what you actually do that is consistent with the Law of God*. In the Parable of the Good Samaritan, the religious leaders who were known for teaching "love thy neighbor" do not *actually do so* when the opportunity arose. But the Samaritan, who was supposed to be *a doctrinal heretic*, obeys the law and loves his neighbor. This message is precisely *identical to the Parable of the Two Sons*.

As a result, the Parable of the Good Samaritan resolves the issue of whether the Parable of the Two Sons implies the disobedient are saved, as the proponents of the Modern Gospel of Cheap Grace (Robertson, Henry) insist must be true. The Parable of the Good Samaritan proves the disobedient religious leaders in the Parable of Two Sons are lost.

For Jesus in the Parable of the Good Samaritan gives the key why the publicans and harlots in the Parable of Two Sons are entering heaven. In context, Jesus tells the Torah-scholar that he was correct that one of the two key commands to obey to enter eternal life was 'love thy neighbor as yourself.' Jesus' point in the Parable of the Good Samaritan which follows is that the one who takes care of his neighbor, and obeys the commandment to 'love they neighbor as thyself' will 'enter life.' The Samaritan corresponds to the publicans and harlots in the Parable of the Two Sons: people regarded as lost by the religious leaders. Yet, the religious rulers who profess the Law and accept its words do not obey what they teach, and due to their disobedience to the Law, they will not 'enter life.' The Samaritan and the publicans and harlots will be promoted over them into heaven.

As a result, because the Parable of the Good Samaritan parallels the Parable of the Two Sons, we know in the latter parable *the disobedient son is in the analogous position of the religious ruler and Levite who both pass by the injured man on the road in the Parable of the Good Samaritan*.

Then because Jesus' meaning in the Parable of the Good Samaritan is that to enter life you *must obey what you teach* about being a good neighbor, we know that the disobedient son does not enter life. The disobedient's failure to obey this command in the Parable of the Good Samaritan makes the religious ruler and Levite both guilty of damning sin. Yet, a sinner who obeys the Law toward his neighbor enters life. *The religious rulers who profess obedience but do not act in accord do not enter life*. Thus, it follows logically that in the Parable of the Two Sons, the disobedient son too does not enter life. The Cheap Grace Gospel is wrong when its defenders, like Robertson and Henry, insist the disobedient son is still saved. That could not possibly be Jesus' point.

Obedience to your profession is crucial. Sincere words of *belief* mean nothing if not followed up by *consistent action* with your belief. Who says so? Jesus.

Now we can understand Kierkegaard's frustration over the incessant glosses to erase Jesus' points. Here is how he expressed this in 1855 from a Lutheran experience:

> And in this my opinion is the *falsification* of which official Christianity is guilty: it *does not frankly and unreservedly make known the Christian requirement* [of costs to salvation]— perhaps because it is afraid people would shudder to see at what a distance from it we are living, without being able to claim that in the remotest way our life might be called an *effort in the direction of fulfilling the requirement*. (Kierkegaard, *Kierkegaard's Attack, supra,* at 38.)

The Samaritans: A Brief Synopsis On Who They Were

Jesus was accused of being a Samaritan (Jn. 8:48). This was a way of saying He was a heretic. "The Samaritans were followers of a corrupt form of Judaism [and the] Jews regarded them as heretics." (Richard R. Losch, *The Uttermost Parts of the Earth: A Guide To Places In The Bible* (Eerdmans: 2005) at 209.) Samaritans were a sect within Judaism in the northern part of Israel. Where they lived came to be known later as Samaria. The name "Samaritan" means "keepers of the Law." They claimed to be the true repository of the authentic Mosaic Law. They had their own schismatic temple in the North. The Samaritan sect also had a strong belief in a coming Messiah. Interestingly, they taught a Millennium would follow, and then conclude in one grand final conflict between God and the forces of evil. Then comes resurrection and judgment. They taught those who did good pass to the Garden of Eden (on earth) and those who did bad go to the Fire. (James Allan Montgomery, *The Samaritans, the Earliest Jewish Sect: Their History, Theology and Literature* (J.C. Winston: 1907) at 246,248-50.)

8 *Jesus' Answer To The Direct Question On How To Obtain Eternal Life*

Was Jesus Ever Point-Blank Asked How To Have Eternal Life?

Jesus was asked twice how to have "eternal life." Once by a lawyer and once by a young rich man. Jesus both times answers that the key to salvation is to obey the Law, in particular the Ten Commandments. Jesus then explains to the apostles this means one must live a life based on self-denial which keeps on following Jesus.

What did Jesus precisely say to the rich young man?

Jesus told the young rich man that if you would "enter life," obey the Ten Commandments. (Matthew 19:16-26; Mark 10:17-31; Luke 18:18-26.) Jesus recited these commands verbatim to the young man.[1] Here is the exchange:

> (16) And behold, one came to him and said, ***Teacher, what good thing shall I do, that I may have eternal life***? (17) And he said unto him, Why askest thou me concerning that which is good? One there is who is good: but ***if thou wouldest enter into life, keep*** [Greek, ***tereo, obey***] ***the commandments***. (18) He saith

---

1. Some think it is significant that the Sabbath command is not repeated. Some have developed an odd hermeneutic that if something is not repeated in the New, it is abolished. Why? Jesus said all the Law, to the least command, remains. (Matt. 5:19.) Also, Jesus did not have to inquire whether the man kept the Sabbath because in that era it was an unavoidable civil duty.

---

unto him, Which? And Jesus said, Thou shalt not kill, Thou shalt not commit adultery, Thou shalt not steal, Thou shalt not bear false witness, (19) Honor thy father and mother; and, Thou shalt love thy neighbor as thyself. (20) The young man saith unto him, All these things have I observed: what lack I yet? (21) Jesus said unto him, *If thou wouldest be perfect, go, sell that which thou hast, and give to the poor, and thou shalt have treasure in heaven: and come, follow me.* (22) But when the young man heard the saying, he went away sorrowful; for he was one that had great possessions. (23) And Jesus said unto his disciples, Verily I say unto you, It is hard for a rich man to enter into the kingdom of heaven. (24) And again I say unto you, It is easier for a camel to go through a needle's eye, than for a rich man to enter into the kingdom of God. (Matt. 19:16-24, ASV.)

Is Jesus Heretical For Teaching Us The Law Applies?

That Jesus says obeying the Law is the key to entering life should not surprise us. The commonly heard idea in the Fable of Cheap Grace that the Law was abrogated for a New Testament believer is itself the clearest heresy. (Or is Jesus the heretic?) For even if a prophet came with "signs and wonders" that "came to pass" but tried to "seduce you from following the way the Lord commanded you to walk in," he would be a false prophet. (Deut. 13:3-5. See Isaiah 8:20.)

What about Paul's language that the Law was abrogated? Luther in his youthful writings relied upon those passages. The young Luther clearly thought the Law was abrogated. These youthful passages in Luther's writings are frequently cited by evangelicals. However, the mature Luther recanted.

The mature Luther realized the lesson to the young rich man and many other passages made it absurd to conclude that the Law had been abrogated in the New Testament. The mature Luther condemned as *the worst heresy* any view that countenances Jesus' coming abrogated the Law. The mature Luther wrote in the *Antinomian Theses* (1537):

> To abolish the Law is therefore to abolish the truth of God....[To] discard the Law would effectively put an end to our obedience to God.[2]

Why did Luther make this reversal? Because the mature Luther realized that if any writing were ever joined to the New Testament which purported to teach the Law given Moses is abrogated, then such a text could not possibly be inspired text. It would be sheer heresy of the highest magnitude.

For the Law given Moses was said by God to be "ordinances" that shall be "*everlasting for all generations*." (Ex. 27:21; 30:21; Lev. 6:18; 7:36; 10:9; 17:7; 23:14, 21, 41; 24:3; Num. 10:8.)

In fact, Luther knew the Bible teaches that any would-be prophet who seeks to "seduce you from [ever following] the Law" given Moses would be the mark of a "false prophet." (Deut. 13:1-5.) If Jesus did so, this passage in the Law says any effort to seduce people from the Law's principles would mark Jesus as a false prophet. Jesus could never be the Messiah even if he had "signs and wonders" if Jesus simultaneously taught the abrogation of the Law which was "eternal for all generations." (*Id.*)

Moreover, several passages say the true Messiah will usher in a New Covenant that revives respect for and obedience to the Law given Moses. If Jesus did anything less, this would be a proof Jesus was not Messiah. For God had said

---

2. Martin Luther, *Antinomian Theses* (1537), reprinted as *Don't Tell Me That From Martin Luther's Antinomian Theses* (Minneapolis: Lutheran Press, 2004) at 32-34.

that when the New Testament arrived, it would come and "inscribe the Law (Torah) on our hearts." (Jeremiah 31:31-33.) What does *inscribe the Law* mean? Isaiah explained those who "know righteousness" are "the people *in whose heart is my Law....*" (Isaiah 51:7.)

Likewise, Isaiah explained Messiah would make the Law better known and practiced. When the Redeemer is sent to Israel to create a new covenant, God promises by Him *"these words* that *I have given you"* (the Law) "will be on your lips and on the lips of your children and your children's children *forever."* (Isaiah 59:21 NLT.)[3]

Likewise, Isaiah wrote that when His Servant (Messiah) comes, God "will *magnify the Law* (Torah), and make it honorable." (Isaiah 42:21 ASV/KJV.)

Jesus proved to be worthy of being Messiah because, contrary to what many suppose, He revived full respect for the Law. In fact, Jesus, for His part, did everything possible to put the Law given Moses by God on our lips and in our hearts forever. Jesus said immediately after just referring to the "Law (given Moses) and the Prophets" (Matt. 5:17):

> Whosoever therefore shall break *one of these least commandments, and shall teach men so,* he shall be called the least in the kingdom of heaven: but whosoever *shall do and teach them,* the same shall be called *great in the kingdom of heaven.* (Matt. 5:19 KJV)

---

3. All commentators agree Isaiah 59:21 is a promise of the New Covenant. Barnes says "these words" or "my words" means God's truth previously given "for the guidance and instruction of the church." Clarke, however, says this means the "words of Jesus." But Clarke overlooks the tense, which is a *past* tense. "These words" were given prior to the coming of the Redeemer. Keil & Delitzch concur, but they try to claim the prior "words" are the words of a covenant given to Abraham in Genesis 17:1 *et seq.* No one wants to accept the simplest solution: Isaiah is saying the same thing as Jeremiah. God intended the Law is on the lips and in the hearts of all those who belong to the New Covenant.

Only in Matthew 19:7-9 does it ever appear Jesus derogates a part of the Law as solely from Moses "due to the obstinacy" of the human heart, permitting divorce when God preferred otherwise.[4] But it turns out that Jesus is not derogating the Law at all, but instead is criticizing the allowance God had to make for man's sinfulness which was never God's plan "from the beginning." Eve was made for man *prior* to the Fall. This explains why Jesus completely reaffirms the divorce principle Moses' uttered as *valid*, namely that a certificate of divorce was appropriate for an "unseemly thing" (Deut. 24:1). Jesus then defines "unseemly thing" as "adultery." (Matt. 5:32, 19:7-9.) Jesus precisely affirms what the Law of Moses previously said. Hence, Jesus was not saying this is a "defective maxim" in the Mosaic Law.

Thus, Jesus never abrogates the Law given Moses. While it is assumed Jesus did so, and this is used to claim Jesus' words to the young rich man had to be merely pulling the young man's leg, the proponents have not thought through the implication. If Jesus were teaching the young man that obedience to the Law was no longer the path to enter life, then this contradicts Deut. 6:25. Jesus no longer qualifies to be God's Messiah. (Deut. 13:1-5.) But He surely was! Which means Jesus was being serious with the young man.

Bonhoeffer: On Necessity To Obey The Law

Dietrich Bonhoeffer, the Lutheran Pastor killed by the Nazis, explains in his *The Cost of Discipleship* (1937) how *obedience* to the Law is part of Jesus' salvation formula. Bonhoeffer says we ignore this passage from Jesus at our peril.

The following is how Bonhoeffer reads the story of Jesus' answering the young rich man's question on how to have eternal life. (Matt. 19:16-22.) Bonhoeffer says Jesus by

---

4. Based on this verse, some affirm Jesus supposedly teaches the Old Testament was "marred by imperfect laws or defective maxims" (George B. Stevens, *The Teachings of Jesus* (1916) at 50.)

quoting the Ten Commandments has changed it from an academic question to a call "to a simple *obedience* to the will of God as it has been revealed." (*Id.*, at 72.) Jesus reaffirms the Ten Commandments "as the commandments of God." (*Id.*, at 73.) Jesus is saying that we must move on from purely academic questions, and "get on with the task of *obedience*." (*Id.*, at 73.) It is "high time the young man began to hear the commandment and *obey* it." (*Id.*, at 73.)

When the young rich man says he has obeyed all the commandments, Jesus tells him that he still lacks one thing to be "perfect." Jesus tells him to sell all that he has and give it to the poor. Bonhoeffer says the point is unmistakable:

> But it is an addition [to the salvation formula] which requires the *abandonment of every previous attachment*. Until now perfection has always eluded his grasp....Only now, by following Christ, can he... practise it aright. (*Id.*, at 76.)

But the young man was attached to his many possessions. He did not heed Jesus' call. He went away grieved by the cost. The young man did not make the commitment Jesus required. The young man *wanted grace* for eternal life, but *only if it came free*. Jesus said it was instead a *costly grace* — one that would cost the young man everything.

Bonhoeffer then excoriates the Christians who use Paul's attack on legalism to undermine Jesus' message:

> We are excusing ourselves from single-minded obedience to the words of Jesus *on the pretext [that this endorses] legalism*....(*Id.*, at 80.)

Bonhoeffer claims that we cannot "trifle" with Jesus' words (*id.* at 81) by reinterpreting them to line up with our favorite doctrine of grace:

> [T]he whole word of the Scriptures summons us to follow Jesus. We must not do violence to the Scriptures by interpreting them in terms of an abstract principle, *even if that principle be*

> **the doctrine of grace** [for fear] otherwise we
> shall end up in legalism. (*Id.*, at 84.)

Thus, Bonhoeffer saw obedience as crucial and integral to the salvation doctrine Jesus taught. Bonhoeffer even says if the bogeyman of legalism and free-grace are used to refute Jesus, these bogeymen must die. The words of Jesus must live and be always boldly taught.

Other Commentators Who Get It Right

The *Bethel Church of God* observes below that Jesus' words to the young rich man are starkly different from the Gospel of Cheap Grace which predominates:

> What are some of the necessary things one
> must do in order to gain **eternal life**? Notice
> this example: [Quotes Matt. 19:16-24.]

> Keeping the commandments of God **certainly
> flies in the face of what many believe today.**
> Yet, Jesus was **very clear.** The Jewish people
> were adamant in observing the first four com-
> mandments, but **lax in the last six**. This is why
> Jesus told this man what he should do. The law
> Jesus referred to was the Ten Commandments.[5]

Yet, our predominant teachers tell us the Law given Moses was abrogated. When we reject the Law as Jesus' tool to disciple us, Bonhoeffer says cheap grace creates a "Christianity without Christ." (*Cost of Discipleship, supra,* at 59.) Without the Law repeated by Jesus, "[t]here is a **trust** in God, but **no following** of Christ." *Id.* Hence, we arrive at faith alone without any need to follow Jesus. But this is a "way of our own choosing...Jesus will certainly reject it." *Id.*

---

5. *The Teachings of Jesus—What We Should Do #11* http://
www.bethelcog.org/art0011.htm (Bethel Church of God)(last accessed
7/5/06).

Bonhoeffer's Explanation Of The Law-Problem Raised By Jesus' Message To The Rich Young Man

Bonhoeffer said Jesus is clear that the Law remains valid for the New Testament church in Matthew 5:17-20. How does he address the Fable of Cheap Grace? **He ignores its reliance on Paul**. For Bonhoeffer, it is not necessary to defend relying upon Jesus only. He leaves it up to the cheap-grace pastor to explain why we should reject Jesus' words.

Bonhoeffer explains the ongoing relevance of the Law of Moses in preference to any other authority.

Bonhoeffer Starts With The Meaning Of Matthew 5:17-20

Bonhoeffer first quotes Matthew 5:17-20. Jesus says that whoever teaches obedience to the Law is the greatest in the kingdom of heaven. Whoever teaches you to relax in the slightest the Law's commands will be least in the kingdom of heaven. Bonhoeffer than explains the passage's import:

> But now comes the surprise — the disciples are bound to the Old Testament Law. This has a double significance. First, it means adherence to the Law is quite different from the following of Christ, and secondly, it means any **adherence to his person that disregards the law is equally removed from the following of Him**. (*Id.*, at 121.)

Bonhoeffer means that Jesus' followers are not free to disregard the Law. It is a distinct obligation that Jesus imposes which is not satisfied by merely 'following' Jesus. This is true because Jesus makes a condition of following Him that His followers follow the Law. Bonhoeffer continues:

> It is Jesus...who points to the Law....Because it is their Lord who does this, **they are bound to acknowledge this**. (*Id.*)

Bonhoeffer's point is subtle. Jesus is Lord. If He says it is so, who can gainsay him? As Paul says, "let every man be a liar, but God be true!" Jesus cannot be lying to us. If we find anyone who says the Law has been abrogated for one who claims to follow Jesus, then *let such a person be the liar, but God (Jesus) be true*.

Bonhoeffer continues in the same vein.

> The question inevitably arises. Which is our final authority? Christ or the Law? To which are we bound?...Now He [Jesus] tells us that *to abandon the Law would be to separate ourselves from Him*. What exactly does He mean?

Step Two: Answer To The Young Rich Man

Bonhoeffer says the meaning of Jesus is clear from our knowledge of His answer to the young rich man on how to "have eternal life." Bonhoeffer says:

> The Law Jesus refers to is the Law of the old covenant, not a new law, but *the same law He quoted to the young rich man* and the lawyer when they [each asked how to have eternal life.] It becomes a new law only because it is Christ who binds His followers to it. (*Id.* at 121.)

Thus, Bonhoeffer is nailing the point home: to be a Christian, Jesus said you must be one committed to following the Law given Moses. Somehow, a contrary view has poisoned Christianity. We have been led to believe if we follow these words of Jesus we are engaging in heretical *legalism*, *i.e.*, a teaching that God wants obedience to the Law.

Bonhoeffer later returns to this odd development where Jesus' words stand in stark contrast to the Modern Gospel of Cheap Grace.[6] Then Bonhoeffer has some scathing

---

6. Of course, this gospel principally relies upon Paul, but Bonhoeffer never identifies what I call *The Problem of Paul*. See Index under *Paul*.

sarcasm for his opponents. Bonhoeffer mentions that when we give all to Christ, it includes a repentance from all our sinful desires. We turn to God's Law for our new direction because Jesus commanded this. Then Bonhoeffer says the Modern Gospel rejects this. It has developed a *rationalization* that one can become a Christian and keep on sinning (*i.e.*, disobeying the Law of God):

> The breach with things of the world [which Jesus demands] is now branded [by the Modern Gospel] as a **legalistic** misinterpretation of the grace of God....Once again, justification of the sinner has become justification of sin. (*Id.*, at 97.)

Bonhoeffer offered a re-interpretation of what the heresy of legalism *should* mean. It would be making the Law itself an idol, letting it take "God's place." But Bonhoeffer says such an error is

Dietrich
Bonhoeffer
1906-
1945

low on the scale of errors. "The disciples were confronted [by Jesus] with the opposite danger of denying the Law its divinity and divorcing God from His Law." (*Id.*, at 122.)

Thus, we can see that Bonhoeffer refused to shy away from Jesus' words on the Law. Bonhoeffer refused to cower under the dominant Modern Gospel. He did not reject Jesus' view merely because such a view is everywhere mocked as *legalism.* Bonhoeffer refused to bow to the forced contorted readings of Jesus' words. This explains why Bonhoeffer begins his book saying the *words of Jesus* have been so "overlaid with human ballast" that if Jesus Himself were here today delivering a sermon, His very words would be rejected by many in the church. (*Id.*, at 35.) We have put up a superstructure of "doctrinal elements" that make it far more difficult for people to accept Christ's message. (*Id.*, at 36).

Jesus Is Asked The Same Question A Second Time & Answers The Same Way

If Jesus' lesson to the young rich man on his need to obey the Law for salvation were not really a sincere teaching, then we would be forced to conclude Jesus answered a Torah-scholar's identical question about eternal life in the same insincere facetious manner. This stretches all credulity.

For on another occasion, a lawyer asked the identical question. 'How do I obtain eternal life?' Jesus answered the identical way, but even more clearly. He asked the lawyer to recite what the lawyer believed is necessary for eternal life. The lawyer answered that it is key to obey the two most elevated commands in the Law given Moses: love God "with all your heart" (Deut. 6:5) and "love your neighbor as yourself" (Lev. 19:18). The lawyer correctly quoted these two laws from the Law given Moses. Jesus then said the lawyer "answered correctly" and if he did them "you shall live." (Luke 10:25-37.) The exchange was:

> (25) And behold, a certain lawyer stood up and made trial of him, saying, **Teacher, what shall I do to inherit eternal life?** (26) And he said unto him, **What is written in the law?** how readest thou? (27) And he answering said, Thou shalt love the Lord thy God with all thy heart, and with all thy soul, and with all thy strength, and with all thy mind; and thy neighbor as thyself. (28) And he said unto him, **Thou hast answered right: this do, and thou shalt live.** (Luke 10:25-28 ASV.)

Jesus did not tell the lawyer that it was not possible to be obedient. Obedience was something God already promised was within grasp. (See the next section.) Jesus did not tell the young lawyer that something shy of obedience to the Law made you acceptable to God. Instead, Jesus said obedience to the Law, which hung on these two central commands, was the right path. There is no reason to believe Jesus is insincere.

God On Humans' Ability To Obey His Law

Some claim it is contrary to human nature to obey God. Hence, God could not set as a condition of salvation that we must obey Him. Therefore, they read into Jesus' words to the young rich man and the Torah-scholar that Jesus must have been facetious — He was allegedly pulling their legs.

However, God in Deuteronomy 30:11 assures us obedience to these commands "is not *too hard* for thee, neither is it far off." (ASV.) Apostle John said: "And his commandments are not burdensome." (1 John 5:2-3.) As Jesus too says, "my burden is light." (Matt. 11:29-30.)

Thus, obeying God's commandments is not too hard or burdensome if we call on the Lord for help. When Jesus points us in this direction, it is a direction God already promised we can follow.

Self-Denial & Following Jesus

Jesus' message to the young rich man on how to obtain eternal life was combined with a related condition of self-denial and bearing your own suffering by following Jesus. (Matthew 19:16-26; Mark 10:17-31; Luke 18:18-26.)

Our Lord explains His meaning to His twelve apostles immediately thereafter. He tells them that if you give up fathers, mothers, and brothers for Him, deny yourself, take up your cross, and "follow Me," you "*shall* have eternal life." (Matthew 19:27-29.) *See also*, Matthew 10:37-39.

It was as Jesus says elsewhere. Those who are following Him and are losing their life in this world to serve Him do so for "life eternal." (John 12:25-26.) This echoed:

> (38) And he that doth not take his cross and follow after me, is not worthy of me. (39) He that *findeth his life shall lose it*; and he that *loseth his life* for my sake *shall find it*. (Matt. 10:38-39 ASV)

What was this self-denial about? It means not following your will but God's will. You have the same choice Jesus faced in the Garden of Gesthemene.

> And he went forward a little, and fell on his face, and prayed, saying, My Father, if it be possible, let this cup pass away from me: nevertheless, **not as I will, but as thou wilt**. (Matt. 26:39, ASV)

As Jesus denied Himself — the human flesh He was inside, we too must deny ourselves and follow God's directions, commands, and requirements.

Self-denial in this context means **obedience** to God, as Bonhoeffer points out. In context, Jesus specifically mentioned to the young rich man obedience to the Law given Moses, in particular the Ten Commandments.

Jesus' requirement that the rich young man give away his wealth to the poor was an obvious reference to repentance from sin. It was a work worthy of repentance.

Cheap Grace View Of Matthew 19:17

You can prove the force of a passage by looking at how weak are the opposing arguments to such meaning.

Here Jesus is blunt in this message to the young rich man. He clearly states "but if thou wouldest **enter into life**, keep the commandments" (Matt. 19:17.) How can this be viewed other than as what it literally says?

Vincent Word Studies makes no comment on this aspect of verse 17. Likewise *Robertson's Word Pictures* ignores it. The Geneva Study Bible dares not touch it.

However, the major commentators such as Clarke, Barnes and Gill cannot ignore it.

For his part, Adam Clarke says Jesus' answer is **no longer valid**. Since the Law is ended (based on cites to Paul), then Jesus' words that to 'enter life one must obey the Law' is abrogated. Because of Paul's declarations, Jesus' words supposedly belong to a defunct dispensation.[7]

However, this directly negates the relevance of the *words* and *message* of Jesus' Himself. How can we do this when Jesus said that even if heaven and earth passed away, Jesus' words would not pass away? (Matt. 25:35.) How can Jesus' words be defunct in the era of grace? For *after* the Resurrection (when that era surely started), Jesus gave the apostles the Great Commission. He told them to teach the nations to "obey all the commandments that I have given thee." If Jesus' words to the young rich man were defunct, why did Jesus order them to be taught to us even in the era of grace?

Make no mistake about the horrible implication of what Clarke teaches. It is known as dispensationalism. This doctrine is a blatant denial of our need to listen and follow the words of the Lord Jesus Christ. If Paul is the sole source of a reason to disregard Jesus' words as irrelevant, then we must re-examine our priorities (or Paul). For Jesus said the "*apostolos* is not greater than the one who sends him."(John 13:16.)

The only virtue in Clarke's argument is that it is consistent with how people view the Fable of Cheap Grace. However, it surely is not consistent with the *words* of Jesus. It depends on negating them in Matthew 19:17. Clarke is directly upholding a message at odds with what Jesus' taught.

Barnes & Gill, other famous commentators, both teach ***Jesus is saying one thing but He means the exact opposite***.[8] Barnes admits Jesus tells the young man that if he wants to enter life, then obey the commandments. However, Barnes says Jesus really meant the *opposite*. Jesus supposedly meant that if you trust in obedience to the commandments for salvation, you are trusting in the wrong thing. ***Barnes has Jesus say one thing and mean the opposite***. He is insincere.

---

7. For extended quotes from Clarke, see "Rebuttal to Jesus' Answer to the Direct Question On How to Obtain Eternal Life," in the supplementary material section available online at http://www.jesuswordsonly.com/JesusWordsonSalvation.html.

8. See "Rebuttal to Jesus' Answer to the Direct Question On How to Obtain Eternal Life," in the supplementary material available online at http://www.jesuswordsonly.com/JesusWordsonSalvation.html.

Barnes rationalizes this on the same point that tripped up the young Luther — the assumption that the Law was abrogated, relying on patently heretical doctrine.[9] The mature Luther recanted from the doctrine of the abrogation of the Law. (See Preface, "i. The Catechisms (1531) and the Antinomian Theses (1537)" on page xiv *et seq*.) Barnes is unaware of what compelled Luther to recant.

For example, the idea that the Law was abrogated for New Testament members directly contradicts Jesus's words in Matthew 5:19. Jesus tells you anyone who teaches you not to follow a command in the Law by the slightest relaxation will be least in the kingdom of heaven, but whoever teaches you to follow the Law will be the greatest in the kingdom. If anyone — whether Luther or Paul — contradicts a "teaching of [Jesus] Christ" such as on the Law's validity or tries to dilute Jesus' words, Apostle John tells us that person when so teaching does not "have God." (2 John 1:9.)

In sum, we see Barnes' first argument to dispel Jesus' teachings on eternal life to the rich young man depends on assuming Jesus rejected the Law's principles. One of those principles is in Deuteronomy 6:25.[10] It says the same thing Jesus literally tells the young rich man: obedience to the Law is the means to be right (justified) in God's eyes.

However, Barnes denies Jesus is merely reaffirming the Law. Instead, Barnes insists Jesus has the view the Law is negated. Jesus is supposedly trying to announce a new means of salvation: faith alone. To lead the rich young man to this conclusion, Jesus allegedly affirms a principle from the Law

---

9. Even if Paul taught this, it would not make a heresy no longer a heresy. God in Deuteronomy 13:1-5 and Isaiah 8:20 tells us that any new prophecy must not undermine the Law. If it does, it is false prophecy — heresy. You are not to "listen" to that prophet any longer.

10. "And it shall be *righteousness unto us*, if we observe to do all this commandment before Jehovah our God, as he hath commanded us." Plaut in his commentary on *Torah* says this means "these are counted as being 'right' in their relation to Him." (Plaut:1368.) Keil & Delitzsch, Lutheran scholars, say likewise. See page 33.

---

which Jesus supposedly *no longer believes is valid*, but has been superseded. Hence, to get the rich young man to this view about faith, Jesus supposedly masks His true meaning by affirming the opposite of what He truly believes.

Barnes and others who make this claim are unwittingly impeaching the validity of Jesus' Messiahship. Even someone who has previously had "signs and wonders that come to pass" is a false prophet once they teach the people of God not to follow His Law. (Deut. 13:1-5; Isaiah 8:20.) If Jesus is intending to abrogate Deuteronomy 6:25 by endorsing it, which is what Barnes is in effect saying, Barnes is affirming an intention in Jesus' mind that would not only make Jesus appear an insincere hypocrite, but, if true, also prove that Jesus was a false Messiah. As *First Fruits of Zion* points out: "Sadly, the ***traditional understanding*** of the Christian Jesus is that he is a prophet attested by signs and wonders, but that ***he also cancelled Torah***." Then FFOZ adds: "Such a person fits Deuteronomy 13:1-5's description of a false prophet perfectly." Then "the conversion to faith in such a person would be a violation of God's own commandments." (*E-Drash* 8/8/2004 FFOZ.) FFOZ means that modern Christianity has portrayed Jesus' teachings so that a Jew is duty-bound to reject Jesus by the command in Deuteronomy 13:1-5.[11] Barnes has overlooked this compelling problem.

---

11. Incidentally, the early church did not agree with our modern view that the Law given Moses, in particular the Ten Commandments, was ever abrogated. Irenaeus (130-202 A.D.), Bishop of Lyon, France, set forth the doctrine of *universal* Christianity as *practiced*: "The decalogue [Ten Commandments] however was not cancelled by Christ, but is always in force: men were never released from its commandments." ("Against Heresies," *Anti-Nicene Fathers*, Bk. IV, Ch.XVI, at 480.) For this reason, Irenaeus insisted that the Sabbath was on Saturday, in obedience to one of the Ten. The early church except the city of Rome and Alexandria, Egypt, all followed Saturday as Sabbath until in 363 A.D., Rome — urged by the emperor — abolished Saturday Sabbath. See my prior book, *Jesus' Words Only* (2007) at 452 n.31.

Barnes has a second argument to support that Jesus is using guile — pulling the young man's leg. Jesus is supposedly asking the young man to do something that was not possible *at all times* (*i.e.*, keep the law without fail). Obedience, if a requirement of salvation, asks us supposedly to engage in a self-defeating enterprise. Barnes did not factor into this the role that repentance covers over the rough spots in obedience. This was in fact the message to the young rich man — Jesus told the young man to 'give your wealth to the poor' — an obvious 'work worthy of repentance.' Instead, Barnes sees Jesus as putting a 100% without-fail obedience on the young man. Barnes then describes this standard for salvation as an impossible standard because any single failure *irreversibly* causes loss of eternal life. Repentance-from-sin is ignored apparently because it too is a hopeless alternative. Thus, Barnes concludes that Jesus' intent was allegedly to *discourage concern of the young man to actually obey the Law to enter life by affirming that it was the principle to enter life.*

Both Gill and Barnes are trying to imply that the Law given Moses meant that if you sin in the slightest, it is all over. You are damned to hell, irreversibly. Consequently, without a flawless perfect obedience, your destiny is supposedly hell. If true, Jesus was pointing the young man to a path *that could not actually save him.* It only would lead to failure.

Therefore, what Jesus allegedly was doing is showing the young man that obedience was the *wrong direction* to go in because obedience must be perfect for eternal life. Any failure supposedly means hell. Thus, obedience to the law is a hopeless endeavor to righteousness. Jesus supposedly made this point by affirming the opposite was true!

However, Jesus' point is not that the young man should follow a standard that was impossible. Jesus was merely repeating Deuteronomy 6:25. It said obedience to the Law maintains an imputed righteousness before God. The same is repeated numerous times in the Bible, *e.g.*, Eze 18:5, 9. Likewise, Habakkuk 2:4 squarely says in Hebrew that the "just shall live by his *faithfulness*" (not *faith*) — a word in Hebrew meaning *obedient living*.[12] Such obedience is affirmed to be quite feasible. God in Deuteronomy 30:11 reassures us that obedience "is not too hard for thee, neither is it far off." (ASV.)

However, in affirming the opposite, Gill and Barnes are grossly misrepresenting the Law and the Prophets. They are suggesting that once you sin, you are irretrievably lost. However, the Law is not a dead end curse, as they assert. Instead, once you sinned, repentance from sin is always an option unless you died too suddenly to repent. This option to repent for lapses is clearly mentioned repeatedly in God's Word. For example:

> And thou, son of man, say unto the children of thy people, The righteousness of the righteous shall not deliver him in the day of his transgression; and as for the wickedness of the wicked, *he shall not fall thereby in the day that he turneth from his wickedness*; neither shall he that is righteous be able to live thereby in the day that he sinneth. (Eze 33:12)(ASV)

Ezekiel teaches when the righteous sin, they lose life, *i.e.*, eternal life. When the sinner repents, he lives, *i.e.*, he has eternal life. Nothing short of the grave is ever irreversible. Therefore, when one repents and is obeying the Law, it is deemed to be imputed righteousness, so says Deut. 6:25.

The principle of repentance from sin and restoration is also reflected in Deuteronomy 30:1-10, which states:

> When all these things befall you...and *you return them to your heart*... and *you return to God*...then God will turn your captivity and take you back in love...God will bring you back...God will return and gather you...then *you will return to hearing God's voice*...And

---

12.For discussion on justification doctrine, particularly in Habakkuk 2:4, see page 34.

God will again rejoice over you...*if you turn to God with all your heart and all your soul*. (Deut. 30:1-10).

Barnes and Gill are wrong to imply that Jesus was teaching an absolute *perfect* obedience to the Law was necessary *and* that if there was any failure, there was never any hope again. Jesus was not insincerely giving an impossible standard. Barnes and Gill are insisting Jesus' intention was that the young man would give up seeking an imputed righteousness from obeying the Law despite God promising this precisely in Deuteronomy 6:25. This is nonsense.

Barnes and Gill are engaging in an *absolutely false caricature of God's word*. It is a blatant misrepresentation of God's Holy Scripture. *It also makes Jesus appear deceitful*. They make Jesus say one thing but mean exactly the opposite. How shameful that these men would endorse such a depiction of Jesus for the paltry purpose of holding onto cheap grace. Instead, Peter says Jesus "did not sin, neither was *guile* found in his mouth." (1 Peter 2:21-22.)

One Group Agrees With Bonhoeffer About Matthew 19:17

There is one Protestant evangelical church that like Bonhoeffer takes Jesus' words seriously in Matthew 19:17 ("but if thou wouldest *enter into life*, keep the commandments") This is the *Active Bible Church of God* (ABCG) in Brisbane, Australia. (What a pity we must scour so far to find a true defender of Jesus' words.)

Even so, this church tries to defend their views are compatible with the gospel of faith alone, as we shall see.

The Mystery Of Lawlessness

In an article entitled *The Mystery of Lawlessness*,[13] the ABCG explains Jesus' doctrine on obedience:

But what does it mean to truly believe in Him? *If we sincerely believe in Him, would we not do whatever He asks us to do?* Did not Jesus say, "If anyone keeps My word he shall never see death" (John. 8:51)? What did Jesus say to do? In Matthew 19:16-17 someone came to Jesus, asking Him, "What good thing shall I do that I may have eternal life?" *His answer: "If you want to enter into life, keep the commandments."*

Thus, the ABCG lets Jesus explain Jesus' meaning. A refreshing change! Jesus says that the way to life is to obey the commandments. He promises in John 8:51 if we keep His word we shall never see death.

However, then ABCG agrees we are saved by "faith apart from works of the Law," citing the cheap-grace refrain. Then, ABCG quickly flips back to Jesus. ABCG insists we still must be "concerned with works." The ABCG then cites Jude and a costly-grace verse ascribed to Paul (as they understand Romans 8:1, 4):

> Jude mentioned that ungodly men had entered into the church, "Who turn the **grace of our God into licentiousness**" (Jude 4). Licentiousness can mean, "Unrestrained by law; lawless." In other words, these ungodly men taught that *if we are under grace we need not have to keep the law*. Yet, this [license teaching] contradicts what we just read in Romans 8:1,4.[14]

---

13. http://www.abcog.org/nh/lawless.htm (last accessed 6/17/06).

14. "(1) There is therefore now no condemnation to them that are in Christ Jesus. (2) For the law of the Spirit of life in Christ Jesus made me free from the law of sin and of death. (3) For what the law could not do, in that it was weak through the flesh, God, sending his own Son in the likeness of sinful flesh and for sin, condemned sin in the flesh: (4) that the ordinance of the law might be fulfilled in us, *who walk not after the flesh*, but after the Spirit." (Rom 8:1-4 ASV.)

Thus, here is a group that defends Jesus' meaning. It interprets Jesus' words as more important to follow than the refrains of cheap grace. This is truly a refreshing focus on Jesus' words in order to deduce doctrine. It is too bad they did not directly confront the validity of the refrain of 'faith alone.'

Other Christians Are Shocked How Jesus Is So Different From The Modern Gospel

James Watkins is a Protestant professor and author, with a keen love of humor.[15]

In 2006, Watkins wrote an article entitled *What Must I do to Inherit Eternal Life?*[16] In it, Watkins notes that Jesus is asked twice on how to have eternal life. Jesus was asked once by a scribe (a lawyer) and once by a rich man. In response to the scribe, Watkins points out Jesus asks the scribe what does he think is the answer. Jesus then comments. It bears repeating how the interchange went, as Watkins recounts it.

> "What is written in the Law?" he [Jesus] replied. "How do you read it?"
>
> He answered: "'Love the Lord your God with all your heart and with all your soul and with all your strength and with all your mind'; and, 'Love your neighbor as yourself.'"
>
> "You have answered correctly," Jesus replied. "Do this and you will live" (Luke 10:25-28).

Watkins notes we would ***answer differently today***, quite unlike what Jesus affirms as correct:

---

15. See http://watkins.gospelcom.net/bio.htm. (accessed 5/29/2007).
16. See http://watkins.gospelcom.net/faith.htm (accessed 5/29/2007).

> Unfortunately, in the modern church, the expert in the law would have said, "**Simply believe, have faith**."

Watkins is pointing out the incongruity between Jesus' affirmation of the *correct* answer to this key question versus how we normatively answer it today.

These passages caused Watkins to focus on what Jesus taught. He put aside what anyone else taught about salvation to hear the Master. Why? Because Jesus is *the way, truth and life.* Watkins explains:

> So, armed with a yellow highlighter pen, I worked my way through the printed-in-red **teachings of Jesus** to understand what He taught we must do to inherit eternal life. After all, He is "the way and the truth and the life. No one comes to the Father except through [Him]" (John 14:6).

Then Watkins tells how he was completely shocked when he found three passages where Jesus teaches salvation depends on more than faith. Watkins explained:

> However, I was surprised (**actually shocked**), to find that three times more yellow-high-lighted passages dealt with putting that faith into practice in tangible, practical ways.
>
> Please read the following passages carefully and ask yourself, **must I go beyond simply faith to experience eternal life?**

First Watkins cites Luke 10:25-28. This is the interchange with the scribe just discussed. Then Watkins quotes the Parable of the Sheep and the Goats in Matthew 25:34-46.[17] Finally, Watkin cites the discussion of Jesus to the young rich man, referencing Luke 18:18-22.

---

17. For discussion, see "Parable Of The Sheep & The Goats" on page 219 *et seq.*

Once Watkins opened his mind to the issue presented by these verses, suddenly he recognized a floodgate of similar passages. These two discourses about "eternal life" with Jesus were not isolated to the young rich man and the scribe. Jesus repeats many times the same answer.

Then Watkins in his article gets out of the way. Watkins finds quote after quote from Jesus. Time after time, Jesus links more than faith to salvation. Watkins cites the salvation-formula passages that are discussed throughout this book.

What is interesting is that Watkins was first stimulated by the fact Jesus was asked the direct question on how to obtain eternal life by the young rich man and the lawyer. These passages led to a turning point for Watkins on how he needed to answer the identical question today.

Watkins pointed out that each time Jesus answered, Jesus gave a law-based (obedience-based) answer. Also, the Parable of the Sheep and the Goats was directly in line with that conclusion. Thus, we can see that here — in Watkins' case — seeing what Jesus taught in answering this direct question opened up his mind to see all the other times that Jesus says, in effect, the same thing.

This passage has powerfully impacted other famous Christians. It is self-evident Jesus' talk to the rich young man played an important role of disabusing the mature Luther[18] and Bonhoeffer from what they previously thought and believed about *belief alone*.

Conclusion

Thus, Jesus was twice asked directly how to have eternal life. He answered each time that obedience to the Law was how to have eternal life. With the young rich man, Jesus

---

18. In the 1531 Catechism, the mature Luther switched his view of the Law and his explanations on salvation in a way quite unlike his youthful doctrine from 1517-1531. See page xvi of the Preface. See also my prior book *Jesus' Words Only* (2007) at 100-01, 106 and 116-17.

did not address *faith* because in context, it appears, the man *believed* in Jesus. At least, the young rich man had a strong trust in Jesus. Otherwise, there is no explanation why the man had *grief* when Jesus told him the cost to obtain salvation was so high. The young man wanted eternal life from Jesus, but only if it was free or easy. ***The man would only take the offer of eternal life if grace was cheap.***

Jesus was telling the young man and ourselves that instead ***grace is costly***. The man had to give away the very thing that was encumbering him with sin. Jesus gave him a work worthy of repentance that implied this young man's sin was greed. The young man lacked charity. Jesus demanded as a price for eternal life obedience to the principle of cutting off the possessions that were ensnaring him in sin. It was as Jesus elsewhere taught: you can go to heaven maimed or hell whole. (Mark 9:42-47.) For a person suffering from greed whose self-control is absent, the only solution is to give away all their wealth. Then they will learn charity.

The importance of this passage cannot be missed. James Watkins is a perfect example of the shock any Protestant drilled on 'faith-alone' will have when he truly digests this passage. When Jesus is your Master and you finally agree to *hear* Him, your normative beliefs crumble.

Thus, the messages to the young rich man and the scribe are key. In these passages, Jesus directly answered the question on how to obtain eternal life. These passages are something to never loose sight of. ***Jesus has answered the most important question of life***. Yet, He answered differently than what we hear today. Watkins could not believe what he read. So he stopped in his tracks. Then Watkins triple and quadruple checked. Yet, the gospel message of Jesus time and time again came up with the same answer which Jesus gave the young rich man. Salvation is ***certainly*** not by belief alone.

9 *Exceeding The Righteousness Of The Shallowly Righteous — Matthew 5:20.*

Introduction

Jesus taught the Pharisees suffered from shallow teaching on the Law. (Matt. 23:23.) They taught the "less weighty matter" of tithing to the neglect of the "weightier matters of the Law." (*Id.*) The Pharisees replaced written commands from the Law given Moses with oral tradition "that makes of none effect" the written Law. (Matt. 15:6.)

However, that understanding has been vigorously fought by the proponents of cheap grace. It turns out that cheap grace must use all its resources — incessant repetition in Sunday sermons and commentaries — to affix the label upon the Pharisees as *legalists.* If the truth were known, the Pharisees were shallow followers of the Law. As John Milton, author of *Paradise Lost*, correctly said, the Pharisees had a "shallow understanding of scripture." (*Prose Works* (1845) at 144.) However, if this truth were commonly understood, it would destroy cheap grace's explanation of Matthew 5:20. Jesus says you can not enter heaven "except your righteousness exceed that of the Pharisees." If Jesus meant for us to do better than a shallow-performing Pharisee, then personal responsibility is at stake in Matthew 5:20. Cheap grace would be falsified once more. Thus, cheap grace had to destroy an accurate perception of the Pharisees as shallow performers. It instead depicts them as superstars in terms of obedience to the Law. (For an example, see page 212-213.) It was a desperate ploy that ***exploited people's lack of familiarity with Jesus' true teachings about the Pharisees***.

In other words, unless one fixes this misunderstanding about the Pharisees as *legalists*, Jesus' words in Matthew 5:20 fall on deaf ears. Jesus in this passage says:

> For I say unto you, that **except your righteousness shall exceed the righteousness of the scribes and Pharisees**, ye shall in **no wise enter into the kingdom of heaven**. (Matt.5:20)

To explain this challenging verse, we are incessantly told Jesus is pulling our leg. He does not want us to correct for any shallowness in the Pharisees' doctrines. No, they were supposedly in full obedience to the Law, and more righteous than anyone. Thus, Jesus allegedly intends by Matthew 5:20 to force us on our knees to accept grace. We can never hope to exceed the supposedly high level of obedience of those who legalistically follow all the Law given Moses.

However, this view is based on a falsehood. It depends upon a misrepresentation of the Pharisees. It is intended to negate this verse and save cheap grace doctrine.

Zeal Knowing No Bounds To Mislabel Pharisees As Legalists

With a vigor almost knowing no bounds, the Cheap Grace Gospel has altered our perception of what Jesus condemned about the Pharisees. The Pharisees are constantly portrayed as "strict legalists." (Hopkins: 444;G.M. Steele:87; Cheyne:57.) This charge of *legalism* is the claim that the Pharisees taught every jot and tittle of the Law, and that they thought one could be right with God by acting obedient to the Law. The cheap grace gospel adherents desire us to think that Jesus supposedly wanted us to know only faith was necessary to be right with God; and that the Pharisees' error was supposedly that they rejected *faith alone,* wrongly relying instead on obeying all the Law.

Legalism is thus portrayed in such a way that it supposedly is the reason why Jesus excoriated the Pharisees. Hence, we learn from this alleged truism about the Pharisees that we too must avoid ever thinking we are made right in

God's sight by obedience to the Law which God had given previously to Moses. We are demanded to believe this despite Deuteronomy 6:25 and many other passages teaching the opposite: if we obey the Law, God imputes righteousness.[1]

However, this portrayal of the Pharisees is a massive distortion of truth. It is absolutely necessary for the Cheap Grace Gospel to perpetuate this myth because the truth about the Pharisees' doctrine means Jesus is condemning key principles taught by the cheap grace gospel itself. Cheap grace would blow itself up if it had to cite Matthew 15:6,9 and Matthew 23:23 on what were indeed the flaws of the Pharisees.

The Truth

The truth is that the Pharisees were *anti-legalists*. This was Jesus' main fault with them. By their oral traditions they made of "none effect" the written precepts of the Law. (Matt. 15:6,9; 23:23.) Jesus clearly said the Pharisees were only big on tithing — a "less weighty matter of the Law," but otherwise "ignored the weightier matters of the Law." (Matt. 23:23.)

Nor was Jesus ever attacking the principle that one was justified by faithful obedience. This principle was clearly taught by God in Deuteronomy 6:25, Leviticus 18:5, Ezekiel 18:5, 9, and Habakkuk 2:4 (correctly translated), as we discuss elsewhere.[2]

Moreover, Jesus Himself said the very same thing about the key role of obedience as pertains to salvation. Jesus taught the young rich man that the means for entering eternal life was obedience to the law. *This is the identical principle which faith-alone Christianity derides as legalism*. Jesus said one entered into eternal life by "obeying the Law."[3]

---

1. See "Justification In the Law of Moses" on page 33 *et seq.*
2. See "The Repentant Goes Home Justified & The Shallowly Righteous Does Not" on page 27 *et seq.*

In a similar vein, Jesus taught that anyone who would teach a kingdom member not to obey in the least a provision in the Law given Moses would be "least in the kingdom of heaven" (Matt. 5:19). And whoever taught kingdom members to "obey the commandments" of the Law given Moses would be the "greatest in the kingdom of heaven." (Matt. 5:19.)

Hence, *Jesus was a legalist if one uses the definition of a legalist as used disparagingly by the Gospel of Cheap Grace*.

Thus, it is crucial to the cheap grace gospel to keep the truth about the Pharisees away from their bewildered flock. Otherwise, their flock will see their cheap grace teachers are, in fact, the modern Pharisees — *anti-legalist teachers who say the Law is no more except tithing*. And their deceived flock will find out that their teachers erred in saying that obedience is not a pathway to enter eternal life.

Yet, the most important aspect of this chapter is that by studying the true error of the Pharisees, we unlock *Matthew 5:20*.

Jesus said the Pharisees were causing their proselytes to be lost. Jesus pointed at the Pharisees' doctrine as the cause. Hence, we need to learn from Jesus what was that false doctrine or doctrines. Jesus is saying that the Pharisees' heresy will cause our loss of salvation. Thus, it is imperative we find out what the Pharisees really taught and treat those doctrines like the plague. It turns out to be highly relevant today because *true* Pharisaism — anti-legalism — is rampant.

> "Are you going to discredit my justice and condemn Me so you can say you are right?"
> God to Job (Job 40:8 NLT)

---

3. This was Jesus' lesson to the young rich man in Matthew 19:16-26; Mark 10:17-31; Luke 18:18-26. For discussion, see page 123 *et seq.*

A Shallow Righteousness Or An Impossible Standard?

Jesus says whoever "relaxes in the least any of the commands in the Law (given Moses) and teaches others likewise shall be least in the kingdom, but whoever does them and teaches you to follow them shall be the greatest." (Matt. 5:19.)(For this translation, see page 173.) Then Jesus said: "For I say unto you, That except your righteousness shall exceed the righteousness of the scribes and Pharisees, ye shall in no case *enter into the kingdom of heaven*." (Matt. 5:20.)

Clarke says these two verses together prove it was the Lawless shallow doctrine of the Pharisees that imperilled them and their followers. This is what the expression "least in the kingdom" meant, proven by the outcome in Matthew 5:20. Clarke — one who often agrees with cheap grace — admits (contrary to his ordinary views) the following:

> He who, by his mode of acting, speaking, or explaining the words of God, sets the holy precept aside, or explains away its force and meaning, shall be called least — *shall have no place in the kingdom of Christ here, nor in the kingdom of glory above*. That this is the meaning of these words is evident enough from the following verse [*i.e.*, 5:20].

Jesus was equating the Pharisees with the priests whom the Prophet Hosea in Hosea 4:6 said were *shallow in teaching* the Law. The people were destroyed as a result:

> My people are *destroyed for lack of knowledge*: because thou hast rejected knowledge, I will also reject thee, that thou shalt be *no priest to me*: seeing *thou hast forgotten the law of thy God*, I will also forget thy children. (Hos 4:6 ASV.)

The "knowledge" the people lack is clearly identified by the end of this passage as *knowledge of the Law.* The priests had "forgotten the Law of God."

Hence, the priests who Hosea excoriates were *no longer teaching the true Law of God*. They had devised their own traditions. The people were, as a result, being spiritually destroyed. The people lacked the knowledge of the Law to follow. This would necessarily lead to disobedience to God due to the people being taught *a shallow version* of the Law.

Faith Alone View Of Matthew 5:20

Jesus' words about entering heaven in Matthew 5:20 is a very blunt and difficult verse for the Fable of Cheap Grace to accept. The typical explanation, especially among faith-alone adherents, is that Jesus meant *the Pharisees were doing an excellent job of keeping and teaching the Law*. If you wanted to enter heaven you had to do better than the best. Jesus was allegedly upholding therefore a standard so *excessive* it must be supposed that *Jesus implied obedience to the Law was an impossible standard.* Why would Jesus do this?

According to these faith-alone theologians, Jesus did so to show you the impoverished nature of works righteousness. Works are supposedly never relevant to salvation. 'Faith alone' is the only path you allegedly can take that will succeed. Any other path that actually takes Jesus literally and expects us to exceed the righteousness of the Pharisees is supposedly a heresy of works-righteousness. Rather than allow Jesus to test their assumption on the relevance of works, they distort Jesus' words to uphold a doctrine never spoken from the mouth of Jesus — the doctrine of faith-alone!

Is this notion of a Pharisee as a highly obedient figure justifiable? No. *It is indefensible*. Jesus excoriated the Pharisees, as we shall see, for several teaching errors:

- The Pharisees teaching selectively from the Law only the lesser commands (such as tithing), leaving the more weighty matters of the Law undone (Matt. 23:23);

- The Pharisees teaching traditions which if followed led to the violation of the Law of Moses (Matt. 15:6,9); and
- The Pharisees expressly teaching that certain wrongs under the Law were acceptable behavior (*e.g.*, adulterous lust if no adulterous act followed).(Matt. 5:27-28.)[4]

Thus, Jesus could not possibly mean the Pharisees were upholding the Law to a very high standard. ***Jesus was saying the very opposite of that.*** The Pharisees were *shallow* in how far the Law was to be obeyed.

In fact, Jesus even identifies this shallowness as precisely why their proselytes were not entering the Kingdom of God. Thus, there is a total parallel between Matthew 5:20 — where ***a righteousness that matches Pharisaic righteousness will never be enough to be saved*** — and the fact Jesus says in Matthew 23:13-15,23 the Pharisees' pupils were lost. Therefore, shallow teaching of the Law of God caused the Pharisees' proselytes to be lost. As Clarke said, this is also necessarily implied from Matthew 5:19-20. To enter heaven, one must do better than the shallow doctrine of the Pharisees.

What was Jesus' principle? It is frightening to consider because the Fable of Cheap Grace so blatantly rejects Jesus' words. Jesus' true meaning was:

> You can never have the righteousness you need for eternal life if you are satisfied following your teachers' ***shallow version of the Law***. Obedience to the true Laws of God is the pathway to enter into eternal life. It is a ***narrow way*** and ***few find it***. People prefer ***shallow teachers of the Law*** than true teachers of all of God's commands. That's why the greatest in the kingdom of heaven is he who teaches obedience to the commands given Moses.

---

4. "People had come to believe that one could lust after a [married] woman, as long as the act of fornication was not committed. But Jesus showed that this understanding was foreign to the actual command by Moses." R.A. Hawkins, "Covenant Relations of the Sermon on the Mount," *Restoration Quarterly* Vol. 12, #1 (explaining Matt. 5:27-28).

Or as Hosea 4:6 said, the people are perishing for lack of the knowledge of the Law because their priests are shallow teachers of the Law.

Did The Pharisees Imperil The Salvation Of Their Pupils By A False Teaching?

One of the ways to know what Jesus preached about salvation is to see what Jesus said was a contrary message which condemned people to being lost. Thus, one of the clearest ways to understand the *affirmative* requirements of salvation is to study what Jesus *negates* as teachings which prevent salvation. As Arthur Pink, a Baptist thinker, says, "the simplest and ***most conclusive way of ascertaining*** of the nature of the righteousness Christ requires from all who shall have a part in His everlasting kingdom is to observe that it is placed in ***direct antithesis*** [to the teachings] from the...scribes and the Pharisees."[5]

Jesus clearly said the Pharisees were zealous evangelists, even going on missionary journeys. However, they held a doctrine that once believed prevented their pupil's salvation. It also prevented the salvation of the Pharisees.

> But woe unto you, scribes and Pharisees, hypocrites! because ***ye shut the kingdom of heaven against men***: for ***ye enter not*** in yourselves, neither suffer ye them that are entering in to enter. (Mat 23:13) Woe unto you, scribes and Pharisees, hypocrites! for ye compass sea and land to make ***one proselyte***; and when he is become so, ye make him twofold more a son of hell than yourselves. (Mat 23:15)(ASV)

5. Arthur W. Pink, *Exposition of the Sermon on the Mount* (Grand Rapids: 1959) chapter eight at http://www.pbministries.org/books/pink/Sermon/sermon_08.htm (Providence Baptist Ministries) (last accessed 6/16/06).

Thus, we see the Pharisees were highly evangelistic. Jesus said do not mistake zealous evangelistic behavior as proof someone is from God. The Pharisees were blind guides. People wanted to enter the kingdom. The Pharisees were abroad evangelizing them. Yet, the Pharisees had a false teaching. It made their proselytes not enter the kingdom of God. Matthew Henry in his famous commentary sees this clearly: "The scribes and Pharisees were enemies to the...*salvation* of the souls of men."

What was this teaching that was a barrier to salvation for the Pharisees and their proselytes?

Josephus And Dead Sea Scrolls Identify The Pharasaical Teaching Jesus Was Attacking

The Dead Sea Scrolls (250-50 B.C.) speak comparably to what Jesus said about the flaws in the Pharisees' doctrine on the Law. The DSS say the Pharisees were "smooth interpreters" of the Law. Horsley says this means the Pharisees' rulings "were lax and liberal" on how to interpret the Law. He says this is ironic, because the DSS give "quite a different picture from the Christian traditional stereotype of [the Pharisees] as strict legalists." (Horsley: 153.)

This notion of the Pharisees as legalists is likewise completely destroyed by Josephus — a Jewish scholar — in his work *Antiquities of the Jews* (78 A.D.)

For Josephus in 78 A.D. will tell there were two primary parties in Judaism in Jesus' day. They were the Sadducees and Pharisees. He will explain the Sadducees taught strict obedience to the Law. The Sadducees rejected the Pharisees precisely for their opposite approach on the Law of Moses. They believed the Pharisees supplanted the Law of Moses with mere traditions of the Pharisees. The Pharisees were *negating* the Law of Moses by their traditions.

Jesus, we shall see, was siding with the Sadducees on this point. Here is Josephus, the First Century Jewish historian, identifying what divided these two parties:

> What I would now explain is this, that the Pharisees have delivered to the people a great many observances by succession from their fathers, which are **not written in the Law of Moses**; and it is **for this reason that the Sadducees reject them**, and say we are to esteem those observances that are in the written word, but are **not to observe what are derived from the tradition of our forefathers**. (Josephus Flavius, *Antiquities of the Jews* 13.10.6 (13.297)(Whiston translation (1841) at 360.)

Thus, Jesus comes and faults the Pharisees primarily on the issue in dispute with the Sadducees. The Pharisees' oral teachings negated the Law and ignored the weightier matters of the Law. (Matt.15:6; 23:23.) Jesus never criticizes the Sadducees for their rigid position of strictly following the Law of Moses without embellishment. Instead, Jesus repeatedly confirms the validity of the Sadducees' position on the Law. Jesus' only express rejection of a Sadducee teaching was

Josephus

that there was no resurrection to eternal life.[6] Jesus says this is a terribly mistaken idea.

Hence, in the quote above, Josephus, unintentionally helps identify the *precise* reason for Jesus' rejection of the Pharisees. The Sadducees taught adherence to the written Law of Moses. The Sadducees rejected the Pharisees' teachings precisely because the Pharisees *added* to the Law of Moses their oral principles, elevating them above the written commands. Jesus did not fault the Sadducees on their rejec-

---

6. Jesus spoke harshly about the Sadducees. "Beware the leaven of the Pharisees and the Sadducees." (Matt. 16:6.) Matthew explains the leaven meant the "teaching of the Pharisees and Sadducees." (Matt. 16:12.) The Sadducees taught "there is no resurrection." (Matt. 22:23.) Jesus did not address other issues that separated the parties. The Pharisees believed in Fate (which means a partial predestination), while the Sadducees believed in free will. (*Antiquities:* 351.)

tion of the anti-legalism position of the Pharisees at all. Jesus only faulted the terrible doctrine of the Sadducees that there is no such thing as eternal life in a resurrection to come.

Chaplain and Bishop Jeremy Taylor (1613-1667) said this variance in doctrine between the two sects is why Jesus in Matthew 5:20 says our righteousness must exceed that of the Pharisees rather than that of the Sadducees. In this verse, "Christ does not name the Sadducees, but the Scribes and the Pharisees." Jeremy traces this back to the shallow doctrine of the Pharisees, for they (not the Sadducees) would "add words of their own" to the Law, but the Sadducees "would admit of no suppletory traditions."[7] This is why Jesus exhorted us to exceed the righteousness of the Pharisees: it was shallow. The Sadducees alone were on the *right track* in terms of the Law.

Is this variance why the Pharisees were dangerous?

What Pharisee Teaching Clearly Imperiled Salvation?

What did Jesus say the Pharisees were falsely teaching which imperiled the salvation of their proselytes (Matt. 23:13)? Ten verses later Jesus said the Pharisees were only teaching tithing from the Law, but not the rest of the Law.

> Woe unto you, scribes and Pharisees, hypocrites! for ye tithe mint and anise and cummin, and have left undone the **weightier matters of the Law** [—] justice, and mercy, and faith: but these **ye ought to have done**, and **not to have left the other undone**. (Matt. 23:23)(ASV)

Matthew Henry again sees clearly what Jesus is reproving. "They [*i.e.*, the Pharisees] were very strict and precise in **smaller matters of the law**, but **careless and loose in weightier matters** [**of the Law**]." However, Henry never puts

---

7. Jeremy Taylor, D.D., "Sermon 1: Righteousness Evangelical," *Discourses on Various Subjects* (Boston: 1816) at III:10.

two-and-two together. He never realizes this *anti-Law* doctrine which Jesus reproved was the very doctrine keeping proselytes of the Pharisees from entering heaven.

What the Pharisees were doing was minimizing what portions of the Law were important to follow. They only were following the ones that could be seen outwardly. "But all their works [from the Law] they do for to be seen of men" (Matt. 23: 5). Tithing fit perfectly into that category. It could be seen by men.

Many Christian commentators get this right. The *Daily Bible Study* says:

> The lesson from the Pharisees' example is...God's true people are to live according to **all** of God's Word, **not just certain parts** that are most convenient or to one's own liking.[8]

Others like the famous Baptist pastor, Pink, agree the Pharisees' error which Jesus exposed was "their observance of the law was a *partial* one: they laid far more stress on its ceremonial aspects than upon its **moral requirements**."[9]

Pharisaic Shallowness In Law Teaching Identifies Salvation-Critical Laws

Jesus in the same vein elsewhere warns about the salvation-threatening teachings of the Pharisees by their *dilution* of the Law of Moses. By way of introduction:

Jesus in the Sermon on the Mount says the Pharisees ignore God's law on **hate and vengeance**. Despite the Bible clearly prohibiting personal vengeance and hate, the Pharisees taught it was permissible to hate your enemies and exact vengeance. They rationalized this by out-of-context proof

---

8. http://www.keyway.ca/htm2002/pharisee.htm (last accessed 6/16/06).
9. "Sermon on the Mount," *supra*, http://www.pbministries.org/books/ pink/Sermon/sermon_08.htm (last accessed 6/16/06).

---

text quotes of the 'eye for an eye passage' and reliance on non-inspired texts. Jesus bluntly corrected them, and paraphrased passages of the Law of Moses against hate and vengeance which the Pharisees glazed over in their analyses.

Jesus also taught in the Sermon on the Mount that the Pharisees are teaching that *the sin of adultery is not in the heart*, but only in action. Just prior to this declaration, Jesus says that to enter heaven, the people must have a righteousness that *exceeds* that of the Pharisees. Jesus then explains what this means. He does not say the people need a *faith* which the Pharisees lack. Instead, the people need to follow *principles* from the Ten Commandments such as the command to not *covet your neighbor's wife* which the Pharisees negated. They taught that adulterous sins were not completed if they remained solely in the heart and not acted out.

The Sermon On The Mount Identifies Soul-Saving Changes To The Pharisees' Doctrine The People Must Follow

In the Sermon on the Mount, Jesus touches precisely on how the Pharisees ignored the commands from the Law which focused on *inward sins* such as coveting a married woman. Jesus says in the same context that if the people want to "enter the kingdom of God" then their righteousness must exceed that of the Pharisees. (Matt. 5:20.) They must *do* the commands of the Law which the Pharisees were ignoring.

Jesus begins the Sermon by saying "you shall in no wise *enter the kingdom of heaven* unless your righteousness exceeds that of the Pharisees." (Matt. 5:20.) By saying this, Jesus is harkening to His theme that the Pharisees had shallow teachings on the Law which were a barrier for salvation. (Matt. 23:13, 15.) In the Sermon, Jesus will explain what is the *missing righteousness* untaught by the Pharisees. Jesus will identify precisely what *righteousness* the Pharisees are not teaching, which if such shallow doctrine were corrected, would allow one to exceed the Pharisees' supposed righteousness. It would permit entry into the kingdom of heaven.

Jesus was insisting the people had to obey the parts of the Law the Pharisees were not teaching them *i.e.*, were *subtracting* from the Law. Jesus was telling the people that their leaders had also misconstrued passages to contradict other passages, *i.e.*, they were *diluting* the Law. Jesus taught them in the Sermon on the Mount the following specific corrections to their errors by the Pharisees regarding the Law.

- The Tenth Commandment prohibiting coveting a married woman was just as much against adultery as the Seventh Commandment that prohibited the *act* of adultery. This is discussed in detail below.

- Do not swear *falsely* at all (whether in God's name or by heaven or anything else).[10]

- Do not use the command which allows public authorities to punish 'eye for an eye' as justification for you to take personal vengeance when personal vengeance is prohibited in the Law.[11]

10.The Greek translation of Matthew inadvertently dropped the word *falsely* from the Hebrew Matthew. This erroneously made it appear Jesus said one is *never* to take an oath. (Nehemiah Gordon, *Hebrew Yeshua v. Greek Jesus* (Hilkia Press, 2006) at 59, **65-66**, 68.) But God commands people to take oaths in God's name. "Thou shalt fear Jehovah thy God;... and by his name shalt thou swear." (Deu 10:20 ASV.) Gordon, a Jewish scholar, notes the Pharisees taught you could violate an oath as long as not sworn in Yahweh's name. The Bible prohibited any *false* swearing in God's name. (Lev. 19:12.) By examining Jesus' criticisms, one can deduce how the Pharisees twisted this verse. The Pharisees obviously said this passage implied you could falsely swear even if you invoked objects closely associated with God, like the Temple. You supposedly would transgress the command only when God's name is used. However, Jesus was invoking the broader principle in Zechariah 8:17 which said "love no **false** oath: for all these are things that I hate, saith Jehovah." Thus, you were not allowed to dupe others if you worded your oath carefully. Thus, the Pharisees diminished the Law once more. Gordon detected the difference in the Hebrew version of Matthew where Jesus corrected them, saying 'do not swear *falsely* at all,' whether by the temple or anything else. The Greek translation dropped the word *falsely*. Then Gordon explains the instruction ending 'anything beyond this is evil' was an Hebraism used in the Original Testament, meaning **anything beyond (added to) the Torah was evil**.

- "You heard it said, hate your enemies" was a reference to teachings by the rabbis from the *non-inspired* portion of Psalms. As surprising as it may be to learn this, the book of Psalms was deemed in Jesus' day (and still today among Jews) as part of the *Writings* section of the Jewish Bible, and hence was not believed then or now by Jews to be 100% inspired. The *Writings* section meant the Holy Spirit *at times* was present in them but not always. However, the rabbis liked to quote from Psalms as if authoritative even when it justified hating your enemies. (Psalm 139:22, "I hate them with a perfect hatred.") Yet, Jesus said rather love your enemies. Jesus then revived the Law's command against hate of your brother and neighbor. (Lev. 19:17.) Jesus later explained in the Parable of the Good Samaritan that any stranger is a neighbor. Jesus then said hate is as wrong as murder.[12] Incidentally, Christian commentators, not knowing what Jesus was saying, actually still rely upon Psalms to justify hating your enemies if you believe them to be God's enemies.[13]

Pink Concedes Jesus Taught Works-Righteousness For Salvation Before Pink Tries To Reaffirm His Grace Doctrine

Once you make this analysis of the errors of the Pharisees, Jesus' point in Matthew 5:20 becomes self-evident. The righteousness required to enter heaven that exceeds the

---

11. The people were being told they could take vengeance because the Bible says 'an eye for an eye.' (Lev. 24:17-21.) Yet, implicit in that authorization was that it was the public authorities who would examine and decide the case. An individual could not unilaterally punish malefactors. Jesus was re-invoking this principle: "Thou shalt not take *vengeance*, nor bear any grudge against the children of thy people; but thou shalt love thy neighbor as thyself: I am Jehovah." (Lev. 19:18, ASV.) Jesus was not saying legal authorities should no longer exact proportionate punishment to the crime committed. Jesus was saying *vengeance* cannot be personally exacted. It belongs to God through the lawful authorities to do so. You *personally* must turn the other cheek.

Pharisees' righteousness is the obedience to the principles from the Law which the Pharisees negated or ignored. As the famous Baptist commentator, Pink, put it:

> [T]he simplest and **most conclusive** way of ascertaining the nature of the righteousness which Christ requires from all who shall have part in His everlasting kingdom is to observe that it is placed in **direct antithesis from the righteousness of the scribes and Pharisees**.
>
> (Arthur Pink, *Sermon on the Mount*, ch. 8.)[14]

Pink was then honest enough to recognize Jesus' obvious message in the Sermon on the Mount even though it contradicted cheap grace. Pink explains Jesus intends us to see the shallow doctrine of the Pharisees is the opposite of the elevated standard of righteousness the people must have. Pink's list is comparable to our synopsis of the Sermon in the bullet outline above. Pink says Jesus teaches in the Sermon:

- The Pharisees failed to acknowledge the Bible does sometimes condemn internal thoughts;

---

12. Leviticus 19:17, the verse prior to prohibiting vengeance (see prior footnote), prohibited hatred. Lev 19:17 states: "Thou **shalt not hate** thy *brother* in thy heart: thou shalt surely rebuke thy *neighbor*, and not bear sin because of him." This equates 'brother' with a 'neighbor.' The rule is that you do not harbor a grudge against your neighbor and hence hate a brother. It was implying you had to treat your neighbor like a brother. (Keil & Deilitzch.) This is why Jesus then says in the Parable of the Good Samaritan that a neighbor is any stranger. Christians, unfortunately, were given a misimpression that Psalms is 100% inspired by dropping the Jewish division of the canon. The Jewish canon in Jesus' day (which Josephus confirms) was divided as Law (the five books of Moses), the Prophets (the recognized prophets) and the Writings. The latter section was not regarded as 100% inspired. Rather, the Holy Spirit's presence was detectable at points. (This is why Daniel was then still in the Writings section, not the Prophets.) This explains why Jesus carefully worded His statement that He fulfilled prophecies "written about me...*in* Psalms" (Luke 24:44). Jesus did not say the prophecies were "as spoken by the Psalmist" which would have implied every word of the Psalmist, even on hating your enemies (which Jesus contradicts), was inspired.

- The Pharisees obeyed only "certain parts of the Law which suited their tastes while utterly ignoring or nullifying other vital features thereof;" and

- The Pharisees obeyed the parts of the Law they favored solely to please men, not God.

Then Pink gets down to the key issue: does obedience to higher principles of God's Law rather than the shallow ones of the Pharisees play a role in salvation? Pink shockingly answers *yes*, at odds with cheap grace.

> This **superior righteousness, then, consists of an obedience to the Divine Law** which would be acceptable to a holy but gracious God. Such an obedience must necessarily spring from the fear of God and love to God: that is, from a genuine reverence for His authority, and from a true desire to please Him. *It must comprise a strict conformity to the revealed will of God*, without any **self-invented** and **self-imposed additions** thereto. It must give particular attention to the "**weightier matters of the law**," namely justice, mercy and faith. It must be a sincere and not a feigned obedience, a filial and

---

13. Christian pastors, not understanding this, insist it is permissible to hate God's enemies. They argue it is only wrong to hate your *own* enemies. Unfortunately, this implies it is permissible to hate your own enemies if you can rationalize they are also God's enemies. These pastors thus teach you to violate Jesus' command. Andrew Sandlin in the *Forerunner* commentary, for example, quotes Psalm 139 as if inspired, and says: "This statement by David, as well as scores of others in Scripture... no doubt sounds strange — perhaps even offensive to the ears of many modern believers....The idea of a Christian's hating...wicked people is largely incompatible with the religious sentimentalism pervasive in modern Western Christianity...." (A. Sandlin, *The Attitude of the Godly Towards God's Enemies*, http://forerunner.com/forerunner/ X0508_Sandlin_-_Gods_Enemi.html (last accessed 11-30-2006).) You can hate the "works" of evildoers. Rev.2:6.

14. Pink, *Sermon on the Mount*, Chapter Eight (Providence Baptist Ministries), http://www.pbministries.org/books/pink/Sermon/ sermon_08.htm (last accessed 11/30/06).

Jesus' Words On Salvation

not a slavish one, a disinterested and not a selfish one. It must be a symmetrical or complete one, having respect to **all God's commandments**. Such an obedience will not puff up or encourage self-righteousness, but will cause the one who sincerely aims thereat to walk softly before the Lord, and will produce humility and denying of self.[15]

Of course, Pink as a Baptist cannot leave this admission alone. Pink must affix a cheap grace verbiage to Jesus' words. Thus, Pink attempts to ascribe all this *work* to the activity of the Holy Spirit acting in you by divine grace. But slapping the word *grace* onto Jesus' doctrine does not change the fact Pink concedes **Jesus teaches obedience to the strict letter of the Law as vital for salvation**. Pink's digression into cheap grace labels is a deceptive comfort.

Thus, our critique here is vital to hold in mind. Without **holding the line on what Jesus teaches**, we would end up committing the very error that Pink admitted Jesus was excoriating the Pharisees for committing. For Pink said the Pharisees taught obedience to only

certain parts of the Law which suited their tastes while utterly ignoring or **nullifying** other vital features thereof (Arthur Pink, *Sermon on the Mount*, chapter eight.)

This nullification of the Law (except tithing) is precisely what the Modern Gospel of Cheap Grace depends upon. As we shall discuss later, most of the modern church teaches only that tithing is still valid from the Law, but nothing else from the Law applies in the era of grace.[16]

---

15. Pink, *Sermon on the Mount* Chapter Eight, excerpted in full at http://www.pbministries.org/books/pink/Sermon/sermon_08.htm.

16. See page 194 *et seq.*

This means *modern grace teaching is identical to the Pharisees' doctrine*. Jesus said that the Pharisees were big on **tithing**, but had set aside the weightier matters of the Law, stressing the less weighty matters of the Law. (Matt. 23:23.)

Deficiency Of Pharisees On Adultery Doctrine

Let's explore in detail the Pharisee error on adultery. We will learn Jesus was excoriating the Pharisees' negation of one of the Ten Commandments. Jesus' point is not self-evident unless you (a) know the Law and (b) become aware of Pharisaic teachings on lust for a married woman.

In the Sermon on the Mount, Jesus explains while discussing adultery what was deficient in the Pharisees' teaching. Jesus says the Pharisees fell down by not teaching the Tenth of the Ten Commandments: thou shall not *covet* thy neighbor's wife. The Pharisees were failing to teach it was wrong to covet your neighbor's wife (*i.e.*, number ten of the Ten Commandments). Instead, they emphasized it was only important not to commit the *act* of adultery, which of course is also *separately* prohibited in the Seventh of the Ten Commandments. The Pharisees focused on only one command touching on adultery to the neglect of another command on adultery that was *equally important* to teach.

Jesus says: "You've heard it said do not *commit* adultery [*i.e.*, the Seventh Commandment], but I tell you that whosoever looks on a [*married*][17] woman to lust after her has committed adultery in his heart" [*i.e.*, the Tenth Commandment]. (Matt. 5:27-28.)

> "[You] believe not [Moses'] writings...." Jesus, speaking to religious leaders Jn 5:47

> "And you have not His word abiding in you...." Jesus, speaking to religious leaders Jn 5:38

---

17. The Greek word only means a *married* woman. See footnote 6 on page 206. Besides, it is the only plausible translation because the Bible never said sex with a single woman was *adultery*. For adultery to take place, a woman had to be already married. (Lev. 20:10.)

The Pharisees taught there is no sin in *thoughts* of lust for a married woman if the act of adultery did not follow. They taught this despite one of the Ten Commandments expressly prohibiting *coveting* of a married woman. As one commentator points out regarding Jesus' meaning:

> People had come to believe that one could lust after a [married] woman, as long as the **act of fornication [i.e., sex] was not committed**. But Jesus showed that this understanding was foreign to the actual command by Moses.[18]

This is likewise understood by a commentator who nevertheless favors Cheap Grace, Deffinbaugh, Th.M.:

> The Jewish interpretation of the seventh commandment was that one was guilty of adultery **only if he or she had committed the physical act.** This was a very narrow and external interpretation of the Law and **ignored the clear teaching of the tenth commandment**: 'You shall not covet your neighbor's house; you shall not covet your neighbor's wife....(Exodus 20:17).[19]

The oral tradition had made of none effect the tenth of the Ten Commandments. The *oral law* of the Pharisees had come to tower over the *written Law given to Moses by God.*

What corroborates this was the Pharisaic oral teaching is current rabbinic thought. Without naming names, a conservative Jewish rabbi on national radio teaches Judaism does not say there is any such thing as adultery in *thoughts*. The only adultery is in action. This rabbi says this principle is true

---

18.Robert A. Hawkins, "Covenant Relations of the Sermon on the Mount," *Restoration Quarterly* Vol. 12, No. 1 reprinted at http://www.restorationquarterly.org/Volume_012/rq01201hawkins.htm (last accessed 6/16/06).

19.*The Fatal Failures of Religion: #2 Legalism* at http://www.bible.org/page.asp?page_id=604 (last accessed 7/4/06).

beyond adultery: there are no sins of the heart in Judaism. There are only sins in physical actions. (He says this is the major difference between Christianity and Judaism.) But that very teaching is *contrary* to the Tenth Commandment: "Thou shalt not *covet* your neighbor's wife." Thus, the error Jesus tried to correct within Judaism still persists. (Catholicism repeated this error in 1567, Pius V ruling "only overt action was to be considered sinful, but not mere desire." Plaut:558.)

The Pharisaical Elevation Of The So-called 'Oral Law'

How can a blatant contradiction emerge that negates one of the Ten Commandments?

Because by Jesus' day, the oral law became so important in Pharisaical Judaism that it was axiomatic that the oral law *had more weight* than the Prophets. For example, Maimonides, a great exponent of the Oral Law, explained in the Middle Ages why there is an appropriate emphasis on rabbinic oral law over the written prophets. Maimonides cites a tradition dating to Jesus' day. He cites Eliezer who was then a famous rabbi. Maimonides synopsizes a lesson from Eliezer:

> If there are 1000 prophets, all of them of the stature of Elijah and Elisha, giving a certain interpretation, and 1001 rabbis giving the opposite interpretation, you shall 'incline after the majority' (Exodus 23:2)[20] and *the law is according to the 1001 rabbis, not according to the 1000 venerable prophets*.[21]

---

20. The Pharisees were notorious for out-of-context proof-texting. The passage Exodus 23:2 is a command not to follow the majority when you testify as a witness; instead, always tell the truth. The Oral-law advocates (*i.e.*, the Pharisees) took it out of context, and read it as a command to adopt majority viewpoints on the meaning of the Law or Prophets even if it violates the actual words of a Prophet. As Nehemiah Gordon (a Karaite Jew and scholar) says, the rabbis read Exodus 23:2 "out of context," and "derive a completely different principle" from it than what it states. (N. Gordon, *Hebrew Yeshua v. Greek Jesus* (2006) at 18.)

This is the attitude Jesus was battling. The Pharisees developed doctrines that cancelled the words delivered by the prophets. The Oral Tradition tragically was being given more weight than God's true prophetic messengers.

This explains how someone so intelligent as this radio rabbi (whom I mentioned above) is still stuck on oral traditions. He in good conscience affirms the difference between Christianity and Judaism is that Judaism does not recognize as sin anything that is not accompanied by action. The only reason this is so is that the oral law supposedly replaced the written law on certain issues, such as this important principle against adulterous lust in the written law.

What the radio rabbi teaches is precisely what Jesus was criticizing 2000 years ago. It continues among sincere Jewish rabbis today. It has never changed. This is the power of *oral* tradition. ***Two thousand years later, and it is still with us***. And somehow, the fact the Tenth Commandment is staring them in the face does not dissuade these sincere rabbis from their doctrines. They have rationalized away the fact their teaching is directly contrary to what the Law says based on the priority of the Oral Law. Even moral, fair, and sensible rabbis rely more on the oral law than the written law.

Incidentally, not all of Judaism agrees with this radio rabbi. So please do not misread that the radio rabbi's views are dominant. Instead, Judaism, like Christianity, is fraught with commentators who are at odds with each other. So the *Encyclopedia of Judaism* can say "covetousness" is defined as *inordinate desire* for another's wife or possessions, and is condemned in Judaism based on the Tenth Commandment.[22]

---

21. Moses Maimonides, *Introduction to the Mishnah* (Jerusalem: 1992) at 27-28 [Hebrew text as translated in Nehemiah Gordon, *Hebrew Yeshua v. Greek Christ* (2006) at 83-84.]

22. "Covetousness," http://www.jewishencyclopedia.com/view.jsp?artid=838&letter=C (last accessed 7/4/06).

The radio rabbi thus represents a strain of thinking identical to what Jesus was trying to correct. It is still alive today. This helps us *corroborate* how to understand what Jesus was correcting. Jesus was confronting oral tradition by the Pharisees which negated the Law. This led to an inferior righteousness *in practice* and *in teaching* by the Pharisees. It did not meet God's standards. *It was shallow.* Jesus said that to enter the kingdom of heaven, the people must have a righteousness that exceeds that of the Pharisees. *One of those higher standards* the people needed is *that they must follow the Tenth of the Ten Commandments* which the Pharisees nullified by the Oral Torah.

The radio rabbi then becomes a contemporary example of what Jesus was up against. No doubt ordinary Jews of Jesus' era were struggling to understand how seemingly moral and devout rabbis (just like the radio rabbi) could be *wrong* in a way that negated the Law. The ordinary Jew who heard there was no sin from mere thoughts unless action followed must have assumed the rabbis learned this truth due to superior study of the Bible. Yet, the people were wrong in this assumption.

To dislodge this assumption which prevailed 2000 years ago, Jesus gave numerous speeches on the hypocrisy and false teachings of the Pharisees. It must have shocked Jesus' audience what He was saying. Only those who truly loved God would have tried to attempt to focus on Jesus' words to see how He corrected the Pharisees' doctrines.

Paradoxically, today the same spiritual airs are assumed by our modern church leaders. We have to dislodge this smugness by the direct and powerful impact of Jesus' words. Thus, in this book we have spared no punches. This book has tried to lay bare the many contemporary foundational doctrines that clearly violate Jesus' words, *e.g.*, the mocking of Jesus' doctrine of repentance and obedience as 'earning salvation,' 'legalism,' etc.

You need to escape these mantras. By dint of repetition, many have accepted a view of salvation that displaces Jesus' doctrine. Listen attentively to Jesus' teachings on this score. Jesus says your very salvation is at risk if you swallow the modern equivalent of the Pharisees' shallow doctrines.

Corroboration Of Jesus' Intent From Jesus' Excoriation Of The Pharisees

There is no mistaking what angers Jesus about the Pharisees' teaching which He says is a barrier to salvation. The Pharisees had a similar teaching about one of the Ten Commandments to *honor your mother and father*. In Jewish interpretation, including by Jesus, this meant taking care of your mother and father if they were poor. If you failed to do so, then you *dishonored* your mother and father. However, the Pharisees taught that if you paid a special *Korban* (gift) to the Temple, this "more sacred" payment excused obeying God's *actual* command to give support to your mother and father.

In the quote below, Jesus refers to this special Korban obliquely in Matthew 15:5. Jesus was quoting what such a Korban payor was allowed to say to his parent: "That wherewith thou mightest have been profited by me is given to God." (This is in Mishnah *Nedarim. See* Edwards, 2002:211.) Jesus teaches this negated the commandment of God. Honoring/supporting your mother and father was your *sacred* duty. It was not to be abandoned by paying sufficient monies to satisfy the human demands of Temple authorities. *See*, Matt. 15:6 ("you have made the commandment of God of none effect by your tradition.") In Matthew 15:2-9, we read:

> (2) Why do thy disciples transgress the tradition of the elders? for they wash not their hands when they eat bread. (3) And he [Jesus] answered and said unto them, **Why do ye also transgress the commandment of God because of your tradition**? (4) For God said, Honor thy father and thy mother: and, He that speaketh

evil of father or mother, let him die the death. (5) But ye say, whosoever shall say to his father or his mother, That wherewith thou mightest have been profited by me is given to God; (6) he shall not honor his father. And *ye have made void the word of God because of your tradition*. (7) Ye hypocrites, well did Isaiah prophesy of you, saying, (8) This people honoreth me with their lips; But their heart is far from me. (9) But in vain do they worship me, *Teaching as their doctrines the precepts of men.* (ASV)

Thus, Jesus excoriates the Pharisees for replacing the commandments of God (*i.e.*, the Law given Moses) with what is merely a *tradition* of men. As the English Reverend

Jeremy Taylor 1613-1667

Jeremy Taylor explains, "they thought they did well enough [with the] corban, and let their father starve." (Taylor, *Discourses, supra*, III:13.) Jesus regarded this doctrine of the Pharisees as *negating* the Law of Moses by means of their own oral law. Jesus was attacking those who make an Oral Law of greater stature than the Written Law given Moses.

Clarke concurs, and comments on this passage, saying: "Pretenders to zeal often prefer superstitious usages...and *human inventions* to the positive duties of [God]."

Barnes likewise concurs that the Pharisees trained the people to trust them over the written Law: "[The commands in the oral law] are, however, regarded by the [Pharisaical] Jews as *more important than either Moses or the prophets*." (The bracketed text is added for the sake of accuracy.)

Robertson's *Word Pictures* concurs too: "The [Pharisaical] rabbis placed tradition (the oral law) *above* the law of God."

Thus, we see Jesus is upset with the Pharisees once more for negating the Law. The Pharisees were giving contrary Oral Law teachings. This was comparable to what we previously noted. For example:

- The Pharisees taught the less weighty matters of the Law (*i.e.*, tithing) had to be followed, but they left untaught the weightier matters from the Law. (Matt. 23:23.) It was in this context that Jesus said they were preventing salvation of their proselytes. (Matt. 23:13, 15.)

- In the Sermon on the Mount, Jesus said the Pharisees taught it was wrong to commit adultery, but they negated the validity of the Tenth Commandment that it was wrong *in itself* to covet a married woman. (Matt. 5:27-29.) Jesus told the people to "enter into the kingdom of God" they had to follow a righteousness higher than this shallow righteousness of the Pharisees. (Matt. 5:20.)

- Lastly, in Matthew 15:2-9, we see the Pharisees' teaching about the special Korban (or Corban) was viewed by Jesus as negating obedience to one of the Ten Commandments. Their human ***oral*** teaching had the effect of causing obedience to the Law to wither. Their teaching was a Law-less teaching. It served to negate the Law.

The Pharisaical Error Pin-Pointed Again By Jesus

If the Pharisees' Lawless teaching is what prevents salvation, then we would expect to find Jesus explicitly giving us direction on this. Does Jesus ever explain that a false guide is one who relaxes in the least any command in the Law of Moses?

Yes, Jesus tells us clearly what He thinks about those who teach us *not* to obey some provision in the Law given Moses by God.

In Matthew 5:18-19, Jesus explains that anyone who "shall teach" others not to follow a command of the Law of Moses (in the least) will be least in the kingdom of heaven:

> (18) For verily I say unto you, Till heaven and earth pass away, one jot or one tittle shall in no wise pass away from the Law [*i.e.*, Nomos], till all things be accomplished. (19) ***Whosoever***

> *therefore shall ~~break one of these least~~ [relax*
> *one of these] commandments [in the least]*,
> and *shall teach men so,* shall be called least in
> the *kingdom of heaven*: but whosoever shall
> do and teach them, he shall be called great in
> the kingdom of heaven. (ASV)[23]

Jesus thus excoriates those (like the Pharisees) who taught commands from the Law given Moses did not necessarily have to be followed. Jesus says, by contrast, in His "Gospel of the Kingdom" that those who are "great in the kingdom of heaven" will be those who teach others to obey the Law given Moses. The antithesis Jesus uses here is borrowed from Proverbs 28:4: "To reject the Law is to praise the wicked; to obey the Law is to fight them." (NLT.)

Thus, we see Jesus taught the Law given Moses had to be followed. The weighty and the less weighty. The moral commands from the Law (*e.g.*, thou shalt not covet) as well as the externally-testable commands (*e.g.*, thou shalt not commit adultery). Jesus taught us the Pharisees failed to teach both. Jesus said their teachings were causing those coming to them for salvation to not enter the kingdom of heaven. Jesus said for us to enter the kingdom of heaven, our righteousness *must exceed this half-hearted shallow effort* to keep the Law. The Pharisees were *lukewarm* about the Law. They were not on fire to obey it: Jesus said they picked and chose what to obey.

We necessarily must understand therefore that Jesus is telling us that *anyone who says obeying the Law is not important for salvation is bringing a false gospel*.

> "Moses gave you the Law,
> but none of you obeys it!"
> John 7:19, Jesus teaching in the
> Temple

---

23. The bracketed text is to correct a mistranslation in the KJV. The Greek verb means *loosing* or *relaxing*, not *breaking*. *See*, Joseph Rotherham, *The Emphasised Bible: A New Translation Designed to Set Forth The Exact Meaning* (1902) at 932. He provides the corrections that appear in the bracketed text. *Cf.* Vulg (411 A.D.) "dissolve."

Overlapping Laws For Jew & Gentile With Different Scope

That said, we must realize that the Law sometimes applies differently to Jews than Gentiles. Yet, the Law is being followed even when the Law makes exceptions or has different patterns for Gentiles (also referred to as *sojourners* or *foreigners*). The Law has far less commands applicable to Gentiles than it has for Israelites. Regardless, when it does apply to a Gentile, it must be followed. Thus, we can say emphatically that anyone who teaches sojourners (Gentiles) that the Law given Moses when it *expressly applies to sojourners* (foreigners/Gentiles) is either unimportant or unnecessary are bringing the false teachings of the Pharisees. Jesus condemns this doctrine and warns of its soul-threatening effect.[24]

Cheap Grace Gospel Claims Fulfilling The Law Abolished The Law

However, as we all know, the Modern Gospel of Cheap Grace says the Law given Moses is no longer applicable. It is nailed to a tree. Abolished. Taken away. It is a shadow of things to come. Yet, nothing from Matthew 5:17-20 says this.

To make Jesus fit the Cheap Grace Gospel, what proponents of this **other gospel** do is lift one word out of context from this passage: *fulfill*. The cheap grace proponents claim Jesus *fulfilled* all the Law for us so we no longer must obey

---

24. Obviously, Jesus' view, if taken seriously, would upset the commonly heard notion that the New Testament replaced the old. This replacement-theory is not a doctrine ever taught by Jesus. Instead, Jesus said that if you tried to make a Gentile (Sojourner) follow commands only applicable to Jews (the old), you can cause the new to spill out (be unduly squeezed out and pressured) and cause their being lost. Therefore, the correct doctrine is to put nothing on a Gentile that was not put on a sojourner/foreigner under the Law. See my prior book, *Jesus' Words Only* (2007) at 102-05.

---

the Law. Thus they make this word *fulfilled* swallow all the principles Jesus just laid down. However, the full context of Jesus' statements speaks at odds with this view:

> (17) Think not that I came to **destroy the law** or the prophets: I came not to destroy, but to **fulfil**. (18) For verily I say unto you, **Till heaven and earth pass away**, one jot or one tittle shall in **no wise pass away from the law, till all things be accomplished**. (Mat 5:17-18.)

Now, the defenders of cheap grace concede Jesus means here primarily that He came to fulfill the prophecies in the Law about a Messiah, *e.g.*, Numbers 24 (the Star Prophecy); Gen. 3:15 (a man will crush the head of the snake); Gen. 49:10-12 (the Shiloh Prophecy of Messiah), etc.

However, what they fail to realize is that, as they also admit, the prophecy in Genesis 3:15 has not yet been fulfilled. This says a man will come who will crush the head of the serpent after having his own heal bruised. Satan bruised Christ's heal at the cross. But Satan is alive and well. In fact, Satan must be loosed at the end of the millennium. Then and only then will he be destroyed. (Rev. 20:10.) Thus, the death blow to the head of Satan mentioned in Genesis 3:15 has not yet happened. Upon its occurrence, a new heaven and earth will replace the current ones. Thus, literally, the prophecies of the Law will *not be fulfilled* until coincidentally the old heaven and earth pass away. At that point, Satan is finally destroyed in the Lake of Fire.

Consequently, when Jesus says the Law continues **until the heavens and earth pass away**, this completely fits the duration for the fulfillment of the Genesis 3:15 prophecy. The Book of Genesis is part of the 'Law given Moses,' and the Law, including this prophecy of Genesis 3:15, continues until Satan is destroyed. This happens to coincide with a date still off in the future — the passing of the old heaven and the earth. And thus the Law does not pass away until all things are fulfilled, which happens when heaven and earth pass away. That has not even remotely yet happened! Hence, the Law is still valid because it is not yet entirely *fulfilled*!

Accordingly, what Jesus said was literally true: not one jot or tittle of the Law given Moses would pass away until the Heaven and Earth pass away. This point coincides with precisely when the Law's prophecies are fulfilled in their entirety.

Thus, Jesus' meaning that He came to fulfill the Law did not mean that His obedience *replaces* any need for individuals to follow the Law prior to the passing of the heavens and earth.

Unfortunately, it is a fact that the Christian dogma of the last four centuries has taught the Law was done away with in 33 A.D. This interpretation does not follow from anything Jesus said about fulfilling the Law. ***Jesus' saying He came to fulfill a prophecy is not the same as saying He came to replace your duty to obey the Law with His perfect obedience***. Such a teaching undermines everything Jesus did teach about obedience to the Law. Such a cheap grace teaching reflects a Pharasaical ***disrespect for the Law*** in contravention to the respect for the Law Jesus said was crucial for salvation. (Matt. 5:20-21.)

The Pharisees Are The Opposite Of Legalists

As we must realize by now, modern Christians are trained to incorrectly understand the Pharisees' error. We are misinformed the Pharisees caused their followers not to be saved because the Pharisees allegedly *insisted upon all the Law* being followed rigorously. Allegedly Jesus was condemning any doctrine that insisted we obey *all* the Law of Moses. For example, *Halley's Bible Dictionary* says:

> Pharisees were the most numerous and influential of the religious sects of Jesus' day. ***They were strict legalists***. They stood for the rigid

observance of the letter and forms of the Law, and also for the Traditions.

However, this is wrong in saying the Pharisees stood for the rigid observance of "the Law." The Pharisees' error was that *they did not teach the entire Law, but only a very small and less weighty part — tithing*. They also *replaced* commandments of the Law with traditions of men. As *Tyndale's Bible Dictionary* (2001) correctly says, Jesus means the "Pharisees...are devoted to their own traditions, which they offer not as supplements but as *rivals* to God's Word [the Law]." (*Id.*, at 870.) Thus, the *Halley Bible Dictionary* blurs this. It implies a different error which is *exactly* the opposite of what Jesus identified as the Pharisee error. *The Pharisees were not legalists*. Instead, they were the opposite: they worked the *negation* of the Law given Moses.

As Robert Thiel correctly points out:

> Some claim that believing in following the laws of God makes one a legalist. However, if legalism is defined as adhering to the ten commandments, then **the Pharisees could not have been 'legalists'** — the Pharisees repeatedly violated the ten commandments and justified these violations by traditions of men (Mark 7:13).[25]

If a legalist is anyone who thinks the Law of Moses is valid, and therefore should be followed by a follower of Christ, *then Jesus is a legalist*. The doctrines we condemn as legalism today, as reflected in the *Halley Bible Dictionary*, make Jesus a heretic. For Jesus applauded the Pharisees' tithing efforts, and then said that *the Pharisees did not go far enough in their obedience to the Law*. They were really good about the less weighty matters of the Law, but they left the weightier matters of the Law undone. (Matt. 23:23.)

---

25. Robert J. Thiel, Ph.D. *Were the Pharisees Condemned for Keeping the Law of God?* (2001) www.cogwriter.com/pharisee.htm (6/17/06).

As Thiel points out, if Jesus' words really had any weight with us, then the sign of the modern Pharisee is someone who "does not actually keep the ten commandments."

Hence, *something is fundamentally amiss in the way we understand the error of the Pharisees*. It's obvious why: we have adopted the Pharisee error as *normative* Christianity. We did away with the Law given Moses. Gone is the Sabbath. It is ignored even though it is one of the Ten Commandments. Most Christians would say they do keep Sabbath on Sunday. However, this is not God's day. We have felt free to move it to a day of our own choosing, just like Jeroboam moved the Feast of Tabernacles by one month. This was a day "of his own invention." (1 Kings 12:33.) The Prophet Daniel pejoratively warns of the one who one day will put down three rulers, and "shall think to *change the times and the Law....*" (Dan. 7:25.) Jesus likewise abhorred such Lawless teachings. Thus, to prevent us from seeing this, we have to be repetitiously indoctrinated to *think* the Pharisee error was exactly the opposite of what Jesus said it was.

How Cheap Grace Differs From Jesus

The dominant dogma of modern Christianity has become identical to what Jesus condemned. To prove this to yourself, simply listen to a clear presentation of the Modern Gospel of Cheap Grace at almost any supposedly evangelical church on Sunday. Here is a perfect example of what you might hear. This is from the *Lectionary Series* wherein it identifies what it thinks is wrong when someone teaches us to obey the Law of God:

> Legalism, the heresy known as sanctification by obedience, can easily undermine our initial 'yes' for Jesus. We begin to believe that *our continued standing before God, his approval and love, and our progress in the Christian life, is gained by obedience to Christ*. This way of thinking undermines "repentance and faith."

So, the initial 'yes' for the journey of faith, *can be undermined* if the believer gets into *the business of law-obedience.* For us today, let us beware that we haven't unknowingly said 'yes,' but have then forgotten the Father's will.

The church today is infested with legalism. The adoption of the heresy of *sanctification by obedience is widespread* and so many church attenders have forgotten their 'yes' and now seek a law-righteousness rather than a righteousness which is *apart from the law of God.* If we are to do what the Father wants, then we must live by grace through faith and not by works of the law. [26]

What is truly amazing is how anyone can think this way if one believes Jesus was God-in-the-flesh. To believe this supposed gospel in the quote above, you must not take Jesus very seriously. For Jesus said you can go to heaven maimed or hell whole. (Matt. 5:30; Mark 9:42 *et seq.*) Yet, what did the *Lectionary Series* just say? The opposite:

[It is heretical to believe] our continued standing before God, his approval and love, and our progress in the Christian life, is *gained by obedience to Christ.*

Yet, what the *Lectionary* condemns as heretical doctrine is exactly the doctrine which Jesus taught. The *Lectionary* insists justification by obedience to the Law of God is a heresy. Anyone who teaches that it is necessary to obey God's moral commandments and thus avoid sin to go to heaven is supposedly a heretic. What are we to think? Are we to feel sorry for 'poor Jesus' who in Mark 9:42-47 did not have the benefit of this insight of modern evangelism? Are we to think Jesus made a mistake when He said in John 15:14 that "you

---

26. "Matthew: The authority of Jesus. 21:23-32," at http://www.lectionarystudies.com/studyg/sunday26ag.html (last accessed 6/21/06).

are my friends *if* you obey my commandments"? For the *Lec-tionary* insists it knows better that "God's... approval and love... is [not] gained by obedience to Christ." If we only knew who was Lord, then this would not be a difficult issue.

The same kind of error about salvation occupied the Pharisees' attention. They taught salvation was by election. They were Abraham's seed. They were saved. Jesus said this misses the key necessity of repentance *from sin.* (Matt. 5:29-30.) Jesus required a repentance that was an active life-chang-ing correction to obedience to the Law which they broke.

If one had their Master's words *first* and *foremost* in their mind, it is amazing what Christians can come to believe is a *Christian* teaching. Yet, here we have progressed to the point that mainstream Christianity teaches what the Teacher vigorously taught against.

When this conflict is exposed between Church doc-trine and Jesus, cheap grace defenders will declare you are a heretic if you insist Jesus' words are still valid. You suppos-edly do not realize that ***Jesus' words belonged to a prior and different dispensation than the Christian dispensation.*** (See *Jesus' Words Only* (2007) at 367 *ff.*) Jesus' words are alleg-edly defunct, but the ***Church doctrine of today which is con-trary to Jesus is supposedly valid.***

Derisive Rebuttals: Awls In Ears, Fringes On Garments & Head Coverings

One of the rebuttals I have received tries to deride me personally as a hypocrite and then deride the good sense behind the Law itself, as if God is not indirectly being attacked. Those who do this also think they are following a pattern that replicates Jesus' approach. It does not.

For example, I am confronted with the argument that I do not supposedly keep the Law. Therefore, I must be a hypo-crite. Then I ask them: 'what Law don't I keep?' Then they respond by making derisive attacks on 'why don't you put awls in ears of servants?' and why 'do you shave your beard?' 'Why are there no fringes on your garments?'

However, these are not commands in the Law I am disobeying, but my verbal pugilist does not know this due to his ignorance of the Law itself.

The implicit assumption behind this argument is that Jesus was so upset with hypocrisy of not keeping these supposed commandments that He abolished the entire Law. Jesus' alleged solution to the Pharisees' hypocrisy was simply to abrogate the Law. Yet, if so, *the Pharisees would no longer be sinners for the many transgressions Jesus had hitherto been hurling at the Pharisees*. They would now have an easy road. The entire thrust of this argument of my verbal pugilist is obvious nonsense.

But what is most disturbing is that this argument is laden with *a derision of the Law given by God.* And this is pernicious because it *attacks the character of God Himself who authorized these supposedly strange commands*. So what about the principles these verbal pugilists denigrate which supposedly come from the Law? They were:

- Awls in ears of a servant.
- No shaving of beards.
- Fringes on garments; and
- Head coverings.

They are actually trying to take these principles, which they assume are in the Law even though they often are not present or are optional, and then use it to *make fun of the Law of God*! They treat God's word as *foolishness*! God only help them!

The verbal pugilist cites these presumed principles from the Law to mock it and denigrate it. What an odd esteem they have for the words of I AM to Moses. *I hate to inform them of this but they are mocking Jesus,* for Jesus said He was the "I AM." Jesus said, "Before Abraham was, I AM." (John 8:58.) Thus, when I find these hurled insults at my adherence to God's Law, it is incongruous that these people can claim they love Jesus — the very same I AM who gave these commands they find so strange and distasteful.

Actually, the alleged silly commands they mock are either:

- Not in the Law at all but are a simple tradition (*e.g.,* head coverings);[27] or

- Are voluntarily imposed (*e.g.,* awls in ears of servants who volunteer to be a servant for life);[28] or

- Are exaggerated interpretations by means of tradition meant to put a hedge around the Law. For example, the notion of not shaving a beard is a modern tradition. The Biblical command is merely a prohibition on — in effect — a Fu Manchu beard. You cannot *simultaneously* cut below the sideburns and cut off the chin-edge of the beard which if done is a Fu Manchu;[29] or

- Limited to Israelites only and not Sojourners (Gentiles), *e.g.,* fringes on garments. Also, the fringes command is not that hard to comply with if you happen to be wearing a four corner long garment. It is even decorative.[30]

How Far Does The Law Apply To Gentiles

James taught us that if the Law given Moses says the command applies to a "child of Israel," it is literal. It does not apply to Sojourners (Gentiles) who are part of the community.

---

27. Nehemiah Gordon is a Karaite Jew, which means a Jew who rejects traditions added to the Law (formerly known as *Kara*). He explains one such accretion of tradition is the *kippah* or skull-cap. See N. Gordon, *Hebrew Yeshua v. Greek Jesus* (Halkiah Press, 2006) at 19-20.

28. Deuteronomy 15:16-17 reads: "16 It shall be, *if he tells you,* 'I will not go out from you;' because he loves you and your house, because he is well with you; 17 then you shall take an awl, and thrust it through his ear to the door, and he shall be your servant forever. Also to your female servant you shall do likewise."

James in Acts chapter 15 read the command on circumcision in Leviticus 12:3 to mention only an imposition on the children of Israel. James thus said as a matter of literal interpretation, it does not apply to non-Jews.

---

29. Friedman's modern translation of the Torah as well as many others make clear that the command was (a) not to cut from your face the hair below the sideburns and (b) cut off the edge of your beard (*i.e.*, hair on the chin). Thus, if you put two-and-two together, the Bible prohibits a Fu Manchu. Friedman translates Leviticus 19:27 "you shall not trim your head's edge, and you shall not destroy your beard's edge." First, this was *not* a command to have a beard. It was how to cut a beard you already had. Second, Friedman's note indicates "your head's edge" means "sideburns." *Pe'ah* means *side*. (Ex. 26:20.) It is obvious that the Bible understands the chin area as the *beard*. The area above the chin on the cheeks is the sideburn area, and is distinct. So the prohibition is on cutting the hair from the sideburn area, thus leaving an empty space between your sideburn area and your chin-beard. Then it says, in Friedman's translation, "you shall not destroy your beard's edge." What does that mean? You were not to cut the chin beard's edge off. If you put the two commands together, it precisely tells you *not to have a Fu Manchu beard*. Some commentators more loosely say it means "trimming of the corners" is forbidden. (*Beard Bible Dictionary.*) However, this prohibition is not against *any* trimming of *corners*. It is against *shaping the beard in two simultaneous ways*: cutting off the hair below the sideburns and cutting down the edge of your beard so that it was short at the chin area. The Satanic world intuitively understands this verse better than we do. Satanists like LaVey wear a Fu Manchu-styled beard. Such a beard naturally has a more sinister aspect. *That's all Leviticus 19:27 prohibits.* If having a beard was mandatory or shaving the sideburns was *always* wrong, then it makes no sense that ritual purification of a leper involved shaving all the hair on his head and his beard. (Leviticus 14:9. See also Nu 8:7.) If the modern practice among some Jews to not shave the beard was understood in earlier times, then it makes no sense why devout pilgrims from Shechem, Shiloh and Samaria "having *their beards shaven* and clothes rent" bring meal-offerings and frankincense into the "house of Yahweh." (Jeremiah 41:5.) People closer to the time these commands were first written thought an act of being more holy and clean was to *shave* all of the beard off. Also, other commentators from the Jewish Karaite tradition make plausible arguments from *Bible texts alone* that the prohibition was against cutting a beard to show mourning. See "Shaving and Sidelocks? The Real Meaning of Leviticus 19:27-28," at http://www.karaite-korner.org/shaving.shtml (last visited 11/30/06).

James' view is clear again later in Acts 21:18-26, when James confronts Paul. James reminds Paul that the decision about circumcision being unnecessary was only true for Gentile Christians. Jewish Christians must still follow the circumcision command.

If you apply the Israel-Sojourner distinction which James employed, then only a very limited portion of the Law of Moses applies to non-Jews.

Gentiles would have to obey primarily the Ten Commandments and Leviticus chapters 19 & 20 & 24:13-24 and part of 17 which Jesus alludes to many times. These are moral commands that do not introduce themselves as commands to only Israel.

In fact, in Chapter 20 of Leviticus, it in particular says it applies not only to Israelites but also to "foreigners" in the land. Chapter 20 had to do with sexual practices.

The fact the Law is sometimes broadened explicitly to include foreigners supports James' method of interpretation. If it always applies to the foreigner, then Leviticus 20:2 and 24:16, 21-22 did not need to say the highlighted portion below:

> Moreover, thou shalt say to the children of
> Israel, Whosoever he be of the children of

---

30. "The Lord also said to Moses: *Speak to the children of Israel,* and thou shalt tell them to make to themselves fringes in the corners of their garments, putting in them ribands of blue: that when they shall see them, they may remember all the commandments of the Lord" (Numbers 15:37-39). The Karaite Jewish position (*i.e.*, strict literalist) is that this command only requires fringes on a garment that has, itself, four corners. You are *not commanded to wear four-cornered clothing,* but whenever you wear four-cornered clothing, you must have fringes to remind you of the Torah. See "Tzitzit," http://www.karaite-korner.org/tzitzit.shtml (last accessed 11/30/2006). This makes sense or otherwise, all underwear, bathing suits, hats, scarves, shirts, etc. would have to have tassels. Thus, in modern usage, if a child of Israel wore a poncho or toga, then tassels are necessary. Since wearing such clothing is no longer common, perhaps it would be appropriate to find other visible means to remind themselves of the Law. Yet, there is no command to do so.

Israel, or of *the strangers that sojourn in Israel*, that giveth of his seed unto Molech; he shall surely be put to death: the people of the land shall stone him with stones. Lev 20:2 ASV

Any Israelite or *any foreigner living in Israel* who curses the LORD shall be stoned to death by the whole community. (Lev 24:16 GNB)

Whoever kills an animal shall replace it, but whoever kills a human being shall be put to death. This law applies to all of you, to Israelites and *to foreigners living among you*, because I am the LORD your God. (Lev 24:21-22 GNB.)

Thus, James is being a literalist. The Law's distinction between Israelite and foreigner/sojourner should apply even in the Christian age. The burdens vary.

However, if you believe there is no more distinction between Jew or Gentile, such a false teaching can lead to a heightened burden on the Gentiles beyond what the Law itself required. That distinction is what James was battling with Paul to preserve and maintain.

In other words, if you say a Gentile is under the same Law that *only* applies to Israelites, these extra burdens on them are in excess of what the Law itself requires.

Thus, if we erased the Jew-Gentile distinction in reading the Law, we would make it harder for Gentiles to be followers of Jesus. Such a doctrine would lead to unnecessary burdens on Gentiles. Instead, we should obey the Law in how it defines its scope on Jews versus on foreigners/sojourners.

In fact, the only commands in the Law specifically addressed to both Jews and *foreigners/sojourners* were in Leviticus 17 (*viz.* 17:8 *et seq.*), all of Leviticus 19 and 20 as well as Leviticus 24:15-22. There are other commands that are *universal*, such as the Ten Commandments (Exodus 20) and the general command against adding to/subtracting from

Scripture (Deut. 4:2, 13:5). Yet, none of these commands are too hard to follow. Most of the rest of Torah is merely history, *e.g.*, all of Genesis, most of Exodus, most of Numbers.

However, despite this narrowness of application, the leading Christian authorities tell Gentiles that Torah-keeping is a pointless burdensome task.

This is mostly done by sneering at the Law as antiquated or as an impossible standard. These theologians make this argument relying upon false interpretations of the Law or assuming burdensome *traditions* are part of the Torah-Law of God. Ironically, this manner of interpreting the Law is precisely what disturbed Jesus and He fought against. Jesus was concerned people would *confuse* these burdensome man-made rules with Torah, and thus hesitate following the Law given Moses by God.

However, look how the theologians of the Modern Cheap Grace Gospel reinvigorate these exaggerations of the Law so as to pour derision on the Law. They disregard how Jesus fought against oral traditions that burdened the people. These theologians instead exaggerate the commands, citing the oral law traditions, so as to denigrate the ongoing relevance of the Law.

How can people read Jesus' words and commit the very same types of distortions of the Law as He was condemning, thereby undermining Jesus' own points? It is astonishing what people who claim to be followers of Jesus can do so at odds with the teachings of Jesus.

Defenders Of The Modern Gospel Even Admit The Pharisees' Error Was Teachings Subversive Of The Law

There are some commentators today who hold to the Modern Gospel of Cheap Grace yet who recognize Jesus' words were not attacking *legalism* as the Modern Gospel typically defines it.

They realize Jesus was attacking those like the Pharisees who taught against keeping the *whole* law.

However, despite Jesus thereby contradicting the Cheap Grace Gospel's doctrine on the Law which should lead a Christian to repent of false doctrines about the Law, these same commentators insist *things changed* later.

They preach the Law was done away with after Jesus' resurrection. Thus, these same commentators say we are in the right if we now adopt the very outlook of the *enemies* of Jesus and His salvation doctrine during His ministry. *These commentators' analysis is a most astounding mental giration to watch*. Here below are some excellent examples of this amazing rationalization of a contradiction between Jesus and their understanding of the Modern Gospel of Cheap Grace.

You know a doctrine is bankrupt when its own proponents unwittingly offer self-contradictory explanations for what they are *willing* to believe.

Deffinbaugh Gets It Right But Still Dismisses Jesus' Lessons as Irrelevant Today

An excellent article on this issue is by Bob Deffinbaugh, Th.M. It is entitled *The Fatal Failures of Religion: #2 Legalism Matthew 5:17-48*. Deffinbaugh recognizes the real flaw of the Pharisees which led people from salvation was the Pharisees did not take the Law seriously enough. The Pharisees' error was not *legalism* as defined today by the Modern Gospel of Cheap Grace.

> The stage is now being set for the contrast Jesus made between Himself and the scribes and Pharisees. The real culprits were the scribes and Pharisees. **They did not regard the Old Testament Law highly enough**. They had **set it aside**, preferring their own rules, regulations and traditions (Mark 7:7-9). The one who was truly great in the Kingdom was he who would **both teach the Old Testament faithfully**

(without watering it down), and who would
live in accordance with this teaching. In the
remaining verses, Jesus demonstrated how it
was the scribes and Pharisees *who failed to
take the Law far enough*, thus loosening and
lowering its requirements.[31]

Bob Deffinbaugh points out that everyone in the
crowd assumed the Pharisees were obedient to the *whole*
Law. But Jesus said they were wrong. The Pharisees had been
selective. For this reason, Jesus warns the crowd in the Sermon on the Mount that they have to have a righteousness that
exceeds that of the Pharisees. Deffinbaugh explains: "His listeners would have to do better than them if they wanted to
enter into God's Kingdom." (*Id.*)

Ironically, then Bob Deffinbaugh signals that the
Modern Gospel of Cheap Grace properly teaches us that this
later all changed. Deffinbaugh then undercuts what he just
said Jesus meant. He says:

> [I]f the best within Judaism could not merit
> entrance into God's heaven, neither can you or
> I. Legalism seeks to win God's heaven by the
> keeping of some code of conduct. (*Id.*)[32]

Yet, Deffinbaugh had just said that the listeners had to
do better than the Pharisees to "enter the kingdom of heaven."
Jesus said the Pharisees were not entering because *they disobeyed the Law* by not teaching all of it or by nullifying parts
of it through oral traditions. It logically follows that Jesus
meant His listeners had to *obey all the Law*, and not trust the
oral traditions that nullified various parts of the Law.

31.http://www.bible.org/page.asp?page_id=604 (last accessed 7/4/06).

32.Deffinbaugh says: "The Old Testament Law was given to men as a
standard of holiness. By its keeping, none of us would ever enter into
eternal life, for it only condemns us." This contradicts Deuteronomy
6:25 which says obedience to the Law imputes righteousness to us —
we are no longer seen as sinners.

Deffinbaugh is actually *contradicting* Jesus by saying that obeying the Law was irrelevant to "entering the kingdom of God." (Matt. 5:20.) Jesus just told the audience this was crucial: to enter heaven, they had to exceed the Pharisees who were failing to follow *all* of the Law.

Let Us Reason: Correctly Understands The Pharisee Error But Then Nullifies This Truth From Jesus Is Any Longer Relevant

Here is another similar example of an article that likewise correctly understands Jesus. It is from *Let Us Reason Ministries* entitled *Beware the Leaven of the Pharisees*.[33] However, by the end of the piece, the author will say Jesus' words no longer apply to us because we live in the era of grace, and the Law is abolished. The fact *Let Us Reason* understands Jesus abhorred that same teaching from the Pharisees of His era does not cause the *Let Us Reason Ministries* to ever hesitate. They feel free to rely upon a Pharisaical doctrine which apparently is bewitching us rather than the teachings of Jesus.

Regardless, what is refreshing is this article does *not* attempt to redefine Jesus' meaning by resort to other sources as a filter to hear Jesus. It is a Jesus'-words-only discussion. This article is absolutely profound even though it is another disturbing example of what irrationality supports the Modern Gospel of Cheap Grace. This article entitled *Beware the Leaven of the Pharisees* begins totally on target:

> If one does a study of who the Pharisees were and what they believed and practiced they *would be shocked to find they are still among us today.* Not just in the Judaism as in the Ultra Orthodox, but in Christianity. And you probably have seen them and *been bewitched by their teachings* and practices and *do not even know it*.

33. http://www.letusreason.org/WF39.htm (last accessed 6/17/06).

The Pharisees tried to correct Jesus with their own **man-made laws that were not from Moses**. They made up **their own laws** that were not from God to correct Jesus. Jesus' whole ministry was in conflict with their teachings, and more often than not he was addressing the religion that **they perpetrated upon the people**. They were very religious and most were in awe of how blessed they were....

If there is anything we can learn from Jesus on this it is to **not submit to man made laws, traditions** of men or **false Bible interpretations** by **famous religious men** who are known by all. The main point is that we are all are to be subject to the same authority and standard, the Word of God....However they have clever ways to convince you by guilt, fear and just plain **spiritual manipulation** just like the Pharisees.

Next, the author recognizes that the Pharisee teachings were destructive because they went *beyond* the Scriptures. They made people follow the *non-Biblical* oral law:

When someone leads people beyond the Scriptures instead of correctly explaining what is contained in them, he is being **spiritually destructive** to himself and others who listen to him. This is no small matter to be shirked at. The Pharisees brought almost the whole nation of Israel into their bondage by **obedience to their non-biblical teachings**.

Let Us Reason Ministries next clearly understands the Pharisees were not teaching obedience to the Word of God either in the person of Jesus or Yahweh's words to Moses:

Intentional false teaching has its source in pride. This is why Jesus warned of the leaven of the Pharisees in both their teachings and practices. **Their own arrogance and pride had them reject Jesus' words.** When the Pharisees disputed Jesus over His claims, *He pointed them to the Word.* Jesus often told them that they did not understand the word. Mark 7:5 Then the Pharisees and scribes asked Him, "Why do Your disciples not walk according to the tradition of the elders." The reason is because *they were following their own law not Moses law the way it was intended;* it was *corrupted* by the Pharisees interpretation. Jesus responded in v.13 "making *the word of God of no effect through your tradition* which you have handed down. And many such things you do."

Let Us Reason Ministries thus is unquestionably aware of what Jesus was condemning: Lawless teachings that nullified the Law given Moses. This appears even more clear in the next quote. However, a notion begins to creep in that Jesus' principles are all passé — a suggestion that Jesus' words were solely for a different era — supposedly the era of the Law that allegedly died at the Cross. We live allegedly in a *distinct* era of grace where the Law is no longer applicable.

This suggestion obviously is in reliance upon **a teaching of a Pharisee that has somehow wormed its way into the consciousness of those who *claim* to follow Christ.** *Let Us Reason Ministries* thus gives us the following mixed message of what things were like *under the law* not grace:

> "But woe to you Pharisees! For you tithe mint and rue and all manner of herbs, and pass by justice and the love of God. These you ought to have done, without leaving the others undone." In Matthew 23:23 Jesus explains they "have *neglected the weightier matters of the law:* justice and mercy and faith." These you ought to have done." Here Jesus makes it clear that living the life of faith toward God included love toward man that was just as important as what you give to God; and *this was under the law, not grace.* However when you see a lack of

grace and mercy in a person's life is often a sign of something wrong. A lack of compassion for the poor and neglecting to help people when you are able shows whom you are serving. We see in the Pharisees the example of false teachers *who majored in the lesser things of the law, and neglected the greater.* As Jesus pointed out "justice and mercy and faith. These you ought to have done, without leaving the others undone" (Matthew 23:23; Micah 6:8). The Pharisees became blind because they *upheld their own laws and interpretations over Moses*, and were stricter at enforcing them.

Thus, this is a brilliant piece. It is regretfully true the author is pointing to the idea that Jesus' words are all passé — meant solely for the Era of the Law. They make this claim based upon their trust in the Modern Gospel of Cheap Grace.

Yet, their adherence to cheap grace is what makes the above *admissions* so compelling to accept. The author does not realize the entire idea that the Law is passé comes from an adoption of Pharisaical principles of Law-negation. **It is as if we embraced a Pharisee into our New Testament and treated his teachings on par with or superior to Jesus' words**. Yet, there is no denying the Modern Gospel of Cheap Grace holds *doctrines on the Law that are as subversive as those held by the enemies of Jesus*. These Modern Gospel teachings are *indistinguishable* from what this author just admitted Jesus condemned the Pharisees for teaching.

Let's recapitulate this author's key *admissions* of what was wrong with the Pharisees. This way we can see that *anyone* who holds to cheap grace should acknowledge Jesus indicts the Modern Gospel of Cheap Grace as false:

- The Pharisees' *"spiritually destructive"* message was that they put "Israel into their bondage by *obedience to their non-biblical teachings*."

- The Pharisees' non-biblical teachings were "their own man-made laws that were *not from Moses*. They made up their own laws."

- The Pharisees' "own arrogance and pride had them reject Jesus' words." What did Jesus teach? Jesus "pointed them to the Word...[but] they were *following their own law not Moses' law* the way it was intended; it was *corrupted* by the Pharisees' *interpretation*. Jesus responded [they were] 'making the word of God of no effect through your tradition which you have handed down. And many such things you do.'"

- "We see in the Pharisees the example of false teachers who majored in the *lesser things of the law*, and neglected the greater. The Pharisees became blind because they *upheld their own laws and interpretations over Moses*, and were stricter at enforcing them."

Cannot this author see the incongruity that he holds today a doctrine which ultimately is *identical* to the Pharisee teaching of yesterday? It is frankly astonishing that people who profess Christ cannot see this. *It is like a blindness has descended over our eyes.*

Yet, this author correctly understands Jesus' point. No doubt about that. Yet, even then, he still accepts for today the very same teaching by the Pharisees that we can select what the church prefers the people to follow from the Law, *i.e.*, tithing, but the rest is not important. It is as if we are rebuffing Jesus by claiming we can follow a teaching of a Pharisee among us. A Pharisee who has teachings at *total* odds with Jesus. This is not merely ironic but also very disturbing.

Before we finish and discuss Matthew 5:20, let's now take a time-out to actually consider how horrifying is our modern doctrine on the Law of Moses in light of Jesus' words. We have duplicated Pharisaical doctrines on the Law.

Modern Gospel Has Identical View of Law as Jesus Condemned — Tithing Valid But Rest Is Optional

In what I call the **Greatest Irony of the Centuries,** the Modern Gospel of Christianity teaches precisely what Jesus condemned 2,000 years ago.

A large percentage of Protestant churches today teach there is only one command from the Law of Moses which needs be followed: the Law of Tithing. However, all the other commands from the Law of Moses need not be followed. They are mere shadows, and have passed away.

Allegedly we now have a Christian morality that only avoids what is "obvious" as wrong. This *obviousness* is measured by *expediency*: "All things are lawful but not all things are necessarily expedient." Thus, even though the Sabbath command is one of the Ten Commandments, you will hear instead "let every man be fully persuaded in his own mind" whether to follow it at all or on a day of our choosing.

However, these same teachers in the modern Protestant church will tell us we are not free from every part of the Law. There is one provision we need still to follow: tithing. This is explained by the highly popular pastor Randy Alcorn, in his mainstream Christian book *Money, Possessions & Eternity* (Wheaton, Illinois: Tyndale, 2003) at 174-75, 181.[34]

Larry Burkett, another mainstream Christian author on financial issues, shares this view,[35] and expressly finds that the command on tithing from the 'Old Testament' clearly remains valid for Christians.[36]

---

34. Randy claims he "detests legalism." He means teaching the Law applies to a Christian. (*Id.*, at 181.) He then acknowledges the strongest argument against tithing is the 'law versus grace' argument. Yet, he says just because we are under grace does not mean we "should stop doing all that was done under the law." (*Id.*) Randy then says "I believe there's ongoing value to certain aspects of the old covenant." (*Id.*, 181.) The only such aspect he finds valid from the Mosaic Law is *tithing*. How can Jesus' words about the Pharisees not burn in his ears?

However, both Alcorn and Burkett are embarrassed to admit they insist this one principle from the Law still applies. They do not want to be accused of being legalistic. Yet, they both concur there is one command from the Law given Moses to follow: tithing. Other than that, Alcorn says the *Old Testament* is passé. No other command than tithing from the Law given Moses supposedly need concern us in the modern Christian church.

Moreover, any of us who regularly attend church in America also know when it comes to offering time, the sermonette is often straight from the Law with little or no hedging on its applicability.

Yet, tithing can never be argued to be a principle that is *obvious*. There is *nothing obviously* immoral for not paying a tithe. It is simply a principle from the Law given Moses. Hence, this is why the tithing principle must be quoted from the Mosaic Law to get people to even think about it.

Thus, mainstream Christian teaching today is ***identical*** to the Pharisaical teaching that Jesus condemned. Jesus specifically said this lukewarm teaching about the Law was keeping people from salvation. Jesus specifically condemned ***stressing only tithing from the Law.*** (Matt. 23:23.) This Pharisaical teaching was causing the prevention of salvation both for the Pharisees as well as their proselytes.

---

35. Larry Burkett, the modern spokesperson on issues of Christian financial duties, similarly explains Matt. 23:23 endorses tithing this way: "Those who encourage Christians to completely ignore the Old Testament and teach that Christians don't need to observe anything that the Old Testament commands are ignoring Jesus' *advice*." http://www.new-life.net/faq212.htm. For Mr. Burkett, this "advice" of Jesus is limited to obeying the command to tithe. But that is the opposite of Jesus' point. That verse has Jesus saying that not only tithing should be followed, but all the commands of God given to Moses, in particular the Ten Commandments.

36. Burkett writes: "The second thing that creates problems for Christians related to the tithe is that most Christians have a misunderstanding of the ***validity of the Old Testament for today***. I think that it's clear that the Old Testament has *some* continuing legitimacy for Christians today." http://www.new-life.net/faq212.htm

---

Jesus' Words On Salvation   **195**

How could we possibly have fallen into the very same error that Jesus condemned? I have to repeat *over and over* that it is **as if some Pharisee's words have been incorporated into Scripture,** and we swallowed him hook, line and sinker. It is **as if a Pharisee who preaches against keeping the Law** has crept into the New Testament.[37]

In light of our doctrines being so identical to what Jesus condemned, don't you think on Judgment Day that Jesus as Judge is going to ask some tough questions. Won't He ask us if we were *listening* even ever so barely to Him? He will ask you point blank *why you followed anyone who came with precisely the teaching that Jesus condemned*! Judgment Day is going to be a disappointing day for many.

In fact, Jesus says this tithe-only doctrine is certainly a perilous teaching for the one who teaches the Law is otherwise not to be followed. Jesus warns the Pharisees in very stern terms only ten verses later about the consequence of a doctrine that stressed only tithing:

> Ye serpents, ye offspring of vipers, how shall ye escape the judgment of hell? (Mat 23:33)(ASV)

The Salvation Message Of Matthew 5:20

Finally, we are ready to listen to Jesus in Matthew 5:20. Knowing the Pharisees were shallow in obedience to the Law (rather than faithful adherents), we no longer will misunderstand what Jesus meant about the Pharisees in this verse.

> For I say unto you, that **except your righteousness shall exceed the righteousness of the scribes and Pharisees,** ye shall in **no wise enter into the kingdom of heaven.** (Matt. 5:20)

37.My book *Jesus' Words Only* (2007) discusses this question in depth.

To help me explicate this passage, I will call upon an audio sermon that everyone should listen to. It was given by Steve Walker, the pastor of a Presbyterian church in northern California. The sermon is entitled *God's Grace for the Impure Heart*. It begins by talking about Matthew 5:6.[38]

To understand the "hunger for righteousness" in 5:6, Pastor Walker explicates Matthew 5:20. In 5:20, Jesus uses the word "righteousness" one more time. This time, however, Jesus says "to enter heaven" our "righteousness must exceed that of the Pharisees."

Could Jesus actually expect *real* righteousness or does Jesus want us to put on *His imputed* righteousness? This is key for it determines whether salvation is *entirely* by *imputed* righteousness or depends, in part, upon our *actual* righteousness. Pastor Walker does not subtract or suppress from Jesus' words. His sermon points were:

- If we are only sorrowful (mourn) about our sin, and are not "exhibiting" a change, we have not gone far enough.

- The truth of what God requires men "suppress" in their hearts or they "suppress the truth" in unrighteousness. Men do not like to hear the need to repent from sin.

- In Matthew 5:20, when Jesus says our "righteousness must exceed that of the Pharisees," it is "pretty clear" that Jesus intends us to understand this "has to do with righteousness *in acts*."

- Walker offers as proof that Jesus gave several illustrations thereafter designed to expose defects in the Pharisees' *actual* behaviors. We must actually do better than the Pharisees' shallow obedience. These passages were: (1) Verses 27-30 tell us the true importance not to lust unto adultery; (2) Verses 31-32 tell us the true nature of the commands not to divorce; (3) Verses 33-37 tell us to keep our promises whether in the form of an

---

38. It is available at http://www.cverc.org/update/sermons.htm (last accessed 7-1-07).

oath or otherwise; (4) Verse 38 tells us to not retaliate, but turn the other cheek; and (5) Verses 43-48 teach us to love our enemies.

What Pastor Walker is saying is hardly remarkable in light of the true nature of Jesus' criticism of the Pharisees. Yet, in this day and age, Pastor Walker is a brave soul for teaching this so bluntly.

What is the opposing argument? I could read you dozens of commentaries that unabashedly say Jesus is not serious. Jesus is supposedly setting the bar so high above even the most righteous people (*i.e.*, the Pharisees), that Jesus could never possibly be suggesting we could enter heaven by obeying the principles He then outlined. You repeatedly hear this argument such as in Willard's *The Great Omission*.[39]

Yet, you see, this argument that Jesus was allegedly being facetious depends crucially on the misleading claims about the Pharisees being very righteous people. This is why we have spent over 50 pages disproving that claim. Otherwise, you cannot hear Jesus' words in the Sermon on the Mount. They are neutralized from being taken seriously.

Thus, the decontamination of our collective consciousness about the Pharisees is one of the most important repairs we need in our thinking. Why? Because **the preservation of what Jesus meant in His most important sermon depends upon erasing the misinformation about the Pharisees**. Unless you obliterate the false indoctrination you have received about the Pharisees' errors, you *never* can see the meaning and point of the Sermon on the Mount.

---

39. These competing arguments are discussed and refuted in the chapter entitled "The Sermon On The Mount" on page 201 *et seq.*

Conclusion

Jesus is clear. He teaches you to make sure you do not have a view of God's written law as shallow as that of the Pharisees. Otherwise, you can never exceed their righteousness and thereby "enter the kingdom of heaven." (Matt. 5:20.) That's it. It was always a verse with a blunt meaning.

The Pharisees were not superstars of teaching and obeying strictly the Law. Instead, the "Pharisees were... shallow... interpreters of the... Scriptures." (John Gorham Palfrey, *The Relation Between Judaism and Christianity* (Crosby, Nichols: 1854) at 108.) Jesus said the Pharisees taught the less weighty principles from the Law, leaving the weightier matters on mercy, justice and faith untaught and undone. (Matt. 23:23.) They nullified the Law by traditions. (Matt.15:6,9.)

The cheap grace gospel skillfully deflected this truth about the Pharisees. They indoctrinated us into thinking the Pharisees were 100% obedient to the Law. By deluding us the Pharisees were perfect morally, we were misled to *think* Jesus' could never demand truly that our righteousness exceed that of the Pharisees to be saved (Matt. 5:20). This teaching by Jesus supposedly was therefore intended to drive us to realize fulfilling such a high moral duty is beyond our grasp; thus faith is the sole means of 110% righteousness.

The truth is much different. Our modern teachers are the ones who misled us about the Pharisees being supposedly great legalists. Rather, the Pharisees were shallow *anti-legalists*, as Jesus repeatedly exposed and denounced them for.

Once we correct that, Jesus' message is self-evident. The Pharisees cannot be justified because they follow a shallow version of the Law. Jesus said they were only good about tithing, but about nothing else in the Law. (Matt. 23:23.)

Before Luther realized this, he taught us in 1525:

> Moses is dead. His rule ended when Christ came. He is of no further service....*[E]ven the Ten Commandments do not pertain to us*.

The sectarian spirits want to saddle us with Moses and all the commandments. We will just skip that....

I dismiss **the commandments given to the people of Israel**. They neither urge nor compel me. They are dead and gone, **except insofar as I gladly and willingly accept something from Moses**...[40]

Yet, the mature Luther woke up and reversed his own earlier doctrine. He denounced such antinomianism (*i.e.*, anti-Law doctrine) in the *Antinomian Theses* (1537).[41] The mature Luther wrote in that work: "To abolish the Law is therefore to abolish the truth of God." (*Id.* at 33-34.) Luther also said anyone who would "discard the Law would effectively put an end to our obedience to God." (*Id.*, at 32.)

The dominant Protestantism of today, however, is going along in reliance on the words of the young Luther. It has still not grown up as its early leader did, to realize that it was wrong to deride *legalism*. **For this word has been used as an arrow of derision at a teaching which is identical to what our Lord Jesus Himself taught**. Luther finally saw this. Will we? Much is at stake. It changes how you hear things. What do you hear when Jesus says a few verses later: "Be ye perfect even as your father in heaven is perfect"? (Matt. 5:48.) Do you think Jesus is merely driving you to have faith to be perfect in God's eyes? Or did Jesus literally mean you must strive to act perfectly *just as God is perfect*? It turns out if you are not listening to Matt. 5:20, you also cannot hear 5:48. "So take care how you listen; for whoever has, to him more shall be given; and whoever does not have, even what he thinks he has shall be taken away from him." (Lk. 8:18.)

---

40. Martin Luther, "How Christians Should Regard Moses," *Luther's Works: Word and Sacrament I* (Philadelphia: Muhlenberg Press, 1960) Vol. 35 at 161-174.
41. Martin Luther, *Don't Tell Me That! From Martin Luther's Antinomian Theses* (Lutheran Press: 2004). See also page xvi *et seq.* of the Preface.

---

10 *The Sermon On The Mount*

*Jesus' Several Calls To Ongoing
Righteousness For Salvation*

Due to the Modern Gospel of Cheap Grace, you never hear that there is a salvation message in the Sermon on the Mount. You are told instead it is a list of impossible virtues. Jesus is supposedly directing you to realize you are irreversibly lost absent faith alone. The virtues He requires for salvation, so clearly stated in the Sermon, just could not possibly be required of sinful man. Only an easy and simple faith could ever be allegedly required by God for salvation.

Thus, even though you have read the Sermon on the Mount many times, you have become de-sensitized to its salvation promises and requirements. Cheap grace gives you a different paradigm on *how* to read its message. What Jesus is really saying alludes you. His message is as foreign to ourselves as it was to the Pharisees. In truth, Jesus was directing them to their faults of virtue (disobedience). He wanted them to repent from disobedience to obedience. The Pharisees were on a failing grade because the Pharisees taught only the lesser commands of the Law, ignoring the more important ones. So says Our Lord Jesus. (Matt.23:23.)

However, now look at the Sermon. See what activities of the heart by you, if performed, Jesus says result in salvation. Notice how "all addressed not the believing faculties, but to conscience, sense of responsibility, power of moral and spiritual decision." (*Congregational Review* (May 1868) at 210.) In Matthew 5:3-12 (KJV), Jesus promises these Blessings (Beatitudes) of salvation for these behaviors:

TABLE 1. **Sermon On the Mount Analyzed From Matthew 5**

CONDITION	RESULT
[If] poor in spirit	Theirs is the kingdom of heaven. (3)
[If] meek	They shall inherit the earth. (5)
[If] merciful	They will obtain mercy. (7)
[If] persecuted for righteousness sake	Then theirs is the kingdom of heaven. (10)

It logically follows that if you are proud or you are not forgiving or you are persecuted due to sinfulness, you are not qualified to receive mercy or inherit the earth. You are lost. But if you are humble, are merciful, and persecuted for doing good (and bear up under it), then yours is the "kingdom of heaven" and you shall "obtain mercy."

The salvation theme of the Sermon on the Mount is underscored in how Jesus began the Sermon on the Mount. Jesus called us to have a "righteousness that exceeds that of the Pharisees," absent which "you shall in no case enter the kingdom of heaven." (Matt. 5:20.) Jesus is making obedience to several principles a condition of entrance into heaven. As discussed in the prior chapter, Matthew 5:20 is not Jesus pulling our leg. We are not free to ignore the literal import of Jesus' words. (See chapter beginning at page 147.)

Rather, it is clear from the verses that follow in the Sermon that these are real directives. Jesus wants them truly performed. Jesus is explaining what it means to have a righteousness that exceeds that of the Pharisees:

- You must not call your brother a fool (5:21-26);
- You must not lust after a married woman (*gunaika*) (5:27-30);[1]
- You must not divorce your wife (*gunaika*) absent adultery by her (5:31-32);[2]
- You must not make false vows (5:33-37);[3] and

---

1. For the correct translation of *gunaika*, see the footnote at page 206.

- You must not return evil for evil (5:38-48).

Jesus is not suggesting these commands are so lofty that you can ignore their literal application to you. Jesus is not opining on faith being the means to acquire this righteousness. Rather, Jesus is directly calling us to obey these principles. By doing so, we shall exceed the shallow righteousness of the Pharisees and "enter the kingdom of heaven." (Matt. 5:20.) The Pharisees obviously committed all these sins. They taught a watered-down version of the Law. (See the chapter on the Pharisees beginning at page 147.) Thus, Jesus was promising "entry...into the kingdom of heaven" (5:20) for obedience to His restoration-of-the-Law principles.

A Good Analysis: Reading Jesus' Words Literally

The lesson of the Sermon is clear but is lost on our modern ears. The best description appears from the pastor who runs *Believe*. When literally understood, Jesus' message is clear:

> Jesus concludes the sermon by setting up certain requirements that relate directly to one's being saved or lost. He divides mankind into three classes: those who (1) follow him (7:13-14, 17, 21, 24-25), (2) do not follow him (vss. 13-44, 26-27), and (3) pretend to follow him (vss. 15-20, 21-23). *To be saved one must actually follow the teachings of the sermon,* but Jesus does *not* say they must be *performed perfectly.* The saved are those *who accept and actually attempt to direct their lives by the sermon*; the lost are those who pretend to follow or who reject these teachings....Mere pro-

---

2. For an arguably more valid variant in the Hebrew version of Matthew, which makes the failure to use a divorce certificate the focus, see my prior book, *Jesus' Words Only* (2007) at 140 fn. 5.

3. On the importance of the Hebrew variant, which contains the word *falsely*, see Footnote 10 on page 160.

---

fession of belief, without the following, will secure Jesus' condemnation, 'I never knew you. You evildoers, depart from me' (vs. 23).[4]

Is Obedience Satisfied By Mere Faith?

Is the response Jesus wants to His sermon a change in personal behavior or simply the adoption of a belief in facts like the atonement, Jesus resurrected, and so on?

As demonstrated in the chapter on the Pharisees, what Jesus is saying is that personal righteousness must start with a *personal change in one's view of the Law.* You must bring back the ***forgotten key commands from the Law of Moses.*** Without personal knowledge of God's commands, you have no compass. Your chance of following the Law's commands is reduced to whatever your conscience can recognize on its own as right or wrong. God always insists conscience alone is insufficient to know God's full will. The very purpose of the Law was to reveal God's will. Knowledge of the Word gave the possibility of life where otherwise people would perish everlastingly. As Hosea 4:6 said, the people of his day were perishing (eternally) because "you [priests] have forgotten the Law" and dispensed a shallow obedience.

Prophet Hosea

This is why in the Sermon on the Mount, Jesus focused on the Pharisees' oral teaching on adultery. They taught adultery was only by committing the actual act of adultery. The Pharisees' Oral Law said that coveting a married woman was only wrong if it led to adultery. If the lust solely remained unacted upon it was supposedly not sin. The Pharisees shallowly insisted adulterous action must follow to make the lusting wrong.[5] Jesus said this Pharisaical teaching

---

4. "Sermon on the Mount," http://mb-soft.com/believe/txw/sermonmt.htm (last accessed 5-24-05).

5. See page 166.

nullified one of the Ten Commandments. Among the ten, God declares it is wrong in and of itself to "covet your neighbor's wife." (Exodus 20:17.)

Jesus was thus restoring the Law's principles. The purpose was to restore the path to life. This is what is behind Jesus' statement that only if your "righteousness exceeds that of the Pharisees may you enter the kingdom of heaven." (Matthew 5:20.)

However, others claim Jesus had no intent to raise respect for the Law. Instead, Jesus supposedly had an opposite goal — to engender disbelief one could satisfactorily ever keep the commands of God. To do this, Jesus in the Sermon supposedly gave impossible commands, such as against lusting against any "woman." From this, it is rationalized Jesus was proving how futile it would be to think obedience to God's commands is the path to life. Supposedly, then only faith can be the sole means of salvation.

However, while Jesus may have been translated to appear to give an impossible command in the King James Bible, Jesus clearly did *not* say what the King James Bible attributes to Him about *lust*.

For in Matthew 5:27-28, Jesus is simply telling *all men*, married or unmarried, to obey one of the Ten Commandments that prohibited lusting after your neighbor's wife — *gunaika*. This word in Greek *only* means "married woman" or "wife."[6] It is everywhere else translated that way in the New Testament. See Matt. 5:32 ("wife"); Ephesians 5:22,33 ("Married woman....") and Romans 7:2-3 ("a married woman is bound....") I can only speculate what motivated the King James Bible Puritan translators to make Jesus *ban* sexual desire for any woman by all men. Jesus did not do so.

With this correction in mind, there is nothing too difficult for a man in not looking in lust at a married woman. Most men would agree that is something they can control. Jesus was not therefore insisting upon something crazily impossible, as some contend. As God tells us: "Now what I am commanding you today is *not too difficult for you or beyond your reach*." (Deut. 30:11.)

Typical Modern Gospel Spins Away From The Original Gospel

The Earliest Gospel On Obedience To The Sermon

As noted above, a popular view today is that the Sermon does not represent principles to obey. Jesus supposedly wants merely to show us we *can never* meet God's standards for salvation. Jesus allegedly wants us to see the absurdity of trying to actually do the principles in the Sermon on the Mount.

Yet, how did the early church which could read the original Greek understand Jesus' words? Did they think the Sermon on the Mount involved principles to obey? Or did the early Greek-fluent church think the Sermon was a lesson on the futility of salvation by obedience? Did the early Greek-fluent church think Jesus, in effect, was pulling our leg?

---

6. The Greek word *gunaika* signifies a *married woman*, not a *woman*. If it had been *gune,* it can mean *woman* or *wife*. (See 1 Cor. 7:4, *wife*.) If it were *gunaikes*, it would mean *women*. (For a thorough and able discussion, see *What Is Adultery?* at http://www.brightfiles.com/findtruth/otherart/adultery.htm (last accessed 8-17-07).) Moreover, *married woman* is the only meaning that fits. Adultery *by definition* cannot be committed with an unmarried woman. (Lev. 20:10, "a man's wife"; Deut. 22:22-24, "a woman married....") Adultery, as defined in the Bible, is not what we typically assume. It always requires a *married* woman to be involved. *A married man could not commit adultery with an unmarried woman.* Instead, if a married man lusts for/has sex with a virgin, this could break either the marriage vow (binding with God—Matt. 12:36, 'judged by every word that comes out of your mouth') or it implicates other provisions in the Law not having to do with adultery. *See,* Exodus 22:16-17; Deut. 22:28-29. Hence, the only proper translation of *gunaika* in Matthew 5:27-28 is *married woman*.

It is important to examine the perception of the early Greek-fluent church to resolve this issue. After all, the early church could read the original Greek. It commented on this question within the lifetime of actual disciples of the apostles. These commentators must be closer to the original meaning. They necessarily enjoy a closer approximation to the apostles' doctrines.

Justin Martyr

The earliest post-apostolic church clearly thought Jesus meant for us to behave according to His commands in the Sermon on the Mount. In 157 A.D., Justin wrote *First Apology* where he quotes the entire Sermon on the Mount as he addresses Emperor Antoninus Pius. To prove to the emperor that Christians take these teachings as *truly* to be followed, Justin Martyr says:

> And many, both men and women, who have been Christ's disciples from childhood, remain pure at the age of sixty or seventy years; and I boast that I could produce such from every race of men. For what shall I say, too, of the countless multitude of those who have **reformed intemperate habits, and learned these things**? (Justin Martyr, *Apology*, 167-8.)

As Dallas Willard says, in this first three hundred years of the faith, Jesus "was the center of attention and devotion in their lives."[7] However, as time wore on, this focus slackened. By our day, the Modern Gospel of Cheap Grace has replaced the gospel taught in that early era. And what was that gospel of the earliest era? Was it consistent with the salvation message of the Sermon on the Mount? Yes, indeed it was.

---

7. D. Willard, *The Great Omission* (San Francisco: Harper, 2006) at 98.

Salvation Message Of Early Church Had Sermon's Message

David Bercot, an attorney, has synthesized the beliefs of the church leaders in the post-apostolic era between 125 A.D. to 325 A.D. He is the author of the 703 page comprehensive *A Dictionary of Early Christian Beliefs: A Reference Guide to More than 700 Topics Discussed by the Early Church Fathers* (Peabody, Mass.: Henrickson Publishing, 1998.) Based on this extraordinary research, Bercot claims "early Christians *universally* believed that works or **obedience play an essential role** in our salvation."[8]

There is a reason for this. When Jesus gets to the end of the Sermon on the Mount, He underscores that works are essential. Then Jesus says He clearly expects us to keep on obeying these principles to avoid the fire and destruction:

> Every tree that does **not bear good fruit is cut down and thrown into the fire**. Thus you will know them by their fruits. Not every one who says to me, 'Lord, Lord,' will enter the kingdom of heaven, but **only the one who keeps doing [*poieo*, continuous tense known as present participle active] the will of my Father who is in heaven**.... Every one then who hears these words of mine and **keeps doing [*poieo*, present participle active] them** will be like a wise man who built his house on rock.... And every one who hears these words of mine and **does not continue to do [*poieo*, present participle active] them** will be like a foolish man who built his house on sand....[whose end is destruction]. (Matt 7:19-21 and 24-27).

---

8. David W. Bercot, *Will the Real Heretics Please Stand Up: A New Look at Today's Evangelical Christianity in the light of Early Christianity* (Texas: Scroll Publishing, 1999) at 57. For a thorough discussion of the actual gospel taught during what is called the Patristic Era of 125-325 A.D., in both the East under the Orthodox and the West under **pre-**Roman Catholicism, see my prior work, *Jesus' Words Only* (2007) at 425 *et seq.*

The Modern Gospel Teaching That The Sermon Is Irrelevant

Those who today believe in the Modern Gospel of Cheap Grace find it necessary to denigrate the value of Jesus' teaching in the Sermon on the Mount.

One argument is that Jesus' words in the Sermon on the Mount are meant for a different dispensation. For example, Pastor Mike Paulson of Touchet Baptist Church in Touchet, Washington, in a sermon entitled *What Would Jesus Do or What Would Paul Do?* boldly dismisses the Sermon on the Mount. He claims its teaching belongs to a different dispensation. Pastor Paulson says it is heretical to teach the Sermon on the Mount literally as applicable today.

> Unfortunately, most 'modern' Christians follow those teachings today—I call them Beatitudinal Christians and a simple reading of the Sermon on the Mount should [show] them that they can NOT live that sermon completely today— no way, not at all—not even close! *The stuff in the Sermon on the Mount actually contradicts Paul's teachings in everything from salvation to doctrinal belief!* You would think folks would see this—but like Jesus said of them, ye err not knowing the Scriptures....[9]

Pastor Paulson is not an aberration, but a normative teaching today. Walvoord published under the Moody Press is likewise typical:

> The Sermon on the Mount, as a whole, is *not church truth precisely*...It is *not intended* to delineate justification by faith or *the gospel of salvation.* [The Sermon involves] *unimportant truth.* (John Walvoord, *Matthew: Thy Kingdom Come* (Moody Press: 1984) at 44, 45.)

---

9. The main page of the Touchet Baptist Church is at http://www.touchet1611.org/index.htm. The sermon quoted is entitled WWJD v. WWPD? and is reprinted at http://www.touchet1611.org/PeterPaulMary2.html (last visited 2005).

This approach found its clearest exposition in the teachings of the founder of dispensationalism — Clarence Larkin. He began the movement by saying there is nothing for a modern Christian to worry about obeying from the Sermon on the Mount. His text, still cited today among dispensationalists, is *Dispensational Truth* (Philadelphia: Larkin, 1918). Based on dispensational logic, Larkin explains Jesus' teachings in the Sermon on the Mount "have **no application** to the Christian, but only to those who are under the Law, and therefore must apply to another Dispensation than this." (*Id.*, at 87.) This notion thus divorces the church from Christ.

Clear Invalidity Of Dispensationalism

However, dispensationalism is clearly an erroneous doctrine as applied to render defunct Jesus' teachings. After Jesus' resurrection when the *atonement* was done and the era of grace had clearly begun, Jesus gave the Great Commission. Nothing in this suggests Jesus wanted His commands in the Sermon on the Mount to expire merely because the era of grace had certainly begun. To the contrary, we read:

> And Jesus came to them and spake unto them, saying, "All authority hath been given unto me in heaven and on earth. (19) Go ye therefore, and make disciples of all the nations, baptizing them into the name of the Father and of the Son and of the Holy Spirit: (20) **teaching them to observe all things whatsoever I commanded you**: and lo, I am with you always, even unto the end of the world." Matt. 28:18-20

The Greek word for *observe* is literally *diligently do* and often is translated as *obey*. It is the Greek word *tereo*.

Jesus was reiterating His commands had ongoing validity. They did not die at the Cross, as dispensationalists insist. Jesus is speaking after the Cross. Jesus is saying His teachings are as much alive as when He delivered them.

In fact, during His earthly ministry, Jesus warned His words would not expire at the cross. Jesus said His words would remain valid even though "heaven and earth pass away" (Matt. 24:35.)

Yet, dispensationalism harmonizes away Jesus' teachings as invalid because it claims to have found a better version of God's grace than the one Jesus taught. Thus, Jesus' words were only supposedly valid for another two years after Jesus spoke them, *i.e.*, they expired at the crucifixion. "It is finished" for the Modern Gospel proponents means *all of Jesus' lessons are cancelled* unless they fit our Modern Gospel doctrine of faith-alone.

Cheap Grace Claims Jesus Does Not Mean What He Says

In the Law God gave Moses, God said that if we obey the law, it is imputed righteousness to us. (Deut. 6:25.) God in Deuteronomy 30:11 then assures us obedience to the Law "is not too hard for thee, neither is it far off." (ASV.) As Apostle John said: "And his commandments are not burdensome." (1 John 5:2-3.)

However, many wed to the Modern Gospel of Cheap Grace argue that since Jesus' teachings about moral action are impossible for anyone (other than Jesus) to comply with perfectly, then His teachings are nothing more than an illustration. Jesus' supposed point in commanding against adulterous lust, keeping your oath, etc., is not because He expects obedience. Rather, Jesus allegedly gave those commands to paint a picture of an unattainable perfection necessary for salvation. Jesus supposedly meant to show us how impossible it would be for us to attain salvation except by faith alone rather than striving to obey Jesus' points. The Sermon on the Mount is thereby eviscerated of any literal meaning. It allegedly only shows how salvation for such imperfect beings is impossible except through the saving grace of faith. In fact, some claim Jesus wanted us to realize the futility of any attempt to obey the commands Jesus actually gave in the Sermon on the Mount.

Dallas Willard in his otherwise great book *The Great Omission* (San Francisco: Harper 2006) says precisely this:

> Thus, for example, Jesus' teachings in the Sermon on the Mount...[are] illustrations of what living from the Kingdom God [should mean]....[However] to live in conformity with them...is like to attempt the **impossible**, and **will lead to doing things that obviously are wrong** and even **ridiculous**. (*Id.* at 105.)

Thus, Willard goes so far as to denigrate Jesus' principles of conduct by claiming they actually reflect an impossible standard of conduct. Willard says it is just too hard to be humble, a peacemaker, and one who does not lust after married women, etc. Willard thinks it is obvious that Jesus does not expect us to actually change our behavior to conform to His teachings.

Not only that, Willard denigrates the Sermon by claiming Jesus would have us do things that are "obviously wrong" (he does not explain how) and "even ridiculous" if we should obey its principles.[10] Oh my! What men cannot convince themselves when they start from a wrong assumption that they are free to ignore Jesus' doctrine.

John MacArthur gives the same explanation.

> Yet Jesus had stunned multitudes by saying, 'Unless your righteousness surpasses that of the scribes and Pharisees, you shall not enter the kingdom of heaven' (Matt. 5:20)—followed by, 'You are to be perfect, as your heavenly Father is perfect' (v. 48). Clearly, He set a standard that was **humanly impossible**, for **no one**

---

10. What is truly ironic is that Willard's book is self-contradictory to the extreme. He claims the *great omission* of the church is the failure to teach obedience to Christ's commands as a matter of obtaining proximity (not salvation). Then how is Willard's mocking of Jesus' commands in the Sermon as "impossible" and "wrong" and "ridiculous" going to correct this omission? It is more of the same problem, perhaps stated even worse than ever stated by any other cheap grace proponent!

---

could surpass the rigorous living of the scribes and Pharisees.[11]

MacArthur's premise that the Pharisees were living obedient to the Law is a false premise in this statement, as we saw in the chapter on the Pharisees.[12] The Pharisees had shallow doctrine on the Law. They were lost because they were teaching the less important aspects of the Law, while ignoring its more important aspects of Justice, Mercy and Faith. (Matt. 23:23). Thus, their followers could never be saved. They were being disobedient to the commands that matter, paying attention only to the lesser commandments. Hence, Jesus was totally serious in saying the listener must have a righteousness that exceeds the Pharisees' righteousness. This is what the Sermon then outlines.

Carl Stange, a famous religion professor at Koenigsberg in 1903 and commentator on the Sermon on the Mount, is another who speaks like Willard and MacArthur. For example, Stange similarly writes of the Sermon on the Mount:

> The teaching about the ideal.... only serves to make plain *the reprehensibility of the human condition*....The meaning of the moral demand is not that it gives us the power for the good but rather that it *shows us our impotence for the good*.[13]

Bauman's Response To Stange's Dismissal Of The Sermon

Clarence Bauman, however, decried this hermeneutic. Clarence Bauman is Professor of Theology and Ethics at the Associated Mennonite Biblical Seminary. Bauman says that

---

11. John MacArthur, "Jesus' Perspective on Sola Fide," (2004) at http://www.biblebb.com/files/MAC/sf-solafide.htm (last accessed 4/8/2007).

12. See page 147.

13. Quoted in Clarence Bauman, *The Sermon on the Mount, The Modern Quest for its Meaning* (Mercer University Press: 1985) at 177.

Stange improperly makes Paul's doctrine elevated above Jesus' words by the Modern Gospel of Cheap Grace, and then the improper lense through which to understand Jesus:

> Stange's central axiom is **derived not from Jesus** but from Paul and reflects not the content of the Sermon on the Mount but **the influence of Reformation dogma**.

> Stange made claims about the Sermon on the Mount which **its content does not validate**. He read into it theories and experiences foreign to its sphere. Stange's misinterpretation of the Sermon on the Mount exemplifies the characteristically Lutheran hermeneutical **incongruity of superimposing upon the teaching of Jesus the theology of Paul**.[14]

Bauman explains how far we have fallen from Jesus: "Jesus' teaching of the Way of the Cross has been replaced by Paul's proclamation of the Word of the Cross...." The Modern Gospel of Cheap Grace tells us it is too hard to actually follow Jesus' commands in the Sermon. Thus, the Cheap Grace Gospel teaches us that it is absurd to hold these commands up as a standard. Rather, this pseudo-gospel tells us these commands were satisfied by atonement. So Bauman concludes "implicit in the logic of most atonement theories" of the Modern Gospel of Cheap Grace is that "**following Jesus is presumptuous and unnecessary**."[15]

In Pastor Paulson's quote above, such a terrible notion is no longer implicit. Paulson openly says it is actually heretical to teach what Jesus taught in the Sermon on the Mount as something to follow. Paulson said: "The stuff in the Sermon

---

14. Clarence Bauman, *The Sermon on the Mount, The Modern Quest for its Meaning, supra*, at 185.

15. Clarence Bauman, *The Sermon on the Mount, The Modern Quest for its Meaning, supra*, at 421.

on the Mount *actually contradicts Paul's teachings* in every-thing from salvation to doctrinal belief!" Paulson then rea-sons that we err in following Jesus' teachings any longer!

Leo Tolstoy, a Russian Christian remembered as one of the greatest authors of all time, likewise decried this mod-ern hermeneutic. He says it is wrong to see Jesus as speaking facetiously rather than seriously. Tolstoy said the Modern Gospel makes Jesus into someone who merely pretends to be insisting on obedience. We are asked to see Jesus as preach-ing things He supposedly thought too lofty to actually per-form. Tolstoy said this is unfair to Jesus. One must take Him at His plain meaning. It is insulting to the Lord to assume He is being deliberately misleading to make His point:

> I accepted the fact that *Christ meant exactly what he said*. The least that can be required of those who judge another man's teaching is, that *they should take the teacher's words in the exact sense in which he uses them*. Christ did not consider his teaching as some *high ideal* of what mankind should be, but *cannot attain to*, nor does he consider it as a chimerical, poetical fancy, fit only to captivate the simple-minded inhabitant of Galilee.[16]

Bonhoeffer (1906-1945), professor at the University of Berlin and pastor of the Pomerania Confessing Church, likewise critiqued this view that denigrates Jesus' words:

> We Lutherans have gathered like eagles around the carcass of cheap grace, and there we have drunk of *the poison which has killed the life of following Christ*. The word of cheap grace has been the ruin of more Christians than any commandment of works.[17]

---

16. Clarence Bauman, *The Sermon on the Mount, The Modern Quest for its Meaning, supra,* at 11 (quoting Leo Tolstoy).

17. Bonhoeffer, *The Cost of Discipleship, supra,* at 44.

Is Obedience An Inherently Absurd Path?

What about John saying we lie if we say "we have no sin" and "have not sinned"? (1 John 1:8,10.) Some read this to mean we never can do righteousness. This then supposedly rules out ever having to do anything in obedience to be right with God. This follows because if we can never truly break off from sin for even a significant time, God could not be just in making our salvation depend on not falling into sin.

If 1 John 1:8,10 means this, it rules out *de facto* all Jesus' commands to be righteous for salvation sake in the Sermon on the Mount. Yet, is this what Apostle John is saying when those verses are read in context? *Absolutely not.*

What John meant in 1 John 1:8,10 is that some thought by the atonement God does not see their sinning. This is how verse nine clarifies *the context* of verses eight and ten. John is declaring it wrong to say that by atonement God does not see them when they sin. John Wesley, the famous pastor, comments on this, pointing out how the context of verse nine dictates the meaning of verses eight and ten: "The ninth verse explains both the eighth and tenth: 'If we confess our sins, he is faithful and just to forgive us our sins, and to cleanse us from all unrighteousness.'"[18]

John means they lie to themselves if they say they do not sin because of *atonement*. Instead, only upon confession, repentance and "walking in the light" does the atonement apply. The quoting from 1 John 1:8 or 1:10 out of context has been used to actually overthrow the meaning of the passage. It is seriously argued based only on verse eight or ten that atonement means God never sees us as sinning. This is precisely what John was refuting in context.[19]

---

18. John Wesley, "A Plain Account of Christian Perfection," *The Works of John Wesley* (ed. by Thomas Jackson)(1872) Vol. 11, at 366-446. On how *cleansing* in verse nine refers to atonement, see "Apostle John's Two-Fold Atonement Principle." on page 14 *et seq.*

19. See page 14 *et seq.*

In other words, John intends us to understand those who say they have no sin (verse eight) stand in contrast to those who are cleansed by the blood of Christ by walking in the light (verse seven). John then says those who say 'we have not sinned' (verse ten) stand in contrast to those who have confessed sin and are now cleansed from all unrighteousness (verse nine). John is not saying we never can stop sinning. Far from it! John says in verse seven as "we walk in the light, the blood of Jesus keeps us clean." Verse seven specifically contemplates obedience. Yet, this message in verse seven appears completely controverted if you lift verse eight or ten out of context. Yet, to lift a verse that says one thing *in context* and use its opposite *out of context* meaning is the grossest of misrepresentation.

Furthermore, if you read verses eight and ten to say we lie if we say we do not keep on sinning and are ever obedient, as faith alone apologists read them, then this creates a second fundamental incongruity. If you start at verse seven through nine, John says if "we walk in the light, we have fellowship with him," but if we "walk in darkness," "we lie" if we say "we have fellowship" (1 John 1:7,9.) He who "abides in [Jesus] ought himself to walk even as he walked." (1 John 2:6.) Hence, if the reading of verses eight and ten really meant we are never free for a moment from sin or we never experience obedience consistently (*i.e.*, walking in the light, walking as He walked), then no Christian is in "fellowship" ever with Jesus. This is the incongruous result of lifting verses 8 and 10 out-of-context from 1 John 1:7,9.

Conclusion

Jesus tells you in the Sermon on the Mount that it is destructive of your salvation if:

- You lust after a married woman.
- You take a false oath.
- You hate your brother.
- You take vengeance in your own hand.

- You divorce your wife without her being guilty of adultery or you fail to use a certificate of divorce.

- You sow discord rather than peace.[20]

- You fail to show mercy (forgiveness) to others.

- You are impatient.[21]

- You collapse under persecution for righteousness sake and for Jesus' name sake.

All those who practice the contrary — who practice the opposite noble virtues — are promised salvation.

If you thus are committed to following Jesus, you will memorize these principles and call them to mind throughout *every* day. The Sermon is not indicating an impossible standard. Nor is it passé. Instead, the Sermon on the Mount is the life-blood of your daily walk. Jesus tied a big promise — salvation — to those who follow His directions. Thus, there is never a moment you can treat these principles as optional.

Those who teach that you can 'skip all that' are bringing you a *false* Gospel. A gospel that cancels the words of Jesus. What is deplorable is they are completely aware of what they are doing yet persist in doing it anyway. In fact, they claim anyone is a heretic who is not willing to cancel Jesus' directions in the Sermon on the Mount as "impossible" (Dillard), "ridiculous" (Dillard), "unimportant" (Walvoord), "wrong" (Dillard), and as having "no application to the Christian." (Larkin.) Oh My! How far we have fallen from Jesus!

20.Jesus, however, taught that peace should not be gained by compromising truth. His message would cause division and a lack of peace within families. (Matt. 10:34-39.) His own message caused divisions between the Pharisees and Himself. Thus, a Christian must sow peace and harmony, but not fail to preach the true gospel in order to keep peace.

21.The verse "blessed are those who mourn" was a Greek translator's error. The original Hebrew Matthew says *who are patient*. See George Howard, *The Hebrew Gospel of Matthew* (Mercer: 1989).

11 *Parable Of The Sheep & The Goats*

*The Parable Of The Sheep And The Goats:
Does Faith Alone Save?*

Jesus tells a parable known as the Parable of the Sheep and the Goats. (Matthew 25:30-46.) Jesus says that one group who calls Him Lord serves Jesus' brothers in need with food and clothing. This group goes to heaven. Another group who calls Him Lord but who fails to do so are sent to hell.

Jesus is commanding charity to his brothers on threat of going to hell if you do not do it. Jesus is promising eternal life to those who do it. Faith that is alone does not save. This parable reads:

> (31) When the Son of man shall come in his glory, and all the holy angels with him, then shall he sit upon the throne of his glory: (32) And before him shall be gathered all nations: and he shall separate them one from another, as a shepherd divideth his sheep from the goats: (33) And he shall set the **sheep on his right hand**, but the goats on the left. (34) Then shall the King say unto them **on his right hand**, Come, ye blessed of my Father, **inherit the kingdom** prepared for you from the foundation of the world: (35) For I was an hungred, and ye gave me meat: I was thirsty, and ye gave me drink: I was a stranger, and ye took me in: (36) Naked, and ye clothed me: I was sick, and ye visited me: I was in prison, and ye came unto me. (37) Then shall the righteous answer him, saying, Lord, when saw we thee an hungred, and fed thee? or thirsty, and gave thee drink?

(38) When saw we thee a stranger, and took thee in? or naked, and clothed thee? (39) Or when saw we thee sick, or in prison, and came unto thee? (40) And the King shall answer and say unto them, Verily I say unto you, Inasmuch as ye have done it unto one of the least of these my brethren, ye have done it unto me. (41) Then shall **he say also unto them on the left hand**, Depart from me, ye cursed, into **everlasting fire, prepared for the devil and his angels**: (42) For I was an hungred, and ye gave me no meat: I was thirsty, and ye gave me no drink: (43) I was a stranger, and ye took me not in: naked, and ye clothed me not: sick, and in prison, and ye visited me not. (44) Then shall they also answer him, saying, Lord, when saw we thee an hungred, or athirst, or a stranger, or naked, or sick, or in prison, and did not minister unto thee? (45) Then shall he answer them, saying, Verily I say unto you, Inasmuch as ye did it not to one of the least of these, ye did it not to me. (46) And these shall go away **into everlasting punishment: but the righteous into life eternal**. (Matt. 25: 31-45, KJV.)

Please note that Jesus clearly divides the sheep from the goats based on works of charity. "[H]e rebukes not because they have not believed in Him, but because they have not done good works." (Augustine, *Fide et operibus*, Cornish:61.) Please also note that there is no doubt Jesus equates the sheep "inherit[ing] the kingdom" with going away "into life eternal." (vv. 34, 46). There is also no doubt that Jesus contrasts this with the fate of the goats who call Him Lord but who failed to do charity. They go into:

- "everlasting fire, prepared for the devil and his angels" (v. 41)
- "everlasting punishment" (v. 45.)

As Gathercole, an evangelical scholar, concedes, Jesus in Matthew 25:31-46 says "***deeds*** of hospitality...are ***certainly*** the criterion for judgment."[1] Let's examine this thoroughly so this very important point is not forgotten.

Jesus' Criterion For Salvation: Charitable Works

Why the different ends of the sheep versus the goats? Is it because one believed and the other did not? Or rather is it because among those who accepted Him as their Lord some served Him by clothing, feeding and visiting the "brothers" of the King while others did not?

Or another way of asking this is to inquire why do the sheep inherit the kingdom. Is it because they are believers who are saved despite failing to do works of charity? Was their faith alone enough? *No.*

Jesus says:

> (35) For I was hungry and you gave me something to eat, I was thirsty and you gave me something to drink, I was a stranger and you invited me in, (36) I needed clothes and you clothed me, I was sick and you looked after me, I was in prison and you came to visit me.

The sheep confess they do not remember doing it for the Lord himself. The King explains: 'I tell you the truth, whatever you did for one of the least of these brothers of mine, you did for me.'

Why are the goats[2] sent to "eternal fire"? Did they lack ever having faith? No, rather Jesus says:

---

1. Simon J. Gathercole, *Where Is Boasting: Early Jewish Soteriology and Paul's Response in Romans 1-5* (Eerdmans: 2002) at 113.

2. There is no negative connotation to the label *goats.* "The goat was not in evil repute in the East, as contrasted with the sheep; on the contrary, the he-goat was a symbol of dignity, so the point of analogy is merely the separation between the sheep and the goats." (*The Gospel According to St. Matthew* (ed. A.Carr)(Cambridge: Univ. Press, 1893) at 195.)

Jesus' Words On Salvation   **221**

(42) For I was hungry and you gave me nothing to eat, I was thirsty and you gave me nothing to drink, (43) I was a stranger and you did not invite me in, I needed clothes and you did not clothe me, I was sick and in prison and you did not look after me.

The goats confess the same error, not ever having seen the Lord in need. And the King replies:

I tell you the truth, whatever you did not do for one of the least of these, you did not do for me. (Mat 25:45.)

The answer is that one group serves the brothers of the King and the others do not, by works of charity. *One has works of charity and one doesn't.* That is the dividing line in being finally saved, as told in this parable. *Both the sheep and goats call him Lord, so both had faith.* One was dead and one was alive.[3]

If you instead believe only the sheep had faith, then you have the incongruous lesson that Jesus is warning people already lost (the goats) that they better do works of charity for His brothers or face hell. This would be a doctrine of *works alone*, which appears incompatible with any of Jesus' teachings.

Because Jesus clearly says works of charity are the dividing line between the two groups, and we know *faithless* works are meaningless to God, then Jesus must be speaking to believers. Jesus insists believers must have works of charity or otherwise they are sent to hell with unbelievers.

Thus, it follows that Jesus wants us to understand the goats who called Him Lord are sincere Christians (*i.e.*, had accepted Him as Lord and Savior). They are goats because they failed to serve Him by works of charity to His followers. The formula is faith and works (of charity). This charitable service then becomes the dividing line in terms of who is and who is not ultimately saved among people who have faith in Jesus.

This is not surprising. In Isaiah 58:7 *et seq.*, God promises "salvation shall come like the dawn" if you bring the poor into your home, give him clothes, etc.

Corroboration In The Epistle Of James

What helps corroborate we are reading Jesus correctly is that James clearly paraphrases this parable in James chapter two. Everyone remembers that James says that "faith alone" does not justify. However, no one seems to remember James says such faith cannot save because it lacks *charitable works*. James is saying *identically* what Jesus says in the Parable of the Sheep and the Goats.

James chapter two is an obvious paraphrase of Matthew 25:30-46. The two passages are virtually **verbatim copies** of each other. Not a single leading commentator mentions

---

3. On the significance that both groups call Jesus *Lord*, fabulists of cheap grace deny it any significance. In doing so, they merely engage in *ad hoc* denial that the lost were at one time Christians. They cite no adequate proof for this reading. *The Expositor's Bible Commentary*—an evangelical text—states: "There is **no significance** in the fact that the goats address him as Lord... for at this point there is no exception whatever to confessing Jesus as Lord." (Vol. 8, at 522.) What does this mean? The argument appears to be that this event occurs on judgment day when *according to their interpretation of Paul* everyone must confess Jesus as Lord. However, Paul *never* said this. It is a pure *myth* he did so, by amalgamating two disparate verses together. The first is Philippians 2:11. Paul says God exalted Jesus so that "every tongue *should* confess Jesus is the Lord." Nothing is said about this actually occurring universally, nor is there any indication this talks about the judgment seat. The second is Romans 14:11-12 where Paul says at the judgment seat "every knee shall bow and every tongue shall confess to God. So that every one of us shall *give account of himself* to God." There confession of *sins*, not of Jesus, is in view. Some amalgamate the two verses to mean "every tongue *shall* confess Jesus is Lord" when "every tongue shall confess" at the judgment seat. Yet, the two verses cannot be combined without violence to the original *context* of each verse. Thus, the *Expositor's* is relying upon a commonly heard amalgamation of two distinct verses. There is thus no basis to suppose non-Christians will ever confess Jesus on judgment day.

---

this. The reason is obvious. If one knew how James understood and applied doctrinally Jesus' Parable of the Sheep and the Goats, this would simply cement the falsity of the Fable of Cheap Grace. James writes:

> (14) What doth it profit, my brethren, if a man say he hath faith, but have not works? *can that faith save him?* (15) If a brother or sister be naked and in lack of daily food, (16) and one of you say unto them, Go in peace, be ye warmed and filled; and yet ye give them not the things needful to the body; what doth it profit? (17) Even so *faith, if it have not works [ergon], is dead in itself* [*i.e.*, if alone]. (James 2:14-17, ASV.)

Now compare this faith that is not completed because it lacks works of charity and thus cannot save in *James* with Jesus' words in the Parable of the Sheep and the Goats. In that parable, Jesus threatens damnation for lacking charity. The parallels are striking:

Parallelism of James 2:14-17 & Parable of the Sheep & the Goats

James	Jesus
"brother or sister without clothes..." (James 2:15.)	"I needed clothes and you did not clothe me."(Matt. 25:36.)
"brother or sister without... daily food..." (James 2:15.)	**"For I was hungry and you gave me nothing to eat." (Matt. 25:42.)**
"faith without works...." (James 2:14.)	"Lord...when did we see you hungering...or naked....?" (Matt. 25:44.)
"is dead [and] can[not] save." (James 2:14.)	**"Be going...into the eternal fire prepared for the devil and his angels." (Matt. 25: 41.)**

Hence, we see Matthew 25:30-46 — the Parable of the Sheep and the Goats — is identical in message and content to James 2:14-17. If James, the Lord's brother, evidently read it this way, we should do so as well.

Why Is Charity So Central In God's Word?

Why would charity toward others be so crucial to salvation, as Jesus says? We could do an entire Bible study on this. It appears that charity toward others is the most significant way you mark departure from your old life of sin. Daniel can tell the king "break off (discontinue) your sins...by showing mercy to the poor." (Dan. 4:27.)

Charity in the Hebrew Scriptures was frankly one of the most elevated commands to obey. One might even say it is central to Torah. It reflects obedience to God's command to *love thy neighbor* in a concrete way. Thus, the Law of Moses said if a brother of God's people is in your midst who is "needy" then "thou shalt surely open thy hand unto him, and shalt surely lend him sufficient for his need in that which he wanteth." (Deut. 15:7-8.) Thirty-six times the Bible then commands the same charity must be shown to the "stranger" in your midst for "you were once strangers in the Land of Egypt." (*E.g.*, Deut. 10:19.)

The charity-principle is one of the most characteristic ways of doing justice in God's eyes. God desires it more than any blood sacrifice. (Prov. 21:3; Mark 12:33.) In Isaiah 58:7 *et seq.*, God promises "*salvation* shall come like the dawn" if you bring the poor into your home, give him clothes, etc. If you are charitable, God promises if you call on Him, then "the Lord will answer." (Isaiah 58:9.) Thus, even the issue of whether God will speed an answer to prayer depends on how charitable you are being to the poor.

Furthermore, if you are charitable, God will guide you "continually" and make you like a watered garden. (Isaiah 58:11.) God promises special blessings to those who give charity to the poor.

Thus, there is no end of verses that elevate charity above almost every other command except to Love the Lord thy God with your whole mind, heart and soul.

Cheap Grace Interpretation Of The Parable Of The Sheep & Goats

Most of the time, proponents of the Modern Gospel of Cheap Grace ignore this parable. One Christian expresses my own experience, and perhaps your own:

> In my Baptist upbringing, and even after becoming a Christian, Matthew 25[:31 et seq.] was NEVER touched on, mentioned, taught, etc. And you'd be surprised how easy it is to gloss over it in your own studies when your own denomination, pastor, teachers, and friends don't give it any notice, either.[4]

Whenever the Parable of the Sheep and the Goats is actually examined, because it is James 2:14-17 stated as a parable, proponents of the Modern Gospel of Cheap Grace lose all semblance of reasonable interpretation.

Dillow mentions the view that the sheep are Christians who ministered with food and clothing and visited in prison *Jews*, Jesus' "brothers." However, they are not just simply any Jew of every generation, but only Jews living in the great tribulation period. (Dillow, *Reign of the Servant Kings, supra*, at 73.) Dillow explains that if we do not choose something like this interpretation which imposes 'faith plus works saves' as true for a very small future historical group, then the present *standard* 'gospel' is ruined for the rest of us. Dillow says that but for a faith-alone explanation, Matthew 25:34 means "that inheriting the kingdom is conditioned on obedience and service to the King, a condition far removed

---

4. http://onefortruth.blogspot.com/2005/09/sheep-and-goats-parable-or-prophecy.html (Ninjanun comment to 9-29-05 blog).

from the New Testament [*i.e.,* the Cheap Grace Gospel] teaching of justification by faith *alone* for entrance into heaven." (*Id.*)

Thus, this spin of the parable defers Jesus' teaching on salvation by works to only those trapped in the tribulation who were never Christians pre-tribulation.

It is absurd to interpret a parable as having a distinct salvation message for only the tribulation period. Why would it change just for those in this seven year period?

Thus, the Modern Fable of Cheap Grace spins this passage so it ends up teaching there is a separate salvation message for a small historical group only in the future who will be required to have works of charity or suffer hell. (Incidentally, their forefathers in this fable tried a similar solution. Back in the 1800s, cheap grace taught the Parable of the Sheep and the Goats was true only from 33 to 70 A.D.)[5]

Therefore, according to the latest cheap grace views, we today are comforted that we do not have to change the cheap grace gospel message until the tribulation is upon us. In this view, reconciling the 'faith alone' gospel to Jesus is not necessary because Jesus' teaching on works and salvation applies in the future when Christians 'are gone anyway.'

In this manner, this parable is neatly swept under the rug to be dusted off when the time is right for non-Christians to find it. (Please note this recognizes that faith-plus-works will one day be a non-heretical doctrine; it just does not fit our time, according to proponents of cheap grace.)

This tribulation-only solution can be dismissed with just one Bible verse. Christ's 'brethren' does not mean ethnic Jews, let alone only Jews of a seven year future period. Jesus asked once "who are my brothers?" Jesus answered that his brothers and sisters should be those "doing the will of God." (Matthew 12:48-50.) (Please note Christians are not defined as *believers* by Jesus, but rather as *doers* of God's will.)

If one must escape this parable with such a nonsensi-cal notion that Jesus' brothers are non-Christian Jews of the tribulation period, the cheap grace gospel is not being held

---

5. The older school of Protestant theologians had a similarly astonishing solution. They limited the parable's validity to only the period of 33 A.D. to 70 A.D. Whittemore summarized the support for this. He can-vassed all the opinions from major theologians that endorsed this idea. He was arguing that this parable was fulfilled at the destruction of Jerusalem. Whittemore claimed it therefore had no further moral meaning for any Christian thereafter. "We think, then, we must have shown to the satisfaction of every individual who shall peruse those pages, that *this whole parable was completely fulfilled at the time of Christ's coming to the Jewish state [at the temple destruction in 70 A.D.*]." His proof is the temple destruction took place "within forty years after the crucifixion" and this is when the goats were supposedly punished. (Thomas Whittemore, *Notes and Illustrations of the Parables of the New Testament* (Boston: J.M. Usher, 1855) at 347.) Even though Jesus speaks of this judgment for the goats being with the same "fire" for the *diabolos* (devil) and his angels, Whittemore claims the *diabolos* can mean simply an "adversary...very often...human beings" and that *fire* can mean simply temporal affliction, not hell. (*Id.* at 350.) Whittemore says the *diabolos* is a reference by Jesus to the Jews of 70 A.D., and the *fire* to the temple destruction that same year. There are a cascade of non-sequiturs to all of what Whittemore claims. This likely explains why what was once a popular 'faith-alone' solution to this parable has withered. Yet, it is worth listing off a few of the non-sequi-turs to give this idea its proper burial. *If nothing else, it is worth men-tioning this old idea just to prove once again how much pressure this parable puts on faith alone advocates*. Whittemore's ideas prove how far into nonsense faith-alone advocates have been willing to reach to solve this particular parable. The first non-sequitur is: Jesus never speaks of the destruction of the temple as a *coming back*. Even if He did, why is the moral of this parable about charity limited to the sup-posed coming of Christ in 70 A.D.? Moreover, the parable says the verdict of eternal life or damnation is at a particular coming where one group is thrown in the "fire of eternal damnation reserved for the devil and his angels." (Matt. 25:41.) To suggest this is temporal affliction of Jews in 70 A.D. is fantastically silly. Instead, this particular coming in final judgment of Jesus is one Jesus spoke frequently about. (See Matt. 12:42-50.) Obviously, that coming, which is in our future, is the only coming in view in Matthew 25:41. Clearly, all of Whittemore's non-sense was an extremely strained reading so as to reign in a parable directly destructive of the fable of cheap grace. After all, it is James chapter two stated as a parable.

---

even loosely based on Jesus' words. The modern view of salvation is being held *in spite* of whatever Jesus teaches.

Bob Wilkin — President Of The Grace Evangelical Society

Finally, others like Bob Wilkin who cannot reconcile the parable to 'faith alone' insist we are forced to do so regardless of the language.

> [I]t follows from the discussion above that the basis of 'inheriting the kingdom' ([Matt.] 25:34) is good works. Since Scripture cannot contradict itself, we know from a host of other passages that cannot mean that these people will gain entrance to the kingdom because they were faithful.[6]

Thus, the final foxhole is the *ad hoc* denial that Jesus can mean what He says because we know what cheap grace otherwise teaches *must remain* true.

Conclusion

The best advice on how to understand the Parable of the Sheep and the Goats is to follow Daniel Fuller's guidance. He exhorts us to allow Jesus to challenge our core doctrines:

> To the objection that...Matthew 25... lead[s] us right back to Rome and **salvation by works**, my answer is twofold. First, we must determine, **regardless of consequences**, what the intended meaning of each of the biblical writers is. We must let each one speak for himself and **avoid construing him by recourse to what another writer said**. Otherwise **there is no**

---

6. Bob Wilkin, *Has This Passage Ever Bothered You? Matthew 25:31-46 - Works Salvation?* http://www.faithalone.org/news/y1988/ 88march1.html (last accessed 11/05).

escape from subjectivism in biblical interpretation. (Daniel Fuller, "Biblical Theology and the Analogy of Faith," *Unity and Diversity in N.T. Theology* (Eerdman's 1978) at 195-213 fn. 22.)

Thus, reading Jesus through the overlay of the Modern Gospel of Cheap Grace is wrong. You cannot press Jesus' words down so they fit your favorite fable. Such conduct is reprehensible. In fact, the duty to construe Jesus free from other writers is an imperative. The very validity of all writers for acceptance in the New Testament turns on whether they *go beyond* or *transgress* Jesus' teaching. As 2 John 1:9 says:

Whoever **goes beyond** and **doesn't remain** in Christ's teaching, doesn't have God [*i.e.*, breaks fellowship with God]. He who **remains** in the teachings [of Jesus Christ], the same has both the Father and the Son.

Jesus' words are thus the standard whether the Gospel of Cheap Grace is valid. Even if it cites Paul, this does not resolve the issue. Balaam was once a true prophet of Christ — he gave the famous Star Prophecy of Messiah (Numbers 24:17). The Magi relied upon it (Matt. 2:1.) But Balaam still later became a false prophet. Jesus says Balaam taught doctrines subversive of the Law given Moses by "I Am." (Rev. 2:14). Jesus said He was "I am." (John 8:58.) By going beyond Jesus' principles in the Law (Matt. 5:19), Balaam went from Christ's prophet to a false prophet. (Deut.13:3.) Thus, Paul is not better than Balaam. His validity, just like Balaam's, rests on consistency with Jesus.

Here, Jesus' meaning is as plain as day in the Parable of the Sheep and the Goats. Even advocates of cheap grace concede the meaning. Jesus tells us that those who call Him Lord and do works of charity *inherit* eternal life in the kingdom. Those who call Him Lord and failed to do works of charity will go to the eternal fire reserved for the Devil and his angels. All the efforts to squirm out of this parable (which refutes faith alone) were disrespectful of Jesus and tortured.

12 *Parable Of The Purchase Of The Field (The Hidden Treasure)*

Parable Of The Purchase Of The Field In Matthew 13:44

Jesus teaches in a one-line parable commonly called the Parable of the Hidden Treasure that you must be willing to sacrifice all that you have in this world to acquire the kingdom. A better name for the parable is the *Parable of the Purchase of the Field.* This name will help keep in our mind the *price* to be paid for the kingdom, as Jesus intends us to see as the *main* point.

Jesus gives this parable in succinct but powerful terms:

> The kingdom of heaven is like unto a treasure hidden in the field; which a man found, and hid; and in his joy he goeth and selleth all that he hath, and buyeth that field. (Matt. 13:44, ASV.)

What underscores this verse's meaning is the next verse. In the immediately following verse, Jesus repeats the same idea in another single-sentence parable. This is known as the Parable of the Pearl of Great Price:

> (45) Again, the kingdom of heaven is like unto a man that is a merchant seeking goodly pearls:

> (46) and having found one pearl of great price, he went and sold all that he had, and bought it. (Matt. 13:45-46.)

Both parables are identical to the message Jesus gives the rich young man.[1] *Jesus told the young rich man that he should have exchanged all that he had in this life as worldly riches to obtain eternal life.*

The German evangelical minister, Frederick Lisco, in *The Parables of Jesus* (trans. Rev. Fairbairn)(Philadelphia:1850) agrees. He cites Calvin in support. Lisco says the meaning of the Parable of the Treasure is obvious. It is like the "mariner in a tempestuous sea" who "readily parts with it all, that he may save his life." *Id.* at 93. The "highest good" is possessed by "self-denial;" hence, sinful attachments are "all abandoned." *Id.* Lisco quotes Calvin saying this verse means that "Christ exhorts his people [to] the renouncement...of those things contrary to piety..." and "postponing every other object" that interferes with the "zeal to obtain" possession of eternal life. *Id.* This self-sacrifice of all that we have in exchange for the kingdom was Jesus' blunt way to identify the cost to acquire the kingdom.

As we shall see below, many famous Christian thinkers concur on this interpretation of the Parable of the Purchase of the Field: Bonhoeffer, MacArthur, and, as Lisco says even Calvin. It is surprising to think Calvin agrees. So many times his doctrines sowed the seed for the gospel of cheap grace. But when it came to this parable, Calvin saw it the same way as did Bonhoeffer, and as does MacArthur.

Commentators Who Agree The Purchase Of The Field Means A Costly Grace

John MacArthur In *Gospel According To Jesus* (1995)

John MacArthur in *The Gospel According to Jesus* says that the clear meaning of this parable is that grace is costly. Jesus is telling us what to do when confronted with

---

1. Matthew 19:16-26; Mark 10:17-31; Luke 18:18-26. For discussion, see page 123 *et seq.*

the offer to acquire the kingdom. MacArthur says the *Purchase of the Field* parable is no different than numerous other messages by Jesus on the same issue.

> Forsaking oneself for Christ's sake is **not an optional step** of discipleship subsequent to conversion: it is the *sine qua non* of **saving faith.** The Savior consistently set forth his gospel on those terms. Faith as he categorized it is nothing less than a complete exchange of all that we are for all that he is. Two brief parables in Matthew 13:44-46 [including the parable of the purchase of the field] illustrate precisely this truth. (*Id.*, at 142.)[2]

MacArthur says the purchase of the field symbolizes that a sinner who wants the kingdom "will gladly yield everything else he cherishes to obtain it." The corresponding truth is that those who hold onto their earthly treasures "forfeit" the treasure of obtaining the kingdom.

John MacArthur

---

2. MacArthur teaches this requirement of giving up all that you have is essential to "saving faith." But MacArthur does not see this as an additional component, but part of the meaning of *saving faith.* Thus, MacArthur imagines repentance-from-sin is indistinguishable from faith alone. MacArthur has thereby tried to defend his views are compatible with 'faith alone.' However, is it really correct to say Jesus taught faith alone for salvation? To say so would appear disingenuous to anyone who later learns you mean by *faith* that it includes *repentance from sin, sacrificing all that you hold dear in this world, obedience to the commandments, etc.* Isn't Jesus' gospel of costly grace compromised by using a misleading label of 'faith alone'? Using such a label matches our prevailing notions and gives room to deflect charges of heresy, but it mismatches Jesus' teachings. One must use labels with precision, or otherwise old wrong-headed notions are never cleared away.

Dietrich Bonhoeffer (Lutheran Pastor): The Cost Of Discipleship (1937)

The Lutheran pastor, Dietrich Bonhoeffer, is a modern Protestant Christian pastor. He claimed that he was teaching the authentic Gospel of Jesus Christ. He said somehow it had been lost in the post-reformation period. Bonhoeffer insisted the modern gospel of free grace, with its emphasis on faith alone, gave us a crippled gospel. It is a Cheap Grace. He claimed it actually *denies* the Words of Jesus.

One of the many key proofs for Bonhoeffer's claim was, in fact, the Parable of the Purchase of the Field. In his chapter entitled *Costly Grace*, Bonhoeffer first defines what he means by Cheap Grace — a term he first coined.

> Yet it is imperative for the Christian to **achieve renunciation**, to **practice self-effacement**, to distinguish his life from the life of the world.....[If free grace is all there is, then let] him rest assured in his possession of this grace-for **grace alone** does everything. Instead of following Christ, let the Christian enjoy the consolation of his grace! **This is what we mean by cheap grace**, the grace which amounts to justification of sin without justification of the repentant sinner who **departs from sin and from whom sin departs**....Cheap grace is the grace we bestow on ourselves. (*Cost of Discipleship, supra,* at 44.)(Emphasis added.)

Accordingly, Bonhoeffer starts out saying there is a high cost to grace. It requires achieving renunciation. It requires a departure from sin. Any other kind of grace is a **false consolation** that we simply are bestowing on ourself. Jesus did not promise salvation without cost.

Bonhoeffer later will say the doctrine of cheap grace has been "disastrous to our spiritual lives." For "instead of opening up the way to Christ *it has closed it*." (*Id.,* at 54.) Because this cheap grace doctrine so abandons the actual words of Jesus, Bonhoeffer calls this *"Christianity without Christ."* (*Id.*, at 59.) He claims those who oppose what Jesus teaches are infected with an "excess of Protestant zeal." (*Id.*, at 68.) What are his Biblical proofs?

The first proof he cites is the *Parable of the Purchase of the Field.*

> Costly grace is the treasure hidden in the field; for the sake of it a man will gladly go and sell all that he has. (*Id.*, at 45.)

The second proof is the Parable of the Pearl of Great Price.

> It is the pearl of great price which the merchant will sell all his goods. (*Id.*)

The third proof is the Heaven-Maimed or Hell-Whole statement of Jesus in Matthew 5:29-30 and Mark 9:42 *et seq.*:

> [Costly grace] is the kingly rule of Christ, for whose sake a man will pluck out the eye which causes him to stumble. (*Id.*)

The fourth is the Parable of the Nets. The disciples will leave their nets and follow the call of their master.

Another proof Bonhoeffer cites is Jesus' message that he who gains his life in this world shall loose it in the next, but he who looses it for Jesus' sake in this life will gain his life in the next world. (Mark 8:31-38.) Bonhoeffer says those who teach to the contrary that Jesus "makes no costly demands" are merely giving you an emotional lift. They are not giving you the Gospel as Jesus proclaimed it. (*Id.*, at 88.)

The next proof was the story of Jesus' answering the young rich man's question on how to have eternal life. (Matt. 19:16-22.) We discussed Bonhoeffer's comments on this previously.[3]

---

3. See "Bonhoeffer: On Necessity To Obey The Law" on page 127 *et seq.*

John Calvin 1509-1564: The Cost To Qualify To Receive Grace

Calvin (1509-1564) interestingly agrees with John MacArthur and Bonhoeffer. Calvin first says Jesus makes clear this parable's meaning by means of the immediately following *Parable of the Pearl of Great Price.* They are the same message. Calvin explains that "in the same manner as a treasure, though it be hidden, [acquiring the kingdom] is preferred to a vain appearance of wealth." [4] Then Calvin directly concurs with MacArthur and Bonhoeffer:

> We now perceive the leading object of both parables. It is to inform us, that none are **qualified for receiving the grace** of the Gospel but those **who disregard all other desires**, and devote all their exertions, and all their faculties, **to obtain it**. (*Id.*)

Clearly, Calvin just said that those who wish to "obtain" the object of the kingdom of God must be "qualified for receiving the grace" of God by complying with the costs to do so laid down by Jesus in this parable.

Then Calvin directly deals with the hard question whether this means we really and truly must turn away from ourselves, including our material possessions, **to obtain salvation**. Calvin does not run to the Modern Gospel of Cheap Grace for his answer. Instead, Calvin says it is unmistakable that Jesus taught elsewhere that the answer is *yes*, that is what we must do — we must turn away from our greed and sinfulness. This means there is no avoiding this parable's meaning about the costliness of grace. Calvin explains this as an unavoidable meaning if we use the "natural meaning" of words:

John Calvin

---

4. http://www.ccel.org/c/calvin/comment3/comm_vol32/htm/xxiii.htm (last accessed 7/2/06).

But it is asked, is it necessary that we abandon every other possession, in order that *we may enjoy eternal life*? I answer briefly. The natural meaning of the words is, that the Gospel does not receive from us the respect which it deserves, unless we prefer it to all the riches, pleasures, honors, and advantages of the world, and to such an extent, that we are satisfied with the spiritual blessings which it promises, and *throw aside every thing that would keep us from enjoying them*; for those who *aspire to heaven must be disengaged from every thing that would retard their progress*. Christ exhorts those *who believe in him to deny those things only which are injurious to godliness*; and, at the same time, permits them to use and enjoy God's temporal favors, as if they did not use them. (*Id.*)

Calvin, a prominent voice within the Protestant Reformation, here refused to change Jesus' obvious meaning into a teaching that salvation can come without "throwing aside everything that would keep us from enjoying" it, including all things "injurious to godliness."

However, then in the next note on the text, Calvin tries to reconcile this with the doctrine of free-grace. In essence, Calvin argues that Jesus means the gift of salvation belongs *freely* to everyone who *buys it* by relinquishing their sinful life. This rationale is how Calvin held onto Jesus' gospel while not relinquishing the key verbiage of 'free-grace.' Calvin writes:

[Matt. 13:]46. And *bought* it. By the word buy Christ *does not mean, that men bring any price, with which they may purchase for themselves the heavenly life*; for we know on what condition the Lord invites believers in the book of Isaiah, (55:1,) Come and buy wine and milk without money and without price.[5] But though the heavenly life, and every thing that belongs to it, *is the free gift of God*, yet we are said to buy it, when *we cheerfully relinquish the desires of the flesh*, that nothing may prevent us from obtaining it; as Paul says, that he 'reckoned all things to be loss and dung, that he might gain Christ' (Philippians 3:8.)

What Calvin appears to imply, which is correct, is that the atonement of Christ pays for sin. None of us can pay anything to redeem ourselves from sin. None of us is a sinless

---

5. This is often read out of context to make it appear salvation is cost-free, without repentance. However, it reads to the contrary in the fuller context: "Ho, every one that thirsteth, come ye to the waters, and he that hath no money; come ye, buy, and eat; yea, come, buy wine and milk without money and without price. (2) Wherefore do ye spend money for that which is not bread? and your labor for that which satisfieth not? hearken *diligently unto me*, and *eat ye that which is good*, and let your soul delight itself in fatness. (3) Incline your ear, and come unto me; hear, and *your soul shall live*: and I will make an *everlasting covenant* with you, even the sure mercies of David. (4) Behold, I have given him [Messiah] for a witness to the peoples, a leader and commander to the peoples. (5) Behold, thou shalt call a nation that thou knowest not; and a nation that knew not thee shall run unto thee, because of Jehovah thy God, and for the Holy One of Israel; for he hath glorified thee. (6) Seek ye Jehovah while he may be found; call ye upon him while he is near: (7) *let the wicked forsake his way, and the unrighteous man his thoughts; and let him return unto Jehovah, and he will have mercy upon him; and to our God, for he will abundantly pardon*. (8) For my thoughts are not your thoughts, neither are your ways my ways, saith Jehovah." Isa 55:1-8 ASV.

Read out of context, the "without price" is typically interpreted to mean one is saved by faith without repentance from sin. Grace is said to be free. However, verse seven *erases* that notion. Instead, "without price" means the items for sale have no price on them you can buy with the world's money. These are spiritual possessions. How are spiritual blessings purchased? Without money and without price. The exchange, instead, is in verse seven. If the "wicked forsake his way, and the unrighteous man his thoughts and return to....Jehovah," then God "will have mercy upon him...and abundantly pardon." There is a spiritual price, not a worldly price. Thus, grace is costly *spiritually*. Yet, it is without a price in worldly terms.

lamb. However, if we claim Calvin was agreeing with the Modern Gospel of Cheap Grace, this would be wrong. The next sentence in the above quote makes this clear.

Calvin cites Paul as someone who actually repeats Jesus' principle that to gain Christ, Paul "reckoned all things [he had] to be loss and dung...." (Phil. 3:8.) Calvin then returns to agreeing that in some sense we do 'buy' salvation— "we are said to buy it, when *we cheerfully relinquish the desires of the flesh*, that nothing may prevent us from obtaining it...."

John MacArthur says the same thing — Jesus speaks of our 'buying' the kingdom, but MacArthur tries to insist He is not contradicting the Modern Gospel's doctrine of grace:

> In a sense, the parables [of the Purchase of the Field and Pearl of Great Price] say the men *did buy their salvation,* but you have to understand what is meant by that.[6]

Then what is meant by this 'buying' of which Jesus speaks? MacArthur says we know a rich man cannot *buy* his way into heaven, citing Matthew 19:24. But that is not what that verse said. In fact, Jesus said, in effect, the sacrifice of money would, for that rich man, have a saving effect in Matthew 19:24. When the rich man was sorrowful and unwilling to give up all his wealth to the poor as *one part* of his price to enter heaven, Jesus in 19:24 said "it is hard for a rich man to enter heaven." The man *also* had to follow Jesus and take up his cross, but *one unmistakable element* was the cost of giving away all his possessions to the poor.

There is no escaping Jesus' point: grace is costly. For men wed to mammon, Jesus has a steep price for repentance.

---

6. http://www.biblebb.com/files/MAC/sg2303.htm (last accessed 7/2/06)

Compare Jesus' Doctrine On Light-Hearted Or Half-Hearted Acceptance

Corroborating proof of what the Parable of the Purchase of the Field means comes from comparing it to other messages of Jesus about the *cost* to follow Him. If we find a persistent doctrine of Jesus about taking the call from Him as involving serious cost and deprivation, then we know more certainly Jesus' meaning in this parable.

For example, in Luke 9:57, a man came to Jesus and called him Lord and wanted to follow Jesus. Yet Jesus responds that the cost is very high. Jesus is seeking to dissuade the man from a light-hearted decision. For the man said: "Lord, I will follow Thee wherever Thou goest." But Jesus responded: "Foxes have holes, and birds of the air have nests, but the Son of man hath not where to lay His head." (v. 58).

In other words, Jesus says "Here's the price for following Me: You give up your comfort of a nice place to sleep and I'll give you My Kingdom." The man did not like the costs. He did not make the transaction. Jesus told him the costs were *higher than the man assumed*, and the man backed off from a serious costly step of following Jesus.

In verse 59, Jesus asked another man to follow Him. The man said, "Lord, permit me first to go and bury my father." (v. 59.) However, the man's father was not even dead yet. The man's words meant he wanted to wait for his inheritance. Jesus said, "Let the dead bury their dead; but go thou and preach the kingdom of God." (v. 60.) That man did not want to give up his inheritance. Thus, he did not make the transaction. The man's intentions were good, but his interest was not serious enough to sacrifice now his opportunities for wealth and comfort.

Finally, a third man, mentioned in verse 61, said, "Lord, I will follow Thee; but let me first go bid them farewell, who are at home at my house." This even appeared to be a reasonable request to act sociable to those at his home.

However, Jesus said, "No man, having put his hand to the plough, and looking back, is *fit for the kingdom of God*." (v. 62.). In other words, "You *can't* plow a straight furrow while looking in the opposite direction and expect to enter the kingdom of God." That man was not willing to walk away from his life with his parents to serve the kingdom, which Jesus repeatedly said was a cost, which if paid, means you will "inherit eternal life." (Matt.19:29.)

Thus, we learn from these true-life examples that Jesus rejected light-hearted acceptance of Himself. Jesus wanted to make sure that each person knew the high cost in human terms of what it *really* means to accept Him. For if you looked back longingly at what you gave up, you were not fit for (worthy of) the kingdom of God. You would fail. You would lose the kingdom. You will not have escaped the kingdom that leads to spiritual death. Thus, every time someone tried to come on board the Jesus-ship, Jesus tried to dissuade them unless they *understood* and *accepted* the high human cost of doing so.

What is the message of the Gospel of Cheap Grace? *The exact opposite message of what Jesus taught.* There is supposedly no cost in human terms of accepting Jesus. It is merely acceptance of a belief. The cheap grace gospel is emphatic that there is no moral cost involved. Because nothing is supposedly sacrificed, you never are looking back feeling sorry for anything you gave up! As a result, in the Gospel of Cheap Grace, you can never become unfit for the kingdom by missing the things that you did before following Christ. Why? *Because you never had to give them up in the first place*! You are supposedly always safe and secure, and loved and accepted "just as I am."

Hopefully, one can now see how stark the difference is between Jesus' words and the gospel that most of us evangelicals have been assuming was true.

Compare Jesus' Doctrine On Denying Yourself And Confessing Christ

Another series of verses repeat the meaning of the Parable of the Purchase of the Field. These passages emphasize the duty to deny yourself and commit your way to obeying Jesus as ruler of your life to receive *life* — a synonym for salvation.

In Matthew 10:37-39, the issue is whether a person is willing to give up everything he has to receive Jesus. The Lord says in Matthew 10:37:

> He that loveth father or mother more than Me, is not worthy of Me; and he that loveth son or daughter more than Me, is not worthy of Me.

Jesus goes on to explain what *worthy* means. If you are not willing to give up something that needs to be given up, such as your family, then you are not going to have life. Instead, you will lose it. *Life* is a synonym here for eternal life in the Kingdom. Jesus next said: "And he that taketh not his cross and followeth after Me, is not worthy of Me. *He that findeth his life shall lose it*; and *he that loseth his life for My sake shall find it*." (Matt. 10:38-39.)

That is the simple transaction: you give up all that you hold dear in this life and receive all that He offers: *life in the world to come*. If you cling to your life here instead, you will lose life in the world to come.

In Matthew 16:24, Jesus likewise said to His disciples, "If any man will come after Me, let him deny himself, and take up his cross, and follow Me." The basic principle in salvation is that a person gives himself up to follow Christ.

Finally, in Matthew 19, as we discuss elsewhere,[7] a rich young ruler came to Jesus and said, "...what good thing shall I do, that I may have eternal life?" (v. 16). Jesus said, "If

---

7. See "Jesus' Answer To The Direct Question On How To Obtain Eternal Life" on page 123 *et seq.*

thou wilt be perfect, go and sell what thou hast, and give to the poor, and thou shalt have treasure in heaven; and come and follow Me" (v. 21). Jesus was saying, in effect, 'If you want My treasure of life in the kingdom, then give away all you hold dear.'

Are these repetitive messages meant to instill obeying only one command of Jesus to *believe* in Him? Hardly. Yet, that is what some insist is the case. ***However, in none of these examples was Jesus talking to a person who did not already want to believe in Jesus***. Rather, each was a person who was hesitating treating Jesus as his immediate ruler — they were reluctant to obey Jesus if it involved too much ***personal cost***.

Jesus was saying that salvation depended on *more than a desire to believe*. You had to pay the personal cost that Jesus required. You had to relinquish all the sin-life which you held dear that could hold you back from obeying Jesus.

Thus, it is no wonder that Bonhoeffer started his book *Cost of Discipleship* by emphasizing the Parable of the Purchase of the Field (the Hidden Treasure). It spells out clearly the costliness of grace.

TABLE 1. Costliness Of Salvation Theme

	Parable of the Purchase of the Field	Parable of the Pearl of Great Price	Luke 9:62 Unfit for kingdom if put hand to plough and look back	Matthew chs. 10, 16, 19 Find life by losing it. Lose life by keeping it.
Salvation	"kingdom of God"	"kingdom of God"	"fit for the kingdom"	"enter life"
Cost	worth all that you have.	worth all worldly wealth that you have.	Give up inheritance, home life, etc. vs. looking back activity.	Give up all that you have, if necessary all worldly wealth, to enter life.
If Not Pay The Cost	Pass up kingdom	Pass up kingdom	Unfit for Kingdom	Will not enter life

Sermonette: Selfish Salvation Programs.

The moral ideal behind Jesus' message on counting the cost is to sacrifice self to God. The opposite vice is protecting yourself from God's demands. Jesus thus impliedly says the kingdom can only be acquired by *sacrificing your selfish desires* so as to obey God's commands. Succinctly, we must lose self-centered principles or we lose the kingdom.

Is it possible to craft a message of salvation which endorses the same selfishness which Jesus condemns? A very insightful article from 1868 explains this takes place when you teach a repentance-free salvation. The salvation message then becomes all about what you get. There is nothing about what you must give up to God and His creation. Such a message is solely selfishness! Here is a snippet from this astute article from 1868 entitled: "The Place of Repentance in Religion and Theology," *The Congregational Review* (Boston: Broughton & Wyman, 1868) Vol. 8, May 1868, at 201,212:

> That faith in his Son which he requires is a holy faith, and this makes it necessary that the soul should first go over to holiness from sin [*i.e.*, repentance]. **As it [*i.e.*, faith] is good for nothing if works do not follow it, so it is if repentance does not precede it**. It is dead being alone. It is no ground of pardon. It has no holiness in itself. Its validity and vitality comes from a moral change elsewhere than in the believing faculties. As a new exercise of the soul it is, **without repentance**, simply putting confidence in God in respect to one's well-being because of the love and work of Christ, **our well-being** remaining the supreme object of regard. **It is utterly selfish**. A sinner's trust in everybody and in everything—God included—is **selfish**, until **selfishness is dethroned by a change of mind** [*i.e.*, repentance from sin].

13 *Forgiven But Not Forgiving*

Introduction

The Parable of The Unmerciful Servant can be found in Matthew 18:23-35. Initially, this servant is forgiven all his mountain of debt — a symbol for sin. However, later this servant is unforgiving to several of his own servants.

The master learns the servant was unforgiving in turn toward the servant's debtors. In response, the master reimposes the prior debt of his unforgiving servant. The master then ordered the unforgiving servant to be sent to the same prison which the servant originally avoided by the master's gracious grant of forgiveness. The master orders the servant to be tortured and tormented until he could pay the enormous (and hence unpayable) previously forgiven debt.

Jesus closes by saying this parable is how the Father will treat each of us if we are not forgiving.

Thus, the message is simple and easy to discern. When we have post-salvation sin of unforgiveness, and we do so repeatedly, the Master will be grieved, and send us to the same prison he had spared us from by graciously granting salvation. There we will be tortured and tormented to pay for our enormous (and hence unpayable) debt.

Luther agreed. Addressing the unmerciful servant directly, Luther says you "should have been... *completely discharged* from all thy debt, *hadst thou*...showed compassion to thy neighbor; but now *God will not forgive thee*, and besides will reckon as strictly with thee, as thou wouldst with thy neighbor." (Quoted in Frederick Lisco, *The Parables of Jesus* (trans. from German by Rev. Fairbairn)(Philadelphia:1850) at 113, quoting Luther, *House-Pos.* 5.239.)

To those who say the unmerciful servant was never a believer forgiven by grace, the mature Luther says *not so*. It is directed precisely at a forgiven believer. In fact, Jesus' point is to warn the forgiven who do not *obey* Jesus' commands. Luther explains:

> The punishment here spoken of is not for the heathen, or for the general mass, who never hear the word of God, but for **those who with the ear receive the gospel, and keep it upon their tongues, but who will not live according to its precepts**. (Luther, *Church-Pos.* 14-251, quoted in Lisco, *The Parables of Jesus* (trans. from German by Rev. Fairbairn)(Philadelphia:1850) at 114 (emphasis added),

The German evangelical minister, Lisco, similarly explained that as "God *first* exercised compassion" with us, He "*afterwords* desires and expects it of us." *Id.*, at 114. The servant's subsequent unforgiveness "forfeits" God's prior exercise of mercy. "The king does not break his promise; but the ungodly person frustrates the purpose of divine goodness." *Id.* Lisco quotes the renown *Bengel's Gnomon* as saying Jesus clearly means "they who have **experienced grace** ought most of all to be **afraid of wrath**." The Master's wrath in this parable means salvation is revoked.

Retroactivity Principle

In the Parable of the Unmerciful Servant in Matthew 18:23-35, Jesus tells us that our forgiving others is **retroactively examined after salvation**. In other words, Jesus explains that if *after* God has forgiven you a mountain of debt, you then turn around and *later* are not forgiving in turn, the penalty for your prior sin is re-imposed and you must pay for it in torment. Those are Jesus' very words. Of course, we cannot pay for our own sin and thus Jesus is threatening damnation if we should commit the sin of unforgiveness *repeatedly* even after initial salvation.

Parable Of The Unmerciful Servant

Do you recall whether in the Parable of the Unmerciful Servant that someone forgiven a huge debt has it reimposed by God the Father? Read carefully the following quote from Matthew 18:23-34 in the KJV to answer the question:

> (23) Therefore is the kingdom of heaven likened unto a certain king, which would take account of his servants.

> (24) And when he had begun to reckon, one was brought unto him, which owed him ten thousand talents.

> (25) But forasmuch as he had not to pay, his lord commanded him to be sold, and his wife, and children, and all that he had, and payment to be made.

> (26) The servant therefore fell down, and worshipped him, saying, Lord, have patience with me, and I will pay thee all.

> (27) Then the lord of that servant was moved with compassion, and loosed him, and *forgave him the debt*.

> (28) But the same servant went out, and found one of his fellowservants, which owed him an hundred pence: and he laid hands on him, and took [him] by the throat, saying, Pay me that thou owest.

> (29) And his fellowservant fell down at his feet, and besought him, saying, Have patience with me, and I will pay thee all.

(30) And he would not: but went and cast him into prison, till he should pay the debt.

(31) So when his fellowservants saw what was done, they were very sorry, and *came and told unto their lord all that was done*.

(32) Then his lord, after that he had called him, said unto him, *O thou wicked servant, I forgave thee all that debt, because thou desiredst me*: (33) Shouldest not thou also have had compassion on thy fellowservant, even as I had pity on thee? (34) And his lord was *wroth,* and delivered him to the *tormentors*, till he *should pay all that was due unto him*.

Is this about how God will treat us? Jesus says emphatically yes, closing the parable as follows:

(35) So likewise shall my heavenly Father do also unto you, if ye from your hearts forgive not every one his brother their trespasses.

Thus, in this parable, Jesus tells a story of a servant who was forgiven a mountain of debt. Ten thousand talents represents a large fortune. The master originally was going to send the servant to prison as a consequence. After being forgiven and being spared prison, the servant still insists others pay their debts to him. He is not being forgiving in turn. Later, the Lord is "wroth" meaning either *angry* or *grieved*. He then orders the servant sent to the "jailers" to "torment him" until he pays the entire debt. (Matt. 18:28-35.)

Jesus explicitly says "this is how my Father will treat each of you" to make it clear this is an analogy to the way God the Father works with us. (Matt. 18:35.)

Thus, Jesus clearly teaches that if after you have been forgiven all your sins, if you are not forgiving in turn to others, your prior forgiveness is revoked, and you will have to pay the entire debt of your own sin in hell.

Reciprocity Principle Stated Elsewhere

This principle is not astonishing. James says "judgment [*krisis*] without mercy" will be applied to anyone who "showed no mercy." (James 2:13 KJV.)

You are offered mercy so you will fear God, not fear him less. "But you offer forgiveness that we might learn to fear you." Psalms 130:3-4 (NLT).

Jesus often stated this reciprocity principle directed at Christians. In Matthew 6:14-15 (KJV) Jesus teaches: "For if you forgive men their trespasses, your heavenly Father will also forgive you. But *if you do not forgive men* their trespasses, *neither will your father forgive you your trespasses.*"

Thereby, in Matthew 6:14-15 Jesus makes our forgiveness expressly conditional.[1] Jesus does so by assuring you that you are not forgiven your sins if you do not forgive others. Thus, there is no denying Jesus threatens God sees a Christian's actual attitude. God will withdraw forgiveness because of it. There is no covering of Jesus for a born-again Christian, as cheap grace fabulists argue, by which God cannot see we are unforgiving.

Likewise Jesus told us to pray: "Forgive us our debts, **as** we also have forgiven our debtors." (Matt. 6:12.) In other words, we ask God to forgive us to the same extent we are being forgiving to others. **Forgiveness is not one-time and permanently applied to all future conduct.**

---

1. Defenders of cheap grace incredibly claim that you are still saved if God *refuses to forgive your sins* due to your unforgiveness. Charles Stanley — the two time President of the Southern Baptists, asks a rhetorical question about Matthew 6:15: "Does this mean that my failure to forgive someone who has wronged me will deprive me of my forgiveness God purchased in my behalf through Christ's blood at Calvary?" (Stanley, *The Gift of Forgiveness* (Thomas Nelson, 1991) at 104.) Stanley goes on: "When Jesus says in this passage, 'Then your Father will not forgive you your transgressions,' He is not implying that our salvation is in jeopardy." (*Id.*, at 105). Only our fellowship supposedly will suffer. Thus, even though Jesus says God will not forgive your sins if you are unforgiving, Stanley incredibly tells you that God will save you despite not forgiving you.

Again, Jesus says in Mark 11:25-26 that our prayers for forgiveness from God are conditional on our forgiving others.

> (25) And whenever you stand praying, **be forgiving**, **if you are holding anything against** anyone, **so that** also your Father, the [One] in the heavens, **shall forgive you** of your transgressions. (26) But **if you do not forgive**, **neither will your Father**, the [One] in the heavens, forgive your transgressions. (Mark 11:25-26 ALT.)

As Coffman, the famous commentator, says about this passage: "This prerequisite of all divine forgiveness of human transgression was most **dogmatically stressed** by the Son of God."[2]

Thus, in Matthew 6:12, Matthew 6:14-15 and Mark 11:25-26, Jesus is clearly saying we can only ask God to forgive ourselves to the same extent we have been willing to forgive others. Therefore, Jesus clearly is saying we are not free to be forgiven by God if we are unwilling to forgive others. Consequently, Jesus taught our forgiveness by God *at all times* depends on our forgiving others. It does not turn upon solely some prior act of regeneration, or a one-time forgiveness received or upon faith alone.

Therefore, it follows that nothing surprising is in Jesus' parable of the Unmerciful Servant. Your initial forgiveness of a mountain of debt is revoked if you later refuse to forgive others. Jesus said the same thing in the three declarative statements quoted above.

In fact, what the parable says is the unmerciful servant did not understand the *conditionality* of his own forgiveness. As a result of unawareness of how the Master held *a condition over the forgiveness*, the servant violated the principle of

---

2. http://www.searchgodsword.org/com/bcc/view.cgi?book=mr&chapter=011 (last accessed 5/5/07).

being forgiving to others. As a result, the servant had his forgiveness *revoked.* Jesus wants us to understand precisely how this *conditionality* works: the unmerciful servant who does not forgive in turn is sent to the same prison he initially avoided, but this time to pay without mercy every last cent of his debt in torture and torment. ***If we do not forgive after being forgiven, we lose forgiveness***. We will pay forever for our sins in the prison of hell. Jesus could not be clearer.

Leading Commentators' Thoughts

Matthew Henry: God Revokes Forgiveness To Non-Christians

One of the clearest ways of knowing the straightforward reading is best is to watch how cheap grace proponents (a) admit key aspects of the parable at odds with their doctrine and (b) fall over themselves in silly ways to escape the implication at odds with their doctrine. Matthew Henry provides us such an example. Henry incongruously claims this parable proves God revokes forgiveness to non-Christians. Yet, that means Henry claims that one can receive forgiveness and not be a Christian. That idea makes absolutely no sense. Yet, it shows you how far one must go to uphold cheap grace in the face of this parable.

Let's hear what Matthew Henry — a clear upholder of the gospel of cheap grace — has to say. Henry is compelled to admit God revokes forgiveness in the circumstances that Jesus outlines and the servant ends up in hell:

> How he ***revoked his pardon and cancelled the acquittance***, so that the judgment against him revived (Matt. 18:34); He delivered him to the tormentors, till he should pay all that was due unto him..... he that would not forgive shall not be forgiven; He delivered him to the ***tormentors***...the ***executioners of God's wrath***...[and] will be their tormentors for ever. He was sent to

Bridewell [*i.e.*, a London prison] till he should pay all.

But in the next breath, Henry says this:

Our debts to God are never compounded; **either all is forgiven or all is exacted**; glorified saints in heaven **are pardoned all**, through Christ's complete satisfaction; damned sinners in hell are paying all, that is, are punished for all.

What Henry is saying (which becomes clearer later, as we will discuss), is this person whose forgiveness was revoked was never a Christian. Then, one must ask: how did he have all his sins originally forgiven? How can God completely forgive someone of all their sins, and that person not be a Christian? This is a puzzle that only gets worse as we continue to analyze Henry's comments.

Henry then makes it clear later that God would never revoke a Christian's forgiveness. This leaves us once more completely puzzled how in the parable the unmerciful servant can be forgiven all his sins initially to have them revoked later, but never have been a Christian. Listen now to how Henry BLATANTLY CONTRADICTS OUR LORD AND HIMSELF:

The danger of not forgiving; So shall your heavenly Father do. (1.) This is **not intended to teach us that God reverses his pardons to any**, but that he denies them to those that are **unqualified** for them, according to the tenour of the gospel; though having seemed to be humbled, like Ahab, they **thought themselves**, and others thought them, **in a pardoned state**, and they made bold with the comfort of it. Intimations enough we have in scripture of the forfeiture of pardons, for caution to the presumptuous; and yet **we have security enough of the continuance of them**, for comfort to those that are sincere, but timorous; that the one may fear, and the other may hope. Those that **do not forgive** their brother's trespasses, **did never truly repent of their own**, nor ever truly believe the gospel; and therefore that which is taken away is **only what they seemed to have**, Luke 8:18.[3]

Henry says here that God "does **not revoke** his **pardons** to any." But what did Henry say earlier was Jesus' point? Henry initially said the passage reveals "how he *[God] revoked his [the unmerciful servant's] pardon* and cancelled the acquittance, so that the judgment against him revived. (Matt. 18:34)." Henry is trapped in a self-contradiction.

Then Henry is telling us — and in this last quote does so several times — that Jesus must intend this unmerciful servant was *never* a Christian. How preposterous — a "servant" was forgiven all his debt of sin but we are supposed to believe he was never a Christian!

Then what is going on? Henry tells us that the servant merely *thought* he was forgiven everything. What on earth is Henry thinking! This is utterly silly. There is no wrong *assumption* by the servant about this issue as Jesus tells the parable. In fact, if the unmerciful servant had not been forgiven everything, then his master would not have been 'wroth' with him. It was only due to the injustice involved over such forgiveness which the unmerciful servant **actually received** that caused the Master to be 'wroth.' The master explains to the servant later that the servant should have forgiven as the master had forgiven the servant.

Henry is simply wrong. The master does indeed forgive the servant. In fact, every other servant of the unmerciful servant knew that to be the case as well. Based on that, they went to the Master and asked for intervention at the *unfair-*

---

3. Notice how the quoted passage does not support the assertion. Jesus' words come to mind: "Take heed therefore how ye hear: for whosoever hath, to him shall be given; and whosoever hath not, from him shall be taken away even that which he thinketh he hath." Luke 8:18 ASV.

ness of the Unmerciful Servant. 'He was forgiven everything, but he won't forgive us.' It is therefore absolute nonsense to suggest what Henry suggests that the unmerciful servant was never really forgiven, but merely *thought* he had been forgiven.

Incidentally, the highly popular author, Max Lucado, in his book *In the Grip of Grace* (Word 1996), says the same thing. He simply tries to improve upon its presentation. Lucado claims that when we are saved we are made perfect forever. This supposedly means no subsequent sin can cause imperfection and loss of salvation. For this Lucado relies primarily upon the unsourced work of the Epistle to the Hebrews 10:14. (*Id.*, at 75.)[4]

Thus, Lucado says Jesus could not possibly mean a saved servant can lose his salvation by later being unforgiving. Lucado concludes that therefore we must believe the unmerciful servant "doesn't believe" he was forgiven. (*Id.*, at 153.) And because this servant never believes it, the unmerci-

---

4. Origen in 225 A.D. said no one is sure who wrote the book of Hebrews. Tertullian in the 200s said he thought it was Barnabas. The verse at issue reads: "For by one offering he hath perfected for ever them that are sanctified." Heb 10:14 ASV. If sanctification turns on obedience, then this quote is consistent with Jesus. If sanctification does not mean obedience, and Lucado reads it right, what should we conclude? Certainly, Jesus says one who is forgiven all their sins is *not perfected forever*, and an examination is coming later for post-forgiveness sin, in particular the sin of unforgiveness. This is His clear point in the Parable of the Unmerciful Servant. What then of this passage in Hebrews which Lucado reads to the contrary? I would say that *if Jesus contradicts an unsourced letter that no one knows who wrote it*, which lacks any prophetic or apostolic credential, then *we have utterly no basis to try to conform and twist Jesus' words to fit a doctrine taught in this unsourced text*. That seems a pretty obvious conclusion. We don't presume Hebrews is authoritative, and then squash down the literal meaning of Jesus' parable to fit such an unsourced work merely because long ago for reasons no one can explain the Epistle to the Hebrews was added to the New Testament.

---

ful servant supposedly never *receives it.* (That's a non-sequitur.)[5] Hence, he was a lost person supposedly who was merely offered forgiveness, but never took it.

Unfortunately for Lucado, there is utterly nothing to support the idea that the unmerciful servant did not receive complete forgiveness. Every other servant, ***including the master,*** believes it was previously given. This is the only reason the master was wroth with the servant. The servant had failed to act forgiving after the servant was (indeed) forgiven.

Yet, both Henry and Lucado have revealed the motivation of ***reading out*** of the Parable the true meaning of Jesus. They both don't want Jesus to ever say a Christian has any responsibility to be obedient after salvation is granted. That would violate the doctrine of cheap grace. Thus, a clear parable of Jesus which refutes cheap grace doctrine simply must be crushed to serve their favorite gospel doctrine. There was no lengths to which these two gentlemen were not willing to go to defeat Jesus' obvious meaning. They twisted and tortured the Lord's word to fit their preconceived notions. Their ideas were sad efforts to defeat the Lord Jesus Christ's clear meaning and purpose. Woe be to the 'lying pen' of the scribes! (Jer. 8:6-9.)

Other Cheap Grace Explanation Of The Parable

Wrath, Torment, And Prison Do Not Reflect Hell

Other cheap grace advocates are preposterous in different ways than Henry and Lucado. Others deflect the passage by explaining the *torment* and *wrath* and *jail* in this

---

5. I can be forgiven a debt regardless of whether I believe I have been forgiven. It can be done unilaterally, and does not require bilateral acknowledgment. As long as the Master believed it was forgiven, then it was forgiven. Therefore, Lucado's logic is a *non-sequitur.*

passage are not in hell. These descriptions are supposedly merely symbols of earthly unpleasantness. They allegedly represent only earthly (temporal) punishment. The rationale for this reading is that the unmerciful servant supposedly will surely go to heaven because he received God's initial grace and forgiveness.[6]

Is this revoked forgiveness only on this earth (temporal) but we remain forgiven in God's heavenly balance sheet? Do we still go to heaven? No.

We are not merely at risk of some chastisement, yet we make it to heaven. Listen to Jesus: we have our ***initial*** forgiveness ***revoked***, which results in prison, torture, and torment to pay ourselves for our huge debt of sin, so says our Lord Jesus Christ! Indeed, in the parable, you end up going to ***the same prison that the original forgiveness spared you from.*** (Matt. 18:28-35.) Thus, the prison can only be hell.

Let's examine this with care.

Was The Prison Avoided Hell?

First, we know that hell was the original prison that the Master's forgiveness spared the servant from because it was an eternal punishment for his debt. How do we know it was eternal? All commentators point out that 10,000 talents in those days would be billions of dollars in today's world. No one servant could ever hope to pay that debt. Thus, the amount tells you the prison would be the servant's eternal home. Commenting on the implication from the amount of talents, the German evangelical minister Lisco said, "he was

---

6. Thus, Dillow gets around this parable by *ad hoc* (just so) assertions in *Reign of the Servant Kings, supra,* at 384: "this passage is ***not*** discussing *eternal* issues. Temporal issues are in view. If we fail to forgive our brother from the heart, God will bring severe discipline on us in time and withhold ***temporal*** forgiveness for fellowship in the family." Likewise, MacArthur in his *Study Bible* (1997) at 1427 makes the same *ad hoc* assertion: "This pictures severe discipline, not final condemnation." *Ad hoc* statements are illogical because they lack proof.

adjudged to an *eternal* and righteous *punishment*." (Frederick Lisco, *The Parables of Jesus* (trans. Rev. Fairbairn)(Philadelphia:1850) at 115.)

We know this prison is hell for a second reason. When the Master revokes the forgiveness, and reinstates the debt, the Master sends the servant for *torture* at the jailers' hands at that prison. We know torture and torment are associated by Jesus elsewhere with *hell*, not earthly chastisement. (Luke 16:28; Rev. 14:11, hell described as place of "torment".)

Lastly, the logic of the parable requires this prison to be hell. Once the prior forgiveness is revoked, the servant is sent to this prison. Since it originally symbolized hell, it must still be hell by the end of the parable. This matches the fact the master's revocation was in *wrath*. Also the amount at stake was enormous, and no human could possible pay the debt if re-imposed. Finally, the master's action of revoking the prior forgiveness makes hell the only logical result. Without forgiveness by God, where could we possibly be but *hell?*

In other words, trying to equate this prison to chastisement on earth does not wash. The enormous load of debt is put back on the person *first*. If mere chastisement were involved on earth, and we remain saved, Jesus would not say the huge load of the prior debt is *re-imposed*. Nor would Jesus mention *wrath, torment, prison* and *non-forgiveness* as the *final state* of the unmerciful servant. Those descriptions are all depictions clearly designed by Jesus to tell us HELL is this servant's fate. This is why this passage is a clear dilemma for cheap grace. Salvation is contingent. Here, it hangs in the balance on whether you are *later* forgiving after you are forgiven.

Furthermore, that is the meaning behind the reciprocity passages. *See*, Matthew 6:12, Matthew 6:14-15 and Mark 11:25-26, discussed *supra* at page 249 *ff*. If you fail to forgive as you were forgiven, then your sins will not be forgiven. These are *all express threats of revocation of forgiveness by God offered to you.* There is no missing therefore the point of the Parable of the Unmerciful Servant. This is an end-of-salvation loss of forgiveness. As James says—"judgment without mercy" is imposed on those who showed no mercy. (James 2:13.)

James has it right. All those who contradict Jesus and James are bringing a blatantly false gospel.

James R. Davis Gets It Right

The correct views by old German evangelicals — the mature Luther and Lisco — of this parable have ended up in the dust bin. The only modern revival of a straightforward reading comes from James R. Davis. He is one of the most prolific Christian sermon writers today.[7] Davis provides a sermon summary of the Unmerciful Servant. His conclusion is based on a straightforward application of the parable:

> This parable teaches that *forgiveness can be revoked*.
>
> James 2:13 [reads] "because judgment without mercy will be shown to anyone who has not been merciful. Mercy triumphs over judgment!" (NIV)
>
> All forgiveness is conditional; the condition in every case is *dependent upon the forgiven continuing in faith and obedience*.
>
> Jesus said, that having received grace, one must show grace or he will *fall from grace*.[8]

Davis goes on and says that clearly Jesus intends us to understand the unmerciful servant ends up in hell:

> *Final punishment* of the unmerciful and unforgiving.
>
> He forfeited his wife and children.

---

7. See http://www.focusongod.com/sermon.htm

8. James R. Davis, "The Unmerciful Servant," http://www.focusongod.com/forgive.htm (last accessed 6/9/2007).

It would have been impossible for him to repay the debt while free, even less of a chance now.

He shall have justice without mercy; **he shall always be paying; yet he shall never pay off the debt**.

That's what **hell** is about.

Accordingly, Davis is reading the elements of the parable with straight-forward spiritual meanings. There is no imagined thought-processes of the unmerciful servant. There is no speculation about a forgiveness that was not real. There is no effort to superimpose preconceived doctrines. Nor are there wild assumptions that forgiveness can be experienced by a person who remains lost (and a non-Christian) after forgiveness, as Henry claimed.

Instead, Davis summarizes Jesus just as the passage reads: the servant who is forgiven everything but later is unforgiving has that forgiveness revoked, to pay for his sin forever in torture and torment in the prison of hell.

Concluding Remarks: The Broad Way Of Cheap Grace

Charles Stanley in the next quote will invite us to go on the broad way that leads to destruction. He will directly teach contrary to Jesus' teaching in the Parable of the Unmerciful Servant. Stanley will open a seductive and easily reached doorway. This door will take us down a path which leads directly to the very pit of hell. Stanley writes:

But a man or woman who has been rescued once from a state of unforgiveness **need not worry**. For once 100% of a man's or woman's sins have been forgiven, **the potential for being unforgiven has been done away with**. The risk factor is zero. There are **no more fires** from which the believer needs to be saved.

(Stanley, *The Gift of Forgiveness* (Thomas Nelson, 1991) at 36.)(Emphasis added.)

Unfortunately for Stanley (because teachers will pay the consequence of false teaching), there is one more fire to be saved from after initial forgiveness by God. It is the pit of hell, including torment, which Jesus says we avoid by being forgiving after we are forgiven. Yet, Stanley's message is inviting you to enter into that flame by telling you to disregard what Jesus just taught you. Stanley says you are forgiven and going to heaven even if you later are not forgiving. The dangers of Stanley's way are obvious because of Stanley's frequent denials of Jesus' very blunt words.[9]

Stanley is not alone in opening up this seductive door to Christians. Stanley is joined by Matthew Henry. And by Max Lucado. These three men are all of great renown and respect. Yet, they are all false sirens calling you to the wrong path.

There is no excuse if you take the path they offer. For Jesus is ***extremely blunt*** in the Parable of the Unmerciful Servant: servants who are forgiven everything but turn to unforgiveness will suffer ***wrath***, ***torment*** and ***imprisonment forever***. Yet, Stanley, Henry and Lucado say to Christians 'don't worry'... 'be happy.' But Jesus says to His followers:

> (14) For ***if ye forgive*** men their trespasses, your heavenly Father ***will also forgive you***. (15) But ***if ye forgive not*** men their trespasses, ***neither will your Father forgive your trespasses***. (Matt. 6:14-15 ASV.)

Jesus warned us of the ways of the likes of Stanley, Henry and Lucado:

> (13) Enter ye in by the narrow gate: for wide is the gate, and ***broad is the way***, that leadeth to destruction, and many are they that enter in thereby. (14) For ***narrow is the gate***, and strait-

9. See for example Footnote 1 on page 249.

ened the way, that **leadeth unto life**, and *few are they that find it*. (15) Beware of false prophets, who come to you **in sheep's clothing**, but inwardly are ravening wolves. (Matt. 7:13-15 ASV.)

Thus, forgive others right now as Jesus directed because God's forgiveness of you depends on it.

Example of Believer Lost Due to Unforgiveness

Some deny Jesus in the Parable of the Unmerciful Servant is warning **believers**. They cannot imagine a **believer** can ever fall into **hell's grip** due to unforgiveness. Yet, we actually have an example in the Book of Acts that a believer became lost due to unforgiveness. We have proof that **a believer** (Simon Magus) fell into hell's grip specifically due to the sin of unforgiveness.

In Acts, Luke tells us about Simon, a sorcerer. He is also known in history as Simon Magus (Simon the Great One.) "Everyone, from the least to the greatest, often spoke of him as 'the Great One—the Power of God.'" (Acts 8:10.)

Meanwhile, Philip was a deacon preaching in Samaria where Simon had practiced sorcery. By Philip's preaching, many were led to Christ: "But now the people **believed** Philip's message of Good News concerning the Kingdom of God and the name of Jesus Christ. As a result, many men and women were **baptized**." (Acts 8:12.)

Philip then also preached to Simon Magus. Luke records Simon too became **a believe**r and was baptized:

> Then Simon himself **believed** and was **baptized**. He began following Philip wherever he went.... (Acts 8:13.)

Later we will learn that Simon Magus came to suffer from *bitterness*. Luke tells of Peter and John healing people. Simon offers to pay for such power, is rebuffed, and then Peter comments that Simon is in the grip of "***bitterness***" and is (thereby) held ***captive by sin.*** We read in Acts 8:18 *ff*:

(18) When Simon saw that the Spirit was given when the apostles laid their hands on people, he offered them money to buy this power. (19) "Let me have this power, too," he exclaimed, "so that when I lay my hands on people, they will receive the Holy Spirit!" (20) But Peter replied, "May your money be destroyed with you for thinking God's gift can be bought! (21) You can have no part in this [*ministry*] [Greek, *logos*], for **your heart is not right with God**. (22) Repent of your wickedness and pray to the Lord. **Perhaps He will forgive your evil thoughts**, (23) for I can see that you are full of **bitterness** [*pikria*, acridity, bitterness] and **are held captive by sin**." (24) "Pray to the Lord for me," Simon exclaimed, "that these terrible things you've said won't happen to me!" (NLT, "bitter jealousy" changed in verse 23 to "bitterness".)

The word *pikria* translated as *bitterness* is comparable to the *unforgiveness* of the unmerciful servant.

Marvin Vincent defines *pikria* or *pikros* as a "bitter frame of mind." (*Word Studies In The New Testament*.)

Simon Magus suffered from *bitterness* and as a consequence was *not right with God*. Yet, he previously believed and was baptized.

Thus, Simon Magus is a perfect example of a believer who suffered hell-gripping *unforgiveness*. Hence, the story of Simon Magus shows us how a ***believer*** can commit *unforgiveness* and the consequence: his heart became *no longer right with God*. He was no longer *just* — justified — in God's eyes. Simon Magus' later doctrine about goddess figures was blatant heresy, proving he remained lost to the end: "The ecclesiastical writers of the early Church universally represent him as the first heretic, the 'Father of Heresies.'"[10]

10."Simon Magus," http://www.newadvent.org/cathen/13797b.htm (accessed 6/10/07).

14 *Parable Of The Ten Virgins*

Synopsis

In Matthew 25:1 *et seq.*, there were ten virgins waiting for the bridegroom to come. Five still had oil for their lamps when the groom came. The other five were running out. Their lamps were beginning to go out just before the groom came. Thus, the second five were not prepared as the crucial time approached. They had the oil for a time, but then they ran out ("their lamps were going out"). So these five determined just before the groom came that they would try to get more oil. To their shock and dismay, the groom came when their oil was barren. They were in the midst of hoping to get more. The door is then shut and they are excluded from the wedding feast.

The moral of the story is it was then too late. Their *good intentions were not enough.* They postponed getting the extra oil too long. The door was shut. When the second five heard the groom arriving, they turned back from their shopping trip. These five tried knocking on the door for entry. However, they found they were excluded from the banquet. They suffer weeping and gnashing of teeth outside. Jesus then says this should teach us "you will not know the day nor hour." So the lesson is we must always be ready for our Lord's return. *We cannot rest on our good intentions to some day get the extra oil we need.* Instead, God will *absolutely* require sufficient oil burning when that time comes.

To whom is this parable directed? A Christian or a non-Christian?

Oil in Scripture typically represents the Holy Spirit.

A *virgin* in Scripture usually symbolizes a blameless person. A saved person. The term *virgin* is never used elsewhere to describe the lost. It also makes no sense to refer to a lost person as a *virgin*.

Jesus closes this parable saying we must be ready and watch for when He returns because you know not the day nor hour of His return. (Matt. 25:13.)

The Passage

Then shall the kingdom of heaven be likened unto ten **virgins**, who took their lamps, and went forth to meet the bridegroom. (2) And five of them were foolish, and five were wise. (3) For the foolish, when they took their lamps, took no oil with them: (4) but the **wise took oil in their vessels [Jars]** with their lamps. (5) Now while the **bridegroom tarried**, they all slumbered and slept. (6) But at midnight there is a cry, Behold, the bridegroom! Come ye forth to meet him. (7) Then all those virgins arose, and trimmed their lamps. (8) And the foolish said unto the wise, **Give us of your oil;** for our lamps **are going out**. (9) But the wise answered, saying, Peradventure there will not be enough for us and you: go ye rather to them that sell, and buy for yourselves. (10) And **while they went away to buy**, the bridegroom came; and **they that were ready went in with him to the marriage feast**: and **the door was shut**. (11) Afterward came also the other virgins, saying, **Lord, Lord,** open to us. (12) But he answered and said, Verily I say unto you, **I know you not**. (13) Watch therefore, for ye know not the day nor the hour. (Matt. 25:1-13 ASV.)

Cheap Grace Spin Of This Parable

The Modern Gospel of Cheap Grace responds by simply denying the Parable of the Ten Virgins has any parabolic meaning. This approach is clearly set forth in the evangelical *The Expositor's Bible Commentary* (1989):

> There is **no point** in seeing hidden meanings in the *oil*...

> The oil **cannot easily apply** to...the Holy Spirit. It is merely an element in the narrative showing that the foolish virgins were unprepared for the delay...

> The **point is not** these girls' *virginity*, but simply that ten...*maidens* [were] invited to the wedding. (Vol. VIII at 512, 513).

So the cheap grace defenders cannot permit any secondary meaning to the word *oil* or the word *virgin*. They try to recast the *virgins* as simply *maidens*. The reason is that *The Expositor's Bible Commentary* states it is aware that otherwise a condition exists upon the virgin being accepted in the kingdom: "there **must be behavior acceptable to the master, the discharge of allotted responsibilities**." *Id.*, Vol. VIII at 512. If this parable had any meaning we could uncover, the *Expositor's Bible* realizes grace would become costly. It would not be free. Thus, only if this parable is left a complete mystery can the gospel of cheap grace survive, and that is where *Expositors* dumps the parable: into the unknown.

However, if we accepted the obvious that the *virgin* represents a Christian, and the *oil* represents the Holy Spirit, we would have a dilemma. The cheap grace defender would have to accept that Jesus expressly taught that a Christian will not go to Heaven absent "behavior acceptable to the master, the discharge of allotted responsibilities." Jesus would contradict the Modern Gospel of Cheap Grace. *Rather than ever question their paradigm thinking that assumes belief alone is correct, these cheap grace defenders would prefer taking the outrageous step of saying Jesus had no parabolic intent in a parable.* This, of course, leaves the parable utterly meaningless. This is frankly shocking.

Conclusion

The solution in this parable is easy: *oil* is the Holy Spirit and the word *virgins* means cleansed and washed Christians.

The meaning is, as the *Bible's Expositor's* reluctantly admitted, that a virgin's "behavior [must be] acceptable to the master, the discharge of allotted responsibilities." *Id.*, Vol. VIII at 512. Otherwise, the virgin is denied entry and denied being known by the Master.

As Frederick G. Lisco (1791-1866), a German evangelical minister from Berlin, taught in *The Parables of Jesus* (trans.from German by Rev. Fairbairn) (Philadelphia: Daniels & Smith, 1850), the "parable of the virgins mainly teaches...there is also necessary a kind of ***working***...because it is only through such ***an exercise of principle in the daily life***, that the disposition [of heart] can be preserved and strengthened, which otherwise would languish and die." *Id.* at 178. He calls this "working" the "***works of faith***."

Luther similarly said in *Miscellaneous Sermons* 18:34 that these (pure) virgins are "fools" because they "hear the gospel, but ***do not follow it***." Luther adds this applies to those in ministry who "possess the highest gifts of God." (Quoted in Lisco, *supra*, at 184.)

Hence, faith with a good beginning (*virginity*) that later runs out of works (*behavior acceptable to the master — the discharge of allotted responsibilities*) does not save. You will be spewed out of Jesus' mouth. Whether we prefer calling these works by the name of *works of faith* or simply *works*, it adds up to the same principle. Following Christ's principles are necessary for salvation. Works of obeying Jesus. Thus, Christ again has falsified the principles of the modern gospel of cheap grace. His is one of costly grace.

15 *The Prodigal Or Lost Son*

The Role Of Repentance-From-Sin

In Luke 15:17-24, we find the Parable of the Prodigal Son. Perhaps it should be called the Parable of the Lost Son. Jesus explains later that this son was "lost" but then found. (Luke 15:24.)

This parable is about being spiritually *dead* and *lost, coming to your senses, repenting, turning around* and *going home to your father.* The Father-God in the Parable says the son was dead but is now *alive again.* Thus, this parable also is a message about the steps to be born again.

We are all familiar with the plot. The younger son wasted his inheritance in riotous living (vv 13,30). He came to be in need and "came to himself" (vv 14-17). He first verbalized repentance and then took all the steps of repentance. Jesus explained:

- The Prodigal acknowledged his error: "I have sinned." (v18).
- The Prodigal no longer believed himself worthy to be called a son (v19).
- The Prodigal decided to go back to the father (vv 18,19). He thereby left the practice of sin (vv 20,21). This decision is a turning around in repentance. (*Cf.* vv 7,10)
- The Prodigal confesses his sin to the father (vv 20,21).
- The Prodigal seeks to appease his father by offering to be just a servant of the father (vv 19,21).

The Father is overjoyed when the son comes home. (vv 20,22-24.) This parallels Jesus statement that there is joy in heaven among the angels when a sinner "repents" (vv 7,10).

This is all about *repentance-from-sin and turning around in obedience and reconciliation.* It involves (1) a decision to turn from sin; (2) taking actual steps to turn around; and (3) an effort to appease his father by an offer of servanthood (reconciliation). This is about what it means to be born again. *Faith is never mentioned!*

Modern Gospel On The Ropes Again

The Parable of the Prodigal Son is extremely damaging to the Modern Gospel of Cheap Grace. Why? Because this parable explains what Jesus meant in John 3:3 by being born again:

> Jesus answered and said unto him, Verily, verily, I say unto thee, Except one be **born anew**, he cannot see the kingdom of God. (John 3:3.)

This passage is typically lifted out of context of John chapter three. This way no one ever sees that repentance (from sin) and obedience is part of the steps to be born again.

For in the nearby verse of John 3:36, we hear standards comparable to those in the Parable of the Prodigal as a means of being born again. John 3:36 says:

> He that continues to obey unto the Son keeps having eternal life, but he that keeps on **disobeying** the Son shall not see life, but the wrath of God continues to remain on him. (John 3:36.)[1]

---

1. This verse has been distorted by those who seek to conform Jesus to the Modern Gospel of Cheap Grace. Thus, even though the word *apeitho* has only one meaning in ancient Greek, *to disobey*, they freely change God's words to say 'not believe' in John 3:36. See page 448 *ff.*

We see in 3:36 that it is the same message as in the Parable of the Prodigal Son. Jesus says the son was dead, *repented from sin*, turned around in *obedience*, and became alive again. He was lost but now is found. Jesus in John 3:3 says unless one is born again, one cannot enter heaven. God in John 3:36 says that obeying unto Jesus, which should give life, is *cancelled* out when we keep on disobeying Him, in which case we will not see life but rather God's wrath remains on us. The Parable of the Prodigal Son, John 3:3 and 3:36 are the same message about repentance-from-sin, obedience, and being born again.

When Does The Father See The Son?

The Cheap Grace proponents have various strategies to circumvent Jesus' meaning in this parable. Some wed to cheap grace try to re-envision the conditions of salvation in the Parable of the Prodigal Son. They want to imagine the Father sees the son *before the son repents or turns around.* Thus, they can still believe salvation occurs totally by mercy of the father without the need to repent from sin or turn from sin to God. For them, the father's comment that the son is alive again and thus saved is *imagined* to take place *before* the son repents from sin or actually turned around and headed home. (In this way, they can insist salvation is by God's mercy at a point where our faith precedes repentance from sin or obedience.)

However, in the story, the son has already repented in his heart about his sin and turned around to return home *when the father first sees him*. Then, and *only then*, does Jesus say the father sees the son afar off and comes running to the son. We cannot change the order of events to satisfy our salvation doctrine. This is the first key part of the actual passage:

> (17) But when he came to himself he said, How many hired servants of my father's have bread

enough and to spare, and I perish here with hunger! (18) I will arise and go to my father, and will say unto him, Father, **I have sinned against heaven, and in thy sight:** (19) I am no more worthy to be called your son: make me as one of thy hired servants. (20) And **he arose, and came to his father.** But while he was **yet afar off**, his father saw him, and was moved with compassion, and ran, and fell on his neck, and kissed him. (21) And the son said unto him, Father, I have sinned against heaven, and in thy sight: I am no more worthy to be called thy son. (Luke 15:17-21, ASV.)

If Jesus wanted us to believe that the father forgave before the son repented from sin or turned around, Jesus used all the wrong words to do so. To convey that message, all Jesus had to do was cut out verses 18 and 19. Then the returning to the father would not necessarily imply any change of heart or direction *preceded* the prodigal's return to his father. Then the father running to the son would be without *repentance* or any period of *obedience* by the once lost son.

Commentaries Which Obscure Jesus' "Alive Again" Terminology

Jesus in the second part of the Parable of the Prodigal is going to identify a lost condition that is equal to spiritual death, and a reversal that is called being "alive again." Jesus says:

> And the son said unto him, Father, I have sinned against heaven, and in thy sight, and am no more worthy to be called thy son. (22) But the father said to his servants, Bring forth the best robe, and put it on him; and put a ring on his hand, and shoes on his feet: (23) And bring hither the fatted calf, and kill it; and let us eat, and be merry: (24) For this **my son was dead, and is alive again; he was lost, and is**

> *found*. And they began to be merry. (Luke
> 15:21-24 KJV.)

Clarke's Commentary

Clarke recognizes that the boy's "coming to his
senses" in verse 17 is repentance. He explains that "repentance is represented [in the Bible] as a restoration to sound
sense." It is quite more than that, but Clarke is identifying
Jesus' symbolism here correctly as meaning *repentance*.

However, in his commentary, Clarke totally ignores
the significant fact the father says this son was "dead, but is
alive again." (Luke 15:24.)

For Clarke, this passage has nothing to say about what
it means to be "born again." It says nothing about having
been a true son, sinning, becoming dead, and then coming
'alive again.' Thus, the most profound part of the passage is
ignored. The reason is obvious: Jesus makes the born-again
experience contingent on repentance-from-sin and turn-
around to God. The son's being "born again" is not linked by
Clarke to either contingency because that would contradict
the Modern Gospel of Cheap Grace. This claims faith alone is
the sole contingency that would make a son "alive again."
That is, born again. But Jesus says *no*. Jesus says instead that
it is repentance from sin and turning to God in obedience that
makes one "alive again" — born again.

Barnes' Commentary Similarly Downplays 'Alive Again'

Barnes also must realize verse 24 ("was dead but is
alive again") is the problem verse for the Modern Gospel of
Cheap Grace. Jesus would be saying repentance from sin and
turning around to God are the preconditions for being born
again.

Thus, Barnes totally downplays the fact the boy is
"alive again." Barnes tries to focus on the word *dead* instead.
He says this can mean either the father "supposed" the son
was dead or the son was in fact "dead to virtue." The reason

Barnes makes these claims is that this young boy never *stopped* being the son of the father. If one believes in the doctrine of eternal security, then how can a true son by sin become dead? Thus, Barnes suggests the father merely *supposed* the son was dead. However, that cannot be true. Jesus says the father directly affirms the son had been *dead* and is now *alive again.*

Barnes realizes this and provides a second alternative escape to salvage the Modern Gospel of Cheap Grace. Barnes claims *dead* means *dead to virtue.* Barnes makes this suggestion because if you believe in Calvinism and eternal security, we are dead in sins, and we can do nothing absent the regeneration *first* by God. Yet, as Jesus tells this parable, the *dead* son in fact *comes to his senses.* Hence, contrary to many commentators, Jesus says spiritual deadness does not mean one is incapable of 'coming to your senses' and repenting in one's mind and turning around.

Consequently, to eliminate the issue, Barnes prefers to see the son as always remaining spiritually alive but he is *dead to virtue.* Thus, the death is supposedly not a complete spiritual death, and the born again experience Jesus describes is not the true born again experience which Jesus describes in John chapter three.

But Barnes' notion misses Jesus' point. The son is "alive again" which means the son is *born again.* The son has had a spiritual rebirth. The father says the son was both "dead" and "lost" prior to becoming "alive again." Thus, the Prodigal must have been spiritually dead, yet capable of repentance from sin and turning around. In fact, this is what Jesus is **encouraging** anyone dead in trespasses and sins **to believe** and **act upon**. It is never too late. You are never too spiritually dead to "come to your senses." The very hopeful point of Jesus' message must be obscured by the proponents of the Modern Gospel of Cheap Grace. They must slavishly protect cheap grace at the expense of the true gospel from the one they call Lord.

Thus, rather than give encouragement to us to turn around while dead in trespasses and sins by "coming to our senses," the modern gospel fabulists typically discourage any such notion. You are so dead that repentance from sin and turning are only possible if God *miraculously* quickens you first. So they tell you to wait on the movement of the Spirit. Any other kind of repentance (they will tell you) is *fleshly* repentance, generated in your own heart's futile attempt to be right with God.

This effort to obscure Jesus' meaning (and encouragement) is even more blatant when Barnes downplays the "alive again" language. Barnes says:

> Hence, to be **restored to "virtue"** is said to be **restored again to life**, Rom 6:13; Rev 3:1; Eph2:1. It is probable that this latter is the meaning here.

Barnes wants us to think Jesus' words 'alive again' merely mean 'restored to virtue,' rather than 'restored to spiritual life.' So you see, Barnes has said *death* does not really mean *spiritual death*, and *life* does not really mean *spiritual life*. Instead, supposedly, *death* means *spiritual defect in virtue* and *life* means *living without such defects in virtue*.

Why all this torture of Jesus' words? Barnes' interpretation is impossible. Jesus says the father says the son was dead and this meant he was **lost.** This is then contrasted with becoming alive again (born again). This necessarily implies the dead son became saved by means of repentance, turning around from sin and heading home. Hence, death meant spiritual death, and life meant spiritual life. Let's read Luke 15:32 again which dispels Barnes' suggestion:

> But it was meet to make merry and be glad: for this thy brother was **dead,** and is **alive again**; and was **lost**, and is found. (ASV)

This passage is thus not merely about finding virtue and being 'restored to (a virtuous) life.' It is about someone who was *lost* and *dead* because they were engaged in riotous living with prostitutes. Now they are alive again. They are found. They are saved. They are born again (alive again). Now we know the true meaning in John 3:3 regarding what it means to be *born again*. It depends on taking the same steps as the Prodigal Son took: repentance and turning in obedience back to the Father.

Conclusion

Let's now chart out the meaning of the Parable of the Prodigal Son. When one lets Jesus' words explain Jesus' words, His message is clear. Salvation is the issue. The son was *lost* but now is *found*. He is born again. Why? The only changes were he *came to his senses, repented of sin, turned around to his father* and *offered reconciliation.* However,

TABLE 1. Parable Of The Prodigal Son

Terms	Meaning
"came to his senses"	Repentance from sin.
"dead"	*"Lost"* (Luke 15:32)
"alive again"	"Found" (**saved**) (Luke 15:32) and hence 'born again'

these steps in being born again are not taught in the Modern Gospel of Cheap Grace. Rather, that gospel insists one goes from *lost* to *found* without any repentance from sin or turning in obedience toward God. (See pages 269-270,483-485.) You are supposedly saved by belief alone. However, Jesus contradicts that — instead sticking a dual condition of repentance and obedient submission into the crevice that separates man from God's salvation. These actions must occur for reconciliation to take place.[2]

Hence, when Jesus elsewhere tells us that unless a man is "born again" he shall not "enter the kingdom of heaven" (John 3:3), we know the steps outlined in the Parable of the Prodigal Son are ignored at our peril.

However, look at what the commentators wed to the Modern Gospel of Cheap Grace (like Barnes) do! They draw you away from realizing the Prodigal was lost. They make you think the Prodigal's being *dead* was less than a *spiritual death*. Then they try to make you think the *spiritual birth* was less than a *spiritual rebirth*. The Prodigal's "alive again" experience was supposedly simply a minor correction to some few virtues that were missing. Frankly, it is frightening to see how little compunction the commentators of greatest repute have when Jesus' words are at odds with the Modern Gospel of Cheap Grace which they prefer.

Thus, it turns out that Jesus' gospel is not all too surprising. What is really shocking is the *extraordinary efforts* to rationalize rejection of Jesus' Gospel from those claiming He is their Lord.

---

2. In a pro-faith alone commentary by Godet, one of the more amazingly bizarre arguments is advanced to deflect this parable. Godet first claims the conversion of the son represents not only repentance, but also "faith," citing Luke 15:18-20a. (Frédéric Louis Godet, *A Commentary on the Gospel of St. Luke* (trans. Edward William Shalders, M. D.) (I. K. Funk & Co., 1881) at 377.) Repentance is then forgotten, and this parable is supposedly all about *faith*. Yet, *faith* is actually never mentioned and entirely absent in this parable. Verses 18-20a do not deal with faith. In them, the son simply verbalizes repentance and then returns home. This clearly represents not only repentance but also obedient submission. There is no mention or suggestion of *faith*. Then Godet repeats again this false claim that reconciliation is *faith*. This time, however, Godet realizes that he has a dilemma. What he is calling faith is in the story really an action of reconciliation. Thus, rather than accept this as proving the parable is not about *faith*, Godet changes *faith* into an *act*: "Faith is not a thought or desire; it is **an act** which brings two living beings into personal contact." *Id.*, at 378. Then, later, this same author bizarrely says "it is **easy to understand**" how "from this parable St. Paul might have **extracted the doctrine of justification by faith**." *Id.* at 381. No! It is the opposite. The puzzle is how anyone could extract justification by faith from a parable that (a) never mentions *faith*; and (b) emphasizes *works of repentance* from sin, including turning around and heading back to the father, which makes one go from being "lost" to being "alive again."

Charles Finney

1792-1875

Leader of Second Great Awakening: Charles Finney Endorses JWOS

"As soon as I learned what were the unambiguous teachings of the [Westminster] Confession of faith upon these points, ... I repudiated and exposed them. Wherever I found that any class of persons were hidden behind these dogmas, I did not hesitate to demolish them, to the best of my ability. When I came to the [Westminster] Confession of faith and saw the passages that were quoted to sustain these peculiar positions, I was absolutely ashamed of it....[When Gale taught them], I raised objections....What did he mean by faith? Was it merely an intellectual state? Was it merely conviction, or persuasion, that the things in the gospel were true?... Brother Gale had imbibed a set of opinions, both theological and practical, that were a strait jacket to him....A nature sinful in itself, a total inability to accept Christ and obey God...and all the kindred and resultant dogmas of that peculiar school, have been the stumbling block of believers and the ruin of sinners.... *Perseverance in faith and obedience ... is ... an unalterable condition of present pardon of past sin, and of present acceptance with God.* The penitent soul *remains justified no longer than his full-hearted consecration continues.* If he falls from his first love into the spirit of self-pleasing, he falls again into bondage to sin..., is condemned, and *must repent* and do his 'first work,' must turn to Christ and renew his faith and love, *as a condition of his salvation.*" Charles Finney, ordained Presbyterian minister explaining why he rejected tenets of Presbyterian church, and became a famous revivalist. *Memoirs* (1876) at 52-53,59-60. See also *Systematic Theology* (2003 reprint) at 739. With this gospel, Finney led 500,000 people to accept Jesus as Lord and Savior.

16 *The Parable Of The Unprofitable Servant*

Introduction

The Parable Itself

Jesus teaches:

> For the kingdom of heaven is as a man travel-
> ling into a far country, who called his own ser-
> vants, and delivered unto them his goods. (15)
> And unto one he gave *five talents*, to another
> *two*, and to another *one*; to every man accord-
> ing to his several ability; and straightway took
> his journey. (16) Then he that had received the
> five talents went and traded with the same, and
> made them other five talents. (17) And likewise
> he that had received two, he also gained other
> two. (18) But he that had received *one* went
> and **digged in the earth, and hid his lord's
> money**. (19) After a long time the lord of those
> servants cometh, and **reckoneth with them**.
> (20) And so he that had received five talents
> came and brought other five talents, saying,
> Lord, thou deliveredst unto me five talents:
> behold, I have gained beside them five talents
> more. (21) His lord said unto him, Well done,
> thou good and faithful servant: thou hast been
> faithful over a few things, I will make thee ruler
> over many things: enter thou into the joy of thy
> lord. (22) He also that had received two talents
> came and said, Lord, thou deliveredst unto me
> two talents: behold, I have gained two other tal-
> ents beside them. (23) His lord said unto him,
> Well done, good and faithful servant; thou hast

been faithful over a few things, I will make thee ruler over many things: enter thou into the joy of thy lord. (24) Then he which **had received the one talent came** and said, Lord, I knew thee that thou art an hard man, reaping where thou hast not sown, and gathering where thou hast not strawed [sown]: (25) And *I was afraid*, and went and hid thy talent in the earth: lo, there thou hast that is thine. (26) His lord answered and said unto him, *Thou wicked and slothful servant*, thou knewest that I reap where I sowed not, and gather where I have not strawed: (27) *Thou oughtest therefore to have put my money to the exchangers, and then at my coming I should have received mine own with interest*. (28) Take therefore the talent from him, and give it unto him which hath ten talents. (29) For unto every one that hath shall be given, and he shall have abundance: but from him that hath not shall be taken away even that which he hath. (30) And *cast ye the unprofitable servant into outer darkness: there shall be weeping and gnashing of teeth.* (Matt. 25:14-30 KJV.)

A More Accurate Name

This parable could also be called the ***Parable of the Servant who Produces Nothing***. Non-productivity is the main point and the focus of Jesus' most important warning. However, sometimes we call it the Parable of the Talents. A better label, and which is used sometimes, is the *Parable of the Unprofitable Servant*. For this discussion, we will use that familiar label so as to keep the point of the parable in sharper focus. The term *talents* in the normal name "Parable of the Talents" has taken an unwarranted meaning that this is a parable of varying *rewards* based on varying *talents* or *abilities*. Such a notion is not the warning thrust of the parable. Thus, it is preferable to call this the Parable of the Unprofitable Servant. This way we will keep the focus on the warning issue in the parable: it is the consequence of failing to produce anything with what riches the master gave the servant.

Synopsis Of Parable Of The Unprofitable Servant

In this parable, Jesus talks about three servants who were each given some gold (or talents). Two invested wisely. One not at all. The latter had nothing to show for having been given the gold.

Was the unwise servant merely punished, but made it to heaven? No. In Matt. 25:14 *et seq.*, Jesus says "now throw this useless [*unprofitable* KJV] servant into outer darkness where there will be weeping and gnashing of teeth." (Matt. 25:30 NIV.) Jesus in Matthew 13:42, 49-50 identifies this place of "weeping and gnashing" as the "fiery furnace" where the wicked are sent by the angels in the day of judgment.

This parable is straight-forward and easy to dissect. The three servants are said to be three servants of the Lord. One produces nothing with the treasures entrusted to him. Two produce varying amounts and receive varying rewards. The one who produces nothing receives no reward and is sent to hell.

Hence the warning of the story is very clear. A servant of the Lord Jesus must produce some fruit or otherwise he will be sent to hell. It is exactly as Jesus teaches in Matthew 7:19: "Every tree that bringeth not forth good fruit is hewn down, and cast into the fire." As Chrysostum (349-407 A.D.) explained, it is not only sinners who go to "outer darkness, but he also who does no good." (Wordsworth:134.)

Finally, this parable also teaches that all Christians who are productive (in the way Jesus means) are rewarded in correspondence with the fruit they produced.

This is probably the easiest of all the parables to dissect. Yet, because it so clearly contradicts the Modern Gospel of Cheap Grace, it suffers twists and turns by commentators eager to bury its meaning. Let's now turn to see how cheap grace teachers interpret this parable so as to solve their dilemma that the Lord clearly refutes their faith-alone gospel.

What is Outer Darkness Where There Is Weeping and Gnashing Of Teeth?

Advocates of the Modern Gospel of Cheap Grace (*e.g.*, Dillow and Charles Stanley) insist the place this servant is thrown outside in darkness is *in heaven*, not hell. This servant thrown in this place of "weeping and gnashing" supposedly remains saved. Jesus allegedly means this servant suffers merely a loss of rewards by being thrown outside.

For example, Charles Stanley insists that this "weeping and gnashing" which is "outside in darkness" is in *heaven*, not hell: "It certainly *does not mean hell*...It clearly refers to being thrown *outside* a building into the *dark*. There is no mention of pain, fire or worms."[1]

In arriving at such a conclusion, Stanley never discusses the Master's words in Matthew 13:42 and 13:49-50. In them, Jesus twice calls the place of "weeping and gnashing" the "fiery furnace." First, Jesus says in 13:42 this place is the "*fiery furnace*" where the angels at the time of final judgment throw those who were "ensnared" in sin. Lastly, Jesus says in 13:49-50 that this place of "weeping and gnashing" is the "fiery furnace" where the wicked are sent after separating them from the righteous.[2] How can this place of weeping and gnashing be anything but a lost condition?

---

1. Charles Stanley, *Eternal Security: Can You Be Sure*, *supra*, at 125.
2. Stanley's claim also disregards God's consistent message that in heaven there is "no more sorrow, nor crying." (Rev. 21:4; *see also*, Isaiah 25:8 "God will wipe away tears from all faces"; Rev. 7:17.)

Because these two 'furnace' passages share implications undermining Stanley's doctrine and he cannot explain them away, he was compelled by his outlook to ignore them.

For had Stanley discussed these verses, Jesus would refute faith alone. Rather than lose the Cheap Grace Gospel, Stanley preferred abandoning Jesus' intention behind His warnings. Thus, Jesus and His meaning are sacrificed to the pyre of the Modern Gospel of Cheap Grace. As Bonhoeffer said of the modern cheap grace gospel: "Jesus is misunderstood anew, and again and again *put to death*." (Bonhoeffer, *Christ the Center* (1960) at 39.)

Can this place of darkness outside really be in heaven? Stanley insists it can. He explains:

> To be in the **outer darkness** is to be in the kingdom of God but outside the circle of men and women whose faithfulness on this earth earned them a special rank or position of authority. (Stanley, *Eternal Security, supra*, at 126.)

But Stanley is again contradicting Scripture in his desperate attempt to hold onto the faith-alone gospel which this simple parable refutes.

For example, in Revelation 22:23, we hear of the New Jerusalem that needs no sun because the "glory" of God and Jesus are the "light" thereof. The New Jerusalem, importantly, is the picture of the kingdom of God. This is thus the same as heaven. Then Revelation says there shall be no "night" there. And there "shall no wise enter into it...[except] they who are written in the lamb's book of life." (Rev. 21:27.) This thus says only those written in the book of life can enter this city. And there is no darkness there. Stanley fails on his claim that there is darkness anywhere in heaven. God says there is no night there. Instead, God's glory provides light throughout.

What about this place *outside*? Can this really mean inside heaven but outside a ruling group of authority as Stanley claims? Clearly the answer is *no*.

Revelation 22:15 says "outside" are the "dogs, and sorcerers, and whoremongers, and murderers, and idolaters, and whosoever loveth and maketh a lie."

These outside are almost verbatim listed again in Revelation 21:8. Listen to their fate:

> But the fearful [cowards] and unbelieving, and the abominable, and murderers, and whoremongers, and sorcerers, and idolators, and all liars, **shall have their part in the lake which burneth with fire** and brimstone, which is the second death. (Rev. 21:8 KJV.)

Likewise Revelation 20:15 says: "And whosoever was not found written in the book of life was cast into the **lake of fire**." Then Revelation 20:10 says the lake of fire is a place of torment for Satan: "And the devil... was cast into the lake of fire...and shall be tormented day and night for ever and ever." (KJV).

Lake of Fire

Thus, those outside in darkness in Revelation are going to hell's fire.

Furthermore, what could be more clear than Matthew 8:12 that outside heaven are those who suffer weeping and gnashing?

> And I say unto you, that many shall come from the east and the west, and shall sit down with Abraham, and Isaac, and Jacob, **in the kingdom of heaven**: (12) but the **sons of the kingdom shall be cast forth into the outer darkness**: there shall be the weeping and the gnashing of teeth. (Matt. 8:11-12 ASV.)[3]

---

3. The parallel in Luke 13:28 (NKJV) is slightly different: "There will be weeping and gnashing of teeth, when you see Abraham and Isaac and Jacob and all the prophets **in the kingdom of God**, and yourselves **thrust out**."

Those "sons of the kingdom" who have fallen into sin are thus thrown into "outer darkness" which is clearly outside the "kingdom of heaven."[4]

Thus, Jesus equates being thrust out of the kingdom of heaven with a place of weeping and gnashing of teeth in Matthew 8:11-12. In the kingdom of heaven is Abraham and all the prophets. Therefore, the kingdom of *heaven* must mean *heaven.* It is inescapable that the place of weeping and gnashing must be *outside* heaven. It can only be a place for those destined to hell.

Hence, honest evangelical scholars admit Jesus' point. For example, Russell in his dictionary writes: "The Greek noun [for gnashing] occurs repeatedly in the sayings of Jesus...concerning the remorseful gnashing of teeth by those *excluded from heaven.*"[5]

---

4. Notice that these "sons of the kingdom" are in "heaven" when thrown "outside" heaven. Jesus says they are "thrust out" of the "kingdom of heaven." (*Cf.* Luke 13:28 in footnote 3 *supra.*) Jesus is thus rejecting eternal security. This is clear here as well as by comparing this to the wedding guest who is thrust outside of heaven in the Parable of the Wedding Garment. (Matt. 22:1-13.) Jesus calls the wedding guest a "friend" who has accepted the invitation, and makes it all the way to the banquet. Yet, just before the celebration begins, it is noted the "friend" is lacking a "proper robe." Jesus says this "friend" is then thrust outside in darkness, thus excluded from what obviously is heaven. This "friend" who accepted the invitation but otherwise made no preparations to be ready was to be torn apart in a place where there is weeping and gnashing of teeth. Thus, sons of the kingdom in Matthew 8:11-12 can mean Christians because Christians can be removed from the banquet-exam inside heaven. This supports regarding "sons of the kingdom" in Matthew 8:12 as a stock phrase of Jesus to mean saved individuals, including Christians. Further proof is that the "good seed" in the Parable of the Tares in Matthew 13:38 are likewise "sons of the kingdom." At the judgment, in that parable, those who are such sons (and have obviously not fallen into condemnation) are preserved in the final judgment. Now note once more that in Matthew 8:12, these same "sons of the kingdom" (hoi huioi tes basileias) are thrown into this "outer darkness" because they have fallen into sin or teach lawless doctrine. Thus, repeatedly Jesus describes "sons of the kingdom" as including believers who are thrust outside of heaven for various faults.

How do Stanley and Dillow in *Reign of the Servant Kings* deal with these countervailing passages in Matthew 8:11-12, and 13:42, 49-50? They ignore them. They never discuss them. In other words, the Modern Gospel of Cheap Grace simply asserts a place of darkness outside where there is weeping and gnashing of teeth is in heaven. The only justification of this is that otherwise Jesus refutes the Modern Gospel of Cheap Grace. These two authors love this other gospel even though it is contrary to what Jesus taught. Hence, Jesus' true gospel is ignored. No contrary evidence is admissible to test the Gospel of Cheap Grace. Why? Because the Modern Gospel of Cheap Grace knows it has no substance if it were properly held up to Jesus' words. Cheap grace proponents prefer a fable to the harsh reality of Jesus' words.

"Weeping & Gnashing"
Sistine Chapel

Is this person in Heaven or Hell?

Isaiah 25:8 says in heaven: "God will wipe all tears from all faces."

Rev. 21:4 says in the New Jerusalem: "No more sorrow or crying there."

Furnace of Fire

But Stanley & Dillow insist that "weeping and gnashing of teeth" is in heaven rather than hell! Yet Jesus says NO! When the Son of Man returns, His angels will gather out of earth all who "commit lawlessness" and:

"will throw them into a furnace of fire; in that place there will be *weeping* and *gnashing* of teeth." (Jesus, Matt. 13:42.)

---

5. Emmet Russell, "Gnash, Gnashing of Teeth," *The Zondervan Pictorial Encyclopedia of the Bible* (Ed. Merrill C. Tenney) (Grand Rapids: Zondervan Publishing House, 1975) at 2:735.

To be absolutely precise in our analysis, let's create a table summary of the verses at odds with Stanley and Dillow to see what they both have overlooked:

TABLE 1. Place Outside In Darkness Where There Is Weeping And Gnashing Of Teeth: Is This Heaven Or Hell?

	"Outside"	"Darkness"	"Weeping & Gnashing"
Jesus says it means:	**Hell** — "outside" are cowards and unbelievers who are to be thrown in "lake of fire." (Rev. 22:15; 21:8; 20:15)	**Hell** — in New Jerusalem, glory of God always present, giving "light," and no more "night." (Rev. 22:23, 21:27.)	**Hell** — "fiery furnace" is place of "weeping and gnashing" that angels throw the 'ensnared' at end of time. (Matt. 13:42, 49,50.) Those "thrust out" into "outer darkness" from the "kingdom of heaven" will suffer "weeping and gnashing." (Matt. 8:11-12; Luke 13:28).
Stanley-Dillow assert this is:	**Heaven**	**Heaven**	**Heaven**

Why is such a preposterous notion put forth by Stanley and Dillow that weeping and gnashing outside in darkness signifies heaven? Because in seven of the nine parables where Jesus warns of weeping and gnashing of teeth, Jesus is clearly warning Christians. Not hypocrites. Not mere professors. But real servants. Real Christians. Among the seven are this Parable of the Unprofitable Servant. The warning here is to a *servant*. Other parables are just as clear — sometimes even clearer — that Christians are in view in these weeping and gnashing parables.

Numerous Other Weeping & Gnashing Parables Aimed At Christians

Dillow in *Reign of the Servant Kings* acknowledges that many parables of Jesus which discuss "weeping and gnashing of teeth" are aimed at Christians. These parables typically threaten such grief on servants of His in the parables who are to be thrown "outside in darkness." These servants' errors were:

- not having interest on their talents given by God. Matt. 25:14 *ff.*
- abusing fellow Christian servants. Luke 12:41 *ff.* Matt.24:48 *ff.*
- failing to have charity to the brothers. Matt. 25:31 *ff.*
- being once virgins who later let their oil burn out. Matt. 25:1 *ff.*
- being once a "friend" who accepts the "call" and is even seated at the great banquet but when the time for examination comes they lack a "proper robe." Matt. 22:2 *ff.*

Stanley and Dillow both confess it is too obvious to deny that the above weeping and gnashing parables are Jesus' threat to true Christians of this place for misbehavior.

The problem that Stanley and Dillow are hoping to solve by insisting this place is in heaven is obvious. Otherwise, Jesus is warning Christians **hell** (weeping and gnashing outside in darkness) if they have the failings of the "unprofitable servant. If they are an "abusive servant." If they are "goats" who call Him Lord but do not provide food, clothing and water to the brethren.

Why did Dillow and Stanley make this admission? Because of the overwhelming weight of textual evidence that the weeping and gnashing parables are aimed at true Christians. This is what forced Dillow and Stanley into the above preposterous assertion to save the gospel of cheap grace. They both amazingly insist a place outside in darkness where there is weeping and gnashing is *inside* heaven. Oh my! What man cannot make himself believe when he will not listen to *all* of Jesus' words!

MacArthur Tries To Say The Servant Never Was A Christian Servant

Apparently lacking familiarity with this overwhelming weight of evidence that these weeping and gnashing parables apply to true Christians, MacArthur is going to insist this *servant* in the Parable of the Unprofitable Servant was *never* a true Christian. Why? Because MacArthur admits this servant was lost in the end. The weeping and gnashing outside in darkness is clearly a reference to judgment in hell. However, why should his fate in hell tell us this person was never a Christian? Because MacArthur knows the Modern Gospel of Cheap Grace says a Christian can never become lost as long as they once truly believed. In other words, faith alone doctrine is used to block any meaning from Jesus that is to the contrary!

However, Jesus' Gospel says that a servant who does not produce on God's gold talents bestowed graciously on him is sent to hell and those servants who do produce are given proportionate rewards. ***Jesus must be wanting to warn servants to be productive in some manner.*** There is no textual reason to say the unproductive servant is a nonbeliever while the other two are believers. It is only circular presupposition in the validity of the Modern Gospel of Cheap Grace that is used to force such a reading on the text.

Let's hear MacArthur's argument to see this exposed.

John MacArthur in his *Study Bible* (1997) attempts to spin this passage in a way that does not conflict with the Modern Cheap Grace Gospel. He says that the three servants are "professing" believers. (Page 1441). That is not accurate. There is a purpose in MacArthur's misdescription. MacArthur wants to say later that the unproductive servant was *never* a true believer but was merely professing to believe. Therefore, MacArthur is planting a false seed that we should think this 'servant' was always lost. However, Jesus gave all three the same designation: ***servants.***

Next, MacArthur concedes that the master in the story is Christ.

With these premises set forth, let's return to the *servant* versus *professing believer* issue. Why would Jesus call someone a servant who professes to believe but is not a believer? Wouldn't Jesus call him an *unbeliever*? This way we would know the unbelief is why he was unproductive. By calling him a servant, Jesus is making us think that he was **not true to his calling as a servant** rather that he was **not true to his belief** as a Christian. Jesus used the wrong terminology if he had the meaning that MacArthur is obviously trying to draw us to accept.

Next, MacArthur says the parable is about "faithfulness," and even says the "parable suggests that all who are faithful will be fruitful to some degree." This is a non-sequitur. This conclusion relies upon concluding the first servant is not a true believer. Yet, MacArthur never has proven that is textually possible.

Meanwhile, this claim that the parable is about *faithfulness* allows MacArthur to perform another slight of hand. Having interjected the word 'faithful' in his spin, which at first he uses to mean *loyal,* MacArthur next switches this so it means 'full of *faith.*' MacArthur concludes: "the fruitless man is unmasked as a hypocrite and utterly destroyed." MacArthur had previously laid this unsubstantiated groundwork to suggest Jesus was saying the unprofitable servant lacked true faith. With that foundation, MacArthur now is deducing **a fruitless person necessarily means he has been exposed as a non-believer.** A hypocrite. He supposedly merely professed faith, but he was not faithful in the sense of not being full of faith. Hence, MacArthur wants us to think the servant was never a believer.

Do Christians really not recognize what MacArthur has done? Our long conditioning to the Modern Gospel of Cheap Grace just accepts this. We never critically examine arguments. This is because we too are hunting for support for our preconceived views of faith alone. We want the easy way. Independent critical thought which questions that assumption is dissuaded. If the result of reading Jesus' words literally defects from the cheap grace gospel, the reaction is not curiosity and self-examination. Instead, it results in twisting and turning Jesus' words. What MacArthur has done is itself shocking: he has stripped the passage of its true meaning and *given us a substitute meaning that satisfies presuppositions about the Modern Gospel of Cheap Grace*. It is then seen as compatible with faith alone — the very doctrine the Parable of the Unprofitable Servant directly refutes.

Conclusion

In the Parable of the Unprofitable Servant, Jesus gave three servants different treasures of the kingdom to use productively. Two do so and one does not. The one who does nothing is condemned to hell. It is that simple.

The Parable of the Unprofitable Servant is not about professing faith and lacking fruit thereby, leading to your exposure as a false believer. The parable is not about a false professor somehow *tricking God into giving him some treasure of heaven to waste*. That doctrinal construct is highly belabored and strained. Such a view is simply a mental overlay solely designed to hold onto the Modern Gospel of Cheap Grace. To hold onto faith-alone doctrine. Its intent is obvious: it wants to justify rejecting Jesus' words whenever on their face they refute the faith alone paradigm.

Instead, this parable is one of the most blatant contradictions of cheap grace from the lips of Jesus. For Jesus says, as He does in many other passages, that the fruitless Christian will not be saved. This is in the Metaphor of the Vine (John 15:1-6); the Parable of the Sower (Luke 8:8 *ff.*); the Parable of the Sheep and the Goats, etc. It fits precisely the non-parabolic and direct statement of our Lord in Matthew 7:19:

> Every tree that bringeth not forth good fruit is hewn down, and cast into the fire. (Matt 7:19.)

The servant with no good fruit on his talent is eventually cast into the fire of hell.

Could Jesus be any more blunt in a parable?

Frederick Lisco (1791-1866), a German evangelical minister in Berlin, explains it likewise, citing Calvin in support. The servant who is lost is the one who did not use the treasure given by the Lord in a "conscientious and faithful" manner. (Lisco, *The Parables of Jesus* (Philadelphia: Daniels & Smith, 1850) at 197.) The other two servants knew the "obligation under which they lie to serve" their Lord, but only "if they acted agreeably to the will of the Lord." *Id.* Calvin says that Jesus gives the parable to believers to "stir themselves up to the **work of a pure and holy life**." *Id.*, at 202. Also, Lisco emphasizes it was not the "sinful" use of the talent, but instead the "slothful indifference" toward it that caused the unprofitable servant to suffer his fate. *Id.*, at 198. God calls him a "wicked and slothful servant." *Id.*, at 200. His fate is clear. He is brought to the "final judgment" which involves the "strictest justice." *Id.*, at 201. The slothful servant for his "negligence and shortcoming" will suffer "everlasting pain." *Id.* This proves the "necessity and importance of **works** of love...." *Id.*, at 202.

Hence, Jesus' warning to those who trust in faith alone to their detriment (by *not having completed works to show* at judgment) is unmistakable. Your doctrine is false.

Will you have any excuse for having no fruit on the talents of gold God gives you? Will you be able to argue you could believe no works were necessary to be saved?

At the final judgment seat, you will not be able to point fingers at John MacArthur, Stanley, Dillow or Paul, and blame them. Jesus was too blunt in the Parable of the Unprofitable Servant as well as in Matthew 7:19. Jesus will grill you on why you did not take His words in their plain sense. You will have no answer. He told you all along He was your "Sole Teacher." (Matt. 23:8-11.) And your sole teacher told you that the unprofitable servant goes to hell. There will be no more excuses then. 'He who has ears to hear let him hear.'

17 *Count The Cost*

Count The Cost Message In Luke 14

Jesus told the rich young man that part of the salvation formula was denying himself and bearing his own cross. For him, Jesus said this meant giving up all his wealth and giving it to the poor. (Matthew 19:16-26; Mark 10:17-31; Luke 18:18-26.) For this young man, Jesus meant you cannot serve God and mammon. (Matt. 6:24.) You will love one and hate the other. The man's love of money put him in the difficult position of hating God's requirement for repentance when it was pressed upon him. The man went away *grieved* at the request to put aside his love of mammon.

Jesus again refers to this requirement of "bearing your own cross" in his famous warning to *count the cost*. Jesus defined "bearing your own cross" to mean that you need "to count the cost" of becoming a Christian or otherwise you would not "complete" the course, but fail to continue and have to sue for peace with your enemy (the Devil). You will be defeated. (Luke 14:28.) The passage reads:

> (27) Whosoever doth not **bear his own cross**, and come after me, cannot be my disciple. (28) For which of you, desiring to build a tower, doth not first sit down and **count the cost**, whether he have wherewith **to complete it**? (29) Lest haply, when he hath laid a foundation, and is not able to finish, all that behold begin to mock him, (30) saying, This man **began to build**, and **was not able to finish**. (31) Or what king, as he goeth to encounter another king in war, will not sit down first and take counsel whether he is able with ten thousand to meet him that cometh against him with twenty thousand? (32) Or else, while the other is yet a great way off, he sendeth an ambassage,

and asketh conditions of peace. (33) So therefore whosoever he be of you that **renounceth
not all that he hath, he cannot be my disciple.** (34) Salt therefore is good: but if even the
salt have lost its savor, wherewith shall it be
seasoned? (35) It is fit neither for the land nor
for the dunghill: men cast it out. He that hath
ears to hear, let him hear. (Luke 14:27-35,
ASV.)

If you fail to count the costs, you will find yourself to
be like a king who goes to battle with 10,000 only to find the
enemy has 20,000 men. You will have to sue for peace terms.
In ancient cultures, this meant the king was captured and
enslaved to his enemy, usually taken back to the enemy's
homeland in chains.

What Are The Costs Of Which Jesus Speaks?

Jesus makes it clear in the same context that the cost
is the "renunciation of all that [you] have." (Luke 14:33.)
This is the cost you must bear.

But what does "renunciation of all that you have"
mean?

Clarke says this cost means "the difficulties" with
being a Christian. Gill, however, says it means you must
assess the cost of the "ordinances" to which you must submit
that go with your profession of Christ. Gill adds other factors
in the *costs*:

> [F]or such a work is chargeable and costly, and
> should be thought of and considered, whether
> he is able to bear it: for he will be called to **self-
> denial**; and must expect to suffer the **loss of
> the favour of carnal relations and friends**;

While these suggestions may be all simultaneously
true apart from this passage, here Jesus Himself defines the
costs as "the renunciation of all that you have." (Luke 14:33.)

Thus, such costs which we must count include the high personal cost of repenting from fleshly sins, *e.g.*, greed, gluttony, envy, anxiety, adulterous lust, etc. This is clearly part of what it means to "renounce all that you have." You must give up all that you hold dear that simultaneously holds you back from following Jesus. The Lord makes this clear not only in the *Count The Cost* lesson, but also in parallel passages.

To understand the *count the cost* passage, let's break it down into two issues. If we can first understand what is at risk if we miscalculate the costs, then this should help us understand what are those costs we must pay.

What Does Jesus Teach Is The Risk Of Miscalculation?

Jesus in the various examples of those who do not count the cost (Luke 14:27-35) underscores that our salvation is otherwise at risk. First, if you did not count the costs of building a tower, then the tower is not "completed," and merely only "begun." It had a beginning without a successful "finish." (Luke 14:28-29.) Others will mock you.

This first example is reminiscent of the Parable of the Sower, where the first seed "believes for a while" and it "sprouted," but in time of temptation it falls away (Luke 8:13), withers and dies. (Luke 8:6.) Because the sower lesson is a parable, death and the loss of life signify the loss of eternal life. Thus, even though the seed like the builder began well, in each case the second seed and the builder later suffer failure. In the Parable of the Sower, this means death and damnation. Thus, it should mean the same thing in the builder example in Luke 14:27-35.

This is corroborated by Jesus' second example in the *Counting the Cost* lesson in Luke 14. In this example, the consequence for miscalculating the costs is surrender to your enemy. Jesus says it is like a king going to war with only

10,000 men and finding out he confronts 20,000. The king miscalculated, and has to sue instead for peace. (Luke 14:31-32.)

Applied spiritually, this teaches that in our battles, if we miscalculate the costs, a Christian ends up being forced to sue for peace with his enemy the Devil. We are defeated. We have to surrender to Satan, and accept his terms. We are *ensnared* by Satan. We are taken prisoner into his domain.

Thus, when these two examples — the builder and king-going-to-war — are combined, Jesus means that the risk of miscalculation is to not finish what you began. It means, as a result, you become surrendered to Satan. Both cases *must be talking about the loss of salvation*.

That salvation is at stake for miscalculating the cost is evident in other teachings of Jesus. In Matthew 16:24–26, we read:

> ... if any man will come after me, let him deny himself, and take up his cross, and follow me. For whosoever will *save his life* shall *lose it*: and whosoever *will lose his life for my sake* shall find it. For what is a man profited, if he shall gain the whole world, and *lose his own soul*?

Clearly, in this teaching Jesus equates *losing one's soul* with *saving your life* in this world. Then Jesus says you have a stark choice: either (a) *gain the whole world (in this life)* and *lose your own soul (in the next)* or (b) *lose your life in this world for Christ's sake* and *gain it in the next*. It is an echo of the *hell whole* or *heaven maimed* principle. (Matt. 5:30; Mark 9:42 *et seq.*) This save-your-life-here-lose-it-in-the-next principle is precisely the same message as in the lesson of *counting the cost* in Luke 14. Salvation is clearly at stake for miscalculations. Salvation is at stake if you fail to give up the whole world when you should have been prepared to sacrifice it, and thus gain eternal life. Grace is costly, not cheap.

Miscalculation In The Young Rich Man's Response

If that is not clear enough, we can see a real life example of a *miscalculation* from the response of the young rich man. He was told by Jesus what he had to do to enter eternal life. More than just obeying the Law, the young man had to give up all his wealth and give it to the poor and then follow Jesus. (Matthew 19:16-26; Mark 10:17-31; Luke 18:18-26.) For the young rich man, this was a steep cost because the young man was very rich.

This lesson to the young rich man identically matches Jesus' lesson that we must count as costs the "renunciation of all that you have." (Luke 14:33.) Therefore, *what is at stake for the young rich man must be identical* to what Jesus intends to be the risk of miscalculation in the *Counting the Costs* lesson: salvation.

However, the cost of salvation was too high for the young rich man. The cost that Jesus required for him to receive eternal life was giving up all his wealth and giving it to the poor. Thus, Jesus taught the rich young man (and ourselves) that *salvation comes at a steep price* — a price the rich young man was unwilling to pay. He was not willing to renounce all that he had in obedience to Jesus' direction. It was a cost the young rich man was not willing to suffer.

Costs Were Properly Calculated By Zaccheus

Another way to understand what the risk represents from *miscalculating the costs* is to look at what is the outcome from properly *counting the costs*. This is reflected in Jesus' approving of Zaccheus' response to Jesus' message. Jesus tells us that Zaccheus did correctly understand and accept Jesus' gospel. Zaccheus is a model of what renouncing all that you have would look like. Zaccheus repents of extortion by paying back fourfold what he stole. He gives the rest of his money to the poor. Then he follows Jesus. After those *works worthy of repentance*, Jesus responds: "Today salvation has come to this house...." (Luke 19:9.)

Thus, while the young rich man was unwilling to do what Zaccheus did, Jesus says that the outcome of what Zaccheus did was salvation. Zaccheus cut off the riches that had ensnared him (Mark 9:42 *et seq.*) This means it was an acceptable *act* of repentance to God. Jesus said salvation arrived for Zaccheus.

Therefore, it is more than obvious that the risk of *miscalculating the costs* is to lose salvation, and the reward for *counting the costs* properly is salvation.

What Are The Costs We Must Bear Which We Can Miscalculate?

Knowing now the risk of *miscalculating* the costs is damnation, we will next study what did Jesus mean by "renunciation of all that you have." (Luke 14:33.) Is this as Gill and Clarke portray it? Is it merely about the difficulties of being a Christian in other's eyes? Is it merely knowing in advance what 'ordinances' a Christian must obey? Or is it instead, at a clear minimum, repentance from sin and actual obedience? Are these the costs which we must count as a personal sacrifice? Must we let go of our sinful desires before confronting our enemy the devil?

Proving salvation was at stake will also give the answer to this question. The *costs to count* are at least the **sinful propensities which we must relinquish**.

Is this only a change in the mind or acting consistently with repentance from your sin?

Jesus and the Bible before Jesus said it must be dealt with by an *act* or *work* worthy of repentance. A thief who steals must repay. (Nu 5:5-8.) The greedy who has hoarded must now share. Thus, Zaccheus made this calculation correctly, but the young rich man was not willing to do so. Jesus told the young rich man the price, but he was unwilling to pay it. However, we see elsewhere Jesus meant *acts* of repentance from sinful desire is at minimum a part of the renunciation of self. You must be willing to "bear your own cross" by *doing* these acts, suffering the loss of your favorite but sinful things. (Mark 9:42-47.)

How The Hell-Whole Message Explains The Meaning Of Counting The Cost For The Rich Young Man

In the *Counting the Costs* lesson, Jesus says the costs we must count are the "renunciation of all that we have." (Luke 14:33.)

We learned above that failing to do this leads to loss of salvation. You will be captured by your enemy, the devil.

Above we discussed that this *renunciation* means likely acts appropriate to one's repentance from sin. Either obedience or works worthy-of-repentance. The encounter with the young rich man showed us that salvation requires a stern repentance that most people *refuse* to entertain. ***They want eternal life but only if it comes free.*** They gravitate to those within the church who arose who preached grace and God's forgiveness is free and without any personal cost — a gospel completely foreign to that of Jesus. (Jesus only taught the gospel must be preached without monetary charge, but it is not a gospel without personal moral cost to accept.)[1]

Thus, while you cannot atone for your own sins, God has set conditions on the receipt of God's mercy. Jesus insists these conditions *do* cost you a lot.

We have also seen how this is true by the contrasting outcome with Zaccheus. In this event, Jesus makes clear what the cost is that the young rich man would not pay, but Zaccheus was willing to pay. This cost involved ***an act*** of stern repentance. For these two men, the act involved money. One had to repay what he stole and the other had to give all his money away. ***These were acts worthy of repentance appropriate for these two men***. They were not identical, but varied.

Jesus gives each of us just as drastic a command. It too may vary depending on what part of your body is leading you to sin.

What proves conclusively that the drastic step given to the young rich man was a work worthy of repentance-from-sin is Jesus' famous *hell-whole or heaven-maimed* statement. Jesus described this as 'cutting off the parts of your body that are causing you to sin.' The Greek reflects a metaphor to an animal-trap from which an animal who is partially-snared can escape only by letting a body part go as the animal breaks free.[2] Jesus says:

> (42) And whosoever shall cause one of these little ones that ***believe on me*** to stumble, it were better for him if a great millstone were

---

1. Jesus says "without cost you have received; without cost you are to give." (Matt. 10:8.) The next verse mentions money in their purses. Thus, in verse eight, Jesus is prohibiting laying any monetary cost burden on hearing the gospel. Jesus likewise referred to the gospel message as a free gift another time. In John 4:10, Jesus addressed a woman by a well: "Jesus answered and said to her, 'If you knew the *free gift* of God and who is the One saying to you, 'Give Me to drink,' you would have asked Him, and He would have given you *living water*.'" What's the free gift? It's the living water. This is precisely repeated in Isaiah 55:1-8. It speaks of "waters" for the thirsty that you receive without any *monetary* cost. You are to "buy *without money*." You are still to *buy it*, but *not pay in human monetary price-terms*. It has only a moral cost component. This is clear in Isaiah 55:7-8. It says the message of salvation (the living water) is repentance from sin and obedience. Cheap grace enthusiasts lift Isaiah 55:1 out-of-context to prove salvation is without repentance or obedience. But if you read Isaiah 55:1-8 (which is quoted in Footnote 5 on page 238), there is still a transaction. You must *buy* the message, but it is without any monetary price. It then spells out clearly that the cost is repentance from sin and obedience — moral costs, not monetary costs. Hence, the cheap grace enthusiasts blatantly lifted one verse from the passage to suggest the *opposite* of what the passage actually says.

Jesus' Words On Salvation

hanged about his neck, and he were cast into the sea. (43) And if thy hand cause thee to stumble, *cut it off*: it is good for thee to *enter into life maimed*, rather than having thy two hands to go into hell, into the unquenchable fire. (44) where their worm dieth not, and the fire is not quenched. (45) And if thy foot cause thee to stumble, *cut it off*: it is good for thee to *enter into life halt*, rather than having thy two feet to be cast into hell. (46) where their worm dieth not, and the fire is not quenched. (47) And if thine eye cause thee to stumble, *cast it out*: it is good for thee to *enter into the kingdom of God with one eye*, rather than having two eyes to be cast into hell; (48) where their worm dieth not, and the fire is not quenched. (Mark 9:42-48, ASV.)

Thus, Jesus makes it abundantly clear that we can go to heaven maimed or hell whole. We can go to heaven blinded in one eye, missing one hand, or hobbling on one leg. Or we can go to hell, prizing both our eyes, hands and legs. *It is an action of a stern repentance that will determine your ultimate salvation*, at least if you trust Jesus' words. As Jesus said: "Unless you repent, you too will all perish." (Luke 13:3,5.)

Hence, the costs to suffer include "the renunciation of all that you have" (Luke 14:33). What you must calculate as a cost to encounter your enemy is such a renunciation. The young rich man, as long as he did not renounce riches, was going to fail in the next encounter with Satan respecting his sin of greed and non-generosity. If you fail to make the right amount of sacrifice appropriate to your personal failings, you will be defeated by Satan. You will be captured and taken prisoner by the Devil.

---

2. For the discussion of that animal-trap metaphor in this passage as well as a full discussion of the passage, see page 49.

Strive To Enter

Jesus elsewhere tells us the cost and effort we must exert is high. Jesus says in Luke 13:24: "Strive [*agonizomai, agonize, use all your strength*] to enter in by the narrow door: for many, I say unto you, shall seek to enter in, and shall not be able [*i.e.*, lack strength]." Cutting off body parts is no easy task. It is painful. It figuratively cuts the skin. It causes your flesh to bleed. But Jesus promises over and over *if you are willing to pay the costs*, you will be saved. If you lack the foresight or the will to make the appropriate sacrifice in advance of your temptations, Jesus warns you will fall and become lost. You will fail to enter the doorway that leads to eternal life.

Strain to enter in by the narrow door

Cheap Grace Commentators' Explanations Of The King's Miscalculation

One of the ways to know one has correctly analyzed a passage is by looking at how hard or impossible it is to accept a competing understanding. We can find the strength of our own conclusion only when "we look at the arguments for alternative conclusions." (Peter Suber, *Stages of Argument*.)

When we study the leading commentators — Clarke, Gill and Barnes — they each try to make Jesus sound like the Modern Gospel of Cheap Grace. Yet, it is transparent that their dogma is dictating the conclusion. For they have made material admissions that, if applied to its natural conclusion, end up with a contrary conclusion to their doctrine.

That is to say, the clarity of the parable forces these men to make crucial admissions which undermine the Modern Gospel of Cheap Grace. They admit the king going to war in Luke 14 is a Christian. A true Christian. They admit the enemy king is Satan. They admit the cost of miscalculating the forces needed to meet Satan was surrender and defeat to Satan. (See Table 1 on page 302 below.)

To explain away these admissions, those wed to the Modern Gospel of Cheap Grace try to change the nature of the *costs* so salvation remains without personal moral cost. They insist we know *a priori* that salvation is without such personal sacrifice, *i.e.*, it is by faith alone. Thus, they rewrite Jesus' words to match that viewpoint. To them, even though Jesus says in context that the costs involved a renunciation of all that you have (Luke 14:33), the faith-alone-commentator says Jesus means you did not pray enough to God. Thus, the *cost* is supposedly that you did not depend entirely on God. You failed to pray — this is the sole cost you supposedly had to sacrifice. In fact, you allegedly did not realize there was nothing you *could do* to be ready other than depend entirely on God through prayer. They insist you did not realize that there was no *personal* moral cost you could sacrifice to meet your enemy.

But what did Jesus really mean? *The exact opposite.* You are not prepared to battle the opposing king because you did not cut off the body parts ensnaring you in sin. (Mark 12:42-47.) You did not renounce all that you have. (Luke 14:33.) You did not take up your own cross and follow Jesus. (Luke 14:27 *cf.* Matt. 10:37-38.) *You assumed salvation is free, without moral cost.* Jesus warns you will suffer certain defeat. Thus, *the Modern Gospel of Cheap Grace is precisely the message Jesus tried to warn you against.* Cheap grace doctrine of faith alone sets you up for defeat.

This is not to say prayer has no role in a Christian life or in following Jesus. However, *we need to pray for the things Jesus told us that we need*: the ability to pay the costs that God requires. Ask God to "lead us from temptation."

We also need to pray for the strength to resist the Modern Gospel of Cheap Grace itself as a foreign pressure. *Its message tells us there are no moral costs we must suffer to gain the kingdom.* When Peter told Jesus that He should not go to the cross (His costs) — that such sacrifice was *optional*, Jesus replied "get behind me Satan." (Matt.16:23.) Jesus is telling us likewise that if we do not accept the costs of **taking up our own cross daily**, and we think instead *they are optional costs*, we are listening to Satan. By not counting the costs in advance of taking up our own cross, Jesus says we will be defeated and captured by Satan. Jesus Himself by example taught us to suffer all the sacrifice necessary to avoid capture of ourselves by Satan. Hence, the message that sacrifice is optional — only for those who want close 'discipleship' with Christ rather than eternal life — is indeed the message of Satan. You need to rebuke it in your heart as strenuously as Jesus did when it came from Peter.

TABLE 1. Parable of King Going to War in Luke 14

Parable Elements	Cheap Grace Filter	Unfiltered by Modern Gospel
King going to war	Admits king is Christian.	Same. King is Christian.
Enemy king	Admits enemy king is Satan.	Same. Enemy king is Satan.
Petition for Surrender	Some suggest only loss of closeness with God at stake. Most are quiet on implication of surrender to enemy king.	Loss of salvation.
Costs that king did not count and underestimated	Failure to pray to God for strength in the battle. Failure to ask other Christians for help.	*Renunciation of all that you have: sinful desires and desire for family/ social approval.*

Is Counting The Cost Repentance-From-Sin Or Failure To Pray In Advance?

Is the failure to count the costs the failure to sacrifice sin which is threatening you with capture by Satan? Or is the failure to count the costs, as some like Gill suggests, the failure to pray in advance?

The failure to count the costs must be the failure to sacrifice the sin that is threatening your defeat to Satan — the failure to repent. How can we be so sure? Because without repenting from sin *first*, God does not hear your prayers anyway! Thus, *it is pointless to argue prayer, by itself, is the 'cost' to initially pay.* This is because a prayer without repentance would not be heard anyway. Thus, to focus on prayer as the necessary sacrifice ignores the fact it has no power unless combined with repentance. So says God Almighty!

God specifically repeats over and over that He refuses to hear the prayers of those who have not *paid the cost* of repenting first. God will not hear the prayers of the unrepentant. (Isaiah 1:15;[3] Zechariah 7:13.)[4] The Psalmist knew this:

> If I regard iniquity in my heart, The Lord will not hear: (Psalm 66:18, ASV.)

The Lutherans Keil & Deilitzsch in their famous *Commentary on the Old Testament* say a correct translation is even stronger on that verse's meaning. They prefer this meaning:

> We render: *If I had aimed at evil in my heart*, the Lord would not hear; not: He would not have heard, but: He would *not on any occasion hear.* (Psalm 66:18.)

Likewise, Jesus tells us that through prayer we can do anything, but a precondition is to first pray for forgiveness, which itself is contingent on our being forgiving to others.

---

3. "And when ye spread forth your hands, I will hide mine eyes from you; yea, when ye make many prayers, I will not hear: your hands are full of blood." (Isa 1:15.) Keil & Deilitsch explain this means that *God would not hear the prayer of unrepentant sinners*. "However much they might stand or lie before Him in the attitude of prayer, Jehovah hid His eyes,...even though they might pray loud and long." In the next verse, Keil & Deilitsch explain the message is that the cure is initial repentance and ongoing repentance (obedience) to be clean in God's sight: "According to the difference between the two synonyms (to wash one's self, to clean one's self), the former must be understood as referring to the one great act of repentance on the part of a man who is turning to God, the latter to the *daily repentance of one who has so turned*." (K&D Commentary, Isaiah 1:16.)

(24) I tell you, you can pray for anything, and if you believe that you've received it, it will be yours. (25) But when you are praying, *first forgive anyone you are holding a grudge against,* so that your Father in heaven will *forgive your sins, too.* (Mark 11:24-25 NLT.)

Jesus is simply echoing the principle that prayer is powerful, *but* first you must forgive others, which then permits God to forgive you. Jesus is implying that your forgiveness from God is a contingency of your prayers, which itself turns (in part) on your forgiving others first.

Clarke on How Doctrine of Prayer Assists Interpreting Passage

This Bible-principle on prayer-linked-to-repentance influenced Clarke in his commentary on the Parable of the King. Clarke realized prayer alone is not what the king lacked. Clarke confesses: "Disobedience to God will *hinder our prayers from being answered*, and may give Satan a legal hold in our lives."

Thus, Clarke is acknowledging that God will not hear any prayer from someone who has not already repented from their sins. (Ps. 66:18; Isaiah 1:15; Zech. 7:13.) Such an unrepentant person, even if they were already a Christian, are like a king who goes to battle only committing 10,000 of his

---

4. In this passage, God says those who will not hear the Law of Moses and the Prophets who cry out to them, God will not hear their prayers: "(12) Yea, they made their hearts as an adamant stone, lest they should hear the Law, and the words which Jehovah of hosts had sent by his Spirit by the former Prophets: therefore there came great wrath from Jehovah of hosts. (13) And it is come to pass that, as he cried, and they would not hear, so they shall cry, and *I will not hear*, said Jehovah of hosts." (Zech. 7:12-13.) Keil & Deilitsch acknowledge God was upset the people were not following the Law, although K&D narrowly describe it as "the moral precepts of the law" so as not to offend our modern teaching that the letter of the Law was abrogated. Then K&D say the consequence is a block on prayer: "As they have not hearkened to the word [*sic*: Law] of God, so will God [not hearken to them], when they call upon Him, namely in distress...."

---

troops but then finds this number is no match for his enemy's troops of 20,000. As a result, you must surrender to your enemy the devil.

Thus, the free and easy cost-free gospel with no corresponding personal repentance/sacrifice of Gill is *wrong*. One cannot bank on prayer for the strength to meet the enemy forces. God does not hear the prayer of the *unrepentant*.

Consequently, if you have not already repented from sin in your heart, then prayer for strength in a battle with Satan does you no good. Your attitude must change before God will agree to help you succeed to follow through on your new attitude. In other words, you cannot call on God in prayer for the strength to resist that temptation if you already have not made up your mind to resist that temptation. You will be powerless going into battle. You cannot depend on the miracle of prayer **when God is not listening**! You must repent from sin first, and then God will hear your prayer to confront the enemy (the devil). This is precisely what Jesus means by counting-the-costs.

Are The Costs To Pay The Price Of Discipleship, Not Salvation?

Many commentators who defend the Modern Gospel of Cheap Grace say the costs Jesus requires includes your personal sacrifice of your creature comforts. Henry is an example. Henry starts out somewhat properly analyzing the import of Jesus' words:

> They [*i.e.*, the prospective Christian] must be willing to quit that which was very dear, and therefore must come to him thoroughly weaned from all their *creature-comforts*, and dead to them, so as cheerfully to part with them rather than quit their interest in Christ.

However, in the same context, Henry starts to inter-ject a notion that these costs are merely the price to be a *super* Christian. These are supposedly the standards to "follow Jesus" and "be Jesus' disciple." Henry and others imply this parable is not about salvation, but about having **a close fel-lowship** as a disciple of Jesus Christ. Henry suggests the mis-calculating Christian will not enjoy the greater "recompense" enjoyed by the super-Christian disciple who does count the cost. Thus, counting the cost is supposedly **optional**, and if you skip these costs, your salvation is as safe and secure as a Christian who counts the costs. You allegedly just forfeit greater rewards (*i.e.*, "recompense").

However, this suggestion that laces Henry's discus-sion ignores that Jesus said the stakes are very high. Jesus said if you do not count the costs, you are like a king who went to war, miscalculated the forces necessary, and you have to **surrender to your enemy** (the devil, in context.) Sur-render means you are *ensnared*. It must mean you are now captured. As Jesus says in John 10:27-28, that whoever *keeps* on *listening* to Jesus and *keeps* on *following* Him can never be snatched. But in the Parable of the King, when you do not count the costs of such *discipleship*, of *listening* and *follow-ing*, you are **snatched away and defeated**. You are captured by Satan. This cannot represent anything but damnation.

Restored Church Of God Has Correct High Cost View Of Parable

The *Restored Church of God* (RCG) sees this parable as at odds with the Modern Gospel of Cheap Grace. The RCG grounds its view in the fact Jesus' message here is so similar to many other comparable teachings of Jesus:

> True Christianity is **not the easy way of life advertised by most professing Christians**. Christ said, "Enter you in at the strait [difficult] gate: for wide is the gate, and broad is the way, that leads to destruction, and many there be

which go in thereat: Because strait is the gate and narrow is the way, which leads unto life, and few there be that find it." (Matt. 7:13-14).[5]

Thus, RCG says Jesus states there is a high cost involved. This teaching of Jesus affirms, in effect, grace comes at a high cost, contrary to what we are told by the Modern Gospel of Cheap Grace.

In addition to personal repentance, the RCG says Jesus' teachings mean that *counting the cost* involves accepting the risk of rejection by your social circle if you follow Jesus. The RCG explains the risk entailed in following Jesus by taking this lesson and comparing it to Jesus' other teachings on such a price to pay:

> Another 'cost' of true Christianity is the forsaking of this world's ways, customs, and traditions: "...COME OUT OF HER, MY PEOPLE, that you be not partakers of her sins, and that you receive not of her plagues" (Rev. 18:4).

> You will find that family, friends and acquaintances will no longer view you in the same way. They will **not be able to accept your new way of life**: "Wherein they think it strange that you run not with them to the same excess of riot, speaking evil of you" (I Pet. 4:4).

---

5. *Q: What is the meaning of Luke 14:28, and 'counting the cost?'* at http://www.thercg.org/questions/p094.a.html (last accessed 7/6/06). The RCG teaches some other interesting points. First, RCG says the ceremonial and civil laws of the Law do not apply to Christians (http://www.thercg.org/articles/acfftoc.html), but that the Law of God, represented by the Ten Commandments, does apply to Christians. (http://www.thercg.org/articles/lg.html.) Luther came around to the same view in his 1537 *Antinomian Theses*. The RCG also believes it is unreasonable to ignore the Saturday-Sabbath command. (http://www.thercg.org/articles/htmtsad.html.) This is comparable to Tyndale's and the Eastern Orthodox view of Sabbath.

You must be willing to accept that *your own family will likely reject you for your beliefs* (Matt. 10:34-38; 19:29; Mark 10:29).

You must also be willing to accept that, ultimately, as Christ stated, "...*you shall be hated of all nations for My name's sake*" (Matt. 24:9).

Thus, if you follow Jesus, teach His doctrine and obey Him, you can expect you will be rejected by your social circle. This may even include the religious circles that claim to be Christian. Losing social acceptance was another cost that Jesus repeatedly emphasized that you must count and accept.

In fact, if you teach Jesus' gospel of salvation in America today, you will be frequently shouted down as a heretic by most of those who profess Christ. This is because, in reliance on Jesus' words alone, you deny the cheap-grace teaching which dominates in America. Unless you are prepared to sacrifice social acceptance as a price of following Jesus, when you suffer rejection by family and friends you will be tempted to fall back into worldly thinking that rejects following Jesus and His words.

For example, even as you read this book and learn what Jesus' Gospel represents (*i.e.*, what Jesus says when you do not *filter* it through anyone else's teachings), you come up with doctrines at *total odds* with the Modern Gospel of Cheap Grace. *Your social circle will insist you should not take Jesus' words seriously. For example, I am repeatedly ridiculed and jibed at by my Christian friends for simply quoting back to them Jesus' principles as serious ones to accept.*

For instance, many in Christendom will urge you to dismiss Jesus' words as intended for the Dispensation of Law, not of Grace. By resisting this pressure on you to ignore Jesus' words, you are going to suffer certain costs. It may be ostracism. It may be subtle ridicule and contempt. It may be the hostility of being called a heretic. Some may even hate you "for my Name's sake." Will you buckle under the pressure or cling to Christ?

Ironically, your greatest enemies, like Jesus' greatest enemies, will be from the group that claims it is closest to God.

Final Analysis

When you take all the commentaries and synthesize them, you come up with a clearer understanding of the parable of *counting the costs*. Those who filter Jesus to sound like the Modern Gospel of Cheap Grace make crucial admissions which undermine faith alone. They admit the king going to war in Luke 14 is a Christian. A true Christian. They admit the enemy king is Satan. They admit the cost of miscalculating the forces needed to meet Satan was surrender and defeat to Satan. (See Table 1 on page 302 above.)

However, those who filter Jesus and read Him so as not to undermine cheap grace try to change the nature of the *costs* so salvation remains free of moral cost. They insist we know *a priori* that salvation is without personal *moral* cost. Thus, they rewrite Jesus' words to match that viewpoint. To them, even though Jesus says in context that the costs involved a renunciation of all that you have (Luke 14:33), the filtering-commentator says Jesus means you did not pray enough to God. Thus, the *cost* is supposedly that you did not depend entirely on God. In fact, you allegedly did not realize there was nothing you *could do* to be ready other than depend entirely on God. They insist you did not realize that there was no moral cost you could sacrifice to meet your enemy.

But to repeat: what did Jesus really mean? ***Again: the exact opposite.*** You are not prepared to battle the opposing king because you did not cut off the body parts ensnaring you in sin. (Mark 12:42-47.) You did not renounce all that you have. (Luke 14:33.) You did not take up your own cross and follow Jesus. (Luke 14:27 *cf.* Matt. 10:37-38.) ***You assumed*** *salvation is free, without moral costs*. You will suffer certain defeat, Jesus warns. Thus, *the Modern Gospel of Cheap Grace is precisely the message Jesus tried to warn you against*. Faith alone doctrine sets you up for such defeat.

Even Calvin admitted this, even though incongruously he otherwise upheld 'faith alone.' Calvin taught: "Lest any one should think it hard to follow Christ on such terms, which *require the renouncement of all his lusts*, a proper admonition is given to meditate beforehand *what a profession of the gospel really requires*." (Quoted by Lisco, *The Teachings of Jesus* (1850) at 281.)

Thus, if you simply let Jesus teach you, then you are prepared for facing Satan. To do this, and lead others to follow Christ, you will have to reject the Modern Gospel of Cheap Grace. But to do this will expose you to abuse and ridicule from the dominant 'Christian' authorities and their followers.

What should you do? *Count the cost, including the loss of friends and social approval.* Jesus is always the better reward. Don't worry. Accept the sacrifices. Following Jesus' words can never jeopardize your salvation. Persecution is just one more cost of following Jesus. Bonhoeffer paid the price for preaching costly grace. You can too. We must handle this as Job did. He spoke up! "Did I fear a great multitude, or did the contempt of families terrify me, that I kept silence?" (Job 31:34.) If you keep silent, you will bear the sins of those deluded. (Eze 33:6-7.) Thus, the cost of silence is deadly.

To repeat, this is not to say prayer has no role in a Christian life or in following Jesus. However, *we need to pray for the things Jesus told us that we need*: the ability to pay the moral costs that God requires. Ask God to "lead us from temptation." We also need to pray for the strength to resist the Modern Gospel of Cheap Grace itself as a pernicious social pressure. It seeks us to believe there are no moral costs we must suffer to avoid capture by our enemy. If we fall for this gospel, Jesus says we are not ready. We must count the costs necessary to avoid capture of ourselves by Satan.

18 *The Parable Of The Sower*

What The Parable Of The Sower Confirms About Faith

Introduction

The Greek verb *pisteuo* is typically translated in Luke 8:13 in the Parable of the Sower as "believes."[1] It is the same word as used in John 3:16 which is likewise translated typically as *believes*. Assuming this is a correct translation, this makes Luke 8:13 one of two passages in the Synoptic Gospels that talks about faith and salvation. (The other is Luke 7:47.)[2]

However, the Parable of the Sower discusses *believing* in a *negative manner*. The Parable of the Sower teaches that the failure of one who "believes for a while" to obey God's commands ("falls into temptation") leads to becoming lost. Thus, faith that later fails in *action* does not save. In fact, the only person saved among the seeds is the fourth seed who *produces fruit to completion*. Hence, in this parable Jesus addresses faith and works in a way totally at odds with the Modern Gospel of Cheap Grace.

Please note this is not a parable that proponents of cheap grace can avoid by claiming its meaning remains a mystery. Jesus explained the parable's symbolic meaning in *excruciating detail*.

Let's analyze with care the Parable of the Sower.

---

1. It can mean also *trust, commit, comply* or *obey*. For the purposes of this chapter, we will assume the Greek verb *pisteuo* here means to *believe* in the Parable of the Sower.
2. For a discussion of Luke 7:47, *see* my prior book, *Jesus' Words Only* (2007) at 157-60.

Analysis Of The Parable Of The Sower

The first seed never believes because Satan snatches the word from his heart before he can believe "and be saved." (Luke 8:12.) Unlike the first seed, the second seed (*i.e.*, the seed on rocky soil) (Luke 8:6) "sprouted." Jesus explains this means the second seed "received the word with joy" and "***believes for a while***." (Luke 8:13.)

In Luke 8:13, the Greek tense translated typically as "believes" is the present indicative active of *pisteuo*. This tense means Jesus is saying the seed on rocky ground "***keeps*** on believing." Jesus then adds an adverb meaning "for a while." In this context, the present indicative is indistinguishable in meaning from the present participle active of *pisteuo* which is used uniformly in John's Gospel.[3] They are both a continuous tense.

Logically, if the first seed would have been "saved" had Satan not prevented faith from forming, this second seed must be "saved." Thus, Jesus is saying the second seed is "saved" (at least) for a while because it believed for a while yet the first seed is never saved because it never believed.

Jesus goes on to say the second seed then "withered away" (*i.e.*, shriveled up). (Luke 8:6). Jesus explains this means it fell into "temptation" (sinned) and "fell away." (Luke 8:13, *aphistami.*) Why did it fall away? It shriveled up "because it lacked moisture." (Luke 8:6.) The Greek of this verb was present active as well, meaning "it did not continue to have moisture." Jesus explains again why, saying the seed

---

3. On the present continuous tenses in Greek, see page 510 *et seq.* See also Appendix A: *Greek Issues* in *Jesus' Words Only* (2007). For discussion in particular on *pisteuo* in Luke 8:13 and John's Gospel, see my prior book, *Jesus' Words Only* (2007) at 171.

"did not have root." (Luke 8:13.) The verb, however, is again present active in Greek (*ecousin*) and means "it *did not keep holding* on to the Root."

TABLE 1. Parable Of The Sower: The Second Seed

Second Seed Metaphor	Jesus' Explanation
sprouted	received the word with joy
	continued to believe for a while
did not continue to have moisture	did not keep holding to the root
withered away (shriveled up)	tempted, fell away

Thus, Jesus teaches that someone who received the word with Joy, "continued to *believe* for a while," thereby "sprouted," but then fell into temptation. This person ends up withered away (dead). Dead means no life. No life means no eternal life. The reason is they "did not keep holding to the Root" and so they "fell away." This was a lesson about faith lacking endurance and being destroyed by sin. Thus, it is a negative message about faith. *It is not an example of faith saving, but how faith can be brought to naught by sin.*

One of the greatest preachers, John Donne (1572-1631),[4] said this parable contains a great warning to Christians. This is because the second seed represents *believers*:

> [Y]et *we* may *relapse into former sins*, or fall into new, and come to savour only of the earth...[W]e may have *received the good seed, and endured for a while,* as St. Matthew expresses Christ's words; *Received it and believed it for a while*, as St. Luke expresses them, and then *depart from the goodness* which God's grace had formerly wrought in us, and *from the grace of God itself*.[5]

---

4. In 1610, Donne publicly renounced Roman Catholicism, and wrote anti-Catholic pamphlets. He was an attorney who was drafted by King James, as it were, into being an Anglican minister in 1615.

Donne is saying this parable teaches a Christian *believer* who "departs from the goodness" wrought in him or her by God *has departed* "from the *grace* of God itself." Disobedience disqualifies *believers* from grace.

Thus, the second seed's source problem is not lack of faith. Its problem was having the wrong expectations of what it costs to follow Christ. As Lisco in *The Parables of Jesus* (1850) explains, the second seed represents those who "seek and expect from Christ an easy life,...[and] will make no sacrifice for it." *Id.*, at 62.

What would have prevented the fall? Jesus said 'keep holding on to the Root.' When you let go, you are opposite of the saints who "keep the commandments of God, and the faithfulness (*pistis*) of Jesus." (Rev. 14:12.)

Parallel To Revelation 2:4-5

There is no missing this point if you see the precise parallel to Revelation 2:4-5. There Jesus tells the Ephesians they have "left your first love," and "art fallen," so "repent" and do your "first works."

The second seed in the Parable of the Sower likewise had "joy" in the word at first, like the Ephesians had "love at first." The second seed "sprouted" and thus had "first works," just like the Ephesians. The second seed then sinned and "fell away," just as the Ephesians "art fallen." The solution, as always, is "repent," as Jesus told the Ephesians in Revelation 2:4-5 and do your "first works."

Third Seed Illuminates Traits Of The Saved Fourth Seed

Now who is the only saved person in the Parable of the Sower? It is the fourth seed, which is the only one who brings forth *fruit* or...dare I use the synonym...works.

---

5. John Donne, "Sermon on 'Easter' 1626," *The Works of John Donne, D.D.* (Henry Alford, ed.)(London: John Parker, 1839) Vol. 1 at 378.

The fourth seed is received by the good and noble heart that hears the word. To understand the fourth seed, we must see the contrast to the third seed. The KJV says the third seed "brings no fruit to perfection." (Luke 8:14, KJV.) However, the translation is lacking.

Rather, the third seed is choked by thorns (*i.e.*, the worries of this world) and so does not *telesphorousin*. This Greek word combines *teleos*, which means *end*, with *phore*, which means *to produce, bring forth*. Together, the two words literally mean "to complete" or "bring to a finish." *Telesphore* is often used with regard to fruit, pregnant women or animals. (*Robertson's Word Pictures.*) *Telesphorousin* is the present active form in Greek. So it means "did not keep on producing to the end" or "did not continue to the finish." **Completion, not perfection, is in view.** They did not *telephorousin, i.e.*, they did not keep on producing **to completion**. They were choked off.

This is likewise reminiscent of the Sardisians whom Jesus tells in Revelation 3:2 that their works are "not complete," *i.e.*, **incomplete.**[6] NASB,GWT,ALT,Darby. (*Cfr.* KJV "works not perfect"). Failure to **complete** your works leads to a loss of salvation.[7] As Jesus tells the parable, Jesus really means the works of the third seed did not reach "completion," but were instead cut off by thorns that stopped their growth, just as Jesus was saying about the Sardisians' works.

---

6. *Pleroo* (from the Greek word *pleres*) means "to complete" or "make full," "to carry through to the end," "to make complete in every particular, to render perfect etc." (Thayer's).

7. I suspect the KJV intends to set the bar as high as perfection for doctrinal reasons. This translation would suggest we have an impossible burden, which the KJV hopes to imply means we can only be 100% perfect if we had the imputed righteousness of Christ to begin with. Yet, the verb is not directly about perfection. This reads far too much into the verb. It is emphasizing the human failing of *not completing* the works given to them. The thorns *choke* growth and maturity (completion).

Knowing the flaws of the third seed opens our understanding of the fourth seed's reason for being saved. The fourth seed, by contrast, "fell into good ground, and grew, and brought forth fruit a hundredfold." (Luke 8:8.) Listen to Jesus' explanation of why this person alone among the four is ultimately saved:

> And that in the good ground, these are such as in an honest and good heart, having heard the word, hold it fast, and **bring forth fruit with patience**. (Luke 8:15 ASV.)

The Greek verb for "hold it fast" is in the Greek present active again. It means "keep on holding down." It is not hold "fast," but hold "down." (*Robertson's Word Pictures.*) This is a significant point. As Jesus tells the parable, the devil swooped down and stole the word from the first sewn seed, depriving it of salvation. By continuing to **hold down the word**, the fourth seed is **guarding itself**. It is doing everything possible to keep Satan from snatching the word away. It is the same meaning behind John 8:51. He who has "kept guard" (*tereo*) over Jesus' word "should never [ever] taste death." (John 8:51, ASV.) Finally, what does it mean that the only saved person in this parable "brings forth fruit with patience" (Luke 8:15, ASV)? Salvation depends on completing works to the end.

Luke 8:15 really means: "who keep carrying on producing fruit with endurance." The Greek verb this time is *karpos* (carrying) combined with *phore* (produce, bear) in the Greek present indicative. So it has a continuous meaning. This is followed by *hupomeno* in Greek. In most translations of this verse, *hupomeno* is rendered as *patience*. However, almost everywhere else *hupomeno* appears in the NT it is translated as *endurance,* which is the more likely intended meaning of Jesus. The combination of *karpos* and *phore* implies fruit-bearing by definition. This parallels Luke 8:8 which mentions "fruit a hundredfold." Thus, literally, Jesus is saying the saved seed "keeps carrying on producing fruit with endurance." This is in sharp contrast with the third seed which was lost because it did not "continue to the finish" or "produce to completion." (Luke 8:14.)

So let's build a diagram of the saved person in the Parable of the Sower.

TABLE 2. Parable Of The Sower: Fourth Seed

Fourth Seed (The Saved)	Jesus' Explanation
good ground	noble and good heart
seed sewn	heard the word
grew	kept holding the word down (protecting it)
keeps on producing fruit a hundredfold	keeps on carrying on producing fruit with endurance. *Cfr.* third seed fails to produce to the finish

Here is Jesus' salvation formula in a nutshell. Producing fruit is never optional. Fruitlessness and being choked are pictures of the lost, even including those who "kept on believing for a while" and who "received" the word with joy at first. In fact, Jesus' point is even more adamant than just that: Jesus is saying partial fruitfulness is not enough. Jesus portends gloom for the one who has growth and then is choked off by thorns. Your initial good works are forgotten if you do not finish and complete well. Instead, you must endure to the end to be saved. This is an echo of Matthew 10:22 once more. It is reminiscent of Ezekiel 33:12. Salvation by faith alone is clearly refuted. Salvation by works alone is not approved either. However, salvation by endurance in good works to the end is crucial besides faith. So says the Lord Jesus Christ.

Once you unlock the Sower Parable, you unlock all the parables. Jesus implied this when He asked: "how will you know all the other parables if you do not understand this one?" (Mk 4:13.) This is why cheap grace strenuously seeks to obscure this particular parable. Yet, it is a parable one cannot claim is *hard to understand*. Jesus already explained it!

Luther Could Not Come Up With A Gloss
To Solve The Parable Of The Sower

No one has ever properly explained how Jesus' Parable of the Sower can even remotely line up consistent with the Modern Gospel of Cheap Grace. Luther's effort is so untenable that it proves how absolutely impossible it is to reconcile the two. Luther must have realized Jesus contradicts the Modern Gospel. Thus, he injects the Modern Gospel's doctrine of faith, not works, into what saves the second seed. Luther then ignores how this mismatches the rest of what the parable means.

Luther begins his commentary properly. The first type who has their seed snatched are those who "hear the word" but do not understand it. (*Sermons of Martin Luther*, Vol. II, at 114.)[8] These "never believe" and never become saved. (*Id.*, at 115.)

Luther then says the second seed knows the correct doctrine of salvation, *i.e.*, "they know the real truth" that they are saved by "faith without works" (the Cheap Grace Gospel). However, "they do not persevere." He adds: "when it comes to the test that they must suffer harm, disgrace and loss of life or property, then they fall and deny it....in times of persecution they deny or keep silence about the Word."

Luther in essence is saying that they lose their salvation because under pressure they deny this truth that salvation is by faith alone. This is a bizarre self-contradiction. If you can lose your salvation by losing faith in the principle of faith alone, then faith alone does not save you. You must *endure* or *persevere* in the doctrine of faith alone or be lost. This is a self-contradiction, because then faith alone did not save you. Faith and ***perseverance in faith alone*** saves you. These two

---

8. Martin Luther, "The Parable of the Sower," *The Precious and Sacred Writings of Martin Luther* (Minneapolis, MN: Lutherans in All Lands, 1906) Vol. 11 reprinted as *The Sermons of Martin Luther* (Grand Rapids, Michigan: Baker Book House) (1983) Vol. II at 113 *et seq.*

ideas are self-contradictory: if you must persist in faith to be saved, then *persistence*, not the faith alone, is necessary for salvation. Hence, Luther's solution is nonsensical. (Anyone who has read eternal security arguments know that they reject Luther's argument precisely because salvation then depends on more than a one-time faith. Luther is actually contradicting the Modern Gospel of Cheap Grace to save it from the Parable of the Sower.)

Martin
Luther
1483-
1546

Luther's comments on the third group are enlightening as well. This group of seeds "always possess the absolutely pure Word...." (*Id.*, at 116.) Their fault is "they do not ***earnestly*** give themselves to the Word, but become ***indifferent*** and sink in the cares, riches and pleasures of this life...." (*Id.*, at 117.) They are thus apparently initially saved. Luther says "these have all in the Word that is needed for their salvation, but they do not make any use of it, and they rot in this life in carnal pleasures." Luther seems to understand Jesus is saying their problem is sin, not lack of proper faith. Luther says that despite the proper knowledge of the Gospel, "they do not bring under subjection their flesh." (*Id.*)

This leads Luther to the correct conclusion why the fourth seed is saved. Luther says they "bring forth fruit with patience, those who hear the Word and *steadfastly retain it*, meditate upon it and ***act*** *in harmony with it*." This leads to as true a statement as you will ever hear by Luther:

> Here we see why it is no wonder there are so few true Christians, for all the seed does not fall into good ground, but only the fourth and small part; and that they are ***not to be trusted who boast they are Christians*** and praise the teaching of the Gospel. *Id.* at 118.

Luther realizes that salvation depends in the Parable, as Jesus depicts it, on *YOU!* It depends on the earnestness of *your response and productivity!*

This is the end of Luther's substantive commentary. What did he do? He explained Jesus' parable correctly. Yet, he pretended it was consistent with the Modern Gospel of Cheap Grace by injecting it into what saved the second and third seeds initially. Luther did so without acknowledging it was self-contradictory nonsense. How can a seed that is saved by faith alone have to persevere and *not succumb to sin*? How can it lose salvation by *being overcome by the thorns* (pleasures) of this life? Nor did Luther try to ever explain away why the saved fourth seed alone had *completed works*.

Luther's response is a perfect example of how people retain the cheap grace gospel even when it contradicts Jesus. Luther is conceding certain unavoidable aspects of this parable are at direct odds with cheap grace. Yet by injecting the Modern Gospel of Cheap Grace into the middle of the discussion, Luther makes it appear that Jesus' words are compatible with it. In this manner, Luther has somehow rationalized away that a conflict exists.

It is as Isaiah prophesied: "the wisdom of their wise men shall perish, and the understanding of their prudent men shall be hid." (Isaiah 29:14.)

How Presuppositional Logic Influenced Luther

A worthwhile side-note is to point out that the young Luther's presupposition which imposed *faith alone* on the Parable of the Sower is not unique. It is how the young Luther erred repeatedly in construing other passages. It is a presupposition the young Luther allowed to permeate all his interpretations of the parables. Warren Kissinger noted this defect in his *The Parables of Jesus: A History of Interpretation and Bibliography* (Metuchen, N.J.: American Theological Library Association, 1979) at 47:

> The central category of his [Luther's] herme- neutic is... *sola fide* [*i.e.*, faith alone], and this is reflected in his interpretation of the parables. It often appears **strained** and as **a presupposi- tion superimposed upon a given parable**.

> Here perhaps Luther does some "spiritual jug-
> gery" of his own, and reflects... a methodology
> which he found so distasteful in the allegoriz-
> ers [of parables].

Thus, the young Luther had a penchant of twisting Jesus' parables so that they fit the presupposition of faith alone. The parable texts did not support Luther's favored con-clusion. The parables, in fact, stood for the opposite. How-ever, to prevent the casual Sunday Christian from learning the parables were all at odds with *faith alone*, the young Luther incessantly injected *faith alone* into *how* to read each parable. He read each one to conform to his presupposition that *faith alone* was true.

The young Luther's decision to do this has had major repercussions on Christian history. It created a tantalizing yet deficient path of salvation for millions of souls.

If the young Luther had not distorted the parables' meanings, then Jesus' parables would have refuted faith alone doctrine long ago in everyone's analysis. Rather than be open to Jesus' correction, the young Luther was constantly redact-ing Jesus' Gospel to fit Luther's youthful endorsement of the Fable of Cheap Grace.

Thankfully, Luther gave up this fable when he was more mature. As an older man, Luther endorsed the costly grace gospel as what Jesus truly taught.[9] See the *Shorter Cat-echism* and *Longer Catechism* of 1531 and the *Antinomian Theses* of 1537. The mature Luther reformulated salvation-doctrine to be one of costly grace yet without bluntly declar-ing his change to anyone.

---

9. See "Tyndale Causes Luther To Quietly Abandon Faith Alone" on page xiii *et seq.*

The Parallel To The Unprofitable Servant

In the Parable of the Sower, Jesus says the seed in good ground sometimes produces different yields. Jesus says "others fell upon the good ground, and were giving fruit, some indeed a *hundredfold*, and some *sixty*, and some *thirty*." (Matt. 13:8, ASV.)

This precisely parallels Jesus' Parable of the Unprofitable Servant. (Matt. 25:14-30.) In that parable, one servant is unprofitable, and produces nothing. Jesus says this one must be thrown outside where there is weeping and gnashing of teeth. The two servants with five and ten talents produced respectively are, by contrast, welcomed in the kingdom.

There are two striking parallels. The unprofitable servant is similar to the second seed in the Sower Parable who "believes for a while" (Luke 8:13) but sins and hence withers (dies) (Luke 8:6), never bearing any fruit. Likewise, the profitable servants produce varying multiples of talents, which clearly parallels the fourth seed in the good ground that produces varying amounts of return.

This tells us Jesus is underscoring a distinction on who is saved and unsaved in the Parable of the Sower, just as Jesus clearly did in the Parable of the Unprofitable Servant. For in the latter, the servant of His Lord who takes the treasure given him but who *produces nothing* is then sent to a place "outside" of weeping and gnashing. Jesus elsewhere says this place is the "fiery furnace" where there is "weeping and gnashing of teeth." (Matt. 13:42.) Of course, there is no weeping in heaven (Isaiah 25:8; Rev. 7:17, 21:4), and thus we know Jesus' imagery is meant to signify damnation for the servant of His who is unprofitable

This means in the parallel Parable of the Sower that the second seed who sprouts initially but *produces no fruit* or the third seed which is choked off and *produces nothing* is meant to symbolize the same thing as the unprofitable servant. Therefore, we know that Jesus intends us to view the seed that produces no fruit and withers (dies) to be spiritually dead even though at first "he believes for a while." (Luke 8:13). Such seed is as damned as the unprofitable servant in the Parable of the Unprofitable Servant.

Hence, when combined, these two parables are clear. Jesus teaches a one-time believer who sins and produce no fruit, and consequently withers and dies (Luke 8:6, 13) is an unprofitable servant who goes to the place "outside" where there is "weeping and gnashing." Jesus specifically says this place is the "fiery furnace." (Matt. 13:42,50.)

Commentaries On The Parable Of The Sower Without Presuppositions

In *Counting the Cost*, subtitled *The Cost of Bearing Fruit With Perseverance*, Mark Dunagan, of Beaverton Church of Christ, correctly explains the Parable of the Sower in Luke 8:11-15. He says:

> Being a faithful Christian is not an easy or effortless task for anyone, including the "good" heart. This person has to **hold on to the gospel**, and **bear fruit with "perseverance."** It is going to take work and effort to live the Christian life.[10]

Amen! Dunagan has the approach Jesus exhorts.

10.http://www.ch-of-christ.beaverton.or.us/Counting_the_Cost.htm (last accessed 7/16/06).

Clarke's Surprisingly Frank Commentary On The Parable Of The Sower

Adam Clarke, the famous commentator, typically does everything he can to twist passages to fit cheap grace. However, in reading the Parable of the Sower, he brings no such presuppositions.

Clarke correctly sees the target of this parable is the one in the crowd who fails to bring forth personal fruit:

> Under the parable of the sower, our Lord intimates, That of all the multitudes then attending his ministry, few would bring *forth fruit to perfection*. (Comm, Matt. 13:3.)

Clarke also correctly understands the problem with the first two seeds is the *deficiency of soil* when one hears Jesus' Gospel. There is the impervious ground "by the way side." There is no room in the soil for the seed to enter. Then there is the stony ground in which the second seed landed. The stony ground only has a thin surface of the earth to grow in. (Comm., Matt. 13:4-6.)

Then Clarke says the difficulty with the third seed is different. It is not the soil *itself*. Rather, it is the surroundings in which the seed is sown. This earth has been "ploughed up," and thus was fertile and accessible for growth. However, this seed was sown where there were already "brambles and weeds" which unfortunately "had not been cleared away." (Comm., Matt. 13:7.)

Then Clarke correctly sees the difference for the fourth seed. It is *prepared to hear* the gospel:

> Good ground — Where the earth was deep, the field well ploughed, and *the brambles and weeds all removed.* (Comm., Matt. 13:8.)

Let's stop there. The Modern Gospel teaches it makes no difference how you prepare the soil of your heart *prior* to hearing the gospel. Nor is it supposedly important after you hear the gospel to clear away the cares and worries of this world as a *precondition* to not later being choked off, and hence bearing no fruit. According to the Modern Gospel of Cheap Grace, your saved-relationship can never turn on *either* *preparing* your heart to listen nor *improving* your chance of being *fruitful* once you are saved. Thus, notice how Clarke is forced to admit Jesus teaches contrary to the Modern Gospel of Cheap Grace by the force of Jesus' words.

Cornelius Exemplifies Perfectly The Fourth Seed

Is there any examples in the New Testament that illustrate what Jesus teaches? Yes. The same person (Dr. Luke) who wrote Luke chapter eight also wrote about the life of Cornelius in Acts chapter ten. Surely, Luke told the story of Cornelius to provide a living example of what Jesus said in Luke chapter eight.

In fact, Cornelius' story proves it is foolish to believe that pursuing God earnestly does not matter to prepare yourself to find the true Gospel. In Cornelius' case, God sent a message to a man who did not know Christ. God's message was that the man's acts of generosity to the poor had been a fragrant odor to the Lord. God now wanted Cornelius to hear the gospel from Peter. Cornelius was the good soil. Yet, Cornelius was still *unsaved* and without the Holy Spirit when he did this generosity and when the Lord brought Peter to Cornelius. (Acts 10:1 *ff.*)

Finishing Up Discussion On Clarke

Clarke has admitted all of Jesus' points about the importance of preparing the soil and our productivity upon hearing the word. Clarke is very close to exposing the falsity of the Gospel of Cheap Grace. That gospel claims the receptivity of our soil makes no difference. All that matters supposedly is the sovereign electing force of God. Clarke gets ever so near to exposing the impact of Jesus' mention of the four *soils* as playing a key role in final salvation. Yet, Clarke does not follow-through. Predictably, when the Gospel of Faith Alone is vanquished in Luke 8:13 — when Jesus says the second seed "believed for a while" but due to sin ends up lost (Luke 8:13) — Clarke is silent. He makes no comment.

Salvation Message Of Revelation Is Straight From The Parable Of The Sower

As we touched on earlier, we can confirm our interpretation of the Parable of the Sower by comparing the parable to Jesus' words in Revelation. In the latter, Jesus once more states His core salvation theology. Jesus does this in Revelation by reproving or commending each church by the criteria that Jesus used in the Parable of the Sower. This is done ever so subtly. Thus, many commentators miss this.

There are some who left their first love. (Rev. 2:4). They correspond to the second seed that starts with joy. This seed "believes for a while" but in time of temptation falls away. (Luke 8:13.) In Revelation, these do not "produce to completion" because of incomplete works. (Rev. 3:2.)

> "So because thou art lukewarm, I will spew thee out of my mouth."
> Rev. 3:16

Then there are believers at another church who are neither hot nor cold but lukewarm. Jesus explains why: "Because thou sayest, I am rich, and have gotten *riches*, and have need of nothing." (Rev. 3:17.) These correspond to the third seed which was choked not only by the cares of this world, but also by "*riches* and pleasures" of this life. Thus, they did not produce to the end. (Luke 8:14.)

Yet, there is one church and one seed that is viewed as on the right path. This is the church of Philadelphia which compares to the fourth seed in the Parable of the Sower. The church at Philadelphia is told "I know thy **works**," and as a result a door is in front of them that no one can shut. (Rev. 3:8.) This church has very little "power" left, but "*did keep*

my word, and did not deny my name." (Rev. 3:8.) This corresponds to the fourth seed which "in an honest and good heart, having heard the word, ***hold it fast***, and ***bring forth fruit*** with patience." (Luke 8:15.) There is an unmistakable parallelism between "keep my word" (Rev. 3:8) and "hold it fast" (Luke 8:15) as well as "thy works" (Rev. 3:8) and "bring forth fruit...." (Luke 8:15).

Hence, Jesus has made re-appear in the Book of Revelation all the criteria for a saved seed versus these lost seeds from his Parable of the Sower. Why?

Precisely because there is no more difficult passage for Cheap Grace doctrine to explain than the Parable of the Sower. Jesus in the Book of Revelation written near 90 A.D. invokes the Sower Parable obviously to rebuff the message Jesus heard in the church pre-90 A.D. that faith alone saves, and works matter not at all. The Sower Parable says those whose faith died due to temptation or whose works were incomplete were lost. Only the one who produces fruit to the end was saved in the Sower Parable.

Conclusion

The Parable of the Sower is an amazing nugget of Jesus' doctrine. For here is the whole *true* gospel of salvation from Jesus' lips. It is all contained in a very unassuming Parable of the Sower. Jesus tells you how to be saved and what is necessary to complete your salvation. Jesus tells you also how to be lost even after you have faith and accepted His word with joy and experience initial growth ("sprouted").

The key starting point is to realize Jesus tells you that the outcome turns crucially on the preparation of the soil of your heart to hear Jesus' Word. Jesus taught in this parable that you must brace yourself to accept the Word's requirements. You will face trials of temptation. Others who are not constantly deliberating on Jesus' words or who are not focused on them will fail. The second seed was foolish, not counting the costs. It quickly "believed," but just as quickly fell into temptation. The third seed began well, but let the world's demands crowd out those of the Lord. Only the fourth persisted in producing fruit and was saved.

Marcus Dods, D.D., in his *The Parables of Our Lord* (Edinburgh: Macniven and Wallace, 1883) at 10-20 aptly explained this parable. The second seed had a "shallow" conception of the costs of the kingdom. The second seed thought he did not have to stay *rooted* to the Words of Jesus — he wondered off to teachers other than Jesus, and thus did not "keep holding to the Root (Jesus)." The third seed went a little further. It had zeal for the word of Jesus. Yet, the third seed's zeal was soon crowded out by the cares and interests of this world. The third seed heard the word, accepted it, but thereafter did not keep the pathway to growth clean by making sure "the field [was left] to itself" — Jesus' words alone.

Thus, as to the first three seeds, even those who believed for a while, Dods says there was a "failure of the gospel." Jesus said the reason had nothing to do with the Word itself. It turned instead upon the varying quality of the soils *before the Word was sown*. It turns on three things: stubbornness (first seed), moral weakness or "shallowness" (the second seed) and lack of maintaining one's clear focus on Jesus' words alone (the third seed).

Then what is the right approach of the fourth seed which Jesus is holding up for us to imitate? Dods says the "good and noble" heart "had deeper character," and "receives the word with deliberation, as one who has *many things to take into account and weigh*." Dods adds: "He receives it with seriousness and reverence and trembling, *foreseeing the trials* he will subjected to, and *he cannot show a light minded joy*." Then, despite these costs, the Word of Jesus is "held fast" by the fourth seed. As Dods closes the point, the "fruitful hearer" realizes Jesus means he "must keep the word." The fourth seed *protects* Jesus' Words as that of its "Sole Teacher." (Matt. 23:8.) If we likewise mirror this focus on Jesus' words *alone*, we are holding to the Root — the doctrines of Jesus Christ — which the second seed failed to do.

19 *Every Tree Without Good Fruit*

The Passages At Issue

But when he [John the Baptist] saw many of the Pharisees and Sadducees coming to his baptism, he said unto them, Ye offspring of vipers, who warned you to flee from the wrath to come? (8) Bring forth therefore *fruit worthy of repentance*: (9) and think not to say within yourselves, We have Abraham to our father: for I say unto you, that God is able of these stones to raise up children unto Abraham. (10) And even now the axe lieth at the root of the trees: *every tree therefore that bringeth not forth good fruit is hewn down, and cast into the fire*. Matt. 3:7-10 (ASV).

(14) For narrow is the gate, and *straitened [narrow] the way, that leadeth unto life*, and few are they that find it. (15) Beware of false prophets, who come to you in sheep's clothing, but inwardly are ravening wolves. (16) By their fruits ye shall know them. Do men gather grapes of thorns, or figs of thistles? (17) *Even so every good tree bringeth forth good fruit; but the corrupt tree bringeth forth evil fruit.* (18) A good tree cannot bring forth evil fruit, neither can a corrupt tree bring forth good fruit. (19) *Every tree that bringeth not forth good fruit is hewn down, and cast into the fire*. (20) Therefore by their fruits ye shall know them. (21) Not every one that saith unto me, Lord, Lord, *shall enter into the kingdom of heaven*;

but *he that doeth the will of my Father who is in heaven*. Matt. 7:14-21 (ASV).

The Warning

Jesus and John the Baptist in the passages above both make the following statement: "every tree therefore that bringeth not forth *good* fruit is hewn down, and cast into the fire." (Matt. 3:10; 7:19.)

John the Baptist explained his meaning by emphasizing the need to have "works worthy of repentance." (Matt. 3:8.) He ridiculed the prevalent idea among the Jews that because they were Abraham's sons (the theory of election of those days), they were somehow a chosen people *for personal salvation*. John the Baptist rejects this, saying *each* individual must bring forth good fruit or be cast into the fire. He made the salvation formula very personal. It was not by national election as some supposed. One could not trust in one's election as Abraham's son. Instead, one had to bring forth personal fruit worthy of repentance.

Jesus makes this very same statement in the context of warning about false prophets: "Every tree that bringeth not forth good fruit is hewn down, and cast into the fire." (Matt. 7:19.) Jesus promises burning in fire for every "tree" that lacks *good* fruit.

What does this expression mean?

What 'Bringeth Forth Good Fruit' Means

The verb tense for "bringeth not forth good fruit" is the Greek present active participle of *poie*. (*Interlinear Scripture Analyzer*.) The verb *poie* means *to do* or *to make*. In Greek, this thus means everyone who "does not *keep on producing* good fruit" will eventually be cut down and thrown in the fire.

Are Trees An Individual Or A Nation?

Some proponents of cheap grace recognize this passage as a problem passage for their doctrine. They argue that Jesus does not intend to establish good fruit as a criterion for salvation. Rather, good fruit is supposedly a criterion whether a people as a nation are to be rejected. Thus, the burning which Jesus threatens allegedly does not mean *hell* fire. It means supposedly persecution for a people group who are lacking good fruit. Therefore, because it is a nation-group, the suffering supposedly can only mean a temporal suffering. It allegedly does not mean such a people group will end up in hell.

Hence, this view argues a *tree* in this verse is not intended to be an individual. It is supposedly intended to be an entire people group. From this, cheap grace advocates deduce the fire cannot be hell fire, and thus we are to suppose 'fire' means merely persecution.

But what does Jesus *really* mean by *tree*? Individuals or nations? In other words, what *object* did Jesus intend to warn?

Jesus in context tells us to test whether a prophet is false or true by means of examining their *fruits*. In Matthew 7:20, Jesus says "surely you will be knowing them from their fruits." (Incidentally, Jesus says the fruit that proves they are false is because they work *anomia*. Matt. 7:23.)[1]

Thus, in context, the warning is about *individuals*, not nations. We are to examine the prophets whether their fruit works *anomia* (*i.e.*, negation of the Law or lawlessness).[2] We

---

1. *Anomia* means either "the negation of the law" or "lawlessness, lawless conduct." (See my prior book, *Jesus' Words Only* (2007) at 61.) Jesus and Deuteronomy 13:1-5 tells us that if a prophet has signs and wonders "that come to pass" yet seeks to seduce us from obeying the Law given Moses, then they have evil fruit. This is how you know they are false. This applies therefore to anyone who proclaims Christ, like Balaam, but who thereafter falls because he "teaches [us] to not follow the least command" in the Law of Moses. (Matt. 5:19.)

2. See footnote 1 *supra*.

---

test their doctrine against the Law given Moses. Was their *personal* doctrine and actions good or bad? God will do the same with *every tree*. Then those lacking *good fruit,* such as those who worked *anomia*, will go into the fire. Hence, *every tree* must mean *every person*. It does not mean *every people group*.

Are Only False Prophets & Not Believers Being Warned?

Some proponents of cheap grace try to argue that Jesus' message in Matthew 7:19 of cutting down trees without good fruit is limited to false prophets. The false prophets are mentioned in 7:20. Then the argument goes that since false prophets could *never* have been one who believed in Christ, Jesus is not warning a believer they must have good fruit. The believer can supposedly trust that Christ's righteousness covers them and they have no *personal* duty to have good fruit. They allegedly will not be sent to the fire of hell for lacking good fruit.

There are several flaws in this argument. Let's start with the last one.

First, the covering of Christ is withdrawn from a sinning Christian, but is re-applied to such a Christian upon repentance from sin. So says Apostle John. (1 John 1:7-9, ASV.)[3] Thus, from Apostle John's statement, one would deduce that Jesus means precisely in Matthew 7:19 that a sinning Christian is a tree without good fruit, and is sent to the fire. Apostle John gives us the reason: in such a case, the blood of Christ *no longer covers* the sinning and unrepentant Christian. (For more discussion, see page 1 *et seq.*)

---

3. "(7) but if we walk in the light, as he is in the light, we have fellowship one with another, and the blood of Jesus his Son *cleanseth us from all sin*. (8) If we say that we have no sin, we deceive ourselves, and the truth is not in us. (9) *If we confess our sins*, he is faithful and righteous to *forgive us our sins*, and to *cleanse us from all unrighteousness*." (ASV)

Second, even if Matthew 7:19 were a warning to false prophets, such prophets were not persons necessarily who never believed in Christ. It is possible to have been a believer in Jesus Christ, even prophesying of Him, but later fall into damnation. This is precisely the case with the prophet Balaam. **Before** he became false by teaching it was permissible to violate the Law (Rev. 2:14), Balaam *was a believer in Christ* and *true prophet of Christ*. In fact, he is one of the greatest prophets of Christ, as discussed below.[4]

This means that Jesus' warning of knowing whether a prophet was false by his fruits meant to direct us to examine even true believers in Christ by this standard. For Scripture actually speaks of a believer in Him (Balaam) — a true prophet of Jesus Christ — who later fell into damnation by working the negation of the commands of God. (Rev. 2:14.)

Let's study Balaam's life briefly.

Moses wrote the account of Balaam being filled with the Holy Spirit (Numbers 24:1-2), and then prophesying that a star would rise over Judea signaling the birth of a king who would rule the world. (Numbers 24:17.) This is known as the famous Star Prophecy.

Balaam - true prophet of Christ later turns false

What Is The Star Prophecy?

This is the messianic prophecy that led the Magi in Matthew 2:1 to find the baby Jesus in a manger. The Star Prophecy brought them to a place to worship Jesus as a baby, bringing gifts of frankincense, gold and myrrh.

However, later, Balaam fell by teaching the negation of the Law given Moses. Balaam told the people they could eat meat sacrificed to idols and fornicate. (Numbers 31:16; Rev. 2:14.)

---

4. You can find a full discussion on this background of Balaam in my prior book, *Jesus' Words Only* (2007) at 53-55, 59, 135 *et seq.*

Because Balaam — a true prophet of Christ — negated the Law and seduced the people from following the Law, Balaam *later* became a false prophet. (Deut. 4:2; 13:1-5.) His work of negating the Law made him have evil fruit. Because he was a tree without good fruit, working *negation of God's commands*, we know Balaam is lost despite once being a true believer and prophet of Christ. (Rev. 2:14.)

Thus, there is such a thing in Scripture as a good believing prophet — even one who proclaims Christ — who later becomes false by teaching people not to follow the Law given Moses. It is therefore wrong to assume *every* false prophet could not originally have been a true prophet and true believer in Christ.[5]

Accordingly, when Jesus in Matthew 7:19-21 says every tree without good fruit is cut down and thrown in the fire, the term "every tree" is not a warning solely to non-believers. It is not only a warning to false prophets who *never knew* Jesus. Rather, by "every tree" Jesus means exactly that. By telling us to test prophets in the same context, Jesus did not mean to say look at only *non-believers* and test their fruit. This same fruit test applies to true believers who proclaim Christ like Balaam did but who later fall by working the negation of God's law. "Every tree" means exactly that: "every tree." Thus, merely believing in Christ, as did Balaam, did not insulate Balaam from Jesus' testing, and finding Balaam turned false. *See*, Revelation 2:14.

Consequently, Jesus did not intend to exclude believers from the warning about sending to the fire every tree that lacks good fruit. Instead, Jesus was serious when He said *every* tree is subject to this test. A believer can be like a prophet who becomes a false prophet by the bad fruit of negating the Law. This is why Jesus identified a true prophet of Christ — Balaam — in Revelation 2:14 later becoming

---

5. *See also*, 1 Kings 13:1-26 (true old prophet deceives young prophet of Judah, lying to him about a supposed new prophecy that negated a prophetic command God previously gave the young prophet.)

false by teaching the Israelites they could eat meat sacrificed to idols and fornicate. Hence, we know anyone of us similarly lacking "good fruit" can be sent to hell's fire.

Similar Lesson In The Parable Of The Sower On Producing Fruit Applies To Individuals

The fact this good fruit-requirement applies to individuals is corroborated in several ways. First, when Jesus tells the Parable of the Sower in Mark 4:20, He says the saved seed are the ones who "are hearing" (present participle active) the word and are "*beside* receiving it" (*Interlinear Scripture Analyzer*) "continuing to *produce fruit.*" The Greek for *produce* fruit is in the present active indicative of *karpophore,* and hence it means *keeps on producing fruit.*

Thus, Mark 4:20 says the one who "receives" (believes) the word and "keeps on producing fruit" is saved. In parallel, Matthew 7:19 says the one does not "keep on bringing forth fruit" ends up in the "fire." The two passages are corollaries of one another, thereby confirming the meaning of each passage. This parallelism allows us to understand Jesus is talking in Matthew 7:19 about the necessity for an *individual* to continue to produce good fruit because an *individual* is clearly in view in the Parable of the Sower in the fourth seed that is saved after producing fruit to the end.

The Parallel Message In The Metaphor Of The Vine Applies To Individuals

Furthermore, in John 15:1-6, Jesus gives a statement about burning non-productive branches that parallels Jesus' threat to burn non-productive trees in Matthew 7:19. This parallel proves Matthew 7:19 is just as much directed to individuals as Jesus' words were in John 15:1-6. In the latter, Jesus tells the apostles that "you" are the branches and Jesus is the vine. These are true *individuals* — people, not nations. Jesus then says the branches that "keep staying" in Jesus are continually kept clean and produce fruit. However, those branches who "do not produce fruit" are "taken away" (15:2). Because they "do not stay"[6] in Jesus, they do not "produce fruit" and are as a branch that has withered. It is cut off, thrown *outside* the vineyard and "is burned." Clearly in John 15:1-6, the branch that is burned is an *individual*. Jesus says the apostles are the branches. They are *individuals*.

Thus, in the Metaphor of the Vine, Jesus warns an apostle they too can be *cut down*, just as the tree in Matthew 7:19 is cut down. Jesus warns the apostles likewise in the Metaphor of the Vine that once cut down they will be "thrown outside" and "burned." Hence, we can be certain that the principle in Matthew 7:19 of being cut off and thrown in the fire for lacking good fruit is one Jesus wants us to understand applies to individuals, even apostles.

The Parallel Passage Of The Parable Of The Fig Tree

In Luke 3:8, after a call to "repent or perish" (Luke 3:2-5), Jesus says in effect "Bear fruit in keeping with repentance." Jesus says:

> (6) Then Jesus told this story: A man planted a fig tree in his garden and came again and again to see **if there was any fruit on it,** but he was always disappointed. (7) Finally, he said to his gardener, "I've waited three years, and there hasn't been a single fig! Cut it down. It's just taking up space in the garden." (8) The gardener answered, "Sir, give it **one more chance**. Leave it another year, and I'll give it **special attention** and plenty of fertilizer. (9) If we get figs next year, fine. If not, **then you can cut it down**." (Luke 13:6-9 NLT.)

---

6. The Greek word is from *meno* which is the root of our word *remain*. It means to *stay* or *continue* in one place.

Thus, Jesus teaches here to have fruit consistent with repentance. God will help through His Holy Spirit and be patient. But an ultimate judgment based on fruit is coming.

What Does 'Cast in the Fire' Mean In Jesus' 'Fruit of the Tree' Message?

What does Jesus mean about "cast into the fire" in Matthew 7:19? Is it a place of smelting Christians so their bad works are burned off but they are otherwise in heaven and not in hell?

Certainly, in context, Jesus means that among those sent to this fire are the false prophets who we will recognize by their lack of good fruits. (Matt. 7:20.) The false prophets who are "cast into the fire" must mean they are sent to hell. However, the warning Jesus gives is broader than merely false prophets. It applies to "*every* tree." Thus, because *persons* who are prophets are clearly one type of *tree* within Jesus' meaning, then when Jesus warns the risk to "every tree," Jesus must mean to warn "every person."

Thus, from context, we know Jesus is *warning everyone who does not have good fruit that they will be cut down and thrown in the fire*. If false prophets are in hell, so is every other tree that lacks good fruit.

Fruit Thrown Outside In John 15:1-6 Corroborates That The 'Fire' In Matthew 7:19 Means Hell

The conclusion that "fire" in Matthew 7:19 means *hell* is corroborated once more by John 15:1-6 — the Metaphor of the Vine. Jesus gives the analogous lesson as in Matthew 7:19. Jesus says the branch that does not produce fruit is to be thrown "outside" the vineyard and then burned.

What is the place *outside* where people wait to be sent into the fire? Is this a place of scolding for the saved? No.

For we know anyone thrown outside to be burned is destined for hell. We know this for several reasons, but the two most important are:

First, Jesus tells us that unprofitable servants who do not produce fruit with the riches (talents) given them are thrown *outside* to a place of weeping and gnashing. (Matt. 25:14-30.) Because we know there are no tears or weeping in heaven (Rev. 7:17; 21:4; Isaiah 25:8), this place *outside* cannot be inside Heaven. Jesus likewise tells us this place of weeping and gnashing is meant to signify hell's fire. (Matt. 13:42, the ensnared are thrown into the "fiery furnace" where there is weeping and gnashing.)

Second, we learn the same thing from Revelation 21:8 and 22:15 — those *outside* waiting to be burned are the ones going to hell's fire. In Revelation 21:8, it says "outside" are the "dogs, and sorcerers, and whoremongers, and murderers, and idolaters, and whosoever loveth and maketh a lie." In Revelation 21:8, we are told these same categories of peoples (cowards, unbelievers, sorcerers, etc.) will be thrown in the "lake of fire." This must be hell because Revelation 19:20 tells us the devil and the beast are thrown into the same "lake of fire."

Thus, the sequence in John 15:1-6 of being thrown *outside* and then *burned* precisely matches Revelation 21:8 and 22:15. These people — those who did various evil things — are thrown outside the New Jerusalem who then are thrown in the lake of fire.

This means that in John 15:1-6, Jesus wants us to understand those "branches in me" who are found "without fruit" are thrown "outside" to be "burned" must mean they are sent to hell. Then when we look back at the parallel warning in Matthew 7:19 about *trees without fruit*, we must conclude Jesus means by "fire" the fires of hell itself as well.

Conclusion

Jesus is beginning to be repetitive on the same issue. Over and over, it is those who do good things that are resurrected. (John 5:29.) It is not those who merely believe who will be saved. (John 12:42, believing but cowardly rulers. See page 445 for discussion.) Rather, for example, those who have added works of charity can expect salvation, while those who have not, are promised damnation. (Matthew 25:30-46, the Parable of the Sheep and the Goats, discussed at page 219 *et seq.*) Jesus repeats it again here in Matthew 7:19 by saying every tree that does not *keep on producing good fruit* will be cut down and thrown in the fire. This is a warning as severe as Jesus can make it.

What makes Jesus' point unmistakable about "fruit" is Jesus gives the same lesson in several obvious parallel statements. See Table 1 below.

For example, Jesus gives the same warning in His Parable of the Unprofitable Servant. That servant does not produce fruit with the riches given him. He is thrown *outside* to a place of weeping and gnashing. (Matt. 25:14-30.) This place of "weeping and gnashing" is the "fiery furnace." (Matt. 13:42.)

A second example is that Jesus gives the identical message in the Metaphor of the Vine. (John 15:1-6.) Those who fail to produce fruit are those who fail to keep staying in the vine. Jesus says they are like a branch that is withered, thrown *outside* and which are later *burned.*

These and the other passages cited below all corroborate that Jesus intends the literal meaning of His statement: "every tree that does not bear ***good*** fruit is cut down and thrown in the fire" (Matt. 7:19).

TABLE 1. Parallels Of Statements On Fruit, Profit Or Good Deeds

CONDITION	RESULT
If not keep on producing good fruit	Then cut down and thrown in the fire. Matt. 7:19-21.
If you fail to produce any interest/profit on God's deposit of talents (riches)	**Then thrown outside where there is weeping and gnashing of teeth. Matt. 25:14-30. Place of weeping and gnashing is the "fiery furnace." Matt. 13:42.**

TABLE 1. **Parallels Of Statements On Fruit, Profit Or Good Deeds**

CONDITION	RESULT
"Every branch in me that beareth not fruit"	"He taketh it away." John 15:2.
"If a man does not continue to stay in me... can do [produce] nothing [i.e., no fruit]. If not stay in me"	**Then "cast forth as a branch, and is withered; and they gather them, and cast them in the fire, and they are burned." John 15:4-6.**
If did "good things"	Then you shall rise to "resurrection to life." John 5:28-29
If did "bad things"	**Then you shall rise to "resurrection of damnation." John 5:28-29**
If to least of brethren of Christ you "gave... meat,...drink, and took... in, and clothed... [or when] sick,...you visited....."	Then "inherit the kingdom" and enter "into life eternal." Matt. 25:34, 45.
If to least of brethren of Christ you did not "give... meat,...drink, and... took... in, [or]clothed... [or when] sick,... you [did not] visit...."	**Then "depart from me, ye cursed, into everlasting fire, prepared for the devil and his angels" and you "shall go away into everlasting punishment." Matt. 25:41,46.**

Why is "good fruit" indispensable? Because it represent the works of a repentant heart. Such works are not mere *proof* of an antecedent repentance of the heart which alone would suffice to save. No! Such works are *the* repentance worthy of the antecedent repentance of the heart. You have stolen? You pay back, like Zaccheus did.

The Bible always required that if you stole, you could not just sincerely say you were sorry. The one who stole but who had not repaid could not ask God to apply atonement. Instead, you have to first pay back what you stole with interest. (Exodus 22:1-15; Leviticus 6:1-5; Numbers 5:5-8; 2

Samuel 12:6.) As Ezekiel says, eternal life[7] is by repentance from the heart combined with actual works worthy of repentance:

> [I]f the wicked restore the pledge, **give again that which he had taken by robbery**, walk in the statutes of life, committing no iniquity; **he shall surely live, he shall not die.** (Eze 33:15.)

This is why Prophet John-the-Baptist told the Pharisees they could expect baptism avail them nothing without first doing *erga axios metanoia — works worthy of repentance.* (Matt. 3:8.) They thus lacked the vital fruit that Ezekiel said was necessary to be cleansed and hence *live.* Prophet John-the-Baptist in a similar vein explained what he meant about "works worthy of repentance." He said that "a tree without good fruit [*i.e.*, works worthy of repentance] is cut down and thrown in the fire." Hence, without works worthy of repentance, one lacks good fruit, and you will go to hell.

Jesus in Matthew 7:19 deliberately quotes John so as to emphasize the *necessity* first to have works worthy of repentance — what John had equated with **good fruit** in the identical expression that Jesus borrowed. Otherwise, the cleansing which baptism represents would have no effect in God's eyes. (Notice neither baptism nor atonement are effective to cleanse without *works worthy of repentance / reconciliation with the one you offended.* See page 5 *supra.*)

This explains perfectly why the evangelical sermon of Jesus and the apostles primarily focused on repentance.

> "And they went out and preached that men should repent." (Mark 6:12.)

---

7. Ezekiel uses *life* to mean *eternal life*, and *death* to mean *damnation.* See, Ezekiel 33:12-16, where Ezekiel says the dead receive life by repentance, and the living go from life to death by sinning and disobedience. Hence, Ezekiel speaks of dying and living in a spiritual, not physical sense.

This explains why Peter's first two sermons that brought the first converts concluded with this exhortation:

> "**Repent** and be baptized, every one of you, in the name of Jesus Christ, for **the remission of sins**." (Acts 2:38.) "**Repent** ye, therefore, and turn around, that **your sins may be blotted out**." (Acts 3:19.)

Note again how *blotting out sins* — atonement — is conditioned upon repentance. Peter clearly understood what Ezekiel and Jesus previously declared.

Peter did not invent this evangelistic speech. For his first two sermons were simply obeying what Jesus in His last message expressly taught was to be the evangelical message:

> And He said to them, "Thus it is written, that the Christ should suffer and rise again from the dead the third day; and that **repentance for forgiveness of sins should be proclaimed in His name** to all the nations, beginning from Jerusalem." (Lk. 24:46-47.)

Repentance was key because without works worthy of repentance, we lack the good fruit which is essential to escape the fire. (Matt. 3:8;7:19.) However, if we have such works worthy of repentance, we shall "live" forever. (Eze 33:15.)

Where have we heard this same message before that faith alone, without works is dead and cannot save? Ah, yes, the message from Jesus' brother in the flesh — James. He said in total accord with Jesus, Ezekiel, Peter, and all the prophets:

> (14) What [is] the advantage, my brothers, if someone is saying he has **faith but is not having works**? Such **faith is not able to save him**, is it?****(17) So also such **faith if alone, is dead if it is not [also] having works****** (24)... [A] person is **justified by means of works and not by means of faith alone**.... (James 2:17-26.)

20 *Metaphor Of The Vine*

Introduction

In the Metaphor of the Vine, Jesus tells us that if we "obey My commandments," then we are abiding in Him. (John 15:10.) Jesus then says this abiding is crucial to salvation. First, Jesus says only by abiding in Him (obeying) can we produce fruit. (John 15:4.) Second, Jesus then says the "branch in me" that does not "keep bearing fruit" (present participle active in Greek) is "taken away." (John 15:1-2, *harpazo*-ed.) This cannot possibly a good outcome on salvation. For Jesus then says the branch that does "not keep abiding in me" (defined as 'obeying' in verse 10) (present participle active again) is as a branch that is "cut off from the vine, withered, thrown outside and is burned." (John 15:1-6.) Yet, verse ten says such abiding is by "obeying My commands."

Hence, it is easy to deduce the point. Jesus teaches if a "branch in me" fails *thereafter* to "obey my commandments," you are not "abiding in Jesus," and you cannot bear fruit which is essential to not being "taken away." Once you are taken away, it is too late. The one in Jesus who failed to keep on abiding in Jesus — which Jesus defines as "obeying my commandments" — will find himself/herself "cut off from the vine, thrown outside, withered (dead) to be burned" in hell. It is rather obvious.

What of the faith alone gospel? Here Jesus explicitly says it does not save. Instead, Jesus directly makes salvation contingent, in part, on works of obedience. Only by keeping Jesus' commands in you and obeying them will you produce the "fruit" (works) necessary for branches "in me" (Christ) to be spared being "taken away," "cut off," thrown 'outside," becoming thereby "withered" (dead) and then be "burned" at the final harvest. In fact, one of those "commands" you need to keep in your mind is *this passage*, which when properly understood should spur the prayer to have such fruit!

Branches In Me: Two Possible Fates

In John 15:1-6, Jesus says He is the Vine and the apostles are the branches. Jesus does not say the apostles' *works* are branches. Instead, Jesus says an apostle — body, mind and soul — is a branch.

Jesus then says a branch "*in me*" that fails to produce fruit will be "taken away." (Verse 2.)[1] This fruitless branch failed to "keep on abiding in me" (Verse 5). Such a branch, if it does not "keep on abiding in me," is cast "outside," and as a result becomes dried up (lost all life/is dead), to be cast into the fire to be burned. Thus, the fruitless branch in Christ — due to its not abiding in Jesus (*obeying him, see verse 10*) — lacks fruit, is taken away, thrown outside, dies and is burned.

The American Standard Version of John 15:1-6,10 reads:

> (1) I am the true vine, and my Father is the husbandman. (2) Every branch *in me* that beareth *not fruit*, he *taketh it away* [*harpazo*]: and every branch that beareth fruit, he cleanseth it, that it may bear more fruit. (3) Already ye are clean[2] because of the word which I have spoken unto you. (4) Abide in me, and I in you. As

---

1. The Greek for "taken away" is *harpazo*. Dillow argues it should mean here *lifted up* to follow vinedresser practice. This appears plausible at first until one does a word study on *harpazo* in Jesus' usage. In John 10:27-28, Jesus says by *listening* and *following*, you will not be "harpazo-[ed]" from His hand. Clearly, *harpazo* has an end-of-salvation meaning. This also fits better the Metaphor of the Vine where Jesus next says the fruitless branch is thrown outside the vineyard.
2. Judas had just left the room. The other eleven alone are present.

---

the branch cannot bear fruit of itself, except it abide in the vine; so neither can ye, except ye abide in me. (5) I am the vine, ye are the branches: *He that abideth in me*, and I in him, the same *beareth much fruit*: for apart from me ye can do nothing. (6) *If a man abide not in me,* he is *cast forth [outside] as a branch*, and is withered; and they gather them, and cast them into the *fire*, and they are *burned*....(10) If ye *keep my commandments*, ye shall *abide in my love*; even as I have kept my Father's commandments, and abide in his love.

Consequently, Jesus teaches those who "keep on abiding" in Him are alone able to produce fruit. (John 15:5.) Jesus then repeats twice that if you fail to "keep on abiding in Jesus," you cannot "bear fruit." (John 15:4, 6.)

The Greek word for *abide* in all three verses is *meno*. It means to *stay* or *continue in one place*. Here it is three times used in the present participle active — a continuous tense. (On how to translate, see page 510 *et seq*.) Thus, Jesus means unless you "keep on staying in me," you cannot "bear fruit." (John 15:4, 6.) By contrast, if you "keep on staying in me," you will bear much fruit. (John 15:5.)

The one who "does not keep abiding in me" is "cast outside" to be "burned."[3] (John 15:6.) Why did this happen? Because by failing to "abide in" Jesus, you could produce no "fruit" (John 15:4,6), and the one who "bears not fruit is taken away." (John 15:2.)

What kind of burning happens to the fruitless branch that was taken away and thrown outside in John 15:6?

Verse six is clearly a reference to the time of burning of the branches. In vinedresser practice, this occurs at the final harvest time. Burning of vine branches is not done during the growing season.[4]

---

3. This is *ballo*, to cast out, with *exo*, outside.

John Wesley, the famous evangelist, saw clearly Jesus' meaning:

> They are burned. It is not possible for words more strongly to declare, that **even those who are now branches in the true vine may yet so fall as to perish everlastingly.**[5]

Jesus is clearly saying that you will be judged for failing to have fruit. The root cause of your failure is failing to "abide in" Jesus. Since *abiding* is crucial to having the fruit without which you will be sent to hell, *it is imperative to discover* Jesus' definition on what it means to "abide in" Jesus. Our Lord defines it in the same speech.

What Does It Mean To Abide In Jesus?

What is the answer to the now perilous question of what it means to "keep on abiding" in Jesus? To repeat, this is crucial to understand. Jesus clearly says if you fail to do this (verse six), you will not have fruit, and you will thus become lost. You will be taken away and thrown outside into the fire to be burned.

Jesus tells you what it means just four verses later:

> **If ye keep (tereo) my commandments** (*entolas*, plural), ye shall **abide in my love**; even as I have kept my Father's commandments, and abide in his love. (John 15:10 ASV.)

So if you keep Jesus' *entolas*, which means *directions*, you "abide in" His love. The verb translated as *keep* is the aorist active subjective. It is the verb *tereo*. It means to *hold fast, observe* or *obey.* As an aorist, it means *kept,*

---

4. For a discussion, see Gary W. Derickson, "Viticulture and John 15:1-6," *Journal of the Grace Evangelical Society* (Spring 2005): 23, 40-41.

5. John Wesley, "Perseverance of the Saints," *Fundamental Christian Theology: A Systematic Theology* (A. M. Hills ed.) (C. J. Kinne), 1931, Vol. II, at 266-281.

---

observed, or *obeyed*. If you *should* have *kept, observed* or *obeyed* Jesus' directions, you "shall" abide in His love. *You are abiding in Jesus*. If you should have failed to keep His commandments, you **no longer are abiding in Jesus' love**. You are **no longer abiding in Jesus (verse six)**. You are disobeying Jesus.

Actually, what Jesus is saying is obvious. ***Obey His commands, and thus you will have the fruit that obedience provides***. Consequently, abiding in Jesus would have to mean obeying Jesus, just as He says. It actually produces the fruit of obedience. Absent such obedience, you are not abiding in Jesus. As a result, you lack the fruit *essential* not to be taken away and thrown outside and be burned in the fire.

This dovetails with John 8:51 which uses similar vocabulary. Jesus says there:

> I tell you the truth, anyone who **obeys** (*tereo*) My teaching (*logos*) will [or *should*] never [ever] die! (John 8:51 NLT.)

> Verily, verily, I say unto you, If a man **keep my word**, he **shall** [or *should*] never see death. (John 8:51 ASV.)

This is simply repeated in John 15:1-6, 10. In John 8:51, Jesus says if you obey His teaching, you should never ever die. Why would that be? Because by obedience to Jesus' teaching you will have the fruit Jesus requires in the Metaphor of the Vine. Absent such fruit of obedience, you will be taken away, be thrown outside, and be burned.

This is re-emphasized one more time in John's Gospel. In John 3:36, it says in correct translation:

> He that **keeps on obeying unto the Son** hath eternal life; but **he that keeps on disobeying the Son shall not see life**, but the wrath of God abideth on him. (John 3:36.)

The first part is typically translated as "believes," but the Greek really says that when you "keep on obeying," you are enjoying eternal life.[6] This is then contrasted with what happens when you "keep on disobeying the Son." The second part says God's "wrath keeps abiding on" such a disobedient person.

Thus, John 3:36 is re-emphasizing John 15:1-10 and John 8:51. As long as you are obeying Jesus, you should never ever die. (John 3:36a; John 8:51.) However, when you are not obeying Jesus' *entolas*, and instead you are being disobedient to His *entolas*, you have the wrath of God abiding on you. You lack the fruit that is essential to not being taken away, thrown outside and then be burned. (John 3:36b; John 15:1,6.)

Is 'Abiding in Me' Distinct From 'Abiding in My Love'?

Can it be argued that "abiding in me" in John 15:5-6 does not mean "abiding in my love" in John 15:10? Is this "abiding in my love" in John 15:10 (which Jesus defines as **obeying His commandments**) something *disconnected* with what Jesus just said was "abiding in me" that you absolutely had to have in order to avoid the final fiery judgment in John 15:6? No. They are identical for a few strong reasons.

First, let's go back to verse five.

> I am the vine, ye are the branches: He that abideth in me, and I in him, *the same beareth much fruit*: for apart from me ye can do nothing. (John 15:5 ASV.)

Here, 'bearing fruit' is anyway likely the result of "obeying my commandments" in John 15:10. The concept of fruit is typically equated by Jesus with good works and obedience. (Matt. 7:16-20; 13:22; 21:43.) Thus, if Jesus later explains the way to abide in "His love" is to obey His commandments (John 15:10), this naturally explains why there is a causal nexus with such abiding and "bearing fruit" in John 15:5. Obedience has fruit — *works of righteousness*.

---

6. See "The Use of Pisteuo By The Greatest Prophet (John the Baptist) In John 3:36 As Obeys" on page 447.

A second proof that "abide in me" (15:5-6) is to be equated with "abide in my love by obeying my commandments" (15:10) comes from other elements within the Metaphor of the Vine itself.

In verse four, Jesus says "Abide in me, and *I in you*." Doesn't this verse demonstrate a synergy between Jesus "abiding in you" and our "abiding in" Jesus? Yes. Jesus explains what it means for Him to abide in us in verse seven.

> If ye abide in me, and *my words* (*rhemata*, declarations, sayings)[7] *abide in you*, ask whatsoever ye will, and it shall be done unto you. (John 15:7)(ASV).

Thus, what Jesus means by "abide in me and I in you" (John 15:4) is that if you abide in Jesus, then Jesus' *words* (*rhema*) are abiding in you. (John 15:7.) Thereupon, Jesus is abiding in you when His words are actively abiding in you.

Obviously, these *rhema* are the words that are the springboard for obedience to Jesus' directions. They are His commandments (*entolas*) in 15:10. The meaning of *rhema* that fits best here and elsewhere is *words of command* or *commands*, not simply *words*. (*See*, Luke 5:4-5; John 6:63;6:68; *cf. NAS New Testament Lexicon* (*rhema* means *inter alia* "words of command").) Hence, John 15:7's mention of *rhema* — commands — abiding *in you* directly ties back into verse ten where abiding in Jesus' *entolas* (directions) means we abide *in His love* (*i.e.*, abide in Him.)

---

7. In John 17:8, Jesus said to the Father that He has "given them the words (*rhemata*) which thou gavest me." Robertson says *rhemata* has a slightly different connotation than the singular *logos*. Robertson says the "plural rhemata refers to every single word of God (John 3:34) and of Christ (John 5:47; 6:63, 68) while the singular *logos* (John 17:6, 14) refers to God's message in its entirety." (Jeffrey Khoo, "Evangelicals and Catholics Together in John 17:21?," *The Burning Bush* 2/1 (January 1996) at 9, 13, citing Robertson, *Word Pictures in the New Testament* (Nashville: Broadman Press, 1933) at 5:276.)

Consequently, it is easy to deduce that abiding in Jesus' love (John 15:10) must be the same as "abiding in" Jesus (John 15:5-6) because His abiding in us (John 15:4) is defined as His commands abiding in us. (John 15:7.) In other words, if what is important about His abiding in us is *His words/commands* (John 15:7), then it makes perfect sense that what is important about us "abiding in" Jesus is our obedience to those very same words (*entolas, rhemata*) in us. (John 15:10.)[8] Hence, it follows that 'abiding in Jesus' in verses five and six must mean "abiding in His love" in verse ten.

To repeat, the latter Jesus defined as "obeying [His] commandments." (John 15:10.)

This brings us all the way back to the answer to the crucial question about salvation in John 15:1-6. Jesus has equated the crucial "abiding in me" in verse six with "abiding in My love" which in turn is defined as "obeying my commandments." (John 15:10.)

Finally, it is spiritually preposterous to suggest one can be abiding in Jesus who is not also abiding in Jesus' love. The two descriptions cannot possibly be distinct. For Jesus says "abiding in His love" is by "obeying my commandments." (Jn 15:10.) "You are my friends if you do whatever I command you." (Jn 15:14.) *It follows that a Christian who disobeys Jesus' commands is no longer abiding in Jesus' love.* It then could never make any sense to say a disobedient Christian is "abiding in" Jesus in the sense required in John 15:6. Thus, Jesus clearly means that a failing to abide in Him is a failure to obey Him, and its consequence is you lack the crucial fruit that will spare you from damnation.

---

8. This is once again corroborated by reading the epistle of Apostle John who is writing these inspired words from Jesus: "See that what you have **heard** from the beginning **stays** in you. If it does, you will also **stay in the Son and in the Father**. And this is what he promised us- even eternal life." (1 Jn. 2:24,25 NIV, with *meno* corrected to mean *stay*, identified in bold). Thus, what you "heard" means the "entolas" (commandments) of Jesus.

This is underscored by John 3:36 which says if one "keeps on disobeying the son, the wrath of God keeps abiding on him." (John 3:36.) It is thus nonsense to say one can "abide in" Jesus and thereby be able to produce the fruit necessary in John 15:1-6 yet be a disobedient Christian who lacks Jesus' love for you.

Consequently, we know Jesus' lesson on "abiding in my love" in John 15:10 is indistinguishable from "abiding in me" in John 15:6. Hence, obedience to Jesus' commandments (John 15:10) is what it means to "abide in me" in John 15:5-6. It follows that *absent obedience you lack the crucial-saving fruit* of John 15:6. You are "cut off" and "burned."

Accordingly, for multiple good reasons, Jesus abides in you when His commandments abide in you. Also, you abide in Jesus when you obey Him. Then only by obeying Jesus will you produce the fruit unto salvation required in John 15:1-6 and enjoy the love of Jesus. (John 15:10,14.)

The Metaphor's Meaning About Connection

This conclusion then makes sense of the entire metaphor. Jesus means by connection to Him that apart from *knowing* Jesus' words (commands, *rhema* & *entolas*), and keeping them in your memory, you cannot produce good fruit. Without this connection, you cannot obey Jesus. Thus, when Jesus in John 15:5 says it is not possible for you to bear fruit if you are not abiding in Jesus, the reason is plain. Without Jesus' commands in you, *you are merely following your own sense of conscience of what is right and wrong*. You will ultimately be disobedient. Like the Pharisees who cherry-picked what to follow from the Law (Matt. 23:23), you will have a shallow set of commands to follow unless all of Jesus' commands are part of your tool set of life.

Thus, in John 15:6, your failure to abide in Jesus (*i.e.,* obeying the words of Jesus) is guaranteed if you do not have Jesus' words in you. John 15:4 and 15:7 say Jesus is in you when Jesus' sayings and commands are in your memory (and you loyally follow them). Apart from having Jesus' commands in you (John 15:4,7) and you obeying them (John 15:10) and thus you abiding in Jesus (John 15:5-6), you can not produce any good fruit. (John 15:4-6.) And absent such good fruit, you are taken away, cast outside to be burned. (John 15:2,6.)

Implications On The Cheap Grace Gospel

Obviously, the Metaphor of the Vine is all about having more than just faith. If Jesus' words are in you and He abides in you, but you do not abide in Jesus by obeying those very same words, then such disobedience will cause the wrath of God to remain on you. (John 3:36.) If you fail to obey Jesus' commands, then you do not abide in Jesus/in the love of Jesus, and you will lack the fruit without which you will be marked as a branch to be thrown outside to be burned. (John 15:1,2,6,10.) Faith without fruit cannot save. Never could and never will. Jesus is merely repeating Deuteronomy 6:25. The Cheap Grace Gospel is clearly falsified by Jesus' Metaphor of the Vine.

What About Jesus' Promise Not To Cast Out In John 6:37?

Yet, some think this view is at odds with Jesus promising to never cast out someone in Jesus. Their argument is based on the common English translation of John 6:37. Based on this, they refuse to acknowledge the literal meaning of John 15:1-10.

However, a correct translation of John 6:37 fits perfectly into John 15:6.

John 6:37 actually says he who "***keep on*** coming" to me "I will in no wise cast out."[9] This implies whoever *stops* coming to Jesus will be cast out. Proponents of faith alone, predestination, etc., admit the *continuous* aspect of the verb

---

9. The Greek word for *cast out* is *ekballo*, which combines *exo* with *ballo*. The Greek word for *coming* is *erchomai* in the present tense, which means "is coming."

tense for *come* in this verse.[10] This is precisely what John 15:6 says. If you do not keep on staying in Jesus, then you bear no fruit, are cut off, become dead and are thrown in the fire.

This is clear in context of John chapter six. Jesus defines this *coming* in verse 40 of chapter six by a synonymous activity to *coming.* It is the activity of *looking.* "For my Father's will is that everyone who *keeps looking* [present participle active] to the Son and *pisteuo eis* Him shall have eternal life, and I will raise him up on the last day." (On the meaning of *pisteuo eis*, see page 428 *et seq.*)

Thus, Jesus teaches that all those who *keep on coming* to Jesus and *keep on looking* to Jesus have the same benefit as those who in John 15:1-6 *keep on abiding* in Jesus and are consequently fruitful.

John 6:37 is merely restating the positive part of John 15:1-6. However, John 6:37 and John 6:40 both are *consistent with the negative warning of John 15:6* that those who stop coming to Jesus and stop looking to Jesus are those who do not keep on abiding in Him, are unfruitful and are cut off from the vine. They are as dead branches which, in the final harvest, are removed and burned.

Hence, there is nothing inconsistent between John 15:1-6 and John 6:37. Jesus will not cast outside anyone who keeps coming to Him, who keeps listening to Him and who

---

10. Dr. James White admits: "Throughout this passage an important truth is presented that again might be missed by many English translations. When Jesus describes the one who comes to him and who believes in him [3:16, 5:24, 6:35, 37, 40, 47, etc.], he uses the present tense to describe *this coming*, believing, or, in other passages, hearing or seeing. The present tense refers to a *continuous, on-going action*. The Greek contrasts this kind of action against the aorist tense, which is a point action, a single action in time that is not on-going.... The wonderful promises that are provided by Christ *are not for those who do not truly and continuously believe*. The faith that saves is a living faith, a faith that *always looks* to Christ as Lord and Savior." (White, *Drawn by the Father: A Summary of John 6:35-45* (Reformation Press: 1999) at 10-11.)

---

keeps abiding in Him. He will cast outside only the ones who do not keep on listening to Him, who do not keep on coming to Him and who do not keep staying in Him. For these are the ones who are disobeying the son upon whom the wrath of God continues to abide. (John 3:36.)

Distortions To Retain The Cheap Grace Gospel

One can be certain what Jesus truly means in John 15:1-6,10 by studying how weak are the competing solutions to make Jesus sound like the Modern Gospel of Cheap Grace.

Therefore, we can deduce the strength of the above conclusions by examining the unsuccessful struggle that Cheap Grace Gospel adherents endure to explain away the Metaphor of the Vine. By way of synopsis, these points are:

- One view holds that a branch is not an apostle. Instead, we are told that the branch is an apostle's *works*. The fire that burns is supposedly in heaven (not hell), and it burns away wooden works, and thus does not imply the fiery judgment of hell. (Dillow, *Reign of the Servant Kings*.)

- Another view simply asserts the *fire* is not a threat of hell. Jesus is not threatening to throw any apostle *outside* where the sinners go *en route* to hell in Revelation 22:15. This is accomplished principally by deleting the word *outside* in the translation. The word for *outside* only appears in the original Greek, the Latin Vulgate, and the Spanish Reina Valera. Its omission in standard English translation helps sustain the *nonsensical* assertion that the fire and burning which Jesus mentions is not hell.

- Another view holds that a branch was never a true believer because the fate in hell proves they were never a believer. If a believer suffered in hell for lacking fruitfulness, this would contradict faith alone doctrine. This means Jesus contradicts Paul. Certainly that cannot be a 'biblical' outcome. However, then dogma from someone other than Jesus becomes the test of how to read Jesus even when the dogma is at odds with Jesus. This view ignores Jesus said the eleven *believing* apostles (Judas had left beforehand) are branches and are 'clean right now.' Jesus' message is clearly directed at believers, not unbelievers. Jesus' warning is to a branch "in me" that does not produce fruit because it does not continue to abide "in me." Jesus' warning of burning unfruitful believers at the final harvest is clear.

The Significance Of the Word *Outside* Missing In Most Translations

Before we discuss the argument some make that the burning in John 15:6 is not hell, we need to know that something is missing in the standard English translations. This omission began at least with the KJV. This omission continues today up through our NIV. Almost every translation in English omits that Jesus says the fruitless branch is cast *outside* despite the Greek word for *outside* being present in every Greek text. *Vincent's Word Studies* says the Greek word here means "outside." Vincent goes on to explain the fruitless branch is thrown "outside" the vineyard.

What would have been the consequence had *outside* been properly translated? Everyone would have seen the link to the "unbelievers, fearful (cowards), and liars" who in Revelation 22:15 are "*outside*" waiting to be thrown in the lake of fire in Revelation 21:8. There you have the identical steps as in John 15:6: the cowards and unbelievers *et al.* are "outside" to be "burned" in the fire of hell. Thus, correctly translating "outside" in John 15:6 would let all Christians easily and readily know Jesus is warning the apostles of being sent "outside." This is the place en route to hell's fire if they do not produce fruit because they failed to abide in Jesus. This failure to abide in Jesus is then equated by our Lord with a failure to "obey [His] commandments." (John 15:10.)

However, as we all know, such an implication would destroy the Cheap Grace Gospel held by the many of those engaged in translation. It would also upset the doctrine of almost every other 'evangelical' group engaged in translation of our English Bible. So rather than translate it correctly, it is obscured by other less readily recognized words such as *forth*, *away*, *without*, etc.

Here is a sampling of the major translations where *outside* is not correctly reflected in the rendering.

> If a man abide not in me, he is cast **forth** as a branch, and is withered; and men gather them, and cast them into the fire, and they are burned. (John 15:6 KJV, ASV, Webster, GB.)

> If any one may not remain in me, he was cast forth **without** as the branch, and was withered, and they gather them, and cast to fire, and they are burned. (John 15:6 YLT.)

> Anyone who does not remain in Me is thrown **away** like a useless branch and withers. Such branches are gathered into a pile to be burned. (John 15:6 NLT.)

Only a few translations render it correctly as *outside.* The Spanish Reina Valera uses "fuera" which means *outside.* The Latin Vulgate uses "foras" which likewise means *outside.* The Good News Bible is adequate, saying "out."

It is hard to explain the behavior of the KJV unless one admits bias is involved. For the KJV renders the same expression in Matthew 21:39 when Jesus is talking of evil servants who kill the son whom the master then fires, having them "thrown **out** of the vineyard." Why not translate similarly the similar expression in John 15:6?

Moreover, there is absolutely no doubt that the word at issue should be translated as *outside* in John 15:6. If we look at the same word's usage throughout the New Testament, this is overwhelmingly obvious.

The same Greek word is used to describe Peter sitting "outside" while Jesus is inside being questioned by the high priest. Matt. 26:69 (NLT, GNB, Vulgate, RV)("outside"). *Cf.* KJV, ASV, YLT, GB ("without").

When Jesus was told that his mother and brothers were "outside" wanting to see him in Matthew 12:46, it was the same Greek word used in John 15:6. (NLT, WEB, RV, Vulgate)("outside");(KJV, ASV, YLT ("without").

The same Greek word is used by Jesus when He says in Matthew 5:13 that the salt that loses its savor is good for nothing but to be cast "outside." (RV, Vulgate. *Cf.* KJV, ASV, NLT, GB, GNB("out");YLT ("without").)

Likewise, in John 6:37, Jesus promises that anyone who keeps coming [present participle active] to Him He will in no wise "cast out" or "outside," using this very same Greek word as in John 15:6.

Thus, why do you think this word for *outside* is not translated in John 15:6 by most English translations? What could be so bad about us knowing a branch in "me" who does not produce fruit and is thrown "outside" is in fact cast *outside* to be burned?

Because, as noted earlier, if *outside* were used, then everyone could have seen the link to the "unbelievers, fearful, and liars" who in Revelation 22:15 are "outside" waiting to be thrown in the lake of *fire* in Revelation 21:8.

> (22:15) **Outside** the city are the dogs—the sorcerers, the sexually immoral, the murderers, the idol worshipers, and all who love to live a lie.

> (21:8) But cowards, unbelievers, the corrupt, murderers, the immoral, those who practice witchcraft, idol worshipers, and all liars—***their fate is in the fiery lake of burning sulfur.*** This is the second death. (NLT)

Thus, when we examine the argument in the next section that says John 15:1-6 does not undermine cheap grace because the burning supposedly is not in hell, this argument is made only palatable due to the standard translations. They all obscure that the word *outside* is present in John 15:6. Such obfuscation by means of translation permits such arguments that the burning is not in *hell* to appear plausible. However, in the original text, it is not even remotely possible.

Nevertheless, even as commonly translated by omitting *outside*, it is self-evident the fires of hell are the threat. Jesus says the branch that does not bear fruit and is taken away (verse two) — the one who does not continue to abide in Him (and hence cannot be fruitful) (verse five) — is ultimately withered, and is to be thrown away (outside) to be burned. It is dead and subject to fire. Laney sees the implication clearly. The final disposition is a "prelude to judgment, not of blessed fellowship with Christ in heaven."[11]

Smith agrees. "In the context, verse 6 describes the taking away in no uncertain terms as a taking away to judgment."[12]

The Fiery Smelt Solution: The Burning Is Supposedly Not Hell

Joseph Dillow contends that we must see John 15:6 in light of Paul's words about a smelt. Paul speaks of our works being burned in a heavenly smelt so God can discern the good works from the bad. (1 Cor. 3:15.) Yet, we will pass through this smelt as if "by fire." Thus Dillow says if we use Paul's picture of a smelt to interpret Jesus' remarks, Paul implies that Jesus means we remain saved after this burning process. Consequently, when Jesus says the branch is thrown outside to be burned, while Jesus literally says *you are the branch*, Dillow says Jesus surely must mean your *works* are the branch. These weak and strong works are supposedly then burned off to reveal the valid works. Something other than *you* is allegedly consumed by fire. Otherwise, Dillow realizes

---

11. J. Carl Laney, "Abiding is Believing: The Analogy of the Vine in John 15:1-6," *Biblioteca Sacra* 146 (January-March 1989): 55, 61.

12. Charles R. Smith, "The Unfruitful Branches in John 15," *Grace Journal* (Spring 1968): 3, 9.

---

the Modern Cheap Grace Gospel's entire edifice of doctrine would be falsified by Jesus. Dillow believes we surely cannot permit that to happen.

Flaws In Dillow's Spin That Fire Is Smelt In Heaven

Unfortunately for this hypothesis, branches in the Metaphor that are burned are "you." Jesus says this is the apostles who are "clean right now." Yet, if they do not continue to bear fruit by staying in Jesus, Jesus warns they will be taken away, cast outside, and be entirely consumed by fire. *Apostles are people, not works*.

Moreover, it is impossible to believe the branches in the Metaphor of the Vine are equivalent to what Paul is discussing. No branch thrown in the fire will survive. If a branch could represent either good or bad works, as this cheap grace hypothesis assumes, there is still no branch that can survive a fire. Burning a branch made of *wood* will never reveal some left over good works. *It will all be ash*.

Thus, the picture Jesus used of branches being burned is a mismatch to what Paul envisions is thrown in the heavenly smelt. The Cheap Grace Gospel adherents are putting a square peg in a round whole. Paul imagines works of precious metal versus wood going into a smelt. Only the metal works survive. The wooden ones are burned off. Paul's picture mismatches the context of Jesus' metaphor which envisions *each and every fruitless branch made of wood is thrown outside and burned*. Thus, Paul's heavenly smelt does not assist us in interpreting Jesus' words.

Also, this argument has one other gaping problem. Jesus' Metaphor of the Vine makes it clear the fruitful branch will be spared *any* burning. But Paul is saying that all Christians are to have their works passed through this heavenly smelt. Jesus and Paul cannot be talking of the same thing. If they were the same, then Jesus would be implying the fruitful branch never sees the smelt of heaven, which leaves only one ridiculous implication. It would mean the fruitful branch is going to hell. This is nonsense. The one spared the fire in John 15:1-6 cannot be lost. Hence, the one whose works are smelted in heaven and are saved must include the fruitful branch in John 15:1-6 who is spared the fire experience which Jesus threatens. Hence, the smelt in heaven cannot contain the fire which Jesus promises to spare the fruitful branch from suffering in John 15:1-6. Thus, it is wholly improper to use Paul's smelt idea to interpret John 15:1-6.

Further Spin That Fire Is Rarely A Symbol Of Hell

Many cheap grace adherents know this smelt notion does not work. Yet, they are undaunted. Dillow goes on to amazingly suggest the word *fire* rarely means God's judgment. Joseph Dillow in *Reign of the Servant Kings* at first concedes that fire is used in Scripture as a symbol of God's judgment, *e.g.*, Isaiah 26:11. However, then he shockingly says: "Only rarely and exceptionally is it associated with the fires of hell." (*Reign, supra,* at 412).

For this amazing statement, Dillow completely ignores Jesus frequent references to hell as a "fiery furnace" or "flames" or "fire." (*E.g.*, Matt. 5:22;13:42,50; Mk 9:43.)

In fact, the "fire" in view in John 15:6 is clear by continuing on in Jesus' same speech. The Metaphor of the Vine (John 15:1-6) leads directly into John 16:1-2. There Jesus explains the prior warnings were so the apostles will not be "ensnared" (Greek *skandalizo*). This tells us the kind of "fire" in view in John 15:6. For Jesus in Matthew 13:41-42 similarly says that when He returns with the angels *all* those who are "ensnared" (Greek *skandalizo*) will be sent to the "fiery furnace." Clearly, in Matthew this means *hell*.

Thus, the warning of the Metaphor of the Vine was given to discourage the apostles from being "ensnared" (*skandlizo*-ed) (John 16:1-2). They thereby avoid being thrown into the fire in John 15:6. Hence, it is clear this fire is the "fiery furnace" of hell. This is because Jesus uses the same Greek word elsewhere — "ensnared" (*skandalizo*-ed)

— and says this group goes into this "fiery furnace" in Matthew 13:41-42 on Judgment Day. It is thus utter nonsense to argue that John 15:6 is talking about a fire other than the fires of hell.

Spin That Branch Thrown In The Fire Never Believed

Others realize both the smelt theory and fire-not-hell theory do not wash. Therefore, another proposal to save cheap grace from John 15:6 is to say the branch thrown in the fire never was a believer.

However, in John 15:1-6, Jesus tells eleven apostles that they are branches. They are all "clean" right now. (Judas had just left.) Jesus is thus talking to eleven *believers* who are branches. However, Jesus warns them that a branch "in me" will be cut off if it lacks fruit on the branch. (Verse two.) Jesus says if you fail to abide in Him (*i.e.*, are disobedient to His word in you), you will become like a branch that is withered (fruitless) and thrown in the fire. This means Jesus threatened a *believing* apostle with damnation for failure to continue to abide in Jesus, *i.e.*, obey His commandments. Hence, Jesus refutes the Cheap Grace Gospel that says there is nothing you need to continue to do to remain saved after you have initial faith in Jesus.

Undaunted by Jesus' clarity, some commentators like John MacArthur adopt the idea that the Metaphor of the Vine solely threatens unbelievers. He does so because he admits the fire described in John 15:6 is hell. MacArthur says "the imagery of burning suggests that these fruitless branches are doomed to hell." (MacArthur, *The Gospel of Jesus* (Zondervan: 1994) at 171.)

However, if the branch is a Christian who goes to hell for "failing to abide in Jesus" (*i.e.*, have His word in you bear fruit), then the Modern Gospel of Cheap Grace is wrong. How then can salvation be by faith alone without works?

To solve John 15:1-6 so the Cheap Grace Gospel is upheld, John MacArthur in his *Study Bible* (1997) in direct contradiction to Jesus makes an *ad hoc* assertion that the branches that do not produce fruit were never true believers. "The branches that do not bear fruit are those who *profess* to believe but their lack of fruit indicates genuine salvation has never taken place and they have no life from the vine." (*Id.* at 1615.)

However, Jesus said a believing apostle who was *clean* right now is a *branch* subject to this threat. Jesus talks about a "branch *in me*" that does not "bear fruit" being "cut off." As the *New Living Translation* words it, Jesus says: "He cuts off *every branch of Mine* that *doesn't produce fruit....*" (John 15:2 NLT.)

Laney points out, this phrase "in me" refers to saved persons elsewhere in the Gospel of John.[13] Dillow too concurs that it would be "inconsistent to say the phrase in 15:2 ['branch in me'] refers to a person who merely professes to be saved but is not."[14]

Furthermore, it only gets worse for MacArthur's view as one reads the passage. Jesus says again the failure of a "branch to keep staying *in me*" (continuous tense of *meno*) will end up making it a useless branch, to be thrown outside and burned. (John 15:6.)

Jesus meant this as a warning to apostles to bear fruit, and to do this they had to continue to abide "in me." Jesus defines this as "obeying my commandments" so that we "abide in my love." (John 15:10.)

The implication of Jesus' Metaphor is clear. The Apostles knew that their failure to abide in Jesus would lead to the failure of fruitfulness and the consequence of the fire for useless branches. This message unquestionably was the same as Jesus gave elsewhere: be fruitful or perish. "Every tree that does not bear good fruit is thrown in the fire." (Matt.7:19.)

---

13. Laney, "Abiding is Believing: The Analogy of the Vine in John 15:1-6," *supra*, at 63.

14. Joseph Dillow, "Abiding is Remaining in Fellowship: Another Look at John 15:1-6,"*supra*, at 45.

Baptist Professor Gary Derickson Concurs MacArthur Errs

That a believer is being warned is confirmed by the careful analysis of Gary W. Derickson, a Baptist college professor, in "Viticulture and John 15:1-6," in *Journal of the Grace Evangelical Society* (Spring 2005). He is blunt that it is incorrect to ignore that the risk in verse six (being burned outside the vineyard) belongs to a believer:

> [Jesus] was clearly addressing His believing disciples. He linked answered prayer to abiding (v 7) and His Father's glory to their fruit bearing (v 8). Both abiding and fruit bearing, developed and defined in vv 4 and 5, are related directly and conditionally to the men standing in Jesus' presence. Both vv 6 and 7 begin with third-class conditional clauses, indicating that *it was possible for the disciples*, undeniably identified by "you" in v 7, *to fail to abide. If they could fail to abide in v 7, they could also be described by and subject to the warning in v 6.* When the fruitfulness that results from abiding demonstrates their relationship to Christ as His disciples (v 8) and is seen in light of the promises of vv 5 and 7, their *usefulnes*s as His disciples must be in view in the *warning* in vs 6. *Id.*, at 41-42.

Derickson then deals with the clear implication of what it means that one who was a branch in Him is then detached.

> How can one be a branch attached to Christ and then become detached without ever having been regenerate or *without losing salvation*?

Yes, indeed. As Derickson says, Jesus just warned that a branch "in me" can become detached by failing to abide in Jesus. This is totally *anathema* to the faith alone gospel.

Derickson then says if you want to hold to the faith alone gospel and see this as a "commentary [by Jesus] on justification," then one solution is to say Jesus was talking of branches that never abided in Him. This is MacArthur's argument. However, not only does this contradict Jesus' words, but also, as Derickson points out, it makes no sense within the passage.

> The problem with this is that it would mean, *strangely*, that Jesus issued *a warning to unbelievers in the middle of encouraging His disciples*, individuals who believed in Him but who needed to be strengthened to **keep trusting** Him in view of what they would experience over the next three days. *If uselessness was not Jesus' point*, then the only interpretation for anyone holding eternal security would be spiritual decline and discipline by death for persistently disobedient believers.

Derickson tells the holders of the Modern Gospel of Cheap Grace how implausible is such a solution. You have to ignore the fact that the ones warned were those presently abiding in Jesus. You have to assume those warned about *failing to abide* were nonbelievers. Also, Jesus

Gary Derickson

would have oddly inserted this message during a discourse clearly talking to believing apostles in positive terms about *abiding in Him.* Also, the context of *uselessness* points to believers, not unbelievers. Yet, if MacArthur's solution is abandoned, there are no more solutions left. The alternatives do not wash, such as a "branch in me" is a Christian who is merely disciplined, not damned. (We discussed earlier about how this solution can not work.)[15]

---

15. "The Fiery Smelt Solution: The Burning Is Supposedly Not Hell" on page 358 *et seq.*

Derickson Is Compelled To Deny The Fire Is Hell But Admits It Is A Final Harvest Analogy

Derickson is a believer in faith alone. He is caught in a dilemma by his carefully studied admissions above. In Derickson's case, due to the admission that a believer is in view, he opts to save cheap grace by saying the fire is supposedly not hell. We already previously disproved that option.

Yet, what is fascinating to watch in Derickson's argument below is how desperate it has become. He makes this claim about a fire not in hell while ignoring evidence Derickson himself provides on how viticulture illuminates the passage. Listen to a man caught in a contradiction.

> That v 6 looks at the *fall, postharvest pruning* is seen in the practice of burning all the wood not attached to the vine....Jesus' message to His disciples...[i]f they chose not to "abide," they would not bear fruit and would therefore not be used by God. (*Id.*, at 42-43.)

Derickson, however, argues this is not judgment:

> In a vineyard anything not attached to the vine is useless and discarded. A *part of the discarding process at the end of the productive season is the burning of dry materials*. The burning *need not describe judgment*; it is simply *one step in the process* being described. It is what happens to pruned materials. Their uselessness, not their destruction, is being emphasized. (*Id.*, at 41.)

Despite his efforts to minimize the viticulture picture, Derickson just admitted this burning is an *end of harvest* process of burning off deadwood. Derickson can try to claim this is 'only the pruned branches' and disclaim this implies 'judgment.' But the viticulture picture Derickson himself provides is an *end of harvest* burning process. Thus, Jesus was looking at the *final harvest.* When it is finished, all the useless branches which are left over are then **burned**. Those who did not produce fruit are dead branches which are burned. Whether Derickson admits it or not, the picture that viticulture paints here is that Jesus must be speaking of the final judgment. There is a fire for the useless branches at harvest time. It is simple. It is not difficult to discern.

Again, the futility of the various foxholes that Cheap Grace Gospel proponents utilize to escape Jesus' meaning is *one of the best proofs* that faith alone is wrong doctrine. This goes for those who like MacArthur claim that the branches "in me" were never believers. It goes just as well for those like Derickson who recognize the silliness of MacArthur's view. He too advances an absurd solution that the burning at the end of harvest of useless branches implies only a disciplinary step on Christian believers. Rather, being burned in a final harvest means precisely that — the judgment of hell.

Conclusion

Jesus' lesson in the Metaphor of the Vine is the same as John 3:36 — you can believe, begin having life for the age, but if you disobey Him, then you "shall not see life." However, if you let Jesus' commands abide in you, then Jesus will live in you and empower you to have the fruit necessary to avoid the final judgment. But if you disobey those words, and thus you do not abide in Him, you can produce nothing. You will be a branch with no fruit. The Vinedresser removes all branches with no fruit in the final harvest and burns them. Damnation is your lot.

Of course this Metaphor refutes the Modern Gospel of Cheap Grace. But who is your Lord? Jesus or the modern fabulist of cheap grace? Choose the Lord! He is your "sole teacher." (Matt.23:8,10.) None can speak in His presence with their words of consolation for mere belief. Jesus says *continue to abide* (obey) *and bear fruit.* Fail to do so and be burned. It is that simple.

21 *John 8:51: Obedience Should Save*

The Nature Of Obedience

Before we discuss what Jesus teaches on obedience for salvation in John 8:51, we need to dispel a myth of the Fable of Cheap Grace. It insists we can not be obedient. We are allegedly too weak. We supposedly can never expect to live obediently. Thus, God would allegedly be unfair if He ever made our salvation depend upon ongoing obedience.

This teaching is a blatant lie of Satan. God tells us: "Now what I am commanding you today is *not too difficult for you or beyond your reach*." (Deut. 30:11.)

God is emphasizing our capacity to respond to His commands so that we take them to heart. From God's assurance that *we can* is how God tells us *we should*. There is no *responsibility* without *capacity* to respond.[1]

Thus, God wants us to be energized by His word toward a reassuring and positive outlook on our duty and ability to obey Him. Only God is Good and without sin. But

---

1. Charles Finney, the famous evangelist, concurred in 1837 in *Justification By Faith,* saying many exaggerate the effect of sin by Adam. We still have a nature created with *capacity* to obey God. Adam's sin causes us merely to be "subjected to aggravated temptation," but it "has by no means rendered [human] nature sinful." Finney says man's nature, "in all its elements...essential to moral agency,... God has made it as well as it could be made, and perfectly adapted to the circumstances in which he lives in this world." (Otherwise, how did Jesus overcome sin while fully in human flesh and exercising no self-control stemming from His divine nature as Son of God?) Finney adds: "The truth is, *man's nature is all right, and is as well fitted to love and obey God as to hate and disobey him*." Those who read various Psalms out-of-context ('no, not one') to prove the opposite make a mockery of God's word. See my prior work, *Jesus' Words Only* (2007) at 268-70.

God wants us to have a positive outlook on our *capacity* to respond so that we should *do* good and call on Him for help to do so.

This is why it is such a heresy of the "deceiver and antichrist" to teach Jesus did not come in "human flesh" (2 John 1:7). A key point of Jesus' life was that during His time on earth, He was fully human yet never would exercise any superior power to avoid sin. As divine "from above," He could have. Satan, in fact, tempted Him to use His divine nature to save Himself from difficulty. (Matt. 4:1-11, "command these stones....") But Jesus refused to use those powers for such purposes. Jesus knew part of His mission was to prove sinless despite living in human flesh. "For we have *not* an high priest which *cannot be touched* with the feeling of our infirmities; but was in *all points tempted like as we are*, yet without sin." (Heb 4:15.) Hebrews makes the point this was not miraculously achieved, but was despite the fact Jesus shared identically our *human nature*. Hebrews says Jesus "partook...of flesh and blood...." and "it was necessary for Him to become like His brothers *in all [respects]*...." (Heb. 2:14,17.) Jesus' death then becomes an inspiration to us: "For in that he himself hath suffered being tempted, he is able to help them that are tempted." (Heb. 2:18.) Jesus "left us an example, that we should follow His steps: who did no sin, neither was guile found in His mouth." (1 Peter 2:21-22.) By our capacity to follow His example and obeying Him, we are saved: "And [Jesus] being made perfect, he became the author of eternal salvation unto *all them that obey him*." (Heb 5:9.) Thereby, Jesus' obedience unto death teaches us our similar capacity to obey. Anyone who teaches you Jesus did not come in "human flesh," and instead had some superior flesh untainted by human nature, Apostle John says is the "deceiver and antichrist." (2 John 1:7). Instead, Jesus showed us the path of righteousness is a path open to any human who prays to God the Father in Jesus' name to avoid temptation. Jesus did this by giving mankind the most perfect example of a human obedience to God under the severest trial.

John 8:51 And The Overlap Of The Great Commission

Jesus told the apostles to make disciples of all the nations, "teaching them to **obey** [*tereo*] everything I commanded you." (Matt. 28:19-20.) Why were these commandments to be taught and obeyed by the nations?

Because Jesus explained in John 8:51 (NLT): "I tell you the truth, anyone who **obeys** [*tereo*] My teaching will never die!"[2] Or another translation would be, "all those who may have kept on obeying My Teaching *should* never ever die."[3]

This is the same message in Jesus' parable about the one who builds on sand. "And every one that heareth these words of mine, and **doeth them not**, shall be likened unto a foolish man, who built his house upon the sand [whose end is destruction]." (Matt. 7:26-27 ASV.)

Jesus similarly told the young ruler. "To enter life, *obey* [tereo] the commandments." (Matt. 19:17).[4]

What Is A Failure To *Tereo* In Jesus' Doctrine?

Is the disobedience which Jesus is concerned about the failure to *believe*? Is it is just one command to believe that He has in mind?

---

2. The King James renders "obey" in this verse as "kept guard." In Greek, the literal meaning is "to attend to carefully" or "guard." Metaphorically it means *obey, observe*, etc. The leading translations of *tereo* are: "obey" (NIV, NLT, GNB), "observe" (ASV, Vulgate, YLT), "observing" (ALT), and "guard" (KJV/SRV).

3. The Greek word for *obey* and *have* are both active aorist subjunctives. See my prior book, *Jesus' Words Only* (2007) at Footnote 15, page 383. This means "obeys" is "should/may have kept on obeying" and "will never" is actually "should never ever." For discussion on how the subjunctive tense is often ignored to serve doctrinal biases, see my prior book, *Jesus' Words Only* (2007) at Footnote 15, page 383.

4. See "Jesus' Answer To The Direct Question On How To Obtain Eternal Life" on page 123 *et seq.*

No. It means obedience to multiple commandments.

First, in Revelation 22:14, it speaks of multiple commandments: "Happy [are] the ones doing His **commandments (entolas)**, so that their right shall be to the tree of life, and they shall enter by the gates into the city." (Rev 22:14.)[5]

Second, when Jesus gave the Great Commission, Jesus told the apostles to teach all the nations to "*tereo* [obey, observe diligently] **all** [things, *panta*, **plural**] that I have commanded [*entellomai*] you." (Matt. 28:20.)

Lastly, Jesus used *tereo* another time, just as He did in John 8:51, to refer to *plural commandments.* Jesus even said the obedience to them gained eternal life. This arose when a rich young man asked Jesus how to have "eternal life." Jesus answered the young rich man: "To enter life, *obey* [tereo] the commandments." (Matt. 19:17). Jesus then quoted nine of the Ten Commandments given by God to Moses.

Meaning Of *Tereo*

The Greek word *tereo* is synonymous with *obey* because of its derivation. It literally means to keep diligent watch. It was a maritime term. On the old sailing ships, they watched the stars for their navigation directions. They would watch the North Star so that they could maintain their correct course of travel. Sometimes a strong wind would blow them off course or clouds might obscure the star, but by keeping careful watch on the stars, they could return back to their correct course. This process of diligently keeping one's course on the North Star was the action of *tereo*. Thus, outside of the maritime context, it came to mean *diligently follow* or *obey.*

What did Jesus mean by *obey* (*tereo*) in John 8:51? We have assistance by reading Revelation 3:3 where Jesus uses *tereo* again to warn Christians who had started well but were now failing. Jesus' usage of *tereo* is very enlightening:

---

5. See "Right To The Tree Of Life" on page 373 *et seq.*

Remember, therefore, what you have received and heard; **obey** it [***keep watch / diligently follow***] (*tereo*) and **repent**. But if you do not ***keep watch*** (lit. wake up), I will come like a thief.... (Rev. 3:3.)

Jesus thus says here 'repent and obey.' What was this a repentance from? A singular failure to believe initially? Hardly. It is abundantly clear from what Jesus told them to repent: the failure to have **completed** works! Jesus said in the prior verse:

Become watching [fig., Wake up], and strengthen the rest which you were about to be throwing out, for I have not found your **works** having been **completed** before My God. (Rev 3:2 ALT.)

Hence, Jesus wants the Sardisians to obey (*tereo*) what He has previously commanded. They obviously started well, and had partial works. Yet, their works were *incomplete.* What did this mean? This is identical to the Parable of the Sower where the second and third seed "believed for a while" (Luke 8:13) but then fell into temptation or were choked by thorns, and did not "produce to completion." (Luke 8:14, ALT.) They did not bear "fruit to the end" as did the fourth seed.[6]

It is this same *tereo-obedience* behavior that Jesus says, if diligently followed, should end up that you "never ever die." (John 8:51.)

Commandments To Remember And Obey

So what are some of these specific commandments from Jesus which lead to life if obeyed in patient endurance, or hell if disobeyed? Here is a small sampling of verses from just the early chapters of Apostle Matthew's Gospel. None

---

6. See "The Parable Of The Sower" on page 311 *et seq.*

are parabolic. Hence, there is no mystery involved. All threaten damnation if certain principles are *disobeyed*. Or they promise eternal life if certain principles are *obeyed*:

- "One who is *angry* with his brother shall be in *danger of judgment*." Matt. 5:22 ASV.

- "Whosoever shall *say 'Fool'* shall be in *danger of Hell fire*." Matt. 5:22 ASV.

- "Every tree that *bringeth not forth good fruit* is hewn down, and *cast into the fire*." Matt. 7:19 ASV.

- "[B]ut I say unto you, that every one that *looketh on a [married] woman to lust* after her hath committed adultery with her already in his heart. And if thy right eye causeth thee to stumble, *pluck it out,* and cast it from thee: for it is profitable for thee that one of thy members should perish, and not thy whole body be *cast into hell*." Matt. 5:28-29 ASV.

- "[B]ut I say unto you, *love your enemies*, and pray for them that persecute you; that you may be *sons of your Father* who is in heaven." Matt. 5:44-45 ASV.

- "And be not afraid of them that kill the body, but are not able to kill the soul: but rather *fear him who is able to destroy both soul and body in hell*...But *whosoever shall deny me* before men, him will I also deny before my Father who is in heaven...He that *findeth his life shall lose it*; and *he that loseth his life for my sake shall find it*." Matt. 10:28, 33, 39 ASV.

- "And behold, one came to him and said, Teacher, what good thing shall I do, that I may have *eternal life*? And he said unto him,... '[I]f thou wouldest *enter into life, keep the commandments*. He saith unto him, Which? And Jesus said, Thou *shalt not kill*, Thou shalt *not commit adultery,* Thou shalt not steal, Thou shalt *not bear false witness*, *Honor thy father and mother*; and, Thou shalt *love thy neighbor* as thyself.'" Matt. 19:16-19 ASV.

Yet, despite the clarity of Jesus' Gospel, how many would teach obedience to Jesus' commands in these verses *actually* are crucial for salvation? Each verse expressly says so. They merely repeat John 8:51: all who obey should be saved. Only wrong doctrine can explain how these passages ever could have been shunted aside or ignored.

22 *Right To The Tree Of Life*

Confirmation Of The Message To The Young Rich Man In The Book Of Revelation

In the Book of Revelation at 22:14, in the middle of two statements by Jesus, we are told the consequence of "doing His commandments" is the "right to the tree of life" and to "enter" the new heavens — the City of the New Jerusalem.[1] In Revelation 22:14, the various versions read:

> Happy [are] the ones ***doing His commandments***,[2] so that their ***right*** [or **power**, *exousia*] will be ***to the tree of life***, and they ***shall enter*** by the gates into the city. (Rev 22:14, ALT.)

> Blessed are they, that ***doe his commaundements***, that their ***right*** may ***be in the tree of life***, and may ***enter*** in through the gates into the citie. (Rev 22:14, Geneva.)

---

1. The ***immediately preceding*** verses are clearly from Jesus: "Look, I am coming soon, bringing My reward with Me to repay all people according to their deeds. (13) I am the ***Alpha and the Omega***, the First and the Last, the Beginning and the End." (Rev 22:12-13 NLT.) And the ***immediately following verse*** is clearly from Jesus: "***I, Jesus***, have sent My angel to give you this message for the churches. I am both the source of David and the heir to His throne. I am the bright morning star." (Rev 22:16 NLT.)

2. For the discussion on how this 'do his commandments' exists in the earliest known Greek manuscripts from the 200s, and was quoted in 208 A.D. by Tertullian and 251 A.D. by Cyprian, see page 382 below. On why the modern translations materially vary the verse in reliance upon a single much later errant and sloppily prepared Greek text — the Sinaiticus — from 330 A.D., see page 384 below.

> Blessed are they that **do his commandments**,
> that they **may have right to the tree of life**,
> and may **enter** in through the gates into the
> city. (Rev 22:14, KJV.)

The only significant difference in these three translations is that one says those who do his commandments
"shall" have the right to the tree of life, and the other two say
those who obey the commandments "may" have the right to
the tree of life. Which is correct?

'Shall' Is The Correct Translation

The verb infinitive at issue is *eimi*.

The future indicative of *eimi* ('to be') is *estai.* The
subjunctive of *eimi* is *ê*.

In Revelation 22:14, *eimi* reads both ways simultaneously — "ina **estai ê** exousia autôn."[3]

How should this odd sequence be understood and
translated? As a subjunctive — *may, should* or *might*? Or as a
future tense — *shall*?

This unusual structure appears four times in the New
Testament. First, we find it in Luke 10:12 — "anektoteron
estai ê tê polei ekeinê." This is translated as "it **shall** be more
tolerable in that day" for Sodom than for that city. Clearly,
Jesus did not mean it *may* be more tolerable for Sodom.
Instead, Jesus meant it *should* be and *will* be.

The combination *estai ê* appears again in Luke 17:30
— "tauta **estai ê** êmera o uios tou anthrôpou apokaluptetai."
This is translated, "even thus **shall** it be in the day when the
Son of Man is revealed." Jesus is not saying it '*may* be business as usual' when He returns. Rather, Jesus clearly means it
should and *will* be just like in the days of Lot.

---

3. *Estai* appears in all compilations of the Greek New Testament texts,
   without variation. See Stephens 1550 Textus Receptus; the Scrivner
   1894 Textus Receptus; the Byzantine Greek text; and the Alexandrian
   (Westcott-Hort (1881).)

This *estai ê* appears again in Mark 12:7 — "**estai ê** klêronomia.**" This is where the scheming husbandmen say to themselves that they will kill the son so "the inheritance **shall** be ours." Their scheme to kill the son is so that it *should* and *shall* be theirs at the same time.

Estai ê finally appears in Romans 15:12 — "**estai ê** riza.**" This is quoting Isaiah as saying "there **shall** be a root" of Jesse, etc.

Obviously, the quote from Romans 15:12 settles the usage issue. It is not conceivable that Isaiah spoke that Jesus *may* be from the root of Jesse.

Hence, the meaning of this future subjunctive structure **estai ê** is something that not only *should* happen but also *will* happen. *Estai ê* cannot be weakly understood as merely something *may* happen.

Thus, Revelation 22:14 properly should be translated as "their right *shall be* to the tree of life, etc."

Obedience To Commandments Is A Conditional Salvation Beatitude

Revelation 22:14 is a conditional beatitude. Only those who do His commandments *shall have* the right to the tree of life and enter the New Jerusalem. *Cf.* Rev. 14:12 (the faithful "keep the commandments of God....")

Therefore, this verse says those who do God's commandments *shall* have a right to the tree of life, and enter into the gates of the New Jerusalem — the new Heaven.

Clarke acknowledges these words mean in Greek they enjoy "an authority founded on right, this *right founded on obedience to the commandments of God....*"

Hence, this passage has a simple meaning. Those who do God's commandments have a right to the tree of life and to enter the New Jerusalem.

What does this tree of life represent?

The Tree of Life

The fruit of that tree was explained in Genesis to impart eternal life. God said in Genesis that if the human Adam who already had fallen into sin were now to eat from the tree of life, Adam would have "lived forever" and "become as one of us." (Gen. 2:9, 3:22 JPS.) To prevent a disobedient Adam from enjoying living forever as "one of us," God had to prevent any uncontrolled access by Adam to the tree of life. Thus, God removed Adam from the Garden of Eden. This was to prevent any further unrestricted access by Adam to the tree of life. Hence, when Jesus says in Revelation 2:14 that those who "do the commandments of God shall have the right to eat of the tree of life," Jesus means those shall receive salvation — the right to "live forever."

Access To The New Jerusalem

That salvation is involved in Revelation 22:14 is also obvious from the fact that those who receive the right to eat of the tree of life shall have a right to "enter the city (*i.e.*, the New Jerusalem)."

What does the city of the New Jerusalem signify? The new abode created by God to share presence with us. (Rev. 3:12.)[4]

Thus, Revelation teaches, like Jesus taught the young rich man,[5] that the path to eternal life with God is by doing God's commandments in the here and now.

---

4. "He that overcometh, I will make him a pillar in the temple of my God, and he shall go out thence no more: and I will write upon him the name of my God, and the *name of the city of my God, the new Jerusalem*, which cometh down out of heaven from my God, and mine own new name." (Rev 3:12 ASV.) "And I saw *the holy city, new Jerusalem, coming down out of heaven of God*, made ready as a bride adorned for her husband." (Rev 21:2 ASV.)

5. Matthew 19:16-26; Mark 10:17-31; Luke 18:18-26.

See Table 1.

TABLE 1. Comparison of Revelation 22:14 and Matthew 19:16-26

Revelation 2:14	Matthew 19:17-18
"Happy [are] the ones *doing His commandments*, so that their *right will be to the tree of life*, and they shall *enter by the gates into the city.*" (ALT)	"(17) if thou wouldest *enter into life, keep the commandments*. (18) He saith unto him, Which? And Jesus said, Thou shalt not kill, Thou shalt not commit adultery, Thou shalt not steal, Thou shalt not bear false witness, etc." (ASV)

A Singular Command Or Plural Commands? A Command Only To Believe?

Those wed to the gospel of cheap grace insist Revelation 22:14 means that the obedience required is solely to the *single* command to believe. (Jamieson, Gill.) There is supposedly no implication that any command more than simply *believing* is necessary to have a right to the tree of life and enter the New Jerusalem.

Is this a sound reading of *this verse*? No.

First, in Revelation 22:14, the obedience which gives us the right to the tree of life is obedience to *commandments* in the plural form.

Second, Revelation 22:18-19 refutes this idea that an obedience to a single command to believe is in view.

This passage comes only four verses after Revelation 22:14. In Revelation 22:18-19, we see a deliberate parallel to Revelation 22:14 by use of the *identical expression* "right to the tree of life and to enter the city."

Revelation 22:18-19 speaks precisely of someone violating Deuteronomy 4:2 (adding or subtracting from God's word). This is then applied specifically to the "words of this *book* of prophecy." The violator of that command will find "his share removed" from the "tree of life and in the holy city...."

Here is Revelation 22:18-19:

> And I solemnly declare to everyone who hears the words of prophecy written in this book: If anyone *adds anything* to what is written here, God will add to that person the plagues described in this book. (19) And *if anyone removes any of the words from this book of prophecy*, God will *remove that person's share in the tree of life and in the holy city* that are described in this book. (Rev 22:18-19 NLT.)

Hence, if someone is doing "his commandments," they enjoy the "right to the tree of life and to enter the gates of the city" (Rev. 22:14). However, if they violate a command such as subtracting from the words of an inspired text (here Revelation), then *"that person's share in the tree of life* and in the holy city" shall likewise be *"removed."* (Rev. 22:18-19.)

Obviously, these commands in Revelation 22:18-19 — the obedience to which is absolutely necessary to retain one's right to the tree — has *nothing* to do with belief alone. It has to do with *not tampering by subtracting from the text of God's word*, which command originates with Deuteronomy 4:2. Thus, one way to understand the scope of "commandments" in Revelation 22:14 is to see their scope just four verses later. The commands are extended just four verses later to something distinctly different than merely disbelieving. Instead, one's share in the tree of life is removed due to violation of Revelation 22:18-19 — wrongfully subtracting from the Book of Revelation itself.

As one Christian scholar notes, Revelation 22:18-19 is the "mirror-image" of the beatitude of Revelation 22:14.

> [I]n a mirror-image of the beatitude in [Revelation] 22:14, the warning to those who remove

anything from the book is of exclusion from the city and the tree of life.[6]

Hence, the way Gill and Jamieson read Revelation 22:14 ignores its plural reference to 'commands.' They also ignore the mirror-image application of 22:14 just four verses later in

John Gill 1697-1771

Revelation 22:18-19. Thus, together 22:14 and 22:18-19 hinge salvation on a violation of a command other than *to believe* by someone who clearly, as a result of their disobedience, is being threatened with having God "remove his share" in the tree of life.

Moreover, Revelation 22:14 says — just as Jesus said in His earthly ministry — that obedience to the multiple *commandments*, in particular the Ten Commandments, are what allows one to "enter life." (Matt. 19:16-26.) This is the "path to the tree of life" which God set up cherubim and flaming swords to guard against access by an unrepentant Adam and Eve. (Gen. 3:24.) Yet, Jesus was *the Way* (John 14:6) and He gave the secret to the "way to the tree of life" for the repentant sons of Adam: *obedience to God's commandments.*

Lastly, the proof that eternal life is not merely by belief alone is self-evident in the Parable of the Sheep and the Goats as well as numerous other lessons and parables of Jesus.[7] In the Parable of the Sheep and the Goats, Jesus says those who obey the duty to be charitable inherit eternal life, but those who disobey this principle are sent to "eternal fire." (Matt. 25:31-46.) Jesus could hardly be more blunt.

---

6. Stephen W. Pattemore, *The People of God in the Apocalypse: Discourse, Structure, and Exegesis* (Cambridge University Press, 2004) at 212.

7. See "Parable Of The Sheep & The Goats" on page 219 *et seq.*

Modern Gospel Of Cheap Grace: How It Views Revelation 22:14

Bob Wilkin, head of the Grace Evangelical Society, is a renown belief-alone teacher. In his article entitled, "Who Are The Outsiders? Revelation 22:14-17,"[8] he provides arguments to allow cheap grace to survive this passage.

By examining how weak is Wilkin's case for reconciling Revelation 22:14 with such doctrine, we will realize just how strong a passage it is for confirming Jesus literally meant what He said to the young rich man.[9]

Wilkin claims the "tree of life" in Revelation 22:14 means *abundant life* for Christians, not eternal life in heaven. Then what about the fact it meant eternal life to Adam? Wilkin's response is that had Adam eaten from the tree, it did not allegedly mean eternal life in heaven. He argues it would have meant *everlasting life* for Adam in *hell.* It is stupefying sometimes to realize what people think is sensible argument.

Then what about those *who have the right to enter the New Jerusalem?* Wilkin's solution is that those who lose the right to enter the New Jerusalem means they are still living safely in heaven *outside* of the New Jerusalem. What about the fact the place *outside* is identified in Revelation as where those are sent preparatory to being sent to hell, including *unbelievers, murderers, liars, cowards,* etc? (Rev. 21:8; 22:15.) Wilkin imagines there is a place *way* outside the New Jerusalem where the lost go en route to hell. But those Christians *outside* the New Jerusalem are still safe *outside*, but somehow are still *inside* heaven. It is nonsense to suggest there is one type of *outside* for Christians and another type of *outside* (further out) for the non-Christian. *Outside* is outside.

---

8. http://www.faithalone.org/news/y1993/93nov3.html (last accessed 4/24/07).

9. An extensive discussion and critique appears online in the supplement section, entitled *Rebuttal Arguments to Right to Tree of Life.*

Obviously, only because this passage refutes the cheap grace gospel — and repeats Jesus' message to the rich young man,[10] this passage is being fought off by the silliest of arguments. If one can believe all such nonsense of the cheap grace gospel enthusiasts, one cares not at all to know the true meaning of this passage. One is simply superimposing faith alone dogma at all costs — even when contrary to Jesus' obvious sense. One has slavish regard for *presuppositions* rather than the Lord. As Jesus said: 'They hear but do not listen. They see, but do not understand.'(Matt. 13:14-15.)

HISTORICAL NOTE: LATER CORRUPTION OF TEXT

Incidentally, there is a modern movement to accept a textual corruption of Revelation 22:14 from the middle 300s. This corruption erases the problem to cheap grace posed by the original wording of the verse. This is worthy of extensive discussion for two reasons:

1. It highlights the fact that modern compiled Greek texts from the 1800s to the present have permitted influences that are illegitimate, in particular from the Sinaiticus (Aleph), which is the source of this variation;[11] and

2. Despite the evidence being overwhelming here that 'obey his commandments' is the original text and that the Sinaiticus is both highly corrupted in this passage as well as generally, no one has lifted their finger to protect the words of Revelation from the loss of this very important verse.

10.Matthew 19:16-26; Mark 10:17-31; Luke 18:18-26.

11.An excellent synopsis in columns of the changes and deletions of verses in the modern compiled Greek texts reflected in the NIV can be found in Richard Anthony, *Comparisons Between the Majority(KJV) and Minority (NIV) Texts* at http://ecclesia.org/truth/m-m.html (last accessed 9-7-07). For example, the NIV deletes/greys out Matthew 12:47 and 21:44 and a host of other passages.

At the same time, a very horrible injunction hangs over the book of Revelation. It is a threat which compilers and translators should never have dared to transgress:

> And I solemnly declare to everyone who hears the words of prophecy written *in this book*: If anyone *adds anything to what is written here*, God will add to that person the plagues described in this book. (19) And if anyone *removes any of the words from this book* of prophecy, God will remove that *person's share in the tree of life and in the holy city* that are described in this book. (Rev 22:18-19 NLT.)

In fact, ironically, this little injunction is the converse of Revelation 22:14, as mentioned above. Those who "obey his commandments" have the right to "tree of life and to enter the holy city," but those who transgress by removing or adding words from this particular book of prophecy would find "that person's share in the tree of life and in the holy city" taken away.

I suggest all compilers of the New Testament, who are true Christians, to give immediate heed to what follows.

The Text Tradition That Has 'Obey His Commandments.

The Majority Greek manuscripts have Revelation 22:14 saying "obey his commandments."

This tradition is documented in the Stephens 1550 Textus Receptus; the Scrivener 1894 Textus Receptus; and the Byzantine Majority Text.[12] It appears in the oldest Latin Vulgate, [411-424 A.D.], the Syriac versions (Peshitta, Harkelian, and Philoxenian), Lamsa's 1936 translation of the Syriac Peshitta, the Coptic Boharic (*3rd* to 4th century), and the Armenian ancient versions

---

12. See http://www.greeknewtestament.com/B66C022.htm (accessed 7-16-07).

Jamieson concedes the King James source is confirmed by the earliest evidence from church commentators who quoted it in the 200s, as well as by very early Bible texts likewise from the ***200s***: "so B, Syriac, Coptic [***3d***/4th Century],

Cyprian

and CYPRIAN [***251 A.D.***] [says 'do his commandments']."

Quotes of Revelation 22:14 in the 200s Solve The Case

Tertullian in 208 A.D. and Cyprian in 251 A.D. both quote the 'obey his commandments' rather than the 'wash their robes' variant.[13] Tertullian quotes Revelation 22:14 in *On Modesty* (208 A.D.):

> [T] Apocalypse [Revelation says]... again "Blessed they ***who act according to the precepts***, that they may have ~~power~~ [***authority***, *potestatem*] over the tree of life and over the gates, for entering into the holy city." "Dogs, sorcerers, fornicators, murderers, out![14]

Cyprian in 251 A.D. quotes Revelation 22:14 as saying:

> In the Apocalypse [Revelation, we read]... Blessed are they that ***do His commandments***, that they may ***have*** ~~power~~ [***authority***, *potestatem*] over the tree of life.[15]

---

13. Cyprian lived in Carthage, and was a pupil of Tertullian.

14. Tertullian, *On Modesty*, Chapter XIX [9], *Objections from the Revelation and the First Epistle of St. John Refuted*, available online http://www.tertullian.org/anf/anf04/anf04-19.htm#P1585_463823 (last accessed 7-21-07). The word translated as "power" is in the original Latin *potestatem*. See, http://www.tertullian.org/latin/de_pudicitia.htm (accessed 7-21-07). In Latin, *potestatem* means "personal power, capacity, force,... virtue,... control,... sovereignty, dominion, rule,... ***authority***...." (Charlton Lewis, *An Elementary Dictionary* (1918) at 630-31.) The word *power* would suggest something exceeding God's position. The Latin meaning which matches most closely the Greek meaning is *authority*.

This would settle almost certainly that the correct translation of the Greek is 'obey his commandments.'

Tradition And How It Changed

For this reason, all Bibles until the modern era have translated Revelation 22:14 as *'obey his commandments.'*[16] Why did this change? Jamieson says:

> But A [Alexandrinus, ca. 450 A.D.], Aleph [Sinaiticus ca. 330 A.D.], and the Vulgate [of 425] read, '(Blessed are they that) wash their robes.'

Aleph means the Codex Sinaiticus. It dates to approximately 330-340 A.D. It is thus the obvious source text of the much later Vulgate and Alexandrinus texts. At the same time, Sinaiticus clearly post-dates commentaries from the 200s by over one-hundred years. Thus, 'wash their robes' is remarkably isolated, late and rare in the Greek text tradition. According to Jamieson, no other earlier Greek text than the Sinaiticus reads 'wash their robes.'

---

15. Cyprian (died 258), *Three Books of Testimonies Against the Jews*, Book II: *That In the Sign of the Cross Is Salvation for All People*, available online at http://www.ccel.org/ccel/schaff/ anf05.iv.v.xii.iii.xxiii.html?highlight=blessed,are,they,that,do,his,com- mandments#highlight (access 7-15-07).

16. The 'obey his commandment' appears in the following translations: Tyndale 1525, Coverdale 1535, the Bishop's Bible 1568, the Geneva Bible 1587, the 1611 King James Holy Bible, Wesley's 1755 translation, Webster's 1833, Luther's German Bible of 1545, the Italian Diodati, Young's 1911, the NKJV 1982, the KJV 21st Century version, Green's Modern KJV 1998, the Hebrew Names Version, World English Bible, the Third Millenium Bible, as well as the Spanish Reina Valera from 1602 - 1909. The Spanish Reina Valera of 1960 changed its text to 'wash their robes.'

The Scribal Error That Explains The Discrepancy

How did this Greek manuscript with the variation 'wash their robes' come about? Did it substitute 'wash their robes' in place of an original expression of 'obey his commandments'? Or was the error the other way around?

It turns out that a transposition of a few Greek letters clearly explains a scribal error took place — in whatever direction it took place. The Trinitarian Bible Society explains how 'obey his commandments' and 'wash their robes' are almost identical in Greek. It is thus obviously a scribal error which explains the errant text:

> [B]ut we desire to be sure that we set down in the printed Scriptures an accurate representation of the words of the Holy Spirit and not the product of an ancient scribal error. There is a close similarity in the Greek between *PLUNONTES TAS STOLAS AUTON* (wash their robes), and *POIOUNTES PAS ENTOLAS AUTOU* (do his commandments). The unfamiliar appearance of POIOUNTES ('do' rather than 'keep') may have led a scribe, whether or not deliberately, to adopt the other form of wording, and so produce the prototype of the manuscripts which underlie the modern rendering 'wash their robes.'

Which Way Is The Corruption Of Revelation 22:14?

In theory, this corruption could be in either direction. It could have been corrupted prior to 200 A.D. If so, then Tertullian and Cyprian in 208 A.D. and 251 A.D. respectively simply quoted the erroneous passage. They might have erred saying 'obey his commandments.'

How would this be evaluated?

If the Sinaiticus is much younger than 208 A.D., then clearly it would be more likely that Tertullian and Cyprian relied upon an errant *later* text. Conversely, if the Sinaiticus is much older than 208 A.D., then Tertullian and Cyprian are relying on the correct text which existed previously. And then 'obey his commandments' is truly the original text.

How old is the Sinaiticus? It was found in 1844 in a monastery in the Sinai. It is dated for textual reasons to the mid-300s. The *Catholic Encyclopedia* in "Codex Sinaiticus" explains why:

> Its antiquity is shown by the writing, by the four columns to a page (an indication, probably, of the transition from the roll to the codex form of manuscript), by the absence of the large initial letters and of ornaments, by the rarity of punctuation, by the short titles of the books, the presence of divisions of the text **antedating Eusebius [died 340]**, the addition of Barnabas and Hermas, etc. Such indications have induced experts to place it in **the fourth century**, along with Codex Vaticanus and some time before Codex Alexandrinus and Codex Ephræmi Rescriptus; this conclusion is not seriously questioned, though the possibility of an early fifth-century date is conceded.[17]

Thus, the Sinaiticus is dated to somewhere in the 300s, probably near 330-340 A.D.

Because this comes too late for Tertullian and Cyprian to have ever known about, it is obvious Tertullian in 208 A.D. and Cyprian in 251 A.D. are looking at the original version. It always read "obey his commandments."

Yet, is there any other evidence that would strengthen our opinion such as proof the Sinaiticus is a poorly prepared copy?

17.http://www.newadvent.org/cathen/04085a.htm (accessed 7-16-07).

The Answer Bears On The Reliability Of Many Modern Translations

Before we analyze the quality of the Sinaiticus, there is a lot more at stake here than just Revelation 22:14.

It turns out the reliability of the Sinaiticus also bears on the very important question whether we are going to change allegiance to modern versions like the New International Version.

For we shall see, numerous Bible texts (such as the NIV) today rely upon the Bible-compilers Westcott and Hort. They were the first to incorporate in the 1800s the variants from the Sinaiticus into their new Greek New Testament compilation. Their compilation included the Sinaiticus' 'wash their robes' for Revelation 22:14. The Westcott Hort compilation of the Greek text became the basis for today's Nestle-Aland compilation. It is published by the United Bible Societies. The Nestle-Aland is on its 26th Edition. It is still going strong. This compilation was the basis for the translation of the New International Version. Thus, because the Westcott-Hort-Nestle-Aland compilation of the Greek adopted the Sinaiticus-variant of Revelation 22:14, that variant is now rampant throughout most modern translations.

For example, the Sinaiticus-version of Revelation 22:14 can now be found in such versions as the NIV, RSV, NASB, ESV, Holman Standard, and Darby. All these versions read: "Blessed are those WHO WASH THEIR ROBES, that they may have the right to the tree of life, and may enter by the gates into the city."

Proof Of Carelessness In Scribes Who Worked On Sinaiticus

So is the Sinaiticus a reliably prepared copy of the Greek New Testament? Eminent Christian professionals who handled and inspected the Sinaiticus concur it is very poor and very rough. These include Burgon and Scrivener.

First, we will start with Burgon's views.

John William Burgon matriculated at Oxford in 1841, taking several high honors there, including a B.A. in 1845 and a M.A. in 1848.[18] In 1860, while temporary chaplain of the English congregation at Rome, he made a personal examination of Codex B (Vaticanus), and in 1862 he inspected the Sinaiticus at St. Catherine's Convent on Mt. Sinai.

In 1883, Burgon wrote *Revision Revised* (London: John Murray: 1883). It was primarily a criticism to the compilation text done by Westcott Hort which in turn was used to translate the *Revised Version of the Bible* (1881).

Burgon often is misused today to prove he thought the King James's source text was infallible and excellent. Burgon not only did not say that, but also denied that was his point. He declared that issue was not the subject matter of his particular book.[19] In fact, Burgon was fully admitting that sometimes the Majority Text collation Greek text upon which the KJV is based could be found to have errors. (See Footnote 19, page 389.) Yet, Burgon's focus was whether Aleph (Sinaiticus) and similar texts were reliable, which in turn formed part of the basis for the *Revised Version of the Bible* in 1881.

Burgon wrote this regarding Aleph (Sinaiticus):

> I insist and am prepared to prove that the text of these two Codexes (B and Aleph) *is very nearly the foulest in existence*... That they exhibit *fabricated texts* is demonstratable....B and Aleph are covered all over with blots — *Aleph even more than B*....[20] On many occasions 10, 20, 30, 40 words are dropped through *very carelessness*. Letters, words or even whole sentences are *frequently written twice* over, or begun and immediately cancelled; while that *gross blunder*, whereby a clause is omitted because it happens to end in the same

---

18. A full biography is at "John William Burgon," *Wikipedia* http://en.wikipedia.org/wiki/John_William_Burgon (accessed 7-17-07).

words as the clause preceding, occurs no less than 115 times in the New Testament.

Next and finally, another scholar of Greek, Dr. F.H.A. Scrivener (1813-1891), was also permitted to examine the Sinaiticus. He wrote a seminal scholarly work on it entitled *A Full Collation of the Sinaiticus Ms. With The Received Text of the New Testament* (Cambridge: 1864). This represented a collation of the Sinaiticus to the Textus Receptus (Majority Text.) Yet, he speaks identical to what Burgon observed about a confusing array of correctional alterations made to the Sinaiticus manuscript:

> The [Sinaiticus] Codex is covered with such alterations...brought in by at least **ten different revisers**, some of them **systematically spread over every page**, others occasional or limited to separated portions of the MS, many of these

---

19. In the King James Only debate Burgon is often cited as if he was a purist about the Majority Text. However, Burgon himself proposed over 100 corrections to the Book of Matthew alone. In his *Revision Revised*, Burgon said he used the Stephanus' Greek Testament of 1550 as a standard. Yet, he wrote, "...by so doing I have not by any means assumed the textual purity of that common standard. In other words, I have not made it 'the final standard of appeal.'" Burgon added that it is simply the "most convenient standard of comparison; not, surely, as the absolute standard of excellence." *Id.*, at xviii-xix, preface. He added later: "Let no one at all events obscure the one question at issue, by asking,— 'Whether we consider the textus receptus infallible?' The merit or demerit of the Received Text has absolutely nothing whatever to do with the question. We care nothing about it. Any Text would equally suit our present purpose." *Id.* at 17. "Once for all, we request it may be clearly understood that *we do not*, by any means, *claim perfection for the Received Text*. We entertain no extravagant notions on this subject. Again and again we shall have occasion to point out (*e.g.* at page 107) that the *textus receptus needs correction*." *Id.*, at 21, footnote 2. "[I]n not a few particulars, the 'Textus receptus' does call for Revision, certainly." *Id.* at 107. Of interest, Burgon discusses the idea whether God promised to protect the textual transmission from error. To this he said: "That by a perpetual miracle, Sacred Manuscripts would be protected all down the ages against depraving influences of whatever sort, — was not to have been expected; certainly, was *never promised*." *Id.* at 335.

Jesus' Words On Salvation

being contemporaneous with the first writer, but the greater part belonging to the sixth or seventh century. (*Id.*, at xix.)

Dr. Scrivener continued and gave a very sobering analysis of the chaos evident in the Sinaiticus text:

> This manuscript must have been derived from one more ancient, in which the lines were similarly divided, since the writer occasionally omits just the number of letters which would suffice to fill a line, and that to *the utter ruin of the sense: as if his eye had heedlessly wandered to the line immediately below*. Instances of this *want of care* will be found (in) Luke 21:8; 22:25, perhaps John 4:45;12;25, where complete lines are omitted; John, 19:26; Heb. 13:18 (Partly corrected); Apoc. 8:16; 19:12; 22:2, where the copyist passed in the middle of a line to the corresponding portion of the line below. It must be confessed, indeed, that the *Codex Sinaiticus abounds with similar errors of the eye and pen*, to an extent not unparalleled, but happily rather unusual in documents of first-rate importance; so that Tregelles has freely pronounced that 'the state of text, as proceeding from the first scribe, may be regarded as very rough.' *Id.* at xv.

Dr. Scrivener exposed that Westcott Hort compiled their famous Greek New Testament using a wrong and conjectural theory. They did not use reliable textual analysis:

> There is little hope for the stability of their imposing structure, if its foundations have been laid on the sandy ground of *ingenious conjecture*. And, since barely the smallest vestige of historical evidence has ever been alleged

---

20. David O. Fuller, *Which Bible?* (Grand Rapids International Publications: 1970) at 93, 126-28.

in support of the views of these accomplished Editors [*i.e.*, Westcott Hort], their teaching must either be received as intuitively true, or dismissed from our consideration as precarious, and even visionary. (Scrivener, Introduction, Vol. 11, at 295.)

In light of this, *Bible Researcher* notes: "The text of Sinaiticus...contains an ***unusually high number of readings which have clearly arisen by transcriptional error....***"[21]

Why Did Modern Bible Translators Not Adjust For This Error In The Texts Used To Translate Revelation 22:14?

It is abundantly clear from the above that the Sinaiticus is in error. It is a mess of chaos. Westcott Hort selected its erroneous language without doing the kind of textual analysis that Bible scholars were expected to do. The complaints, however, of Burgon and Scrivener — men of excellent credentials — fell on deaf ears. At least, it seems that's what has happened. For what else can explain why the error in Revelation 22:14 persists in each edition of the Nestle-Aland of the United Bible Society which contains "wash their robes"?

Do modern authorities explain themselves, or even identify the question? Generally not. For example, the *New International Greek Testament Commentary* is typical of a number of recent commentaries. It makes no mention of the variant reading for Rev. 22:14. It fails to disclose "do His commandments" is the alternate to "wash their robes."[22] Others mention it, but try to suggest the case is equally plausible either way.[23] In truth, instead, it is decidedly in favor of 'obey his commandments.'

Unfortunately, this silence or misleading presentation has a tragic explanation.

21."Codex Sinaiticus," http://www.bible-researcher.com/codex-aleph.html

Revelation 22:14 is one of the most important verses that explains *obeying multiple commandments* are what gives you the right to enter the kingdom of heaven. ***It is a verse (among many others) that refutes clearly the belief alone doctrine of our modern era***. One need only look at the commentators falling over backwards to try to explain how cheap grace is still valid when faced with the original text 'obey His commandments.' For example, listen to Jamieson, Faussett and Brown and how they try to truncate *do his commands* to the single command *to believe*:

> The English Version (King James Bible) reading is quite compatible with salvation by grace; for God's first and grand Gospel "commandment" is to believe on Jesus. Thus our "right" to the tree of life is ***due not to our doings***, but to what He has done for us. The right, or privilege, is founded, not on our merits, but on God's grace.

Yet, that is completely contrary to the text. It says *commandments*. Not command! It says our doing of the commandments do give us the right to enter. It is no different than when Jesus said those who do "good things" (plural) shall rise to resurrection and those who "do evil things (plural)" shall rise to condemnation. (John 5:28-29 KJV.)(For a thorough discussion of that passage, see page 395 *et seq.*)

22.G.K.Beale, "Revelation is The Book of Revelation, a Commentary on the Greek Text," *The New International Greek Testament Commentary* (Howard Marshall and Donald A. Hagner, Editors) (Wm. B Eerdmans: 1999) at 1139. Without mentioning the variation, Beale sloughs off the concern by saying 'wash their robes' is another way of speaking about an enduring faith. Yet, there is a stark elevation of meaning by 'obey his commandments' that even the proponents of 'wash their robes' know the latter does not contain.

23.See Bruce M. Metzger, *A Textual Commentary on the Greek New Testament, Second Edition, A Companion Volume to the United Bible Societies' Greek New Testament* (Fourth Revised Edition) (Stuttgart: German Bible Society, 1994) at 690. The systematic refutation of the UBS explanation is Stephen Goranson's article, "The Text of Revelation 22:14," *New Testament Studies* (1997) Vol. 43 at 154-157.

Thus, Revelation 22:14 is a clear problem passage (like all the others cited in this book) for *modern doctrine*.

Yet, not in the Sinaiticus version. No! All the problems go away! It's like a dream come true for the cheap grace enthusiast. There is a scribal error that erases the problem. If you go with it, you don't need to offer any more lame explanations.

This is not merely my surmise. Many concede this is precisely the real reason that 'wash-their-robes' is preferred over 'obey his commandments.' For example, Gaebelin says the "correct" reading is "wash their robes" because we know "obey his commandments" is the wrong salvation doctrine.

> "The Authorized Version [KJV] is faulty. Instead of 'blessed are those that do his commandments' the correct reading is 'blessed are they that wash their robes.....***Eternal life and eternal glory cannot be obtained by keeping commandments, by the works of the law.***" (A.C.Gaebelin, *The Annotated Bible* (available online at http://www.biblecentre.org/commentaries/acg_70_revelation.htm.)

Pastor Saxe likewise says "it becomes clear that an alternate reading to the majority [*i.e.*, 'washed their robes] is accepted by many" because it "upholds the Biblical [*sic*: faith-alone] view [of salvation without obedience]."[24]

However, the Trinitarian Bible Society correctly critiques using doctrine to make the decision on the right text:

> The substitution of 'wash their robes' for 'do his commandments' was adopted by textual critics of the 19th and 20th centuries and is now found in many modern versions. It has ***proved attractive to many conservative evangelicals because of a mistaken [?] fear***

---

24. "A Conditional Beatitude, Rev. 22:13-14," www.fellowshipbibleannarbor.org/BibleStudies/nt/rev/PastorSaxe/RevelationCh22Vv13to14.pdf.

> *that the old reading savoured of justification
> by works.*[25]

This use of doctrine to dictate picking a rare, isolated and late variant is specious. A professor who works on translating confessed this dilemma, and that a professional must resist such temptation. When there are two choices — one errant text and one true, a quandary of decision presents itself: "I am unceasingly exposed to the temptation of retrenching, modifying, or adding something to the Scriptures." (Gaussen: 115.) Gaussen says the "foolhardy" response is to use dogma as a guide, telling the Lord that this "is worthy of thee, [but] this [other text] is not worthy of thee!" Gaussen means the true text should drive doctrine, not doctrine determine the true text.

Here, there is thus no secret what has impelled the acceptance of a corrupt text. The corruption subtracts words inimical to cheap grace. Faith alone doctrine ends up crushed if the earliest and obviously most reliable text is retained.

This episode involving Revelation 22:14 is just one more proof that the greatest weapon of Satan today to keep Christians in the dark is the use of compilations of the Greek New Testament. For the compilers hide in anonymity and are shielded by presumed scholarly-purpose and detachment.

There is no doubt what is the fate of these compilers absent repentance. They have removed words from this book of prophecy and added new ones. God warns them in Revelation 22:18-19 that such a *"person's share in the tree of life and in the holy city"* will be "removed."

There was never any excuse in the face of Tertullian's and Cyprian's quotes from 208 A.D. and 251 A.D. Hence, it is long overdue to now fix the Nestle Aland text of Revelation 22:14 which has influenced the NIV, RSV, etc.

---

25. Article No. 38, http://www.holybible.com/resources/Trinitarian/ article_38.htm.

Jesus' Words On Salvation

23 *Those Who Have Done Good Things Are Resurrected*

Ever Notice This In John's Gospel?

Perhaps you have read John's Gospel dozens of times, but never have given any thought to these words of Jesus:

> Marvel not at this: for the hour is coming, in the which all that are in the graves shall hear his voice, And shall come forth; **they that have done good [things], unto the resurrection of life**; and **they that have done evil [things]**, unto the resurrection of **damnation.** (John 5:28-29 KJV)[1]

We all glaze over this. We trust our Modern Gospel has the better truth. We read this verse but we somehow block its truth from penetrating our minds. Yet, so far, we see Jesus here is saying the same thing we saw in His answer to the young rich man and the Torah-scholar. It is the same message Jesus gave John about those who do God's commands and thereby enjoy the *right* to eat of the tree of life and enter the New Jerusalem — the abode of God. (Rev. 21:14.)[2]

---

1. Compare: "For God shall bring every **work** into judgment, with every secret thing, whether it be **good**, or whether it be **evil**." (Eccles. 12:14.) Compare also Jesus' statement after talking of the "good things" or "evil things" that come out of the mouth from the heart says: "every **idle word** that men shall speak, they shall give **account thereof in the day of judgment**. For by thy words thou shalt **be justified,** and by thy words thou shalt be **condemned**." (Matt. 12:36, 37.) Thus, the "good things" and "evil things" include the words of your mouth.

2. See "Right To The Tree Of Life" on page 373 *et seq.*

Let's break John 5:29 down to see its blunt but rather surprising meaning.

TABLE 1. **John 5:29 Analyzed**

Condition	Result
If have done good things (plural)	Resurrection to Life.
If have done evil things (plural)	Resurrection of Damnation.

The word for *good* is *agathos*. It is in the accusative *plural* of a word meaning *good thing*. Thus, more literally, this passage says those who have done "good things" will rise to eternal life. In contrast, Jesus says those who have done "evil things" — the plural of *phaulos* meaning *bad thing* — rise to damnation.

These plurals are important because some wedded to the Modern Gospel of Cheap Grace try to spin Jesus so He means the saved were resurrected because they did *only one good thing* — *believed*. However, that is only permissible because our English translations lack the clarity that the underlying Greek word for *good thing* is in the *plural*. Jesus is talking about those who did *good things*, not *merely* one good thing, such as *believe*.

Then, of course, the cheap grace reading is ignoring something even more fundamental. Jesus contrasts the ones who did "evil things" with the ones who did "good things." Jesus says salvation precisely turns on whether you did "good things" or "evil things." Jesus' message was blunt.

Interpretation

Gathercole is an evangelical scholar. He acknowledges in John 5:29 that "John's Jesus [says]...the criterion for whether one is punished or receives life at the *eschaton* [*i.e.*, the age to come] is the 'doing' of good or evil."[3] Actually, to repeat, Jesus said it is whether one was doing *good things* or *evil things* that will make the difference.

Jesus does not say the criterion is whether you believed one time or not. The criterion, and the only criterion mentioned, is that you have done *good things* as opposed to *evil things*. If taken literally, this means **Christians are not shown any favoritism over non-believers in the judgment-by-works process**. Apostle Peter precisely had this same understanding. He wrote in 1 Peter 1:17: "And if you call on the Father, the One *judging impartially according to the work of each* [one], conduct yourselves *in fear [during] the time of your sojourn* [fig., life on earth]." (ALT)

In fact, Jesus later gave Apostle John a vision of this final judgment process. John sees *all* the dead, including those listed in the book of life, uniformly *judged* by this criterion of *works*:

> And I saw the **dead**, the great and the small, standing before the throne; and books were opened: and another book was opened, which is **the book of life**: and the **dead were judged out of the things which were written in the books, according to their works**. (Rev 20:12 ASV.)

---

3. Simon J. Gathercole, *Where Is Boasting: Early Jewish Soteriology and Paul's Response in Romans 1-5*. (Eerdmans 2002) at 114. However, Gathercole claims that John's Jesus does not equate "doing good" with "obeying Torah" because of Jesus' answer in John 6:26-29. (*Id.*) Gathercole means if faith is a good work in John 6:26-29, then it *alone* is what Jesus meant by "good things" that cause one to be resurrected in John 5:28-29. Salvation remains supposedly by *faith alone*. However, the word *work* in John 6:26-29 disproves *pisteuo* represents *believing* there. Paul's usage in Romans 4:4-5 & Eph. 2:8-9 proves when *pistis* means *faith*, it stands in contrast to *works*. Thus, Jesus did not use *pisteuo* to mean *believes* in 6:26-29 if Jesus equated it with a *work,* as Gathercole reads the verse. The only *work*-meaning of *pisteuo* that fits is when *pisteuo* means *obey*. See 422 *ff* for this translation of *pisteuo*. Thus, in 6:26-29, the work of *pisteuo* is not *believing*, but *obeying*. This translation alone avoids the incongruous definition of *faith* as a *work*. Even if that were rejected, John 6:26-29 cannot solve John 5:28-29 for the simple reason that Jesus said the plural *do good things* in John 5:28-29. Jesus in John 5:28-29 did not tie resurrection to just one work — belief. Jesus tied it clearly to the plural *good things*.

The Key Of The Book Of Life: Personal Responsibility

Moses previously spoke of this same *book of life* mentioned in Rev. 20:12. God's response explained the process by which names are added and *erased*, and judged. Moses asks God to forgive the people's use of the golden calf during Moses' trip up the mountain:

> Yet now, if you will, forgive their sin; and *if not, blot me, I pray you, out of your book* which you have written. And the LORD said unto Moses, *Whosoever has sinned against me, him will I blot out of my book*. (Exo 32:32-33.)

God's response above explains that names are in this book, but when you sin against God, your name is *erased*. Once in, however, absent God's blotting your name out, you have *life*.[4] Moses offered to lose entry in this book in solidarity with Israel's fate to move God to forgiveness, *i.e.*, making himself an offering to appease God's wrath. God responded by saying obedience is an individual responsibility. Personal sin is the criterion of who is in and who is blotted out.

Then how does atonement interplay with judgment? If what God told Moses is true, *no one can offer their own damnation as a substitute* to save another from the consequence of *unrepentant disobedient* behavior. How do we then understand the interplay of *personal judgment-by-works* and *substitutionary atonement*?

This is an area of confusion. The solution is to stop confusing *judgment by-works* principles with *atonement* principles. *Substitutionary* atonement is simply the *payment* which God offers to those who have need of forgiveness of sin (which is everyone). At the same time, Jesus explained

---

4. See: "And... there shall be a time of trouble, such as never was since there was a nation even to that same time: and at that time thy people shall be delivered, *every one that shall be found written in the book*. (2) And many of them that sleep in the dust of the earth shall awake, some to *everlasting life*, and some to shame and everlasting contempt." (Dan 12:1-2 ASV.)

---

atonement applies to *only a person who has properly repented from and appeased the one whom they offended by sinning* (*i.e.,* reconciled with the one offended). See page 1 *et seq.* As a result, atonement by Jesus does not let you pass the judgment by works on a personal review by God. Rather, if you pass the judgment by works where failure is mitigated by prior repentance from sin, *then* atonement applies!

As Apostle John explained Jesus' message on atonement, Christ's atonement only applies as we *walk in the light* including *confessing sin* when we fail to *walk in the light*:

> (7) but *if we walk in the light*, as he is in the light, we have fellowship one with another, and *the blood of Jesus his Son cleanseth us from all sin*. (8) If we say that we have no sin, we deceive ourselves, and the truth is not in us. (9) *If we confess our sins*, he is faithful and righteous to forgive us our sins, and *to cleanse us from all unrighteousness*. (1 John 1:7-9, ASV.)

Thus, whether these sins are overlooked and atoned for depends on the *walking in the light* characteristic that represents *personal* cleanness — *works* of obedience that God requires! Atonement cleans you of sins in your past. In other words, atonement *alone* does not allow you to pass through the judgment by works. Hence, if you have *unrepented sin where you did not reconcile with the one you offended by works worthy of repentance* you will come into condemnation. Your name will be blotted out of the book of life! It's that simple! For example, in Revelation 3:5, Jesus gives this *conditional* statement: "He that *overcometh*, the same shall be clothed in white raiment; and I will *not blot out his name out of the book of life*, but I will confess his name before my Father, and before his angels." The logical corollary, and implication, is that the one who does not overcome and instead denies Jesus will have his name *blotted out of the book of life.* Jesus stated that negative corollary bluntly in Luke 12:4-5,8-9. Jesus taught sin leads to being blotted out.

Paul Concurs

Paul repeats Jesus' point about a judgment by individual works in Romans 2:6-10. It does not turn on whether someone was merely ever a *believer*. Paul says the final criterion is *"works"*— those who do good receive eternal life. Those who do evil are damned.[5] This may seem odd in light of other teachings by Paul. Yet, Paul's words are identical to Jesus in John 5:28-29. Paul correctly paraphrased the Master.

What is interesting is the early church saw Paul's words on a judgment-by-works in Rom. 2:6-10 as clearly refuting cheap grace—specifically faith alone. Origen in 246 A.D. was combatting Marcion who in 144 A.D. proclaimed Paul's faith-alone verses were the only Gospel. Marcion rejected many of Jesus' teachings as legalistic, and intended for an earlier dispensation. Marcion insisted in his *Antithesis* #19 that God now saves those who merely "believe," and God no longer judges any for "disobedience." But Origen said Paul in Romans 2:6-10 teaches to the contrary that "God pays back to each one not on his nature but *on account of his works*." (Origen, *Commentary on the Epistle to the Romans* (Ed. Scheck) at 2:4:7 at pg. 111.) Then Origen saw an implication at odds with Marcion' faith alone dogma: "in the second place, let believers be edified so as to *not entertain the thought that, because they believe, this alone can suffice for them*." *Id.*, at 111-12. We may be shocked to read passages like John 5:28-29,1 Peter 1:17 or Romans 2:6-10. We *never* sincerely believed that any *personal* obedience (good works) was required at the judgment seat. We were simply wrong.

---

5. "God (6) who will render to every man according to his **works**: (7) to them that *by patience in doing good works [ergon agathon] seek for glory and honor and incorruption, eternal life*: (8) but unto them that are factious, and *obey not* the truth, but *obey unrighteousness*, shall be *wrath* and indignation, (9) *tribulation and anguish, upon every soul of man that worketh evil*, of the Jew first, and also of the Greek; (10) but *glory* and honor and peace to every man that *worketh good*, to the Jew first, and also to the Greek." (Rom 2:5-10.) See discussion of this passage at 474 *ff* & 526. Note Paul like Peter says this is impartial.

24 *Incomplete & Lukewarm Works*

Incomplete Works In Revelation 3:1-3

In Revelation, Jesus is going to repeat almost verbatim twice what we read in the last few chapters. Judgment is by works, just as Jesus said: "every tree therefore that bringeth not forth *good fruit* is hewn down, and cast into the fire." (Matt. 3:10; 7:19.)

First, in Revelation 3:1-3, Jesus tells the church at Sardis:

> And to the angel of the assembly in Sardis write: 'These [things] says the One having the seven spirits of God and the seven stars [i.e., Jesus is speaking]: I know your *works*, that you have a name that you live, and you are *dead.* (2) 'Become watching [fig., Wake up], and strengthen the rest which you were about to be throwing out, for I have not found *your works* having been *completed* before My God. (3) Therefore, be remembering how you have received, and be keeping [*tereo*, *obey*] it, and repent. Therefore, if you will not watch, I will come upon you like a thief, and you shall by no means know what hour I will come upon you." (Rev 3:1-3 ALT.)

It is obvious that the Spirit is present, but the Spirit is going out. What is bringing about the Sardisians' spiritual death is their works *were not complete in God's sight.* In fact, Jesus says they have a reputation for being alive, but they are "**dead.**"

The Sardisians' spiritual condition is similar in one respect to the third seed in the Parable of the Sower. This seed has thorns choke it. Jesus says the third seed did not *telesphourousin*. (Luke 8:14.) This means the third seed fails to produce to the end, or fails to bring its fruit to ***completion***. (For more discussion, see my prior book, *Jesus' Words Only* (2007) at 171.)

The picture of the Sardisians is very interesting:

- They are dead.
- Something still flickering in them is about to be quenched.
- Their works are not complete.

Let's make a reasonable inference on what these points mean. The first point means their faith is dead. The second point means the Holy Spirit is about to be quenched and depart. The third point means they have no completed works or mature fruit to show.

The threat is implicit that damnation will follow unless they "repent" and "obey." The spirit will be utterly gone soon, and they will be totally dead spiritually.

We know this explicitly from the parallel Parable of the Ten Virgins. It tells us that when the spirit departs — when the "virgins" (innocent born-again Christians) suffer the oil (Holy Spirit) in their lamps being finally quenched — then damnation results.[1] The foolish virgins are excluded from the banquet with Jesus. They are left "outside" which Jesus elsewhere describes as a place of darkness for the lost *en route* to hell.[2]

---

1. For discussion of the parable, see the chapter "Parable of the Virgins" on page 263 *ff.*
2. See "What is Outer Darkness Where There Is Weeping and Gnashing Of Teeth?" on page 280 *et seq.*

So Revelation 3:1-3 sounds a lot like a dead faith without completed works does not save. Where have we ever read that before?

Jesus' Rejection Of Faith Alone In Revelation 3:15-18

Where else does Jesus say a Christian without deeds has a faith that is dead and such faith cannot save? That a tree without good fruit is sent to the fire to be burned?

Jesus says it again just a few verses later addressing believers of Laodicea on what they lack.

> I know thy **works**, that thou art neither cold nor hot: I would thou wert cold or hot. (16) So then because **thou art lukewarm**, and neither cold nor hot, I will **spue thee out of my mouth.** (17) Because thou sayest, **I am rich**, and increased with **goods**, and have **need of nothing**; and knowest not that **thou art wretched**, and **miserable**, and **poor**, and **blind**, and naked: (18) I counsel thee to buy of me gold tried in the fire, that thou mayest be rich; and **white raiment**, that thou mayest be clothed, and that the **shame of thy nakedness do not appear**; and **anoint thine eyes with eyesalve**, that thou mayest see. (Rev 3:15-18 KJV.)

Jesus unequivocally rejects faith alone here. He is talking to believers at Laodicea. He is equating them to the third seed from the Parable of the Sower. In the parable, the third seed has gone further than the second seed in growth. The second seed "believed for a while." (Luke 8:13.) Yet, while the third seed started similarly but grew more, it was later choked by the "cares, riches and pleasures of this life," bringing no fruit to completion. (Luke 8:14.)

In Revelation 3:15-18, Jesus identifies similarly that "riches" have led the Laodicean church to become lukewarm in works, just like happened to the third seed in the parable.

Jesus tells you that He is cutting off those who have luke-warm works, ***spewing them out of His mouth***. Unless they repent, their nakedness will be visible. This is a lost condi-tion, because they lack the proper garment — the white rai-ment. (Rev. 3:18.) Jesus previously disclosed how crucial that white raiment is to salvation:

> He that overcometh, the same shall be ***clothed in white raiment***; and I will ***not blot out his name out of the book of life***, but I will confess his name before my Father, and before his angels. (Rev 3:5 KJV.)

Hence, Revelation 3:15-18 is all about the essential necessity of zealously adding works to faith. It refutes clearly that a faith which started well can suffice if alone later.

Is There A Familiar Echo To Jesus' Words?

Where else have we heard this same message that faith without works does not save? Indeed, it is familiar to all of us. It is in the often resisted James 2:14-25 passage. James 2:17 reads: "Even so faith, if it hath not works, is dead, being alone." James asks rhetorically "can such faith save?" which calls for a negative answer. Thus, faith without works, James says, cannot save.[3] (For more on this, see page 492.)

In Revelation 3:1-3 and 3:15-18, what must those with a faith that has become dead and who lack completed works do to awaken spiritually?

Revelation 3:3 says they must "remember what you have received and heard; ***obey*** it and ***repent***." In Revelation 3:18, they must 'buy eye-salve' from Jesus so they can see.

---

3. Scholars in ancient Greek who are Christians admit that James' mean-ing is that faith without ***completed*** works cannot save, *i.e.*, works are not merely a forensic proof of your already saved condition. James means works (besides faith) are ***indispensable*** for you to be saved. See my prior work, *Jesus' Words Only* (2007) at 250 *et seq.*

They are blind and in darkness. The latter verse says the way out of darkness is going to cost them. They will have to chew on the words of Jesus — in fact, upon these harsh words about the shallowness of their works (lack of obedience).

Melding These Passages With The Parable Of The Virgins

Accordingly, Jesus is teaching in the Parable of the Ten Virgins and Revelation 3:1-3 and 3:15-18 that *faith without works is dead*. You are spiritually about to have the Spirit totally quenched. Jesus gives a precisely parallel message in Revelation 3:1-3 and 3:15-18 that duplicates the Ten Virgins Parable. However, this time Jesus speaks plainly in *declarative* statements. While in the parable we are not sure what it means for "virgins" (born-again Christians) to have the spirit flickering out, Revelation 3:3 tells us precisely: the *Sardisians are lacking completed works.* Revelation 3:15-18 then tells us those with "*lukewarm works*" among the Laodicean church members will be spewed out of Jesus' mouth. Their condition is lost because they lack the proper garment — the white robe which zealous works would have given them.

Furthermore, those statements in Revelation 3:1-3 about not completing your works contain one more piece of crucial information. It says that despite the Sardisians' reputation for being alive they are *dead.* They have "incomplete works." Something is flickering out in them. These additional facts let us see a precise overlap to James 2:14-17 which was written prior to the Book of Revelation. Jesus was obviously aware of His brother James' epistle. Jesus was clearly affirming James' position that faith without completed works is dead and cannot save. Jesus used virtually identical language. Therefore, Jesus intended in Revelation 3:1-3 and 3:15-18 to affirm the correctness of James 2:14-17.

So what do these three passages mean? They boil down to James' message that *faith alone...cannot save.* Jesus is endorsing James' principles. Hence, if you do not add works of charity which James mentions, your faith is dead. The Spirit is about to leave you. Quicken what little remains. If not, you will suffer spiritual death and be left outside the New Jerusalem with the unbelievers and sinners, to be sent on judgment day to hell itself. Jesus' warning is to be ready and watching as well as to repent and obey. Bring the works assigned to you to "completion."

Has God given you a task that is only half-completed? Then finish it!

Jesus Says The Final Judgment Is Based On Your Practices

In accord with these passages, Jesus in Matthew 16 states:

> For the Son of man shall come in the glory of his Father with his angels; and then he shall **give ~~reward~~ every man according to ~~his~~ the practice ~~works~~** of each. (Matthew 16:27)

The ordinary translation is lacking in two respects. The word translated commonly as *reward* is actually "give" or "pay." In Greek, it is *apodidomi*. Also, the word rendered as *works* is not the word for *works* used in the New Testament. Everywhere else, the word *works* in the New Testament is *erga* in Greek. Here, instead, the word is *praxis*. It means *practice*. On Judgment Day, Jesus will give to each according to "the practice of each." ***Jesus promises to judge by your practice, not according solely to your faith***. It is the pattern (practice) of your life that Jesus will judge.

In sum, Jesus judges by the practice you had for works. He will reject you for lack of fruit. You will be judged by your practices, not your faith. You are judged by your faithfulness, not your beliefs. This is the same message Jesus gave in His warning of a judgment by works on everyone in John 5:28-29. For a thorough discussion of this passage in John, see the chapter beginning at page 395.

25 *Eternal Life: Based On Good Works Or Faith Alone?*

Jesus' Normal Salvation Passages Versus "Eternal Life" Passages

In most of the salvation passages to this point, Jesus has not used the words *eternal life*. Jesus said those who "kept" (*tereo*, obeyed) His word "should never ever die." (John 8:51). Jesus has said those who "endure to the end shall be saved." (Matt. 10:22.) Jesus has said you can go "to heaven maimed" or "hell whole." (Mark 9:42-47.) Jesus has said if you are unforgiving after being forgiven a mountain of debt (initial salvation), your forgiveness is revoked. You are sent back to the jailers to be "tortured" at the prison that the master originally spared you from. You must pay every last penny of your previously forgiven debt. (Matthew 18:23-35.)

In other words, Jesus often does not use the expression of *eternal life* when Jesus talks of salvation.

Outside the book of John, we find the term *eternal life* mentioned only rarely. Jesus says those who have given up homes, family, etc., for the "kingdom of heaven **shall** inherit eternal life." (Matthew 19:16, 30.)

Problem For Cheap Grace: 'Eternal Life' Is Frequently Tied To Works & Obedience

Dillow is a chief proponent of the gospel of cheap grace. He realizes, however, that the translated term 'eternal life' is in verses which frequently directly tie it to good works, such as in Matthew 19:16, 30, just quoted. This very serious difficulty for faith alone doctrine is infrequently mentioned. However, Dillow confesses this truth:

> The phrase eternal life (Gk. *zoen aionion*) occurs forty-two times in the New Testament. Its common meaning... entrance into heaven... is well documented. However, many are not aware that ***in eleven of those forty-two usage***s (26 percent) ***eternal life is presented to the believer as something to be earned or worked for.*** Mt. 19:16, 19:29; Mk. 10:17, 30; Lk.10:25, 18:18, 30; Rom. 2:7; Gal. 6:8, Jn. 12:25-26; Rom. 6:22. (Dillow, *Reign of the Servant Kings, supra,* at 135-36.)

Thus, 26% of the time "eternal life" is clearly linked to works or obedience. What a dilemma for cheap grace that says instead belief alone is what one needs to be saved!

As a solution, Dillow argues that in forty-two passages except these eleven passages, the Greek *zoe ainon* means 'entrance into heaven.' However, in these eleven problem verses, Dillow says we must switch *zoe ainon* to mean instead a *happy and abundant life* starting in the here and now, but never implying 'entrance into heaven.' Why?

Otherwise, Jesus is laying down conditions of good works, obedience, etc., for *entrance into heaven.* Because this would violate *cheap grace*, and its belief alone position, Dillow says we must change the meaning from *eternal life* into *happy abundant life* in just those eleven verses.

However, that means Dillow is varying the meaning based on preconceived notions of which doctrine is correct. Dillow is putting doctrine ahead of the text. ***Dillow is not letting the text shape doctrine***. Instead, he is blatantly biasing the text to fit preconceived doctrine.

However, if *eternal life* means *entrance in heaven* in thirty-one passages, it should mean *entrance into heaven* the eleven other times that Dillow disputes the meaning merely because it is conditioned on good works, obedience, etc.

Most important of all, Dillow never reveals that there is nothing in *zoe ainon*'s meaning that includes the idea of a *happy and abundant life*. That is not a dictionary meaning. It is an invented *ad hoc* (a just-so made up meaning) idea to fix the problem posed by *zoe ainon*.

The Dilemma Posed If Zoe Ainon Does Mean Eternal Life

The correct conclusion, however, as demonstrated below, is that *zoe ainon* is about salvation every time it appears. The fact this means there are eleven verses that tell us obedience and works are simultaneously conditions of *zoe ainon* does not change this. Our doctrine is formed by the verses' actual meaning. We don't make verses fit our pre-ferred doctrine. If we make our doctrine force a foreign meaning upon an expression like *zoe ainon*, we are putting our doctrine beyond testing by the original Greek language. We are imagining a realm of doctrine that is above the inspired words of Jesus.

For example, we cannot use the commonly heard idea that *salvation is by faith alone* to squash out of existence con-trary verses from Jesus. Rather, Jesus' contrary verses to faith alone doctrine dictate, as we will prove in the next chapter,[1] that we need to re-evaluate how we translate the word *pistis* as *faith*. That word has permissible alternative meanings such as *faithfulness, pledge, trust*, etc. It should force us also to re-evaluate how we translate the verb *pisteuo* as *believe* instead of the permissible alternative meaning of *obey*.

In fact, we shall see this dilemma reaches its climax with John 3:16. In the next chapter, we will prove that we should have translated the key verb in John 3:16 — *pisteuo*

---

1. See "John 3:16: Obeying Unto Christ Should Save?" on page 417 *et seq.*

— with these eleven verses in mind. This verb *pisteuo* can mean *believe* certainly, but with equal validity it can mean *obey, comply, trust,* etc.[2] In other words, these eleven works-obedience-*eternal-life* passages are simply more proof that *pisteuo* in John 3:16 means *obey,* not *believe,* as we will thoroughly prove in the next chapter.

Thus, Dillow is wrong to use these eleven works-obedience-eternal life verses, which are quoted below, to rationalize a meaning of *zoe ainon* which is unknown in any dictionary — a *happy and abundant life.* This concocted meaning is solely invented to satisfy the doctrine of *faith alone.* Rather, these eleven verses are a leading clue that we must overhaul our understanding of the Greek word *pistis* (noun) and *pisteuo* (verb). While *pistis* and *pisteuo* are almost everywhere translated in the KJV as *faith* and *believe,* they equally signify in a Greek dictionary the respective meanings of *faithfulness* (obedient living) and *obey.*

Let's now examine why eleven passages cause such turmoil for the belief-alone adherents. In each, *zoe ainon* is contingent on good works or obedience.

The Eleven Works-For-Eternal Life Passages

Dillow — one of the staunchest *belief alone* advocates today whose books are evangelical seminary classics — admits that if *zoe ainon* (translated typically as *eternal life*) really means *entrance into heaven,* then there are numerous passages that tie it to good works and obedience. Dillow's list of the eleven obedient-works-for-eternal-life passages are:

---

2. See "John 3:16: Obeying Unto Christ Should Save?" on page 417 *et seq.*

- Matthew 19:16, 19:29: "(16) Someone came to Jesus with this question: "Teacher, what *good deed* must I do to have *eternal life*?...(29) [Jesus responded:] And everyone who has given up houses or brothers or sisters or father or mother or children or property, for My sake, will receive a hundred times as much in return and *will inherit eternal life*." (NLT)

- Mark 10:17, 30: "As Jesus was starting out on His way to Jerusalem, a man came running up to Him, knelt down, and asked, 'Good Teacher, what must I do to *inherit eternal life*?'....(29)'Yes,' Jesus replied, 'and I assure you that everyone who has given up house or brothers or sisters or mother or father or children or property, for My sake and for the Good News, (30) will receive *now in return* a hundred times as many houses, brothers, sisters, mothers, children, and property— along with persecution. And *in the world to come* that person *will have eternal life*."

- Luke.10:25[-28]: "One day an expert in religious law stood up to test Jesus by asking Him this question: 'Teacher, what should *I do to inherit eternal life*?' (26) Jesus replied, 'What does the law of Moses say? How do you read it?' (27) The man answered, 'You must love the LORD your God with all your heart, all your soul, all your strength, and all your mind.' And, 'Love your neighbor as yourself.' (28) 'Right!' Jesus told him. '*Do this and you will live*!'" (NLT)

- Luke 18:18, [29-]30: "(18) Once a religious leader asked Jesus this question: 'Good Teacher, what should I do to inherit eternal life?'.... (29) 'Yes,' Jesus replied, 'and I assure you that everyone who has given up house or wife or brothers or parents or children, for the sake of the Kingdom of God, (30) will be repaid many times over *in this life*, and will have *eternal life in the world to come*." (NLT)

- Rom. 2:7: "He will give *eternal life* to those who *keep on doing good [work]* [*ergon agathon*],[3] seeking after the glory and honor and immortality that God offers." (NLT)

---

3. Oddly, translations like the KJV, ASV and NLT translate *ergon agathon* so as to omit it says *good work* while everywhere else *ergon* is translated as *work*. See, e.g., Ephesians 2:9 ("not of *erga*," plural).

- Gal. 6:8: "Those who live only to satisfy their own sinful nature will harvest decay and death from that sinful nature. But *those who live to please the Spirit* will harvest *everlasting life* from the Spirit." (NLT)

- John 12:25-26: "He that loveth his life loseth it; and he that hateth his life in this world shall keep it unto *life eternal*. (26) If any man serve me, let him follow me; and where I am, there shall also my servant be: if any man serve me, him will the Father honor." (ASV)

- Rom. 6:22: "But now being made free from sin and become servants to God, ye have your fruit unto sanctification, and *the end eternal life*." (ASV) "... you have *your fruit* [*result*] *in sanctification*, and the *outcome* [*is*] *eternal life*!" (literal).

Without even examining Dillow's case that *zoe ainon* means *happy and abundant life*, these eleven verses in their very own context prove Jesus is talking of *salvation-life* in heaven. These passages speak of sacrificing *life* here and now to receive a *zoe ainon-life* in heaven. See John 12:25-26; Mark 10:30. This contrast proves *eternal life* is the gain.

Thus, Dillow's argument fails *in context* that *zoe ainon* means a happy life in the here and now in all eleven passages. Yet, what is Dillow's case built upon? Is it based on anything more than circular logic? Let's see his proof.

Zoe Ainon As Something Different Than Eternal Life

Dillow argues his case as follows for the meaning of *an abundant life* (not *eternal life*) in these eleven passages:

> Life (Gk. zoe) is often used of an ***abundant quality of life*** beyond regeneration which is the possession of those who 'persevere in doing good.' Rom. 2:7...Therefore, not just a counterbalance to death is meant, *i.e.,* regeneration, but an ***abundant life***, a vibrant experience with Christ.

However, Dillow offers no proof except the doctrine of faith alone for such a meaning. He realizes that unless his substitute-translation is used — an *abundant quality of life* — the faith-alone doctrine is falsified. Yet, Dillow *never* offers any proof that the words *zoe ainon* have the meaning he suggests from *a Greek dictionary!* Instead of admitting faith alone is falsified, Dillow accepts a false translation!

However, let's see if Dillow could have made his case better than this. In a sense, Dillow is correct there are other possible meanings. In particular, the adjective *eternal* is not always a correct translation choice. The expression can mean literally "life for the ages" or "life lasting for an age."

Blatant Denial Of Dictionary Meanings To *Zoe Ainon*

Vincent's famous work of 1905 entitled *Word Studies in the New Testament* has self-contradictory claims about *ainon*'s true meaning. Vincent taught in the second volume (on John's Gospel) that *zoe ainon* meant to "live forever." (Vincent, *Word Studies* (1905) Vol. II at 99.) He said it was "a characteristic phrase of John for *lives forever.*" However, Vincent by the time he wrote volume four must have seen a problem. He obviously became aware of the dilemma posed to faith alone doctrine by the eleven troublesome passages referenced above. If *ainon* truly means *eternal* or *forever,* salvation is not by faith alone. To save belief-alone doctrine, Vincent in volume four of his *Word Studies* of 1905 made the following extraordinary reversal about the meaning of the Greek adjective *ainon*:

> The **word always** carries the notion of time, and **not of eternity**. It always means a period of time. Otherwise it would be impossible to account for the plural, or for such qualifying expressions as this age, or the age to come. It **does not mean something endless or everlasting**.... The adjective *ainos* in like manner carries the idea of time. Neither the noun nor the adjective, in themselves, **carry the sense of**

> ***endless or everlasting****...Zoe ainon...*is not end-
> less life, but life pertaining to a certain age or
> aeon, or continuing during that aeon...[It] car-
> ries...a sense of quality. (*Vincent's Word Studies
> of the New Testament* (1905) Vol. IV, at 58-61.)

However, this volume-four-Vincent is wrong. The
volume-two-Vincent is right. First, the most authoritative
Greek dictionary — the Liddell Scott — says *ainon* by itself
means sometimes *eternal* or *perpetual.* (No dictionary ever
says it implies a present quality of life.) Also, the highly
authoritative work by James H. Milligan and George Moulton
entitled *Vocabulary of the Greek Testament* (London:
1930)(reprint Hendrickson Publishers 1997) at 16 says of
ainon:

> [W]e must note that **outside the NT**, in the ver-
> nacular as in the classical Greek... ***it never
> loses the sense of perpetuus*** [*i.e.,* perpetual]....

All other authoritative Greek dictionaries concur on
ainon having this meaning of the *perpetual*: "without end"
(Bauer, BAGD); "without end, never to cease, everlasting"
(Thayer); and "eternal" (*Theological Dictionary of the New
Testament*). Confirming this usage is that the Hebrew word
for *eternal* was *olam*, and it was translated in the Septuagint
in 247 B.C. by *ainon.* (*E.g.*, Dan. 12:2.)[4]

In fact, what volume four of Vincent *Word Studies*
was claiming was preposterous. Yet, the volume-four-Vincent
surely must have realized by then if one does not chip away at
ainos, there is no escaping that *faith alone* doctrine is falsified
by Jesus! (Vincent must have not been able to go back and
alter volume two at page 99 to avoid a self-contradiction.)

---

4. Chr. Wordsworth, Chr. D.D. (Canon of Westminster), *The New Testament of Our Lord and Savior Jesus Christ, In the Original Greek, With
   Notes* (Part I) (London: 1856) at 135.

Nevertheless, unless numerous dictionaries all conspire to promote a false point despite it undermining their favored doctrine of faith-alone, then the volume-four-Vincent appears to have been willing to deny a word its true meaning to save faith-alone doctrine! Yet the volume-four-Vincent must have known Jesus makes a clear use of *ainon* to mean *eternal* in Matthew 25:46, saying: "These will go away into **eternal punishment**, but the righteous into **eternal life**." The meaning of *ainon*'s usage there as *eternal* is undoubtable.[5] For Jesus describes clearly "eternal punishment" in verse 41 as punishment by "eternal fire which is prepared for the devil and his angels." Thus, when this is contrasted in verse 46 with *zoe ainon*, the latter clearly must mean *eternal* life.

Therefore, certainly the volume-four-Vincent could not seriously believe what was being written for the masses. Vincent may have suffered from a temporary apoplexy to save faith-alone doctrine. Whatever the reason, somehow this volume-four-Vincent's bias in favor of belief-alone is what obviously usurped the truth he confessed in volume two. The only reason we can still read his frank opinion in volume two is that it was already in print when Vincent must have noticed the destruction of faith alone doctrine if *zoe ainon* means "eternal life."

> "And if they [Gentiles] shall diligently learn the ways of My People...they shall be built up in the midst of My People. But if they will not obey, I will utterly pluck up and destroy that [Gentile] nation, saith the Lord." Jeremiah 12:16-17 (KJV)

---

5. The volume-four Vincent dismisses *eternal* in this verse, only weakly saying it "is the punishment peculiar to an aeon other than in which Christ is speaking." *Id.* at 60. In other words, the punishment is supposedly only for a period of time other than the epoch in which Jesus spoke. The suggestion is it could be a decade later; the tribulation, etc. Vincent had to know this could not wash. For it would mean the righteous receive only a temporary epoch of life, and the evil receive only a temporary epoch of punishment. That certainly is not Jesus' meaning.

Conclusion

Thus, we have eleven *undisputed* verses that condition *zoe ainon* (eternal life) upon works and/or obedience. Dillow — one of the leading voices in evangelical seminaries today — confessed this. Yet, Dillow's effort to claim *zoe ainon* means something other than eternal life is unavailing. The eleven verses clearly reference salvation, promising that losing one's life here will cause one to "inherit eternal life" in the next. See John 12:25-26. Salvation is the clear import of *zoe ainon* even in the eleven problem passages.

Moreover, Dillow tries to supplant this meaning of *eternal* life with the meaning *abundant* life. Yet, not a single dictionary ever suggests such a meaning. *Ainon* means either *eternal* or *age-enduring*. *Zoe* means *life*. Dillow is making up a meaning out of thin air when *zoe ainon* is plain as day.

We saw other reputable men (the volume four Vincent) are so desperate to withdraw these eleven verses from the salvation-debate that they are willing to downplay that *ainon* itself can ever mean *eternal*. Yet, all the other most reputable dictionaries say to the contrary that it does often mean *eternal*. Even the volume-two Vincent said likewise! Thereby, the volume-four Vincent is an example of what lengths to which cheap grace advocates are willing to go to save their precious doctrine of faith alone. ***The faith alone advocates are brought to utter desperation by these eleven problem passages.*** Yet, the truth is staring back at us: there are eleven passages, including mostly from Jesus, that tie *eternal life* to actions, works, obedience, and factors which cheap grace rejects as ever a condition of *eternal life*. Who do you heed? Jesus or cheap grace? The eternal consequence of your decision is all in your hands.

26 *John 3:16: Obeying Unto Christ Should Save?*

Introduction

When the English translations of the Greek New Testament were made in the 1526-1611 period, the "difficult Greek in which the New Testament is written...still held mysteries for" English scholars. (Nicolson: 224.) One of those mysteries was the Greek word *pisteuo* in John 3:16. In over 200 instances of *pisteuo* in the New Testament, not once did the King James Bible render it as *obey*. (See *Strong's Concordance*.) However, scholars now realize *obey* was a common meaning of *pisteuo* in ancient Greek. *Obey* certainly was the meaning of *pisteuo* in John 3:36 (see page 448). Yet, this *obedience* salvation formula is identically repeated in John 3:16.

Besides John 3:36 helping, one can more easily accept *pisteou* means *obeys* in John 3:16 when one looks at Apostle John's many quotes of Jesus about obedience. Jesus in John 8:51 says "whoever keeps on **obeying** (*tereo*) My Teaching should never ever die."[1] In John 15:1-10, Jesus says a "branch **in me**" that does not "bear fruit" is "taken away," "cut off from the vine," thrown "outside and burned."[2]

John likewise quoted Jesus saying in total accord:

> Marvel not at this: for the hour is coming, in the which all that are in the graves shall hear his voice, And shall come forth; **they that have done good [things], unto the resurrection of life**; and **they that have done evil [things]**, unto the resurrection of **damnation.** (John 5:28-29 KJV).[3]

---

1. See "John 8:51: Obedience Should Save" on page 367 *et seq.*
2. See "Metaphor Of The Vine" on page 343 *et seq.*

We saw again that Apostle John was told that those who obey the commandments (plural) have *the right* to the tree of life. (Rev. 22:14.) John writes:

> Happy [are] the ones *doing His command-ments*, so that their *right* will be *to the tree of life*, and they *shall enter* by the gates into the city. (Rev 22:14)(ALT)[4]

We also saw Apostle John writing Jesus' words to the Sardisian Christians. They are dead due to having "incomplete works." They can prevent the Spirit leaving by repenting and obeying. Through John's pen, Jesus tells them:

> And to the angel of the assembly in Sardis write: 'These [things] says the One having the seven spirits of God and the seven stars [i.e., Jesus is speaking]: I know your *works*, that you have a name that you live, and you are *dead.* (2) 'Become watching [fig., Wake up], and strengthen the rest which you were about to be throwing out, for I have not found *your works* having been *completed* before My God. (3) Therefore, be remembering how you have received, and be keeping [*tereo*, *obey*] it, and repent. Therefore, if you will not watch, I will come upon you like a thief, and you shall by no means know what hour I will come upon you." (Rev 3:1-3 ALT.)[5]

John another time relays Jesus as saying that luke-warm works by Christians at Laodicea will cause Jesus to spew them out of His mouth.

> I know thy *works*, that thou art neither cold nor hot: I would thou wert cold or hot. (16) So

---

3. See "Those Who Have Done Good Things Are Resurrected" on page 395.
4. See "Right To The Tree Of Life" on page 373 *et seq.*
5. See "Incomplete & Lukewarm Works" on page 401 *et seq.*

> then because **thou art lukewarm**, and neither
> cold nor hot, I will **spue thee out of my mouth.**
> (Rev 3:15-16 KJV.)

Finally, we saw among the many verses that tied *eternal life* (*zoe ainon*) to obedience and works was the following words of Jesus recorded by Apostle John:

> He that loveth his life loseth it; and he that
> hateth his life in this world shall keep it unto
> **life eternal**. (26) If any man serve me, let him
> follow me; and where I am, there shall also my
> servant be: if any man serve me, him will the
> Father honor. (John 12:25-26 ASV.)

These passages from the writings of John quoting Jesus are but echoes of what we find in Matthew, Luke and Mark. John is repeatedly emphasizing themes of obedience.

Hence, besides John 3:36, these passages from John make the proposed translation of John 3:16 as about *obedience* appear far more sensible than translation tradition would suggest. This change, incidentally, will unite what scholars call the Synoptic-Jesus with the Johannine Jesus. It turns out there are no separate portrayals of Jesus in the mind of Matthew-Mark-Luke versus the mind of John. Rather, the translators have improperly given Jesus **two doctrines** and **two personalities** by erroneously translating John 3:16 in a manner which suits cheap grace doctrine to leave uncorrected.

However, we shall see that the leading evangelical scholars who dared write on this question begrudgingly admit *pisteuo* means *obey* in John 3:16. It is only the translators who, for some inexplicable reason, continue to hesitate to make this now compellingly-obvious correction.

Three Interpretive Issues

John 3:16 is the most commonly cited passage from Jesus to prove one is saved by faith alone. This faith is usually described as *believing* that Jesus is Lord and Savior. Or sometimes it is said that you must simply *believe* that Jesus died for your sins. (Stanley, Spurgeon.) Sometimes it is said you must also *believe* that Jesus resurrected.

Whatever is the *belief* one must hold to be saved, typically it is also claimed John 3:16 conveys the idea of a *one-time* belief. In fact, Charles Stanley in *Eternal Security* (1995) at 95 says the verb *believes* in the standard translation implies a one-time belief (that Christ died for your sins, *id.*, at 33-34). Hence, such a one-time belief is supposedly all that you need to be saved. Therefore, it is allegedly irrelevant whether one repents from sin or not. Stanley says it is a good idea to change, but it only improves your fellowship with God. The Lord will supposedly save the disobedient believer anyway based on faith alone.

In fact, Stanley says your salvation is such a foregone conclusion once you sincerely believe Christ died for your sins that even if you for all practical purposes were later an unbeliever in thought and deed, your salvation is never in jeopardy: "Even if *a believer* for all practical purposes *becomes an unbeliever*, his salvation is not in jeopardy." (Stanley, *Eternal Security, supra*, at 93.) Salvation is supposedly by faith alone, from start to finish.

However, there are three defects in the popular *English* translation of the original Greek which in turn feed these interpretations of the verse. (These defects also appear in the German *Luther* Bible of 1522.) The correction of these defects turn on answering these three questions:

- Does the verb *pisteuo* translated in English as *believes* in the KJV mean *believe* or instead *obey, comply, trust*, etc.?
- Is it *pisteuo* "in" Jesus or "for (unto)" Jesus" in the original Greek?
- Is the verb form taken for *pisteousin* translated in the KJV as *believes* (the English simple present tense) instead in Greek a continuous tense meaning? In other words, is the meaning *keeps on* or *continues to* in front of whatever the verb means for *pisteuo*, i.e., keeps on *obeying, etc.,* or keeps on *believing*?

Two of these three issues are readily apparent if you compare common translations of John 3:16, in particular the **bolded** portions below, on the left with those on the right.

TABLE 1. John 3:16: Importance Of Translation

KJV-NIV	Alternative Translations
For God so loved the world, that he gave his only begotten Son... (KJV)	For God so loved the world that He gave His only-begotten [or, unique] Son (ALT)... [Essentially the same.]
that whosoever *believeth* in him (KJV) *cf.* NIV (*believes* in him)	so that every [one] believ*ing* [or, *trusting*] in Him (ALT)
should not perish (KJV)	*should* not perish (ALT)[same]
shall have eternal life (NIV)	*may* have life age-enduring (YLT); *should* have eternal life. (Reina Valera, mas *tenga* vida eterna; Vulgate, *habeat* vida eternum).

Does It Matter If John 3:16 Is About *Obedience* Not *Belief*?

There is a huge difference theologically between *obey, comply, trust* on one side and *belief* on the other.

Jesus discussed once this distinction. Jesus said it is incongruous to *think* you can say you believe in Him as Lord but feel free to *disobey* Him. Jesus said: "Why do you call me 'Lord, Lord,' and do not do what I tell you?" (Luke 6:46.) Jesus therefore declares it is unfathomable that one thinks it is enough to believe in Him but not obey Him.

Another proof of a large chasm of difference between mere belief and obedience comes from the gospel accounts about demons.

Demons believe Jesus is Lord and Savior. (Mark 1:24; Luke 4:34. See also, James 2:19.) The demons, however, do not obey Jesus as Lord. They do not act in compliance with their acknowledgment of the fact of who Jesus is. They do not trust Him. They do not obey Him.

Pastor Stedman, an evangelical scholar who believes in 'faith alone,' unwittingly admits this distinction:

Remember that back in the Gospel accounts there were demons that **acknowledged the deity of the Lord Jesus**? When he appeared before them they said, 'We know who you are, the Holy One of God.' (cf, Mark 1:24, Luke 4:34.) They **acknowledged** what the Jews were too blind to see, the full deity of Jesus Christ, as well as his humanity. But, though demons **acknowledged this, they never confessed it**. They **never trusted** him. They did **not commit themselves** to him, they did not *live* by this truth.[6]

Yet, we are told that John 3:16 proves that if you *believe* Jesus is Lord, Messiah, died for your sins, etc., then you shall have eternal life. If this were true, then the demons should be saved because they believe and know these things are true. (Mark 1:24; Luke 4:34.) James made a similar point in James 2:19. He says the demons believe the facts about God, but they are not saved thereby.

Hence, when we consider Jesus' dismay that people think they can call Him Lord but that obedience is optional, we are justified questioning John 3:16 in standard translation because it licenses that doctrine for so many.

Reliable Dictionary Meanings Of Pisteuo In John 3:16 As **Obey**

The most exhaustive dictionary of ancient Greek is Liddell-Scott's Lexicon. It is by far the most reliable.

There are six meanings offered in Liddell-Scott's Lexicon of the Greek verb *pisteuo* at issue in John 3:16.[7]

One meaning in Liddell-Scott for the verb *pisteuo* is *comply*. A synonym is *obey*. (See Footnote 7, page 423.)

The *NIV Theological Dictionary of New Testament Words* (Zondervan: 2000) has this likewise to say of *pisteuo*:

---

6. Ray C. Stedman, *When Unbelief is Right* (1967), reprinted at http://www.pbc.org/dp/stedman/1john/0161.html (last visited 2005).

Similarly, *pisteuo* means to trust something or someone; it can refer to and confirm legendary tales and mythical ideas. **With reference to people, pisteuo means to *obey*;** the pass[ive] Means to enjoy trust...

This is likewise mentioned in the highly authoritative *Theological Dictionary of the New Testament* (TDNT) 6 (1968): 4-7, in an entry by Bultmann (1884-1976) — the eminent Lutheran scholar — in which he says the verb "pisteuo means" (among other things) "'to trust'" and "also 'to **obey**.'" (It is both enlightening and disturbing to watch how 'cheap grace adherents cope with this dictionary entry despite the TDNT being one of the most authoritative and scholarly dictionary references within *Protestantism*.)[8]

What If It Only Looks Like A Dictionary? It Still Is Not One

Yet, do not be surprised when you go to the evangelical bookstore, and you open up a Greek word study on *pisteuo*, and you find "obey" and "comply" are not even identified as *possible* meanings. For example, in Spiros Zodhiates, *The Complete Word Study — New Testament* (Chatanooga, TN: AMG, 1993) at 1160-62 — on my local Christian bookstore shelf in 2007 — you will see what appears to be a comprehensive entry on *pisteuo*. Yet, not once does it

---

7. Liddel Scott defines *pisteuo* as:

"1. ***trust***, put faith in, rely on a person, thing, or statement,

2. Pass[ive], to be ***trusted*** or believed

3. ***comply***.

4. c. infinitive., ***believe that***, feel confident that a thing is, will be, has been

5. c. dat. and inf., toisi episteue sigan to whom he ***trusted*** that they would keep silence

6. have faith II. (1) p. tini ti ***entrust*** something to another (2) Pass., pisteuesthai ti to be ***entrusted with a thing***, have it committed to one."
This is available online or in a library in the Liddell & Scott *Greek Lexicon* (Oxford: 1869) at 1273.

---

mention "obey" or "comply" as a definition. It is obvious what is happening. Zodhiates never calls his word study a dictionary, and thus you cannot accuse him of misleading anyone. He called it a word study, not a *dictionary.* Unfortunately, the average Christian does not know the fine distinction.

The same problem holds true of the *Strong's Concordance.* Its title — a concordance — means it is only a reference to how the King James Bible translated every Greek word listed. It does not purport to be a dictionary. However, most Christians think because it is laid out as a dictionary, that in fact it is a dictionary. However, *Strong's* is not a dictionary, and never purports to be one. Yet, if you rely upon its 'entries' under *pisteuo,* you never once see the meaning *obey* or *comply.* Don't be fooled. If it does not say it is a *dictionary,* it is not purporting to be one.

How Negative Prefixes Aid Translation

One can further confirm *pisteuo*'s meaning by adding a negative prefix in front of *pisteuo* — the letter *a,* and then see what are the word meanings of the Greek word formed thereby — *apisteo.* Liddell-Scott points out that *apisteo* means, among other things, "to **disobey**...refuse to **comply**." (Liddell-Scott, *Greek Lexicon.*)

---

8. Bing is critical of translating *pisteuo* as *obey.* Rather than deal properly with the issue, he barely mentions the authoritative sources that directly define *pisteuo* as sometimes meaning *obey.* When he discusses Bultmann's entry in the TDNT, Bing claims *obey* is merely a "suggestion." Bing then says Bultmann's theology is driving this "suggestion" rather than Greek. Bing then makes it sound like Bultmann is relying on weak lexical aids. What Bing never does is explore what Greek dictionaries (not concordances or word studies) include among the definitions of *pisteuo.* On that score, Bultmann would have been a poor scholar had he omitted *obey* as one definition. See Charles C. Bing, *Lordship Salvation — A Biblical Evaluation and Response* (Ph.D. Dissertation) (Dallas Theological Seminary, 1991), reprinted at http://www.forerunner.org/bing/LS-chap2.htm (accessed 7-21-07).

Apisteo is clearly used in this way in 1 Peter 2:7. See KJV-Geneva "disobey." See also 2 Tim 2:13 ("if we are *apisteo* disobeying" is antithesis to God's *pistos* or *faithfulness*). In the Septuagint of 247 B.C., *apisteo* "several times answers to the Hebrew [word for] *rebellious*." (Parkhurst, 1829:71.)

Of course, *apisteo* can still mean *disbelieve*, just as *pisteuo* can still mean *believe* in a fact or truth. Nevertheless, the point is that to a Greek the idea of a *belief* alone is not necessarily the correct meaning. A competing and valid meaning of *pisteuo* is *obey* or *comply*. This is demonstrable not only from the dictionary meaning of *pisteuo*, but also from the definition of its opposite — *apisteo*.

Thayer and Parkhurst On *Obedience* Meaning Of Pisteuo

This *obedience*-meaning for *pisteuo* is also reflected by other evangelical lexicographers. These reputable Christian scholars are evidently trying to gently disabuse Christians from the idea of *belief* alone as the *primary* meaning of these words in the New Testament. For example, J.H. Thayer is the most highly honored lexicographer of New Testament Greek. Nevertheless, Thayer noted *pistis* — the noun formed from *pisteuo* — is "used **especially** of the faith by which a man embraces Jesus, *i.e., a conviction*, full of joyful **trust**....**conjoined** with **obedience** to Christ." (Thayer, *Greek-English Lexicon* (T. & T. Clark: 1958) at 511.) Likewise, Parkhurst, who enjoys similar repute, said in 1829 of *pisteuo* in John 3:16 that it simultaneously means a "cordial reception [belief] ... and **obedience**....." (Parkhurst: 683-84.)

'Obey' Fits Other Passages

If *pisteuo* means *obey* here, then John 3:16 would be merely repeating Hebrews 5:9 which explicitly says: "He became the author of eternal salvation unto all of them that are **obeying** Him." (*Obey* is *hoopakouo* in continuous tense.)[9]

---

9. It literally means *to listen attentively.*

Likewise, if *pisteuo* means *obey* in John 3:16, it would fit John 8:51 which says: "anyone who keeps on **obeying** (*tereo*, 'diligently following' in a continuous tense) my teaching should never ever die."

It would also perfectly match Peter's declaration to the High Priest in Acts 5:32: "And we are witnesses of these things; and so is the Holy Spirit, whom God hath given to them that [keep on] **obey[ing]** (*peitharcheo*, continuous tense) him."(Act 5:32 ASV.) *Peitharcheo* means literally *submission to a judge*, and its typical usage means *obey.* Here, Peter says God's Holy Spirit is given to those who "keep on obeying [Jesus]."

Thus, translating *pisteuo* in John 3:16 as *obey* or *comply*, if truly the intention of Jesus, would match other Greek synonyms which are used to mean *obey* and which likewise appear in salvation-formula statements. These equivalent statements which conditioned salvation on obedience use distinct but yet synonymous verbs for *obedience: tereo* — diligently follow or obey; *petharcheo* — submit to a judge or obey; and *hoopakouo* — listen attentively to or obey. (John 8:51; Acts 5:32; Heb. 5:9.)

Hence, the translation of *pisteuo* in John 3:16 as *obey* has serious possibilities. It is a true dictionary meaning. It is not merely a suggestion or contrived idea. Moreover, if intended in John 3:16, we see it fits well into other verses which explicitly emphasize obedience for salvation-sake as used by Jesus, the Apostle Peter and the writer of Hebrews.

'Trust' Meanings Of Pisteuo

There are still other translation options of *pisteuo* to consider. In Liddell-Scott, four of the other six meanings of the verb *pisteuo* center on *trust or entrust.* See Footnote 7, page 423.

These words *trust* or *entrust* are not to be confused with "trust in some fact." Some like Stanley accept *pisteuo* really means *trust,* but then immediately try to dilute the meaning of *trust* so it is indistinguishable from *belief alone.* Instead, *trust* implies *follow* and/or *obey,* and is distinguishable from *believe in a fact.* Based on accepting *trust* as the meaning here, Stanley dilutes it to a trust that Jesus' atonement is sufficient without any works of obedience ever necessary on our part. (Stanley, *Eternal Security, supra,* at 33-34.)

Instead, the meaning of *pisteuo* as *trust* is not so shallow. Another eminent Protestant scholar of the Greek, W. E. Vine in his *An Expository Dictionary of New Testament Words* (Nashville: Thomas Nelson Publishers, 1984) explains when *pisteuo* means *trust,* then *pisteuo* means "not mere credence" (belief alone) but instead, "reliance upon." He means a reliance like you would rely upon your doctor's orders. You would follow or obey your doctor's guidance.[10]

Thus, to *trust Jesus,* if the correct translation, would mean to *trust* Him as the doctor of your soul. If your doctor pays you a visit, gives you a sermon on how you need to live differently, *e.g.,* be a peacemaker, not lust adulterously, not make false vows, etc., in order to have a "righteousness" greater than all the teachers you had before and "enter heaven" (Matt. 5:20, 23:23), you mean by such *trust* to say you are going to trust the doctor's prescriptions. You will **obey** the doctor's orders.

"Belief In Facts" Meaning Of Pisteuo

Nevertheless, in one usage identified in Liddell-Scott, *pisteuo* can be translated as someone *believes* that something is true. Or it can mean to be confident in a fact. (See Footnote 7, page 423.)

This *belief-in-a-fact* usage out of six possible meanings leaves open the door — ever so slightly — that the speaker (Jesus) in John 3:16 could mean potentially *belief* in some fact or truth. This *belief*-usage does not imply, by itself,

---

10.An online reprint is at http://www.bibletexts.com/glossary/belief.htm
(accessed 7-5-07).

by itself, obedience or compliance is what should lead to eternal life. Thus, the *belief alone* option has to be on the table at the outset.

How Was Pisteuo Used In The Immediate Context?

One of the most famous evangelical scholars — Vincent — was one of the first to note the significance of *eis* following *pisteuo* in John 3:16. He said its effect in the sentence required reading *pisteuo* not to mean mere belief in facts. It required the meaning of *obedience*. Vincent says:

> "'believe **on**' (*pisteuosin eis*) is **more than mere acceptance of a statement**. It is so to accept them practically....Hence, to believe **on** the Lord Jesus is not merely to believe the facts of His historic life or His saving energy as facts, but to accept Him as Savior, Teacher, Sympathizer, Judge; to rest the soul upon Him for present and future salvation; and **to accept and adopt His precepts and example and binding upon the life**." (Marvin R. Vincent, *Word Studies in the New Testament* (C. Scribner's: 1905) Vol. 2 at 49-50.)

Background on Vincent's Claim

What Vincent is saying is that it is often overlooked in John 3:16 that *pisteuo* is followed by the words "*eis autos*"[11] — *eis* meaning "**unto**, into, towards, **for**." (Thayer's *New Testament Lexicon*.) *Autos* simply means *him*. The word *pisteuo* is not followed by the Greek word for *in* which is *en*.

---

11. Westcott-Hort, Nestle-Asland 26 (http://www.thenazareneway.com/ greek_new_test/john.htm); Stephen's Textus Receptus 1550; Scrivner 1894; Byzantine Majority (http://www.awmach.org/webo/BGR/ joh.htm#3:1(accessed 7-4-07).

Meaning of Eis

Liddell-Scott's Lexicon provides us once more the most authoritative analysis of the meaning of the word *eis*. In its standard usage, *eis* means "into" or "more loosely, to."[12] Liddell-Scott, however, will explain carefully its usages where it changes to the meaning of *for*. (An English synonym of *for* is *unto* with non-motion verbs. The word *unto* is listed by Thayer above as an optional translation of *eis*, which will be important later.)

However, before discussing Liddell-Scott's detailed examples of the nuanced meanings of *eis*, up front we need to note the word *eis* is never offered to be translated as the English word *in* by either Thayer's or Liddell-Scott.

Yet, the King James felt free to render *eis* with our English word *in* on **138 occasions**, including John 3:16. Yet, **the English word *in* is impermissible**. There is a Greek word for *in*, and not surprisingly it is the word *en*.

With that caution in mind, let's study *eis* in Liddell-Scott — the most thorough and reliable Greek lexicon ever assembled.

Liddell-Scott starts out by distinguishing the possible meaning of *eis* if a verb expresses motion or not.

Liddell-Scott says *eis* with verbs of motion or direction means "into." Thus, one would say you go 'into' (*eis*) a place. This is the typical usage of *eis* — it follows a verb of motion.[13]

Eis With Verbs Lacking Sense Of Motion Or Direction

On the other hand, if the verb "has no sense of motion to or into a place," Liddell-Scott says then the translation should be "for."

---

12. http://www.perseus.tufts.edu/cgi-bin/ptext?doc=Perseus%3Atext%3A1999.04.0057%3Aentry%3D%2331236 (last accessed 7-4-07).

13. Another use of *eis* is to express relations such as "in regard to."

In such a case, *eis* is rendered as *for* because the sentence intends to express *purpose* or *object*. *Eis* as a preposition likewise, when standing alone, often has this function. Liddell-Scott explains:

> of Purpose or Object...*for* good, *for* his good...to live *for* show...to be pertinent, to the purpose...to cause fear [*eis phobon*]

(Incidentally, this *for* meaning is distinguishable from the Greek word *gar* which means *for* in the sense of *because*. "Repent, for (Greek, *gar*) the kingdom of heaven is at hand." Matt. 3:2.)

We find this *for* meaning of *eis* in many places in the New Testament writings.

The *eis* of purpose, meaning *for*, is how Paul spoke in Ephesians 4:11, 12. Paul said: "And he gave some prophets, some evangelists, some pastors and teachers toward (Greek, *pros*) the equipping of the saints *for* (Greek, *eis*) the work of ministry *for* (Greek, *eis*) the building of the body of Christ."

The same usage of *eis* as *for* (an *object*) is found in 1 Peter 3:21. Apostle Peter says "baptism... does now *save us* — not the putting away the filfth of the flesh, but the answer of a good conscience *eis* — **FOR** — God." Peter means when during the washing of baptism you answer and truly repent FOR God's sake (*i.e.*, the answer of a good conscience), this aspect of baptism is what "saves us" (not the washing of the water).

Apostle Peter uses *eis* the same way again when Peter says in Acts 2:38 the following:

> And Peter said unto them, **Repent** ye, and be baptized every one of you in the name of Jesus Christ **FOR** (Greek, *eis*) the remission of your sins; and ye shall receive the gift of the Holy Spirit. (KJV).

Peter intends us to understand that the water has no magic for salvation sake (1 Peter 3:21), but that a good conscience by repentance from sin is **FOR** the remission of sins.

Hence, we see numerous uses of *eis* in Scripture to mean *for* a purpose or object, including *for* God. We saw examples where it is spoken of as having a *good conscience* FOR GOD or as having *repentance* FOR the remissions of sins. (Incidentally, please do not overlook Peter's salvation statements just quoted at odds with cheap grace.)

Eis Can Crucially Change Meaning

Kenneth Wuest (1893-1962), formerly a professor at Moody Bible Institute, makes the point that translating *eis* into English **incorrectly** has misled the reader in other contexts. His remark below is just as applicable to what happened to John 3:16 due to the English mistranslation of *eis* as *in,* as we shall see below:

> A careful study of the Greek preposition [*eis*] discloses **some precious truth** that would otherwise be **obscured** by reason of **a wrong interpretation put upon an English preposition**, and at the same time **saves the expositor** from arriving at **a wrong interpretation**.[14]

With all of that in mind, let's examine the possibilities of how to translate John 3:16.

Is *Pisteuo* A Verb Of Motion?

Considering what Liddell-Scott explained, the correct meaning of *eis* here should be *for* (or its English synonym *unto*) with the sense of purpose or object. The verb *pisteuo*, whether *obey, comply, trust, etc.*, or *believe* (some fact) is **not a verb of motion**.

Some suggest *pisteuo* has a sense of motion by paraphrasing it to mean '*place* one's faith in or on Jesus.' Yet, that is adding words to make *pisteuo* appear a verb of motion. However, if *pisteuo* is being used to mean *believe*, it not only

---

14. Kenneth Wuest, *Practical Use of the Greek New Testament* (Chicago: Moody Press, n.d.) at 61 and 62.

lacks any motion, it lacks any sense of motion, as even the proponents of that meaning intend. If *pisteuo* means instead *comply, obey, commit*, or *trust*, it likewise signifies *no motion — no physical placing*. No one is *going* anywhere, and hence it is not a verb of motion. Thus, one can see the suggestion that it means the motion of *placing* something *in* someone else is a motion activity not present in the verb meaning itself. What drives this?

Some Christian scholars suggest that we must either "***supply a missing idea of motion***" or "recognize a negligent use of *eis*" in certain contexts.[15] If the meaning is metaphysical, "it is left to the interpreter to decide which meaning is best suited to the context in every particular case." (Butmann, *id.*) While never saying so, such a lesson can only be addressed to the problem presented by *eis* in John 3:16. If you want the meaning of *eis* in John 3:16 to come out as *in* due to a preconceived notion about salvation, you simply must supply the "missing meaning" to the verb involved (*i.e.*, 'placing'), so *pisteuo* now appears a verb of motion. Then you can rationalize *eis* to mean *into*. Then it is a short leap — although itself unjustifiable — to truncate this down to *in*. With that *in* placed where it does not belong, you can then peg *pisteuo* to mean *believes.*

However, may I suggest this idea that translators are free to supply a "missing meaning" or suppose "negligent use of *eis* " is doctrine speaking. It is no longer objective analysis. Objective scholars would readily see Butmann's reasoning is used to help justify the translation of *eis* as *in* rather than as *for*. In other words, some describe the verb in such a manner of 'putting faith in someone' *solely* to justify the habitual English rendering of *in* within John 3:16. This is how they force *eis* to mean *in* — by conforming the verb meaning to justify their preferred understanding of *eis*. Yet, it is the

---

15. Alexander Buttman, *A Grammar of the New Testament Greek* (Andover: Walter Draper, 1873) at 333 (available from Google books).

nature of the verb that controls the meaning of *eis*. It is not the preferred rendering of *eis* which drives us to change and mold the verb. These translators have it backwards.

Let's turn to objective scholars for help. Malcolm D. Hyman of Harvard provides useful analysis in *Greek and Roman Grammarians On Motion Verbs and Place Adverbials* (January 4, 2003) (available online).[16] His study provides us an objective source of information. He says a motion verb means an intransitive verb which "denotes *a change of place*." You will find it often in conjunction with "a spatial adverbial — a prepositional phrase or adverb." Hyman points out that ancient Greek grammarians spelled out these rules with precision. Such a grammarian was Apollonius Dyscolus. Apollonius explained adverbs' meanings change in relation to whether a motion or non-motion verb is used. Thus, *ano* means *above*, but after a motion verb it means *upwards*. Apollonius described this phenomenon in Greek where "semantic categories are represented by the same linguistic form." In other words, the preposition's meaning changes by the nature of the verb involved. Latin has the identical grammar.

What are verbs of motion? Hyman explains that if the verb signifies one is *going* somewhere, it is a verb of motion, and adverbials (including prepositions) take on a different meaning. For example, "I start," "I proceed," or "I make my way" are motion verbs. When used with motion, Hyman mentions *eis* means *into*.

When the verb is not of motion, such as here — where it is *obey, commit, trust* or *believes*, Liddell-Scott says the sense of *eis* is *for*. Also, one can see the verb followed by *eis* and a pronoun *him* (indicating Jesus) is identifying an object or purpose in view. It is comparable to the example Liddell-Scott gave of *for (eis) his good*. The verb activity is thus for the sake of Jesus. It is *for Him*.

16.http://archimedes.fas.harvard.edu/mdh/motion.pdf (accessed 7-18-07).

Vincent in volume two of his work agrees on the impact of *eis* in the sentence. In fact, Vincent says *eis* drives the meaning so that *pisteuo* means *obey*, not merely *believes* when Jesus speaks in John 3:16. Vincent says the *eis* requires *pisteuo* to mean "to accept and adopt His precepts and example as binding upon" one's life — the true predicate to *eternal life* in John 3:16.[17] *Pisteuo* is thus *unto* Him — *for His benefit, for His service*. It means *obedience* results in eternal life.

Unto's Meaning In English

In rendering John 3:16, we will prefer rendering *eis* as *unto* rather than *for*. It simply sounds better. In English, *unto* is a word that when change in "place is not the sense" (*i.e.*, a motion is not involved in the verb), *unto* means "in order to or with the purpose that."[18] In short, it means *for* in the sense of purpose. Thus, if the verb involved is not a verb of motion from place to place, *unto* is a perfect synonym for the English word *for*. Sometimes it just sounds better to use *unto* in place of *for*. See for example Romans 1:16 RSV ("power of God unto (*eis*) salvation..."); Romans 6:10 ("Christ died unto (*eis*) sin once....")

Having Solved Eis' Meaning, What Is The Best Meaning Of The Expression?

Now let's put Vincent's claim in volume two of his famous work that *pisteuosin eis* in John 3:16 means to *obey* Jesus. We will take the previously established meanings of

---

17. As quoted previously above, Vincent in his Prologue of volume two emphasizes that *eis* in expression of *pisteuosin eis* means *obeying* Jesus. See quote at 428 *supra* from Marvin R. Vincent, *Word Studies in the New Testament* (C. Scribner's: 1905) Vol. 2 at 49-50.

18. Edward Byrd, "Unto what then were ye Baptized?," *The Reminder* Volume No. 23 Issue No. 07 (November 1983), available online at http://www.anabaptist.com/ReminderTemplate.cfm?ReminderID=3 (accessed 7-21-07).

---

pisteuo, and then combine each with *unto* as the best English synonym for *eis*. The result should allow us to test which of the following statements reads best. (The verb tense is continuous which is reflected below by adding 'keeps on.')[19]

- "whosoever keeps on trusting **unto** him...."
- "whoever keeps on obeying/complying **unto** him...."
- "whoever keeps on believing (that a thing is, will be or has been true) **unto** him."
- "whoever keeps on committing **unto** him."

The interesting thing here is no matter what meaning you give *pisteuo* among these, when you remove *in* and replace it with the sense of *for* (*i.e.*, 'unto'), the emphasis of the sentence changes. The verb activity now has a purpose that validates it. This is what the word *eis* does to the sentence. As Vincent said, *this little preposition is the key that unlocks the verse*.

Unfortunately, the preposition *in* which the KJV used only obscures this purpose.

As Professor Wuest said as to other passages, the wrong English translation of the Greek preposition *eis* can cause "*some precious truth*" to be "*obscured* by reason of *a wrong interpretation put upon an [erroneous] English preposition*" used to translate *eis*. The repair of such an error "*saves the expositor* from arriving at *a wrong interpretation*." See page 431 *supra*.

Thus, in John 3:16 *eis* makes clear that whatever the activity it is that *pisteuo* represents, it is *for* Jesus' sake. It is not a verb activity you have *in* Jesus. It is something you are *doing* FOR Jesus — "unto" our Lord. That's the point of John 3:16. That activity, whatever it might be, is done FOR Jesus. We now *pisteuo* **unto** or **FOR** Jesus.

---

19. See "Issue #3: Continuity Or One Time Pisteousin?" on page 509 *et seq.*

Once you have that *for* meaning in mind, the decision on which of the meanings best reflects Jesus' intention is clearly *obeying* or synonymously *committing*. You are serving *for* Christ and His sake alone. You are not obeying to be "seen by men." (Matt. 6:1.) It is not *for* others. It is not obedience *for* obedience-sake alone. Instead, you have taken on a commitment *for* Him to serve only Him. This is an obedience which you will keep on honoring and doing *for* Jesus' sake, just as a good servant should be doing.

This completely lines up with John 8:51: "whoever keeps on **obeying** (*tereo*, diligently following) My Teaching should never ever die."

Thus, John 3:16 is a synonymous way of saying what is clearly said in John 8:51.

You are keeping to your obedience *for* Jesus' sake, and hence you "should receive eternal life."

Contrast this with how many read John 3:16. For example, many belief-alone advocates say salvation is for those who "believe in *the fact* that Christ died for your sins." Or that salvation is for the one who "believes in the *fact that* Jesus was Messiah." Thus, Stanley says you are saved if you ever once believe or trust in the fact that "Jesus died for your sins." (*Eternal Security, supra,* at 33-34.)

Yet, that is not the point at all of John 3:16. It is not what *faith* you place *in* Jesus. It is instead about what you are doing *for* Jesus.

The Context And Meaning Of John 3:14-15

There is another key to knowing what Jesus meant in John 3:16. Verse sixteen begins with the conjunction *gar,* rendered "For" or better "Wherefore." ("**For** God so loved.....") This means John 3:16 is intended to explain the preceding verses — verse 16 is going to tell us the meaning of John 3:14-15. Thus, by parallel reasoning, John 3:14-15 tells us the meaning of John 3:16 — because verse 16 is meant to reflect 3:14-15. These preceding words were:

> And as Moses lifted up the serpent in the wilder-
> ness, even so must the Son of man be lifted up;
> (15) that whosoever keep on *pisteuo*-ing may in
> (*en*) him have eternal life. (John 3:14-15).[20]

Jesus in these two verses is equating the story about the way the snake healed people in the Mosaic account and how those who *pisteuo* today will find eternal life in Jesus when He is lifted up.

Jesus in John 3:14-15 is referring to Numbers 21:4-9. There we learn that after the Israelites were led from Egyptian bondage into the wilderness of Sinai, many of them began to murmur against Yahweh. Accordingly, the Lord sent fiery serpents among them as a mode of punishment to bite them. When the people acknowledged their sin of rejecting the manna and sought deliverance, God instructed Moses to fashion a serpent out of brass, and set it upon a standard. Any person who "looked" upon the serpent would live.

This concept of *repentance from rejecting manna* and then *continuing to look* in one direction upon the lifted-up serpent is merely another way of saying *repent* and *obey.*

F.F. Bruce, an evangelical scholar and professor of Greek for many years, concurs.

F.F. Bruce says in his *The Gospel of John* (Wm. B. Eerdmans: 1994) at 89:

> It was the saving grace of God that healed the
> bitten Israelites when they believed his word
> and **obeyed his command.**

One can see this *looking* implies obedience when you study together two verses: John 1:1 and John 5:19. The verse John 1:1 usually is translated to say that the Word was *with* God. However, the Greek preposition was *pros — towards —*

---

20. Please notice this time it is "*in* him have eternal life." It is still not "believe *in* him." Here, the "in him" means eternal life is located in Jesus. The one who is *pisteuo*-ing "may in [Jesus] have eternal life." Vincent *Word Studies* points out that the "*in him*" formula of John 3:15 "*occurs nowhere else in John.*" (VWS, Romans 4:5.)

God. Jesus was *towards* God. Jesus' whole being was directed to the Father. Then John 5:19 tells us what it means to be ***looking*** *towards* the Father:

> Jesus therefore answered and said unto them, Verily, verily, I say unto you, The Son can do nothing of himself, but what he **seeth** [Greek, ***blepo***, looking] ***the Father doing***: for what things **soever he doeth**, these the **Son also doeth in like manner**. (John 5:19 ASV.)

Thus, when we are looking towards the Son lifted up on the cross, we should be likewise doing whatever we know Jesus was doing on the cross. This is the necessary effect that Jesus' looking at the Father had on Him. Thus, by our looking at Jesus on the cross lifted up like Moses lifted up the brass serpent, we will necessarily plan to imitate Jesus. What was Jesus doing? When we look at the cross, we see Christ's ***obedience*** to the Father. "Not my will, but thy [will] ***keep being done***." (Luke 22:42, translated by Robertson, *Word Pictures*.)

Elsewhere, Jesus makes this plain, saying our ***imitation*** of what He did on the cross — losing one's own life for the sake of someone else — is *crucial* for us individually to later receive *life* (eternal life):

> And he that ***doth not take his cross and follow after me***, is ***not worthy*** of me. (39) He that ***findeth his life shall lose it***; and he that ***loseth his life for my sake shall find it***. (Matt. 10:38-39.)

Hence, John 3:14-15 is about a repenting-from-sin people who now want to turn to God and by *looking* up at the healing standard are obeying God. They have to look upon the serpent raised on a standard high just as Moses' instructed them. These repenting humbled people were *pisteuo*-sing just like we are supposed to be *pisteou*-sing. Jesus too will be "lifted up" for us (John 12:32) and like the serpent, when we "look on" the Son and imitate His costly sacrifice, we will be healed and live. He who ***like Jesus*** loses his life for Christ's sake "shall find" life. (Matt. 10:38-39.)

It is also as Jesus says in John 6:40: all who "keep on looking" — present participle active — "on the son and should be *pisteuo eis* Him should be having eternal life." This is a parallelism further accentuating *pisteuo eis* means *obey unto*. The *looking* and the *pisteuo*-ing are synonyms for obeying in that context.

Thus, John 3:14-15 says if we *pisteuo* the way the Israelites did, we too should be healed and live. The *pisteuo* of the Israelites in the story cited one verse prior to John 3:16 is not *mere belief alone*. Rather, it is *repenting from rejecting the manna, turning back to God and then obeying Moses' instruction to look at the object of healing and life.* The whole process is repentance and obedience. With Christ, the looking upon the cross is also meant to imply you must imitate His obedience on the cross.

One cannot misread the Israelite passage to which Jesus refers as salvation by the **shallow physical act** of looking at the serpent. We cannot reduce salvation to simply looking at the Cross in our mind's eye, knowing it was the work of redemption. This would be pure gnosticism.

Yet, this is essentially how Bruce Demarest views it in *The Cross and Salvation: The Doctrine of Salvation* (Wheaton, Illinois: 1997): "For the healing to occur, **no religious work was involved**; a person **simply looked** in faith and lived." (*Id.,* at 259.) Demarest says for us that looking is mere *knowledge* (in Greek *gnosis*) about Jesus and His work: "Foundational to saving faith is *knowledge* of Christ's person and saving work...." (*Id.*) Demarest is emphasizing salvation by **looking at the cross** and **knowing of Jesus' person** and the work at the cross. Demarest thus teaches salvation by mere *gnosis*.

Now we are beginning to see why the early church taught it was heresy for Marcion to proclaim salvation by *gnosis* (belief in facts-faith alone) without obedience.

Therefore, Jesus in John 3:14-15 means only those who have the characteristic of the Israelites who repented from rejecting the manna, who asked God for mercy, who heartily now ate the manna again without grumbling, who then obeyed Moses to look up at the raised serpent, and who finally *pisteuo*-ed and continued to do so (the verb is in the continuous tense) will receive life.

Hence, John 3:16 is an explanation of John 3:14-15. The *gar* that begins 3:16 directly ties into 3:14-15 as an explanation. The word *pisteuo* is used in 3:14-15 again. Because Jesus is analogizing *pisteuo* to the *obedient* looking up by the repentant Israelites on the serpent in the Numbers account, we again know that *obey* should be the translation of *pisteuo* in John 3:16.

Jesus' Other Uses of Pisteuo and Pistis,-os

In five passages, in particular, Jesus' usage proves He meant *obeys* by the word *pisteuo* and *obedience* by *pistis*.

Pisteuo Destroyed by Temptation. The second seed in the Parable of the Sower keeps on *pisteuo*-ing for a while, but in time of temptation, falls away and withers (dies). (Luke 8:13.) It thereby becomes lost due to disobedience. Its *pisteuo*-ing was destroyed. Hence, "falling into temptation" is the opposite force that destroys *pisteuo*-ing. Among the various dictionary possibilities for *pisteuo* in Luke 8:13 which best contrasts to *temptation* is the meaning *obey*. For *disobedience* (falling into temptation) is the direct antithesis to *obedience*. Hence, Luke 8:13 should be translated that the "second seed keeps on obeying [*pisteuo*] for a while but in time of temptation falls away...." The word *obey* is the correct and hence intended antithesis to the *temptation*.

Heaven-maimed or hell-whole. We have seen Jesus warned the twelve apostles about those who "*pisteuo* unto" Him who become ensnared. (Matt. 18:6; Mark 9:42.) Such *pisteuo*-ing people and the apostles only have two options when so ensnared: they can go to heaven-maimed by cutting off body parts ensnaring them in sin (*i.e.*, causing them to violate

God's commandments) or they will go to hell whole. (Mark 9:42-47.) *Pisteuo* is thus being brought to nothing by *disobedience* in this passage. Hence, this antithesis proves *to obey* is the meaning of *pisteuo* in Matthew 18:6 and Mark 9:42.

The Work of God is Pisteuo. In John 6:27-29, Jesus speaks of *pisteuo* as a work. Obedience is a work; faith is not, even as Paul's usage proves. (Eph.2:8-9.) See discussion on Footnote 3, page 397. Hence, *pisteuo* means obey in John 6:27-29.

The Servant Who Is Pistos. In a parable of a prudent and faithful servant who ends up suffering weeping and gnashing with the *apiston* (disobedient), Jesus calls the servant initially *pistos*. Every Bible renders *pistos* as *faithful*. That is, the *obedient*. After sin, this servant is punished with the disobedient — those who are *a* + *pistis*. See page 57. In Rev. 2:10, the *faithful* "pistos" receives the "crown of life."

Another Key Factor: The Wider Context Of Jesus' Other Words

The object in view in John 3:16 is that Jesus wants you to have eternal life, correct? The question then is whether Jesus intends you to receive eternal life either:

- by merely *believing* in the fact that you are a sinner and He died for your sins? That is what Charles Stanley and dominant evangelical doctrine insists is the only requirement for you to be given *eternal life*. (Stanley, *Eternal Security, supra,* at 33-34.)
- or by *obeying unto Him* as a good servant should.

Here is where this entire book *Jesus' Words on Salvation* serves as mere prologue to make this wider contextual analysis of *pisteuo* in John 3:16. For we have seen Jesus repeatedly emphasized obedience to His commands for salvation-sake. Here are few highlighted passages to consider.

Atonement Is No Benefit Without Appeasement of the One Offended. Jesus said before you bring the "atoning sacrifice" to God's heart for your plea of mercy you MUST ABSOLUTELY have first appeased the one you offended (whether God or man). (Matt. 5:23-24.) (See page 1 *et seq.*)

Jesus said leave your "sacrifice" (*doron*) offering at the "sacrifice altar" and be first "reconciled." Then and only then "bring the sacrifice" back to God's altar. Only then will you have atonement *cleanse* you from all sin! Jesus' doctrine was the same teaching as all the prophets before Him. The prophets taught the ineffectiveness of the atonement for those who had not first repented and been *actually* reconciled to the one whom they had offended. (Jer. 7:22-23; Mic. 6:6-8, Joel 2:13, Hos. 14:1-2; & Mal. 1:10, 3:3-4. Cf. Isaiah 27:9.) Jesus was also simply teaching the principle of "works worthy of repentance." John the Baptist — the "greatest Prophet" (Matt. 11:11) — also taught these were necessary before one could expect baptism to be effectual. (Matt. 3:7-10). Hence, Jesus gave a *works-worthy-of-repentance* condition to claim the atonement. This directs *pisteuo* in John 3:16 to more likely be rendered as *obey* than *believe* to fit this truth.

Weeping and Gnashing Parables. All the weeping and gnashing parables are likewise similar warnings of hell to God's servants who suffer from disobedience or lack of fruit.

For example, in Matthew 25:14-30, the servant to whom God gives a talent of gold but who — when the time for examination comes — has produced no fruit is sent to the outer darkness where there is weeping and gnashing of teeth. Jesus defines this place elsewhere as the "fiery furnace" where sinners are sent by the angels on Judgment Day. (Matt. 13:42.) As Jesus bluntly stated elsewhere, "the tree without good fruit shall be cut down and thrown in the fire." (Matt 7:19.) Or as Jesus clearly taught in the Metaphor of the Vine — a "branch *in me*" that produces "no fruit" is to be "taken away" and "cast outside" and "burned." (John 15:2,5-6.)

Sheep and Goats. Another important example is that Jesus says those who call Him Lord, but on the day of judgment are exposed as not having done charity to the brethren will be called to account, and sent to "eternal fire" due to their lack of charity. (Matt. 25:31-46, *viz.* v. 41.) Jesus in direct contrast says those who call Him Lord and do the works of charity "inherit the kingdom." (v. 34.) (See pages 219 *et seq.*)

Thus, unmistakably Jesus teaches in the Parable of the Sheep and the Goats that only those who do works of charity go to heaven, and all others go to "eternal fire."

Dillow concedes in this parable that "inheriting the kingdom is conditioned *on obedience* and *service* to the King...." (Dillow, *Reign of the Servant Kings, supra,* at 73.) Dillow then further concedes that Jesus' words "are a condition far removed from the New Testament [*i.e.*, the shallow belief-alone translation of Jesus] teaching of justification by faith alone for entrance into heaven."

Dillow fails to use these facts as an impetus to re-analyze the translation of *pistis* and *pisteuo* in his favorite verses. Instead, faith-alone apologists give us a nonsensical re-interpretation of the parable. They resolve this conflict between Jesus' teaching of salvation-by-obedience and our modern belief-alone doctrine by relegating this parable to only being true during the tribulation period *after* all Christians are gone. Such apologists thereby dismiss it for now.

However, the solution to this dilemma is patently obvious. The doctrine of 'faith alone' needs to be re-evaluated in light of the underlying Greek. Thus, this parable directly points out there must be an error in the common translation of *pistis* and *pisteuo* — *at least when Jesus is teaching. Pisteuo* in Jesus' thinking is frequently not only *believes*. He often must intend *obeys* as His meaning.

Obedience Doctrine in Jesus' Words. Finally, Jesus in several other places makes obedience indispensable, and not something that *belief* alone allows to be recognized as satisfied:

- If you call Jesus 'Lord,' but 'do not do His will,' He will tell you that He never knew you. (Matt. 7:21.)

- "And why call me Lord, Lord, and do not do what I say?" (Luke 6:46.)

- The faithful and good steward who later becomes **disobedient** is assigned a place along with the unbelievers/unfaithful outside in darkness where there is weeping and gnashing of teeth. (Luke 12:42-46.) See "The Parable Of The Good Servant Turned Evil" on page 55 *et seq.*

Evangelical Experts' Opinion

Next, we will explore what was the predominant usage throughout the New Testament of the verb *pisteuo* and its noun form, *pistis*.

What do evangelical or Protestant scholars say?

If you listen to one of the foremost evangelical specialists on the meaning of these Greek terms predominantly in the New Testament, this specialist once more vindicates what we have so far established. For in Vine's *Greek Commentary*, he delineates the "***main*** elements in faith [*pistis*]... and the corresponding verb, *pisteuo*" so that it connotes the following:

> (1) a firm **conviction**, producing a full acknowledgment of God's revelation or truth, e.g., 2 Thess. 2:11,12: (2) a **personal surrender** to Him, John 1:12; (3) a **conduct inspired by such surrender**, 2 Cor. 5:7 (Vine, *id.*, at 411).

Vine's means *pistis* (noun) or *pisteuo* (verb) share these characteristics at the very same time. His elements correspond to: 1. trust; 2. striving to obey (compliance); and 3. obedience. Vine's is hence indicating that the *main* meaning in the New Testament is not *credence* alone. Consequently, rarely does *pisteuo* or *pistis* solely mean *belief, faith alone* or mere *intellectual assent* or *knowledge* about *a truth or fact*, whether of great spiritual importance or otherwise.

To the same effect is *The Dictionary of Fundamental Theology*. It tells us that in the New Testament *pistis* and the verb *pisteuo* meant primarily to convey salvation by something more than mere belief. It ordinarily means that compliant trust and obedience or strong commitment (surrender) is integral and directly intended as part of the word meaning of either *pisteuo* or *pistis*.

> [F]aith is a process involving the entire human person — knowledge and commitment — as he or she advances toward the person of Jesus Christ. The interpersonal aspect of this faith [in the New Testament] makes it akin to the faith of the O[ld] T[estament]. It is **both trust and surrender** to God... it is **obedience** that assimilates the person to the crucified and risen Jesus and bestows the Spirit on the children of God.[21]

With that said, now let's examine texts other than when Jesus speaks that use the word *pisteuo* or its cousins, like *episteusan* in the next discussion.

Apostle John's Personal Usage of Pisteuo

In John 12:42, Apostle John is speaking. In the KJV, it reads:

> Nevertheless among the chief rulers also many **believed** [*episteusan*] on [*eis*] him; but because of the Pharisees **they did not confess him**, lest they should be put out of the synagogue: (43) For they loved the praise of men more than the praise of God. (John 12:42-43 KJV.)

---

21. Gilles Langevin, "Faith," *Dictionary of Fundamental Theology*. (ed. Rene Latourelle & Rino Fisichella)(New York: Crossroad Publishing Company, 1994) at 309 (emphasis added).

In John 12:42, Apostle John uses the verb *episteusan,* which is a word built on *pisteuo*. The prefix *epi* connotes *above the norm, above, on* or *upon.*

The correct translation should be these rulers "zealously/completely obeyed unto" Jesus.

The prefix *epi* is used to intensify the meaning of what follows. For example, when *epi* precedes *ginosoko,* to know, Vine's says its primary meaning is "to know ***thoroughly*** (epi, 'intensive' [of] ginosko, 'to know.')"[22]

These rulers therefore deeply and thoroughly had *pisteuo* unto Jesus, but they would not confess Him. As a result, those who prefer *believe* as the translation cannot dispute these were true believers. Robertson, a Baptist scholar, in his *Word Pictures* says John 12:42 means these were rulers who "***actually*** 'believed on him' (*episteusan eiv auton*) in their convictions...." (Whether it means *believed* or *obeyed* is postponed for later comment.)

If Robertson — a Baptist scholar — were correct that *pisteuo* meant *believes,* then faith alone doctrine is anyway in perilous trouble. For if true, here are rulers who had truly believed, but clearly were cowards later. Why does this pose a problem for faith alone? Because disobedience to Jesus — failing to confess Him — leads to loss of salvation. How do we know this? Because as moral cowards, God tells us the "cowardly" rulers who once "believed" will be thrown into the "lake of burning sulfur" with "unbelievers." (Rev.21:8.) Thus, those who *pisteuo* for a time but later turn into cowards go to hell just like any non-believer.

Yet, the true difficulty for faith alone doctrine is that John 12:42 presents an *antithesis* between *episteuosan* and the disobedient failure to confess Jesus. In John 12:42, Apostle John says that this *epi + pisteuo* has ended. He uses the *aorist* verb tense. This means their *pistis* existed intensely for a while and then ended. This is just like happened to the second seed in the Parable of the Sower who at first had *pistis*

22.Vine's Commentary on *epiginoska*'s usage in 2Pe 2:20 and 22.

with *joy* but later falls into temptation, withers and dies. (Luke 8:13.) The *aorist* tense in John 12:42 means an event that lasts for a while has ceased. It does not continue past a finite point. Here *epi* + *pisteuosan* continued intensely but then ended, replaced by a failure to confess Jesus.

Because in John 12:42, the *pisteuo* stopped upon *cowardice, w*e know a moral weakness marked the end of whatever *pisteuo* represented. The *pisteuo* should have saved them had it continued. Hence, this antithesis proves what translation of *pisteuo* here is correct. For *epi* + *pisteusan* is destroyed by cowardice. *Pisteuo* in this verse does not mean *believed*. Instead, it means *obeyed*.

The confirming proof is familiar. Again, as in John 3:16, the preposition *eis* is directly following the verb — here *episteusan*. Thus, as established previously, *eis* means *for* with non-motion verbs and is wrongly translated as *in* after *pisteuo* — a non-motion verb. The English word *unto* conveys the sense of *for*. Which means the Greek verb *pisteuo* within *episteusan* before *eis* means *obey* or *comply*. John 12:42 should likely read in a better translation:

> Nevertheless, still also many of the rulers [once] ***zealously obeyed unto*** Him, but because of the Pharisees they were ***not confessing*** [Him publicly], so that they should not be expelled from the synagogue. (John 12:42.)

Hence, we can see here that *episteusan* must mean these rulers had obediently followed Jesus at one time. They obeyed joyfully unto Him just like any other valid servant would do. But then they became afraid. They saw their friends and religious associates would scorn them for doing so. So they pulled back. They ***betrayed*** their earlier commitment to Christ by ***disobeying*** Him. By not confessing Him openly.

The Use of Pisteuo By The Greatest Prophet (John the Baptist) In John 3:36 As **Obeys**

Evangelical Protestant scholars such as F.F. Bruce will explain that *pisteuo* in John 3:36, which is verbatim the words in John 3:16, means *obey.*

In John 3:36, the speaker is John the Baptist. Jesus said John was the "greatest prophet" before Him. (Matt. 11:11.) Thus, Jesus tells us emphatically what we are about to read is something given under inspiration of the Holy Spirit.

In John 3:36, we will see another *pisteuo eis* (for) Jesus — identical to John 3:16 — is in the first half of John 3:36. We refer to it as John 3:36a. This clause is then *negated* in the second half by *disobedience.* We call this clause John 3:36b. As F.F. Bruce will explain, this direct contrast of 3:36a to 3:36b tells us that the speaker intends you to understand *pisteuo* as *obey. Pisteuo eis* is identified as something directly destroyed by *disobedience.* Because the direct opposite of disobedience is *obedience,* it tells you that *pisteuo eis* in John 3:36a means *obey,* not *believe.* In other words, disobedience to Jesus does not destroy *belief* in His atonement or Jesus as Messiah. Rather, disobedience destroys obedience. Hence, the contrast in John 3:36 clearly identifies *pisteuo eis* as meaning "obey unto," standing in contrast to the verb meaning *disobey* in John 3:36b.

Let's now look carefully at John 3:36 to see this.

Analysis Of John 3:36

First, John the Baptist is clearly amplifying 3:16 in 3:36. He repeats verbatim the salvation formula of John 3:16 but then John provides a competing contrast. John contrasts *pisteousin eis* with *disobeying* as a warning to the one who is *pisteuo*-ing. Here is what John 3:36 says literally in a correct translation:

> He that keeps on **obeying unto** the Son keeps on having eternal life [*cf.* the 3:16 formula], and he that keeps on **disobeying** [*apeitheo*] toward

[*to* in Greek] the Son shall not see life, but the wrath of God keeps on remaining on him.

In 3:36b, the Greek verb *apeitho* has **one and only one** meaning in Greek: *to disobey.*[23] *Cf.* Acts 26:19 ("Oh king Agrippa, I was not **disobedient** (*apeithes*) to the heavenly vision."); Titus 1:16 (*apeithes*, "**disobedient**" (KJV).)

F.F. Bruce says it is clear in the sentence structure that the *pisteousin eis* in the first part of John 3:36a is used "here in antithesis" to *disobedience* in the second part — in John 3:36b. (Frederick Fyvie Bruce, *The Gospel of John* (Wm. B. Eerdmans: 1994) at 98.) He says as a result of this antithesis in 3:36, "saving faith comprises believing and **obeying**." Bruce adds that those who "will **not obey** the son cut themselves off from the benefits of His sin-removing work," and their "**persistent impertinence** leaves them exposed to the wrath of God...." (F.F. Bruce, *The Gospel of John, supra,* at 98.)

F.F. Bruce's conclusion about John 3:36a is highly significant. If you read Bruce with care, he touches little on the issue of what *pisteuo eis* in John 3:16 means about salvation on the page where he directly discusses John 3:16. (*See, id.,* at 89.) Yet, here, when Bruce finally reaches John 3:36, and the same salvation formula is repeated verbatim, Bruce reveals a blockbuster fact. Bruce sees clearly there is more to the *pisteuo*-formula of John 3:16 which re-appears *verbatim* in 3:36a. Bruce precisely relies upon the antithesis between

---

23. *Apeitheo* only has one Greek meaning: **disobey.** (Liddell-Scott.) This is followed in ASV, RSV, NASV, WEB and GNB. *Cfr.* KJV and Luther's Bible ("not believe"). Why the difference in the KJV & Luther Bibles? Because Pauline dictionaries of ancient Greek, while admitting "not believe" is a meaning "not found outside our literature," claim the word *apeitheo* must mean disbelieve when used in Christian literature. (*Greek Lexicon of the New Testament* (eds. Bauer, Arndt, Gingrich, and Danker) at 82.) But why? Because unless we adopt an idiosyncratic meaning 'just for us Christians' that matches the accepted doctrine of cheap grace, then John 3:36 would undermine our favorite notions about salvation by 'faith alone,' and our favorite verse to prove it: John 3:16.

---

pisteuo in 3:36a and *apeitho* in John 3:36b to come to the conclusion *pisteuo* means *obey*, not merely *believes*.

Who is F.F.Bruce? This is the same F.F. Bruce (1910-1990) who impressed evangelicals with his work *New Testament Documents: Are They Reliable*? He taught Greek for years at the University of Edinburgh. He was the editor of the *Evangelical Quarterly*.

Yet, what Bruce is revealing in his penultimate book before he died was the most profound revelation of all. He sees the *pisteuo* of John 3:16 in the light of John 3:36. He says salvation must depend crucially not just on belief, but on *obedience*. It is John 3:36 that illuminates John 3:16 for F.F. Bruce.

This is also the message of John MacArthur. In his *The Gospel According to Jesus* (Zondervan: 1994), John MacArthur recognizes John 3:36 proves the 'believing' in John 3:36a is ended by the disobedience in John 3:36b. MacArthur says this proves salvation depends on a lasting obedience to Christ's authority, not on a one-time 'believing.' (*Id.* at 39 fn.) Hence, disobedience to Jesus' commands means God's wrath rests on you. MacArthur recognizes this disobedience in John 3:36b is directly a negation of *pisteousin eis* in John 3:36a.

Therefore, when John 3:36b says God's wrath rests on the disobedient, it does so in contrast to those in John 3:36a who keep on *pisteuo*-sing and who otherwise would have kept on having an "eternal life." Prophet John-the-Baptist in John 3:36b meant therefore to put in jeopardy those *pisteuo*-sing in John 3:36a who fall into temptation, thereby breaking the *pistis* they have. It is Luke 8:13 all over again — the seed that is *pisteuo*-ing for a while (typically translated as *believes*), then falls into temptation, withers and dies.

Consequently, we can deduce the meaning of *pisteuson eis* in the first part of John 3:36 as *keep on obeying unto the son*. **Only an obedience unto Jesus is in direct antithesis to disobedience to the son in 3:36b.**

Hence, this lesson from John the Baptist proves the word *pisteuo* clearly meant only *obey* in John 3:16. For only twenty verses later — John 3:36a — an undeniable prophet of God repeats the very same salvation formula as in John 3:16 but this time the context conclusively demonstrates *pisteuo* means *obeys*. This proves the *pisteuo* back in John 3:16 must have had the same meaning. Thus, the "greatest prophet" (before Christ) did His Lord the greatest service of all. John the Baptist uttered John 3:36 so that all the misconstruction of John 3:16 could easily be removed once an objective and patient examination was made.

Cheap Grace Deflects John 3:36 By Mistranslation

Incidentally, cheap grace translators have deflected John 3:36 from destroying cheap grace by the simple step of mistranslation of *apeitheo*. Please remember that *apeitheo* only has one meaning: *disobey*. Even the evangelical seminary dictionaries which defend *disbelieve* as a meaning admit the translation as *disbelieve* is "unknown outside our literature."[24] In the table below, you can readily see this key difference between the inaccurate "believe not" translations and the accurate "obey not / disobey" translations.

TABLE 2. John 3:36 — Yet Another Mistranslation?

"Believes Not"	"Obeys Not"
He that believeth on the Son hath everlasting life: and he that ***believeth not*** the Son shall not see life; but the wrath of God abideth on him. (KJV)	He that believeth [continuous tense] on the Son hath eternal life; but he that ***obeyeth not*** the Son shall not see life, but the wrath of God abideth on him. (ASV)
He who is believing [N.B. reflects continuous tense correctly] in the Son, hath life age-during; and he who is ***not believing*** the Son, shall not see life, but the wrath of God doth remain upon him. (YLT)	And anyone who believes [continuous tense] in God's Son has eternal life. Anyone who ***doesn't obey*** the Son will never experience eternal life but remains under God's angry judgment. (NLT)

---

24. See Footnote 23, page 449.

TABLE 2. John 3:36 — Yet Another Mistranslation?

"Believes Not"	"Obeys Not"
El que cree en el Hijo, tiene vida eterna; mas el que *es incrédulo* al Hijo, no verá la vida, sino que la ira de Dios está sobre él. (Reina Valera)	Hee that beleeueth in the Sonne, hath euerlasting life, and hee that *obeyeth not* the Sonne, shall not see life, but the wrath of God abideth on him. (Geneva Bible 1599)
Chi crede nel Figliuolo ha vita eterna; ma chi *rifiuta di credere* al Figliuolo non vedrà la vita, ma l'ira di Dio resta sopra lui. (Italian Riveduta Luzzi)	One who believes [continuance tense] in the Son has eternal life, but one who *disobeys* the Son won't see life, but the wrath of God remains on him. (World English Bible)
He that believeth on the Son, hath everlasting life: and he that *believeth not* the Son, shall not see life; but the wrath of God abideth on him. (Webster Bible 1833)	Whoever believes [continuous tense] in the Son has eternal life; whoever *disobeys* the Son will not have life, but will remain under God's punishment. (Good News Bible.)

Why this erroneous translation on the left side of the column? This alteration makes it appear that *disbelieving* in Jesus is what brings wrath, not *disobedience* to Jesus. By this alteration, you would then naturally infer that the intended contrast by John the Baptist is between *disbelieves* on one side (3:36b) with *believes* on the other side (3:36a). Hence, by altering *disobey* to *disbelieve*, this is how the translators supported rendering *pisteuo* as *believes* in 3:36a. Yet, it is built on a complete falsification of what John the Baptist said. As noted before, *apeitho* only has one meaning in Greek: *to disobey*. It bears repeating that even the scholars who defend this replacement of *disobeys* with *disbelieves* admit that in **all literature outside the Christian scripture**, *apeitho* **only has one meaning**: *disobey*.[25]

Yet, we are not free to conjecture about a Christian-only meaning to *apeitho*. We especially cannot do so when the only virtue of imagining an idiosyncratic meaning is to insulate the cheap grace gospel from a verse that falsifies it.

25.See Footnote 23, page 449.

Thus, the translations on the left in the table above protect cheap grace doctrine. They do so by falsifying the translation. How can this be honoring God? He told us that we are ***never*** permitted to "subtract" from His Holy word. (Deut. 4:2.) Only the translations on the right are true to God.

What About Paul's Use Of Pistis And Pisteuo?

Introduction

As mentioned above, to understand John 3:16, the Master and Sole Teacher has the privilege of interpreting His own words. We looked at the context of John 3:16. We looked at the context of other lessons of Jesus. We looked at inspired prophets like John the Baptist. We looked at the words of Apostle John — the writer of John 3:16 — who injected his own thoughts in John 12:42. There we saw Apostle John discusses the rulers who had *pisteuo* but contrary to that *pistis* later refuse to *confess* Jesus. The evidence repeatedly proves John 3:16 should have been translated as *"obey* unto Him" (Jesus). The verse gives no support that mere belief alone saves or mere belief is all there is to salvation.

The Problem Of Paul

There is no secret here what is the problem weighing against us from changing our perceptions to Jesus' intentions. Many impose their views of Paul's doctrines upon Jesus' words. ***They translate Jesus to most closely follow the doctrines they perceive Paul is teaching***.

However, we are not free to invert the relationship between Jesus and Paul so that Paul becomes the Master used to undermine the words and clear meanings of Jesus.

As Kierkegaard pointed out in 1855 in his work *My Task:* "It is of great importance, especially in Protestantism, to straighten out...[the] *inverting* [of] the relationship, and in effect *criticizing Christ by Paul*, the Master by the disciple."[26]

Nevertheless, we will now demonstrate that Paul clearly *often* intends *pistis* to mean a *faithfulness* which is destroyed by *disobedience*, unto damnation of even Christians.

We will also see that Paul sometimes means by *pistis* a *faithfulness* in the 'Old Testament' sense of *faithful (obedient) living*.

We will also see that Paul *often* teaches that justification is by *obedience* or *faithfulness*, not *belief alone* — a truth hampered from your notice by minimizing translations of Paul's words.

This is not to deny there are *just two or three* problem passages where Paul affirms *pisteuo* or *pistis* in such a way that the meaning is *belief* alone. This is particularly the case in Romans 4:5.

We will address these verses later, in particular the significance of Romans 4:5. We will see how the early church confronted this very problem of the words of Christ versus Paul. We will see clearly how the early apostolic church solved the dilemma. It will no doubt surprise many of you.

---

26. This inversion is usually done by not distinguishing Paul from Jesus, and simply labelling anything from Paul as "the Bible," without any sense of *priority* for Jesus. For example: "As with any single verse or passage, we discern what it teaches by *first filtering* it through what we know the **Bible** [*i.e., Paul*] teaches on the subject at hand. The **Bible** [*i.e., Paul*] is clear that salvation is by grace through faith in Jesus Christ, not by works of any kind....(Ephesians 2:8-9). So, *any interpretation* which comes to the conclusion that *any... act*, is necessary for salvation, is *a faulty interpretation*." http://www.gotquestions.org/baptism-Acts-2-38.html.

Regardless of how the early church resolved this problem, what remains unaltered is that there are abundant proofs that *ordinarily* — except for two or three passages — Paul means *faithfulness* (obedient living) for *pistis*, not *faith* or *belief alone*. This assists us once more in corroborating how Jesus was likely using the noun *pistis* and its verb cousin *pisteuo*.

Romans 10:11 Translates OT "Trust" With Pisteuo

Let's start with Romans 10:11.

Paul uses *pisteuo* in Romans 10:11 to translate a verb in an 'Old Testament' passage which in Hebrew only meant *trust*. Because of the force of the original Isaiah passage, the NIV renders *pisteuo* in Romans 10:11 as *trust* rather than *believe* even though *believe* is how the NIV everywhere else translated *pisteuo* in the New Testament.

> As Scripture says, 'Anyone that **trusts** in him will never be put to shame.' (NIV) (Rom. 10:11)

Paul is quoting from Isaiah 28:16.

Why did the NIV translate *pisteuo* in Romans 10:11 into *trust* rather than *believe*? Because the NIV realizes its own version of Isaiah 28:16 renders the word in the underlying OT as *trust* (rely upon and follow). The NIV translates Isaiah 28:16 as "the one who *trusts* will never be dismayed..."

Why didn't the NIV render the Hebrew word as *believes* and then render Romans 10:11 as *believes*, so as to prevent an inconsistency in translating *pisteuo* when used by Paul elsewhere in the New Testament? Because the Hebrew word here was limited to *trust*. It was not *faith* or *believing*. The Hebrew word is not about intellectual assent in a fact about God or belief in a promise. But this then means that the NIV accepted that Paul here used the verb *pisteuo* to mean *trust*. The NIV left us to supposedly believe that Paul intended *pisteuo* everywhere else to mean merely *believing* in some fact about Jesus/the atonement, but here, and here alone, to mean *trust*.

Instead, it should have been a monumental fact that Paul uses in Romans 10:11 *pisteuon* to translate the 'Old Testament' word that meant *trust*. Because if this is true, then why should we not have used Romans 10:11 to enlighten us on translating *pisteuo* elsewhere in Paul's writings? To make a comparison to how Jesus likely used *pisteuo*?

Romans 10:11 is an important link back to the 'Old Testament.' It unlocks the normal meaning of the word *pisteuo* in the New Testament. The Greek word has variable meanings. We cannot presuppose we know it means the most shallow meaning among all possible options: *belief in* or *intellectual assent to* a fact or truth. It can also mean *trust*, which implies *obedience*. Thus, how to translate *pistis* and *pisteuo* in Jesus and even in Paul's writings is unlocked by witnessing first-hand Paul's own rendering of the word for *trust* in the 'Old Testament' by the Greek verb *pisteuo*.

Thus, we know that because the OT equivalent word in Isaiah 28:16 only meant *trust*, and Paul rendered this 'Old Testament' word for *trust* by *pisteuo,* we can deduce the correct usage *throughout the New Testament* would primarily be at least *trust* (which connotes obedience anyway), not **faith** (which connotes mere belief or intellectual assent).

Romans 3:3: Another Proof That *Pistis* Does Not Mean Faith

We read in the American Standard translation of Romans 3:3 the following:

> For what if some were without faith? shall their want of faith make of none effect the **faithfulness** [*pistis*] of God? (Rom 3:3 ASV.)

Another meaning for *pistis* is proven here. This verse proves it sometimes certainly must mean *faithfulness*. It would be utter nonsense to render this the "faith of God" or even the "trust of God." God has no faith in Himself or trust in Himself, which even hard-core Pauline scholars admit.[27]

Here, *pistis* has only one meaning that fits in Romans 3:3: *faithfulness,* which here means 'consistent righteous behavior.' It is comparable to the human activity of *faithfulness* toward God. *Pistis* certainly has nothing to do with *belief* here.

One comment on Romans 3:3 is insightful:

> It seems quite clear to me that Paul does not mean by PISTIS what Luther meant by "Glaube" (faith). PISTIS can certainly mean "faith" or "trust," but it can also mean "faithfulness" as it must in Romans 3:3.[28]

There is more in Romans 3:3 to learn regarding *pistis.* It also impacts translation of the *apistia* in the first part of the sentence. Ordinarily, and in the ASV quote above, it has *apistia* as "want of belief." Yet, this is wrong. It mismatches the direct contrast to the *pistis* of God. Thus, the *apistia* — formed by the negative prefix *a* in Greek in front of *pistis* — should be seen as the contrast to the *pistis* of God. Thus, the *pistis* of God, which has to mean *faithfulness* of God, is being contrasted to *apistia* — obviously the *unfaithfulness* of men. This is translated correctly in the American Literal Translation:

> For what if some were unfaithful? Their **unfaithfulness** [*apistia*] will not make the **faithfulness** of God useless, will it? (Rom 3:3 ALT.)

---

27. The King James prefers a rendering that makes no sense, and renders this the "faith of God." Fortunately, this is an isolated phenomenon. See GNB ("faithful"). In fact, those who believe Paul virtually always uses *pistis* to mean *faith,* concede in Romans 3:3 *pistis* must mean *faithfulness.* "The translation 'faithfulness' is dictated by the parallel terms as well as the reference to God's *pistis.*" (Karl P. Donfried, "Paul and the Revisions: Did Luther Really Get It All Wrong?," *Dialogue: Journal of Theology* Vol. 46, No. 1 (Spring 2007) at 31, 34 (available online).

28. Michael Palmer (April 1999) posted at http://lists.ibiblio.org/pipermail/corpus-paul/19990403/000132.html (accessed 7-1-07).

Yet, there is even one more key within this verse that makes certain *apistia* means *unfaithful* in the sense of disobedient.

Where the ALT has "if some were *unfaithful*" the Greek verb is *apisteo*. This combines the *negative* prefix *a* with *pisteuo* which latter verb we find in John 3:16. When the prefix and verb are so combined, the word means in ancient Greek either *to disobey* or *disbelieve*. In context, one can see here it means *disobey*. The ALT changed this into "were unfaithful;" while satisfactory, another more precise meaning that fits the context is *disobey*.

With this background, now look at the entire passage with the underlying Greek verbs and nouns exposed. Here we see *pistis*, *apistia*, and *apisteo* are all dancing around giving us an entirely different concept about *pistis* and *pisteuo* in other contexts. Here *pistis* certainly is not talking about *belief* as *mental assent* for God does not have that about Himself. This *pistis* of God is contrasted with the disobedient unfaithful behavior of men.

> For what if some *apisteo*-ed [**disobey-ed**]?
> Their *apistia* [**unfaithfulness**] will not make
> the *pistis* [**faithfulness**] of God useless, will it?
> (Rom 3:3 ALT.)

Thus, the *pistis* of God is the faithful righteous behavior of God. Paul teaches it is not useless merely because men are disobedient and unfaithful. Hence, *pistis* certainly in this context meant *faithfulness*, with an emphasis on *righteous* behavior. We know this because it is contrasted against *disobedient* behavior. We also saw that *a-pisteuo* meant "not obeying" here which re-emphasizes that *pisteuo* should ordinarily be translated to mean *obey* in the New Testament.

Romans 3:22: More Proof *Pistis* Means Faithfulness

A reputable Christian scholar, N.T. Wright (Bishop of Durham, England), in 2005 pointed out that Luther erred in translating *pistis* as *faith* in Romans 3:22. Because it is speaking of the *pistis* "of Jesus," it can only mean once again *faithfulness*. This is because the text has in Greek a subjective genetive ("faithfulness *of* Christ") not an objective genetive ("faith *in* Christ").[29]

Wright is backed up by George Howard's scholarly analysis of the Greek. He demonstrated that in the twenty-four times the genetive is used in Paul's writings, it is used in the *subjective genetive* sense, which means *of*.[30]

In other words, because it says *of*, not *in*, within the *genetive* used in Greek, Wright explains Romans 3:22 must be speaking of Christ's *faithfulness*, not Christ's *faith* in Himself or God. The idea of *pistis* as *faith* when spoken *of Jesus* would be totally incongruous anyway within the verse. Only *faithfulness* makes sense when we speak of *pistis* as *of Christ*.

This notion of Jesus' "faithfulness" here likewise totally matches how Paul speaks elsewhere of "one man's obedience" (Rom. 5:19) as a synonym for the faithfulness (obedience) of Christ. Hence, Paul uses *pistis* in Romans 3:22 to mean *faithfulness (obedience) of Jesus*, not the *faith of Jesus*.

Indeed, in the Gospel accounts we learn Jesus' faithfulness was an obedience unto death to the Father's will. (Matt. 26:39, "if it be possible, let this cup pass away from me: nevertheless, not as I will, but as thou wilt.")

Weak efforts have been offered in reply to dispute Wright's reading of Romans 3:22, but they are sophistic.[31]

Wright was correct. In fact, Luther could never have been translating properly because he openly defended his translation of Romans 3:22 based upon the Latin text, not the Greek text.[32] Even so, Luther actually acknowledges in the quote in Footnote 32, page 461 that the Latin too has a gene-

---

29.N.T. Wright, *Paul in Fresh Perspective* (Minneapolis: Fortress, 2005) at 47.

30.George Howard, "On the "Faith of Christ," *Harvard Theological Review* Vol. 60 No. 4 (Oct. 1967) at 459, 459.

---

tive *of*, not *in*. Then how did Luther translate *pistis* as meaning *faith* when the *pistis* "*of* Jesus" in Romans 3:22 could not possibly be translated as *faith* "**in**" Himself? If the genetive is revealed, it had to be *faithfulness* (not *faith*) "*of* Jesus."

The explanation by Luther is astonishing. In one of the most stunning glosses of a Scripture text, Luther simply suggests he is free to replace the words *of* with *in,* because he prefers an entirely different structure to the sentence. It is unabashed! See Footnote 32, page 461.[33]

This is how Luther changed the *faithfulness* **of** Christ into *faith* **in** Christ. This is how an example of *pistis* meaning *faithfulness* was erased by Luther, and made into *faith*. Thus,

---

31. One recent dissent is Karl P. Donfried, "Paul and the Revisions: Did Luther Really Get It All Wrong?," *Dialogue: Journal of Theology* Vol. 46, No. 1 (Spring 2007) at 31 (available online). Donfried's argument has numerous flaws, and no valid points. First and most important, Donfried does not deny there is a subjective genetive here — the key issue. Instead, he claims that he reads Luther as saying there is none in the quote in Footnote 32, page 461. But Luther does not say that. In fact, Luther is quoting *Latin*, not Greek which the scholar (Wright) is citing and whom Donfried opposes. Nor does Donfried note that Luther is confessing he is wishing the Latin read differently than it actually reads. The Latin reads exactly as Wright reads the Greek! It is a mystery how Luther came about with his translation even from the Latin! Next, Donfried quotes translations of early church 'fathers' who in allusions and paraphrases are translated as talking about 'faith' in this verse. However, these English translations of the early Greek and Latin 'fathers' prove nothing. The original Latin word *fides* in some of those texts has as much ambiguity as the Greek word *pistis*. One translation error does not support later error. Thus, because these 'fathers' were translated as talking about *faith* does not prove Romans 3:22 was translated as *faith* correctly. Finally, Donfried says Wright's view of *faithfulness* as the correct translation has led to frightening theologies. He cites Bondros' recent work as an example of where this translation must take you: "The extreme consequences of Wright's misinterpretation of Paul can be seen in the recent volume by David Bondros, *Paul on the Cross*...." *Id.*, at 35. He then explains Bondros teaches Paul did not believe Christ made atonement for sin, but Christ was merely obedient to being used as an instrument of redemption. This is the big smear by means of a fallacious non-sequitur. Yet, Donfried never actually addressed the key issue: the Greek meaning of the text.

---

for generations, we lost one clear usage example from Paul that *pistis* meant *faithfulness*. Thanks to Bishop Wright in 2005, this original meaning has now been restored.

We should note that the KJV is correct *grammatically*, revealing the *genetive* construction "**of** Jesus Christ" in Romans 3:22. However, it mistranslates *pistis* as *faith*. It reads "faith of Jesus Christ." Yet, again, it is incongruous to speak about the "faith of Jesus" because Jesus cannot make Himself the object of His own belief. He knows who He is.

'Faithfulness Of Jesus' Appears Seven Times In Paul's Writings

By the way, Luther's erroneous translation of Paul talking about a "faith in Christ" in Romans 3:22 is a translation error which reappears in six other passages in the English New Testament. Luther's errors in these passages influenced English translations to follow Luther's lead. This has misled millions on the nature of justification in certain passages. *Pistis Christou* appears not only in Romans 3:22, but also in Romans 3:26, Galatians 2:16,20, 3:22, Phil. 3:9, and Ephesians 3:12.

---

32. Luther unabashedly tried using the Latin version to understand the Greek, but it is incoherent because the Latin genetive is the same as the Greek. Luther wrote: "when it says the faith of Christ (*fides Cristi*) [the LATIN], we must understand faith in Christ (*fides in Cristum*)." (Luther, *Works* (American edition; ed. Jaroslav Pelikan and Helmut Lehmann; Philadelphia and St. Louis: Muhlenberg and Concordia, 1955ff) 25, 242 (Lectures on Romans). This makes no sense even on its face. *Fides Cristi* in Latin means the *faith* or *faith-fulness* of Christ. Luther apparently feels free that he can change this by a gloss of interpretation into *fides **in** Cristum*. How can you do that? Perhaps we should say that Luther is actually rewriting the verse to say what he would prefer it would have said. But neither does the Latin nor the Greek say what he wishes Romans 3:22 would say about *pistis*.

33. Interestingly, Luther was not always consistent in wiping out the *of* in the translation of the same expression elsewhere. In Galatians 2:20, Luther translated it "dem Glauben ***des*** Sohnes Gottes." That is, the "faith ***of*** the Son of God."

Justification Impacted

Thus, instead of Paul saying God "justifies him who believes *in* Jesus" (Rom. 3:26 KJV), it says God "justifies him who has the *faithfulness of* Jesus" (Romans 3:26) — a major reversal in meaning. If you have the *obedience* Jesus exhibited, God justifies you.[34]

If Paul had meant instead to say "faith in Jesus" in this verse on justification, he knew how to do it. Paul speaks elsewhere of those who have a *"pistis en Cristos Iesous."* (Gal. 3:26; Eph. 1:15; Col. 1:4.) Similarly, others in the New Testament expressed such a thing as *"pistis en Cristou."* [35] However, Paul never did that in these seven examples. He used a subjective genitive, and did so in particular in this justification verse. When rendered properly, it means you are only justified if you have the "faithfulness *of* Christ."

---

34. Similarly, Galatians 2:20 should read that "I live in faithfulness, the *faithfulness* which is **of** the son of God." Had Paul not used *pistis...of the Son of God,*" then we would not have been sure how to translate his first use of *pistis* which talks of his own *pistis.* We would not know whether he meant *faithfulness* or *faith.* Yet, by Paul equating it to the *pistis of the Son of God,* we know the latter usage is *faithfulness.* (It is absurd to speak of Jesus having a *faith* in Himself.) Thus, the first *pistis* is intended the same way as the second *pistis,* to demonstrate the similarity between the way Paul says he is living and the way Jesus lived: obediently. Incidentally, in a bizarre argument, Chambers claims Galatians 2:20 has to be read the other way around, so it is "I live in faith, the faith which is *in* the son of God" (*i.e.,* an objective genitive). He claims this avoids *clashing* between how *pistis* reads for "believers" versus how it reads for Jesus. That's totally false. It is the opposite. His reading claims that I have the same faith that was in Jesus Christ. However, that rendering clashes with common sense. Jesus does not have a faith in Himself that I then duplicate. He KNOWS who He is. He doesn't have to have a faith (like myself) in what is not seen. (Rom. 8:24.) Also, it is a subjective genitive, meaning "of"; it does not mean "in." Hence, it is Chamber's argument that causes a ridiculous clash, while *faithfulness* makes perfect sense in both cases. For Chambers' argument, see Steven L. Chambers, "'Faith in Christ,' or the 'Faith of Christ? Pistis Cristou in Paul," *Lutheran Theological Review* XII (1999-2000) at 23-24.

Hence, the only somewhat correct translation of Romans 3:26 — each rendering the genitive (possessive) properly — appears in Young's Literal, New Revised Standard (1989), Darby's, Douay Rheims ("faith *of* Jesus") and the Spanish Reina Valera (RV "justifica al que es de la fe *de* Jesús").The only error is that these Bibles each incongruously still translate *pistis* as *faith* (of Jesus) as if Jesus could be believing in Himself or the Father rather than having a *faithfulness* (of Jesus) toward the Father.

Another interesting point is that the KJV has it *faith **in** Jesus* in Romans 3:26 while in every other of the seven verses, the KJV has the possessive correct in saying *faith **of** Jesus*. As Steven L. Chambers notes, "the King James version preserved 'the faith *of* Christ' in every instance except Romans 3:26."[36] Obviously, the KJV was concerned that any more accurate translation of 3:26 would upset justification doctrine. Because that is not at stake in the other six verses, the KJV correctly revealed the possessive "of" meaning.

35.Chambers offers up the argument for consideration that twists this fact around to favor a reading of it as "faith *in* Christ." This argument says Paul is entitled to have an idiosyncratic (isolated) meaning from all others who express the same thought differently. This argument says: "Paul never uses that construction; he never makes Christ (or God) the object of a preposition following *pistis*. Thus, *pistis Cristou* may well be an alternate, and **uniquely Pauline**, way of expressing 'faith in Christ.'" (Steven L. Chambers, "'Faith in Christ,' or the 'Faith of Christ? Pistis Cristou in Paul," *Lutheran Theological Review* XII (1999-2000) at 23 (available online).) Chambers cites (and apparently realizes it is a valid point) Williams' claim that this argument represents a fundamental logical error. Merely because "Paul does not use *pistis en* or *eis* when he seems to mean 'faith in Christ' does not lead to the inverse conclusion that he does mean 'faith in Christ' every time he speaks of *pistis Cristou*." (Chambers, *supra*, at 25, citing Sam K. Williams, "Again Pistis Christou", *CBQ* 49 (1987), 431-447, at 433-34.) Chambers appears to have a misunderstanding that Paul never says *pistis en Cristou*, which he does in Gal. 3:26; Eph. 1:15; Col. 1:4. What Williams is saying is that sometimes Paul appears to mean *in Christ* even when he only says *pistis Cristou,* but this docs not support reading *in* into it every time. This is particularly true because Paul in those four cited passages does prove he knows how to say *pistis en Cristou*.

How Justification In the "Old Testament" Can Assist

Yet, the KJV's effort to change justification into *faith in Jesus* is an unnecessarily strained translation in light of Hebrew scripture. The Scripture taught in Deuteronomy 6:25 that justification was by ***obedience*** to God's law.[37]

This is also what Habakkuk 2:4 says in a proper translation: "the just shall live by his *faithfulness.*" Apparently Paul is being mistranslated whenever it is claimed he taught justification by *faith* in his quotes from the Habakkuk passage.[38] The underlying Hebrew word meant only *faithfulness.*

This concept of justification is also what Ezekiel taught about justification. "But if a man be ***just***, and do that which is lawful and right.... [and] hath walked in my statutes, and hath kept mine ordinances, to deal truly; he is ***just***, he shall ***surely live***, saith the Lord Jehovah." (Eze 18:5,9 ASV.)

Then why translate Paul in Romans 3:26 in a highly dubious way ***as if*** Paul said one is 'justified if one has faith ***in*** Jesus' rather than what it truly says — God 'justifies those who have the ***faithfulness of*** Jesus'? The 'faith in Jesus' construction is *at total odds* with not just normal Greek grammar, but also it is *contra-indicated* by every prior clearly *inspired* Scripture on justification. This includes the parable from Jesus of the Prodigal Son (Luke 18:9-14).[39]

This was the point of two scholars in the late 1950s on how to translate Romans 3:26: Herbert and Torrance.[40] They emphasized the Hebrew meaning of *faithfulness* in the original word that is ambiguously translated as *pistis* or *pisteuo* in the New Testament. When rendered into English, they said we should opt for *faithfulness* rather than *faith.* The ambigu-

---

36. Steven L. Chambers, "'Faith in Christ,' or the 'Faith of Christ? *Pistis Cristou* in Paul," *Lutheran Theological Review XII* (1999-2000) at 20, 22. (available online).

37. "And it shall be righteousness unto us, if we observe to do all this commandment before Jehovah our God, as he hath commanded us." Deut. 6:25 ASV.

ity inherent in *pistis* and *pisteuo* was lacking in the original Hebrew which was sometimes being quoted (Hab. 2:4). In fact, the Hebrew texts which explained justification made it absolutely certain justification was by *faithfulness*, not *faith*.

That such a choice was necessary was particularly true in Romans 3:26. As Chambers explains: "If *pisteuo*, they argued, actually had the preferred Greek translation of *faithfulness*, as distinct from *faith*, then Paul's expression would mean that God was continuing" His prior lessons about justification by faithfulness.[41] It was a point well-taken, especially in light of Deuteronomy 6:25 and Habakkuk 2:4, properly translated. The King James translators claimed they were following such pass-through principles — old to new.

Yet, more important, the only suitable meaning of *pistis* when spoken "*of* Jesus" is *faithfulness*. That is **the beginning and end of the issue**. It is nonsense to say Jesus believes in Himself. It is also ridiculous to say He believes in God. Thus, instead Paul teaches in Romans 3:26 that justification is

---

38.This is extensively discussed in my prior book, *Jesus' Words Only* (2007) at 274-76 and 507-08. This raises the question whether Paul really meant by *pistis* in translating Habakkuk 2:4 *faith* or *faithfulness*. Because the underlying Hebrew *exclusively* meant *faithfulness* (obedient living), it may be simply an *English* translation error which misperceives Paul as saying *faith* not *faithfulness* in Romans 1:17 and Galatians 3:11 when Paul quotes Habakkuk 2:4. Thus, it is conceivable Paul meant that justification is by *faithfulness* (*obedience*), not belief (faith) alone even in these two passages. If Paul meant *faithfulness* in both Romans 1:17 and Galatians 3:11 is what justifies, we have all been misled by the erroneous translations of Romans 1:17 and Galatians 3:11. This would mean that it was not Paul who was mistranslating the sense of Habakkuk 2:4, but it was the English translators who were mistranslating Paul. Regardless of who is mistranslating whom, even had Paul meant we were justified by belief alone (*mental assent*), this does not permit us to overthrow prophetic statements from Habakkuk, Ezekiel and Moses in Deuteronomy on what *causes* justification. This is the point exhaustively demonstrated in *Jesus' Words Only* (2007).

39.The twist on Romans 3:26 to 'faith in Jesus' also is contra-indicated by Jesus' doctrine on justification by repentance in the Parable of the Publican and the Pharisee. See page 27 *et seq.*

---

for anyone of us who has the "faithfulness (obedience) of

---

40. A. G. Herbert, "Faithfulness and 'Faith,'" *Theology* 58 (1955) at 373-79 and Thomas F. Torrance, "One Aspect of the Biblical Conception of Faith," *Expository Times* 68 (1957) at 111-14. Chambers claimed that their arguments were refuted by James Barr, saying Barr established that *faith*, not *faithfulness* 'everywhere dominates in the New Testament.' (See James Barr, *The Semantics of Biblical Language* (Oxford University Press, 1961; repr. London: SCM Press, 1983) 201, *viz.*, at 161-205.) This exaggerates Barr's claims and the validity of his proof. What Barr said instead was that Torrance was wrong to equate *pistis* necessarily with all the meanings that *emet* had in Hebrew. For the Hebrew concept of *faithfulness* in *emet* had wider implications than *faithfulness* in Greek. Barr means it is improper to read into a Greek definition a wider meaning that only exists in Hebrew. Thus, nothing in Barr says it is wrong to *infer* that Paul meant the meaning of *faithfulness* which is a permissible meaning in Greek when Paul quotes Habakkuk 2:4. The reason is clear: we should probably infer Paul used *pistis* as *faithfulness* because Paul *should* have known it meant *faithfulness* at minimum in the Hebrew of Habakkuk 2:4. Paul's orientation most likely had to be to the Hebrew. (W.D. Davies, *Paul and Rabbinic Judaism* (1970).) Even if Paul thought only in Greek terms, nothing in the Septuagint Bible's normal usage conveyed *faith* in the word *pistis* to Paul. As Bishop Robertson said: "the Septuagint... probably never uses *pistis* in our sense of 'faith'... [s]o at least we can say that *pistis* by itself would not primarily suggest the idea of 'faith'...." D. W. B. Robinson, "'Faith of Jesus Christ'—a New Testament Debate," *The Reformed Theological Review* Vol. 29, no.3 (Sept.-Dec. 1970) at 71-81. For this reason, other scholars point out that Hebert and Torrance are still correct contextually on the meaning of *pistis* being *faithfulness* in Romans 3. See Richard B. Hays in *The Conversion of the Imagination: Paul as Interpreter of Israel's Scripture* (Eerdmans: 2005). He explained: "Barr's cogent criticisms of Torrance and A.G. Herbert do not however apply to the present exegetical observations about Romans 3. Barr's basic objection is directed against the linguistically naive assumption that there is a distinctive (Hebraic) 'fundamental meaning' that governs the semantic range of... *pistis* in the NT without regard to context and usage." *Id.*, at 54. Hays, who agrees with my view of *pistis* as *faithfulness* in Romans 3, ends: "My observations here, rather than resting upon an alleged fundamental linguistic equivalence, proceed from the evidence of Paul's *usage* of these words as functionally equivalent terms within this particular discourse." *Id.* In scholarly circles, the reading of "faithfulness of Christ" has gained acceptance, following the seminal work in 1981 by Richard Hays entitled *The Faith of Jesus Christ* (2d Ed. 2001). Hays argues that Paul's wording is not faith *in* Christ, but faithfulness *of* Christ.

Jesus." Paul here is expressing a doctrine of justification by obedience in imitation of Jesus.

After this digression, let's return to our proofs that Paul frequently uses *pistis* to mean *faithfulness*, not faith.

2 Thessalonians 1:3-5,8,11: Pistis Must Mean Faithfulness

Paul says God will punish two types with His ever-lasting vengeance. One type is "those who do not know him" and the second type is "those who ***do not obey*** (*hupakou-ousin*) the gospel of our Lord Jesus." (1:8) Paul prays the Thessalonians, by contrast, will be "***counted worthy*** of your calling, and fulfill every desire of ***goodness*** and every ***work*** of *pistis*, with power." (1:11.) Paul glories in their *pistis* "in all your persecutions" that "you endure." (1:4.) He then importantly says this persecution is "a demonstration (evidence) of the just judgment (*krisis*) of God, to the ***end*** (*eis*) that you may be counted ***worthy of*** the kingdom of God, for which you also suffer." (1:5a ALT; 1:5b ASV.) *Cf.* 2 Tim.2:12 ("If we endure with Him, we shall also reign with Him.")

Verse 1:5 tells you *pistis* means *faithfulness* in the three uses in this passage. For it ends saying God permits persecution to test them to *make* them "***counted worthy of the kingdom of God***, for which you also suffer." Nicholl admits Paul says afflictions "function to purify them so that they will be counted worthy of the kingdom and so [they] can inherit it." (Nicholl-2004: 149-50.) Paul wanted them to "be worthy of their calling." (1:11.) Jesus said He rejects the many He invites whom He "called [yet] were not worthy." (Matt. 22:8.) Hence, you are not simply *worthy* by the initial blood-cleansing by Christ or His call. Salvation is not guaranteed by faith alone had no persecution come your way. Rather, Paul says God allows persecution with the "end" or "objective" that by suffering "you may be counted worthy of the kingdom of

---

41.Steven L. Chambers, "'Faith in Christ,' or the 'Faith of Christ? Pistis Cristou in Paul," *Lutheran Theological Review XII* (1999-2000) at 22 (available online).

God."[42] If faith alone instead were true, no amount of the testing of your endurance in doctrinal belief is necessary to make you worthy of the kingdom. You would in theory be already worthy by faith alone before any persecution. Thus, something other than *faith* alone must be on Paul's mind of what is being tested. Only *faithfulness* as the meaning of *pistis* makes sense in this passage each time it appears.

Twelve Proofs On Paul's Usage Of Pistis As Faithfulness

We clearly have seen *twelve* total times that the only meaning of *pistis* in a passage from Paul is *faithfulness*. See, Romans 3:3 ("faithfulness of God"), Romans 10:11 (the quote of Isaiah where it means "trust"), and seven other verses talking of the "faithfulness of Jesus." (Romans 3:22, but also in Romans 3:26, Galatians 2:16,20, 3:22, Phil. 3:9, and Ephesians 3:12.) We saw that three times Paul extols the "faithfulness" of the Thessalonians under persecution, who are tested by God so they will be "counted worthy of the kingdom of God." (2 Thessalonians 1:3-5,8,11.)

These twelve examples are just more proofs of how the word *pisteuo* (related to its noun form *pistis*) should be translated in John 3:16. *Pisteuo* means those who "obey for/ unto Him" should have eternal life.

Paul's Doctrine On Disobedience Means He Often Understood Pistis And Pisteuo As Faithfulness/Obey, Not Belief/Believe

Is there further confirmation that in Paul's understanding *pistis* and *pisteuo* were negated by disobedience? If so, then we know Paul ordinarily meant these words respectively meant *faithfulness* (obedient living), not *faith,* unless

---

42. Most faith-alone advocates explicate this passage by illogical statements. Calvin for example simply makes an ad hoc statement that "No persecutions can make us worthy of the kingdom of God." Yet, this is a direct contradiction of what Paul just said was God's plain purpose!

---

the context dictates otherwise, as what saves. Otherwise, disobedience could never be relevant to salvation if faith alone is all there is to salvation.

In other words, did Paul ever say a person who had *pistis* could fall by disobedience and lose their salvation/ inheritance in heaven? If so, then we would know the correct translation of *pisteuo* (verb) and *pistis* (noun) in Paul's writings is ordinarily *obey* and *faithfulness*, not *believe* and *faith*, unless — to repeat — the *context* makes clear otherwise.

If so, then the impact on our conception of salvation even as sometimes taught by Paul, and **certainly as taught by Jesus in John 3:16**, would be monumental. If salvation is by *faith*, then it is simple, easy and cost-free. If it is by *obeying* and *faithfulness*, it is precarious and costly.

Paul Teaches Disobedience Negates *Pisteuo*

Paul several times expressly stated a Christian who was morally disobedient would lose his salvation. Paul, in fact, feared for himself that unless he cut off the body parts that ensnared himself in sin, he would go to hell whole.

Of course, Paul learned this lesson from Jesus. Our Lord told the apostles that each of them had a stark choice. You can go to heaven only if you maim yourself by the self-discipline of cutting off body parts ensnaring you in sin. Or, you can fail to take such measures to buffet your body, and you will certainly go to hell whole. (Mark 9:42-47.)

Paul says the *very* same thing in 1 Corinthians 9:27. Paul states:

> I buffet my body, and bring it into bondage, lest by any means, after I have preached to others, I myself should be disapproved (*adokimos*). (1 Cor. 9:27.) (YLT)

Disapproved or *rejected* is the most literal Greek meaning of *adokimos*. Instead of "disapproved," the KJV has it "castaway." Regardless, it is a serious negative condition.

Sometimes it is translated as "reprobate." Every other time the Greek word *adokimos* is used, it is always talking about the lost. (2 Cor. 13:5,6,7, 2 Tim. 3:8, Titus 1:16.)

Thus, Paul held the fear that he might be rejected by God and thus be lost unless he buffeted his body. Consequently, in this verse, Paul shared Jesus' view on salvation. Jesus taught you can go to heaven-maimed or hell-whole. (Mark 9:42-47.) You can cut off the body part ensnaring you in sin, and have eternal life (heaven maimed) or you can fail to "buffet" your body in such manner, and go to hell whole. Paul in this verse had Jesus' view that sin, unaddressed by self-discipline over fleshly desire, will cause one to go to hell whole. Even Calvin read Paul's words in the same way. He said it matched Jesus' doctrine that one who begins as a believer must engage in "strenuous perserverance," and it "would be of no avail to have set out boldly on the Christian race if they did not continue to the end." (Calvin quoted in F. Lisco, *The Parables of Jesu*s (Philadelphia:1850) at 119.)

Unquestionably, in this passage, Paul applied this principle of heaven-maimed or hell-whole to someone like himself who already had initial *pistis.* Yet, Paul also clearly implied here that his own prior *pistis* is not the sole determinant of salvation. Hence, Paul's concept of *pistis* is ordinarily not *faith*, but *faithfulness*, which can be negated by disobedience — the very thing Paul says in 1 Cor. 9:27 will make him *adokimos* — disapproved, rejected, a castaway, a reprobate. In other words, a lost soul.

While few who sit in the pews of a cheap-grace church ever learn this truth about this passage, an Atlantic Baptist University article says its meaning is clear:

> To become disqualified (**adokimos**) is to be **disallowed from obtaining eschatological salvation because of failing to meet its condition, obedience to God** (see 2 Cor 13:5-7; 2 Tim 3:8; Titus 1:16; see also Heb 6:8). Implicit in Paul's comments about himself is his warning to the Corinthians that they will likewise become dis-

qualified if they continue their misuse of their freedom [by sinning].[43]

Titus 1:16. In the same vein, Paul in Titus 1:16 says of those who disobey God's commands yet confess — *homologeo* — God, their good works are *adokimos*. Paul uses this identical expression to say if you *homologeo* that Jesus is Lord, you shall be saved. (Rom. 10:9.) But here Paul says the very same *homologeo* for God is negated by disobedience.

> They confess (*homologeo*) that they know God; but in works they deny him, being abominable, and **disobedient** [*apeithos*], and unto every good work reprobate [*adokimos*]. (Titus 1:16, KJV.)

The Young's Literal has this: "Unto every good work *disapproved*." In the literal Greek, it means "to every good work *rejected*." Thus, you can confess God, but if your works disobey Him, you deny God and all your good works are dis-

---

43.This article is entitled: "The Spirit, The Necessity of Good Works and Final Judgment," http://www.abu.nb.ca/courses/pauline/Works.htm (last accessed 11/25/2006). This Atlantic Baptist University course article cites in support G. D. Fee, *The First Epistle to the Corinthians* (NICNT; Grand Rapids: Eerdmans, 1987) at 433-41; C. K. Barrett, *The First Epistle to the Corinthians* (2d ed.; London: Black, 1971) at 218. However, not all agree. The Atlantic Baptist article continues:

"According to J. Gundry Volf, Paul uses the term 'disqualified' (adokimos) in relation to apostleship or service, not in relation to his final salvation (*Paul and Perseverance: Staying in and Falling Away* (Louisville: Westminster/Knox, 1990) at 233-47). In 1 Cor 9:27a, what Paul renounces is [supposedly] his apostolic rights and Christian freedom, and this not for the sake of obtaining final salvation, but for the sake of obtaining a reward."

In response, the Atlantic Baptist University piece says: "Her argument, however, is not convincing."

More important to us, why would Gundry Volf try to make Paul not repeat what Jesus so clearly teaches in Mark 9:42-47? Why subtract a passage where Paul is in clear agreement with Jesus by spinning it to not be about salvation? The reason is obvious: Paul does not endorse cheap grace here, as he is often read to endorse in other passages.

---

approved/rejected by God. (They become like filfthy rags.) You must be lost despite having confessed God. Paul does not say this proves you never truly "believed." He says instead you "deny" God by disobedience.

Galatians 6:7-9. Paul speaks likewise in Galatians 6:7-9. He says that salvation depends upon not sowing to the flesh — even for a Christian. If you have *pistis* in the next quote, it does not satisfy the *obedience* requirement that Paul simultaneously insists upon. This implies that Paul here understood *obedience* was implied in the meaning of the word *pistis*. Obviously, Paul ordinarily meant *faithfulness* (obedient living) not *faith* when he used *pistis*. Paul says:

> Do not be deceived: God cannot be mocked. A man reaps what he sows. The one who **sows to his sinful nature**, from that nature he will reap **destruction**; the one who sows to please the Spirit, from the Spirit will reap **eternal life**. Let us not become weary **in doing good**, for at the proper time we will reap a harvest **if we do not give up**. (Gal. 6:7-9 NIV).

CONDITION	RESULT
What you sow	You reap.
If you sow to the sinful nature	**You reap destruction.**
If you sow to the Spirit	You reap eternal life.
If you do not become weary in doing good = if you do not give up	**You will reap a harvest.**

The meaning of this passage is clear if you simply notice the conditions and the outcomes. See Table above. Paul is addressing Christians. If they sow to the flesh, they will suffer "destruction." In contrast, if they "sow to the Spirit," which is paralleled by the phrase "not become weary in doing good," they will reap "eternal life."

Romans 6:22. Another passage to consider is Romans 6:22. Here Paul says the benefit of becoming God's servant is it should "lead to *holiness*, and the *result is eternal life*."[44]

On this verse, the Atlantic Baptist University article says the meaning is unequivocal:

> Paul continues by saying that **the result ("fruit") of being enslaved to God is holiness (*eis hagiasmon*), by which he means practical righteousness or habitual *obedience* to God.** The *result ("fruit") of holiness, moreover, is eternal life.* In other words, in Rom 6:20-22, Paul gives expression to the familiar Jewish idea that eternal life is *conditional upon practical righteousness*; it is significant that Paul does *not say* that the condition of receiving eternal life is *imputed righteousness* or the "righteousness of God"....

Please note here the purpose or object use of *eis*. This is the preposition we emphasized in John 3:16 means *for*. John 3:16 says he who is *pisteuo*-ing *eis* Christ should be saved. Here in Romans 6:22, becoming God's servant is the first step whose purpose is to lead to an object: holiness. It is *for* the purpose of making you holy. This is not a one-step of belief that transforms you into a holy person. Becoming God's servant has the *eis* purpose of making you *holy*. Then the result is *eternal life*.

Romans 2:13. In another passage, Paul ties justification to obedience. Paul writes:

> For not the hearers of the Law are just before God, but the **doers of the Law shall be justified**. (Rom 2:13.)

44."But now that you have been set free from sin and have become slaves of God, the benefit you reap leads to holiness, and *the result is eternal life*." (Romans 6:22 NIV.)

Incidentally, compare this to our prior discussion of Romans 3:26. Paul there said God justifies whoever has the *faithfulness of Jesus*. This means those who imitate Jesus' obedience are thus justified. (See page 462 *supra*.) This is identical to what Romans 2:13 quoted here literally says in all translations.

Romans 2:6-7. In yet another passage — Romans 2:6-7 — Paul most remarkably of all says that God

> will render to every man according to his works: to them that **by patience in well-doing** [*i.e.*, lit. **'endurance in good works'**] seek for glory and honor and incorruption, **eternal life**.

The Greek words translated as 'patience in well-doing' more correctly say *endurance in good works*. Paul thus says 'to those who endure patiently in doing good works, God **will** render eternal life.'

Here, the Atlantic Baptist University article once more comments how clearly this spells out a doctrine contrary to what most suppose Paul taught. The Atlantic Baptist University article states:

> **Paul clearly affirms that believers will be judged based on what they have done, not on what they have believed.** It should be noted that the eschatological judgment to which Paul refers does not presuppose that **the criterion of receiving eschatological salvation** is perfection, but rather **habitual obedience**.[45]

Thus, this passage adds more support to re-interpreting the word *pistis* in Paul's writings to *ordinarily* mean *faithfulness*, not *faith*. This supports the idea that Paul spoke this way in reliance on Jesus likewise teaching these principles.

---

45. "The Spirit, The Necessity of Good Works and Final Judgment," http://www.abu.nb.ca/courses/pauline/Works.htm (last accessed 11/25/2006).

Colossians 1:22, 23. Similarly, Paul says that *pistis* leads to presenting you holy and blameless unless you fail to continue in *pistis*, and you lose your *steadfastness* in *pistis*. Paul's aim is

> to present you holy, and blameless, and above reproach in His sight IF INDEED YOU CON-TINUE[46] IN ***PISTIS***, grounded and steadfast, AND ARE NOT MOVED AWAY from the hope of the gospel... Colossians 1:22,23.

One can see that again *pistis* here must mean *faithfulness*. The *pistis* can be ruined by losing *steadfastness* in the *pistis*. This is how one speaks of *faithfulness*. This is not how you speak about mere *belief* in facts about Jesus or the atonement. Moreover, this passage negates the idea that a *belief* one-time saved you. Instead, Paul says your salvation is tied up in an activity of *pistis* that must continue or otherwise it is in vain or for nothing. *Faithfulness* or *trust*, not *faith*, best fits those characteristics. Finally, the idea of a *mental assent* in the sense of *faith* in the doctrine of *faith alone* cannot be what Paul intended for *pistis* **here** because he just said *pistis alone* did not save you. Steadfastness or continuance are *also* necessary. To repeat, only *faithfulness* (*obedient living*) if read into *pistis* can contain a sufficiently broad meaning to make sense of **this** verse.

Thus, while everyone succumbs to translating *pistis* as *faith* here, the notion of *mental assent* does not fit. It should be translated here as *faithfulness*, not *faith*. Paul says it is destroyed by losing *steadfastness* and *not continuing* in the *hope* of salvation. When you lose hope in salvation, Paul is concerned you will no longer bother being faithful anymore. Paul is telling us to remain faithful and do not give up on the hope of salvation. Be steadfast. Be *faithful.*

---

46. The Greek word is *epimeno*. It also means "to stay at or with, to tarry still, still to abide, remain, to persevere."

1 Timothy 5:8. Paul likewise shows how a true Christian's misbehavior denies *pistis* and makes you worse than an unbeliever in this quote:

> But if anyone does not provide for his own and
> especially his household, he has **denied the
> faith** [*pistis*, trust, pledge] and **is worse than
> an unbeliever.** (1Ti 5:8 ALT.)

Thus, once again, we see how the better translation choice for *pistis* is not *faith*, but *pledge*. When a Christian does not provide for his family, he denies the *pledge* of faithfulness you gave to Jesus as Lord. If *pistis* meant *faith*, how would you deny your acceptance of facts (*belief*) by simply misbehavior? But if *pistis* means here *pledge*, you surely deny such a trusting faithful relationship or pledge by misbehavior.

1 Timothy 5:11-15. Paul speaks again similarly about *pistis* in 1 Timothy 5:11-15. In fact, here Paul certainly uses *pistis* not to mean *faith* in the sense of belief in facts about Jesus. In fact, most translations of this passage do not render *pistis* as *faith*, but instead translate *pistis* as *pledge*. This is a reasonable rendition. Yet, if you translate *pistis* here as *pledge* in this next quote, then why not thoroughly revise all of Paul's passages on *pistis* to be about salvation by a *pledge*? A firm *commitment*, *trust* or *faithfulness*? The word *pledge* is a synonym for a most solemn *trust*. When you pledge your honor to a king, it is a promise of *compliance* with the will of that king.

Let's now read 1 Timothy 5:11-15 where we find *pistis* is no longer translated by even the leading translations as *faith* but as *pledge*:

> But younger widows refuse: for when they
> have **waxed wanton against Christ**, they
> desire to marry; (12) having condemnation,
> because they have **rejected their first pledge
> [pistis].** (13) And withal they learn also to be
> idle, going about from house to house; and not

only idle, but tattlers also and busybodies,
speaking things which they ought not. (14) I
desire therefore that the younger widows
marry, bear children, rule the household, give
no occasion to the adversary for reviling: (15)
for *already some are turned aside after
Satan*. (1Ti 5:11-15 ASV.)

Paul says that this wanton sensual desire in them
makes them wax *against Christ*. By doing so, they have
rejected their *first pistis*. Here Paul is talking identical to
Jesus who says in Luke 8:13 that after the second seed hears
the word, it at *first accepts* the word with Joy. Then the second seed keeps on *pisteuo*-sing for a while (translated typically as *believes*), but in time of temptation falls away,
withers and hence dies. The noun form — *pistis* — in 1 Timothy 5:11-15 and the verb form — *pisteuo* —in Luke 8:13
must be talking of the first *pledge to obey* unto Christ which
these persons initially made.

Thus, 1 Timothy 5:11-15 is just one more proof that
dictates we can no longer construe Paul's usage of *pistis* or
pisteuo to always mean faith. Rather, Paul is obviously saying
in these passages that salvation turns upon *nothing so shallow as mere faith*. Instead, Paul in these passage must be saying salvation turns on *faithfulness*, trust, a pledge or promise
of compliance — which are legitimate alternative Greek
meanings in standard lexicons.

One can concede that Paul is not always consistent in
his usage of *pistis* and *pisteuo*, as we shall discuss. That is
not, however, a problem in how to interpret Jesus. It is a problem in how to understand Paul! Nevertheless, Paul clearly
often states salvation is not by the shallow notion of *faith
alone*. Hence this at minimum gives us further *confirmation*
that our choice of how to translate *pisteuo* in John 3:16 con-
forms to even how Paul *sometimes* (or even often) spoke and
taught. *Jesus does not have to strictly agree with every mode
of meaning of Paul.* Rather, Paul must strictly always agree
with Jesus. If Paul does not, this is proof that Paul is not

speaking at that moment with inspiration. A conflict in Paul's usage can never be used to gainsay Christ's meaning. Yet, when Paul agrees with Jesus, it shows how Jesus' meaning even penetrated into *some* or most of the writings of Paul.

The clearest examples are the following four inheritance warnings by Paul. They repeat the true gospel of Jesus Christ, as we previously have seen.

Paul's Four Inheritance Warnings

As the final proof that Paul's concept of *pistis* often must mean *faithfulness*, not *faith*, is Paul's *inheritance* warnings. In four passages Paul clearly said that if a Christian commits various sins (which are cognizable as moral rules from the Mosaic Law), such as covetousness, adultery, etc., this means you shall "not inherit the kingdom of God." (1 Cor. 6:9, Ephesian 5:5-7, Galatians 5:19-21, and 1 Thessalonians 4:6-8.) Jesus said those who "inherit the kingdom" means they have "eternal life." (Matt. 25:34,46. See page 219-20.)

We will discuss these four passages in a moment. The point is, if this is true, then this proves again that Paul *often* is not using *pistis* with its shallow meaning of *faith*. Rather, Paul often instead used it with a more strenuous meaning of *faithfulness*, which includes the notion of ***faithful obedience***.

Let's take, for example, 1 Thessalonians 4:6-8, from among these four passages. It clearly is addressing Christians, and says when you act disobediently you "reject God" who has given you His Holy Spirit:

> [For] each of you to know how to be acquiring his own vessel [fig., wife] in sanctification and honor, (5) not in lustful passion of desire, just as also the Gentiles, the ones not knowing God, (6) [so as] ***not to do wrong and take advantage of his brother*** in this matter, because the Lord [is the] avenger concerning all these [things], just as ***also we forewarned you*** and solemnly testified. (7) For God did not call ***us*** to

impurity [or, immorality], but in sanctification. (8) Therefore, the one rejecting [this] [or, regarding [this] as nothing] **does not reject a person but God, the One having also given His Holy Spirit to you**. (1Th 4:4-8 ALT.)

Or 1 Corinthians 6:8-10, we read similarly:

But **you act unjustly, and you defraud, and these [things to] brothers [and sisters]**! (9) You know that **unrighteous [ones] will not inherit [the] kingdom of God**, do you not? **Stop being led astray** [fig., being deceived]; neither sexual sinners nor idolaters nor adulterers nor passive partners in male-male sex nor active partners in male-male sex (10) nor covetous [ones] nor thieves nor drunkards nor slanderers [or, abusive persons] **nor swindlers will inherit [the] kingdom of God**. (1Co 6:8-10 ALT.)

In this 1 Corinthians passage, Paul clearly says that these Christians are acting unjustly toward brothers and sisters. Paul understands these malefactors *have truly* accepted Christ. He then sternly warns them that ***anyone misbehaving will not inherit the kingdom of God***. Actually, someone was leading them astray. Some taught that they safely could act unjustly toward brothers in the faith, or commit this list of sins, and still inherit the kingdom of God. Paul is sternly warning them that the opposite is true.

The passages of Ephesian 5:5-7 and Galatians 5:19-21 are to the same effect. In these two epistles addressed to the "brethren," Paul warns, as he says he warned them before, that anyone who practices various moral sins "shall not inherit the kingdom of God."

Clearly all these passages prove that Paul had an idea that whatever he thought elsewhere about *pisteuo* or *pistis* **often enough** he taught *obedience* was implied in their word meanings. Yet, the only definition of *pistis* that works like this is the option to translate it as *faithfulness, trust,* or *pledge*. Those translations alone connote *obedience*. The meaning of *faith* for *pistis* in these passages, while conceivable, is certainly too shallow to convey what Paul must have intended *in these passages*.

Even in Passages Where Paul Means Intellectual Assent.

Finally, even when Paul does use *pistis* to mean *faith*, in the sense of *doctrine*, almost every time he uses the word that way, Paul also says in the *very same context* that the *faith* (doctrine) is denied or negated by **disobedience to moral rules**. 2 Tim.3:6-8; 2 Cor. 13:5. Thus, Paul was even then still harkening back to a fuller more strenuous meaning about what the *faith* (correct doctrine) entailed.

This is not to deny Paul has verses which teach salvation is by *pistis* without *works* (obedience). (Eph. 2:8-9; Romans 4:4.) But to repeat, this does not raise a problem how to *interpret* Jesus's usage of *pistis* or *pisteuo*. Nor would such evidence in just **two** passages refute that Paul clearly **ordinarily** used *pistis* and *pisteuo* to mean *faithfulness*.

Rather, the fact Paul has a different program of salvation in these two passages merely raises a problem on how to explain the *contradiction* within Paul's view of salvation. In a moment, we shall discuss the solutions employed by the early Christian church to this dilemma. See "The Problem Of Paul's Belief-Without-Obedience Verses" on page 481.

Conclusion On Ordinary Meaning Of Pistis And Pisteuo In Paul's Writings

As a result of the overwhelming evidence above, unbeknownst to most Christians in the pew, evangelical scholars now agree it is impossible to believe Paul **consistently** taught *faith alone* saves. Rather, Paul often taught *faithfulness* saves. As T. Schreiner wrote in *The Law and Its Fulfillment* (Grand Rapids: Baker, 1993) at 203:

> Even though Paul asserts that no one can attain salvation by good works, he also insists that **no one can be saved without them**, and that **they**

> **are necessary to obtain an eschatological inheritance.**

As the evangelist Charles Finney similarly said: "But he [Paul] has everywhere insisted on good works springing from faith, or the righteousness of faith, *as indispensable to salvation.*" (Finney, *Justification by Faith* (1837).)

Consequently, the entire conception of salvation has been negatively impacted for centuries by translating *pisteuo* (the verb) and *pistis* (the noun) *consistently* as *believe* and *faith* respectively. The primary sense in Jesus' teachings, let alone in other portions of the New Testament, of the word *pisteuo* was always *obey, trust, compliance, etc. Pistis* normally means *faithfulness*, not *faith.* This is why Paul could say disobedience (i) was a denial of *pistis* and (ii) was a denial of God who gave His Holy Spirit to you and (iii) causes the loss of the inheritance of the kingdom of God.

The Problem Of Paul's Belief-Without-Obedience Verses

Paul two times teaches salvation by *belief* even if one is still disobedient and has commenced no obedience whatsoever. (Eph. 2:8-9; Rom. 4:4-5; *cf.* Romans 10:9.)[47]

Specifically, as evangelical scholars appear all to concur, Paul teaches in Romans 4:5 that a mental assent to a belief without repentance from sin — while you are still ungodly — saves you. (Romans 4:5.)

These two instances of a usage of *pistis* to mean *belief-only* are clear as long as Paul meant by *erga* (works) a synonym for *obedience.* This appears to be Paul's intent.

Yet, the only way to reconcile Paul fully to Jesus is to always read *pistis* as *faithfulness.* Unfortunately for Paul (if we wish to regard him as always inspired), this has serious difficulties within these two passages. Nevertheless, there is one plausible way to read Ephesians 2:8-9 this way so as to fit Jesus. The weight of Romans 4:5 in the opposite direction may make it a Quixotic venture to solve Ephesians 2:8-9 this way. Yet, if Romans 4:5 can ever be reconciled to Christ's teachings, here is a solution to Ephesians 2:8-9.

Ephesians 2:8-9: Can It Fit Jesus' Words?

As to Ephesians 2:8-9, it can fit Jesus' teaching if you read *erga* in Eph. 2:8-9 to mean **visible** *works.* As a result, then the clause "lest any man should boast" is no longer meant to require the most shallow meaning to *pistis* to keep the risk of boasting to the smallest minimum. Instead, the *boasting* clause would be directed at *erga* as explanation.

---

47. These verses support salvation by a mental belief without obedience, if "works" means *obedience.* If you are saved by *pistis*, not *erga* (Eph. 2:8-9, 'faith' not 'works') so no one can boast, it sounds like God is so concerned boasting may happen that He has debased salvation so mere *belief in facts,* as distinct from obedience/faithfulness, saves you. Similarly, if you *pisteuo* that God raised Jesus from the dead in Romans 10:9b, then this is condition b of what saves you. This 10:9b says if you believe this fact (*i.e.*, the resurrection) is true, you are assured salvation. The salvation statement in Romans 10:9a, however, runs counter to belief alone. It adds the requirement that if you also *homologeo en stoma* — confess with the mouth — that Jesus is Lord, then you are saved. Confession is often admitted by Paulinists to be a *work.* An action. At least it is not *faith alone.* So there is a quandary hanging over Romans 10:9a versus10:9b. Finally, in Romans 4:4-5, if you *pisteuo*, but do not have *erga*, Paul shockingly say God justifies you while you are *still* "ungodly." (This apparently says God justified a man who was *unrepentant-about-sin* — at least that is how most Paulinist commentators read it, as we shall see.) *See also* Phil. 3:8-11. There are various solutions that argue these verses teach salvation by faith and works and not by works alone. (Stulac.) Others claim *erga* means works of the ceremonial law cannot save. However, Paul's negative view about the *entire* law makes that an unconvincing argument. See my prior book, *Jesus' Words Only* (2007), chapter five. Others try to make the case Paul does not *ever* have a "cheap grace" gospel, relying heavily upon Romans 3:7-8. See, Lebedev, "Paul, the Law, Grace and … 'Cheap Grace,'" *Quodlibet Journal* Vol. 6 No. 3, July - September 2004 (available at http://www.quodlibet.net/lebedev-grace.shtml.) Yet, if there is no means of resolution, I offered what I regard is the correct solution about the doctrinal conflict between Jesus and Paul (and Paul with Paul) in my work *Jesus' Words Only* (2007). The title is succinctly the point.

Thus, Paul would be saying you are saved by "faithfulness, not by works (to be seen by men) lest any man should boast." This means you are saved by obedient living (to internal moral rules from Jesus) rather than by *visible* works. If salvation were by visible works, Paul means God would be tempting you to boast. Hence, God allegedly created a salvation formula that does not invite boasting because it depends on *internal* faithfulness that only God sees.

The problem is even if you read Ephesians 2:8-9 that way, there is the seemingly impossible hurdle posed by Romans 4:5 where Paul says he who "works not (*ergazomai*), but believes (*pisteuo epi*)[48] [on] the one justifying the irreverent — ungodly — is being accounted the *pistis* of Him unto [*eis*] righteousness."

In other words, what this verse says is the one who lacks obedience (works) but is *pisteuo epi* on the One who justifies the ungodly is being reckoned with the faithfulness (*pistis*) of Jesus for righteousness' sake.[49]

Pisteuo In Romans 4:5a

Here in Romans 4:5a, *pisteuo* by being contrasted with *ergazomai* is contrasting *working* against *pisteuo*-ing. This antithesis would support an *intellectual assent-belief* meaning to *pisteuo* in this verse.

Most troubling of all, Paul in Romans 4:5b says God "justifies the ungodly."

---

48. Vincent sees a small nuance in the fact this says *pisteuo epi*. It carries the idea of "*mental direction* with a view to resting upon."

49. Please note Romans 4:5 is another instance where *pistis* means *faithfulness*. Paul speaks again about the *pistis* of Jesus. It again must mean faithfulness. It was Jesus' obedience unto death to which Paul is referring by *pistis* here. However, it is the usage of *pisteuo epi* in the first part of Romans 4:5 that poses the difficulty

In light of the fact *works* are irrelevant in this verse, and most concur *repentance-from-sin* is a work, every commentator agrees Paul directly affirms justification *without repentance from sin.*

As Robertson's *Word Pictures* says: "The man is taken **as he is** and pardoned." Wesley concurs, saying God had to justify a man while he was "**at that very time, ungodly.**" Gill insists that Paul means Abraham (in context) was "in **his state of unregeneracy...an ungodly person**" when God justified him. The Geneva notes likewise say: "That makes him **who is wicked in himself** to be just in Christ." Clarke concurs that Paul speaks of Abraham, and according to Paul: "Abraham...was called **when he was ungodly, i.e. an idolater**; and, on his believing, was freely justified." Clarke says we are to understand this is the model: justification comes about **without any interior repentance from sin.** The only requirement Paul has in this verse is belief in the goodness and mercy of God. Clarke says:

> Abraham's state and mode in which he was justified, are the plan and rule according to which God purposes to save men; and **as his state was ungodly,** and the mode of **his justification was by faith** in the goodness and mercy of God.

Thus, it is Romans 4:5 which is the **sole basis to ridicule repentance-from-sin as a requirement for salvation** among most evangelicals.

For example, the famous *Ryrie Study Bible* says repentance from sin is "a false addition to faith" when added as a condition of salvation."[50]

Likewise, Frederick Bruner, on the faculty with the Fuller Theological Seminary, and a prolific evangelical author, insists in his book *Theology of the Holy Spirit* that

---

50.Charles Ryrie, *The Ryrie Study Bible* (Chicago: Moody Press, 1976) at 1950.

receipt of the Holy Spirit is "not conditional." Confession of sin and repentance from sin are "works" which supposedly only hinder simple faith. Bruner insists that repentance is "not something to be done." Rather, it is God's gift which enables a person to follow Christ and decide to be baptized.[51] Again and again Bruner berates Pentecostal Christians in particular who seek more than Christ's forgiveness at conversion. Bruner declares it is wrong to insist that a convert has some responsibility for meeting conditions such as repentance, obedience, eagerness and the like. All such arguments from Bruner hang principally on Romans 4:5.

Does Genesis 15:6 Support Paul's Dispensing With Repentance?

When Paul in Romans 4:5 makes such a radical departure from Jesus' doctrine of "justification" by repentance from sin,[52] Paul must have the very best support. Otherwise, we must reject any doctrine, even from Paul, which subtracts from the words of the Lord Jesus. (Deut. 4:2.)

Paul claims he has clear support in Genesis 15:6, citing it in Romans 4:3 to rationalize Romans 4:5.

Yet, Paul relied upon a ***mistranslation*** of Genesis 15:6 in the Greek Septuagint of 247 B.C.

Twice, Paul quotes from the Septuagint version of Genesis 15:6 — saying "it [faith] was accounted to him for righteousness...." (Romans 4:3; Gal.3:6.) However, ***it does not say that in the original Hebrew***! This verse was one of the very many translations errors in the Septuagint.

---

51. Frederick D. Bruner, *A Theology of the Holy Spirit* (Grand Rapids: Wm. B. Eerdmans Publishing Co., 1970) at 115, 116, 166.

52. See the discussion of the Parable of the Publican and the Pharisee in "The Repentant Goes Home Justified & The Shallowly Righteous Does Not" on page 27 *et seq.*

In 247 B.C., the Hebrew Bible was translated into Greek. It is known as the Septuagint Bible. Jewish scholars acknowledge "the Septuagint was translated by *very bad translators*" and "very often the [Septuagint] translators *did not even know what they were reading* and created nonsensical sentences by translating word for word."[53] Jerome in the Fourth Century shared Gordon's harsh view of the unreliability of the Septuagint translation, providing numerous proofs of its fallibility in his correspondence with Augustine.[54] Scholars likewise note: "Often...the words of the Septuagint do not faithfully reproduce the meanings of the Hebrew Scriptures." (Nicolson, *God's Secretaries* (2004) at 82.)

Then what does the Hebrew say in Genesis 15:6? It is translated more-or-less correctly in the King James:

> And he believed in the LORD; and he counted it to him for righteousness. (Gen 15:6 KJV.)

Well, there is one little license that the King James took. There is no second *he* in the verse. That is an interpolated *he,* as Professor Hamilton will explain in a moment. (There is also no *semicolon.*) It really reads:

> And he believed in the LORD and counted it to him for righteousness. (Gen 15:6.)

---

53. Nehemiah Gordon, *Hebrew Yeshua vs. Greek Jesus* (Jerusalem: 2006) at 33-34. Gordon is a Jewish scholar who is sympathetic to Jesus.

54. On the issue of the Septuagint, Jerome had strong views of its rampant error. Thus, in the 4th Century, as he prepared the Vulgate Bible, Jerome told Augustine repeatedly that the Septuagint Greek Bible was rife with deletions (Messianic prophecies quoted by Matthew) and additions from the Hebrew original. He insisted upon using the Hebrew original. For example, Jerome wrote: "[T]he former translation is from the Septuagint; and wherever obelisks are placed, they are designed to indicate that the Seventy have said more than is found in the Hebrew." See "Letters of Jerome (No. 112)," in *A Select Library of Nicene and Post-Nicene Fathers of the Christian Church, Translated into English with Prolegomena and Explanatory Notes under the Editorial Supervision of Henry Wace and Philip Schaff.* (Oxford: Parker; New York: Christian Literature Co., 1890-1900).

Who then is the subject of the verb *counted*? Abraham. He is the one *counting* or *reckoning* the promise of a child in old-age in Genesis 15:5 as a righteous deed of God. English syntax is the same as Hebrew syntax. ***The subject of the second clause is the subject of the first clause: here Abraham***. Thus, this verse never had anything to do with justification ***by God*** of Abraham. God is not the one doing any of the reckoning in the Hebrew version of Genesis 15:6. Rather, this verse is how Abraham viewed God's promise as righteousness — as a faithful act of God.

The Septuagint changed the subject of *count* to "it," making it unclear who was *counting* what to whom.

Professor Hamilton, an evangelical scholar of impeccable credentials, concedes Paul relied upon a verse which in the original Hebrew can be read that Abraham is the one doing the reckoning, which ***but for*** Paul's *understanding*, would have been the correct understanding of the verse.

In Professor Victor P. Hamilton's *New International Commentary on the Old Testament* (Eerdmans 1990), we read in Vol. I at 425:

> The second part of this verse records Yahweh's response to Abram's exercise of faith: 'he credited it to him as righteousness.' But even here there is a degree of ambiguity. Who credited whom? Of course, one may say that the NT settles the issue, for Paul expressly identifies the subject as God and the indirect object as Abram (Rom. 4:3). ***If we follow normal Hebrew syntax, in which the subject of the first clause is presumed to continue into the next clause if the subject is unexpressed, then the verse's meaning is changed...*** Does *he*, therefore, continue as the logical subject of the second clause? ***The Hebrew of the verse certainly permits this interpretation***, especially when one recalls that *sedaqa* means both 'righteousness' (a theological meaning) and 'justice' (a juridical meaning). The whole verse could then

be translated: "Abram put his faith in Yahweh, and *he [Abram] considered it [the promise of seed(s)] justice*."

Thus, in the Hebrew original version of this verse, it had nothing to do with justification of Abraham *by God* based upon faith. It was Abraham counting the promise of God in Genesis 15:5 as righteousness (justice) by God. Professor Hamilton was being honest despite how a true translation would upset Hamilton's own Protestant theology.[55]

Jewish Scholars Concur On Genesis 15:6

Several Jewish scholars concur that in Genesis 15:6b, it is Abraham reckoning God's promise as righteous. It is not God reckoning Abraham as righteous. These scholars were not writing anti-Christian diatribes. Rather, these comments were spoken in ordinary Jewish commentary and lessons.

First, let's examine the analysis of Ramban (Nachmanides, 1194-1270 A.D.) His explanation appears in what is known as *Rabbinic Bible* (Mikraoth Gedoloth).[56]

Ramban says reading God as the *reckoner* of righteousness to Abraham makes no sense in the context. For this would require we find a great faith which God sees as worthy to impute justification. Yet, Ramban asks: "How should [Abraham] not believe in the good tidings?" In other words,

---

55. Victor P. Hamilton's background is formidable. He is Professor of Bible and Theology at Asbury College. He has a B.A. from Houghton College 1963, a B.D. from Asbury Theological Seminary 1966; a Th.M. Asbury Theological Seminary 1967, an M.A., Brandeis University 1969; and a Ph.D. Brandeis University 1971. Hamilton's commentary is based on his complete translation of Genesis itself.

56. The discussion here derives from an article by the Presbyterian Minister and later professor at various Christian collages, Lloyd Gaston. The article is entitled "Abraham and the Righteousness of God," in the *Horizons in Biblical Theology. An International Dialogue* (1980) Vol. 2. It was revised and republished as Lloyd Gaston, *Paul and Torah* (UBC: 1987). An excerpt posted with permission of Mr. Gaston can be found at http://www.jcrelations.net/en/?id=752.

---

no great faith is involved in accepting a beneficial promise. As the Protestant Pastor and Professor, Gaston, comments: "There is certainly no merit in accepting good news." Thus, the more normal reading of the text, clearly indicated by Hebrew syntax, is to see Abraham as the subject who reckons it (the promise) as God's righteous deed. The opposing view is counter-indicated because there is no momentous struggle for Abraham to believe a promise which he was already wishing to be true.

Ramban says for these reasons he favors the reading put forth above. He explains: "What would be correct in my judgment is that it is said (or, is to be interpreted as follows): 'that he believed in the LORD and thought [*i.e.*, counted] that [it represents] the righteousness of the Holy One.'" [57]

This view is shared by the famous Talmudic-era commentary on Exodus known as *Mekilta de Rabbi Ishmael*, Beshallah 4 (ed. Jacob Lauterbach)(Philadelphia: Jewish Publication Society, 1933) Vol. I at 220. This dates back to the fourth or fifth century A.D.

The *Mekilta* explains Genesis 15:6 in a series of questions and answers by various rabbis. Shemaiah has God explain why He parted the Red Sea: "The faith with which their father Abraham believed in Me is deserving that I should divide the sea for them," for it is said, "And he believed in the Lord [Gen 15:6a] and "he counted it **unto him**

---

57. Gaston mentions that Calvin knew of Ramban's reading but rejected it. Here is Calvin's analysis: "They also, no less skillfully, corrupt the text, who say that Abram is here ascribing to God the glory of righteousness, seeing that he ventures to acquiesce surely in his promises, acknowledging Him to be faithful and true; for although Moses does not expressly mention the name of God, yet the accustomed method of speaking in the Scriptures removes all ambiguity." (Calvin, *Genesis* (London: Banner of Truth Trust, 1965) at 406.) Pastor/Professor Gaston comments correctly: "Whether Calvin is apt to be more familiar with the 'accustomed manner of speaking in the Scriptures' than Ramban is to be doubted." (Lloyd Gaston, "Abraham and the Righteousness of God," *Horizons in Biblical Theology. An International Dialogue* (1980) Vol. 2.)

for (doing) charity [with his offspring]."[58] That is, the *Mekilta* means the one who is counting is Abraham. He is counting the promise by God as charity (righteousness) toward his children.

Frequent Mention In Scripture Of the Righteousness Of God

Ramban's and the Mekilta's view of Genesis 15:6 fits well with the many passages where the psalmist gives a praise for God's righteousness. That's all Abraham was doing in Genesis 15:6. He was simply reckoning the promise from God as more proof of the righteousness of God.

One example is Psalm 7:17: "I will give to the LORD the thanks due to his *righteousness*, and I will sing praise to the name of the LORD, the Most High." (*See also* Ps 5:7-8; 22:30-31; 31:1; 35: 28; 26:5-6,10; 40:11; 51:13-15; 69:27; 71:14-15a, 18b-19, 24; 88:12; 143:1,11).

Also, Ramban's view matches how God speaks often of His own righteousness: "I will uphold you with the right hand of *my righteousness*." (Isaiah 41:10.)

Most important, Ramban's reading fits both Micah's and Nehemiah's depiction of God's "faithfulness" and "stead-fast love" and "righteousness" toward Abraham. This then makes sense of Genesis 15:6 as merely Abraham praising God for the same trait which is prophetically recognized.

Thus, first we read in Micah: "Who is a God like thee, pardoning iniquity and passing over transgression?... Thou wilt show *faithfulness* to Jacob and *steadfast love* to Abraham, as thou hast sworn to our fathers from the days of old." (Micah 7:18-20.) God will show righteousness to the sons.

58.Lloyd Gaston, *Paul and Torah* (UBC: 1987) at 205, quoting from A. Marmorstein, *The Doctrine of Merits in Old Rabbinical literature* (New York: KTAV, repr. 1968) at 37. *Cfr.* Maureen W. Yeung, *Faith in Jesus and Paul* (doctoral thesis, Aberdeen, University 1999) (Mohr Siebeck, 2002) at 259 (omits "he counted it unto him for (doing) charity [with his offspring]").

Lastly, we read in Nehemiah, this account of God's dealing with Abraham:

> Thou art Jehovah the God, who didst choose Abram, and... gavest him the name of Abraham, (8) and foundest his heart faithful before thee, and madest a covenant with him to give the land of the Canaanite,...., to give it unto his seed, and hast performed thy words; for *thou art righteous*. (Neh 9:7-8 ASV.)

The pattern is identical between Genesis 15:6, Micah and Nehemiah: there is mention of the promise of seed to Abraham which is then followed by praise of God as "faithful," having "steadfast love" and He is "righteous." Thus, it makes perfect sense that Genesis 15:6 is saying Abraham believed God about the promise and then he (Abraham) reckoned it to Him (God) as righteousness.

Similarly, the Apocryphal book of Jubilees has a reference to Abraham as the recipient of God's righteousness. It follows the normal Hebrew structure of Genesis 15:6 that Hamilton noted. However, this time, there is no room to argue. The text reads: "And Isaac blessed the God of his father Abraham, who had not withdrawn his mercy and *his righteousness* from the sons of his servant Isaac." Pastor/Professor Gaston interprets this to mean "Abraham and his seed were the recipients of God's *righteousness*."[59]

All these commentaries and scriptural references simply repeat what the textual evidence and grammar dictates is the meaning of Genesis 15:6. Abraham was noting God's righteousness. There was nothing more profound in the passage than that. Hence, it was never a passage having anything to do with God's imputing any righteousness to Abraham.

---

59. See Lloyd Gaston, *Paul and Torah* (UBC: 1987) at 205 n.45.

The Offering Of Isaac Was A Condition Of God's Promise

Furthermore, it is impossible that God imputed justification to Abraham in 15:5 in any completed irrevocable sense. For those who teach faith alone, unless justification is irrevocable, and disobedience cannot destroy it, there is no point anyway to fight for the reading they prefer of Genesis 15:6. Yet, in Genesis 22:16-18, God makes it abundantly clear that the promise and any justification were both revocable had there been disobedience. Since that is the case, as we shall prove in a moment, the strained reading to make 15:6 prove faith justifies without repentance or need to obey later is a quixotic venture not worthy of any more wasted effort.

For God later makes it clear the promise of Genesis 15:5 will only be fulfilled because Abraham passed the test of his obedience. This destroys any notion that faith alone merited the fulfillment of the promise to Abraham, which has crucial implications on modern justification theory. God says:

> By my self I have sworn, says YHWH, *because you have done this* and have not withheld your son, your only son, I will indeed *bless you and I will multiply your seed*[60]... and by your seed shall all the nations of the earth bless themselves, *because you have obeyed my voice*. (Gen 22:16-18.)

If faith in the promise of a blessing and offspring given in Genesis 15:5 supposedly gave permanent justification for Abraham, as some read 15:6, then why did God tell Abraham that had he failed the test with Isaac the promise would have been revoked? In other words, if the belief in the promise made Abraham permanently justified, it must follow that the promise itself was permanent, and not conditional.

60."And he brought him forth abroad, and said, Look now toward heaven, and number the stars, if thou be able to number them: and he said unto him, So shall thy seed be." (Gen 15:5 ASV.)

However, this cannot be true for God says He would have denied what supposedly was a permanently *justified* man the promise had he (Abraham) been later disobedient.

There can be no dispute about this conditionality in Genesis 22. There are two *because's* in the quoted passage. "Because you have done this" and "because you have obeyed," God will keep His promise of Genesis 15:5. "I will indeed bless you and I will multiply your seed...." The negative implication, and hence the message to us, is that had Abraham failed the test, he would have lost the promise. It also follows that a faith which remains alone would never justify. For if God takes back the promise for disobedience, He surely would take back the justification that went with it.

Now it makes perfect sense what James means when he teaches that Abraham was "justified by works" in offering up his son Isaac. Had Abraham failed the test over Isaac, Abraham would have no right to be called just. Hence, justification turns on obedience, and not faith alone, just as James explained.

> Was not Abraham our father *justified by
> works*, in that he *offered up Isaac his son*
> upon the altar? (22) Thou seest that faith
> wrought with his works, and by works was
> faith made perfect;... (24) Ye see that *by works
> a man is justified*, and not by *faith alone*.
> (James 2:21-22,24.)

Conclusion On Genesis 15:6

Given all these facts, do we have any basis to reject that Jesus is correct that justification initiates by repentance from sin? That's what the Lord Jesus taught in the Parable of the Publican and the Pharisee.[61] That's what the Bible always taught in the 'Original Testament.'[62] That's what James was explaining about Abraham. It is also self-evident when you

---

61.See page 27 *et seq.*

examine Genesis chapter twenty-two. Or are we suppose to rely upon Paul merely because he relied upon a mistranslation of Genesis 15:6? Of course not.

Thus, we cannot permit Romans 4:3 and Galatians 3:6 to overturn the original Hebrew reading of Genesis 15:6, the Prophets, and most important of all, the words of Jesus.

The Struggle For Mastery Over Doctrine: Jesus Or Paul?

Here is a key juncture for a Christian to make a decision. Who will you trust? Jesus or Paul?

On one side, you have Jesus saying 'justification' comes by repenting from sin in the Parable of the Publican and the Pharisee. (See page 27 *et seq.*) Jesus in Luke 18:14 uses the same Greek work for "justified" that Paul uses in Romans 4:5: *dikaio*. (See *Interlinear Scripture Analyzer*, free for download off the Internet.)

However, on the other side, you have Paul saying in Romans 4:5 — and most of modern evangelical Christianity insists it is true — that one is *justified in an ungodly state without repentance from sin by mere belief alone*.

Who is right? Jesus or Paul?

The Case For Paul's View of Justification

Well, Paul's proof from Genesis 15:6 cited in Romans 4:3 turned out to be based on a mistranslation! Protestant scholars of pre-eminent status concur with Jewish commentators that the original Hebrew of Genesis 15:6 has *Abraham* as the one doing the reckoning, not God. The only exception to this is *if we are compelled to let Paul serve as authority to rewrite Scripture*. Yet, God prohibits anyone from having such authority. (Deut. 4:2; 13:1-5.)

---

62. See "Justification In the Law of Moses" on page 33 and "Justification In The Prophets" on page 34 *et seq.*

The Case For Jesus' View Of Justification

What is the case for Jesus' words about justification by repentance-from-sin being more important than Paul's views? That should be easy. Unfortunately, this is where so many are tripped up. *They do not follow Christ as pre-eminent over Paul.* So let's go through this analysis carefully.

We know Jesus is above all. Even the greatest prophet (John the Baptist) compared himself to Jesus and realized his own words were nothing but as a mere man "speaking from the earth" in comparison to the words from Jesus. Prophet John explained why: the words from Jesus — the One who came "from above" — is "above all." (John 3:31.)

In other words, Jesus' words are superior to every other prophet from God! God thereby tests our allegiance.

Can We Reconcile This By Treating Paul As A More Valid 'Dispensation'?

If you think instead that Paul has any equal or greater stature than your Lord, you have inverted things. You are using the "disciple to criticize the Master," as Kierkegaard pointed out in 1855. This involves a fundamental error of how to regard Jesus in relation to anyone else.

It is clearly error to treat Paul's words equally as important or more important than Jesus' words. Jesus told you not to do this even as to a true apostle. (John 13:16, "the *apostolos* is not more important than the one who sent him.")

To those who balk, and still insist they must force an agreement between Jesus and Paul, I reply: you absolutely have no Biblical basis for doing so. For Jesus *never* called Paul an apostle. It is a pure myth that Jesus ever did so! Tertullian pointed this out in 207 A.D.

Tertullian On The Lack Of Corroboration To Paul's Claim Of Apostleship

Tertullian was confronting heretics (Marcion) who were citing Paul to prove salvation by mere belief without obedience. (See page 578 *et seq.*) Tertullian said it was troubling that such reliance was being put upon one (Paul) of whom there is not the slightest proof in the four Gospels or Acts that Jesus ever called him (Paul) *an apostle*. Yes, Jesus called Paul a witness (*martus* in Greek). But Jesus never once called Paul an apostle (*apostolos* in Greek).[63] Thus, there is no basis to give Paul whatever authority is assumed to be enjoyed by the twelve apostles.

Here is Tertullian in book five, chapter one, of *Against Marcion* (207 A.D.) rebuffing this zeal for Paul's words ahead of Christ's words:

> I desire to hear from Marcion **the origin of Paul the apostle**. I am a sort of new disciple, having had instruction from no other teacher. For the moment my only belief is that **nothing ought to be believed without good reason**, and that is believed without good reason which is believed without knowledge of its origin: and **I must** with the best of reasons **approach this inquiry with uneasiness when I find one affirmed to be an apostle, of whom in the list of the apostles in the gospel I find no trace.** So **when I am told that he [i.e., Paul] was subsequently promoted by our Lord, by now at rest in heaven, I find some lack of foresight in the fact that Christ did not know beforehand that he would have need of him**, but after setting in order the office of apostleship and sending them out upon their duties, considered it necessary, **on an impulse and not by deliberation, to add another, by compulsion so to speak and not by design** [i.e., on the Road to Damascus]. So then, shipmaster out of Pontus [i.e., Marcion], supposing you have never accepted into your craft any smuggled or illicit merchandise, have never appropriated or adul-

---

63. This is thoroughly examined in my prior book, *Jesus' Words Only* (2007) at 215-220 and 408-421.

terated any cargo, and in the things of God are even more careful and trustworthy, will you please *tell us under what bill of lading you accepted Paul as apostle, who had stamped him with that mark of distinction, who commended him to you, and who put him in your charge*? Only so may you with confidence disembark him [*i.e.*, Paul]: only so can he avoid being proved to belong to him who *has put in evidence all the documents that attest his apostleship. He [i.e., Paul] himself, says Marcion, claims to be an apostle*, and that not from men nor through any man, but through Jesus Christ. *Clearly any man can make claims for himself*: but his claim is *confirmed by another person's attestation*. One person writes the document, another signs it, a third attests the signature, and a fourth enters it in the records. *No man is for himself both claimant and witness.* Besides this, you have found it written that *many will come and say, I am Christ.* If there is one that makes a false claim to be Christ, *much more can there be one who professes that he is an apostle of Christ....* [L]*et the apostle, belong to your other god*:....[64]

Luke Too Denies Paul The Very Office Paul Claimed

Luke likewise in Acts made it evident there were only twelve apostles for all time, and this excluded Paul. *Never does Paul claim in Acts to be an apostle of Jesus. Never do the apostles in Acts describe Paul as an apostle. Nor does Jesus in the three vision accounts in Acts chapters 9, 22 and 26 ever call Paul an apostle.* Jesus says Paul will be a *martus* — a **witness**, not an *apostolos* — which means *messenger.*

64.Tertullian, *Against Marcion* (Oxford University Press, 1972) at 509, 511, reprinted online at http://www.tertullian.org/articles/evans_marc/evans_marc_12book5_eng.htm.

The self-serving flaw in Paul's claim to being an apostle has been recognized by reputable Pauline scholars. For example, John Crossan and Jonathan Reed, in their latest work of 2004 explain:

> [I]n all his letters, Paul sees himself as an apostle sent from God through Christ. The very vocation for which Paul lives is **denied him by Luke**. He is, to be sure, an important missionary....But **he is not an apostle** equal to the Twelve.[65]

Furthermore, Crossan & Reed make the point that Luke's story of how Matthias replaced Judas excludes the possibility of a thirteenth apostle such as Paul. They write:

> Luke insists in Acts 1 that, after Jesus' resurrection, there were still, **always, and only** 'the twelve apostles.'...For Luke, **Paul is simply not an apostle**.[66] Without Matthias' explicit selection, one might have imagined that Luke's Paul was at least implicitly Judas' replacement as the twelfth apostle. With it, **Luke implies that Paul was not an apostle** and **could never be one**....[H]e could never be the one thing Paul always insisted that he was, namely, an apostle sent by God through a revelation of the risen Lord. (*Id.*, at 29.)

---

65. John Crossan & Jonathan Reed, *In Search of Paul: How Jesus' Apostle Opposed Rome's Empire with God's Kingdom* (San Francisco: Harper San Francisco, 2004) at 29.

66. Luke does describe Paul and Barnabas as messengers from the church at Antioch. In Acts 14:4 and 14, the Greek word for *messenger* is used for them, *apostoli*. However, as the Christian historian Ben Witherington explains: "The use of the term *apostoli* in [Acts] 14:4 and 14 seems to indicate that Paul and Barnabas are being viewed as agents/apostles of the Antioch church (cf. 2 Cor. 8:23), *not apostles with a capital A*." (Witherington, *New Testament History* (Baker Academic: 2001) at 229.) In fact, the context clearly shows Paul with Barnabas were merely messengers (*apostolos*) of the church of Antioch.

Jesus Agrees That Twelve Is the Only Number of Apostles

Years after Paul is already dead and after the original eleven apostles already selected Matthias as the twelfth, Jesus reveals to Apostle John in the Book of Revelation that *twelve is the number of apostles for all time.* This verse in Revelation 21:14 follows the mention of the twelve gates of the New Jerusalem. Each gate has a name of the twelve tribes of Israel on it. Revelation 21:14 then says:

> The city was built on ***twelve*** foundation stones. On each of the stones was written the name of one of the Lamb's ***twelve apostles.*** (Rev. 21:14 CEV.)

There is a clear correspondence of one apostle for each of the twelve tribes, gates, and foundation stones. The number each time is only *twelve*. It implies there are not supposed to be more than twelve apostles. You cannot have thirteen or fourteen apostles judging the twelve tribes. Jesus made this clear during His earthly ministry as well. Jesus said the role of the *twelve* apostles was to "sit upon *twelve* thrones, judging the *twelve* tribes of Israel." (Matt. 19:28.)

What Weight Do Paul's Self-Serving Statements Have?

Thus, the only person to say Paul is an apostle *of Jesus Christ* in the entire New Testament is Paul himself.[67]

Yet, we know that Jesus said if He alone bore witness to Himself, then His witness would be untrue. (John 5:31, "If I bear witness of myself, my witness is not true.")

Jesus was extending the Law's principle, so that two witnesses were necessary to establish not only a wrong, but also anything as important as God sending someone for a spe-

---

67. *See, e.g.,* 1 Cor. 1:1; 2 Cor. 1:1; Galatians 1:1; 1 Ti. 1:1. *See, viz.,* "For I am the least of the apostles, that am not meet to be called an apostle, because I persecuted the church of God." (1 Cor. 15:9, ASV) and "For I reckon that I am not a whit behind the very chiefest apostles." (2 Cor. 11:5, ASV.)

---

cial role.[68] In fact, Jesus in Revelation 2:2 clearly agrees a self-serving claim to be His apostle is insufficient proof that you are His apostle.[69] Therefore, Paul's claim to being an apostle suffers from being self-serving. By a *Biblical* standard from *Jesus* Himself, Paul's self-witness "is not true."

Hence, the notion that Paul is an apostle solely comes from Paul's own epistles. But Jesus told us no one can be their own self-witness for then their witness is "not true." (John 5:31, "If I bear witness of myself, my witness is not true.")

NT Era Solution To Paul's Verses On Belief Alone

An early answer within the church to this identical quandary of Paul's *belief alone* verses (at least as 'twisted by some') was to regard such problem verses in Paul as "***difficult to understand***." (Self-contradiction causes uncertainty.)

Hence, the early church taught these belief alone passages were an impermissible basis to stray from what Jesus — our Sole Teacher (Matt. 23:8,10) and Divine Lord — taught us. Second Peter bluntly provides this solution.

---

68. The Law said that no crime or wrong could be established by a single witness. (Deut. 19:15, "any crime or any wrong"). Jesus taught in event of a dispute over a wrong, obtain witnesses so by "the mouth of two witnesses or three *every word* may be established." (Mat 18:16.) Why must this principle apply to would-be apostles? Because without two witnesses with *competent knowledge*, one's claim is entirely *self-serving.*

69. Revelation 2:2 specifically says the persons on trial "said" they were apostles and the Ephesians properly found these persons were *nevertheless* still liars. Thus, Jesus implied such a self-serving statement of being His apostle does not suffice. Jesus says the claimants were appropriately found to be liars. Therefore, Jesus' own words in Revelation 2:2 agree that self-serving testimony cannot ever be the basis to treat someone as an apostle of Jesus Christ.

Second Peter warned us that Paul says many things that are "difficult to understand" (2 Peter 3:17) and many people twist Paul's words so that they fall from their "steadfastness in Christ" to their own destruction.[70]

Second Peter continues and makes clear that it is *talking about* the doctrines of Paul that are a *cheap grace* — that lead Christians to think accepting Christ one time allows you to sin later and still go to heaven.[71] If you follow the belief alone implication that lets go of obedience for salvation, Second Peter says you stop following Jesus. You lose your "steadfastness" in Christ.

In fact, what is remarkable is how *clear* this is explained in Second Peter 2:20-21. For it unequivocally says in Greek that it would have been better you never had *accepted* (*epi-ginoska*, not merely *ginoska*) the Lord Jesus Christ than to have *accepted* (*epi-ginoska*) Him, and then be overcome again later by sinning.[72]

Apostle John likewise used *epignosei* to refer to a saving *epi-gnosis* as long as it continues. Apostle John said anyone who "***epignosei*** [continuous tense, *present participle active*] — keeps on *accepting* — the Son also has the Father." (1 John 2:23.)

This tells us that Second Peter — which uses the same *epignosei* — says it would be better to have never had the Son and Father by *epignose*-ing the Son than to have had them but then be tripped up by a doctrine that licenses sin as salvation-wise safe, and then become lost again.

---

70. Second Peter says:

"And account that the longsuffering of our Lord is salvation; even as our beloved brother Paul also, *according to the wisdom given to him*, wrote unto you; (16) as also in all his epistles, speaking in them of these things; wherein are *some things hard to be understood*, which the ignorant and *unstedfast wrest*, as they do also the other scriptures, *unto their own destruction*. (17) Ye therefore, beloved, knowing these things beforehand, beware lest, being carried away with the error of the wicked, *ye fall from your own stedfastness*." (2Pe 3:15-17 ASV.)

Unfortunately, rather than heed Second Peter, most evangelicals are subjected to translators who torture Second Peter 2:20-21 so it is neutralized from undermining their 'free to sin and yet be saved' doctrine. This teaching is known as Eternal Security which they deduce from Paul's writings.

---

71. Second Peter goes on and clearly specifies what is the wrong teaching of those who 'twist' Paul. They promise that you have *liberty in Christ to sin and remain saved.* Second Peter says: "(17) These are springs without water, and mists driven by a storm; for whom the *blackness of darkness hath been reserved.* (18) For, uttering great swelling words of vanity, they *entice in the lusts of the flesh*, by lasciviousness, *those who are just escaping from them that live in error*; (19) *promising them liberty*, while they themselves are bondservants of corruption; for of whom a man is overcome, of the same is he also brought into bondage. (20) For if, *after they have escaped the defilements of the world through the* **epignosei** ~~knowledge~~ [*acceptance*] *of the Lord and Saviour Jesus Christ*, they are *again entangled therein and overcome*, the *last state is become worse with them than the first.* (21) For it were *better for them not to have* **epiginosko** ~~known~~ [*accepted*] *the way of righteousness*, than, after knowing [sic: accepting] it, *to turn back from the holy commandment delivered unto them.* (22) It has happened unto them according to the true proverb, The dog turning to his own vomit again, and the sow *that had washed* to wallowing in the mire." (2Pe 2:17-22 ASV.) The word *epignosei* and *epignosko* used in verses 20 and 21 is often mistranslated as *knowledge* and *know* respectively. Yet, not one dictionary definition of *epignosei* includes *knowledge.* The Greek prefix *epi* is meant to convey 'above the norm, over and above.' The prefix *epi* thus intends to intensify *ginosko*. Thus, Vines says its primary meaning is "to know *thoroughly* (*epi*, 'intensive' [of] ginosko, 'to know.'") Thus, the definition is some meaning beyond *mere* knowledge. Moreover, to suggest these people "escaped...through [mere] knowledge" of Jesus the evils of the world is silly. These people escaped the *miasmata*, meaning "defilement, stain of guilt" of the *kosmos.* These must be Christians. Thus, *epignosei* obviously is intended to convey that meaning. What *epignosei* means in the *LSJ Middle Lexicon* is essentially (1) to look upon, observe; or (2) "recognize, know again, to *acknowledge or approve*...[iii] to *come to a decision, to resolve, decide.*" The most obvious English synonym that fits the context is "acceptance" and "accept" in verses 20 and 21. Incidentally, Paul uses *epignosei* in the same manner in Titus 1:1 about what saves. There the KJV translates it correctly as "acknowledging [*i.e.*, accepting] the truth." The same is true of 1 John 2:23 which is discussed in the text.

Translation Of Second Peter To Obscure Its Meaning

For Second Peter is translated typically so that it no longer speaks about those who "accepted" Jesus. Second Peter really says those accepting Him are falling from salvation due to demoralizing doctrine. In 2 Peter 2:20-21, it ordinarily is translated so that supposedly people who merely *knew* about Jesus fell away by being taught there is a "liberty" to sin as a Christian. Yet, if Second Peter had meant that persons who merely *knew* about Jesus are at issue, the proper word to use would have been *ginoska* (know). It certainly would not be *epi-ginosko*. A Greek would understand the verb *epi-ginosko* due to the prefix *epi* is intended to intensify the verb *to know*.[73] Hence, it could only mean *accept* or *acknowledge* in this context.

Moreover, it appears suspiciously inconsistent to render 1 John 2:23 to say the one who is "***acknowledging*** the Son also has the father," but rendering the same word in 2 Peter 2:20-21 as '***know***.' The effect of the inconsistency is that the reader is misled. The uninformed Christian is led to think Second Peter is concerned about those who never have accepted/acknowledged Christ but merely *know* about Him. Yet, Second Peter is truly warning those who have accepted Christ unto a saving relationship with the Father and Son that they do not realize that it would be better never to have accepted Christ than to listen to a 'twisting of Paul's words,' and be seduced thereby to think that sinning is salvation-safe. Second Peter means it is not possible for a Christian to safely accept such a liberty to sin even when Paul appears to say so.

How Could It Be Better Never To Have Accepted Christ?

Then what does Second Peter mean? Obviously, the only way it would be better never to have accepted Christ is that you not only go to hell, but also you receive extra lashes

---

72. See Footnote 71, page 502.
73. See Footnote 71, page 502.

for *knowingly* flaunting Jesus' commands based on being led astray by passages in Paul's writings. Did Jesus ever teach this extra-lashes principle, thus strengthening this reading? Yes, He did!

Jesus taught this in Luke's Gospel. He spoke about what will happen to disobedient servants of His. Jesus says the ones who actually knew His will but did not do it receive more lashes than the ones who are disobedient but ignorant of His will. Both types of disobedient servants are in hell, but the ones who receive a worse whipping are the ones who *knew* their Lord's will and still disobeyed:

> And that servant, who **knew his lord's will**, and made not ready, nor did according to his will, **shall be beaten with many stripes**; (48) but he that **knew not**, and did things **worthy of stripes**,[74] shall be beaten with few stripes. And to whomsoever much is given, of him shall much be required: and to whom they commit much, of him will they ask the more. (Luke 12:47-48.)

What should have been the modern response to Second Peter? It should have put us on alert to any and everything Paul says. There is a fatal and destructive message that can be construed from Paul's writings, Second Peter says. This message is identified as a message of "liberty." In context, it is obvious the misleading message is what we call today faith alone doctrine. This *alone* part of the label signifies that no disobedience can destroy your salvation. Faith *alone* supposedly does it all for you. Second Peter yet warns a double dose of damnation for those so duped. For you have accepted the Son, but later became seduced by passages in

---

74. We need to tremble because this teaches *ignorance of the Law is no excuse*. As Lisco says, "even sins which are committed in ignorance are punishable for ignorance itself is guilt. All the subjects of a kingdom are **under an obligation to make themselves acquainted with its laws**, and misconduct from neglect is punishable guilt." Lisco: 254.

Paul to break "the holy commandments." (2 Peter 2:21.) Yet, you knew *the Lord Jesus' will* was very different. You knew Jesus said 'repent or perish,' and 'heaven maimed or hell whole' (Mark 9:42-47). Now, for flagrantly disregarding the Lord's will, you will suffer a double portion in hell. That's what Second Peter is bluntly saying.

Jerome's Low View Of Paul's Writings Akin To Second Peter

Another confirmation that we are reading Second Peter correctly is to examine Jerome's comments about Paul. Jerome translated the Greek NT in 411 A.D. into the Latin Vulgate. Jerome in his Commentary on Galatians and Ephesians wrote: "***Paul*** does not know how to develop a hyperbaton [*i.e.*, a change of normal word order for emphasis], nor to conclude a sentence; and having to do with rude people, he has ***employed the conceptions***, which, if, at the outset, he had not taken care to announce as spoken after the manner of men, ***would have shocked men of good sense***." (Gaussen: 119 quoting *Comm. Galatians* Bk 11, titl. Bk 1, i.1; and *Comm. Ephesians* Bk. 11: 3.1.) In other words, unless you read Paul with extreme care, he is unintelligible and appears contradictory of good sense. One can untangle it, Jerome seems to imply. Yet, Jerome also implies it is very difficult treading to do so. Obviously, basing doctrine on Paul was regarded as precarious in the early church.

What Do We Do With Paul's Cheap Grace Verses?

Then what of the cheap grace verses in Paul such as Romans 4:5? For the one following Christ, this is no problem. For we follow Christ, and always remember His words are above all — as the great prophet John the Baptist said.

Thus, we can take the wise path laid out by Second Peter. It warned us that we can never safely reject Jesus' doctrine. If we do so, even if it is in reliance on Paul's "difficult to understand" cheap grace verses, we will fall from our steadfastness in Christ.

Second Peter was telling us that twisting the costly-grace Paul to become the cheap-grace Paul is a waste of a Christian's time and energy. Study the Master — your one and only Teacher (Matt. 23:10) — just as the Master taught. To spend time trying to make the Master who taught a costly-grace Gospel to match a disciple (Paul) when the disciple cheapens the price of salvation is to invert their relationship. Such an approach makes the disciple the Master, and the Master his inferior, as Kierkegaard warned. God forbid!

Recap On Issues Number One and Two

The big battle is over. *Pisteuo* means *obey* in John 3:16. However, we have other issues to resolve in John 3:16.

Let's review what we have established so far on the translation. Remember what was issue number one as an intepretive issue about John 3:16?

> Does the root of the verb *pisteuo* translated in English as *believes* in the KJV and NIV mean *believe* or *obey, comply, trust,* etc.?

And the second issue was related to the first:

> Is it *pisteuo* "in" Jesus or "for" Jesus" in the original Greek?

We have demonstrated clearly that the verb at issue in John 3:16 means *obey* in this context. It does not mean *believe.* The proofs were:

- Vine's, TDNT, the NIV Dictionary, and Liddell-Scott say the meaning of *pisteuo* can be *obey, comply, trust, commit,* etc. However, one meaning of the verb *pisteuo* does mean *believe* in a fact or assertion. Yet, when the context here has a verb *not of motion* — *pisteuo* — followed by *eis,* the word *eis* is to be translated as *for/unto.* The function of *pisteuo,* whatever it means, is *for* Jesus, not *in* Jesus. The meaning that makes the best sense is *obey* FOR/UNTO Jesus, as Vincent explained.

- The conservative *Fundamental Dictionary of Theology* said that 'faith' in the New Testament was meant to correspond to the 'Old Testament' concept of faith, which inextricably connects *believing* to *surrender* (compliance) and *obedience*. Jesus' doctrine connects OT concepts of obedience to the NT *pistis*.

- Jesus' usage of *pisteuo* in Luke 8:13 showed the seed who is *pisteuo*-ing for a while, then "falls into temptation," withers and hence dies. *Pisteuo* is ended by disobedience.

- John the Baptist — the Greatest Prophet before Christ — said in John 3:36 that those who "keep on *pisteuo*-sing" would keep on having eternal life, but those who "keep on *disobeying* the son have the wrath of God continue to abide on them." As F.F. Bruce maintained, this contrast demonstrates an inspired understanding that those with *pisteuo* should be forewarned that *disobedience* destroys *pisteuo*. The only logical choice for the meaning of *pisteuo* in John 3:36a is *obey*. As Bruce said, all who keep obeying the son are having eternal life, but all those who keep on disobeying the son continue to have the wrath of God abide on them. Thus, John the Baptist used *pisteuo eis* to mean *obey*, not *believe*.

- The usage of other NT writers was comparable. For example, John in John 12:42 spoke of rulers who *epi-pisteuo*-ed for a while, and then their *pistis* ceased due to the sin of cowardice and an unwillingness to confess Christ. John likely meant *obeyed* when he used *epi-pisteuo*, not *believed*.

- Paul in Romans 10:11 used the Greek verb at issue in John 3:16 to render the word *trust* in an 'Old Testament' passage from Isaiah. The word in Isaiah's Hebrew exclusively means *trust*.

- Paul in Romans 1:17 and Galatians 3:11 quotes Habakkuk 2:4. He used *pistis* to translate a word in Hebrew which *only* meant *faithfulness*, not mere belief. Thus, Paul should have understood *faithfulness* as the meaning he was using for justification by *pistis* in those quotes, assuming Paul had a Hebrew knowledge of Habakkuk. Faithfulness means obedient living, not faith. It does not mean belief in some fact or promise.

- Paul in eight passages speaks of the "faithfulness of God" or the "faithfulness of Jesus" by using *pistis:* Romans 3:3; Romans 3:22; Romans 3:26, Galatians 2:16,20, 3:22, Phil. 3:9, and Ephesians 3:12. The alternative notion of *faith* of God or *faith* of Jesus would be a preposterous reading.

- Throughout Paul's other writings, it is obvious his ***primary*** intention is to use the same verb *pisteuo* and its noun form *pistis* to mean *faithfulness* (obedient living). Paul's frequent conception of salvation was that it was lost due to disobedience. This tells us Paul ***primarily*** meant you are saved by *obedience for Christ.* This is a *faithfulness* which entails *obedience.* Paul accordingly must have used the Greek words *pisteuo* (verb) and *pistis* (noun) ***primarily*** to mean *obey* and *faithfulness,* etc., not to mean *believe* and *faith.* If salvation were by a mere mental belief in some facts about Jesus, then it could not be negated by disobedience in these passages from Paul. However, if salvation was by an *obedience* for Jesus, it would be destroyed by disobedience to Him. Since Paul clearly taught in numerous passages that disobedience causes the loss of salvation, Paul used *pistis* to mean *faithfulness,* not *faith,* in these particular passages.

- It is true Paul had some "difficult to understand" passages, as Second Peter described them, which read differently. This is true in particular of Ephesians 2:8-9 and Romans 4:5. However, Second Peter marginalized such "liberty" doctrines as "difficult to understand," and stressed the importance of instead following Jesus' doctrine — so as to not "lose our steadfastness in Christ." Thus, even if Paul had *two* verses that were exceptions to his own typical usage, this does not discount the proof of his common usage of *pistis* to mean *faithfulness.* Moreover, the target we are striving to understand is what ***Jesus (not Paul)*** meant. Jesus is our only "Master" and our "Only Teacher." Consequently, it matters little that a couple of stray problematical verses from a non-apostle cause bewilderment to understand.

Conclusion On Issues One And Two

Thus, when John 3:16 is translated as "believing in the son," it more accurately means *that whosoever keeps on obeying unto Jesus* should have eternal life.

The verse is exhorting obedience to His commands, with a reward of eternal life. Consequently, a true definition of the Greek words *pisteuo eis* in John 3:16 rejects any implication that salvation is by belief in any kind of facts about Jesus. Such a faith has nothing do with salvation *in this passage.* ***This verse assures no one of salvation who simply believes in the facts of the resurrection, that Jesus is Lord and Savior, etc.*** That is not what John 3:16 is talking about. It is talking about obedience, compliance, trust, etc.

Issue #3: Continuity Or One Time Pisteousin?

The third issue we identified at the outset was:

> Is the verb form taken for *pisteuo* which is translated in the KJV as *believes* (the English simple present tense) instead in Greek a continuous tense meaning? In other words, is the meaning *keeps on* or *continues to* in front of whatever the verb means for *pisteuo, i.e.,* keeps on *obeying/complying* or keeps on *believing*?

So is the verb activity of *pisteuo* (whether obey/comply/trust or believes) which 'should lead to eternal life' in John 3:16 merely a *one-time* experience or *continuous*?

Stanley and many others insist it is one-time, not continuous. They claim it is heresy, in fact, to insist anyone who loses *pistis* (whether obedience or belief) could be lost.

Yet, this argument ignores that Jesus in the Parable of the Sower teaches in Luke 8:13 that the seed who "*pisteousin* [obeys or believes] for a while" ends up in temptation, becomes withered and hence dead. It is lost. It is obvious that pisteuo *one time* did not save the second seed.

Thus, let's ask experts how to translate the verb tense in John 3:16. The question is highly narrow: is it a one time *pisteuo* or is it a continuous activity that is required for salvation to be realized?

Synopsis Of Appendix A in *Jesus' Words Only* On The Greek Present Active

Appendix A of my prior work *Jesus' Words Only* (available free online at www.jesuswordsonly.com) discussed the verb tense in John 3:16 in extensive detail. The discussion here is more by way of synopsis than a complete discussion.

In John 3:16, the verb *pisteousin* is in the Greek verb form of *pisteuo* known as the *present participle active.* It is not in the *aorist* tense. Why is the latter fact of importance?

Unlike English, Greek has a specific verb tense for a one-time action. It is known as the *aorist* tense. This can be rendered in English by use of the English Simple Present Tense, *e.g.,* "obeys" or "believes." We can read "believes" in English to mean a one time expression of faith. In fact, Stanley relies upon the fact *believes* is used in common English translations of John 3:16 to prove salvation must be by a one-time *belief* in Jesus, the atonement, etc.[75] Stanley is correct that the English Simple Present Tense has this potential one-time meaning. Thus, the use of *believes* in John 3:16 by many translations **corresponds to the aorist participle** in Greek.

By contrast, in Greek, the **exact opposite** meaning from the *aorist* tense is conveyed by the Greek *present indicative active* or *present participle active.* In Greek, these two forms of the present active tense mean the action is continuing. It is best translated into English using "continues to" or "keeps on" in front of the English gerund.[76]

For example, "he who *continues* to obey" or "he who *keeps on* obeying" is a correct translation of the present participle active of the Greek verb *pisteuo* (if it means *obey*).

---

75. Stanley says "believes" in John 3:16 means a one-time faith. Stanley explains "believes" — the English simple present tense of *to believe* — can mean a one-time event that does not have to continue. From this, Stanley deduces a one-time faith saves. (Stanley, *Eternal Security of the Believer* (Nelson: 1990) at 95.)

The present participle active in NT Greek reflects an "habitual behavior."[77] It signifies a "process [that is] continuous."[78] (This also is still true in modern Greek grammar. *See*, Adams, *Essential Modern Greek Grammar* (1987) at 81.)

This distinction has been recently confessed by a leading Calvinist who is yet a staunch faith-alone advocate. Dr. James White writes about the verb tense in John 6:35-45 (as well as John 3:16) in *Drawn by the Father: A Summary of John 6:35-45* (Reformation Press: 1999) at 10-11:

> Throughout this passage an important truth is presented that again **might be missed by many English translations.** When Jesus describes the one who comes to him and who **believes** in him [3:16, 5:24, 6:35, 37, 40, 47, etc.], he uses the **present tense** to describe this coming, **believing**, or, in other passages, hearing or seeing. The present tense refers to a **continuous, on-going action**. The Greek contrasts this kind of action against the **aorist tense**, which is **a**

---

76. See Appendix A: *Greek Issues* to my prior work *Jesus' Words Only* (2007) for a full discussion. Young's Literal Translation always renders the Greek present indicative active or the present participle active with "[to be] [verb root] + ing" (*e.g.*, "is going."). This is the English Present Continuous tense. It is satisfactory. However, to catch the nuance of the Greek, the NIV was correct to use "keeps on" or "continues to..." as it did so often. However, only *Young's Literal* translation has had the courage so far to fix John 3:16 to read more accurately.

77. Louise Wells, *The Greek Language of Healing from Homer to the New Testament Times* (New York & Berlin: Walter de Gruyter, 1998) at 136 (speaking of the present participle in Matthew 4:23 and 9:35, she say it is "most probably" intended to "describe Jesus' **habitual behavior** while traveling from village to village.")

78. John Eadie, *A Commentary on the Greek Text of Paul to the Colossians* (T&T Clark 1884) at 223 (in Colossians 3:10, the Greek for *renew* is present participle active, meaning "man must be brought back to his original purity, but **the process** of renovation is **continuous**, as the use of the **present participle** indicates.") *Cf.* Edwin Abbott, *Johannine Grammar* (A&C Black: 1906) at 219 ("the present participle means continuousness").

> **point action**, a single action in time that is **not on-going**.... The wonderful promises that are provided by Christ are **not for those who do not truly and continuously believe**. The faith that saves is a living faith, a faith that **always looks** to Christ as Lord and Savior. *Id. at 10-11.*

Yet, those obstinate that grace is cheap, like Dillow, make absolutely desperate claims that the present participle active in Greek lacks *any* continuous sense.[79] This is certainly dogma speaking, not New Testament Greek.

Dillow is fully cognizant of the impact of a continuous tense translation upon salvation doctrine. Salvation would hang upon the individual's persistence, not *faith alone*. Thus, Dillow fights off the continuous tense meaning with aggressive words. Yet, these shoot himself later in his foot:

> That [those claiming a continuous sense] have to hang so much of their argument on the supposed durative force of the present [participle] tense can only be a source of concern. *A theological system which depends on such things*

---

79. Dillow at first admits that "it is true the present tense *sometimes* carry a durative force ('continue')." (*Servant Kings, supra,* at 200.) Then he claims the "present participle... *rarely*, if ever, has durative force...." Next, he says a continuous meaning for the present tense "is not only foreign to normal Greek usage but to usage in English as well." (*Id.*) Dillow is going from one outrageous statement to another. He next says: "The notion that the present tense [in Jn 3:16 having a continuing aspect] is not only contrary to the normal conventions of any language but is not supported by Greek grammar." (*Reign of the Servant Kings, supra,* at 200). Besides this being false for Greek, Dillow is also clearly wrong as to English. "Continuous verb forms [in English] combine a form of *be* with the present participle...to indicate an action in progress or a continuing action, *e.g.,*...I am reading." (Elizabeth Coehlo, *Adding English: A Guide to Teaching in Multilingual Classrooms* (Pippin: 2004) at 76.) I have not misconstrued Dillow. For later he says the Greek present participle active really only has the meaning of a noun. No action is involved. "It acts simply as a noun. So when John refers in [1 Jn] 5:1 to 'everyone who believes,' it is simply a misuse of Greek grammar to insist that John means 'everyone who continues to believe." (*Reign of the Servant Kings, supra,* at 470.)

> *is leaning on a broken reed.*" (*Reign of the Servant Kings, supra,* at 470-71.)

But Dillow's notions of the present participle active, evidently driven by his desire to protect *faith alone* doctrine, are what stand on a broken reed.

Hence, John 3:16 should read instead that God so loved the world that all who "***keep on*** obeying" or "***continue to*** obey" should be having eternal life.

Is It 'Should' Or 'Shall' Have Eternal Life?

Another interpretive question about John 3:16 includes whether the verb for *have eternal life* is preceded by *shall* or *should.* The NIV says John 3:16 is about a promise that you "shall" have eternal life. Yet, the YLT, RV, and Vulgate spell out clearly that it is "should" have eternal life. The word *shall* in English conveys certainty. The word *should* in English conveys a degree of uncertainty.

As explained in my prior book, *Jesus' Words Only* (2007), at 381, the correct translation is *should.*

Source Of Assurance

If salvation is no longer by a simple affirmation of beliefs about Jesus, whence comes assurance of salvation?

Jesus said if we "keep on ***listening*** and keep on ***following***" then "we should not perish" and "***shall*** not be taken away (*harpazo*-ed) from my hand." (John 10:27-28.)[80]

---

80. Compare this to John 15:2 which says the "branch in me" that does not produce fruit is "harpazo-ed" — taken away, later to be thrown outside and burned. (See John 15:2,6.) In John 10:27-28, this same result is avoided by *listening* and *following.* In John 15:5, this same result is avoided by being fruitful which in turn requires that you must "stay in" Jesus, which Jesus then defines as His "word" is abiding in us and His love is abiding in us by "obeying His commandments." (John 15:7, 10.) Hence, *listening* and *following* means *obeying* with *knowledge* of Jesus' precepts, commands and teachings.

Notice the verbs in John 10:27-28 are *listening* and *following*. Assurance relies upon principles of endurance in synonyms for ongoing obedience: *listening* and *following*.

Conclusion

"For God so loved the world that He gave His only begotten son that whosoever keeps on obeying unto Him should not perish but should have eternal life." (John 3:16.)

This was identical as well as a companion verse to John 8:51:

> Most positively, I say to you, ***if anyone keeps on obeying (tereo) My word***, he should never ever see death into eternity (*ainon*) [fig., forever]! (John 8:51.)

Unfortunately, this beautiful message from Jesus has been utterly mangled in modern translations of John 3:16. It is obvious this error persists due to a reluctantcy to admit the doctrine exuberantly discovered in 1517 in Paul's writings needs to be toned down to make room for Jesus' doctrine.

Thus, the majority who call themselves Christians today have walked away from the ***true Jesus***. They cannot face Jesus in all His bluntness, even when He said, "Every tree without good fruit is cast in the fire" (Matt. 7:19). They insist, Jesus must save them without any good fruit. They often rely on John 3:16 to demand of God that obedience can play no role in salvation. Consequently, one of the greatest tragedies in Biblical translation is that John 3:16 has become ***a salvation-deadening*** verse, by reading it the opposite of its true meaning, rather than a salvation-invigorating verse.

27 *Faith Alone*

William Paley's Explains Problems With Faith Alone Doctrine

At this juncture, let's turn to no less a figure than Reverend William Paley (1743-1805) — someone you all know and trust — to address the most thorny of issues in Christian history: is Jesus' salvation message one of faith alone?

Paley was a famous Christian preacher in his day. The Chambers *Cyclopedia of English Literature* (1844) under "Dr. Paley" at page 651 *et seq.* says "he was the greatest divine of the period," gifted with "remarkable vigor and clearness of intellect, and originality of character." Paley's 1794 *View of the Evidences of Christianity* gave him his initial fame. Chambers comments on the many subsequent and popular writings of Paley. Chambers notes that Paley's "perspicacity of intellect and simplicity of style are almost unrivaled." Paley later became well-known as the formulator in 1802 of the watchmaker argument in favor of God as designer of the universe.

However, William Paley was much more than this. He realized the tension between Christ's Gospel and the faith alone gospel. Paley decidedly came out in favor of the Gospel of the Lord Jesus in contrast to that of faith alone. There were others to follow in Paley's footsteps, such as Kierkegaard and Bonhoeffer. But Paley was among the loudest voices ever to take on *faith alone* doctrine despite the possible social repercussions. He argued *faith alone* was contrary to the doctrine taught by Jesus. Paley offered many substantial proofs. This argument is put forth in Paley's Sermons in *The Works of William Paley* (1825) volume six at page 201 *et seq.* You can download this book from books.google.com for free, and read the entire original text at your leisure. It is linked at my website. Here, for your consideration, is a synopsis.

Paley's Dismantling Of Faith Alone Doctrine

First, Paley disarmed the faith alone doctrine by quoting Paul's own words that contradict faith alone. From Romans 2:7-8, he quotes: "To them, who by patient continuance in well-doing [*lit.*, "endure in *good works*"] seek for glory and immortality eternal life: but unto them that are contentious, obey not the truth, but *obey unrighteousness*, tribulation and anguish upon every soul of man that *doeth evil*." Again in Galatians 5:21, Paley quotes Paul saying: "Of the which," namely, certain enumerated sins, "I tell you before, as I have also told you in time past, that they, which do such things, shall not inherit the kingdom of God." (Sermon 209, *The Works of William Paley* (1825) Vol. 6 at 204.)

Then Paley drives home the point that this proves the "necessity of virtue" and the "danger of vice." Paley says:

> These are amongst many texts of the same effect, and they **such as can never be got over**. Stronger terms cannot be devised than what are here used. Were the purpose, therefore, simply to prove from Scripture **the necessity of virtue, and the danger of vice**, so far salvation is concerned, **these texts are decisive**. *Id.*, at 204.

Paley then admitted that indeed there are many "strong passages" in Paul that stand for faith alone. Paley quotes them at length, thereby fairly presenting the dilemma to "serious persons." Then he says: "These, no doubt, are strong

Paley

texts, and...they have led many *serious persons* to lay such a stress upon them, as to exclude good works from being considered even as a condition of salvation." *Id.* at 213.

Paley then concedes if these passages were taken *alone*, then the point of faith alone is established. Yet, this is not the end of the matter. "Scripture is to be compared with Scripture; particular texts with other particular texts; and especially with the main tenor of the whole." *Id.*, at 214.

Paley then sets forth his thesis on Paul's writings as not truly endorsing faith alone (or at least that a follower of Christ cannot accept faith alone as a sufficient point):

> He [Paul] did not mean to lay it down as an article to be received by his disciples, that a man leading a wicked life, without change and without repentance, ***will nevertheless be saved at the last by his belief of the doctrines of the Christian religion***; still less did he mean to encourage any one to go on in a course of sin, expressly and intentionally ***comforting and protecting himself by this opinion***. *Id.*, at 214.

Paley's proof was clear that for Paul to be construed as teaching faith alone would be contrary to all other Scripture (Jesus) and contrary to what Paul himself said in the quotes above (and the other passages Paley will cite below):

> He, the Apostle, could not mean to say this; because if he did, he would say what is expressly and ***positively contradicted by other texts of at least equal authority with his own***; he would say what is contradicted by the very drift and design of the Christian constitution; and would say, lastly, ***what is expressly denied and contradicted by himself***. *Id.* at 214.[1]

Paley then provides proof first from Jesus — whom Paley calls "the ***very highest authority***." Of course, Paul, being a mere man when compared to Jesus, must have his doctrines tested by those of Christ Jesus. As Luther once said if any contradiction exists between a mere man and an unquestionably *inspired* source, the mere man must fall:

"Now [if] [*inspired*] Scriptures and the doctrines of men are contrary one to the other, the one must lie and the other be true." (*Luther Works*, Vol. 35: 153.)

Paley quotes and comments on what the "very highest authority" — Jesus — had to say on salvation:

> For instance, what words can be **plainer, more positive, or more decisive of this point** than our Saviour's own? "Not every one that saith unto me, Lord, Lord, shall enter into the kingdom of Heaven, but he that doeth the will of my Father which is in Heaven." [Matt. 7:21.] **There can be no doubt but that they who are here introduced as crying out to Jesus Christ 'Lord, Lord,' are supposed to believe in him**; yet neither their devotion, nor their faith which prompted it, were sufficient to save them. *Id.*, at 214-215.

As another commentator says: "[In] Matthew 7:21-27...[n]o fault is found with the *faith* of those that were cast out, but for disobedience they were condemned."[2]

After discussing Matthew 7:21, Paley next explains how Jesus re-emphasizes the same point in the very next sentence. Jesus speaks unquestionably of those who had faith (*i.e.*, workers of prophecies and miracles in Jesus' name), but whose faith alone did not suffice:

> Nay, farther our Lord, in the same passage, proceeds to tell his hearers, that many will say to

---

1. Reverend George Horne (1730-1792), later Dean of Oxford, spelled out the same case. After establishing Jesus' clear doctrine on the necessity of works in the Parable of the Sheep and the Goats, and Jesus' assurance of a judgment by works (Matt. 12:36; Rev. 22:12), Horne preached: "Marvellous would it be if, after this, we should find the great apostle of the Gentiles **preaching a contrary doctrine**. But having made our ground good thus far, we shall easily be able, by a short state of that case, to show that he doth not, but harmonizeth in every respect with his brother apostle [*i.e.*, Matthew]." (*Discourses of the Right Reverend George Horne* (London: 1824) III at 185.)

---

him in that day, "Have we not prophesied in thy name, and in thy name have cast out devils, and in thy name done many wonderful works?" [Matt. 7:22.] *It cannot be questioned but that they who do these things in Christ's name believe in Christ.* Yet what will be their reception? "I will profess unto you I never knew you." And who are they who shall be thus repulsed and rejected? No others than *the workers of iniquity.* "Depart from me, ye workers of iniquity." [Matt. 7:23.] *Id.* at 215.

Paley had copious proofs, and found in John the one we emphasized earlier on those who do good things are resurrected. See page 395. Paley quotes and comments this way:

The *difference* between *doing good and doing evil* according to another declaration of our Saviour, is no less than this: "They that have done good shall come forth unto the resurrection of life; they that have done evil, unto the resurrection of damnation." [John 5:29] *Can a greater distinction be made, or expressed in words more plain*? *Id.,* at 215.

Paley goes on to say the entire tenor of the Sermon on the Mount is to require obedience to enter into heaven. To deny this is to deny the point of the sermon itself:

---

2. *Free Will Baptist* (January 1860) at 78. The hypocrisy which Jesus always condemned was having a belief in Himself or legal principles that was not matched by obedience to Himself or those principles. Jesus asked why do you call Him "Lord, Lord" but do "not keep my commandments?" (Luke 6:46.) The Parable of the Good Samaritan emphasized the hypocrisy of the Levite who taught the Law properly about murder but then when the situation arose to aid a dying assault victim, the Levite continues on his way. Jesus then made the point by exalting, by contrast, the one with somewhat incorrect belief (the Samaritan sect member) who obeyed the Law! Thus, correct belief does not save you if you do not obey. Slightly wrong belief (the Samaritan) does not damn you if you later correctly obey.

All the preceptive part of our Lord's teaching, especially his whole **Sermon upon the Mount**, may be alleged on the same side of the argument. And to **substitute belief in the place of the duties there enjoined**, or as an expiation for the offences there forbidden, even when persevered in, **would in effect set aside the authority of the lawgiver.** And did our Lord command and forbid these things (or indeed any thing), if he did not require obedience as a condition of salvation? *Id.*, at 215.

Paley then goes into the question of what Jesus meant by *repentance*, which was Jesus' repeated theme: repent or perish. Paley said this implied good works as a condition of salvation. If this meaning to repentance is denied, Paley says this denies the mission and message of Jesus:

Again, every thing which we read concerning **repentance implies the necessity of good works to salvation**, and the **inconsistency of bad works with salvation**: for **repentance is a change from one to the other,** and can be required upon no other supposition than this. But of repentance we hear continually in the New Testament, and from the first to the last of the great mission of which it contains the history.

Paley began his proof of this sub-point by citing John the Baptist demanding "works worthy of repentance." (Matt. 3:8.) Paley then alludes to Jesus' message to the young rich man and the torah-scholar who asked how to have eternal life. Paley says Jesus' response to these men was each had to repent from the sins to which they had succumbed, *i.e.*, greed and failure to love everyone:

When particular classes of men come to inquire of their teacher [Jesus] what they should do, his answer was **a warning against those particular sins to which persons of**

> *their class and character were most liable*,
> which is his own application of his own princi-
> ple. *Id.* at 216.

All of which goes to prove that repentance is not in
the mind alone, but in deeds too. Paley concludes the point:

> All proves that a moral change, *a moral
> improvement, practical sins, and practical
> virtues, and a turning from one to the other*,
> was what he included in the awful admonition
> which he sounded in the ears of mankind. *Id.*,
> at 216.

But many faith alone advocates say Jesus' salvation
doctrine only applies to a distinct pre-Ascension dispensation
of Law. Jesus' soteriology was allegedly replaced by faith
alone at the Ascension — which ushered in the era of Grace.
Paley says in response *no*.

Paley points out that Peter's first sermon after Jesus'
departure had the same message of repentance in the era of
grace that Jesus taught before the Crucifixion. Quoting Peter
from Acts, Paley says: "*Repent* and be baptized, every one of
you, in the name of Jesus Christ, for *the remission of sins*."
(Acts 2:38.) "*Repent* ye, therefore, and be converted, that
your sins may be blotted out." (Acts 3:19.) *Remission of sins*
and *blotting out sins* are obvious synonyms for salvation.

Incidentally, forty years after Jesus' ascension, Apostle John still had the same idea about how repentance (with
obedience) blots out sin: "But *if* we *walk in the light*, as he is
in the light [*i.e.*, obey Jesus' commandments], we have fellowship one with another, and *the blood of Jesus his Son
cleanseth us from all sin*....(9) *If* we *confess our sins* [*i.e.*,
repent from sin], he is faithful and righteous to *forgive us our
sins*, and to *cleanse us* [by Jesus' blood] from all unrighteousness." (1 John 1:7,9, ASV.) James too had the same idea
twenty years after the Ascension, when he wrote that if a
"brother" should "err," but you "turn back a sinner from the
error of his way, [you] will save a soul from death, and will
hide a multitude of sins." (James 5:19-20.)

In light of this clear consistency of salvation-messages before and after the Cross, Paley says the Apostle Peter's meaning and Jesus' meaning (as well as Apostle John's and James' meaning) were identical: repentance unto good works and obedience saves. Nothing changed after the Cross. The same gospel Jesus preached before the Cross was the gospel preached by His *true* apostles after the Cross:

> This is the explicit language the Apostle [Peter] held upon the subject of repentance; which, as hath already been observed, **has a precise reference to a good and bad life**; and these texts deliver no other judgement concerning the matter than what their great teacher had pronounced before. *Id.*, at 217.

We brought out all such evidences about the meaning of *repentance* in a prior chapter on "Repent or Perish." See page 87 *et seq.*

Thus, contrary to what dispensationalism doctrine teaches today, the twelve apostles had the same gospel Jesus preached about repentance from sin *after* Pentecost in Acts chapter one (and even much later) as Jesus taught prior to the cross. The salvation message of Jesus was not solely for a prior era under a law covenant. Rather, the identical gospel to Jesus' gospel continued into the so-called era of grace. Paley with great wit and wisdom demolished the popular dispensational argument of our era.

Finally, Paley says Paul must be compared to James — one of at least equal stature to Paul:

> By comparing Saint Paul's words with other Scriptures, **we cannot overlook that well-known text of Saint James**: "What doth it profit, my brethren, though a man say he hath faith, and not works; can faith save him?" [James 2:14.] Saint James doth not here suppose the man hypocritically, and for some sinister purpose, to pretend to believe what he does not believe. The illustration which fol-

lows *plainly supposes the belief to be real*, for he compares it to the case of the devils, who believe and tremble. Now we are to remember that *Saint James's words are Scripture, as well as Saint Paul's*. Here, *therefore, is a text, which precisely, and in the most pointed terms, contradicts the sense which the Solifidians put upon Saint Paul's words. Id.*, at 217.

Paley's view of the weight and purpose to give James is in line with Augustine's historical account in *Faith and Works* (*De Fide et operibus*) from 413 A.D. Augustine explained that three letters — the epistles of James, Peter and Jude — were early on written with the "deliberate aim" of refuting the "treacherous" view of those who had "the illusion that *faith alone* was sufficient for salvation."[3]

Incidentally, the weight and purpose of the Epistle of James undeniably was to address a perceived claim in the earlier epistles of Paul in favor of faith alone. This fact is highlighted by Reverend Jeremy Taylor (1613-1667)'s comparing and contrasting the two main points of James against Paul's two points to the contrary:

But that this justification is wrought by faith without works, "to him that worketh not, but believeth," saith St. Paul: that this is not wrought without works, St. James *is as express for his negative as St. Paul was for his affirmative*; and how both these should be true, is

---

3. Quoted in David R. Nienhuis, *Not By Paul Alone* (Baylor University Press, 2007) at 87. Augustine also says that when faith-alone doctrine arose, the epistles of James, Peter, Jude, etc. "direct their aim chiefly against it, so as *with vehemence to maintain that faith without works profits not....*" (Augustine, *Fide et operibus*, trans. Cornish:57.) Augustine explains this is why Second Peter 3:11-18 talks of Paul's "obscure sentences" which evil men used to argue one can "*secure...salvation...[by] faith*," relying on Paul's passages which are "difficult to understand," being thus *perverted* unto their own destruction. (*Id.*, Augustine, trans. Cornish:58.)

something harder to unriddle. But,... "he that affirms must prove;" and, therefore, St. Paul proves his doctrine by the example of Abraham, to whom faith was imputed for righteousness; and, therefore, not by works. And what can be answered to this? Nothing but this, that **St. James uses the very same argument to prove that our justification is by works also** "For our father Abraham was justified by works when he offered up his son Isaac." [James 2:9] Now which of these says true?[4]

Thus, the point of Paley and Taylor was that if the higher authority of Jesus' words needed any corroboration, they come from His brother James. That epistle of James addresses the tension between all of Jesus' teachings and the faith alone view found sometimes in Paul. James' epistle, speaking *after* Paul's writings, gives a decided nod to Jesus' doctrines over that of Paul's sometimes-stated faith alone view.

Where does this tension lead? Paley concludes from these proofs above that Paul's words, if interpreted to set aside the "obligation and necessity of good works" cannot then "be the true sense of Saint Paul's words" or otherwise "it is *contrary to... Christianity itself.*" That is, Paul would be contrary to the Master — "the very highest authority" in the church. And Paul would be contrary to the true twelve apostles who were clearly calling Christians to Christ's *true* and *unmistakable* doctrine of the necessity of repentance/fruit/works for salvation-sake.

Paley then addresses the counter-argument that he is wrongly rejecting Paul's plain sense of faith alone. Paley responds by saying the paramount consideration is whether

---

4. Rev. Jeremy Taylor, *Fides Formata* in *The Whole Works of the Right Reverend Jeremy Taylor, D.D.* (London: 1851) II at 20.

faith-alone, if Paul's true meaning, would contradict even *higher authority.* This is a dilemma for the faith alone adherent, not Paley, because

> such sense [of faith alone] is **inconsistent with** what is delivered by authority as great as his own, and **greater,** and **inconsistent also with the main drift and purpose of that very institution [founded on Christ's doctrine]**....*Id.,* at 219.

Paley then says the problem is resolved by noting Paul's self-contradictions require a firm resolution in favor of Jesus' doctrine. To this end, Paley remarks on how important it is to note these self-contradictions by Paul come in the same epistle where faith alone is apparently endorsed, thereby creating the quandary. (Paul never uses the words "faith alone," and hence it is always dependent on one's *inference* that 'faith alone' was Paul's doctrine.)

It is one thing, Paley says, for Paul to contradict himself on faith alone in two different writings, but it is a wholly different dilemma when the contradiction is in the *very same epistle* where 'faith alone' is deduced. The only solution is then to spare Paul the charge of self-contradiction by construing him consistent with the higher authority (Jesus):

> For though a man may advance what is contrary to sound reason, what is contrary to other authority, nay, what is contrary to his own professions at other times, and in other writings, yet **surely his words ought not to be interpreted, if there be any fair way of avoiding it, in such a manner as to make him contradict himself in the same discourse.** *Id.,* at 219.

Paley then starts by drawing out the conflicting passages on good works in Romans.

> Again: though it be true that Saint Paul in this epistle concludes "that a man is justified by faith without the deeds of the law" [Romans

3:28], yet *in the same epistle he had before told us*, that "God will *render to every man according to his deeds*; to them, *who by patient continuance in well doing*,[5] seek for glory, and honour, and immortality, *eternal life*; but unto them that are contentious, and do not obey the truth, but *obey unrighteousness*, indignation and *wrath*, tribulation and anguish, upon every soul of man that doeth evil, of the Jews first, and also of the Gentiles." [Rom. 2:6-7.] Therefore, his expression concerning faith, in the third chapter of this epistle, though strong, *must not be so construed as to make the author assert the direct contrary of what he had asserted just before in the second chapter.*

Paley cites another example of self-contradiction on faith alone in Romans.

Nor is it possible to reconcile with this opinion [of faith alone] the two following texts, taken out of the *same epistle*: "The wages of sin is *death*;" chap. vi. verse 23. "If ye live after the flesh, ye shall die; but if ye, through the *spirit*, *do mortify the deeds of the body*, ye shall *live*;" chap. viii. verse 13.

Death and life in 8:13 obviously speak of damnation and salvation. For even a disciple of Christ must physically die. Thus, this means if you "mortify the deeds of the body," then you shall have eternal life. If, to the contrary, you "live

---

5. Paley constrained himself to use the KJV translation of *erga* as "deeds" in Romans 2:6 rather than *works*. Yet, *erga/ergon* is rendered everywhere else in Paul's epistles as *works/work*. Paley also suffered to permit the KJV's rendering in Romans 2:7 of the exchange of eternal life for *ergon agathon*. The expression means he who endures (*hupomeno*) in "good work" does so to receive eternal life, in Paul's own words. Yet, the KJV rendered *ergon agathon* as "well-doing." Despite the KJV's effort to obscure the contradiction of Paul with Paul by means of shifting the translation, Paley brought the contradiction to light.

---

after the flesh," you shall be damned. Paul here has a clear echo of Jesus' heaven-maimed or hell-whole message. (Mark 9:42-47.)

Paley then moves on to Galatians to demonstrate another similar contradiction. Paul appears again to endorse faith alone but then he says salvation is by moral obedience:

> The same species of observation applies to the epistle to the Galatians; in which epistle, it is true, that the Apostle hath used concerning faith these ***very strong terms***: "Knowing that a man is not justified by the works of the law, but by the faith of Jesus Christ, even we have believed in Jesus Christ; that we might be justified by the faith of Christ, and not by the works of the law; for by the works of the law shall no flesh be justified." [Gal. 2:16.] Nevertheless, ***in another place of this same epistle***, we have the following ***plain, clear, and circumstantial denunciation***: "The works of the flesh are manifest, which are these—Adultery, fornication, uncleanness, lasciviousness, idolatry, witchcraft, hatred, variance, emulations, wrath, strife, seditions, heresies, envyings, murders, drunkenness, revellings, and such like; of the which I tell you before, as I have told you in time past, that they which do such things shall not inherit the kingdom of God." [Gal. 5:19-20.] ***No words can be more positive than these, and the last words are the most positive of all***, "shall not inherit the kingdom of God." Sinners like these may have been justified in a certain sense; they may have been saved in a certain sense; that is, they may have been brought into a state of justification or salvation for the present; ***but they shall not be finally happy***, "they shall not inherit the kingdom of God." *Id.*, at 221.

Then, most ironically of all, in the epistle where Paul endorses 'faith, not works' (Eph. 2:8-9), Paul also says you lose salvation for misbehavior. Paley continues:

> In the epistle to the Ephesians, **we acknowl-edge the same observation, namely,** that [Paul] hath spoken strong things concerning faith; yet hath **at the same time, and in the same writing, most absolutely insisted upon a virtuous life, and most positively declared that a life of sin will end in perdition**. Con-cerning faith, he hath said this: "By grace are ye saved through faith; and that not of yourselves, it is the gift of God: not of works, lest any man should boast." [Eph. 2:8-9.] Concerning **a life of sin, he makes this declaration**. After having enumerated certain species of sins, he adds these cautionary words, which **show his opin-ion as manifestly as words can show it**: "Let no man deceive you with vain words; for because of these things, even the sinful prac-tices before recited, cometh the wrath of God upon the children of disobedience." [Eph. 5:6-7.] *Id.*, at 221-22.

John Locke's Elaboration On Paley's Argument

To Paley's list and argument about Paul's self-contra-dictions, John Locke (1632-1704) would like to now add his elaboration on Romans 8:13. John Locke was a physician and philosopher as well as the famous author of *The Two Trea-tises on Government* (1690). Locke also did commentaries on much of the New Testament in a most serious manner.

To Paley's case, Locke elaborates on Romans 8:13 to prove salvation is not by faith alone. Locke then goes on to explain the seeming contradiction within Paul's thought. In Romans 8:13, Paul implies works-of-obedience are needed for eternal life: "for if ye live after the flesh, ye must die; but if by the Spirit *ye put to death the deeds of the body, ye shall live*." (Rom 8:13 ASV.) The antithesis is clear: the wages of sin to the flesh is eternal death, but sowing to the spirit reaps eternal life. Paul says this again even more clearly in Galatians 6:8 KJV: "For he that *soweth to his flesh* shall of the flesh reap corruption; but he that *soweth to the Spirit shall of the Spirit reap life everlasting*." Thus, salvation in Romans 8:13 (and Galatians 6:8) is correlated directly to disobedience vs. obedience. John Locke saw the apparent contradiction to Paul's doctrine on works, and proposed a solution. Locke said Romans 8:13 clearly means those who "are actually under the covenant of grace, *good works are strictly required*, under the *penalty of the loss of eternal life*."[6] This was Tyndale's doctrine of double justification. (See page v.)

Three More Internal Contradictions in Paul's Doctrine

Repentance unto Salvation. I would also like to add three more self-contradictions from Paul to the list. The first is on *repentance unto salvation.*

Paul contradicts himself by saying repentance *from sin* is unto salvation. However, this is directly contrary to *faith alone* to salvation. These problem verses start with Paul in 2 Corinthians 7:9-10 (ALT) saying "I now rejoice... because you were caused *sorrow to repentance*... (10) For the sorrow according to God *produces repentance to salvation*, free from regret, but the *sorrow of the world produces death*." Hence, mere sorrow without repentance is not godly sorrow, and leads to death, but sorrow *with repentance* leads to salvation. This is precisely what Jesus taught. Mere sorrow or a change in mind about sin does not save. But sorrow that leads to repentance, *i.e.*, a reform of behavior, is unto salvation.

Paul reiterates the centrality of such reform-of-character repentance when he says in Acts 17:30 ALT: "Therefore indeed, [these] times of ignorance having overlooked, God is

---

6. *The Works of John Locke* (London: Thomas Tegg, 1828) Vol. VIII at 415 (available Google Books)(emphasis added.)

now giving *strict orders to all people everywhere to be repenting.*" Or as the NLT renders it, God "commands every-one everywhere to *repent of their sins and turn to Him.*" Obviously, anything less disobeys God and cannot be the "repentance to salvation" God requires, as expressed in 2 Corinthians 7:9-10.

However, Paul in Romans 4:4-5 says upon mere belief God "justifies the ungodly." All commentators — Rob-ertson, Gill, Clarke, Ryrie, etc. — agree this verse means faith alone justifies you *without repentance from sin and any reform of one's life*. See page 481 and "Pisteuo In Romans 4:5a" on page 483. The young Luther relied upon this to say one was justified "regardless of what your contrition might be" because of your faith alone. (Luther, *Sermon on Indul-gences* (1517).)

Consequently, Paul's view of repentance is another contradiction within Paul's thought. In one passage, he agrees with Jesus that repentance from sin leads to salvation (2 Corinthians 7:9-10), while in another Paul is in seeming dis-sent by claiming that faith (alone) leads to salvation without repentance, even for an ungodly (unrepentant) person. (Romans 4:4-5.)

Faith Without Charity Makes You Nothing. A second self-contradiction by Paul I would add to Paley's list is Paul's *dim* view of faith in comparison to the importance of charity. Paul repeated Jesus' point from the Parable of the Sheep and the Goats that faith alone does not suffice for the goats: "though I have all *faith* so that I could remove mountains, and have *not charity*, I am *nothing*." (1 Cor. 13:2.) Consistent with this, Paul says when charity and faith are compared, "the greatest of these [virtues] is charity." (1 Cor.13:13.)

If Paul's two statements are true about *faith*, and you are nothing without charity, then faith alone without charity makes you *nothing,* and hence profits you nothing, including salvation. Hence, charity is more important than *faith* because it is indispensable to make you *something,* and hence capable of being saved. On the other hand, if instead faith without charity could save, then faith alone would make you at least *something*. Thus, it must follow, if *faith alone* makes you nothing, as Paul says, then faith alone cannot save while you are yet *nothing*.

Moreover, if faith alone saves, then faith always would be the superior virtue to charity. Yet, if charity were indispensable to add to faith to be saved, as Jesus clearly teaches in the Parable of the Sheep and the Goats, then charity would be the superior virtue to have between faith and charity. But if charity were optional to be saved, faith would always have to be the superior virtue to have. Yet what is Paul's view? Paul precisely confirms Jesus' greater emphasis on charity over mere faith. Hence, faith alone cannot be what saves because if true, then Paul could not view faith as a virtue of lesser value than charity. If Paul thought faith **alone** saves, faith would always have to be of superior value in every respect because it *alone* imparts justification and salvation which is the supreme good from God among all things which He bestows. Instead, charity, Paul says, is superior in every respect. Hence, Paul cannot possibly believe faith alone saves. At least, not in these passages.

Yet, in Ephesians 2:8-9, the implication is the opposite. It appears, faith not works (evidently including works of charity) is what saves. Thereby we have another self-contradiction in Paul's reasonings. Paul in one passage (1 Cor. 13:2,13) agrees with Jesus on the essential nature of charity for salvation, just as Jesus teaches in the Parable of the Sheep and the Goats, but then, in another passage, Paul undermines the Master's point, making faith, not charity, of exclusive importance.

Justification Is Uncertain Until Death. I would note one final cluster of contradictions within Paul's writings. It is a decisive cluster. Paul speaks about "justification" as even uncertain for *himself* and something for a believer to *fear* losing. This passage is rarely taught. This is because the typical evangelical sermon claims that Paul's doctrine on *faith alone* is to liberate us from fearing God when we sin if we just have faith and hence assurance. For example, Presbyterian Pastor Huneke, in a classic formula I heard in many sermons during my tutelage in a reformed church, scares non-believers away from ever fearing God. If we fear God about punishing our sin, we supposedly can never be saved. He says: "Guilt keeps us from faith, its fear turns our hearts from Christ, and its shame prevents us from being... disciples of Christ."[7] This is the same teaching we saw previously from the famous pastor, Max Lucado. (See page 65.)

Yet, Paul encourages *believers* repeatedly to the contrary — to precisely have such fear. In fact, Paul says in Romans 11:20-22 that a fearless attitude about assurance is "high minded." His words are "be not high-minded, but *fear*: for if God spared not the natural branches, neither will he spare you." Paul is threatening believing Gentiles about being cut off the tree that represents the body of believers. Likewise, in Philippians 2:12-13, Paul says "continue to **work out** your **salvation** with **fear** and trembling to its completion, for it is God who energizes (*energeo*) you to do and to will according to what pleases Him." Most telling of all, Paul in 1 Corinthians 4:2-5 says it is wrong to assure anyone of their justification before the day of judgment, including himself! He writes:

> Here, moreover, it is **required** in stewards, that a man be found **faithful** [*pistos*, noun nominative]. (3) But with me it is a very small thing that I should be judged of you, or of man's judgment: yea, *I judge not mine own self*. (4) For *I know nothing against myself*; yet am *I not hereby justified* [*dikaioo*]: but he that judgeth me is the Lord. (5) Wherefore **judge nothing before the time**, until the Lord come, who will both bring to light the hidden things of

---

7. His sermon *Guilt and Grace: Cheap or Costly* (May 2002).

darkness, and make manifest the counsels of the hearts; and then shall each man have his praise from God. (1Corinthians 4:2-5 ASV.)

Clarke explains Paul means here that while at that moment Paul knows nothing sinful in himself, he is not "hereby justified," using the same Greek term when Paul speaks of Abraham's justification. Paul then says before judgment day, no one should judge himself *justified*, for all secret things will eventually be revealed. Paul says in verse two what will be required is *faithfulness* (*i.e.*, obedient living) from every servant. Paul actually uses a Greek word which means that every servant must be found to have been a *faithful* person.

Hence, Paul clearly contradicts the concept deduced from Romans 4:3-5 and Ephesians 2:8-9 that faith justifies without faithfulness to follow. In 1 Corinthians 4:2-4, if words have meaning, Paul in fact says to assure yourself that you will be justified in God's eyes before the time of judgment is *presumptuous* and *high-minded*. It is PRIDE — the number one sin of the devil himself.[8] Thus, a great part of the evangelical church teaches a justification which Paul himself, in effect, said was presumptuous, prideful and of the devil!

Returning Now To Paley's Argument On Faith Alone

Paley then astutely comments that in light of such clear teachings from Paul on the necessity of obedience and good works, and the salvation-danger of sin to a Christian (to which one must add Paul's warning against the pride and folly of fearless assurance), we may never know what Paul meant by his faith alone verses. Yet, what *we can eliminate*

---

8. There is one more contradiction, at least if Paul is read correctly in places distinguishing "salvation" from "sanctification." It is a common reading of Paul that obedience is for sanctification, not salvation. Paul contradicts that distinction in 2 Thess. 2:13 when Paul equates sanctification with salvation: "God chose you from the beginning unto *salvation in sanctification of the Spirit* and *belief* of the truth."

as a possibility is that Paul meant good works and obedience were optional for salvation. Paley means Paul is just too clear too often in that opposing direction to deny Paul meant good works and obedience were essential for salvation. Paley infers hence that the deduction of faith alone from Paul is necessarily a wrong deduction. As Reverend Jeremy Taylor similarly taught a generation before Paley, "from [Paul]'s mistaken words much noise hath been made in this question" to prove faith alone. (*The Whole Works of the Right Reverend Jeremy Taylor, D.D.* (London: 1851) at 22.)[9]

---

9. The young Luther had a different hermeneutical approach, which made Paul the key to Scripture rather than treating Jesus as the SOLE TEACHER. This led to subjective and arbitrary results which marginalized Jesus. In his 1522 *Preface to the New Testament*, Luther rejected James' Epistle as canon due to its direct conflict with Paul. Luther also rejected Revelation as canon for obviously the same reason. Luther also expressly minimized the salvation-message in the Synoptic Gospels because they did not speak as clearly about the "glorious" gospel of Paul. (See my prior book, *Jesus' Words Only* (2007) at 33.)

What of Jesus' contrary teachings to Paul's faith-alone verses? The young Luther said if those passages from Jesus are not as clear as Paul's faith alone view, Paul's view stands above them. Fisher explains Luther's logic: "Those Scriptures in which the truth [of faith alone] — considered to be the substance of the gospel — had the central place, furnished the criterion for gauging the relative value and the degree of inspiration to be attributed other sacred writings." (George Park Fisher, *The History of Christian Doctrine* (T&T Clark: 1896) at 280.) Yet, as Fisher points out, when you use the doctrine of *justification by faith* in Paul's writings to reject other passages (predominantly Jesus' words in the Synoptics and Revelation), you are relying upon a subjective and arbitrary standard. You have abandoned *the objective higher standard* — Jesus' words. You are using a subjective appreciation of Paul's ideas and arguments to subvert *clear* passages from Jesus. This is an arbitrary and unprincipled rejection of Christ's words. What Paley is further doing is showing that Paul's words on *faith alone* can never be clearer than Jesus' words because Paul repeatedly contradicts *faith alone*, making Paul's message inherently ambiguous in *full* context. You can only say Paul is clear if you quote Paul *out-of-full context*. Yet, Jesus never has such ambiguity, never once endorsing *faith **alone*** for salvation. Hence, Paley defeats Luther's argument over hermeneutics. Paley says Jesus is the "higher authority," and that is our only *objective* standard. Paul may edify and teach, but he is not the source of truth.

Paley's Conclusion

Paley concludes that "although we were not able to settle, to our satisfaction, the first question, namely, what it was he [Paul] did mean [by faith alone passages]," we know "good works could [not] be dispensed with; or that a life of continued unrepented sin would end in salvation." *Id.*, at 222. The only other alternative is to say if Paul really meant *faith alone*, then we must

> suppose, that Saint Paul delivered a doctrine **contrary to that of our Saviour and of the other Apostles, destructive of one declared end of the Christian institution itself** (and the end and design of any system of laws is to control the interpretation of particular parts); **and lastly**, what is most improbable of all, at the same time and in the same manner, **directly repugnant to what he himself has solemnly asserted and delivered at other times and in other places**. *Id.*, at 222.

In other words, if Paul truly taught faith alone, and we could not refute that, then Paul contradicts Jesus and the twelve apostles. Paley did not have to tell us what that means: Paul would be a false apostle and false prophet. So you have only two choices: either (a) if Paul meant faith alone, then he is a false apostle and false prophet or (b) Paul did not mean faith alone, and instead endorsed Jesus' gospel of faith, works and obedience. Those are the only two logical choices.

A third option in the early church was to be polite. If one insists Paul is inspired, then as Augustine said because Jesus' words on the necessity of works and obedience have "no doubtful sense," then "we must look for another interpretation" of Paul; if we cannot find it, then we must follow Second Peter's directions on Paul, and simply account the 'faith without works' doctrine we perceive in Paul to the fact Paul's "writings [are] hard to be understood, which men ought not to pervert unto their own destruction." (Augustine, *Fide et operibus* [*Faith and Works*] 413 A.D. trans. Cornish:62.)

Therefore, as Paley says, because Paul often enough teaches salvation turns on good works, obedience, fear-and-trembling, and Paul insists it is pride that assures oneself of justification now,[10] we cannot selectively quote Paul on faith alone. Paley — with Protestant vigor and Tyndalian outlook, along with unassailable proof — utterly destroyed the faith alone doctrine in 1825.

Ezekiel's Warning About Diluted Standards for Salvation

Everyone who preached Paul's sometimes-appearing faith alone gospel who otherwise lived a righteous life unfortunately will pay the consequences of their teachings. *If your elevating Paul's doctrine above Jesus' doctrine misled even a single soul to not perceive Jesus' repetitious warnings were about hell for disobedience (hell-whole), i.e., God's absolute requirement that everyone enter heaven-maimed based on repentance from sin or not at all, you will pay with your spiritual life for the disobedience of each such misled soul*. God already warned of this through Ezekiel:

> In My saying to the wicked, 'O wicked one — thou dost surely die,' And thou hast **not spoken** to **warn the wicked** from his way, He — the wicked — in his iniquity doth die, And **his blood from thy hand I require**. (9) And thou, when **thou hast warned the wicked of his way**, to turn back from it, And he hath not turned back from his way, He in his iniquity doth die, And **thou thy soul hast delivered**. (Ezekiel 33:8-9 YLT.)

---

10. Romans 2:6-7; 3:31; 7:12; 8:13;11:20-22; Philippians 2:12-13; 1 Corinthians 4:2-5; 13:2,13; 2 Corinthians 7:9-10; Ephesians 5:6-7 and Galatians 5:19-20; 6:7-9, etc.

Jesus said this too, when He warned that anyone who causes "a believer in me to become ensnared" would find it better to have "a millstone put around his neck and thrown in the sea" than suffer God's aggravated wrath. (Mark 9:42.)

Jesus elsewhere spoke of this "greater damnation" wherein some will be singled out to suffer in hell more than others due to the greater and clearer warning they received. (Matt. 23:14.)

Jude (another brother of Jesus) elucidates Mark 9:42, by similarly referring to a group who will suffer God's aggravated wrath. These teachers seduce Christians by teaching "grace is a license" to sin with no repercussions on salvation. Jude says they will suffer the "blackness of darkness" (Jude 1:4,13).[11] Scholars concur this phrase is meant to identify a place far worse than a normal region in hell. Instead, it represents "the worst darkness one can imagine" where "no light penetrates," identical to "the outer darkness of eternal night" to which Jesus refers in Matthew 22:13 as the fate of the "unprofitable servant." (Paul V. Harrison & Robert E. Picirilli, *The Randall House Bible Commentary* (Randall House: 1992) at 283.)

Jude's place of 'blackest darkness' parallels Jesus' millstone warning: both Jesus and Jude threaten those who seduce Christians into sin by false assurance as suffering the the worst darkness of the deep sea in damnation. Jude says it is caused by a false grace teaching which assures a Christian that God's grace is irreversible. Jude warns of teachers who say a Christian does not risk "eternal fire" (Jude 7) if we engage in "immorality." (Jude 4, 7.) To prove his point, Jude gives several examples where sin caused eternal damnation to angels in heaven and God's people after being saved.[12]

---

11. Second Peter 2:17 likewise speaks of the false teachers who draw you from a "steadfastness in Christ" by a belief in a "liberty" to sin; they are destined to suffer the "blackness of darkness."

12. For more on Jude's letter, and whose doctrine he was condemning, see my prior work, *Jesus' Words Only* (2007) at 104 *et seq.*

Faith Alone: The Oldest Heresy From Christ's Doctrine

'Faith alone' was the first heresy. It was long ago refuted by James, Peter, and Jude.[13] Jesus approved their critique in Revelation chapters two and three. Faith alone was revived by Marcion in 144 A.D., and refuted again by Tertullian in 207 A.D.[14] and all the early church commentators, *e.g.*, Origen, Hermas, Hippolytus, Cyprian, and Lanctatius.[15] Then in 410 A.D., Pelagius revived "faith alone" in his *Commentary on Romans* (410 A.D.)[16]

In reply, Augustine in 413 A.D. refuted faith alone again in his treatise *Faith and Works*. Augustine noted that the faith-alone movement relied upon "not understanding certain obscure sentences of...Paul." Augustine then said these false teachers "maintain that he saves himself who *only believes* in Christ, although he continues in what scandalous sins whosoever he will, even unto the profession of adultery." Augustine says Jesus explained differently to the torah scholar about how to obtain eternal life. Jesus said it was by obeying two fundamental laws, where the love of God comes first (faith), but the love of your neighbor necessarily comes second, and this implies "moral rules of life and conversation." Augustine continues: Jesus likewise spoke contrary to

---

13. See *Jesus' Words Only* (2007) at 94-95, 239*ff.* On Peter, see page 503.

14. See "Post-Script: Importance of Protestants Coming to Grips with the Early Heretic Marcion's Cheap Grace Doctrine" on page 578-585.

15. See my prior work, *Jesus' Words Only* (2007) at 443 *et seq.*

16. *Id*, at 437. Pelagius' other heresy was that "man... can easily obey the divine commands if he pleases" *without* "divine assistance." (Neander:583.) By contrast, Jesus said you can do "nothing" without connection to Him. (John 15:5.) This led to Pelagius teaching that man, who begins sinless, "without Christianity...may avoid sin and earn immortal blessedness, and that they have often done so." (Rainy:470.) Thus, Pelagius heretically taught even though faith alone saves any sinful person, a non-sinful person (of whom many supposedly exist) does not need faith or any connection to Jesus/God to be saved.

---

those who teach by "*believ[ing]...alone* [makes] man come to life" when Jesus instructs the rich young man that eternal life is by obeying "commands of morals." Works alone do not save, but instead "both are connected the one without the other because the love of God cannot exist in a man who does not love his neighbor." (Augustine, *Fide et operibus*, in *Seventeen Short Treatises of Augustine* (trans.C.L. Cornish)(John H. Parker: 1847) at 48,49,51,56,57.)

Faith alone doctrine then laid dormant and dead until 1517. Then it revived. Alas! All the efforts of James, Peter, Jude, Tertullian, Augustine and many others were forgotten.

Heresy based on selective quotes from Paul has revived. It is a renewal of the main teachings of the heretic Marcion. Now, Paul, selectively quoted, is emphasized almost universally in evangelical churches to the detriment of Jesus' doctrine. The discarding of the Lord's teachings are not given any second-thought by those claiming to love Christ. Believers are assuaged by misleading commentaries and false translations. They are blatantly told to dismiss the Lord's words as no longer relevant in a dispensation of grace. Yet, every lover of Christ must necessarily be offended by faith alone doctrine, at least if one takes the time to study *Jesus' Words on Salvation*. We must now more than ever repent from ever teaching the gospel of faith alone. It seduces those coming to Christ away from Him. It leads its deluded adherents to follow a mere man named Paul. Yet Paul never died for anyone's sins. Nor did he proclaim a gospel as brilliant and as superb as the one delivered by the Lord Jesus.

Christ or Paul

As Reverend Vincent Holmes-Gore — also a serious Christian scholar[17]— said in *Christ or Paul* (C.W. Daniel: 1946), the confusing disciple (Paul) has misled many:

> Let the reader contrast the true Christian standard with that of Paul and he will see the *terrible betrayal of all that the Master taught*....

> For the surest way to betray a great Teacher is to **misrepresent his message**.... That is what Paul and his followers did, and because the Church has followed Paul in his error it has **failed lamentably to redeem the world**....The teachings given by the blessed Master Christ, which the disciples John and Peter and James, the brother of the Master, **tried in vain to defend and preserve intact** were as utterly **opposed to the Pauline Gospel** as the **light is opposed to the darkness**.

Soren Kierkegaard (1813-55) spoke likewise. He was a Lutheran and very devout. In the quote below from Kierkegaard, you also hear the clear echo of Bonhoeffer's statement in *Cost of Discipleship* (1937) that we have developed a "Christianity without Christ." Kierkegaard wrote in *The Journals:*

> In the teachings of Christ, religion is completely present tense: Jesus is the prototype and our task is to imitate him, become a disciple. But then through Paul came **a basic alteration**. Paul draws **attention away** from imitating Christ and fixes attention on the death of Christ the Atoner. What Martin Luther, in his reformation, failed to realize is that even before Catholicism, **Christianity had become degenerate at the hands of Paul**. Paul made Christianity the religion of Paul, not of Christ. **Paul threw the Christianity of Christ away**, com-

---

17. Rev. Holmes-Gore was a serious Christian scholar besides a pastor. His writings include "The Thorn in the Flesh," *Theology* Vol. 32 (1936) 111*ff.*; "The Ascension of the Apocalyptic Hope. The Significance of Acts 1:6-8," *Theology* Vol. 32 (1936) 356*ff.*; "The Parable of the Tares," *Theology* Vol. 35 (1937); *These We Have Not Loved* (1942)(Christian-basis to vegetarianism); *The Churches of St. Thomas and All Saints Lymington* (Gloucester: 1947); and "New Morals for Old: Being an Attempt to Restate and Defend the Christian Ideal of Marriage," *Journal of Theological Studies* (1949) 1*ff.*

pletely turning it upside down, making it just the **opposite** of the original proclamation of Christ.

The Lutheran William Wrede (1859-1906) in his book *Paul* (1904) spoke likewise. Wrede was a brilliant New Testament scholar and a Lutheran seminary student. He was also later a tutor at a theological college. Wrede wrote in *Paul* — obviously in sincere respect for Jesus — the following quote:

> The moral majesty of Jesus, his purity and piety, his ministry among his people, his manner **as a prophet**, the whole concrete ethical-religious content of his earthly life, **signifies for Paul's Christology nothing whatever....** The name 'disciple of Jesus' has little applicability to Paul.... **Jesus or Paul**: this alternative characterizes, at least in part, the religious and theological warfare of the present day.

Regarding our modern era, Wrede then says the deplorable situation is that Paul is in ascendancy over the one whom Paul claimed was his Master:

> This second founder of Christianity [*i.e.*, Paul] has even, compared with the first, **exercised beyond all doubt the stronger**—not the better—**influence**. True, he has not lorded it everywhere, especially not in the life of simple, practical piety, but.... **he has thrust that greater person [i.e., Jesus],** whom he meant only to serve, **utterly into the background**.[18]

Test Wrede's claim. Listen to almost any Sunday Sermon. Then count how many times Jesus is quoted or His teachings on salvation are explained. It is rare. Then compare the number of times Paul is quoted. The advantage for Paul's

---

18.William Wrede, *Paul* (1904)(reprinted as Lexington: American Theological Library Association Committee on Reprinting, 1962) at 180–182.

words quoted over Jesus' words is staggering. Jesus' doctrine is unquestionably left in the background. Amazingly, this advantage given to Paul can even be maintained when a parable of Jesus is the subject of exposition! Once you are alerted to the issue, you will become sickened at this forced submission of Jesus to Paul.

Wrede clearly sees the irony of holding onto Paul, and trying to fit Jesus into Paul's doctrine. The teachings of Jesus necessarily must be crushed if you hold onto all of Paul's doctrines. This is because otherwise they don't mesh well. Wrede goes on:

> The older school is no doubt convinced that with Paul it enters, for the first time, into possession of the whole and genuine Jesus; and it is also able, to a certain extent, to take up the historical Jesus into its Pauline Christ. Still, *this Christ must needs for the most part crush out the man Jesus*. (*Id.*)

Wrede's main thesis has never been refuted.[19]

---

19. As John G. Machen recalls for us, the critics of Wrede responded that Jesus had more influence over Paul than Wrede supposed. However, this was not a real answer. The question Wrede posed was whether Paul was a trained disciple of Jesus. The evidence was lacking because rarely do any words of Jesus appear in Paul's Epistles in even a close paraphrase. Certainly we never find Paul quoting Jesus except a misquote of the Lord's Supper. Some ideas are similar at times, as we have seen, but only when Paul speaks of a costly grace. Otherwise, no attention is ever given by Paul explictly to Jesus' doctrine or deeds. In fact, Paul wanders so far from them, many agree he speaks so different from Jesus that Paul represents an entirely new dispensation of truth from that of Jesus. As John G. Machen explained, many thought "Wrede... is refuted already" because there is more connection between Paul's thought and Jesus' thought than Wrede supposed. Yet, the fact is "Wrede was entirely correct" that Paul was no disciple because if Paul had been, then "the Epistles [of Paul] would be full of the words and deeds of Jesus." (Machen, *The Origins of Paul's Religion* (Macmillan: 1921) at 166.) Since Paul's Epistles are barren of any quotes from Jesus and contain very few arguable paraphrases from Jesus' teachings, Paul is at best a poor disciple of the Christ we see in the Gospels.

What has happened? The true Christ, just as Bonhoeffer said, is sacrificed anew and crushed by our adherence to a cheap gospel of salvation. We developed a "Christianity without Christ," as Bonhoeffer lamented.

Antidotes To Faith Alone Doctrine From Bonhoeffer & Kierkegaard

Bonhoeffer on Justification

Bonhoeffer says there is no such thing as being justified by Christ without following Christ.

> The only man who has the right to say that he is justified by **grace alone** is the man who has **left all to follow Christ**. Such a man knows that the **call to discipleship** is a gift of grace, and that the call **is inseparable from the grace**. But those who try to use this grace as a **dispensation from following Christ** are simply **deceiving themselves**. (Bonhoeffer, *Cost of Discipleship* (1937) at 35-47.)[20]

What prevented us from seeing this? The lying pen of the scribes in Jeremiah's day were to blame then. (Jer. 8:6-9.) The lying pen obviously has come back by means of misleading commentary and even alteration of God's word. It teaches you that you can be justified by a grace that dispenses with following Christ. They are incessant in undermining God's warnings. The aim of Satan is always to dilute the warnings of God. To make you safe and comfortable in the very thing that separates you from God — sin. *If Satan can convince you to believe the doctrines about Jesus that his demons already know and make you think you can safely stop there*

---

20. "Costly Grace," excerpt of pages 35-47 at http://www.present-truthmag.com/archive/XIII/13-3.htm (accessed 6-30-07).

and still be saved, then Satan keeps you ensnared in his kingdom. If it were otherwise and were correct that belief alone really saves you, why then do "we read in the Gospels that the devils...confessed Christ and were rebuked by Him" for saying "the same thing which obtained praise in the confession of Peter"?[21]

Thus, Satan suffers no harm if you make solely a sincere statement of *belief* that Jesus died for your sins without repentance. For the same reason, you gain nothing thereby. You are still under the wrath of God if you do not also repent from your sins and thereafter keep on obeying unto Jesus, including all His teachings, commandments and sayings. (John 3:16,36.) As long as you "walk in the light," then the "blood of Jesus" keeps you clean; but if you sin, then only when you "confess your sin" does that same blood wash you again anew. (1 John 1:7-9.) John's point is unmistakable: the atonement ("blood of Jesus") only keeps you clean when you "confess" (repent of sin) and "walk in the light" (obey). It's that simple. But it is also that hard. Jesus had a gospel of costly grace, just as Bonhoeffer said.

Kierkegaard On Whether Salvation Is By A Mere Right Opinion About Jesus.

Because true Christianity is the following of the Messiah, salvation can never be by accepting a set of dogmas on *how to be saved*. When salvation is reduced to having a *right opinion* about Christ or having the *right salvation-formula*, it is no longer Christianity. It is a phantom imitation. As Kierkegaard, speaking from a Lutheran experience, wrote in the 1850s:

> What... [modern] theology understands by faith is really what is called *having an opinion*, or what in everyday language we call *'to believe.'*

---

21. Augustine, *Fide et operibus*, in *Seventeen Short Treatises of Augustine* (trans.C.L. Cornish)(John H. Parker: 1847) at 59.

> Christianity is thus made *into a teaching*.
> Then the next stage is to *'comprehend' this
> teaching*, and this philosophy and theology are
> supposed to do. All this would be entirely
> proper *if Christianity were a doctrine*. But it's
> not. Faith is related to the God-man, *not a doc-
> trine*. (Kierkegaard, *Provocations* (2007) at
> 274.)

Thus, you are not saved by finally reading this book
and understanding correctly Jesus' doctrine on salvation. This
is because *belief* in the right doctrine is not the Way of salvation. Correct knowledge of the path of salvation can help *lead*
you *to* the Way of salvation. Wrong doctrine on salvation can
help *lead* you *from* the Way of Salvation. *But the belief or
mere knowledge of the right path has no intrinsic meaning
unless you take the right Path*.

Hence, Christian people can be saved who have no
idea of what is the right doctrine of salvation. Thank the
Good Lord.

One cannot say the following truth more emphatically: you are not saved by right doctrine about how to be
saved. You are saved by following Jesus! By obeying Him for
His sake! (John 3:16.) By trusting Him because He is worthy.
By enduring to the end, you "*shall* be saved." (Matt. 10:22.)
By denying yourself, counting the cost in advance of what
you will lose by following Him, you "*shall* inherit eternal
life." (Matt. 19:29.) This is a narrow way toward which you
must "*strive* with all your might" — *agonize* is the word in
Greek. (Luke 13:24.)

Facts To Believe Are Relevant

Jonathan Edwards (1668–1759) was a famous faith
alone advocate who raised a hue and cry about a gospel based
on repentance. He said if salvation is by repentance from sin,
even if that is what Jesus and Peter preached, then it is a gospel of paganism. "Some say...salvation [is] by repentance and

reformation, as preached by Christ." Edwards said this necessarily means it is a "salvation to the penitent." Then Edwards says why not go a step farther and say "salvation by Seneca and Cicero?" For they too "taught the necessity of good morals and reformation." Thus, if you preach repentance for salvation, this means you are giving "up the whole of it,... return[ing] to the religion of the pagans." Edwards claims any teaching that salvation is by repentance necessarily gives up the truths of the "divinity of Christ, the trinity, and the atonement." ("Thoughts on the Atonement," *The Works of Jonathan Edwards* (1854) Vol. I at 507.)

Edwards' engaged in an obvious use of the fallacy of the false dilemma. It is a false dichotomy to say salvation is either by works alone (*i.e.*, abandoning belief in the divinity of Christ, etc.) or faith alone. There is always the third possibility that it is by faith and works, just as James said. Or, to be more precise, it can be by a faith or belief in facts which activates one's repentance from sin and one's turn toward obedience. As Hebrews 11:6 says, "without faith it is impossible to please God." The author of Hebrews explains why: "for he who comes to God must believe that He is, and that He is a rewarder of those who seek Him." The choice in salvation doctrines is thus not the false dilemma of choosing either to preach faith alone or to preach a pagan idea of repentance divorced of any faith in God, Jesus or the efficacy of atonement.

Consequently, even though Jesus teaches belief alone cannot save in many parables (*e.g.*, Parable of the Good Samaritan, the Sheep & the Goats, etc.), Jesus did not say *faith* plays no role. It is still highly important to use factual details in an invitation to prove Jesus is the Messiah, Son of God, and died for our sins and rose from the dead. One can never please God *without faith*. But if it ends there, it is no more than the belief that demons share about God, Jesus and the efficacy of the atonement. They know all these things, yet do not turn to God.

In Acts chapter two, Peter uses these factual details in an invitation which were clearly designed to engender the response that Jesus wants, *i.e*, repentance from sin and turning around to God, and going on the path of obeying Jesus.

Peter used these facts of the crucifixion and the prophecies of the Christ in his first invitation to a large crowd where 3,000 "repented" and "received this word...." See Acts 2:14-41.

How and why are these facts used in an invitation? Jesus told us that these facts about the cross would serve to draw "all" men to Him.

> And I, if I am lifted up from the earth, I will draw *all* [*pantas*, plural] TOWARDS [Greek, *pros*] Myself. (John 12:32.)

The story of the crucifixion will draw *all* peoples. Not some kinds of people. Not certain people. *ALL PEOPLE*. Thus, the word *draw* there must mean *attract*. It is not an irresistible story that causes universal salvation. The point Jesus is making is that this story about the crucifixion has the capacity to attract any and everyone to Christ.

This emphasis on the fact of the atonement, however, does not change the Gospel steps which Jesus wants in response to this message of the Cross. Jesus did not mean everyone is saved who believes in the fact of the crucifixion, its power to atone for sins, or His resurrection, etc. *For Jesus taught atonement could not be appropriated without appeasing first anyone you had offended.*[22] This reconciliation Jesus said that must come before you appropriate an atoning sacrifice meant not only *repenting of sin*, but also *doing affirmative acts necessary to reconcile with each person you offended.*

22.See "Atonement: Be Reconciled First To The One You Sinned Against Or Otherwise No Effect" on page 1 *et seq.*

Conclusion

Jesus' Gospel is not faith alone. Paul's Gospel is sometimes faith alone and sometimes the opposite. What possibly explains Paul's apparent inconsistency is irrelevant to decide. Such inconsistency makes him inherently ambiguous. Second Peter simply states common sense: you cannot rely upon someone's teaching that is hard to understand. Here it is *incomprehensible*. You cannot take Paul out-of-context for faith alone when Paul just as clearly says the opposite.

As Paley says, when we are confronted by Paul's self-contradictions, then we must follow Jesus' clear directive on His gospel. It is decidedly a gospel of not only faith but also repentance and obedience to His commands as *necessary* and *indispensable* to salvation. It is "repent or perish." It is "heaven-maimed or hell-whole." It is "every tree without good fruit is cut down and thrown in the fire."

The fact the young Luther gave weight to faith alone does not deter us. Our task is to discover Jesus' doctrine, not Luther's. Faith alone doctrine suited Luther's task in a time of excitement and good purpose. It no longer bears up under a closer scrutiny when examined by Jesus' doctrines. Nevertheless, what we are recovering in this book does appear to be the evidence in Christ's words which convinced the earliest reformers in the end to modify their views on salvation. In 1530, Tyndale realized faith alone was incorrect for the Christian. Erasmus too. It even appears Luther starting in 1531 began to realize faith alone was wrong doctrine for the Christian. That explains why Luther wrote the *Catechisms* the way he did. That's what explains why Luther's agents — Melancthon and Bucer — at the 1541 Regensburg Diet adopted Tyndale's idea of *double justification*. See "Encouragement From Tyndale: His Stunning Reversal On Faith Alone" on page v *et seq.*

Thus, if we needed encouragement, it is good to know we are not alone in rejecting faith alone. We have sterling company in Tyndale, Erasmus, and even the mature Luther.

28 *Conclusion: Jesus' Salvation Doctrine*

Jesus' Gospel of Salvation

Jesus on Repentance

Jesus said you can go to heaven-maimed or hell-whole. (Mark 9:42-47.)[1] You can repent from sin, turning in abhorrence from it, or you will perish. (Luke 13:2-5.)[2]

Atonement: Unconditional or Conditional Covering?

You will ask: 'Can I at least depend on Christ's atonement covering me if I *believe* I am a sinner and the blood of Christ washes me?'

Jesus says *emphatically no!* Atonement is not magic. Salvation is not by verbal incantations.

Jesus taught instead you can appropriate atonement only if you first obtain reconciliation with the ones you have offended. (Matt 5:22-26.)[3]

Jesus' Doctrine on Justification

You are only right with God — "justified" — when you have repented from sin and are walking in full obedience, rather than walking shallowly due to ignorance of God's principles, like the Pharisees walked. Jesus said this in the Parable of the Pharisee and the Publican.

---

1. For extensive discussion, see page 45 *et seq.*
2. For extensive discussion, see page 105 *et seq.*
3. For full discussion, see page 1 *et seq.*

First, Jesus said it was the repentant publican who went home "justified." (Luke 8:14.)

Why did the Pharisee go home unjustified? The Pharisee was only able to tout his obedience to one written command — tithing (the lesser part of the Law) and to one command of the (unauthorized) oral law on fasting. (Luke 18:9-14.) Jesus previously faulted the Pharisees for (a) obeying only tithing from the Law, neglecting the more weighty matters of the Law (Matt. 23:23) and (b) following the oral law to the neglect of the written law. (Matt. 15:6.) The Pharisee in the parable was proud of keeping to just these two shallow and law-negating principles. Jesus means that justification is not maintained by an insufficient shallow obedience. This is why the Pharisee goes home unjustified. The Pharisee was being destroyed by his shallow *belief* in what laws applied to himself. This was precisely what God said destroyed the people in Hosea 4:6. God said in Hosea that because the religious leaders were no longer teaching the full Law, the people were being destroyed. This is the same reason why the Pharisee went home unjustified.[4]

Thus, only when your "righteousness exceeds the righteousness of the Pharisees can you enter the kingdom of heaven." (Matt. 5:20.) Hence, only when you keep bearing fruit (obeying) does God keep cleansing you by means of atonement. (John 15:2.) Only as you "keep walking in the light" does the "blood of Jesus keep you clean." (1 John 1:7.)[5]

Jesus' Doctrine On Rebirth By Repentance

In fact, it is only by repentance from sin and turning back to your father that you go from being "dead and lost" to being "alive again." (Parable of the Prodigal Son. Luke

---

4. For full discussion, see page 27 *et seq.*
5. For full discussion, see page 14 *et seq.*

15:17-24, *viz.* verse 24.)[6] Repentance from sin is thus the condition for the synonymous expression that "to enter heaven" one must be "born again." (John 3:3.)

Jesus' Doctrine on Works

Jesus said if you do not have "good fruit," you are going to be cut down and thrown in the "fire." (Matt. 7:19.)[7] A branch "in me" without "fruit" is "taken away," thrown "outside" to be "burned." (John 15:1-6.)[8]

What kind of good fruit is required? One example Jesus clearly taught is that if you do not have charity for others, you go to "eternal fire," but if you are charitable, you are resurrected to "eternal life." (Parable of the Sheep and the Goats. Matthew 25:30-46.)[9] Hence, faith avails nothing salvation-wise if you lack charity.

It was just as Jesus elsewhere said: those who do "good things" resurrect to eternal life, but those who do "evil things" go to eternal damnation. (John 5:28-29.)[10]

Jesus' Doctrine Of Perseverance And Completed Works

Then if you "have **endured** to the end, you shall be saved." (Matt. 10:22.)[11] The only seed in the Parable of the Sower which was saved was the fourth which "kept on producing fruit with **endurance** to" completion.[12] Its endurance was in producing fruit, or synonymously, *works*.

---

6. For full discussion, see page 267 *et seq.*
7. For extensive discussion, see page 329 *et seq.*
8. For extensive discussion, see page 343 *et seq.*
9. For extensive discussion, see page 219 *et seq.*
10. For extensive discussion, see page 395 *et seq.*
11. For full discussion, see page 81 *et seq.*
12. For full discussion, see page 311 *et seq.*

If instead Jesus finds your "works are incomplete" (Rev. 3:1-3), then Jesus says you are spiritually dead and the Spirit is about to depart from you. (Jesus means faith without works is dead, just like His brother James said in James 2:14-17.) Jesus warns 'repent, obey, and do your first works.'[13]

As to those whose works are "lukewarm," because they are rich and say "I need nothing," Jesus warns He will "spew you out of my mouth." (Rev 3:15-18.)[14] Those with lukewarm works are precisely like the third seed in the Parable of the Sower. The third seed was choked by riches. That seed had substantially more growth than the second seed which had "believed for a while" but in "time of temptation" had fallen and died. (Luke 8:13.) Hence, even though the third seed progressed much farther than the *believing* second seed, the third seed was choked later by "riches and the pleasures of this life." It thus did not produce any mature fruit. The third seed therefore too withered and died.[15] Consequently, the third seed is identical to the Christian in Revelation chapter three with lukewarm works. Jesus will "spew" that seed out of His mouth. The third seed will then die. It is lost.

The same goes for the seed which "***believes/obeys*** for a while" (Luke 8:13) but produces nothing. Such a seed in the Parable of the Sower is just like the servant in the Parable of the Unprofitable Servant "who produces nothing" on the talent given him. Such an useless servant of the Lord in the parable is sent to a place of "outer darkness where there is weeping and gnashing of teeth."[16] In other words, the unproductive "***believing***" second seed is identical to the unproduc-

---

13. For full discussion, see page 401 *et seq.*

14. For full discussion, see page 403 *et seq.*

15. For full discussion, see page 311 *et seq.* The translation of *pisteuo* is arguably better as "obeyed/trusted for a while."

16. For full discussion, see page 277 *et seq.*

tive servant of the Lord who has no good works and as a consequence is sent to hell. Jesus says this "believing" seed withers and dies due to temptation. (Luke 8:13.)

Accept the Costs Up Front to Jesus' Way of Salvation

Therefore, the Way of Salvation is clear. However, Jesus sternly warns not to embark on the path of obedience to His commands unless you already have calculated the costs of what it will take to reach the finish. Otherwise, if you do not know in advance what you need to sacrifice — all your sinful pleasures — you will be re-snatched by your enemy the devil. You will be vanquished. (Parable of Counting the Cost. Luke 14:27-35.)[17]

Yet, if you do suffer all the costs which the kingdom requires of you, Jesus promises you eternal life. It is a *costly* grace, for Jesus says: "And every one that hath left houses, or brethren, or sisters, or father, or mother, or children, or lands, for my name's sake, shall receive a hundredfold, and ***shall inherit eternal life***." (Matthew 19:29.)

The Final Reward And Pleasure Of Friendship With Jesus

You final reward of obedience is that all who obeyed Jesus' commandments "shall have the right" to eternal life and entry into heaven.

> Happy [are] the ones ***doing His command-ments***, so that their ***right*** will be ***to the tree of life***, and they ***shall enter*** by the gates into the city. (Rev 22:14)(ALT)[18]

If you were obedient, you also will be friends of Jesus:

---

17. For full discussion, see page 291 *et seq.*
18. For full discussion, see page 373 *et seq.*

> Ye are my friends, if ye **do whatsoever I com-
> mand [*entellomai*] you**. (John 15:14 KJV.)

Jesus' Doctrine on Obedience (Effect of Sin)

What kind of evil things lead to damnation?

Jesus said if His servant does an evil thing like "fail to
forgive" as did the Unmerciful Servant, God will treat you
precisely like the master treated that servant in the parable.
That means, once God has already forgiven you, if you then
do not forgive others, God will revoke your forgiveness. He
will then send you to Hell and punish you in torment, making
you pay forever the previously forgiven debt of your sins.
(Matthew 18:23-35.)[19]

Another example is what happens if you are His servant but do an evil thing like starting to "beat" your fellow
servants and "eat and drink with the drunken." Jesus says
your prior service as a good servant is forgotten. Instead you
will be sent "outside in darkness" to "suffer weeping and
gnashing of teeth" with "unbelievers/the disobedient." (Luke
12:41-48; Matthew 24:44-50.)[20] *Beating* can include any
kind of *unjustified* physical or emotional abuse.

Jesus' Doctrine Of Obedience To The Law Given Moses

What must one do then to obtain eternal life? When
asked that same question, Jesus said "to enter life obey the
commandments," and He rattled off nine of the Ten Commandments which I AM spoke to Moses on Mount Sinai.
(Matthew 19:16-26; Mark 10:17-31; Luke 18:18-26.)[21]

This is obviously why Jesus says those who teach you
to obey the Law are the "greatest in the kingdom of heaven"
but those who teach you not to follow the Law are "least in

---

19. For extensive discussion, see page 245 *et seq.*
20. For extensive discussion, see page 55 *et seq.*
21. For full discussion, see page 123 *et seq.*

the kingdom of heaven." (Matt. 5:19.) You are the greatest for teaching obedience to the Law because Jesus told the young rich man this is the path of salvation. Likewise, you are the least if you deny the necessity to obey the Law because you seduce people from the path of salvation.

Clarke begrudgingly admits, as it goes against modern doctrine, that Jesus means the anti-legalist will be damned. Clarke says Jesus means by "least in the kingdom" that those who teach against keeping the Law are damning themselves thereby. It does not mean they still go to heaven but in last place. "Least in the kingdom" means they are the lost as viewed by those inside the kingdom — observers in heaven looking out at them. Clarke says this is clear from Jesus' remarks in the very next verse: Matthew 5:20.[22]

In that verse, Jesus says the Pharisees, whom Jesus repeatedly describes as anti-legalists, cannot "enter the kingdom of heaven." Jesus explains precisely why — their lessons about the Law are shallow. The people must "exceed the righteousness of the Pharisees" to enter heaven. (Matt. 5:20.)

Jesus' Doctrine On Salvation-Ending Heresy Of Anti-Legalism

What does Matthew 5:20 mean?

As the Protestant classic text, *Theological Dictionary of the New Testament* (1985) at 574 says of this verse, Jesus means "those who erode the Law while supposedly protecting it will ***not even enter*** the kingdom."

Jesus reiterates this elsewhere in Matthew 23:23. Alexander Bruce admits this verse means the Pharisees "care more for the little than the great commandments [Matt.23:23], [which] has no moral worth and [they are thus] ***not in the kingdom at all***."[23]

Therefore, Jesus is threatening all ***anti-legalists*** with damnation — all who proclaim the Law is of no effect are lost. Jesus is merely repeating Isaiah 50:10-11 when the coming Messiah-Servant attacks self-righteousness — a righteousness conforming to one's own ideas of right-and-wrong rather than the Laws given by God. "Who among you fears the Lord and obeys His servant [Messiah]?... Watch out, you who walk in *your own light* and warm yourselves by *your own fires*. This is the reward you will receive from me [Messiah]: You will soon lie down in great torment." (Isaiah 50:10-11 NLT.)

This no doubt is what Tyndale realized in 1530. This is why Tyndale became such an avowed legalist. (See page v *et seq.* of Preface.) Yet, today we have ignored Tyndale. We also ignored the mature Luther. He was under the obvious influence of Tyndale. In 1537, Luther strongly changed his doctrine on the Law given Moses. Luther became just as

---

22. See page 151. This is even more clear when one compares two of Jesus' threats of an aggravated warning of the darkest *level* of damnation. First, Jesus says one will suffer the "millstone around the neck and be thrown in the sea" in Mark 9:42 — deepest damnation — for the person "causing who one believes in me to be ensnared." (Mark 9:42.) Second and lastly, Jesus speaks similarly in Matthew 5:19. He says those who "teach others" to violate the Law given Moses (hence ensaring them in sin) will suffer a punishment of being "least in the kingdom of heaven." Hence, both the one who suffers the "millstone" and the one who is "least in the kingdom" are those who SEDUCE "believers" from following the Law, causing them to fall into sin. Hence, those deemed "least" share the same quality of wrongdoing as those suffering the "millstone" in Mark 9:42. Therefore, clearly 'least in the kingdom' signifies a lost condition — even the meaning of darkest damnation. Then what does "least in the kingdom" mean? It means one is 'least' viewed by someone inside heaven — the furthest possible distance from heaven. James Blair, a famous theologian, in 1722 gave an insightful discourse which recognized this aspect to 5:19. He said: "The expression of *least in the kingdom* [must] signify to be *totally excluded* from it." For Jesus is warning about the "corruption of others," which Jesus puts (elsewhere) in a "higher pitch of wickedness than only transgressing ourselves." (Note: Mark 9:42-47.) Then of course, in 5:19, there is the "second aggravation" of "doing ill things ourselves." Such disobedience is "countermining our Blessed Savior." Consequently, "least in the kingdom" must mean "in the day of Judgment [they shall be] accounted the *very worst* of all those who have given up their Names to Christ, and profess Christianity." James Blair, *Our Savior's Divine Sermon on the Mount* (5 vols.)(London: 1722) quoted in Edward L. Bond, *Spreading the Gospel in Colonial Virginia: Sermons and Devotional Writings* (Lexington: 2004) at 193-196.

---

much of an avowed legalist as Tyndale with the publication of Luther's *Antinomian Theses*. (See Preface, page xiv.) We are upside down doctrinally today. The very doctrine Jesus condemned — anti-legalism — is now standard doctrine. Its opposing force — the Law's validity — is considered heresy in most evangelical circles. Nothing Tyndale nor Luther realized to correct this error is ever repeated today. Nothing from what Jesus ever said on the Mosaic Law's continuity and the necessity to teach it to be "greatest" in the kingdom — which obviously persuaded Tyndale and Luther — is ever repeated.

How Prophecies Of Messiah Condemn Modern Anti-Legalism

However, when we turn to Jeremiah's and Isaiah's prophecy of Messiah, it is *crucial* to recognize Jesus was a legalist. If it were any other way, Jesus would have been a false Messiah! Jesus had to proclaim the Law as still abiding, never abrogated, and applicable in the New Testament, to fulfill an essential criteria of *who* is the prophesied Messiah in the New Testament. Anything less — any derogation of the Law by Jesus — and Jesus would have been a false Messiah.

---

23. Alexander Bruce, *The Kingdom of God: Or, Christ's Teaching According to the Synoptical Gospels* (Scribner's 1897) at 66. Ironically, then Bruce defends the position he just said caused the Pharisees to not enter the kingdom "at all." Bruce claims that once Jesus fulfilled the Law of sacrifice that Jesus thereby "inaugurates a new time" that does not "formally" abrogate the Law, but allows it to "fall eventually into desuetude [disuse]," making Jesus the one of "greatest" worth. Thus, Jesus' fulfilling (the law of sacrifice) "may at the same time be more or less an undoing" of the entire Law. (*Id.*, at 67.) Accordingly, Bruce admits Jesus is saying anti-legalism is a damning heresy before the Cross. However, after the Cross, Bruce wants us to accept anti-legalism is saving doctrine; in fact, Bruce is saying it is necessary to adopt anti-legalism to make Jesus the one of "greatest" worth. Yet, wouldn't giving Jesus' the greatest glory be by treating His teaching on the Law's continuity as above anyone else's lesson on the Law?

Prophecies Of Messiah Require Him To Reinvigorate The Law

Upholding the Law given Moses[24] versus anti-legalism is God's litmus test for a true prophet. God says any would-be prophet with "signs and wonders that come to pass" who nevertheless "tries to seduce you from the way commanded you" in Torah (the Law given Moses) is a "false prophet." (Deut. 13:1-5.) Any would-be prophet, if his words "contradict" the commands in the Law or the Ten Commandments, "is in complete darkness." (Isaiah 8:20 YLT & NLT.)

Thus, the Torah (Law given Moses) is the mechanism God chose long ago to allow us to verify whether the source of new messages was from God or the devil.

What about Messiah?

Isaiah prophesied that the suffering servant (Messiah) "should increase [God's] Torah [Law] and glorify it." (Isaiah 42:21DSSB.) Thereby, God's people will be those "who know righteousness and have my Law (torah) *in their hearts*." (Isaiah 51:7 DSSB.) It will be the job of Messiah in the New Covenant to "inscribe the Law [given Moses] on our hearts." (Jeremiah 31:31.)[25]

> **" To the Law and the Testimony! [*i.e.*, the Ten Commandments, Ex. 31:8]. If they contradict them, they are completely in the dark." Is. 8:20 YLT & NLT**

24.Under the Law given Moses, God said obedience to the Law was the means by which God reckoned us as "righteous." (Deut. 6:25; see pages 33-35 *supra*.) Typically, this principle that one is justified by obeying the Law is frequently condemned today as heretical *legalism.*

25.Jeremiah 31:31-34 (ASV) reads: "Behold, the days come, saith Jehovah [*i.e.* Yahweh], that I will make a *new covenant* with the house of Israel, and with the house of Judah:...This is the covenant that I will make with the house of Israel after those days, saith Jehovah: *I will put my Law* [Torah] *in their inward parts*, and in their heart will I write it; and I will be their God, and they shall be my people: and they shall teach no more every man his neighbor, and every man his brother, saying, Know Jehovah [*i.e.*, Yahweh]; for they shall all know me, from the least of them unto the greatest of them, saith Jehovah: for I will forgive their iniquity, and their sin will I remember no more."

The placing of the Law on our hearts in the New Covenant in Jeremiah 31:31 merely would fulfill God's command in the Law itself. For the Law given Moses commanded that the Law be placed "in you hearts." (Deut. 6:6-7; 10:12 and 30:6.)

Since the New Covenant simply fulfills this Old Covenant command, can it possibly be true that the principles, ordinances, and commands of the Law were to be abandoned in the New Covenant? Obviously not. Only a mind corrupted to reject God's Prophets could even suggest that idea. Rather, Jeremiah's prophecy meant the exact opposite. Messiah would put the Law in a place (the heart) where the individual would appreciate it more intimately by virtue of knowing it more *correctly* than ever before — a place "less vulnerable to violation."[26] In doing so, Jesus would be basing the New Covenant upon placing *correctly* the Law on our hearts, as commanded in Deut. 6:6-7; 10:12 and 30:6.

Hence, this better and more intimate proximity of the Law to our hearts would be thanks to Messiah. Through his glorifying and extolling obedience to the Law (Isaiah 42:21), the people who are listening to Him would finally fulfill the Law's command to place the Law on their "heart." (Deut. 6:6-7; 10:12 and 30:6.)

In other words, what God is saying about the New Covenant is the same in Isaiah as in Jeremiah. The New Covenant being put "on our hearts" (Jeremiah 31:31) is not something radically different from the Mosaic Law's commands of where to place the Law. By the New Covenant inscribing the Law on our hearts, it would simply fulfill the command in the Law itself to place the Law on our hearts. (Deut. 6:6-7; 10:12 and 30:6.) Messiah would personally make the prophecy of a New Covenant finally come to pass by "increasing" knowledge of the Law and "glorifying it." (Isaiah 42:21)

---

26. Jacob Neusner, William Scott Green, Alan Jeffery Avery-Peck, *Judaism from Moses to Muhammad: An Interpretation: Turning Points and Focal Points* (Brill, 2005) at 58.

Another New Covenant Passage in Isaiah.

Then in Isaiah, God gives us one more prophecy of the nature of the New Covenant. This re-emphasizes the same point about the continuity of the Mosaic Law. This explains why Messiah will glorify and elevate the Law. God says:

> (21) And as for Me, *this is my* [new] *covenant* with them [*i.e.*, the "ones who turn from transgression" v. 20] says the Lord: my spirit that is upon you and *the words that I have put in your mouth* will not depart from your mouth, or from the mouths of your children, or from the mouths of your children's children, from now on and forever. (Isaiah 59, Dead Sea Scrolls Bible.)

Hence, the "words that I *have put* (N.B. a past tense) in your mouth" are the prior commands delivered by God. This is why God invites into the covenant, as Henry notes, the penitent about the Law: "This covenant is here said to be made with them, that is, with *those that turn from transgression*; for those that cease to do evil shall be taught to do well." Therefore, the beneficiaries of this New Covenant are the contrite about breaking God's Law. All others are excluded. Hence, the past tense that says these *words in your mouth* were previously given, but now are the basis of the New Covenant, mean obviously the neglected commands from the Law. A New Covenant is necessary to revive them.

This is mirrored by Messiah's role to revive respect for the Torah/Law. (Isaiah 42:21.) Jesus's words confirm precisely the fulfillment of Isaiah 42:21 and 59:20-21. Jesus perfectly delivered the commands to be contrite and righteous — "repent or perish" and "heaven-maimed or hell-whole" while elevating the importance to teach the Law given Moses. (Matt.5:19.) Only if these commands are followed will we be engaged in the "turning from transgression" from the Law which Isaiah 59:20-21 clearly stated was the prerequisite to be a member of the New Covenant. Jesus thus was giving us the Way to enter the New Covenant. Jesus revived the Law given Moses.

But Henry says what Isaiah 59:21 means is: "The word of Christ shall *always continue* in the mouths of the faithful." Does this mean we need to find Jesus' words represent a wholesale new teaching that replaces the Law? If so, why would Jesus do this for Jesus identified Himself with I AM (Jn 8:58)—the same one who delivered the Law in the first place to Moses? Ex. 3:14-15.

In other words, are these teachings from Jesus intended to replace the Law God gave Moses? Would a Christian's obedience to the Law given Moses ever conceivably be regarded by God as cutting ourselves off from Christ, which we are often told is true? Such a notion is impossible. For God speaks of the "words I have put in your mouth" (Isaiah 59:21) that precede the New Covenant spoken of in verse 59:20, and are to be its permanent basis. Moreover, Jesus gives us the clear answer. He *precisely reaffirms the Law in the New Covenant.* For Jesus taught the greatness of those who uphold the Law which God gave Moses. (Matt. 5:19.) Jesus then gave the sternest warning of damnation on those who teach against the Law's continuity in the New Covenant. Jesus said the latter are the "least in the kingdom of heaven"—meaning the furthest possible distance from those inside the kingdom of heaven. (Matt. 5:19.) Jesus meant damnation is the lot of anyone who either abrogates, relaxes, or replaces the Law, as Clarke reluctantly conceded.[27]

Meaning of the New Covenant in Jeremiah 31:31

Thus, if the New Covenant does not mean to abolish the *principles* of the earlier covenant with Moses, what does *new* mean? It turns out that the Hebrew word translated *new* in the phrase *New Covenant* in Jeremiah 31:31 is inapt. It has been twisted by some to imply the old was worthless and going to be abrogated. This interpretation of *new* violates the intended meaning in Jeremiah. Thus, as Dr. Kaiser points out,

---

27. See page 555 *et seq.*

the Hebrew expression more appropriately and permissibly should be translated in Jeremiah 31:31 as a *renewed* or *restored* covenant rather than a *new covenant.* Dr. Kaiser says this clearly fits the context, which repeatedly emphasizes the continuity of prior principles and relations. Dr. Kaiser says such a revision in translation would prevent the contextually impossible idea that *new* means to abrogate all Mosaic legal principles that came before.[28]

This *renewal* understanding also matches precisely how God in Isaiah and Ezekiel describes the nature of the *new covenant.* In Isaiah 54, the new covenant clearly means a re-union to an abandoned wife-Israel — a renewal of God's covenant relationship with Israel. God in anger previously expressed His intent to abandon Israel. (See Isaiah 50:1; Hosea 2:4,9; Ezekiel 16:35-40.) However, now in the new covenant, the "Holy one of Israel...Adonai has called you back *like a wife abandoned*... 'A *wife married in her youth cannot be rejected*,' says your God.'" (Isaiah 54:6 CJB.) God intends to "woo her [Israel]... I will speak to her heart." (Hosea 2:16.) "Briefly I abandoned you, but with great compassion I am taking you back." (Isaiah 54:7 CJB.) "*I am taking you back*." (Isaiah 54:8 CJB.) Just like the promise after "Noah's flood," God says "I swear [to Israel] that... *my [new] covenant* of peace will not be removed." (Isaiah 54:9-10.) "Instead of being told 'You are not my people,' it will be said to them, 'You are the children of the living God.'" (Hosea 2:1.) "I will satisfy my fury against you, but after that...I will calm down and no longer be angry." (Ezek. 16:42.) This is a new covenant which God promises to the nation Israel and to no other. It is a *renewed* covenant relationship.[29] "I will not

---

28. Dr. Walter C. Kaiser, Jr., in *Toward an Old Testament Theology* (Zondervan: 1991) at 234 explains: "Thus the word 'new' in this context [of Jeremiah 31:31-34] would mean the 'renewed' or 'restored' covenant...." For more on Dr. Kaiser's analysis, see footnote 31 *infra.*

29. Compare most Christian doctrine is that God has divorced Israel to marry the "Church" of Christ. Such a teaching violates prophecy.

do as you have done — you treated the oath with contempt by breaking the covenant. Nevertheless, I will *remember* the *covenant* I made with you when you were a girl, and will establish an ***everlasting [new] covenant*** with you....I will ***re-establish my [old] covenant*** with you." (Ezek. 16:59-62 CJB.)(Bracketed text added for clarity.)

Now we can understand why Tyndale, as he worked over the translation, came to realize that the "Old and New" make "one gospel."[30]

Consequently, the stress in Jeremiah's phrase "inscribe the Law on our hearts" is a promise that Messiah will *continue* the Covenant at Sinai. This covenant was based upon the Law given Israel. However, the Messiah will woo Israel by clarifying the Law, thus bringing it glory. Hence, the new covenant is a renewal of that original covenant at Sinai with Israel. This is why Messiah will put the Law from the first covenant on the heart in a new covenant. By doing so, He will put the Law in a place the Law commanded it should anyway reside. In our "heart," the Law is more apt to be followed and obeyed. The true Messiah could never be one whose mission would be to abrogate the Law given Moses from the first covenant. Messiah can never be one to seduce anyone not to follow the Law. Thus, these prophecies in Jeremiah and Isaiah are crucial to assess the validity of any would-be Messiah — even to determine whether Jesus was Messiah.[31]

Jesus Vindicated As Messiah Due To His Position On The Law

Accordingly, we could never follow Jesus if He ever seduces us from following the Law. Yet, we can see Jesus did preach and teach obedience to the Law given Moses. The fault of thinking Jesus taught otherwise does not belong to Jesus. It is our fault for ignoring these passages, and high-

---

30. William Tyndale, *Tyndale's Old Testament* (Ed. David Daniell) (Yale University Press, 1992) at xxiii (describing Tyndale's doctrine).

lighting only those from Paul which speak differently than Jesus' lessons on the Law. (See 2 Cor. 3:11-17.) Both Tyndale and Luther realized this, and grew up.[32] They wisely chose Jesus over Paul. There is no other choice. The conflict on the Law between Jesus and Paul has no other resolution. You must pick one over the other. Take the avenue that Tyndale and the mature Luther picked. Jesus is King. Paul is not.

Therefore, it is essential to crack the books open on God's Law applicable to Gentiles. Fortunately, the Law applicable to Gentiles is a relatively short list of commands.[33] We do not have to obey commands applicable only to Jewish believers, as James' astute ruling in Acts 15 proves. This is because if we teach Israel-specific commands as binding on Gentiles, such doctrine actually violates the Law itself.

The Impoverished Modern Church's Doctrine on the Law

So, can I rely upon religious leaders of today to give me the true answers on what are God's commands? Jesus said in His day *absolutely not*!

Jesus put the Pharisees down as repeatedly minimizing the Law given Moses. They replaced it with oral teachings that made of none-effect the written law given Moses at Sinai. (Matt. 15:6.) The Pharisees taught the lesser command

---

31. Christian commentators who have analyzed Jeremiah 31:31-34 with care concur. Dr. Walter C. Kaiser Jr. in *Toward an Old Testament Theology* (Zondervan: 1991) at 233 explains: "The structure of Jeremiah 31:31-34 was best analyzed by Bernhard W.Anderson ["The New Covenant and the Old," *The Old Testament and Christian Faith* (New York: Harper and Row, 1963) at 230 n.11]....When the *items of continuity* found in the New Covenant are tabulated in this passage, they are (1) the same covenant-making God, 'My covenant,'; (2) *the same Law, My Torah (not a different one than at Sinai)*; (3) the *same* divine fellowship in the ancient tripartite formula, 'I will be your God'; (4) the *same* 'seed' and 'people,' 'You shall be my people'; and (5) the *same* forgiveness, 'I will forgive their iniquities.'"

32. See page vii and page xiii (Tyndale); page xvii (Luther).

33. See "How Far Does The Law Apply To Gentiles" on page 182 *et seq.*

---

of tithing, while neglecting all the weightier principles from the Law given Moses such as justice, mercy and faith. (Matt. 23:23.)

Yet, look how much is in common between our religious leaders of today and the Pharisees, particularly on the issue of the Law's abrogation. It is obvious that history is repeating itself. It even sounds like *some Pharisee has wormed his way into the New Testament to proclaim abrogation of the Law (except tithing)*. It is as if the religious leaders of the fourth century made this allowance of space alongside our Lord's word for a Pharisee. They apparently did not recognize the need to protect us from Pharisaistic law-negation![34] But Jesus says you must not listen to such religious leaders, and their proffered voices that negate the Law. They are making you "twice the sons of hell as they are." (Matt. 23:15.) Instead, *you must do better* to enter into eternal life than the righteousness of *these shallow Pharisaical law-negating teachers!*

In fact, Jesus bluntly said you have to "have a righteousness greater than the Pharisees to enter the kingdom of heaven." (Matt.5:20.)[35] *Sadly, that was not a very hard challenge as Jesus describes the Pharisees*. They were extremely shallow on their doctrines from the Law given Moses.

In the Sermon on the Mount, Jesus then outlined the virtues you must have to become a "son of God" which virtues the Pharisees lacked: be a peacemaker; do not make false oaths; do not be anxious; do not commit adultery in your heart; do not take personal vengeance; love your enemies as well as anyone in need; etc.[36]

---

34. Indeed, that is one of the main theses of my prior book, *Jesus' Words Only* (2007).

35. For full discussion, see page 147 *et seq.*

36. For full discussion, see page 201 *et seq.*

Faith Alone

But you ask: 'Won't believing *alone* save me instead?'

No, it won't. If you "keep on obeying unto" Jesus, then you "should not ever ever die" (John 8:51)[37] and "should not perish, but should have everlasting life." (John 3:16.)[38]

In fact, Jesus was adamant that professing belief in Him as Lord is meaningless unless you also obey Him. Jesus asked "why do you call me 'Lord, Lord' but **do not do what I say**?" (Luke 6:46.) Such have a flawed concept of what it means to sincerely say that He is Lord. If you call Him Lord "but do not do His will" Jesus will tell you "I never knew you." (Matt. 7:21.) Jesus said those who profess to want to obey Him, but do not actually do so are lost. But those sinners who repent and obey will enter heaven instead of those who say they will obey Him but end up not doing so. (Parable of the Two Sons. Matthew 21:28-31.)[39]

Jesus means obedience is not optional for those who call Him Lord. Salvation is gained or lost depending on actual obedience to Jesus' commands, not mere profession no matter how sincere when made.

In fact, Jesus taught one who has some wrong belief, such as a member of the Samaritan sect, still has "eternal life" when they obey God's commandments such as to save a life along the road. But those such as the Levites who presumably had correct belief in the true God and taught correctly God's commands, Jesus says in the Parable of the Good Samaritan are lost. The reason is they do not *actually* practice what they believe and teach from the Law. (Parable of the Good Samaritan. Luke 10:25 *ff.*)[40]

---

37. For full discussion, see page 367 *et seq.*
38. For full discussion, see page 417 *et seq.*
39. For full discussion, see page 105 *et seq.,* and pages 465 *ff.*

This parable has a blunt point: salvation depends in crucial part on whether you obeyed God's commands. However, it does not mean obedience without *any* faith qualifies. Rather, it means partial incorrect faith on some matters such as the Samaritans had when combined with proper obedience does qualify. Thus, faith alone does not suffice. But one is not disqualified by merely a minor defect in faith or doctrine which God can overlook. Thank the Lord!

Choosing A Simple Message Over A Tortured Message

Truly, Jesus' gospel is obvious. It is not difficult to uncover it. Nor is it hard to explain. You simply take all of Jesus' lessons in their most plain sense. It is actually far harder to explain why a follower of *Jesus* ever abandoned it to adopt faith alone doctrine. To make Jesus' match the faith alone idea repeatedly requires torturing and tormenting of His words, condensing them into a fifth of their meaning. It requires forcing faith to do it all, and necessarily so. If faith alone were true, then Jesus never had to say "repent or perish," or "heaven-maimed or hell-whole." He should have simply said "believe or perish." Instead, Jesus' words were well-chosen to convey the precisely opposite message. He gave us a warning that *repentance from sin* was an essential unwavering salvation-condition. Jesus also told us *obedience* must follow. Grace is costly, not cheap.

40.For full discussion, see page 118 *et seq.* Jesus does not mention Pharisees or Sadducees in the Parable of the Good Samaritan, whom He taught had wrong doctrine. Jesus never said the Levites had wrong doctrine. Thus, presumably the Levites taught all the Law and did so correctly. They just did not do what it required. Hence, the contrast is between the Samaritan with partially wrong doctrine (*i.e.*, they had a schismatic temple "and you worship what you don't know" John 4:22) who obeys the Law versus a Levite with correct doctrine yet who does not obey the Law.

Hence, you must stop wondering off track to others' ideas. Jesus said He was the Way, the Truth, and the Life. (John 14:6.) As God-Yahweh spoke from heaven at the transfiguration, "***Listen to Him!***" (Matt. 17:5.) Anyone who gives you a "different way" to salvation than Jesus laid out is "a thief and robber." (John 10:1.) Do not follow them.

Warning To Not Run Outside Of Jesus' Teachings

Do not follow even Paul. God-the-Father did not speak from Heaven and tell you to listen to Paul like God-the-Father did twice with Jesus — once at His baptism and the second time at Jesus' transfiguration. On Paul's side of the ledger, there is not a single lick of essential corroborating proof that Paul was ever even an apostle of Jesus Christ. For in all three accounts of Paul's encounter with Jesus, the Lord only appoints Paul a *witness* (*martus*), not a *messenger* (*apostolos*). See page 495 *et seq.* There is a huge difference.

We need to follow Tyndale's and Luther's examples in this respect.

Implicit in the sea change of both Tyndale and Luther on salvation and the Mosaic Law[41] is a change in their perception of the *weight* to be given Paul. Both men after 1530 changed their shared belief in the doctrine of justification by faith alone. At about the same time (Tyndale first, Luther second), both men came to realize that such justification doctrine, if valid at all, was true only up to a certain point: the point of initial salvation. Both men recognized that the doctrine of salvation for the Christian hinges on more — it hinges upon obedience to the Law (at minimum the Ten Commandments), and repentance if transgressed. This is the doctrine of *double justification*.[42]

---

41. See page v *et seq.* of the Preface.

Yet, more fundamentally, Tyndale and Luther both jointly changed their view that the Law given Moses had faded away. They must have both realized that no true Messiah could bring such a message. Both men then blatantly reversed course on this point — Tyndale first, then Luther. By doing so, both men implicitly revealed a fundamental shift on the *value* of Paul's words. For Paul's contrary doctrine no longer mattered when compared to Jesus' words and the necessity that they be unfettered by Paul. Otherwise, if Tyndale or Luther had become stuck on Paul's words, Jesus would be falsified as Messiah. Jesus did not deserve such a fate because Jesus exhorted obedience and continuity of the Law given Moses. Tyndale and Luther both implicitly realized holding onto Paul as valid any longer would have meant losing the validity of Jesus as Messiah. They knew that was not worth the price. The reformers then reformed themselves.

Tyndale made the sea change boldly clear. Luther made his change more quietly, first in the Catechisms of 1531 and then more plainly in the *Antinomian Theses* of 1537.[43]

Thus, anyone — whether Paul, Luther or a true apostle — who "goes ***beyond the teachings of Christ***...does not have God." (2 John 1:8-11.) As the NIV puts it: "Anyone who runs ahead and ***does not continue in the teaching [didache] of [Jesus] Christ*** does not have God; whoever ***continues in the teaching [of Jesus]*** has both the Father and the Son." (2 John 1:8-9.)

---

42. Double justification is essentially indistinguishable from what Jesus teaches. Yet, this formula is still not precisely Jesus' words and is potentially misleading. While the double justification formula has the virtue of melding Paul's doctrine with that of Jesus, it is a mismatch. It misleads potentially because if you tell someone that if you 'believe' you are justified, but they cut off listening to you, and do not hear the need for repentance and obedience, then they continue unjustified in the next instant. Thus, Jesus' simpler and more precise salvation formulae (which Peter uses in Acts) are the correct ones to teach.

43. See page xiii *et seq.*

Consequently, if any person transgresses Jesus' doctrines and teaches you not to follow Jesus' doctrine, you are listening to a deceiver. He could be the king, the president or even Paul. There is no immunity from this test of what is true or false doctrine. Jesus' words are a crucial *litmus test* of what is correct for New Testament believers to follow.

Personal Danger To Those Teaching Faith Alone

How severe will God deal with the deceivers who call you to another way? We have seen they are Marcionites modernized, as Scheck notes.[44] They have no compunction against twisting and torturing the words of the Lord Jesus Christ. They show Jesus utter disrespect. They love only Paul or more correctly, they only love Paul when he slackens Jesus' conditions for salvation. ***They ignore Paul just as much as Jesus when Paul agrees with Jesus' costly grace gospel.***[45] They love only the easy way. The Gospel of Cheap Grace.

But the final verdict will be extremely harsh on them. For they knew their Lord's will but excused themselves from doing it! (Luke 12:47.) They thereby caused believers in Jesus to adopt their false doctrine, often leading believers to be "ensnared" by *lack of proper warning*.

In fact, they affirmed that the threats of Christ on His servants of weeping and gnashing for disobedience never apply to the 'true' Christian. They have reassured us incessantly that we are eternally secure based on faith alone. Or

---

44. Thomas Scheck aptly states he found "real and apparent similarities between certain Protestant theological formulae, especially those of Calvinism and [early] Lutheranism, and the assertions of Gnostic and Marcionite exegesis...." (Thomas Scheck, *Origen: Commentary on the Epistle to the Romans* (Washington DC: CUA, 2001-02) at 1.23-4.)

45. See page 522 *et seq.*

---

that we are predestined to 100% success if we were ever a true believer regenerated by the Holy Spirit. Yet, the consequence of such a garbling of Jesus' Way will have its inevitable fruit.

Just as Jesus' conditional promises and stern warnings were designed to lead to righteous behavior for salvation-sake, we know the lopping off of Jesus' conditions to promises or the dilution of His warnings will have the opposite effect. As Reverend Jeremy Taylor said in the 1660s: "If we did believe the promises upon their proper conditions, or... that the threatenings were as really intended as they are terribly spoken,— we should not dare to live at the rate we do." (Rev. Jeremy Taylor, *supra*, at 22.)

Thus, if one "believer in [Jesus]" should be "ensnared" in sin due to the misleading nature of faith-alone salvation doctrine, it would have been better for these religious voices to have had a "millstone put around their neck and [been] thrown in the sea" than face the horrible wrath of God for the harm they caused. (Mark 9:42.) They presented a ***diluted false gospel*** to the masses who were seeking Christ. As the early church lamented in 413 A.D. over the Marcionites (see page 578) whose faith alone gospel still lingered on: "How long then are they to go on being deceived who of...faith [alone] promise unto themselves life everlasting?"[46]

Jesus' millstone warning in Mark 9:42-47 is simply a reflection of Ezekiel's message about the watchman. If you fail to give God's warnings, and you instead dilute His conditions for salvation, the blood of all lost souls due to your teaching fall on your head. All goodness and righteousness you ever did is negated by your dereliction of giving a proper warning:

> But if the watchman see the sword come, and blow not the trumpet, and ***the people be not warned***, and the sword come, and take any

---

46. *Fide et operibus* [413 A.D.], in *Seventeen Short Treatises of Augustine* (trans.C.L. Cornish)(John H. Parker: 1847) at 59.

person from among them; he is ***taken away in his iniquity***, but ***his blood will I require at the watchman's hand***. (7) So thou, son of man, I have set thee a watchman unto the house of Israel; therefore hear the ***word at my mouth***, and ***give them warning from me***. (Eze 33:6-7 ASV.)

Make A Choice to Follow Jesus' Way Instead

Now, if instead you don't want to fail at the judgment seat, then follow the Way Jesus spelled out. William Paley quoted Jesus' many relevant passages to you in the prior chapter. Likewise, the mature William Tyndale identified the identical path to salvation for believers we outline here.[47] Luther likewise set forth the same path in his *Catechisms* of 1531, and the *Antinomian Theses* of 1537.[48] We have also thoroughly summarized above Jesus' salvation doctrine. If you are following what Jesus taught, you are never on the wrong path. You cannot help but be saved when you obey Jesus' teachings. That's the surest way to salvation. In fact, it is the only Way.

The Shortest Possible Synopsis of Jesus' Doctrine

To spell out the gospel of Yeshua (Jesus) in the most simple formula (for everyone loves a formula), it is three successive yet interconnected steps. If you fail, you repeat the

---

47. See page vii *et seq* of the Preface.
48. Luther did so in such a coy imperceptible manner that many Lutherans do not recognize the doctrinal implication from these documents.

steps each time. His Way assumes one already has *knowledge* of and *belief in* Jesus' work on the cross, the atonement, His perfect innocence and divinity, and that the alternatives are "hell whole" or "heaven maimed," etc. Demons know these things too, so don't stop there! Then, if you are convinced of these *facts* — I repeat! 'Don't mistake such *knowledge* (*gnosis*) as saving *faith*!'[49] — here are the steps to salvation:

- Repent from sin. (Luke 13:5.) Make a firm decision to turn from it and in fact turn from your sin. This includes mortify the sources of sinful acts. (Mark 9:42-47.) Repentance implies reconciling with the one you sinned against (Matt. 5:22-26), which signifies "works worthy of repentance." This brings you initial salvation. Repentance brings justification, as it did to the publican. (Luke 18:9-14.) And as Peter says, repentance "blots out sin." (Acts 2:38; Acts 3:19.)

- Trust not only that God is, but also believe He is "the rewarder of those who diligently seek Him." (Heb. 11:6.) Pray daily (or more often) in Jesus' name that God leads you from temptation. (Matt. 6:9-13.) If you seek God on this, He will give you the power to resist sin. See John 1:11-12 discussed below.

- Obey Jesus' commandments, including His incorporation from the Law given Moses. (John 3:16,36; 8:51.) This is only possible by doing step two (trust God and pray to Him for help), and only meaningful if you take step one (repent from error).

Hence, you can see each step is interconnected, and cannot be isolated from the other. It is a *synergy* — a cooperation — just as James taught. (James 2:20-24.) What then is

---

49. This *gnosis* or *knowledge* is everywhere today mistaken for *faith*. This is due to the influence of Paul's meaning of *faith* in Romans 10:9 (*i.e.*, 'believe Jesus rose from the dead'). This is not the meaning of *faith* when Jesus speaks. Instead, the Lord has the Hebrews 11:6 meaning in mind: you must believe God exists, and "He rewards those who diligently pursue Him." Mere *gnosis* (knowledge) is the polar opposite of *faith* in the sense Jesus means it. This is one aspect, often overlooked, to what Origen was criticizing in *gnosticism*.

the role of a true Hebrews 11:6 faith? Faith makes you lean on God in your failures, and believe He will answer your prayers for power to resist temptation in the future.

Empowerment From God, Not Merited Without His Work In You

This is what Apostle John means when he says, "as many as received Him, to them He gave *power* (*exousia*) to become *sons of God*, even to them that *believe* on His name." (John 1:11-12 KJV/Tyndale/Websters.)[50]

---

50. *Compare* how Jesus makes your status as *sons of God* elsewhere contingent on *your* behavior, and then one can see the correct translation of John 1:12 as "power" is self-evident. *See,* Matthew 5:9 (peacemakers "shall be called *sons of God*"); Matt. 5:44-45; Luke 6:35 ("love your enemies....so that you *may* be *sons of your Father* in heaven"). *Cf.* Rev. 21:7 ("he that *overcomes* shall inherit all things, and I will be his God, and he shall be *my son*.") The early church read John 1:11-12 as Jesus empowering us to love our enemies, to be peacemakers, etc., so as to become sons of God. The early church did not read this as your belief in Christ giving you the unconditional *right* to demand God make you a son based on faith alone. For example, Athanasius in *Discourses against the Arians* para. 766 says that "those having received the Word, have gained from Him the *power* to become the children of God....To bring this about, the Word became flesh so that He *might make man capable*" of this. (Quoted in W.A. Jurgens, *The Faith of the Early Fathers* (1979) at 329.) However, many modern translations tamper with the meaning, changing *power* in John 1:12 into *right*. This changes the verse from an *anti-faith alone* verse to a *pro-faith alone* verse. Those changing *power* into *right* are: ASV, NASB, NIV, and God's Word. Due to this falsification, a faith alone advocate celebrates that "these two verses only bring forth rejoicing from Christians" because they supposedly "affirm concretely once again that salvation...is *conditional only upon receiving (believing in) Christ* as your savior." (*Systematic Bible Studies*, http://www.bibleone.net/sbs.html.) Yet, this conclusion is based on a false alteration of Scripture.

This verse reveals a key relationship between *believing* and *becoming sons of God.* As the *Free Will Baptist* of January 1860 explained this verse: "This passage proves something must be done **subsequent to faith** to make us sons of God." For it clearly says "believing on His name did not make them sons of God, but placed this honor **within reach**, gave the privilege and opportunity to become sons." (*Id.*, at 79.)

Erasmus of Oxford (1466-1536) — a great reformer in his own right — likewise explained this verse. He was the most learned man on the meaning of ancient Greek in his day. His reading is the correct one. Erasmus said John 1:12 means we are not "suddenly" made sons of God; rather we are "empowered" to become such children of God by Jesus' "message."[51] Hence, our obedience is never by merit. It is by empowerment infused in us by God's answering of our prayer to resist temptation.

Obedience &Prayer Brings Empowerment; Sin Takes It Away.

What exactly does John 1:12 mean by God giving us the "power to become sons of God...."?

Samson was a type of servant of the Lord who is strong while he obeys the Lord, but loses his strength once he begins to disobey. (Judges 16:1, sleeps with harlot.) Samson thereafter is too weak to resist the badgering of Delilah to know the key to his physical strength — his Nazirite vow. (This optional vow is given by God to Moses in Numbers chapter six.) By telling Delilah the secret, Samson tacitly permits Delilah to break his Nazirite vow that his hair cannot be cut. (Judges 16:17.) This disobedience leads to Samson's blindness and imprisonment. (Judges 16:21.) When he con-

---

51. Erasmus pointed out this verse implies "we do not become sons of God suddenly, but first we are given the **power** which is offered us by the message of grace." (*Hyperaspistes*, book 2, excerpted in J.K.Sowards, et al., *Controversies* (University of Toronto: 2005) at 687.)

---

tinues back on his original path of obedience to his Nazarite vow and prays to God for restored strength (Judges 16:22,28), God gives Samson his greatest victory.

Hence, obedience and prayer empowered Samson. Before that repentance, Samson's sin against his vow to God had taken such power away. This is what John means in 1:12 about empowerment. We are given power to become sons of God when we obey. This is what God promises to give if we pray earnestly for this power.

Empowerment Through Jesus

Jesus says we are from now on to pray to the Father in the name of Jesus (Yeshua). This is important. While Samson returned to obedience — letting his hair grow without cutting it (obeying once again his Nazirite vow), his obedience was combined thereafter with prayer. Then God gave Samson his great victory. Prayer is the connection to Jesus we need daily to have our victories. Jesus says we are to pray daily to "resist temptation." Hence, when we obey God, it is never done on our own power *alone*. It is God answering our prayer.

Hence, the requisite obedience is never your own merit *by itself* that will lead to salvation. Rather, it is only obedience **empowered** by God that causes atonement to apply. (See page 1; Matt.5:22-26.) Jesus in the Metaphor of the Vine clearly says "the branch cannot bear fruit *by itself*..." (John 15:4.) Then as you obey Jesus, you abide in His love. (John 15:10.) This love from Jesus no doubt empowers you to further obedience.

Why Then Is Jesus' Gospel Rejected?

Jesus told us why many reject His message:

> Why don't you understand what I am saying? Because **you cannot bear to listen to my message**. You belong to your father, Satan, and you **want to carry out your father's desires**. From

> the start, he was a murderer, and he has never
> stood for the truth, because there is no truth in
> him. When he tells a lie, he is speaking in char-
> acter; because he is a liar — indeed, the inven-
> tor of the lie! But as for me, ***because I tell you
> the truth you don't believe me***. Which one of
> you can show me where I am wrong? If I am
> telling you the truth, why don't you believe
> me? (John 8:43-47 CJB.)

People do not accept Jesus' message, He says, because they
want to carry out the desires of Satan. They want to break
God's Law, and feel no remorse. Jesus' message insists on
regret, repentance and obedience. No one can prove Jesus'
message is wrong. Instead, they drive around His doctrine,
exploiting out-of-context quoting, and relying upon false
prophets who lie and create myths.

Final Thoughts

Once you know the true gospel from Jesus' lips, you
can finally understand why His very last words on earth were:

> Go ye therefore, and ***teach all nations***, baptiz-
> ing them in the name of the Father, and of the
> Son, and of the Holy Ghost. Teaching them to
> **obey** (*tereo*, diligently follow) ***all things what-
> soever I commanded you***, and, lo, I will be
> with you always until the end of the world.
> (Matt. 28:19-20.)

This means our job is to remain the tireless watchmen
on the wall, ceaselessly giving His warnings of hell by sinning to Christians and non-Christians alike. As long as we
teach *obedience* to Jesus who will judge everyone impartially, we will be innocent of the blood of those whom we
warned. Otherwise, if we fell silent, the guilt of their sins falls
to our tally sheet as well. The Great Commission was fore-
shadowed in Isaiah where God declares:

> I have posted watchmen on your walls, Jerusa-
> lem; they will never fall silent, neither by day
> nor by night. You who call on the Lord, **give
> yourselves no rest**; and give him no rest until
> he restores Jerusalem and makes it a praise on
> earth. (Isaiah 62:6-7 CJB.)

However, the gospel of faith alone caused us to chase
after instilling *beliefs alone* and not *behaviors* as of *equal
importance.* As a result, Jesus' Great Commission makes no
sense any more. As Bonhoeffer said, we have a "Christianity
without Christ." Once we put Christ back into Christianity,
the gospel can truly have its full *intended impact* by the One
who paid with His blood the right to author its terms.

Post-Script: Importance of Protestants Coming to Grips with the Early Heretic Marcion's Cheap Grace Doctrine

Has the last four hundred years been a waste? Has the
descent into cheap grace at odds with Jesus' doctrine all this
time been an unprecedented error? No. This has been a valu-
able period of cleansing of doctrinal errors. However, our
response to those errors ended up in over-reaction. We need
to come back to Jesus. It is that simple. We can take encouragement from the fact that this very same error happened
once before. Let's see how the early church escaped, and perhaps we can simply repeat the measures taken back then.

Most Protestants are utterly unaware that Paulinism,
in particular faith alone doctrine, previously threatened to
overwhelm Jesus' salvation doctrine and destroy it. In 144
A.D., there arose a ship-builder from Pontus named Marcion.
He founded a church system that rivaled in numbers and
influence that of the orthodox Christian church. By 150 A.D.,

Justin wrote that Marcionites had expanded "to the uttermost bounds of the earth."[52] It required three hundred years for the orthodox church to eventually rout out the heresy of Marcion.

Marcion was not battling the Roman Catholic church. It did not yet exist. Instead, there was a large orthodox church led from Jerusalem. The Roman bishop was just one bishop among many throughout the Mediterranean. Even if Peter was in Rome at one point, there was no effort to exercise superiority from Rome until many centuries later.

What happened is that Marcion declared in 144 A.D. that Paul alone was the true apostle for the era of grace; the twelve apostles, in particular their gospel of Matthew, were tainted by legalism; the Jesus of the twelve belonged to the God of the Old Testament; and the Jesus of Paul represented the son of a loving Father who now accepted us by faith alone.

In Marcion's book known as the *Antitheses*, which exists only in fragments quoted by others, we find endorsement of everything Pauline, including faith alone. Marcion's primary antithesis involved faith and law. On one hand, there was the Law given Moses, which the apostolic twelve endorsed in Matthew's gospel. On the other hand, there was the faith alone doctrine of Paul. To solve this antithesis, Marcion invented the idea that Christ had two personages — the one of the twelve and the one presented by Paul. The Jesus of the twelve represented the Creator-God of the Old Testament. The Jesus of Paul represented the Good God or the Father of the New Testament. The *Antitheses* of 144 A.D. reads:

> 18.The Jewish Christ [of Matthew *et al*] was designated by the Creator [*i.e.,* the God of the Old Testament] solely to restore the Jewish people from the Diaspora; but our Christ [present in Paul's writings] was commissioned by the

---

52. B. Aland, "Marcion, Marcionites, Marcionism," *Encyclopedia of the Early Church* (Cambridge: James Clarke & Co. 1992) Vol. 1 at 524.

---

good God [of the new testament] to liberate all mankind.

19. The Good [God] [of Paul's Jesus] is good toward all men; the Creator [God of the Jesus of the twelve], however, promises salvation only to those who are obedient to him [*i.e.*, legalism]. The Good [God of Paul's Jesus] redeems those who **believe** in him, but **he does not judge those who are disobedient** to him; the Creator [God of the twelve's Jesus], however, redeems his faithful and judges and punishes the sinners.

29. The Christ [of the Creator God represented by the twelve] promises to the Jews the restoration of their former condition by return of their land and, after death, a refuge in Abraham's bosom in the underworld [*i.e.*, Sheol/hell]. Our Christ [of the Jesus presented by Paul] will establish the Kingdom of God, an eternal and heavenly possession.[53]

The Jerusalem church previously replied to anti-Law and faith-alone doctrine by saying Paul was an apostate and did not represent true Christianity. As Professor James Dunn notes: "The most direct heirs of the Jewish-Christian groupings within earliest Christianity [*i.e.*, the early Jerusalem church] regarded Paul as the great apostate, an arch enemy," citing *Epistula Petri* 2.3; *Clem. Hom.* 17:18-19.[54]

The Jerusalem church's response is directly reflected in our New Testament. As Augustine noted in 413 A.D. in his treatise *Faith and Works*, the epistles of James (the first

---

53. Dr. Peter M. Head (New Testament Research Fellow, Tyndale House), *The History of the Interpretation of the Apostle Paul* (2001), reprinted at http://www.tyndale.cam.ac.uk/Tyndale/staff/Head/ Lent_01_Handout.htm (accessed 1/5/08).

54. James D. G. Dunn, *The Cambridge Companion to St. Paul* (Cambridge University Press, 2003) at 2.

---

bishop of Jerusalem), Jude (the second bishop of Jerusa-lem),[55] and Second Peter were specifically written to destroy "faith alone" doctrine as inferred from Paul's epistles. (See page 523n *supra*.) Second Peter even said many would fall from their "steadfastness in Christ" by relying upon "difficult to understand" passages in the writings of Paul. These pas-sages were seen as giving a "liberty" that Second Peter said was foreign to the true gospel. (See pages 500-504 *supra*.)

Tertullian, an orthodox church member in Carthage, Africa, wrote in 207 A.D. his famous rebuttal to Marcion. In it, Tertullian raised every ground possible to dispute whether Paul was truly an apostle of Jesus Christ. Tertullian even sug-gested Paul was a false prophet as warned of by Jesus Christ. We previously quoted this daring analysis from Tertullian. (See pages 495-500 *supra*.) In that passage, Tertullian says that Paul's claim to apostleship is totally self-serving, and by Jesus' standards is invalid. Scholars generally now recognize this is a valid criticism of Paul's claims. In the end, Tertullian even suggested "[Paul] is the apostle of the heretics." (Tertul-lian, *Adversus Marcion* 3.5, "haeritcorum apostolus".)

Often, Protestant historians try to obscure the real nature of Marcion's heresy. They focus on every other dispute than the problem of Marcion's teaching of *faith alone*. While it is true that Marcion said there was a different God for the new versus the old testaments, and this claim was battled vig-orously by Tertullian, they ignore what was at stake. ***Mar-cion's goal behind that argument was to justify two different salvation doctrines***. Once he divided salvation into two dis-pensations — the old and the new, Marcion could defend the new is by faith alone and the old one is by obedience. Mar-cion hence was trying to rationalize Paul's doctrine of faith alone as belonging to a distinct dispensation of Paul's Jesus. Thereby, it could be valid despite contradicting Jesus' salva-

---

55.On James & Jude as bishops, see "Appendix to the works of Hippoly-tus," *The Ante-Nicene Fathers: Fathers of The Third Century* (ed. Donaldson, Roberts & Coxe) (1886) Vol. V at 255.

tion doctrine in the gospel of Matthew and John (properly translated). As Arthur Cushman McGiffert, in *A History of Christian Thought* (C. Scribner's Sons: 1949) at 59 explains:

> For the gospel of the free grace of God and salvation by ***faith alone*** had been substituted [by the twelve apostles in their gospels], so Marcion believed, [by] a legalism of a genuinely Jewish character.

Hence, to destroy the significance of the different salvation doctrine in the twelve apostles' gospels, Marcion claimed Paul had the right to proclaim a superseding one.

Thus, Marcion represented a vigorous effort to erase any role of repentance and obedience in the Christian doctrine of salvation.

> Marcion expounded his main position in a work entitled *Antitheses*....[The God of the New Testament] was the God of grace who offered salvation to all by ***faith alone***;.... (T. Alec Burkill, *The Evolution of Christian Thought* (Cornell University Press, 1971) at 42.)

> After Simon Magus, it was Marcion above all whom the Fathers regarded as the arch-heretic:... the law is discarded and salvation depends on ***faith alone***. (Hans Kung, *The Church* (Image Books: 1976) at 316.)

Tertullian in rebuttal to Marcion conceded that the ceremonial law of the old testament was abrogated, but the moral commandments in the Law remained. To this end, Tertullian taught repentance and obedience remained absolutely essential to salvation.[56]

When I encountered this history, I was shocked and in disbelief. David Bercot, a Protestant attorney like myself, was as equally startled by encountering Marcion as I was. After Bercot did a comprehensive survey of the doctrines of the

---

56. See my prior work, *Jesus' Words Only* (2007) at 405-425.

early Church in his exhaustive 705 page *Dictionary of Early Christian Beliefs* (1998), he wrote *Will The Real Heretics Please Stand Up* (1999). In that work, Bercot admits he discovered that the early church, in "contradiction to many of my own theological views," taught doctrines that universally rejected teachings which we all recognize as part of modern accepted Pauline teaching. When Bercot discusses Marcion, he expresses the same shock I experienced when I first read what Marcion taught:

> As surprising as all of this may be to you, **what I'm about to tell you is even more bizarre.** There was a religious group **labelled as heretics** by the early Christians, who strongly disputed the church's stance on salvation and works [*i.e.*, that salvation depended on works]. Instead, they [*i.e.*, the heretics] taught man is totally depraved. That we are **saved solely by grace.** That **works play no role in salvation.** And that **we cannot lose our salvation once we obtain it**.... (*Will The Real Heretics Please Stand Up, supra,* at 66.)(Emphasis added.)

It is obvious that Marcionism has revived. Many Protestants likewise today argue a dispensational division exists between old and new, so that Jesus' contrary salvation doctrine to Paul's doctrine can be *honestly* dismissed as *irrelevant.* (See dispensationalist claims on pages 209-210 *supra.*)

Jesus and the early church had a solution to prevent Paul's teachings from overturning those of Jesus. They were:

- The release of the epistles of James, Jude and Second Peter;
- The release of the Revelation of Jesus Christ, with its heavy emphasis on works required for salvation, including a re-affirmation of James' principles in Revelation 3:1-3; and
- Tertullian's brilliant examination in 207 A.D. of the lack of authenticity to Paul's claims of apostleship and even Tertullian's suggestion that Paul was a false prophet predicted by Christ.

These various attacks on Paulinism were vigorous and well-sustained. Marcion was defeated. These critical analyses must be re-published for a new generation. For four hundred years, we have been entrapped within revived Marcionism. Because Christ's words were so powerful, Christianity lived on despite this albatross hanging on, weighing down His words in the wrong direction. Yet, by our dereliction of duty, Christ's message is obscured. How did this happen?

What took place in the early Protestant Reformation is that this history about Marcion was forgotten. It was primarily Erasmus and Tyndale who initially realized that the reformation had made a significant major mistake. It had treated Paul's doctrines regarding 'faith alone' as a necessity to follow even when at odds with the salvation doctrine of Jesus Christ. These two men bravely changed course. They even obviously caused Luther to change course. He too adopted *double justification* (*i.e.*, salvation begins by faith but requires works and obedience for final salvation) which essentially matches Jesus' doctrine.[57] Unfortunately, Luther's heroism of 1517-18 was not matched by a later bold declaration that he realized this error. Luther tried to make this change quietly, through an ecumenical conference with the Catholic Church in 1541. Upon Luther's death, he left it to Melancthon to continue this effort. Melancthon did so, causing the Lutheran church to adopt double justification as an official doctrine. It lasted until a short while after Melancthon's death. And thus the true gospel expired from being present in any major Protestant denomination. It survives primarily only in the Pentecostal and Mennonite churches.

Consequently, we need spiritual and historical revival. We need to repent of the misleading 'faith alone' doctrine. We also need to refuse anyone else from taking Jesus/ Yeshua's place as our "sole teacher" (Matt. 23:10). We need to repent from the stain of Paulinism upon Christ's message.

---

57. See "A Parade of Witnesses Includes Tyndale and Shockingly The (Mature) Luther Too" on page iv *et seq*.

Bibliographical References

_____. Article No. 38, http://www.holybible.com/resources/Trinitarian/article_38.htm.

_____. "Atonement," *Jewish Encyclopedia* at http://jewishencyclopedia.com (last accessed 10/22/2007).

_____. "Beware the Leaven of the Pharisees," *Let Us Reason Ministries* at http://www.letus-reason.org/WF39.htm (last accessed 6/17/06).

_____. *Book of Concord* (1580).

_____. "Codex Sinaiticus" *Catholic Encyclopedia* in http://www.newadvent.org/cathen/04085a.htm (accessed 7-16-07).

_____. "Codex Sinaiticus," http://www.bible-researcher.com/codex-aleph.html

_____. "Covetousness," http://www.jewishencyclopedia.com/view.jsp?artid=838&letter=C (last accessed 7/4/06).

_____. "The Daily Bible Study," at http://www.keyway.ca/htm2002/pharisee.htm (last accessed 6/16/06).

_____. "Does God Want Christians Freed from the Law?," *New Horizons* (January-February 2001) http://www.abcog.org/nh/free.htm.

_____. "[John Donne]," http://www.luminarium.org/sevenlit/donne/donnebio.htm (accessed 5/6/2007).

_____. "Dr. Duboses' Gospel in the Gospels," *Sewanee Review* (University of the South: 1907) at 111 *ff.*

_____. "John William Burgon," *Wikipedia* http://en.wikipedia.org/wiki/John_William_Burgon (accessed 7-17-07).

_____. E-Drash 8/8/2004 (First Fruits of Zion).

_____. "The Lectionary Series," http://www.lectionarystudies.com/studyg/sunday26ag.html (last accessed 6/21/06).

_____. "The Mystery of Lawlessness," http://www.abcog.org/nh/lawless.htm (last accessed 6/17/06).

_____. "The Place of Repentance in Religion and Theology," *The Congregational Review* (Boston: Broughton & Wyman, 1868) Vol. 8, May 1868, at 201 (googlebooks).

_____. "Matthew: The authority of Jesus. 21:23-32," *Lectionary Bible Studies and Sermons* at http://www.lectionarystudies.com/studyg/sunday26ag.html (last accessed 6/21/06.)

_____. "Nature and Relations of Faith," *Free Will Baptist Quarterly* (January 1860) Vol. 8, No. XXIX at 68 (downloadable at books.google.com).

_____. "Pelagius," *Catholic Encyclopedia*, available at http://www.newadvent.org/cathen/11604a.htm (last visited 2005).

_____. "Simon Magus," http://www.newadvent.org/cathen/13797b.htm (accessed 6/10/07).

_____. "Sermon on the Mount," http://mb-soft.com/believe/txw/sermonmt.htm (last accessed 5-24-05).

_____. "The Spirit, The Necessity of Good Works and Final Judgment," http://www.abu.nb.ca/courses/pauline/Works.htm (Atlantic Baptist University)(last accessed 11/25/2006).

_____. *Theological Dictionary of the New Testament* (TDNT) (1968).

____. "Tzitzit," http://www.karaite-korner.org/tzitzit.shtml (last accessed 11/30/2006).

____. "What Is Adultery?" at http://www.brightfiles.com/findtruth/otherart/adultery.htm (last accessed 8-17-07).

____. "What is the meaning of Luke 14:28, and 'counting the cost?' at http://www.thereg.org/questions/p094.a.html (last accessed 7/6/06).

Abegg Jr., Martin. Flint, Peter. Ulrich, Eugene. *The Dead Sea Scrolls Bible: The Oldest Known Bible Translated for the First Time Into English* (Harper San Francisco: 1999)(DSSB).

Abbott, Edwin. *Johannine Grammar* (A&C Black: 1906).

Adam, Rev. Richard. *The Religious World Displayed: Or, a View of the Four Grand Systems of Religion* (London: Seeley, 1823) Vol. I.

Adams, Douglas Q. *Essential Modern Greek Grammar* (Courier Dover Publications 1987).

Aland, B. "Marcion, Marcionites, Marcionism," *Encyclopedia of the Early Church* (Cambridge: James Clarke & Co. 1992) Vol. 1 at 523.

Alcorn, Randy. *Money, Possessions & Eternity* (Wheaton, Illinois: Tyndale, 2003).

Allison, C. F. *The Rise of Moralism: The Proclamation of the Gospel from Hooker to Baxter* (London, S.P.C.K., 1966).

Anthony, Richard. *Comparisons Between the Majority (KJV) and Minority (NIV) Texts* at http://ecclesia.org/truth/m-m.html (last accessed 9-7-07).

Augustine, *Fide et operibus*, in *Seventeen Short Treatises of Augustine* (trans.C.L. Cornish)(John H. Parker: 1847)(downloadable from books.google.com).

Avis, Paul D. L. *Anglicanism and the Christian Church: Theological Resources in Historical Perspective* (Continuum International Publishing Group, 2002).

Barnes, Albert. *Notes Explanatory and Practical on the Gospels: Designed for Sunday School* (Harper & Brothers, 1853).

Barr, James. *The Semantics of Biblical Language* (Oxford University Press, 1961; repr. London: SCM Press, 1983).

Bauer, Walter; Danker, Frederick; Arndt, William; Gingrich, F. Wilbur. *A Greek-English Lexicon of the New Testament and Other Early Christian Literature.* (Third Edition. Chicago, Ill: The University of Chicago Press, 2000) (BDAG).

Beale, G.K. "Revelation is The Book of Revelation, a Commentary on the Greek Text," *The New International Greek Testament Commentary* (Howard Marshall and Donald A. Hagner, Editors) (Wm. B Eerdmans: 1999).

Bercot, David W. *A Dictionary of Early Christian Beliefs* (Bercot ed.)(1998).

Bercot, David W. *Will the Real Heretics Please Stand Up: A New Look at Today's Evangelical Christianity in the light of Early Christianity* (Texas: Scroll Publishing, 1999).

Buttman, Alexander. *A Grammar of the New Testament Greek* (Andover: Walter Draper, 1873).

Bing, Charles C. *Lordship Salvation — A Biblical Evaluation and Response* (Ph.D. Dissertation) (Dallas Theological Seminary, 1991), reprinted at http://www.forerunner.org/bing/LS-chap2.htm (accessed 7-21-07).

Bonhoeffer, Dietrich. *Christ the Center* (1960).

Bonhoeffer, Dietrich. *A Testament to Freedom: The Essential Writings of Dietrich Bonhoeffer* (Harper Collins, 1995).

Bonhoeffer, Dietrich. *The Cost of Discipleship* (1937)(reprint N.Y: Simon & Schuster, 1995).

Bruce, Alexander Balmain. *The Kingdom of God: Or, Christ's Teaching According to the Synoptical Gospels* (Scribner's 1897).

Bruner, Frederick D. *A Theology of the Holy Spirit* (Grand Rapids: Wm. B. Eerdmans Publishing Co., 1970).

Burgess, Joseph A. Gross, Jeffrey Gros. *Building Unity: Ecumenical Dialogues with Roman Catholic Participation in the United States* (Paulist Press, 1989).

Burgon, John. *Revision Revised* (London: John Murray: 1883).

Broadus, John A. *Commentary on Matthew* (1886) (Kegel Classics: 1990).

Bromiley, G.W. *The International Standard Bible Encyclopedia* (Eerdman's 1995).

Bruce, F.F. *The Gospel of John* (Wm. B. Eerdmans: 1994).

Bruce, Alexander Balmain. *The Kingdom of God: Or, Christ's Teaching According to the Synoptical Gospels* (Scribner's 1897).

Burkett, Larry. *Frankly Answered Questions* http://www.new-life.net/faq212.htm (last accessed 8-16-07).

Byrd, Edward. "Unto what then were ye Baptized?," *The Reminder* Volume No. 23 Issue No. 07 (November 1983), available online at http://www.anabaptist.com/ReminderTemplate.cfm?ReminderID=3 (accessed 7-21-07).

Calvin, John. *Commentary on the Treasure Hidden in the Field* at http://www.ccel.org/c/calvin/comment3/comm_vol32/htm/xxiii.htm (last accessed 7/2/06).

Campbell, Alexander. *The Christian System* (2d Ed. 1839).

Carr, A. (Reverand). *The Gospel According to St. Matthew* (editor)(Cambridge: University Press, 1893).

Chambers, Steven L. "'Faith in Christ,' or the 'Faith of Christ? Pistis Cristou in Paul," *Lutheran Theological Review* XII (1999-2000) at 22 (available online).

Chambers, Robert. "Dr. Paley," *Cyclopedia of English Literature: A History, Critical and Biographical, of British Authors From the Earliest To The Present Times* (Edinburgh: 1844) Vol. II at 651 *et seq.*

Child, L.M.F. *The Progress of Religious Ideas, Through Successive Ages* (C.S. Francis, 1855).

Clarke, F. L. *The Life of William Tyndale* (W. Swan Sonnenschein, 1883).

Clebsch,William A. *England's Earliest Protestants, 1520-1535* (Yale University Press, 1964).

Coehlo, Elizabeth. *Adding English: A Guide to Teaching in Multilingual Classrooms* (Pippin: 2004) (text searchable at books.google.com).

Coffman, James B. *Commentaries* available at http://www.searchgodsword.org/com/bcc/view.cgi?book=mr&chapter= 011 (last accessed 5/5/07).

Crafts, Wilbur Fisk. *The Sabbath for Man* (Funk & Wagnalls, 1885).

Cross, Claire. *Church and People: England, 1450-1660* (Blackwell Publishing, 1999).

Crossan, John. *In Search of Paul: How Jesus' Apostle Opposed Rome's Empire with God's Kingdom* (San Francisco, Harper: San Francisco, 2004).

Cyprian *Three Books of Testimonies Against the Jews* available online at http://www.ccel.org/ccel/schaff/anf05.iv.v.xii.iii.xxiii.html?highlight=blessed,are,they,that,do,his,commandments#highlight (access 7-15-07).

Davies, W.D. & Allison, Dale C. *A Critical and Exegetical Commentary on the Gospel According to Saint Matthew,* volume 2 of *The International Critical Commentary on the Holy Scriptures of the Old and New Testaments* (Edinburgh: T&T Clark, 1988-1991).

Davis, James R. *The Unmerciful Servant* at http://www.focusongod.com/forgive.htm (last accessed 6/9/2007).

Deffinbaugh, Bob. Th.M. *The Fatal Failures of Religion: #2 Legalism Matthew 5:17-*at http://www.bible.org/page.asp?page_id=604 (last accessed 7/4/06).

Demarest, Bruce. *The Cross and Salvation: The Doctrine of Salvation* (Wheaton, Illinois: 1997).

Derickson, Gary W. "Viticulture and John 15:1-6," *Journal of the Grace Evangelical Society* (Spring 2005): 23

Dillow, Joseph. *Reign of the Servant Kings* (2d ed.)(Schoettle Publishing,1992).

Dods, Marcus D.D. *The Parables of Our Lord* (Edinburgh: Macniven and Wallace, 1883).

Donaldson, James. Roberts, Alexander. Coxe, Arthur Cleveland. *The Ante-Nicene Fathers: Fathers of The Third Century* (1886) Vol. V at 255.

Donne, John. "Sermon on 'Easter' 1626," *The Works of John Donne, D.D.* (Henry Alford, ed.)(London: John Parker, 1839) Vol. 1.

Donfried, Karl P. "Paul and the Revisions: Did Luther Really Get It All Wrong?," *Dialogue: Journal of Theology* Vol. 46, No. 1 (Spring 2007) at 31.

Dunagan, Mark. *Counting the Cost,: The Cost of Bearing Fruit With Perseverance* (Beaverton Church of Christ) at http://www.ch-of-christ.beaverton.or.us/ Counting_the_Cost.htm (last accessed 7/16/06).

Dunn, James D. G. *Jesus Remembered* (Eerdmans: 2003).

Dunn, James D.G. *The Cambridge Companion to St. Paul* (Cambridge University Press, 2003).

Dunning, H. Ray. "The Divine Response, Habakkuk 2:4," *Beacon Hill Commentary* (Kansas City, Mo.: Beacon Hill Press, 1966) Vol. 5 at 277 *et seq.*

Eadie, John. *A Commentary on the Greek Text of Paul to the Colossians* (T&T Clark, 1884).

Edwards, Jonathan. "Thoughts on the Atonement," *The Works of Jonathan Edwards* (Boston: 1854) Vol. I.

Edwards, James R. *The Gospel According to Mark* (Wm. B. Eerdmans Publishing, 2002).

Epstein, Rabbi. *The Babylonian Talmud* (Rabbi Dr. Epstein)(London: Socino Press, 1935-1938).

[Erasmus] *Holy Scripture Speaks: The Production and Reception of Erasmus' Paraphrases of the New Testament* (ed. Hilmar M. Pabel & Mark Vessey) (University of Toronto Press, 2002).

Erasmus, *Exposition on the Psalms* (Univ. Toronto Press, 2003).

Finney, Charles G. *Justification by Faith* (1837) http://www.gospeltruth.net/1837LTPC/ lptc05_just_by_faith.htm (last accessed 8-18-2007).

Finney, Charles G. *Memoirs of Rev. Charles G. Finney* (A.S. Barnes & Company, 1876).

Finney, Charles G. *Lectures on Systematic Theology* (reprint 2003)(Xulon Press).

Fisher, Edward. *The Marrow of Modern Divinity* (Boston: John Bryce: 1766).

Fisher, George Park. *The History of Christian Doctrine* (T&T Clark: 1896).

Fletcher, John. *The Works of the Reverend John Fletcher* (B. Waugh and T. Mason, 1833).

Fortner, Dan. *God Sees No Sin* at http://www.pristinegrace.org/media.php?id=297 (accessed 8-25-07).

Friedmann, Robert *Anabaptist Theology* by http: // anabaptistchurch.org/ anabaptist _theology.htm (last accessed 9-26-07).

Fuller, Daniel. "Biblical Theology and the Analogy of Faith," *Unity and Diversity in N.T. Theology. Essays in Honor of George E. Ladd* (R. A. Guelich (ed.)) (Eerdmans: 1978) at 195-213, available at http://www.fuller.edu/ministry/berean/analogy.htm (last accessed 9/4/2007).

Fuller, David O. *Which Bible?* (Grand Rapids International Publications: 1970).

Gaebelin, A.C. *The Annotated Bible* available online at http://www.biblecentre.org/commentaries/acg_70_revelation.htm (last accessed 9-7-2007).

Gaebelein, Frank E. *Expositor's Bible Commentary* (Ed. Gaebelein) (Grand Rapids, Michigan: 1989). Vol. VII.

Gaston, Lloyd. *Paul and Torah* (UBC: 1987).

Gathercole, Simon J. *Where Is Boasting: Early Jewish Soteriology and Paul's Response in Romans 1-5* (Eerdmans: 2002).

Gaussen, S.R.Louis. (Professor of Theology, Geneva, Switzerland.) *Theopneusty, or the Plenary Inspiration of the Holy Scriptures* (trans. Edward Kirk)(New York: John S.Taylor & Co., 1844) (downloadable from books.google.com).

Gerstner, Jonathan. "Legalism and Antinomianism: Two Deadly Paths Off the Narrow Road," *Trust and Obey* (1996) 118 ff.

Godet, Frédéric Louis. *A Commentary on the Gospel of St. Luke* (trans. Edward William Shalders, M. D.) (I. K. Funk & Co., 1881).

Goranson, Stephen , "The Text of Revelation 22:14," *New Testament Studies* (1997) Vol. 43 at 154-157.

Gordon, Nehemiah. *The Hebrew Yeshua vs. The Greek Yeshua* (Jerusalem: Hilkiah Press, 2006).

Hagner, Donald. *Matthew: World Bible Commentary* (Dallas Word Books, 1993-1995).

Hamilton, Victor P. *New International Commentary on the Old Testament* (Eerdmans: 1990) Vol. 1.

Hardwick, Charles. *A History of the Christian Church During the Reformation* (Macmillan, 1865).

Harrison, Paul V. & Picirilli, Robert E. *The Randall House Bible Commentary* (Randall House: 1992).

Hawkins, Robert A. "Covenant Relations of the Sermon on the Mount," *Restoration Quarterly* Vol. 12, No. 1 reprinted at http:// www.restorationquarterly.org/Volume_012/ rq01201hawkins.htm (last accessed 6/16/06).

Hays, Richard. *The Faith of Jesus Christ* (2d Edition) (Eerdmans: 2001).

Hays, Richard B. *The Conversion of the Imagination: Paul as Interpreter of Israel's Scripture* (Eerdmans: 2005).

Head, Dr. Peter M. (New Testament Research Fellow, Tyndale House), *The History of the Interpretation of the Apostle Paul* (2001), reprinted at http://www.tyndale.cam.ac.uk/Tyndale/staff/Head/Lent_01_Handout.htm (accessed 1/5/08).

Herbert, A. G. "Faithfulness and 'Faith,'" *Theology* 58 (1955) at 373-79 (also appearing in the *Reformed Theological Review* (June 1955)).

Herzog, Johann J. *The New Schaff-Herzog Encyclopedia of Religious Knowledge* (1909).

Hollerich, Michael J. *Eusebius of Caesarea's Commentary on Isaiah: Christian Exegesis in the Age of Constantine* (Oxford University Press: 1999).

Horne, George, D.D. *Discourses of the Right Reverend George Horne* (London: 1824) III.

Horsley, Richard A. *Hearing the Whole Story: The Politics of Plot in Mark's Gospel* (Westminster John Knox Press, 2001).

Hopkins, Edward Washburn. *History of Religions* (MacMillan: 1918).

How, Thomas Yardley. *A Vindication of the Protestant Episcopal Church: In a Series of Letters* (Eastburn, Kirk, & Co, 1816).

Howard, George. "On the "Faith of Christ," *Harvard Theological Review* Vol. 60 No. 4 (Oct. 1967) at 459 *ff*.

Howard, George. *Hebrew Gospel of Matthew* (Mercer University Press: 1995).

Huneke, Douglas K. "Guilt and Grace: Cheap or Costly," (Westminster Presbyterian Church of Tiburon)(May 5, 2002) (http://www.wpctiburon.org/sermons/sr20020505.html)(last accessed 10/3/2007).

Hunt, David. *In The Defense of the Faith* (Harvest House: 1996).

Hylsop, James Hervey. *Logic and Argument* (C. Scribner: 1899).

Hyman, Malcolm D. *Greek and Roman Grammarians On Motion Verbs and Place Adverbials* (January 4, 2003) http://archimedes.fas.harvard.edu/mdh/motion.pdf (accessed 7-18-07).

Josephus. *Antiquities of the Jews* (Whiston translation).

Josephus, Flavius. *The Works of Flavius Josephus, the Learned and Authentic Jewish Historian* (Whiston translation)(Simms & M'Intyre: 1841).

Jülicher, Adolf. *An Introduction to the New Testament* (trans. Janet Ward) (N.Y.: G.P. Putnam's, 1904)(dowloadable at books.google.com).

Jurgens, W.A. *The Faith of the Early Fathers* (1979).

Kaiser Jr., Dr. Walter C. *Toward an Old Testament Theology* (Zondervan: 1991).

Kelley, Shawn. *Racializing Jesus: Race, Ideology and the Formation of Modern Biblical Scholarship* (Routledge: 2002).

Kendall, R.T. *Once Saved Always Saved* (Chicago: Moody Press, 1985).

Keil & Delitzsch. *Commentary on the Old Testament* (10 Vols.) (Hendrickson, 1996).

Kierkegaard, Soren. *Provocations: Spiritual Writings of Kierkegard* (ed. Charles E. Moore) (Orbis Books, 2007).

Kierkegaard, Soren. *Kierkegaard's Attack Upon 'Christendom' 1854-1855* (Trans. and Introduction by Walter Lowrie)(Princeton, N.J.: Princeton University Press, 1972).

Kissinger, Warren. *The Parables of Jesus: A History of Interpretation and Bibliography* (Metuchen, N.J.: American Theological Library Association, 1979).

Kittell, Gerhard. Friedrich, Gerhard. Bromiley, Geoffrey William. *Theological Dictionary of the New Testament (TDNT)* (Eerdman's 1985).

Knox, David Broughton. *The Doctrine of Faith in the Reign of Henry VIII* (London, 1961).

Köstlin, Julius. *Life of Luther* (Scribner's, 1893).

Laney, J. Carl. "Abiding is Believing: The Analogy of the Vine in John 15:1-6," *Biblioteca Sacra* 146 (January-March 1989): 55.

Larkin, Clarence. *Dispensational Truth* (Philadelphia: Larkin, 1918).

Lauterbach, Jacob. (Editor.) *Mekilta de Rabbi Ishmael: ritical Edition on the Basis of the Manuscripts and Early Editions with an English Translation, Introduction, and Notes* (Philadelphia: Jewish Publication Society, 1933).

Lea, Henry Charles. *A History of the Inquisition of Spain* (MacMillan: 1907).

Lebedev, "Paul, the Law, Grace and … 'Cheap Grace,'" *Quodlibet Journal* Vol. 6 No. 3, July - September 2004 (available at http://www.quodlibet.net/lebedev-grace.shtml).

Lewis, Charlton. *An Elementary Dictionary* (1918).

Liddell, Henry George & Scott, Robert. *A Greek-English Lexicon* (1940) available online http://www.perseus.tufts.edu (last visited 2007)

Liddell & Scott, *Greek Lexicon* (Oxford: 1869).(The 1891 abridged edition is downloadable at books.google.com).

Lisco, Frederick. *The Parables of Jesus* (trans.from German by Rev. Fairbairn) (Philadelphia: Daniels & Smith, 1850)(downloadable at books.google.com).

Locke, John. *The Works of John Locke* (London: Thomas Tegg, 1828) Vol. VIII.

Losch, Richard R. *The Uttermost Parts of the Earth: A Guide To Places In The Bible* (Eerdmans: 2005).

Lucado, Max. *In The Grip of Grace* (Word: 1996).

Luther, Martin. *Antinomian Theses* (1537), reprinted as *Don't Tell Me That From Martin Luther's Antinomian Theses* (Minneapolis: Lutheran Press, 2004).

Luther, Martin. *Against Antinomianism* (1539) available online at http://www.truecovenanter.com/truelutheran / luther_ against_ the_ antinomians.html#note01.

Luther, Martin. "How Christians Should Regard Moses [given August 27, 1525]," *Luther's Works: Word and Sacrament I* (Philadelphia: Muhlenberg Press, 1960) Vol. 35 at 161-174.

Luther, Martin. *Commentary on the Epistle to the Galatians* (1535) (trans. Theodore Graebner)(Grand Rapids, Michigan: Zondervan Publishing House, 1949) at 48-60 (at http://www.iclnet.org/pub/resources/text/wittenberg/luther/gal/web/gal2-04.html)(last accessed 9-6-07).

MacArthur, John. *The Gospel According to Jesus.* (Zondervan, 1994).

MacArthur, John. "Jesus' Perspective on Sola Fide," (2004) at http://www.biblebb.com/files/MAC/sf-solafide.htm (last accessed 4/8/2007).

MacArthur, John. *The Study Bible* (1997).

Machen, John Gresham. *The Origin of Paul's Religion* (MacMillan, 1921).

Marcion. *Antitheses* at http://www.geocities.com/Athens/Ithaca/3827/antithesis.html (last visited 2005).

Maimonides, Moses. *Introduction to the Mishnah* (Jerusalem: 1992).

Marmorstein, A. *The Doctrine of Merits in Old Rabbinical literature* (New York: KTAV, repr. 1968).

Mathew, P.G. *Self-Delusion Exposed: Matthew 7:21-2* (Grace Valley Christian Center) (Sermon October 12, 1997), available online at http://www.dcn.davis.ca.us/~gvcc/sermon_trans/1997/Self_Delusion_Exposed.html (accessed 7-01-07).

McGrath, Alister E. *Iustitia Dei: A History of the Christian Doctrine of Justification* (Cambridge: 1998).

Menno (Simons). *A Foundation and Plain Instruction of the Saving Doctrine of Our Lord Jesus* (1556).

Metzger, Bruce M. *The Canon of the New Testament: Its Origin, Development, and Significance* (New York: Abingdon, 1965) and (Oxford: Clarendon Press, 1987).

Metzger, Bruce M. *A Textual Commentary on the Greek New Testament, Second Edition, A Companion Volume to the United Bible Societies' Greek New Testament* (Fourth Revised Edition) (Stuttgart: German Bible Society, 1994).

Milligan, James H. and Moulton, George. *Vocabulary of the Greek Testament* (London: 1930) (reprint Hendrickson Publishers, 1997).

Milton, John. *Prose Works* (Westley & Davis, 1845)(downloadable at books.google.com).

Montgomery, James Allan. *The Samaritans, the Earliest Jewish Sect: Their History, Theology and Literature* (J.C. Winston, 1907).

Moreau, Scott *et al. Evangelical Dictionary of World Missions* (Baker, 2000).

Mosheim, Johann Lorenz. D.D. *Historical Commentaries on the State of Christianity During The First Three Hundred and Twenty-Five Years from the Christian Era* (trans. Robert S. Vidal and James Murdock) (N.Y.: Converse, 1854).

Mosheim, Johann Lorenz & Gleig, George. *An Ecclesiastical History, Ancient and Modern: From the Birth of Christ to the Beginning of the Eighteenth Century* (London: 1811) Vol. IV.

The NAS New Testament Lexicon available online at http://bible.crosswalk.com/Lexicons/Greek/grk.cgi?number= 4487&version=nas (last accessed 7-22-07).

Neander, August. *General History of the Christian Church* (trans.J. Torrey) (Crocker & Brewster: 1854)(downloadable from books.google.com).

Neusner, Jacob. Green, William Scott. Avery-Peck, Alan Jeffery. *Judaism from Moses to Muhammad: An Interpretation : Turning Points and Focal Points* (Brill, 2005).

Nicholl, Colin. *From Hope to Despair in Thessalonica: Situating 1 and 2 Thessalonians* (Cambridge: 2004).

Nicolson, Adam. *God's Secretaries: The Making of the King James Bible* (Perennial Edition, 2004).

Nienhuis, David R. *Not By Paul Alone* (Baylor University Press, 2007).

NIV Theological Dictionary of New Testament Words (Zondervan, 2000).

Origen. *Commentary on the Epistle to the Romans Books 1 to 5* [246 A.D.] (trans. Scheck)(Washington D.C.: Catholic University Press, 2001).

Paley, William. *The Works of William Paley, D.D. With Additional Sermons* (London: C& J. Rivington, 1825) Vol. VI. (downloadable at books.google.com).

Parkhurst, John (1728-1797). *A Greek and English lexicon to the New Testament* (1829)(Ed. Hugh James Rose) (available via books.google.com).

Pattemore, Stephen W. *The People of God in the Apocalypse: Discourse, Structure, and Exegesis* (Cambridge University Press, 2004).

Paulson, Mike (Pastor Touchet Baptist Church). *What Would Jesus Do or What Would Paul Do?* available at http://www.touchet1611.org/PeterPaulMary2.html (last visited 2005).

Pelagius. *Pelagius's Commentary on St. Paul's Epistle to the Romans* (trans. & introd. by Theodore De Bruyn)(Oxford University Press: 2002).

Pink, Arthur W. *Exposition of the Sermon on the Mount* (Grand Rapids: 1959) chapter eight at http://www.pbministries.org/books/pink/Sermon/sermon_08.htm (Providence Baptist Ministries) (last accessed 6/16/06).

Piper, John. *Thoughts on Jesus' Demand to Repent* (April 19, 2006), reprinted online at http://www.desiringgod.org/ResourceLibrary/TasteAndSee/ByDate/2006/1780 _Thoughts _on_ Jesus _Demand_to_Repent/ (last accessed 4-17-2007).

Piper, John. *Let Us Walk In The Light of God* (February 3, 1985), reprinted at http:// www.desiringgod.org/ResourceLibrary/Sermons/ByDate/1985/ 476_Let_Us_Walk_in_the_Light_of_God/ (last accessed January 12, 2008).

Plaut, Gunther W. *The Torah: A Modern Commentary* (N.Y.: Union of American Hebrew Congregations, 1981).

Purves, Andrew. *Pastoral Theology in the Classical Tradition* (Westminster: John Knox Press, 2001).

Rainy, Robert. *The Ancient Catholic Church: From the Ascension of Trajan to the Fourth General Council (A.D. 98-451)* (N.Y.: Charles Scribner's, 1902).

Robinson, D. W. B. "'Faith of Jesus Christ'—a New Testament Debate," *The Reformed Theological Review* Vol. 29, no.3 (Sept.-Dec. 1970 at 71-81, reprinted http:// www.presenttruthmag.com/archive/XLIV/44-3.htm (last accessed 9-24-07).

Rotherham, Joseph B. *The Emphasised Bible: A New Translation Designed to Set Forth The Exact Meaning* (London: Bradbury, Agnew & Co., 1902).

Russell, Emmet. "Gnash, Gnashing of Teeth," *The Zondervan Pictorial Encyclopedia of the Bible* (Ed. Merrill C. Tenney) (Grand Rapids: Zondervan Publishing House, 1975) at 2:735.

Ryrie, Charles. *The Ryrie Study Bible* (Chicago: Moody Press, 1976).

Sandlin, A. T*he Attitude of the Godly Towards God's Enemies,* http://forerunner.com/fore-runner/X0508_Sandlin_-_Gods_Enemi.html (last accessed 11-30-2006).)

Saxe, Pastor. *A Conditional Beatitude, Rev. 22:13-14* at www.fellowshipbibleannarbor.org/ BibleStudies/nt/rev/PastorSaxe/RevelationCh22Vv13to14.pdf.

Schaff, Philip. *A Religious Encyclopedia* (1894)(downloadable at books.google.com).

Schaff, Philip. *A Select Library of Nicene and Post-Nicene Fathers of the Christian Church, Translated into English with Prolegomena and Explanatory Notes under the Editorial Supervision of Henry Wace and Philip Schaff.* (Oxford: Parker; New York: Christian Literature Co., 1890-1900).

Schaff, Philip. D.D., *The Renaissance: The Revival of Learning and Art in the Fourteenth and Fifteenth Centuries* (Putnam, 1891).

Schaff, Philip. *Creeds of Christendon* (1919).

Scheck, Thomas. *Origen: Commentary on the Epistle to the Romans* (Washington DC: CUA, 2001-02).

Schreiner, Thomas. *The Law and Its Fulfillment* (Grand Rapids: Baker, 1993).

Schreiner, Thomas. "Did Paul Believe in Justification by Works? Another Look at Romans 2," *Bulletin for Biblical Research* 3 (1993) 131-158 (available at http:// www.sbts.edu/docs/tschreiner/BBR_3.pdf).

Scott, John. Milner, Joseph. Milner, Isaac. *The History of the Church of Christ* (R.B. Seely and W. Burnside, 1829).

Scott, John. Milner, Joseph. Milner, Isaac. *The History of the Church of Christ* (R.B. Seely and W. Burnside: 1828).

Scrivener, F.H.A. Phd. *A Full Collation of the Sinaiticus Ms. With The Received Text of The New Testament* (Cambridge: 1864)(downloadable from books.google.com).

Smith, Charles R. "The Unfruitful Branches in John 15," *Grace Journal* (Spring 1968): 3.

Sowards, J.K., et al., *Controversies* (University of Toronto, 2005).

Springer, Michael Stephen. *Restoring Christ's Church: John A Lasco and the Forma AC Ratio* (Ashgate Publising, 2007).

Stang, Willliam. *The Life of Martin Luther* (Pustet, 1883).

Stanley, Charles. *Eternal Security: Can You Be Sure?* (Thomas Nelson, 1990).

Stanley, Charles. *The Gift of Forgiveness* (Thomas Nelson, 1991).

Stedman, Ray. *When Unbelief is Right* (1967), available at http://www.pbc.org/dp/stedman/1john/0161.html (last visited 2005).

Steele, McKendree. *Outlines of Bible Study* (1889).

Stevens, George B. *The Teachings of Jesus* (N.Y.: MacMillan, 1916).

Suber, Peter. *The Clinical Attitude.* Department of Philosophy, Earlham College, Richmond, Indiana. (http://www.earlham.edu/~peters/courses/inflogic/clinical.htm)(last accessed 9-5-07).

Suber, Peter. *The Stages of Argument.* Department of Philosophy, Earlham College, Richmond, Indiana. (http://www.earlham.edu/~peters/courses/argstages.htm)(last accessed 9-5-07).

Swindol, Chuck. *The Problem of Defection* (audiotape YYP.6A).

Taylor, Jeremy. *The Whole Works of the Right Reverend Jeremy Taylor, D.D.* (London: 1851).

Taylor, Jeremy, D.D. *Discourses on Various Subjects* (Boston: 1816)(3 vols).

Tertullian, *Adversus Marcionem* (ed. trans.) (Oxford: Oxford University Press, 1972) available at http://www.tertullian.org (last visited 2005).

Tertullian, *On Modesty* online http://www.tertullian.org (last accessed 7-21-07).

Tertullian. *Scorpion's Bite (Scorpiace) (Antidote to the scorpion's sting)* available online at http://www.tertullian.org/works/scorpiace.htm (last accessed 8-15-07).

Thayer, J.H. *Greek-English Lexicon* (T. & T. Clark: 1958).

Thiel, Robert J. Ph.D. *Were the Pharisees Condemned for Keeping the Law of God?* (2001) http://www.cogwriter.com/pharisee.htm (last accessed 6/17/06).

Thiel, Robert J. *The Apostle Paul* (2006) at http://www.cogwriter.com/paul.htm.

Trueman, Carl R. *Luther's Legacy: Salvation and English Reformers, 1525-1556* (Oxford Univ. Press, 1994).

Torrance, Thomas F. "One Aspect of the Biblical Conception of Faith," *Expositary Times* 68 (1957) at 111-14.

Tyndale, Robert. *Tyndale Bible Dictionary* (Walter E. Ewell and Philip Wesley Comfort) (Tyndale House, 2001).

Tyndale, William. *Doctrinal Treatises and Introductions to Different Portions of the Holy Scripture, by William Tyndale, Martyr, 1536* (Henry Walter ed.)(Cambridge: The Parker Society, 1848).

Tyndale, William. *The Works of the English Reformers: William Tyndale and John Frith* (Ebenezer Palmer, 1831).

Vincent, Marvin R. *Word Studies in the New Testament* (C. Scribner's, 1905).

Vines, W. E. *An Expository Dictionary of New Testament Words* (Nashville: Thomas Nelson Publishers, 1984) An online reprint is at http://www.bibletexts.com/glossary/belief.htm (accessed 7-5-07).

Wallace, Daniel B. *Greek Grammar Beyond the Basics* (Zondervan, 1997).

Walker, Steve. *God's Grace for the Impure Heart* (audio sermon) at http://www.cverc.org/update/sermons.htm (last accessed 7-1-07).

Walvoord, John. *Matthew: Thy Kingdom Come* (Moody Press, 1984).

Watkins, James. "What Must I do to Inherit Eternal Life?" See http://watkins.gospelcom.net/bio.htm. (accessed 5/29/2007).

Watson, Richard. Bangs, Nathan. *A Biblical and Theological Dictionary: Explanatory of the History, Manners and Customs of the Jews* (Carlton & Porter, 1832).

Wells, Louise. *The Greek Language of Healing from Homer to the New Testament Times* (New York & Berlin: Walter de Gruyter, 1998).

Wesley, John. "A Plain Account of Christian Perfection," *The Works of John Wesley* (ed. by Thomas Jackson)(1872) Vol. 11, at 366-446, excerpted at http://gbgm-umc.org/Umhistory/Wesley/perfect2.html.

Wesley, John. "Perseverance of the Saints," *Fundamental Christian Theology: A Systematic Theology* (C. J. Kinne, 1931), Vol. II, at 266-81.

Wesley, John. *Works of The Reverend John Wesley* (London: 1840) (seven volumes).

Wordsworth, C. *The New Testament of Our Lord and Savior Jesus Christ in the Original Greek; with notes by C. Wordsworth, Canon of Westminster* (London: 1857).

White, Dr. James. *Drawn by the Father: A Summary of John 6:35-45* (Reformation Press, 1999).

Whittemore, Thomas. *Notes and Illustrations of the Parables of the New Testament* (Boston: J.M. Usher, 1855)(downloadable at books.google.com).

Willard, Dallas. *The Great Omission* (San Francisco: Harper, 2006).

Wilkin, Bob. *Repentance and Salvation: A Key Gospel Issue* (1988) available at http://www.faithalone.org/news/y1988/88june4.html (last visited 2005).

Wilkin, Bob. *Has This Passage Ever Bothered You? Matthew 25:31-46 - Works Salvation?* http://www.faithalone.org/news/y1988/ 88march1.html (last accessed 11/05).

Wilkin, Bob. *Who Are The Outsiders? Revelation 22:14-17*, at http://www.faithalone.org/news/y1993/93nov3.html (last accessed 4/24/07)

Witherington, Ben. *New Testament History* (Baker Academic, 2001).

Wordsworth, Chr. D.D. (Canon of Westminster). *The New Testament of Our Lord and Savior Jesus Christ, In the Original Greek, With Notes* (Part I) (London: 1856).

Wrede, William. *Paul* (Lexington: American Theological Library Association Committee on Reprinting, 1962).

Wright, N.T. *Paul in Fresh Perspective* (Minneapolis: Fortress, 2005).

Wuest, Kenneth. *Practical Use of the Greek New Testament* (Chicago: Moody Press, n.d.).

Yeung, Maureen W. *Faith in Jesus and Paul* (doctoral thesis, Aberdeen, University 1999) (Mohr Siebeck, 2002).

Young, Brad. *The Parables: Jewish Tradition and Christian Interpretation* (Massachusetts: Hendrickson, 2000).

Zodhiates, Spiros. *The Complete Word Study — New Testament* (Chatanooga, TN: AMG, 1993).

Software-Resources

E-Sword and its modules were also used in preparing this book. This software is free and can be downloaded at http://www.e-sword.net. The resource modules relied upon from within E-Sword were: various Bibles (GNB, ASV, KJV, YLT, RV, JPS, Webster's, Vulgate, GB) and Commentaries (Gill, Henry, Wesley, Vincent Word Studies, Barnes, Clarke, Keil & Delitzsch, JFB, and Geneva Notes.)

Google Books

Almost any book cited above dated prior to 1917 is fully accessible, downloadable, and searchable online at books.google.com. A special thank you to Google for its scanning project. I wish to also offer a special praise. Beginning in 2004, five major libraries allowed Google to scan their shelves. More libraries have joined Google's project since then. By 2014, Google believes it will have scanned all the books at Oxford, Harvard, Stanford, Michigan, the New York Public Library and most of the rest. Each month, tens of thousands of books are being scanned. There are now over 1 million titles available at books.google.com. This is not merely a fantastic tool for research. It is ***revolutionary***. There is no scholarly endeavor of the past that needs to be forgotten. The highest quality information thereby becomes accessible to everyone. As a result, a carefuly crafted word-search, and a dose of patience, will often dig up a reliable answer to even the most obscure issue. An observant reader of *Jesus' Words on Salvation* should recognize what kind of fruit Google Books can yield. It should provide you a burst of optimism that ***there is nothing hidden that cannot become known***. (Luke 8:17.) You can find out both sides of any issue. You can weigh the evidence, no matter how obscure or difficult to find. You can solve mysteries of Greek or Latin translation that you thought you never had the resources to resolve. You can also find works in other languages. If you have the language skills or Google's advanced language tools at hand, even foreign resources are now accessible on everyone's computer. Nothing is beyond the grasp of investigation with Google's extraordinary tool. Most important of all, *readers now can verify quotes' accuracy and check the facts themselves with ease!* Google Books ultimately puts pressure on authors and scholars to themselves not make claims they have not *fully* checked and verified. For now their audience is much more capable than ever before to expose errors. Thank you Google. One day Google may be remembered as much for Google Books as it is now for its web indexing tools.

Printed in Dunstable, United Kingdom

66048699R00362